FAUST

VOLUME 2

GOETHE

FAUST

Edited with Introduction by

R-M. S. Heffner
THE UNIVERSITY OF WISCONSIN—MADISON

Helmut Rehder
UNIVERSITY OF TEXAS

W. F. Twaddell
BROWN UNIVERSITY

VOLUME 2

The University of Wisconsin Press

Published by
The University of Wisconsin Press
Box 1379, Madison, Wisconsin 53701
The University of Wisconsin Press, Ltd.
70 Great Russell Street, London

First Wisconsin printing, 1975

Complete and unabridged

Originally published in three volumes
by D. C. Heath and Company

Printed in the United States of America
ISBN 0-299-06884-6 ; LC 75-12216

NOTES

In these explanatory notes we have sought to give full information concerning each point of probable difficulty to an American college student. We have tried to give rather too much than too little, without allowing the notes to become too voluminous to be usable.

It has not been our purpose to discuss questions of textual criticism. We have instead made our choice of the various alternatives at each of the textual cruces and have then allowed our text to stand on its own merits without discussion. Only in the case of an unsatisfactory textual solution have we discussed the problem in our notes, in order to explain why the text as we print it is unsatisfactory.

We have not undertaken to present the many literary analogies, parallel passages, and "influences" which Goethe's text constantly suggests, unless it has seemed to us that a reference to these matters would help make the meaning of the text more apparent.

The complete vocabulary which we have prepared for FAUST has made it unnecessary for us to offer translations of individual words in our notes, but the student will find many paraphrases designed to make clear the over-all meaning of difficult lines, as well as an occasional direct rendition of the text into English.

Scholarly opinion is divided concerning the meaning of a number of passages in FAUST. We have not given the history of such divisions of opinion, but have tried to say what we believed the correct interpretation to be, and have then indicated the other opinions which seem to us tenable. In those few cases in which we could not ourselves agree, we have given all the interpretations which appear reasonable to any of us.

These notes do not attempt to deal with the many intricate problems of FAUST interpretation which are raised, particularly, by the second part of the poem. Our primary purpose is to make the text accessible to the student. We have endeavored to provide interpretation only when this appears to be needed for a first-level understanding of the text. Our efforts at higher-level interpretation are to be found in the introduction we provide, not in the notes.

Only one abbreviation which might be unfamiliar is used in these notes. This is SD which, when prefixed to a line number, indicates the stage direction at that place.

Bibliographical references are few and as a rule self-explanatory. The following list may, however, be useful:

URFAUST   The earliest preserved form of Goethe's FAUST.

FRAGMENT   The first form of FAUST published by Goethe, 1790.

Eckermann   GESPRÄCHE MIT GOETHE IN DEN LETZTEN JAHREN SEINES LEBENS by Johann Peter Eckermann, Leipzig, 1836–1848. The pertinent passages for FAUST are also to be found in Gräf, H. G., GOETHE ÜBER SEINE DICHTUNGEN, 2. Teil, 2. Band, Frankfurt a. M., 1904.

Hederich, Benjamin: GRÜNDLICHES MYTHOLOGISCHES LEXIKON . . . , verbessert von J. J. Schwabe, Leipzig, 1770.

FAUST I

These four elegiac stanzas were first written in the summer of 1797, probably on June 24, seven years after the publication of FAUST: EIN FRAGMENT (see Introduction, p. 39), when Goethe had decided to resume work on this drama. The dedication is not an integral part of the FAUST play, but belongs to it as a mood-setting preliminary chord belongs to a pianist's performance of a masterpiece. The title, 'Dedication,' can only be considered a reflection of the mood of the author, since the poem is not explicitly dedicated to any person or persons. Indeed, one may almost say that this dedication is the dedication of the poet to his theme.

1 **schwankende Gestalten** The 'figures' of the play — Faust, Gretchen, Mephistopheles, and the rest — not clearly seen in the poet's imagination, but uncertainly 'wavering,' as they return after years in which he has been otherwise occupied. The poet had once before seen them in his youthful (*früh*) and less lucid imagination. This reference to the *trüben Blick* (line 2) is the poet's criticism of his conception of these figures in his earlier work. Goethe's first interest in the Faust materials appears to have been aroused in 1769 (*cf.* the letter to Zelter, June 1, 1831).

4 **Wahn** 'fanciful idea': his youthful project of putting the figures of the Faust legend into a great drama, of catching these creatures of his imagination and giving them artistic form (*festzuhalten*).

5 **mögt ihr walten** The figures of this tale crowd upon the poet's mind, and he resolves to let them hold sway in his imagination rather than to try to put them away.

6 **Dunst und Nebel** Equivalent to *Nebeldunst*, 'misty haze.' The two nouns connected by the conjunction *und* are used instead of a compound or a modified noun in the figure of speech called hendiadys. This reference to *Dunst und Nebel* (also in a letter to Schiller, June 22, 1797), as the medium from which the figures of his play arise before his mind's eye, seems to imply not merely the dimness with which the persons of the tale are seen, but also the obscurity of the age to which they belong, when alchemy and sorcery flourished, as compared with the clarity and serenity of classic antiquity, as this is conventionally depicted.

8 **umwittert** A magic emanation seems to envelop the moving procession of these figures from the old story.

10 **Schatten** The shades of youthful friends, now dead or departed from the poet's life, the memories of youthful love and first friends, whose passing once caused him great pain.

13 **Klage** His present lament, as it recalls to his mind the names of these departed friends, causes him to retrace in memory the tortuous, labyrinth-like path of his early life.

15 **um schöne Stunden getäuscht** 'deprived of happy hours' (by a trick of fortune).

16 **hinweggeschwunden** Here, as very frequently, the auxiliary of

tense must be supplied from the context. In this case it would be *sind*, to make the present perfect tense '(they) have vanished away.'

17 **Gesänge** 'cantos.' The poet refers to his work as if to an epic poem in the traditional form of Milton's PARADISE LOST, or Dante's DIVINA COMMEDIA. This is a metaphor, since none of Goethe's FAUST has the form of epic poetry.

18 **die Seelen** Those friends and acquaintances in Frankfurt and in Weimar to whom Goethe had read his first FAUST scenes.

19 **Gedränge** The friendly crowd of enthusiastic young people, with whom Goethe associated in Frankfurt, Strassburg, and Wetzlar, and in whose response to his poetic creations his own feelings found an echo.

21 **Leid** The poem is thought of as the expression of the poet's deepest passion, his sufferings. In his youth he had read some FAUST scenes to friends who understood him; now, when his poem, with this dedication, is printed and published, it will be open for all to read and to hear. The use of *Leid* here is analogous to that in the distich, written but never published by Goethe, concerning his novel, DIE LEIDEN DES JUNGEN WERTHERS:

> Ach, wie hab' ich so oft die törichten Blätter verwünschet,
> die mein jugendlich Leid unter die Menschen gebracht.

[From the first version of the second "Römische Elegie," *Jubiläums-Ausgabe*, I, 351.]

22 **Beifall** The approval of the unknown multitude disturbs the poet. He fears that general public approval of his poem may indicate that it is less worthy than he had hoped, see lines 59–62. The phrase, *vielen gefallen ist schlimm*, reflects Goethe's aristocratically aloof attitude toward the literary taste of his time.

23 **was** Refers (like *es*, line 24) to anyone who may have enjoyed the early FAUST scenes, 'whoever . . . he.'

25 **längst entwöhntes Sehnen** The poet's youth lies far behind him (Goethe was now forty-eight years old). For years he has not allowed himself to indulge in reminiscent longing for those very happy early days, see lines 184–197. Now he longs again to be with the kindred souls, the *freundliche Gedränge* (19), who are but spirits in the silent realm of ghosts (26). As the dim figures of the past crowd upon his imagination, the poet's emotions are aroused and he feels himself transported far from present realities back into this remembered past.

28 **lispelnd** In poetry, the attributive adjective after an *ein*-word in the nominative or accusative neuter singular is quite frequently without the expected ending *-es*. — **Lied** This dedication, as the poet sings it, seems to him to fade away, to become faint like the whispering, uncertain sounds of the Aeolian harp, while the vanished past assumes for him increasing reality.

1. VORSPIEL AUF DEM THEATER

The underlying fiction of this scene is that these three persons, the theater director, the poet, and the clown, are about to undertake the production of a play, the FAUST, which is to follow. Goethe uses the scene to exhibit three attitudes toward dramatic poetry, that of (1) the director, who wishes action with variety, in order to bring crowds to his theater, (2) the comedian, who wants a romantic piece with shifting emotions and a direct bond with contemporary life, and (3) the poet, who wishes not to be constrained to write for the uses of the vulgar crowd, but rather in composure to form his work for posterity. The director prevails, and, so to speak, drives the poor poet to his task.

SD 33 **Direktor, Theaterdichter, Lustige Person.** The manager, the poet, and the comedian. The better theater companies employed a writer, whose job it was to prepare the scripts for the various plays presented, to compose occasional prologues and epilogues and, incidentally, a number of original plays each year. The comedian represents the performers of these plays, particularly the player of comic parts, such as the roles of the Fool in Shakespeare's plays.

35 **in deutschen Landen** The implication here is that this is one of those international traveling companies, notably groups of English, Dutch, or German players, who, toward the end of the sixteenth century, performed in the cities and at the courts of princes throughout Europe. This one appears to be uncertain about German conditions and the ensuing dialogue considers the problems posed by German audiences; yet the reference to *unsern deutschen Bühnen*, in line 231, appears to identify this company as a German troupe of the late eighteenth century.

39 Where no theater building existed, these troupes set up their own stages wherever they could — often in a barn, a warehouse, in the town hall, or in a temporary wooden structure (*Bude*, line 50), which they erected on the market place.

41 **Augenbraunen** Another form of *Augenbrauen*, used here for the rime.

46 This audience expects to be astonished (42), and this is the more difficult as its reading is extensive. It will not be easy to find something new for these people.

51 **Wehen** The throes of struggling in the crowd.

52 **Gnadenpforte** The entrance to the theater, which is compared by this allusion to the "gate . . . which leadeth unto life," Matthew 7.14.

53 **vor Vieren** Dative plural of *vier*, now no longer usual. The performances in Weimar usually began at half-past five or six o'clock. This crowd has gathered well in advance: indeed, the play for the evening has not yet been put together.

55 This line, like 104, 117, 119, 126 and a number of others is an Alexandrine: that is, it has six beats, with a caesura (a slight pause) after the third beat (*Hungersnot*). For further details see Introduction p. 140. — Goethe wrote two youthful plays in this French verse form. The effect of the line in the present context is something like that of the ornamentation of rococo architecture.

SD 59 This may be the same poet who spoke the dedication. At any rate he uses the same stanza form. He says that he cannot compose if he thinks of the motley crowd for whom his work will be performed.

62 **Strudel** 'whirlpool,' the symbol of distraction.

63 **Himmelsenge** A place of retreat, which will be like Heaven to the poet.

64 **wo nur** 'where alone.'

66 **Götterhand** The plural form *Götter*, 'of the gods,' is reminiscent of the usage of the Greek and Latin poets. It usually means simply 'divine,' with no direct reference to the Christian God.

67–69 The inspirations of the poet's heart, shyly and tentatively murmured, sometimes fail, sometimes succeed in achieving poetic form.

70 **verschlingt** The subject is *Gewalt*, the object is those thoughts (67–69) to which the poet has tried to give poetic form.

71 **durchgedrungen** Supply *ist*; see note to line 16.

71–74 The poetic product is valued in accordance with the conditions of the moment when it appears. Often a work which is not highly esteemed when first brought forth is found by later audiences to have high excellence. Here and now, brilliance may have a momentary effect; genuine artistry will be recognized even by a remote posterity, however blind the contemporary audience may be to its merits.

79 **Gegenwart** The future, or posterity, may have its values. But the present is worth something too, particularly the present of the fine young fellows whose patronage largely supports these actors.

82 The momentary whim of the public will not embitter the artist who knows how to say his say easily. The larger and less intimate his audience, the more certainly will such an artist find a ready response.

85 The comedian urges the poet to be a good fellow and give them an exemplary play for the evening.

86–88 It has been suggested that there is in these lines an allusion to allegorical figures such as appeared in the baroque plays of Daniel Caspar von Lohenstein, and in the plays of Andreas Gryphius. This does not appear to be altogether likely, since it is evident that no such allegorical figures do appear in our play. It seems rather that the poet is being urged to summon his own powers, his imagination, his reason, his common sense, his emotions, and his passions for this task, and admonished not to omit the comic element. One may compare here Goethe's *Maxime*: "Ein dramatisches Werk zu verfassen, dazu gehört Genie. Am Ende soll die Empfindung, in der Mitte die Vernunft, am Anfang der Verstand vorwalten und alles gleichmäßig durch eine lebhaft-klare Einbildungskraft vorgetragen werden."

93 **in der Breite** 'among the masses.'

99 **Stück:Stücken** A pun. When you give a 'play,' give it right off 'in pieces,' never mind about unity (*ein Ganzes*, 'an artistic whole'). — This is a satirical reference to the then prevalent custom of European theaters of giving performances in which only a series of

effective excerpts from a play, or even from several plays, was presented. Goethe quips at this frailty again at lines 4215–16. He deals with the matter more fully in WILHELM MEISTERS LEHRJAHRE, V, 4.

103 **zerpflücken** 'pick apart' into those portions which it (*das Publikum*) likes best. The director does not credit the general public with any sense for the unity of the play, even if there may be unity in it.

104 **sei** Like *zieme* (105), subjunctive in a subordinate clause of implied indirect discourse, introduced by *ihr fühlet nicht*. This use of the subjunctive after an introductory verb in the present tense has become comparatively unusual in present-day German, but it is very frequently found in Goethe's works. This subjunctive may be said often to have little distinctive meaning and the forms may be translated as if they were indicative forms.

106 **saubern** 'nice.' Used sarcastically to mean something quite different. There were a number of such play-smiths active in Germany in Goethe's day, and he was pretty vigorous in his contempt for them.

111 The poet's task, as described by the Director, is to present something fresh and new, something that will please the audience, while it also gives them something to think about (47–48). That task is here compared to the splitting of wood, and in this case, of soft wood. The people of his audience are without powers of concentration. Some come because of boredom; others come loaded down with overeating; still others come from the distraction of magazine reading. None of them are in any condition to appreciate a work of real artistic merit. They do not wish to be edified: they wish to be still further distracted. That, says the realistic Director, is easy, if only enough is made to happen on the stage.

117 **Maskenfesten** 'carnivals': the great masquerade parties, particularly at Shrovetide, just before Lent. These were especially gay in Cologne, Paris, and Rome. The spirit of such celebrations is well reflected in Berlioz' *Roman Carnival Overture.*

119 The ladies in their finery become an important part of the attraction which brings the audience to the theater, although they are not paid for thus contributing to the success of the evening.

121 **was** = *weshalb, warum,* as frequently; see 122, 127.

127 **ihr armen Toren** This poet and others like him, who think of their plays as works of high art, are thus classed by the realistic actor.

132 The dashes indicate interruption due to a gesture by the poet, perhaps a despairing glance toward Heaven.

135 **sollte** Expresses an intention or an expectation of someone else with respect to its subject: 'You expect the poet, I suppose, to . . .' or 'The poet is expected, I suppose, to . . .'

136 **Menschenrecht** 'Man's right' to perceive and describe the relationship between individual phenomena as these present themselves to his mind and the totality of the world as an entity: the right to philosophize, the right to think.

139 **Element** of nature.

140 **Einklang** That overpowering 'harmony' which springs from the poet's bosom and, encompassing the world's multiplicity of often unrelated events, sweeps these back into the poet's heart as a harmonious whole.

142 **Fadens** Nature is thought of as spinning a thread out of the events of life, eternally spinning, twisting this thread indifferently, and winding it on a spindle. All of these events involve beings which make sounds, and these sounds are unrelated and discordant, therefore vexing to the ear. The process seems endless and meaningless until the poet, perceiving the basic 'harmony' of life, organizes the form of these sounds, arranges the symbols of these events, so that a rhythm results. In this way the poet infuses life, interest, or reason into the dissonant jangle produced by nature.

148 **Weihe** The individual thing or happening has artistic importance only as it is a part of a whole. Only the universal element in the individual event consecrates it, relates it harmoniously to other events. Poetic art, if it is to be significant, must present an individual event in such a way that the universal truth which makes that event important can be perceived intuitively. This done, the individual event does indeed 'strike splendid chords' (149) in the hearts of discerning listeners.

150 **zu** 'as accompaniment to.'

154 **Blätter** The leaves of laurel are insignificant in themselves. But made into a wreath of honor and accompanied by a proper dedicatory or commemorative poem, they become a fit reward for any merit.

156 **Olymp** The seat of the Greek gods, a symbol for the highest aspirations of men, some kind of heaven. The force which creates this heaven, or which sustains and consolidates it, is the peculiarly human power of insight, revealed in the poet.

158-183 The comedian, urging the poet to action, to put together a piece for the evening, suggests that he start with anything that comes to mind (*zufällig* 161), and then let his emotions direct the further course of events. Take any subject from real life (167), he says, and your fine poetic insight will give you power to make your play a revelation to everyone, and then it will be interesting. Of course, you have to work through symbols (*Bildern* 170), and these need to be lively and somewhat perplexing, or at any rate not too clear: you need a lot of human error and a bit of truth to make a brew that will be at once refreshing and edifying. Go about it this way; then the young, the tender of heart, will find in your play the things they themselves have most in their own hearts. Don't try to write for the people who have ceased to grow; no one can please them.

181 **Schwung** The grand gesture, the soaring flight of the imagination, characteristic of the heroic drama of the seventeenth century. Examples abound in the plays of Gryphius and of Lohenstein.

182 **wer fertig ist** The antithesis of *ein Werdender*. People who have ceased to learn have ceased to grow, are 'finished.' They will not feel any attraction to such a play, but that can't be helped: they

don't approve of anything. Hence, write for the young, disregard the perfect, or those who think they are perfect.

184–197 These lines will find an echo in the heart of any man near or past fifty, as Goethe was when he wrote them. They belong intimately by mood to the dedication, and they say that to write for the young the poet needs to be young. This the comedian at once denies.

186 **gedrängter** 'crowding close, one upon the other.'

193 **Wahrheit . . . Trug** Neither of these words is easily defined, as Pilate discovered (John 18.38). Life is full of both things. Truth, however, is something apprehended by the mind, by the human intelligence; *Trug*, be it illusion or delusion, is something apprehended by the senses. The world of truth is a world of abstractions; the world of phenomena, from which these abstractions stem, is perhaps the world of delusion to which this poet refers. Because it appears in this context, this line also has a meaning more closely associated with the world of the theater. Hence *Wahrheit* can be taken to mean 'fidelity to nature,' and *Trug* to mean the 'sham of the stage.'

The two ideas of *Drang* and *Lust* are overtones of the contrast between *Wahrheit* and *Trug*, and suggest the conflict between the activating force of inner drive and the opiate of enjoyment which leads to passivity. This conflict is found in the lives of all and is especially exemplified in the story of Faust.

202 **Kranz** It was customary to hang the wreath intended for the winner of the race upon the goal, where approaching runners could see it.

204 **Wirbeltanz** The violent folk dances, which are physically exhausting, by contrast with the sedate minuet of the princely court.

206 The writing of poetry or of a play is compared to the playing of a lyre or harp, to the accompaniment of which ancient poetry was recited.

209 **mit holdem Irren** The comedian suggests that the poet may wend his way, unmethodically and leisurely, toward his self-set goal, and that the audience will find his meandering pleasant.

212 This *Vorspiel* was probably written in 1797, when Goethe was 48 years old. If there is any personal reference behind these lines, coupled with those of the poet at 184–197, it is to a Goethe who was mature and who needed a bit of urging to take up the task of completing his Faust. He is an *alter Herr* (210) in the sense that he is a senior, not a junior, writer, but not in the sense that he is an old man.

218 **Stimmung** No one has mentioned 'mood' up to this point. But it is evidently expected that the poet will remonstrate and say that he has to find the right mood before he can compose his play. In his conversations with Eckermann (March 11, 1828) Goethe described two kinds of aesthetic productivity: one, the highest attainable, is beyond any poet's control. "Jede Produktivität höchster Art, jedes bedeutende Aperçu, jede Erfindung, jeder große Gedanke, der Früchte bringt und Folge hat, steht in niemandes Gewalt und ist über aller irdischen Macht erhaben. Dergleichen hat der Mensch

als unverhoffte Geschenke von oben . . ." The other kind of productivity is more subject to the will of the poet. "In diese Region zähle ich alles zur Ausführung eines Planes Gehörige, alle Mittelglieder einer Gedankenkette, deren Endpunkte bereits leuchtend dastehen; ich zähle dahin alles dasjenige, was den sichtbaren Leib und Körper eines Kunstwerkes ausmacht." This is the kind of productivity the director understands and urges his poet to undertake.

224 **braut . . . dran** 'set about brewing.'

228 **beim Schopfe fassen** Lysippos, a Greek sculptor (about 330 B.C.) made a statue of Kairos (Opportunity), in which this figure was depicted as having a lock of hair in front and being completely bald on the back of the head. Hence one seized Opportunity by the forelock or not at all, according to tradition based on this statue. Determination (*der Entschluß*), therefore, is to regard the possible as its opportunity. Having seized the possible by the forelock, determination will not let go, but will proceed from this beginning. In short, the director says: Take some subject at hand and begin; the rest will follow, because it has to do so.

232 The reference is to the unrestricted use of all sorts of apparatus and effects on the German stage, in contrast to the classic economy of the French plays of Corneille and Racine. There was no well established tradition in Germany to restrain the ebullient zeal of producers, and every device to surprise and overawe an audience was tried. Thus, *das groß' und kleine Himmelslicht* (235) are the stage properties which represent the sun and the moon, respectively.

238 **an Tier' und Vögeln**, for *an Tieren und Vögeln.* Rather frequently Goethe drops a suffix or an inflectional ending from a word joined by *und* to another which has the omitted morpheme, e.g., *das groß' und kleine Himmelslicht* 235, *von Sonn' und Welten* 279.

242 This need not be taken literally as an itinerary. It is a list of the stopping places in the *Kreis der Schöpfung* which the poet is to traverse. Faust does get into all of these places before he is finished, but not in this order. This whole scene is designed, perhaps principally, to prepare the audience for a most unusual variety in the sequence of scenes to follow.

2. PROLOG IM HIMMEL

The dramatic purpose of this scene is to state the problem of Mephistopheles and Faust. The issue is whether or not Mephistopheles can lead Faust away from the service of the Lord. The Lord appears to be in an indulgent mood, in that he permits, indeed encourages, Mephistopheles to attempt to lead Faust astray.

The analogy of this scene to the Biblical story of Job is evident. There the Lord points to his servant Job as an "upright man" and Satan proposes to destroy Job's character by destroying his possessions. The God of the Old Testament gives his approval to Satan's undertaking, and Job is subjected to grievous torments. In FAUST

Mephistopheles proposes to win Faust away from God, not by persecution, but *sacht* (314) by easy allurements and by pleasures.

By locating this scene in Heaven and using God, Mephistopheles, and the Archangels as speaking characters Goethe achieves something of the atmosphere of the Mystery plays of the Middle Ages.

SD 243 **Der Herr** As this is usually produced on the stage, the Lord does not appear where the audience can see Him, but converses with the others through an opening into an inner court of Heaven. Conventionally this opening is overhead, and a great shaft of light falls from above while the Lord is present. It is cut off when the inner court is closed, line 349. — **Die himmlischen Heerscharen** are the Heavenly Hosts of Luke 2.13. — **Die drei Erzengel** We may assume that there are numerous archangels in Heaven, of whom these three step forward. The Bible mentions only Michael (Jude 9) as an archangel. The name of Raphael occurs in the apocryphal Book of Tobit (12.15). Gabriel is mentioned in the Book of Daniel (8.16) and in the Gospel of Luke (1.19, 26). Neither Gabriel nor Raphael is called an archangel in the Bible.

243 **die Sonne tönt** Aristotle says that some Pythagorean philosophers believed that the heavenly bodies produced musical notes as they moved along their courses. Those which moved slowly produced a low note, those which moved more rapidly produced a high note; so that there was a chance for harmony, if the relative speeds of the stars on their courses were integrally related. This idea has frequently been used by poets and musicians.

244 **Brudersphären Wettgesang** The mention of 'spheres' seems to indicate that Goethe was making poetic use of the ancient Ptolemaic cosmography as the basis for the relationships here presupposed. This doctrine envisaged the earth as a stationary sphere located at the center of the finite universe. This universe was viewed as a structure of hollow, concentric, transparent spheres around the earth: the closest easy analogy to this structure is that of a large onion. The sphere nearest the earth is that of the moon. Within each of the six spheres next outside the moon one of the planets moved on its own (epicyclic) course. Nearest the realm of the moon was the sphere of Mercury, then came the spheres of Venus, the sun, Mars, Jupiter, and Saturn, in that order. Beyond the sphere of Saturn was the sphere of the fixed stars. It is probably the spheres of the planets which are here thought of as 'brother spheres' to the sun. Each sphere as it revolves makes a sound and the whole is viewed as a friendly rivalry. In this Ptolemaic system, God resided outside the finite universe, beyond the *Primum Mobile*, in the Empyrean, the "tenth heaven" of Dante, "the abode of the blessed."

246 **vollendet** The sun cannot be said ever to complete its journey, in the sense that it arrives and ceases to travel. However, it does rotate on its axis and presumably travels around an orbit. It appears that at line 243 the sun was remote enough for its movement to sound a musical note (*tönt*), whereas at line 246 it has come close enough to the observer to produce a thunderous roar, rather than a musical tone.

248 **wenn** = *obwohl,* or perhaps *während.* — **sie** = *die Sonne.* — **mag** = *kann.*

249 **Werke** The works of Creation, described in the first chapter of Genesis, and referred to in Genesis 2.2: "Und also vollendete Gott am siebenten Tage seine Werke, die er machte . . ."

251 **schnell, schnelle** The adverbial form is *schnelle; schnell* is the adjectival form, used as an adverb, as almost any adjective may be used. — A point at the surface of the earth's equator is moving around the earth's axis at a speed of approximately 1000 miles per hour.

252 **dreht** The earth is seen to revolve, and rapidly. This means that the observer is not too remote, and that he is watching a point on the earth's surface move through space. It is apparent that the Ptolemaic cosmography, which viewed the earth as motionless, is not the basis of the conception here represented. It is not known how fully Goethe understood the true relationships of the sun to the other components of its galaxy, but it may be observed that what he here says can be understood to apply to the universe as we know it with less contradiction than it can be applied to the Ptolemaic system.

253 **Paradieseshelle** Daylight is apparently the norm in Paradise; see line 1782.

255 The sea is seen to strike violently in broad currents against a rocky coast, and then the whole — the sea and the coast — is whirled from the view of the archangels as the earth revolves.

261–262 **Kette der . . . Wirkung** The storms of the earth are seen as a series of events which are linked together by a causal connection, one event being in part at least the effect of those which have preceded it and the cause of those which follow.

263–264 **flammt . . . vor** The flashing devastation of lightning goes flaming before the path of the thunder.

265 **doch** Although the tremendous power of these natural forces is impressive, still the angels (*Boten*) are more deeply moved by the even, gentle movement of God's day. What is really impressive in the universe is its relative immutability, the regularity of the laws of nature amidst all movement and change.

267–270 These lines are to be compared with lines 247–250. There the angels derived strength from the sight of God's works, in particular the sun, *although* they were unable to understand them completely. Here the angels are strengthened by the sight of the gentle progress of God's day, *because* they know they cannot comprehend God directly.

SD 271 The name Mephistopheles, in one form or another (Mephostophilus, Mephistophilis, Mephistophiel), belongs to the Faust legend. Goethe's form is that of the FAUSTBUCH DES CHRISTLICH MEINENDEN (about 1725). A satisfactory explanation of the derivation of the name has not yet been found.

271 **wieder nahst** The assumption appears to be that God is making one of His periodic tours of inspection in Heaven, and that Mephistopheles, whose normal field of operations is not in Heaven, has come there expressly to see the Lord. However, he appears to identify

himself *(bei uns)* with the angels of this particular region of Heaven, and to have his place among them as one of the Lord's servants *(Gesinde)*.

273 **sonst** Although Mephistopheles is engaged in the business of seducing souls from God's ways, he has in the past usually been well treated by God upon the occasion of such visits as this. He therefore makes bold to appear now. See lines 337–343.

277 **Pathos** Any attempt on the part of Mephistopheles to exhibit deep feelings *(hohe Worte)* of the sort shown by the archangels.

279 **Sonn' und Welten** See note to line 238.

281 **der kleine Gott** Man was created in God's image, but on a much smaller scale.

282 **wunderlich** In line 250 it was *herrlich*. One has to expect satire from the *Schalk* (339) Mephistopheles.

285 **Vernunft** This was the watchword, the new divinity, of the men of the French Revolution of 1789; and the two lines 285–286 may be taken as an allusion to this Revolution.

287 **Euer Gnaden** A fixed phrase used to address persons of high degree, 'Your Grace.'

288–292 Mephistopheles compares man's use of his intellectual powers in the effort to understand the workings of the universe with the vain leapings of the grasshopper, who, no matter how often or how high he leaps, lands once more in the grass from which he sprang. So man, despite his efforts, remains no better than before. But then, to be sure, man is so constituted that even if he stopped his leaping and lay always 'in the grass' — says Mephistopheles with disgust — he would still 'stick his nose' into everything, because of this peculiarly human inquisitive drive to understand.

294 **nur** There is a certain impatience with Mephistopheles in these lines. 'Do you always come here solely to complain, don't you ever find anything right on earth?' The earth is one of God's pet projects; He made it and, after making it, He peopled it with human beings.

297 **dauern** This is a bit of cynical, scornful irony.

298 **selbst** 'myself.'

299 The parallel here to the Book of Job is evident. There also when the "sons of God came to present themselves before Jehovah," Satan came along. Satan had been "down" on earth, "walking to and fro in it." Job 1.8: "And Jehovah said unto Satan, Hast thou considered my servant Job? for there is none like him in the earth, a perfect and upright man, one that feareth God and turneth away from evil." Satan replied that this fear of God was due to the special care God bestowed upon Job, and that if this were taken away, Job would renounce God openly. Jehovah then granted Satan permission to take away all Job's material wealth, saying (Job 1.12): "All that he hath is in thy power; only upon himself put not forth thy hand." The rest of the book tells of Satan's efforts and Job's sufferings, and his final victory, when God "blessed the latter end of Job more than his beginning," and permitted him long life (Job 42.16): "And after this Job lived a hundred and forty

years, and saw his sons, and his sons' sons, even four generations. So Job died, being old and full of days."

300 **Euch** The shift from *du* to *Ihr* (*Euch*) reflects a change in the attitude of Mephistopheles toward God. This is not a change from lesser to greater respect, but from sympathy to antipathy, — from the feeling that there was some bond between them to the awareness of the irreconcilable difference which sets Mephistopheles apart from the others.

301 **irdisch** 'of the earth, earthy,' — perhaps with some reminiscence of I Corinthians 15.47: "The first man is of the earth, earthy: the second man is of Heaven." This Faust is not the "natural" man, but is driven by a great ferment in his soul to seek the remote, the ultimate. Mephistopheles views this as a mad quest and reports that Faust is at least partially aware of the madness of his strivings. Goethe's problem here was to make Faust a very special case without thereby making him non-human, to make him exceptional but not atypical.

306 'And all things near and all things remote' which Faust is able to acquire or to achieve.

308 **Wenn . . . auch** = *obwohl*, 'even though.'

309 **bald** Just how 'soon' is not clear. Neither is it quite clear what *in die Klarheit führen* means, for it is reasonable to believe that this contrasts with *verworren*, and that both describe conditions under which Faust serves or is to serve the Lord. From lines 315–318 it would appear that clarity cannot be a state of human life on earth but must be a condition attainable only after death. Yet how Faust is to serve the Lord in Heaven is neither clear nor aesthetically important. The solution of the problem raised here might give important information concerning the state of Goethe's plans for Faust at the time he wrote these lines.

310 Supply the subject and read: *Es weiß doch der Gärtner*.

314 **meine Straße** Probably the "broad way that leadeth to destruction." (Matthew 7.13).

315 The Lord restricts the attempts of Mephistopheles to lead Faust astray. As long as Faust lives on earth, Mephistopheles may tempt him.

317 **strebt** Man's striving is the positive drive which leads him to seek his own highest development, the perfect realization of his potentialities. The guiding force in this striving is reason, the goal of which is truth. The negation of this drive, the acceptance of any state as satisfactory, is the most irrational of all errors; and the man who falls into it is in the gravest danger of losing his essential human attributes.

318 Mephistopheles evidently has to deal with numerous dead, presumably those whom he has succeeded in leading along his way (314); but he doesn't enjoy that, any more than a cat enjoys a dead mouse. He now has definite permission to attempt to win Faust over to his way, but no wager has been agreed to by the Lord.

320 **mir** The dative of the personal pronoun is frequently used to refer to its antecedent as the person particularly interested in the action, either in his mind or emotions (the "ethical dative," as

here), or in a practical way (the dative of interest or of advantage). The ethical dative is frequently best omitted from an English translation.

324 **Urquell**   God.

326 **herab**   'down' (to perdition).

328 **ein guter Mensch**   The attribute *guter* is positive, not negative. A good man is a man who strives toward truth and self-perfection. — **in seinem dunklen Drange** 'in the confusedly (308) directed drive' which carries such a man through the errors to which all are subject (317).   Such a man may go astray, but he will discover that he has done so, and he will also know when he is on the right track.   So long as he continues to fight the good fight he remains *ein guter Mensch*, and he may expect to come out all right in the end.

330 **nur**   Mephistopheles concedes that this good man (Faust) knows the right way; only, he says, it won't take long to lead him away from it.

335 **Muhme**   The serpent of Genesis 3, whom Mephistopheles claims as a relative.   The degree of relationship intended by *Muhme* is not clear; it may mean 'aunt,' 'first cousin,' or some more remote (female) relative. Mephistopheles also calls the *Trödelhexe* (4110) "*Frau Muhme.*" — The punishment meted out to the serpent of Genesis 3 was that it should go upon its belly and eat dust all the days of its life.

336 **auch da**   With respect to the celebration of this predicted victory. — The interpretation of this line depends on how one takes *nur.* Some take it to qualify *frei* and to mean 'not otherwise than free, quite freely.'   Others take it to qualify *erscheinen* and to mean 'only appear to be free.'   If one reads *nur* with *frei*, then *erscheinen* means 'to appear,' presumably before God as Mephistopheles is appearing at the moment. God gives permission to Mephistopheles to triumph or to appear to triumph freely in the event that Faust should succumb to his wiles.   God knows Mephistopheles will fail (325–327), but Mephistopheles does not accept this as inevitable.

339 **Schalk**   The crafty, ironical knave who irritates and confuses the good man by impugning the validity of his reason.   There are other forces of evil which the Lord finds it more difficult to condone, but we are not told what these are.

343 **als Teufel schaffen**   Probably the same idea, basically, as at 1336, where Mephistopheles himself admits that, although he always wishes to bring about evil, he always does bring about good.   The present line justifies God's permitting this spirit of negation to try to entrap his servant Faust.   Even with devilish intent, Mephistopheles will be obliged to produce good, because, in the sight of God, the only unforgivable sin of man is the lapsing into a state of unconditional repose (340–341).

344 **ihr**   God turns from Mephistopheles to the archangels who surround His throne and calls them 'true, genuine' (*echt*), to distinguish them from Mephistopheles, who is one of the fallen angels and no longer deserves this approval.

345 **Schöne**   An old form of the abstract noun, like *Länge, Breite, Tiefe. Schönheit* is now the usual form.

347 **umfass'** Optative, 'may the world of becoming (*das Werdende*) encompass you with the gentle bonds of love.'

349 **befestiget** Imperative; the archangels are instructed to give permanence to the unsteady world of phenomena by fixing it in lasting thoughts. They are to observe the things and events of the universe. From these, by means of their "pure" reason, they are to abstract the enduring part — the "ideas" (*noumena*), the principles, laws, relationships.

SD 349 **Der Himmel** The inner sanctum, where God has been. See note to SD 243.

353 **menschlich** 'humanely, like a human being, man to man.' — **mit dem Teufel.** The notion that Mephistopheles is *the* Devil is not consistently adhered to throughout the play. At times he is *a* devil, merely one of many evil spirits.

DER TRAGÖDIE ERSTER TEIL

3. NACHT

In the Prologue in Heaven Goethe has stated the problem of his FAUST. Can Mephistopheles lead this man Faust from the paths of righteousness into eternal damnation, or will Faust, because of his inner qualities, remain invulnerable to the wiles of the Devil? There is a specific criterion of man's fall: his acquiescence in *die unbedingte Ruhe*, and the cessation of that striving which is the mark of man.

In the present scene we meet the chief protagonist, Faust. The method of the poet is primarily that of the soliloquy. There is very little dialogue in this scene, and no action in the usual sense. First we find the scholar Faust in his study, sunk in despair because of his inability to penetrate beyond the outward appearance of things to their reality, and sick of his cloistered life. By means of magic, of which he has become a practitioner, he attempts to find a way to transcend the limits which confine him. He feels himself momentarily exalted into the realm of spirits, evokes an apparition of one of them and, being rebuffed for his presumption, sinks back into his despair. He then conceives the idea that by committing suicide he may gain access to the realm of the spirits beyond this earth. He is about to drink poison when the sound of the Easter carols in the nearby church restrains him and he puts down the poison cup.

SD 354 **gotisch** Gothic architecture is the symbol of the medieval and romantic. The scene is characteristic of the age of the Reformation in sixteenth-century Germany. This is the period of Luther, Dürer, Erasmus, and Hans Sachs. The Gothic style of architecture, although it was developed during the fourteenth century, had not yet been superseded by later forms.

354 **Habe** Supply the subject *ich*. This kind of omission is not infrequent in FAUST. — **Philosophie.** The German university was or-

ganized in four major units or colleges called faculties. These were Theology, Jurisprudence, Medicine, and Philosophy. The effect of this organization can still be seen in the kinds of doctoral degrees granted in our own universities. We still have doctors of theology, of law, of medicine, and of philosophy, the last including almost every type of scholarship not named in the other three classes.

355 **Juristerei** = *Jurisprudenz*. The word here has none of the derogatory connotation now associated with the suffix *-erei*.

356 **leider auch** Faust is particularly disappointed in his study of theology, because he had expected from it the greatest satisfaction of his hunger for truth. Instead he had got from it only unsatisfactory answers to his questions.

357 **Bemühn** Rimes with *Medizin*. In Goethe's rime practice there is no difference between rounded and unrounded vowels of the same type. The vowels *ü* and *i* belong to the type called "high front vowels" and may be rimed with each other, e.g. *Zügen:liegen* 440–441. The vowels *ö* and *e* are "mid front vowels" and may be rimed with each other, e.g. *Bergeshöh'n:gehn* 392–393, *näher:höher* 461–462. The diphthongs *ei* and *eu* may be rimed, e.g. *Zweifel:Teufel* 368–369; see Introduction, p. 144.

360 **Magister, Doktor** The two higher degrees in the sequence: *Baccalaureus, Magister, Doktor*.

361 **ziehe schon** A present tense where in English we should use a progressive present perfect 'I have now been leading.' — **an die zehen Jahr** 'almost ten years.' The accusative indicates approach toward a limit. *zehen Jahr* is archaic for *zehn Jahre*. Goethe used a plural form *Jahr* as well as the normal plural *Jahre*.

364 **wissen** Not merely 'to know,' but 'to know completely and with certainty.' This kind of use, in which more is implied than the words express, is called a "pregnant use" of words.

366 **Laffen** Faust holds his colleagues in contempt, regardless of their positions, enumerated in 367.

367 **Doktoren, Magister, Schreiber, Pfaffen** All are men of academic training. *Doktor* is the highest academic rank; *Magister* is next in order of eminence. *Schreiber* is a man learned in the law, a jurist perhaps; and *Pfaffe* is a member of the clergy. The word *Pfaffe* as used here does not of itself imply disrespect.

376 **möchte** = *könnte*. The verb *mögen* in older German usually meant 'to have the physical power to,' and in that sense 'to be able.'

377 **Magie** Not *magia diabolica*, the black art or necromancy, but *magia naturalis*. This was a craft of conjuration which did not involve an appeal to Satan or other evil spirits, but to the planetary and other good spirits, who were called upon to aid the sorcerer in his efforts to find out the secrets of nature. This dealing with spirits was not of necessity bad or sinful, but it involved some risk that the operator might be deceived by Satan and led to eternal damnation and hellfire (369).

378 **ob** 'to see whether.'

379 **Geheimnis** Faust seeks answers to his questions about the mysterious nature of things. He wants to teach his students things

which will make them better and less sinful men (373), but the truth he seeks remains a mystery to him.

383 Faust wishes to know the nature of the inner cohesive force which holds the universe together. — There is a great gulf between the methods of alchemy and the methods of atomic fission, but the difference is rather in the tools than in the driving force of man's search for truth, which animates both quests.

384 Ostensibly technical terms of alchemy; *Wirkenskraft*, the energy of a living being; *Samen*, the primordial substances out of which things are formed. It seems likely that Goethe invented the term *Wirkenskraft*, while *Samen* is a well-known term in alchemy.

385 **tu'** An auxiliary verb here, and best not translated. — **kramen**, as a small shopkeeper retails small items from his stock to his customers, so Faust feels that he has been dealing out mere words to his students instead of real knowledge. Others take the verb *kramen* to mean 'rummage about in' and construe the line to refer to Faust's feeling of frustration when he finds himself manipulating mere words rather than fundamental facts in his studies.

386 **Mondenschein** Like *Sonnenschein*, a compound with the *-en* of the weak noun declension; now commonly *Mondschein*.

387 **zum letztenmal** Faust wishes that his vain search for truth might come to an end, and that he might join the spirits (394) who float about mountain caverns and meadows in the moonlight. In his imagination he does just that, only to be rudely awakened by the real things his eyes see about him (398).

389 **den ich . . . herangewacht** 'which, sleepless, I have watched approach.'

398–417 The target of this tirade is dead knowledge, the unorganized and meaningless heaping up of learning which generates no living, vital power. Faust's study has become his prison, into which the light of Nature's sun shines but dimly.

403 **Würme** An archaic plural form, now replaced by *Würmer*. Goethe uses both forms; see line 2176.

405 **ein angeraucht Papier** A collective singular: a mass of smoke-browned papers, bundles and rolls of manuscripts, lecture notes, and the like, piled and thrust into the shelves. The smoke came principally from the lamp in which much midnight oil has burned. Concerning the lack of adjective ending, see note to line 28, *lispelnd*.

408 This had been his father's study and laboratory. Faust's father had been an alchemist and a physician, and had possessed the equipment required for these arts (see 1034–1055). *Urväter* suggests that the contents of the room may have come in part from still earlier generations of Faust's family.

410 **du** Faust addresses himself.

415 The world of nature into which God put men, when He created them.

420 **Nostradamus** Latin form of the name of Michel de Nostredame (1503–1566), an astrologer and physician, a contemporary of the historical Dr. Faust (see Introduction, p. 18 f.). No such book as this from the hand of Nostradamus is known to us. Many of the features of the following conjurations have been traced to the ARCANA

COELESTIA (1749) of Emanuel von Swedenborg (1688–1772), the Swedish spiritualist, or *Geisterseher*.

424 The power to become a spiritualist, and thus to hold converse with the many spirits who people the regions around the earth, will be given him by revelation.

426 The intellectual explanation of the cabalistic symbols of his book does not bring him into communion with these spirits. According to Swedenborg's doctrine, such communication is accomplished through the senses, which are opened to the world of spirits by an act of divine or supernatural compassion.

SD 430 **Makrokosmus** The great world, the universe as a whole, contrasted with the microcosm, or man viewed as the epitome of the universe. The symbol of the macrocosm is to be thought of as a drawing which depicts the universe as a mechanism with intricately integrated parts, driven by a unitary force, moving harmoniously in a predestined course. Just which one of a number of such symbols Goethe may have had in mind is not known. None of the known symbols corresponds in detail to what follows here.

431 **Sinnen** Plural of *der Sinn*. Present-day German uses *Sinne*; see line 611.

433 **Nerv' und Adern** for *Nerven und Adern*. See note to line 238.

442 **der Weise** It is not likely that Goethe meant to refer to any single person here. In any event, no satisfactory identification of this sage or of the pretended quotation 443–446 has been made.

446 **Morgenrot** Not the 'dawn,' but "Aurora," in astrological literature a symbol for intuitive knowledge of the universe.

447–453 This vision is mystic and mysterious. Celestial powers ascend and descend on wings fragrant with blessing. They hand each other golden vessels and together they make harmonious sounds. Just what is supposed to be in these golden vessels is not revealed.

454 This symbol of the *Makrokosmus* is, after all, only a spectacle, not reality; it is not nature itself.

455–456 Faust hungers after truth as an infant hungers for nourishment. The metaphor is often compared with that of Isaiah 66.11. In seventeenth and eighteenth century books on natural science, "Nature" is often pictured as a statue of a goddess (Isis) with many breasts. See also lines 1892–1893.

458 **dahin** Equivalent to the relative, *wohin*.

SD 460 **Erdgeist** The *Welt- und Tatengenius*, the tutelary spirit ('genius') of the acts of this world. The Earth Spirit may be taken here as an alchemistic, spiritualistic notion, a spirit which can be caused to appear by the utterance of an appropriate incantation. We do not know precisely what Goethe intended the function of this Earth Spirit in the economy of the Faust play to be (see Introduction p. 90).

464 The effect of Faust's contemplation of the symbol of the Earth Spirit differs from the effect of his contemplation of the symbol of the macrocosm. The latter excited Faust's soul to climb to transcendent heights of the world of spirit, the former moves him to plunge actively into the affairs of the earth. The two images sym-

bolize respectively man's drive toward understanding and his drive toward action.

478   These 'new feelings' are referred to in lines 614–621.

SD 481   A magic formula accompanies the symbol of the Earth Spirit in the book. When this is spoken by the right person under the proper circumstances, the spirit will appear. — In the theater, as Goethe planned it, a much enlarged "transparency" (a lantern slide) of a bust of Jupiter was to be thrown upon the wall of Faust's study. This image was to have flaming eyes and flaming hair.

483   The capacity of men to attract spirits and of spirits to attract men is assumed in the spiritualistic philosophy of Paracelsus and his followers. Swedenborg describes this attraction as "suction," *attractio seu suctio.* — Each spirit is supposed to have its own sphere (484).

488   **mächtig** for *mächtiges;* see note on *lispelnd* line 28. Similarly: *erbärmlich* 489, *wechselnd* 506, *glühend* 507, *griechisch* 523.

490   **Übermenschen** The Earth Spirit recognizes in Faust an unusual human being, a man of great and sincere longing to become like God in knowledge, to become an equal of the spirits of the earth and of the universe. But Faust's terror at the sight of the apparition moves the Earth Spirit to scorn. *Übermensch* is here used as a term of irony.

494   **des** Older form of the genitive case of the relative pronoun, for which *dessen* is now usual.

495   **sich . . . drang** Now usually *sich . . . drängte.*

501–509   Here the Earth Spirit indicates what he is: the guardian spirit, or "genius of deeds" in which the deity is made manifest. Just as clothes condition the outward appearance of their wearer, so life conditions the outward appearance of God.

510   In these words Faust may be said to betray his lack of comprehension of the Earth Spirit, who does not flit about, but is rather indwelling in all phenomena, and who is not restlessly busy *about* things, but universally active *within* living Nature.

519   **Glück** The joy of communing with spirits. The line is somewhat out of harmony with Faust's disappointment expressed in lines 514–517.

521   **Schleicher** The reference is to slow rather than to surreptitious movements of Wagner. He is honest enough, but not inspired, as Faust sees him.

524   **Kunst** The art of reading aloud effectively. The course of study in the liberal arts of the medieval university comprised two divisions with a total of seven fields: (a) the *trivium,* comprising grammar, dialectic, rhetoric, and (b) the *quadrivium,* comprising arithmetic, geometry, music, and astronomy. The *trivium* is concerned with the proper and effective use of language, and Faust, as a university teacher, may be supposed to have been interested in it. The reading of ancient Greek tragedy is to be thought of as an exercise in dialectic or rhetoric, in which Wagner believes Faust to be engaged as a part of his studies.

527 **Komödiant** Not 'comedian' in our modern sense, but rather any theatrical player, including even 'tragedians.' The essential factor of the comparison here is that the actor speaks lines written by someone else as though they were his own thoughts. When Wagner suggests that actors could well teach preachers how to declaim, Faust's immediate response (528–529) is that this is true enough, if the preacher has nothing of his own to say, but merely mouths the words of others. Of course, Wagner is interested in declamation as a part of the art of persuasion (533), necessary to any man in the public eye.

530 **Museum** The name once generally given to a scholar's study. The word, which was borrowed from Greek by way of Latin, originally meant 'dedicated to or belonging to the Muses.'

531 **einen Feiertag** The accusative, meaning about what English 'on,' in the phrase 'on a holiday,' would mean; the genitive case would be more natural in such a sentence and would mean 'of' (a holiday), but the rime with *mag* 529 prevented the use of *eines Feiertags* or *feiertags*.

532 **von weiten** Now usually *von weitem*, with the dative singular of the adjective *weit*. Goethe's form *weiten* is an archaic uninflected adverbial form. This phrase occurs again in lines 3094 and 8160.

533 **durch Überredung leiten** Wagner is thinking only of dialectic, of the art of persuasion. — Johann Christoph Gottsched (1700–1766) did much to improve German practice in this field through his book AUSFÜHRLICHE REDEKUNST. Although most of Goethe's references to Gottsched are uncomplimentary, there is little doubt that the arguments of Gottsched's book were in his mind as he composed this dialogue between Wagner and Faust.

534 The *es* of **ihr's** and **werdet's** represents the means of persuasion which Wagner seeks to understand. The only source of really persuasive arguments is one's feelings, one's heart or soul; purely external arts are not likely to be effective.

536 **mit urkräftigem Behagen** 'with the delight which comes from the vigor of spontaneous utterance.'

538 **leimt zusammen** 'Compile,' as Germans say, "*mit Kleister und Schere*," by pasting together clippings from other people's (or indeed from one's own earlier) writings.

539 **andrer** Genitive plural of the pronoun: 'other people's.'

542 **Affen** Probably the same persons who were called *Laffen* 366. — The syntax of this clause and the dependent clause which follows it is incomplete. This phenomenon is called "anacoluthon," and there is a great deal of it in Goethe's FAUST. One can here supply the missing connection by inference from what follows. The meaning is: 'You can perhaps obtain the admiration of children and fools by the methods suggested, if your taste tends to such things.'

544 **Herz zu Herzen schaffen** 'work heart to heart' (with others).

546 **Allein** is ambiguous. It may mean either *nur* 'only,' or *doch* 'but.' We understand this line to mean: 'However, in spite of all you have just said, the success of the orator does depend upon his style of delivery.'

548 **Er** One of the three pronouns regularly used to address one person. Of these three the most intimate was *du*, next in degree of formality was *Er*, and most formal was *Ihr* with a plural verb. The shift from one form to another is often an effective device to indicate a change of mood. Faust has been speaking in general terms, as if to a group of Wagners, using the plural forms *ihr* 534, *euer* 541, and *euch* 543. *Er*, with the third person verb *Such'*, is correctly formal in address to Wagner but carries a hint of vexation, which seems to have disappeared at 568, where *du* is used. Only once (3524) in FAUST does Goethe use the modern "polite" form with *Sie* and a plural verb to a single person. — **redlichen Gewinn** This is contrasted with *Vortrag* 546. What is to be won by mere external qualities of style, as Wagner understands it, is contrasted with what is to be won by sheer honesty of utterance.

549 **schellenlaut** The cap and bells are the traditional insignia of the jester. Court fools in Shakespeare's times, and later, wore exotic costumes and weird caps, to which tiny jingling bells were attached.

550 **Verstand und rechter Sinn** are to be taken as the logical subject of *trägt*. The two are enough of a unit to justify the singular verb, though the singularity of the act of utterance rather than the nature of the subject probably determined the choice of the verb form.

552 **euch** Faust reverts to his general form of address, as if to a class or group of persons.

555 **Schnitzel kräuseln** A well-known pastime for the entertainment of children, the crimping and folding of odd and insignificant baubles out of pieces of paper. However, the ambiguous case-form of *der Menschheit* makes difficult a definitive interpretation of this line. Some take *der Menschheit* as genitive with *Schnitzel*, meaning 'Man's poorest shreds,' and thence understand the line to mean that such orators as Wagner admires serve up to their audiences mere baubles crimped from the remnants of humanity. We prefer to take *der Menschheit* as a dative, and to understand it to mean: 'curl paper baubles for humanity.' Such orators think their efforts should affect all men, but the curly gewgaws of their discourse are devoid of life and freshness. Paper flowers have no fragrance.

558 Wagner is a learned man. He quotes the first aphorism of the physician Hippokrates, which is universally known in its Latin form: *Ars longa, vita brevis,* or, as Longfellow put it: "Art is long, and time is fleeting."

It may be observed that Goethe here permits Wagner a good deal of *Schnitzel kräuseln* in the form of alliteration: *Kunst, kurz, kritisch, Kopf; Mittel, man, man, muß; lang, Leben; Bestreben, Busen, bang; erwerben, erreicht; steigt, sterben.* The rime scheme is artful: abbacddc.

560 **kritischen Bestreben** The labors of a philologist, the interpreter of ancient documents, whose first task is to establish by critical procedure the genuine or original text of the document and the history of its transmission. — Wagner here represents eighteenth century rationalism, the Age of Enlightenment, which was exceedingly proud of its own achievements (570–573). Judged by modern standards, the men of this day were very careless of historical ac-

curacy in their treatment of the past. Herder, and after him Goethe, were eloquent critics of this laxity, and sharply scornful of this pride.

561 **Kopf und Busen** The seats respectively of the intellect and the emotions. The preposition *um* is to be taken here in the local sense: 'around, in the neighborhood of.' The line thus means that Wagner feels both intellectual and emotional anxiety as he pursues his critical endeavors, not that he is worried about his head and his heart.

562 **Mittel** First, the knowledge of ancient languages (here Greek, Latin, and Hebrew), by means of which the sources become accessible to study; second, the books and manuscripts which contain these sources.

566 **Bronnen** A play on the meaning of *die Quelle,* 'source, fountain.' The word *Bronnen* belongs to a more elevated style of diction than the usual form *Brunnen.*

570 **Ergötzen** is all Wagner understands of *Erquickung* 568. *Ergötzen* is a receptive, passive experience, the effects of which soon pass away; *Erquickung* is a productive, activating experience, the effects of which are lasting.

576 The allusion is to the book with seven seals in the Revelation of John, Chapter 5.1 — Chapter 8.1.

577 Faust includes Wagner in his criticism of the historians of the *Aufklärung* (Age of Enlightenment), *die Herren* of 578.

583–585 **Haupt- und Staatsaktion** The "Tragedy of Blood," in which the rise and fall of princely tyrants was portrayed. This came to be a favorite theme for the puppet plays, many of which Goethe saw as a boy in Frankfurt. In these plays, as well as in many stage plays of that time, the actors were made to voice moralizing comments on human life, or "golden texts" conveying rules for the proper conduct of life.

587 **was** = *etwas.*

589 **das Kind** The truth as revealed by insight.

593 **gekreuzigt** Notably, Jesus Christ. — **verbrannt** The popular means of exterminating prophets or heretics in Faust's time. Some famous victims were: John Hus, burned at the stake in Constance 1415, Giordano Bruno, burned at the stake in Rome 1600. Girolamo Savonarola was strangled before his body was burned, in Rome 1498.

598 **als** 'since it is' Easter Sunday (*der erste Ostertag*). Easter Monday is *der zweite Ostertag.*

599 **ein' und andre** 'one or another.' An indefinite number, or 'this or that,' an indefinite kind of question.

605–606 This is one of the imperfect joints in the composition of the play. What follows was written many years, perhaps more than twenty years, after what precedes, and there are logical conflicts between the two conceptions of Faust's relationship to the Earth Spirit which cannot wholly be resolved. What is said after line 605 is in harmony with the *Prologue in Heaven.*

607 **Geisterfülle** A reference to the presence of the Earth Spirit and the other spirits (493) associated with it (520).

613 **sollte** Faust's feelings were determined by the will of another, the *Erdgeist:* 'I was made to . . .'

614–622 These lines describe in some detail the new feelings alluded to in lines 477–481.

615 **gedünkt** Supply *hatte.* — **Spiegel** This reference to truth reflected in a mirror suggests the *Monadology* of Leibnitz, who speaks of souls as living mirrors or images of the universe of creatures, while spirits are images of Divinity itself, capable of knowing the system of the universe. The pertinent passages of the *Monadology* are conveniently translated in Benjamin Rand's MODERN CLASSICAL PHILOSOPHERS, New York, 1908, p. 213.

616 **sein** Genitive of the reflexive, with *genoß*, instead of the now more usual accusative, *sich.*

617 **abgestreift** Supply *hatte;* 'and who had stripped off all earthly attributes' (*den Erdensohn*).

618 **Cherub** In the generally accepted hierarchy of spirits, the seraphim stand nearest to God. The cherubim are kept somewhat more remote from the deity, while mere angels are restricted to regions still farther from God. — The antecedent of **dessen** is *ich.*

619 A violent anthropomorphic metaphor, which sees Nature as a physiological organism through whose veins the free creative power of the deity flows: 'I, whose free strength presumptuously, with awed emotion, made bold to flow through nature's veins.'

622 **Donnerwort** See lines 512–513. The *du* of the following lines is the *Erdgeist.*

631 **jenem Drang** The impelling urge, exemplified in lines 455–459, to seek actively the source of all life.

632 **Taten : Leiden** The two terms are complementary, 'what we do, and what is done to us.'

634 **Geist** Antithesis to *Stoff.* Our most precious conceptions suffer the restrictions imposed by the fact that we belong to the world of matter. The more exalted the *Geist*, the more foreign and incompatible the *Stoff.*

635 **immer fremd und fremder** Involves two devices for emphasizing the increasing of the quality *fremd.* Either *immer fremder* or *fremder und fremder* would serve. The omission of the suffix *-er* from the first *fremder* is a trick often found in Goethe's poetry.

636–637 Our earth-bound, practical reason bids us accept and be content with that which is good. What appears to our imagination to be better, is likely, this practical reason tells us, to be a delusion. This doctrine is crystallized in sayings such as: "The grass is always greener in the other fellow's yard."

638 **Leben** Here in the pregnant sense: 'real life, life worth calling life,' which results only from exalted sentiments.

640 **sonst** 'formerly': prior to Faust's experience with the Earth Spirit.

643 **Glück auf Glück** 'one happiness after another.'

644 **die Sorge** This conception interested Goethe greatly and he has expressed himself about it in many places. Compare here Part II, lines 11 383 ff. — **gleich** = *sogleich.*

651 **nie : stets** The very fact that one might lose a thing which one greatly treasures, though one does not in fact lose it, causes one to worry about its possible loss and often even to imagine that one has lost it.

656 **Wand** Accusative. The *Fächer* are the shelves and compartments, or pigeonholes, into which are stuffed the *Urväter-Hausrat* of line 408 (the *Trödel* of line 658), which make the room seem oppressive to Faust.

666 **leicht : schwer** The day is contrasted with the dusk as light is contrasted with heavy. To a person who seeks the illumination of truth (the day), the obscurity of human understanding (dusk) is heavy, or difficult to bear. Goethe expressed the sentiments of lines 665–667 more directly in a *Gespräch* with the Jena Professor of History, Luden (1806), when he said of human life:

". . . daß es zu allen Zeiten und in allen Ländern miserabel gewesen ist: die Menschen haben sich stets geängstigt und geplagt, sie haben sich und anderen das bißchen Leben sauer gemacht und die Schönheit der Welt und die Süßigkeit des Daseins weder zu achten noch zu genießen vermocht. Nur wenigen ist es bequem und erfreulich geworden."

It should be observed that at least two recent editors [Max Hecker, in the *Welt-Goethe-Ausgabe* (1932 and 1937) and Ernst Beutler (1939 and 1950)] have replaced *leichten* by *lichten*. They believe *leichten* to have been a printer's error for *lichten*, overlooked by everyone, including Goethe.

669 To think here of primitive electrostatic machines, as some do, is to charge the poet with a not too serious anachronism. The historical Faust was a personage of the sixteenth century. The electrostatic machine, with rotating disc and comblike collectors, was invented by Otto von Guericke (1602–1686) in the mid-seventeenth century. Goethe owned a large machine of this type. It is more probable, however, that the instruments here referred to were mechanical, rather than electric, for 'wheel, cogs, cylinder, bridle' are all terms of mechanics.

670 **Tor** The gateway to the mysteries of nature.

672–673 **Geheimnisvoll** An attribute of *Natur* 673. Faust says that the only avenue to the secret mysteries of Nature is that of revelation to the intellect or soul of an inspired man; that no mere plodding, methodical research will lead to the solution of these mysteries. The veil suggests the veiled statue of Isis, the Egyptian goddess, which stood in the temple at Sais, in Egypt. Schiller used this goddess as a symbol of truth in his ballad, *Das verschleierte Bild zu Sais* (1795).

678 **Rolle** Of paper; see 405. Because the lamp has burned dimly and with much smoke all these years, the roll of papers is becoming covered with soot.

682–683 **ererbt hast : besitzen** Many things which are inherited remain apart from one's own active interests. One may have such things, but unless one actively works with them, they are not one's very own. This *hast* may be taken independently of *ererbt*, and read:

'what you have, having inherited it from your forebears . . .' The sentiment is analogous to that of lines 11 574–11 576.

684–685 The reference here is not to antique furnishings, but to the things of the intellect. The mind can use at a given moment only the things which it creates at that moment. One can make use of the wisdom of the past only when one has won this wisdom for oneself. Then one's mind will produce it when confronted by the need of the moment, and thus it will be useful. — **nützt, nützen** instead of *benützen*, 'to make good use of.'

690 **einzige** = *einzigartige* 'unique,' hence 'very precious, highly treasured.'

692 **Kunst** Equivalent to *Menschenkunst*.

698 **Flutstrom** The intense emotional excitement under which Faust has been: the *Streben* of 697, the *Drang* of 631.

701 Faust, holding in his hands a phial of deadly poison, is contemplating suicide. Therefore the 'new day' is the life beyond death, where he hopes to find new shores, new lands to explore.

702 **Feuerwagen** The time is at dawn on Easter Sunday, and what Faust sees is the radiance of the rising sun. This he thinks of as a fiery chariot, such as that which was driven between Elijah and Elisha (II Kings 2.11) or such as Milton describes (PARADISE LOST VI, 748 ff.):

"And the third sacred Morn began to shine,
Dawning through Heav'n: forth rushed with whirlwind sound
The Chariot of Paternal Deity,
Flashing thick flames . . ."

705 Faust thinks of death as the avenue to new spheres of activity, uninhibited by the presence of the earthly *Stoff* of which he complained at 635, and thus 'pure.'

710 **Vermesse** A weak imperative form instead of the normal *vermiß*. Forms of this kind are not unusual in Goethe's verse. — **Pforten** The gates of death (Job 38.17).

712–713 Suicide is spoken of as a deed which will prove the dignity of man to be sufficient to stand in the exalted presence of God. The demonstration will show the power of man to defy the divine commandment which forbids man to kill (Deuteronomy 5.17).

714 **Höhle** Perhaps the cavern into which the souls of the departed go, the place where fancy condemns itself to its own torment. — In Dante's *Inferno* the punishments meted out represent allegorically the sins themselves, in accordance with the Wisdom of Solomon 11.17: ". . . wherewithal a man sinneth, by the same also shall he be punished." Faust attributes such ideas to the imagination. He does not expect to arrive in any such place; rather he expects to enter new spheres of higher activity.

716 **Durchgang** The passageway from this life to the next. To deter men from voluntarily attempting to go through this passage, the fires of hell burn brightly about its entrance. The penalty for suicide, according to Christian belief, is hell-fire. — **hinzustreben** Depends upon *Hier ist es Zeit* 712.

718 **diesem Schritt** Suicide, the drinking of the death-potion. — **zu entschließen** Depends upon *Hier ist es Zeit* 712.

719 Faust believes that he will pass through his death into new spheres of pure activity (705). But he recognizes the risk he runs: he knows that he may destroy himself completely.

720 **Schale** A costly goblet on which various groups of figures or scenes are engraved or embossed (726).

723 **Freudenfeste** A dative singular rather than the plural form which one might expect, since many such festivities are remembered; see 729.

725 **zugebracht** Supply *hatte.* — *zubringen* is used in the technical sense of proposing a toast while holding out the cup toward the person in whose honor the toast is given. At these banquets the person who proposed the toast and who then drank from the goblet was obligated (727) first to explain one of the scenes thereon in verses (as Keats did in his *Ode on a Grecian Urn*), and having done so, to drink the cup at a single draught.

736 **Morgen** Of the new day (701), which is also Easter Sunday morning, whose sun is now rising.

SD 737 **Chor** In the following lines Faust, in his study, hears the Easter morning service in a nearby church. This service is in the form of a cantata of Easter antiphons, with three choruses: the angels, the women with spices, and the eleven disciples. The songs they sing, however, are Goethe's own, and not the traditional Easter songs of the church.

738 **dem Sterblichen** Mortal man, who was caught in the toils of deadly, insidious, hereditary sin, is offered a means of release therefrom in the resurrection of Christ.

742 **Summen** The low-pitched reverberations of the sounds of the bells (SD 737). The bright *Ton* is that of the choral song which the angels sing.

747 **einst** Reference is to the dawn of the first day of the week after the crucifixion of Christ. No chorus of angels is described in the gospel narratives of this scene; but an angel did say to Mary Magdalene and the women who were with her: "He is not here; for he is risen, even as he said." (Matthew 28.6).

748 **Gewißheit** 'making certain' (a new covenant). The resurrection of Christ was to be the guaranty of the covenant which Jesus made with his disciples (John 14.3): "And if I go and prepare a place for you, I come again and will receive you unto myself, that where I am, there ye may be also."

SD 749 **Chor der Weiber** These are the women who came to visit the sepulchre of Christ and found it empty: Matthew 28.1, Mark 16.1, Luke 24.10, John 20.1.

749 **Spezereien** See Mark 16.1: "And when the Sabbath was past Mary Magdalene, and Mary the mother of James, and Salome, brought spices that they might come and anoint him." John 19.39: "And there came also Nicodemus . . . bringing a mixture of myrrh and aloes, about a hundred pounds. So they took the body of

Jesus, and bound it in linen cloths with the spices, as the custom of the Jews is to bury."

758   **der Liebende**   Christ, who has withstood the test of mortal life. Human life is spoken of as a trial, a test, which is distressing but beneficial, since it provides training for the life after death, for those who pass the test.

763   **am Staube**   'earth-bound,' not *im Staube* 'in the dust.' 'Why do you seek me among the earth-bound? Proclaim your message among more easily persuaded (*weiche*) people.'

765   **Botschaft**   The news of the resurrection of Christ.

771   **sonst**   In earlier years, while the faith of his youth was still alive.

780   One rite of Spring, Easter Sunday, brings joy to many, as is shown in the next scene: *Vor dem Tor*. The 'free joy' is more fully set forth in lines 903–940.

787   **lebend Erhabene**   In apposition to *der Begrabene*: 'he who in this life was exalted.'

789   **Werdelust**   'joy of becoming,' becoming again something which he has not recently been: the Creator, one with the Creator.

790   **schaffender Freude**   Dative with *nah*. Christ is thought of as passing through a change from his mortal condition to that of the godhead, where he will have the joy of creating, and will be again one with God the Father and the Holy Ghost.

793   **die Seinen** = *uns* 794.

795–796   The apostles weep at the departure of Christ from their midst, even though this departure means happiness to Christ in Heaven.

799   **Banden**   The bonds of earthly cares and the fear of death.

801–805   The weak participles are used absolutely, as would be the case if Goethe had written: "*ihr tätig ihn preisenden*," 'you who praise him with your deeds, you who do all these things . . . to you the Master is near.' — In substance, the two great commandments of Christ to his disciples are here represented: (1) "This is my commandment, that ye love one another, even as I have loved you." John 15.12. (2) "Go ye into all the world and preach the gospel to the whole creation." Mark 16.15.

4. Vor dem Tor

Concerning the genesis of this scene there is some uncertainty, although it is clear that it got its present form in the period between 1797 and 1801. Concerning the function of the scene in the economy of the play there is no doubt. It forms the necessary contrast or relief in the long sequence of discourses in Faust's study (354–807), (1178–1529), (1530–2072). More importantly, it motivates the change in Faust's behavior. Held back from suicide by the return of memories of youthful religious fervor, Faust finds among the simple folk of the village the kind of credulity and faith of which he himself is no longer capable. His doubts and his yearning for truth amidst the error of the world return to him, and his mind goes back to thoughts of spirits, with whom he may ascend to fuller and brighter life. As he thinks of these spirits, a poodle appears, which presently reveals itself as indeed a spirit.

The scene is difficult theatrically. Proper effects can best be approximated by means of a revolving stage, since the action moves without stop from the crossroads just outside the town gate, to the nearby village, thence to an adjacent hill, and then back to town again. The characters are types rather than individuals, as the naming of the *personae loquentes* indicates; and much of the scene is operatic rather than dramatic. There are, finally, a few inconsistencies and contradictions which may be observed, but which are of no importance in the over-all understanding of the poem.

SD 808 **Vor dem Tor** The scene lies outside the wall of a small medieval fortified town.

809 **Jägerhaus** Goethe, as he wrote this scene, remembered pretty accurately a similar terrain near his native Frankfurt. But it is clear that he did not mean to permit his readers to recognize the place. This could be any university town in central Germany (Franconia or Thuringia). The forester's lodge was a favorite place to which to walk, because it usually was beautifully situated. One may think of benches and perhaps tables under the trees, where people might picnic.

810 **Mühle** Old mills were favorite dancing places because their floors were made very smooth by the constant dragging of sacks of grain and meal across them. The millers made capital of this asset by operating their properties as resorts on holidays.

811 **Wasserhof** Probably an inn beside a river.

814 **Burgdorf** Probably a village atop a hill; it seems to have an unsavory reputation.

818 **das Fell** We say in English: "I'll tan your hide!" German: "*Ich gerbe dir das Fell! Ich komme dir aufs Fell!*" 'I'll let you have it.' Hence this line means: 'Are you itching for a third tanning?' It appears that the Fourth Apprentice has already had a couple of unsuccessful encounters at *Burgdorf*.

SD 821 **Andre** The feminine form with natural gender, instead of *Andres (Dienstmädchen)* with grammatical gender. So also *Erste* instead of *Erstes*.

824 **Plan** A hardwood floor set up out of doors for dancing. This word, used in the sense of *Tanzplatz*, is Franconian, which indicates that the town is in Central Germany.

827 **sagt** Present tense. Lively interest in what one is reporting often induces a shift from a past to the present tense.

SD 828 **Schüler** Used instead of *Student*. This is a calculated adaptation of the language to the time of the action. When Goethe wrote his first FAUST scenes he used *Student*, but in 1790 he changed all these forms to *Schüler*, which is the older term and which is still used in translating *vagans scholasticus, der fahrende Schüler*.

832   **mir** The dative indicates the person to whose advantage, or at any rate in accordance with whose wish, the action is done. See note to line 320.

842   **geniert** 'restrained by the fear of committing a social error.' The First Student prefers the laxer social code of the servant girls to the stricter etiquette of the middle-class young ladies.

846   **Burgemeister** A colloquial form, used instead of *Bürgermeister*. Although the word now has the effect of an archaic expression, it was not so felt in Goethe's time, but was a well-known word in the spoken, colloquial language.

852   **guten, schönen** Weak adjective forms, as is usual in the vocative case after the pronoun.

856   **leiern** The beggar has some kind of a mechanical music box which he operates by turning a crank. Probably it is a hurdy-gurdy (*Drehleier*), which has the general shape of a lute and the strings of which are made to vibrate by a rotating rosined wheel. Or it may be a barrel-organ (*Leierkasten*).

862   In the sixteenth and seventeenth centuries the Turks repeatedly disturbed European peace of mind. In 1529 they laid unsuccessful siege to Vienna, and thoroughly frightened everyone in Europe. In 1570 they drove the Venetians out of Cyprus. But from this time on their power declined, although they again laid siege to Vienna in 1683. The probable parties to the war here alluded to are Russia and Turkey, which were remote enough from this little German town to permit comfortable discussions of tactics and of the latest news by people of limited, philistine insight.

863   **Völker** is probably to be taken in its older sense, 'armies.'

871   **bleib's** = *bleibe es* 'may it remain' (optative).

872   **Das junge Blut** Equivalent to *der junge Mensch*, who may be either male or female; or *Blut* may be collective, referring to several young persons. The reference here is to the young *Bürgermädchen* of 832, who have apparently remained at the crossroads, waiting for escorts.

874   The girls evidently show their distaste for the old woman, who reacts thereto by saying first that they need not be so proud, second that they must not be offended, and that she will say no more.

875   The Old Woman seems to be something of a procuress.

876   **Agathe** The name of one of the *Bürgermädchen*; it has an "upper-class" flavor.

878   **Sankt Andreas' Nacht** The night of November 29–30. Popular superstition had it that if on this night a girl recited the proper verses and looked in the right kind of a crystal ball, sword, or mirror, she would see her future husband. The assistance of a fortune teller was deemed helpful.

881   **soldatenhaft** 'in soldier's uniform.'

883   **will** This verb does not say anything about the willingness of the future lover to meet the lady. It personifies the chance which stubbornly refuses to bring the two lovers together. Translate: 'But it seems I'm never to find him.'

892   **werben** 'We let the trumpet summon us, both for the joy and for the destruction of a soldier's life.'

893–894 The soldiers sing of two conquests which seem to them similar. Both bring pleasure to the victor and ruin to the vanquished.

905 **Hoffnungsglück** A neologism, like *Hoffnungsdunst, Hoffnungs-fülle, Hoffnungsglut, Hoffnungsgrün;* as Jean Paul wrote: "Mancher Schnee ist geschmolzen, und wir sehen das Hoffnungsgrün des teuern Bodens." The word implies: 'The early plants of Spring, with their promise of happiness to come, are showing green in the valley.'

912 **Bildung und Streben** Things in nature are taking shape and beginning to grow.

914 **Revier** Since this is indeed a river-landscape, the word *Revier,* Italian *riviera,* perhaps still had its more literal meaning of 'a district along a river's bank.' Otherwise, the word may be taken to mean simply 'countryside.'

915 The sun, as the painter of this scene, is said to abhor white and to have used people in their bright Sunday clothes instead of flowers (which were not yet in bloom) to give color to the whole. — Goethe was an unusually acute observer of color and other phenomena of light. In the years from 1790 until his death these problems occupied him more continuously and more completely than any other of his interests. His FARBENLEHRE (1810) was a source of greater pride to Goethe than any of his poetic creations.

937 **schon** The strollers, Faust and Wagner, are approaching a country village some distance from the university city from which they have come.

952 **Linde** The village linden tree was the center of social functions in Spring and Summer.

954–955 **Juchhe, Juchheisa, Heisa** These are interjections, of long literary tradition, which connote noisy jubilation. They are roughly equivalent to our "Hurrah!" or "Whoopee!"

964 This line is part of the girl's remonstrance, spoken to the shepherd, as are also lines 973–975. — According to another view, these lines are spoken by the author of the song to the characters in it.

984 **Hochgelahrter** This form, rather than *Hochgelehrter,* is the form natural for the old peasant.

987 **bring' . . . zu** 'I present it to you with this toast.'

995 **doch** 'indeed, as everyone will testify.'

996 **bösen** The reference is to the evil days of the great plague.

998 In the Faust Chapbook, Faust's father is a peasant. Goethe makes him a physician, the predecessor and teacher of his son (as was the father of Paracelsus); see lines 676–677. The whole incident of the plague and Faust's part in it was introduced into the story by Goethe, to whom it was perhaps suggested by a somewhat similar incident reported in accounts of the life of Nostradamus, a contemporary of the sixteenth century historical Dr. Faustus.

1000 **gesetzt** Supply *hatte.*

1009–1010 Faust judiciously replies to the peasants in stereotyped language which they can understand. He realizes that his own philosophical doubts have no place in these circles.

SD 1010 **Wagnern** An inflected form of the name, no longer in use.

1014 **Vorteil** The advantage, as Wagner sees things, of being revered by these people.

1021 **das Venerabile** The Holy Host, the sacred wafer of the sacrament in its monstrance. When the Holy Host was carried through the streets, the people were expected to kneel as it was carried past them. This practice is still observed in those parts of Germany which are strongly Roman Catholic in their faith.

1034 **ein dunkler Ehrenmann** A man of honor who shunned the public eye, or an honest man of solitary habits.

1035 **Kreise** A property of a circle is that if one follows its line one arrives finally at the place from which one started. The obvious cyclical nature of some natural phenomena is here attributed to all life.

1037 **grillenhafter** Here 'capricious,' without steady, rational control.

1038 **Adepten** The technical title given to the most advanced practitioners of the art of alchemy.

1039 The alchemist's laboratory is called a kitchen because fire and heat (in ovens) were its basic means of effecting changes in materials. It was called 'black' because alchemy was a 'black art,' from the Latin name, *nigromantia*.

1042–1047 There seems to be no point in attempting to identify the technical jargon of these lines with passages in the works of alchemists, though this is to some extent possible. — The theory on which these men proceeded was that the elixir, the great panacea, would be produced, in the form of a bright-colored precipitate, by mixing two substances in a tepid medium and then treating the mixture in heated retorts. The fancy of the alchemists conceived this chemical union as a marriage, and the production of a new substance as a birth. So here the red suitor-lion (reddish mercuric oxide) is 'wed' with the white bride-lily (hydrochloric acid), and the offspring (the sublimate, a solid substance) is called the young queen, the sought-for panacea. Inasmuch as mercury was a favorite substance for these alchemistic experiments, it is easy to understand that many of the products of these black kitchens were indeed deadly poisons.

1053 **Gift** Here masculine, though usually it is neuter.

1056–1063 Wagner's attitude is by no means contemptible, as is sometimes alleged. But he is no genius, — just the hard-working, intelligent scholar, content to make progress in his field when he can, and not disposed to suicide if he can't. He will never reach the top bracket of his profession, though he does come close to it, as Faust's successor. He will not be in the lower brackets at all.

1064–1067 Faust's words are related to Wagner's argument but not a direct reply to it. He is back at the point of pessimism from which he started in line 354.

1073 The sun is earth's source of energy and as it moves along to shine upon other quarters of the earth it fosters new life and growth there. Faust wishes he might fly aloft (*Flügel*) to follow the sun, so that he might see more of the beauty of nature in the evening light. In his study (392–397) he had been moved by the sight of the moon to wish to fly aloft in its soft light. These impulses are symbols of a strong drive to escape, and suggest frustration.

1078 After the light of the setting sun leaves the valleys it still gilds the tops of the adjacent mountains. What follows is reported as if it were seen by Faust in his flight toward the light.

1079 **Silberbach** Some take this word as the name of some particular stream. Since Faust is imagining all mountain heights and every valley, it is more likely that this is a generic singular form, meaning every silvery brook. — From his great elevation Faust sees the brooks flowing into golden rivers far away.

1084 **Göttin** The sun, the symbol of the divine. For a moment it seems that the flight over the sea has deterred Faust. The sun appears about to sink from his sight after all.

1085 **der neue Trieb** The impulse to fly after the sun, to seek divine truth, regardless of the horizon, or sea, or land, always to fly towards the day, leaving night forever behind.

1100 **grillenhafte** Here equivalent to *wunderliche* 'strange, fantasy-filled.'

1110–1117 Mephistopheles described these two driving forces in lines 304–305. The one requires the satisfaction of the highest ambitions and desires of the individual among his fellows; the other, which Wagner is said not to know, requires the satisfaction of the highest aspirations of the human spirit for universal truth, transcending the world of the senses. Faust feels these two driving forces to be incompatible: the one clings with primitive passion to this earth, while the other seeks to rise to a new and richer life beyond this earth.

However, it must not be believed that Goethe here was thinking of anything so simple as a dichotomy between sensuous and intellectual impulses. There is, first of all, the basic fact that Faust has both of these driving forces, Wagner only one. It is not possible to say that Wagner has only sensuous impulses (944–948), and it will not do to identify his intellectual interests with the spiritual flights of Faust. Wagner says, in fact, that he has never had such an impulse (1101).

The drive which Faust has in common with Wagner is the thoroughly respectable, earth-centered drive which seeks the highest satisfactions and the greatest successes for the individual man among men (305).

The drive which Faust has and Wagner lacks is the drive toward universal knowledge and insight, the drive to be "like God." This drive rests upon Faust's capacity to imagine the indescribable, the reality behind phenomenal things and events, the achievement of the humanly impossible. It is the drive of the genius and it is frustrated by the earth-bound nature of man. It reveals itself in the desire to fly, which Faust several times feels: it puts the cup of poison into his hand (735), that he may shake off this burden of his earthly nature, and it is frustrated then by the symbol of the most celebrated case of *caritas, Menschenliebe.* See also the *Chorus mysticus* (lines 12 104–12 111) of Part II. In the present passage, this drive toward the humanly impossible is symbolized by the urge to fly *zu den Gefilden hoher Ahnen*, the abodes of great departed spirits, who have achieved some insight or knowledge denied to their more average fellow mortals.

1118   **Geister**   Not to be identified with the great departed spirits, the exalted forebears of line 1117. These are the intermediary, elemental spirits who intervene in the affairs of men with magic carpets, magic cloaks, and the like. The sphere beneath the cavity of the sky was believed to be ruled over by the moon. This sphere was looked upon as the abode of these elemental spirits. Faust reverts to his hope that such spirits might transport him out of this world into the higher realm to which he again aspires, or that they might at any rate provide him an escape from his present earthly limitations. — The Faust of the legend and Chapbook made frequent use of a magic cloak (1122).

1120   **steiget**   The two parts of this sentence do not fit the normal pattern. *gibt es* 'if there are,' would usually be followed by a third person appeal, 'then let them descend.' Instead, we have the direct, second person, imperative addressed to these spirits. This is another case of anacoluthon, used by Goethe to indicate that Faust's excitement is rising; see note to line 542.

1125   **nicht feil**   To be taken with both *um die köstlichsten Gewänder* and *um einen Königsmantel*. This is a trope called "apo koinou."

1126–1127   Wagner deprecates Faust's impulse to invoke these elemental spirits. Everyone, he reminds Faust, knows the evil spirits who on the slightest hint bring biting winds with sleet and hail from the north, drought from the east, scorching heat from the south, and deluging downpours from the west. In western and central Europe, wet weather is often accompanied by west winds, bringing moist air from the Atlantic; east winds, from the Eurasian landmass, often bring dry air. — Wagner has no insight into Faust's purpose in summoning a spirit to transport him to another world, but thinks only of the numerous evil spirits which plague mankind.

1140   Take *sich* with *stellen* and read: *sie stellen sich, als ob sie vom Himmel gesandt wären.*

1141   **englisch**   'like angels,' not 'like Englishmen.'

1147   **Saat und Stoppel**   A field in which the fresh young grain has begun to show green amidst the stubble of the former season's crop.

1150   **Pudel**   A French poodle, with dense curly hair tightly crimped.

1154   **Feuerstrudel**   Faust, who is sensitive to spirit manifestations, perceives the phosphorescence left in the air behind the circling poodle. In the path taken by the dog he sees a figure, drawn according to the rules of magic, intended to involve the two men.

1167   **pudelnärrisch**   *Pudel* is used as an intensive prefix in words like *pudelnackt* 'stark naked,' *pudelnaß*, 'wet as a drowned rat.' So here, with a Wagnerian pun, it may mean 'very droll, very amusing,' or simply 'as amusing as a trained poodle.'

1177   Wagner guesses that the poodle has been well trained by a group of students. The form *Skolar* here, and *Skolast* in line 1324, are medieval Latin forms characteristic of the learned speech of the sixteenth and seventeenth centuries.

5. STUDIERZIMMER (I)

This is the first of two scenes called *Studierzimmer*. The room is the *gotisches Zimmer* of the scene *Nacht* (354–807), and the action follows immediately after that of the scene *Vor dem Tor*.

The function of the scene is to introduce Mephistopheles into the life of Faust, so that the attempt to lead this servant of God (299) away from his spiritual heritage (324–329) may begin.

The germ of the idea which leads to the compact between Faust and Mephistopheles is put into Faust's mind in this scene (1414), but the actual agreement and with it the initial impulse to the dramatic action of this conflict between Faust and Mephistopheles is left to the second *Studierzimmer* scene.

1180–1181 The subject of *weckt* is *eine tiefe Nacht* (1179), but the connection between the two clauses is not expressed. The night is covering the fields and meadows; and, as it does so, it arouses the better soul of the human observer. — **mit ahnungsvollem, heil'gem Grauen** 'with awed and sacred dread.'

1184–1185 With the coming of night we see the transition from the active life of the preceding scene to the contemplative mood of Faust as he sits down in his study. His thoughts turn to the love of his fellow men and the love of God.

1187 Faust will discover later (1395) why the poodle is sniffing at the threshold.

1197 **sich . . . kennt** This is the heart of a philosopher. Socrates said: 'Know thyself!' and regarded this imperative as the sum of all philosophy.

1198–1201 The feeling is that of deeply religious contemplation and reflects the thought of Spinoza, for whom the highest good was the *amor intellectualis Dei*, man's knowledge and love of God: reason is the instrument, hope the support, and the love of God the motive power of philosophy. — **Vernunft** (1198) may be understood to mean the intellectual power of arriving at truth by reflection, without the assistance of empirical proof.

1200–1201 **Bächen . . . Quelle** There is a progression here. From the stream of life one longs to move toward the source, upstream into the feeder brooks, indeed into the very springs which feed these feeder brooks. The phrase *des Lebens Bächen* is not Biblical, but was widely used by the religious poets of Goethe's day. The phrase *des Lebens Quelle* is Biblical in origin. Both phrases were favorites with the mystic and pietist poets of the seventeenth and eighteenth centuries. Hence there is some reason to believe that the phrases here refer to the revelations of truth in the Bible.

1204 **will** This verb does not attribute volition to the animal noise which is its subject. *will nicht passen* means no more than 'just isn't suited to.'

1212 **der Strom** The feeling of satisfaction with which he has returned from his afternoon walk, and which welled up from his heart as a stream wells up from a spring. This metaphor continues that of *des Lebens Bächen, des Lebens Quelle* in lines 1200–1201.

1215 **dieser Mangel** The lack of the spontaneous flow of the feeling of satisfaction. This can be made up for by turning to divine revelation as this is found in the Bible.

1220 **Grundtext** The theologian turns to the Greek text of the New Testament. What troubles Faust is the meaning of "logos" in the first verse of the first chapter of the Gospel of John.

1237 **Tat** Faust's reasoning has brought him back to the position of the Old Testament, where we read (Genesis 1.1): "In the beginning God *created* the heavens and the earth."

1238 The dog, who has shown signs of distress each time God was mentioned or implied, is thrown into paroxysms of protest by this translation of the Biblical text.

1247 'What's this I see?'

1257 **halbe** Not a full-fledged demon, direct from hell, but some sort of witch or wizard or semi-infernal creature.

1258 **Salomonis Schlüssel** The *Clavicula Salomonis*, a conjurer's book of spells and incantations for the holding, evoking, or exorcising of spirits. This book was widely circulated in the sixteenth, seventeenth, and eighteenth centuries.

SD 1259 **Geister** Subordinate spirits, rallying to the aid of their captive master. They do not enter the study, lest they be trapped as he has been. At line 1447 they sing the song which lulls Faust to sleep and allows Mephistopheles to depart. Faust appears not to hear what these spirits say (1259–1270).

1262 **Höllenluchs** = Mephistopheles. There is irony in this designation: the lynx is the symbol of keenness of vision; yet Mephistopheles is trapped because he failed to see clearly the form of a pentagram on the threshold.

1272 **Spruch der Viere** Against the four spirits of the four elements of Paracelsus, designed to force each to appear in its proper form, revealing its true nature. Faust now reads, or recites, from the conjurer's book (1258).

1273–1276 **Salamander** Fire, because this animal is supposed not to be harmed by fire. It is conjured to glow, thus revealing its nature. — **Undene** Water, a generic name for water nymphs (also *Undinen* 10 712). This spirit is to show its true nature by swimming. — **Sylphe** Air, since the sylphs, according to Paracelsus, dwell in the air, either invisible to man, or glowing like meteors. This one is bidden to vanish (into the air). — **Kobold** Earth. The earth spirits are either kindly or inimical to man, as the mood strikes them. They are *Kobolde, Wichtelmännchen, Pygmäen, Gnomen,* or *Incubi*. One of the latter is called upon in line 1290. This one is told to show its true nature by working (1276).

1291 **Tritt hervor** The imperative is addressed to whichever one of the four spirits may be hiding within the poodle.

1300 **Zeichen** The symbol of Christ. This is a conjurer's diagram in Faust's book, perhaps a picture of a crucifix, perhaps a monogram of the letters J.N.R.J. representing the sign set by Pilate at the head of Christ's cross (John 19.19). These initials come from the Latin text: *Jesus Nazarenus Rex Judaeorum* 'Jesus of Nazareth, King of the Jews.'

1302 **die schwarzen Scharen** The black hosts of Hell.

1305 **ihn** By synecdoche, the name of Christ, who is spoken of as being never born, never described, omnipresent, and wickedly transfixed (see John 19.34).

1319 **Licht** A symbol of the Trinity, possibly an equilateral triangle with the flaming eye of God in the center. — **dreimal glühend** Because it derives light from a threefold source, the Trinity.

1326 **machen** 'made.' Since this verb is here treated as an auxiliary, synonymous with *lassen*, it is put in the infinitive form, as *lassen* would be.

1328 An allusion to line 1226.

1330 **Tiefe** Accusative, the goal which Faust's spirit strives to reach. — This is an ironical reference to Faust's efforts to attain to an understanding of the nature of things by turning away from the world of appearance (*Schein*).

1331 **Herrn** Plural; spirits, who may and sometimes do assume human form as this one has done.

1334 **Fliegengott** This is a translation of "Beelzebub." — **Verderber** is a translation of Greek "Apollyon," Hebrew "Abaddon," of Revelation 9.11. In Exodus 12.23 the Destroyer is spoken of as a spirit whom Jehovah controls. Probably the same spirit is referred to in Job 15.21 and I Corinthians 10.10. — **Lügner** John 8.44 refers to the Devil as a liar. — There is no evidence to show just what Goethe intended by the two words *Verderber* and *Lügner*. The most likely guess is that he used the two words as designations of evil spirits.

1335–1378 Mephistopheles' problem now is to work his way into the good graces of Faust. He endeavors to awaken Faust's interest in dealing with him, first by posing riddles as to his identity. He begins by describing himself (1335–1336) as a devil in the sense of the optimistic philosophy, let us say, of Leibnitz. Then he describes himself (1338) as the spirit of negation in the sense of an active pessimism. Then he depicts himself (1349–1354) as the son of Chaos and the opponent of order, in the sense of a dualistic philosophy. Finally, by way of reducing himself to Faust's level, and even exciting some measure of sympathy in the heart of one also foiled and frustrated, Mephistopheles (1362–1378) tells of the futility of his efforts.

The first proposition (1335–1336) implies that there are two forces: the force of evil, of which Mephistopheles says he is a part, and the opposition to this force, presumably the force of good. It further implies that out of the conflict between these two forces only good results. This is not exactly the same thing as was said in lines 342–343, but both statements are compatible with Leibnitz' optimistic doctrine that ours is the best possible world.

1338 In the Prologue in Heaven, God refers to Mephistopheles as *one* of the spirits of negation (338), the crafty knave. Here, Mephistopheles says he is *the* spirit of negation. Here the two principles of good and evil are thought of as the force of affirmation and the force of negation, and these are then identified with creation and destruction, respectively. The pessimistic judgment expressed by Mephistopheles is designed to appeal to the pessimistic Faust. Mephistopheles is always primarily concerned with the effect of his words on others, never with the truth as truth.

1347 **Wenn** = *während*, or perhaps *wenn auch* 'although.' — **die kleine Narrenwelt** Mephistopheles parodies the phrase: *Der Mensch — die kleine Welt*, in which the view is expressed that each man's spirit is a microcosm, a living mirror of the macrocosm, or universe. This microcosm, or *kleine Welt*, as Mephistopheles sees it, is a 'silly microcosm.'

1350–1358 The doctrine that a dark chaos was the source, by separation, of fire, and hence of light, was taught by Paracelsus. — The argument of these lines is that light is effective only as a property of bodies and hence has no more permanence than they.

Mephistopheles says that he is a part of the force of darkness and, as such, engaged in a conflict with the force of light. This force of light, however, is able to operate only through 'bodies.' Mephistopheles hopes that, when all bodies are destroyed, chaos will be restored (1358).

1359–1361 Faust scorns Mephistopheles' duties of allegiance to the cause of destruction — *würd'gen* is to be taken as ironical. He taunts this evil spirit with the derogatory slur that Mephistopheles can do nothing against the created universe on a major scale, or wholesale, and is therefore obliged to operate only on the individual item — at retail, so to speak — by attacking a single *Körper*. Mephistopheles concedes (1362–1378) that his job seems hopeless at times.

1364 **Etwas** The earth, a 'something' created by the force of affirmation. The *Nichts*, to which this *Etwas* is opposed, is Chaos, — the non-corporeal, non-organic, formless state in which no thing can exist. — **diese plumpe Welt** suggests woodcuts of the seventeenth century, in which the terrestrial globe is represented as a being with pudgy little legs, and in which reference is made to the "crooked and tortuous ways of the world."

1369 **Zeug** Mephistopheles refers to the amazing pertinacity of living species, with their fantastic capacities for the reproduction of their kind.

1374–1378 In the philosophy of Paracelsus there were four elements (see line 1272), one of which, fire, Mephistopheles claims as his own. The four elements, fire, water, air, and earth, were recognized by ancient philosophers (Empedocles, Aristotle) long before Paracelsus. — Mephistopheles claims fire as his own element, since it is the one which destroys all forms of organic life. Yet no life can exist without some heat.

1376 The four qualities of the four elements: air = warmth + moistness; water = cold + moistness; fire = warmth + dryness; earth = cold + dryness.

1381 **kalte Teufelsfaust** 'Cold,' because it is the fist of death, of negation. This is a good example of the aesthetic value of the adjective. Despite Mephistopheles' immediately foregoing assertion that fire is his peculiar element, the poet's choice of attribute is 'cold' rather than 'hot,' because of the association of 'cold' with death, and of 'warm' or 'hot' with life.

1383 **suche** Optative, not imperative. — Faust is not interested in Mephistopheles' account of his failures. If he is to listen to this spirit, it will have to offer something more than pessimistic talk.

1386 At this point we have another of the joints in the composition of the poem. Mephistopheles makes the unmotivated assumption that there will be other interviews between himself and Faust, and the poet permits him to excuse himself now without telling us why he does so. To be sure, we can find a reason in the situation: It is clear that Mephistopheles has maneuvered Faust into a positive, superior frame of mind (1379–1384) and that it would be disadvantageous to try to deal further with him while he is in this mood. In the Chapbook, the contract between Faust and Mephistopheles is signed after the third "disputation" between the two parties.

1395 **Drudenfuß** The five-pointed star was a symbol credited with the power to keep out evil spirits. This one had failed to keep out Mephistopheles, because it had been imperfectly drawn. — The figure occurs on old Greek coins, was used as a symbol of perfection, or of the universe, by the Pythagoreans and others.

1406 **hereingesprungen** Supply *ist.* See 1187, where the poodle becomes aware of his predicament after he has entered.

1418 **das** The business of arranging a compact between a man and the Devil is not a simple business and requires discussion.

1439 **Geister** These spirits begin to sing now at their master's command. Faust sinks into a trance during which he will see what the spirits suggest in their song.

1441 **leeres** Devoid of tangible, physical effect upon the spectator. These images, which are *nicht leer,* not only appeal to the imagination, they also stimulate the senses, the sense of smell, the sense of taste, so that in the end Faust is enraptured.

1448 **Wölbungen** In the imagination of the sleeping Faust the Gothic arches of the walls and ceiling of the study are to melt away, revealing the sky — at first clouded, then clearing to reveal the stars and the entrancing spectacle of angels hovering and bending over the sleeper as he floats past. The singing spirits give orders (imperative *schwindet*) to the Gothic walls, and more politely request, even suggest, the changes in the heavenly scene (optative *schaue,* potential *wären zerronnen*). Thereafter they narrate (present indicative).

1461 **Neigung** With longing the sleeper follows the angels through the sky, and the fluttering ribbons of angelic robes spread out over the landscape as he floats past the rows of bowers, each with its pair of embracing lovers. These bowers are covered with heavily laden vines, the grapes of which fall into wine presses, from which brooks of bubbling wine, trickling through beds of jewels, flow into the valley, where they become lakes at the feet of the hills.

1482–1483 **Genügen grünender Hügel** A violent metaphor which has been variously understood, according to the meaning attributed to *Genügen.* Some take this to mean 'sufficiency,' others take it to mean 'satisfaction.' Probably the orthodox solution is that which understands *Genügen* to refer to the feelings of the observer and takes the whole to mean: 'at the feet of pleasant hills turning green with spring.' Others take *Genügen* to be the satisfaction of the hills which are washed by the waves of these lakes of wine: 'spread themselves into lakes to the quiet satisfaction of the newly green hills.'

1484 **das Geflügel** The birds sip this flowing wine and fly jubilantly toward the sun and the bright isles of the blest, toward which the eyes of the dreamer turn. There he hears people far away joyously shouting and dancing all over the rustic scene. Some even hover in the air, as the scene fades into the more remote distance of those stars which provide them life, love, and protection, and the dreamer drops into a deeper slumber.

1516 Mephistopheles calls himself Lord of rats and mice and various other vermin; see also lines 6592 ff. The Devil is associated with pestiferous, ugly, or uncanny animals, particularly with those of nocturnal habits.

1520 The pentagram which guards the threshold has to be opened by cutting through one of the points on the room side of the figure. By applying oil to the appropriate portion of the lines Mephistopheles induces the rat to gnaw the figure so that a break will release him. The most likely way in which Mephistopheles could get the oil he uses is to dip his finger into the oil of Faust's study lamp.

1525 **Fauste** A vocative, and in the Latin form, as is appropriate in university conversations and as is usual in the chapbook versions of the story.

1526 **abermals** The first disappointment was his encounter with the Earth Spirit.

1527 **der geisterreiche Drang** The throng of spirits which he has just seen in the vision induced by the song.

1528 **daß** 'so that,' in such a way that he must conclude that all this has been a dream and that nothing has really happened except that the poodle has escaped from his study.

6. STUDIERZIMMER (II)

The latter part of this scene (from line 1770 onward) was incorporated into the FRAGMENT of 1790. The first part was written around 1800, and first printed in 1808. Old and new materials have been fused into the present form of the scene and the process has left a number of inconsistencies.

The primary reason for separating this scene from the preceding scene in the study is the fact that for some time Goethe planned to write a *Disputation*, or Ph.D. Examination scene, in which Faust and Mephistopheles were to match wits. It was to have come between the two *Studierzimmer* scenes and is alluded to indirectly in line 1712. In the first Study scene Mephistopheles appears as a wandering scholar (1324); here he appears as a young nobleman.

The departure of Mephistopheles from the preceding scene has only the inner motivation — too subtle for theatrical purposes — that Mephistopheles has maneuvered Faust into a proud, positive frame of mind and can make no further progress in his negotiations with him until this attitude is destroyed. The dramatic reason for separating the two *Studierzimmer* scenes, as the text now stands, is therefore the need to throw Faust into a state of depression.

There is no indication of the length of time which may be supposed to have elapsed between Mephistopheles' escape from the study (1525) and his return at line 1530. His first words to Faust (1533–1543) seem to imply intervening meetings between the two with some talk of a "deal" or agreement and some talk about what 'life,' as Mephistopheles sees it, might do for Faust. Yet this is only an implication, not a clearly defined fact of motivation.

The discussion between Mephistopheles and the new student is one of the oldest parts of the Faust play. Yet it is episodic and without external relation to the action of the play. It is an interlude of acid satire directed at the less likable aspects of university life in Goethe's own day. It is internally related to the Faust problem insofar as the student is analogous to Faust in his natural make-up, a potential Faust about to begin his career.

The major dramatic function of the second *Studierzimmer* scene is to bring about the conclusion of the pact between Faust and Mephistopheles, which sets the terms of this contest for the soul of Faust and establishes the framework of motives for the subsequent adventures of the two great adversaries.

1530 **wieder** Faust is in a somewhat petulant mood as a result of having been disturbed by someone in some way or ways not indicated. Usually he is thought of as sitting at his desk, deep in thought.

1531 Mephistopheles makes Faust repeat his invitation to come in. He is pleased to find Faust not unwilling to join in his hocus-pocus.

1534 **Grillen** 'cares, melancholy thoughts.' Mephistopheles knows that Faust is depressed. How he knows this can be guessed from lines 1581–1582, but not answered on the basis of the current text. Probably he refers to Faust's whole way of life as 'melancholy.' At any rate his first problem as he sees it is to get Faust out of the environment of his discontent. See Introduction pp. 74–75.

1535 **Junker** A cavalier in court dress of Spain. This was a favorite form of incarnation attributed to Satan. In this guise he had ready entrée into the best social circles.

1541 Faust is urged to put aside his professor's garb and with it his professor's way of life and to take on the raiment and the way of life of a gay cavalier.

1549 **Entbehren** There are two points of view open to an individual who finds the fulfilment of a wish impossible. He may revolt against the forces which, as he sees it, deprive him of this thing he desires; or he may renounce the desire. — Faust at this point is on the verge of revolt.

1566 The God within him, who rules his entire being, is unable to change anything outside him. His God is an entirely subjective experience.

1573 **er** = *der Tod.*

1577 **des hohen Geistes** Of the Earth Spirit, lines 482–513.

1580 A direct reference to the events described in lines 737–784.

1583–1587 **Wenn . . . so** 'If . . . still.' The meaning is, substantially: 'Granted that I was deluded, still I curse . . .' — **Gewühle** The tumult of his emotions (354–736).

1584 The form *süß* is ambiguous. Either this is an adjective with the omission of case ending from the first of two or more correlative attributes = *ein süßer, bekannter Ton,* or the form is an adverb, limiting *bekannter.* Either this is a 'sweet (and) well-known tone' or it is a 'sweetly well-known tone.' One can decide such questions only on the basis of the relative appropriateness of the two possible meanings. The reference here is to the Easter music of lines 737–807.

1587–1606 The following tirade is well organized. Faust curses and reviles the physical body which limits the soul, man's overweening pride of intellect, the blinding effect of phenomena which obscure ideas, the illusory hopes of fame, the transitory world of possessions with which man surrounds himself, the solace of wine, the ecstasy of love, and, finally, the qualities which make this life possible to live: hope, faith, and patience to endure. As he reaches the conclusion of this bitter denunciation of things as they are, Faust has reached the pinnacle of his confusion.

1588 **Lock- und Gaukelwerk** Hendiadys for *lockendes Gaukelwerk* 'alluring jugglery.' Similarly, 1590 *Blend- und Schmeichelkräften* for *blendenden Schmeichelkräften* 'deluding powers of flattering persuasion.'

1589 Among the religious poets of the seventeenth and eighteenth centuries, *Trauerhöhle* was a standard metaphor for "body," just as *Jammertal* and *Tränental* were metaphors for "earth." This, therefore, is the body in which Faust's soul is confined.

1591 **Verflucht** Supply *sei.* — **voraus** 'first and foremost.' Man's confidence in the power of the intellect to solve the world's problems appears to Faust to be the first source of evil.

1593 The world of phenomena which occupies our senses blinds us to the reality which transcends that world.

1607 These spirits do two things: (1) they lament the fact that Faust by his renunciation of patience, faith, and hope has destroyed beyond repair the foundations upon which the beauty of this world once rested; (2) they exhort Faust to build with a clear head a more stately world in his own heart, a new world in which he can start on a new course in life. That is, these spirits appeal to Faust's will. Mephistopheles 1627–1630 claims that these voices are those of his own minions, presumably the same spirits who sang Faust to sleep (1447–1505). Some critics believe Mephistopheles; others think that, with his usual crafty guile, he is turning to his own uses the utterances of spirits which might represent Faust's guardian genius, or his better self. The poet's intention is by no means clear.

1616 **die Schöne** = *die Schönheit.* See note to line 345.

1617 These spirits speak of Faust as a 'demigod' (1612), and as a 'mighty one among the sons of earth.' This appears to mark them as earth-spirits, in a friendly rather than an inimical mood.

1619 **prächtiger** Comparative adverb with *baue,* or a predicate adjective correlative with *sie.*

1633 **Säfte** 'humors,' vital juices. — In medieval physiology four fluids were conceived as entering into the constitution of the body and determining by their relative proportions a person's health and temperament. Abundance of blood conduced to sanguine temperament, predominance of phlegm made a man phlegmatic, too much yellow bile made a man choleric, too much black bile made him melancholy.

1635–1638 Faust is urged to put aside his solitary grief and to seek the company of other men. Even the least distinguished of such associations will, he is assured, restore his sense of human values. Mephistopheles' use of *spielen* is an allusion to the "joy of grief," which was a topic of interest in Goethe's Weimar. Literary reflexes of the idea can be seen in Karl Philipp Moritz' novel ANTON REISER (1785 ff.). — The vulture (1636) is an allusion to the story of Prometheus.

1641 Mephistopheles' description of himself here as a lesser familiar spirit, rather than as Satan himself, accords with the tradition of the chapbook Faust story rather than with Goethe's later conception of his character.

1652 **um Gottes willen** 'as a matter of charity, without recompense.' The choice of this form of expression produces a secondary antithesis, or an antithetical overtone, because of the word *Teufel* in 1651.

1656–1659 The contrast between this world and the next is in the Christian tradition. Faust immediately says that the life after death (1660) does not interest him. His joys arise in *this* life, his sufferings are lighted by the sun he knows. Only if this world were to be destroyed would he perhaps be interested in another. This does not imply skepticism concerning the reality of the world beyond.

1665 **kann** 'If I find it possible sometime to give up these joys and sufferings, then . . .'

1669 **jenen Sphären** This is *das Drüben* of 1660. Faust has said that only if this world is destroyed or if sometime he finds it possible to renounce this world will he concern himself about another. He does not now wish to listen to a discussion of the putative conditions in that other world, whether it knows emotions or differences of degree or rank, whether it contains a Heaven and a Hell.

1672 **in diesen Tagen** Probably implies 'right away,' 'in the immediate future'; possibly it implies 'in the days you live on earth.'

1677 **gefaßt** 'understood.' *fassen* echoes *erfassen* of 325. What the Lord called (328) 'the obscure striving of a good man,' Faust calls 'the lofty striving of a human spirit.'

Notes

1678 Food which does not satisfy, red gold which melts away like quicksilver, a game one cannot win, love which is not true, honor which is
not lasting — Faust concedes (*doch* = 'indeed') that Mephistopheles
can produce these things. But they cannot afford satisfaction to a
striving human spirit. They are as unsatisfactory as fruit which
rots before it can be picked or as trees which daily burst into leaf,
but never get beyond that stage. After Faust has enjoyed some
of the things Mephistopheles can provide, he repeats with greater
definiteness the thought which underlies these lines (3240–3246):
the conviction that nothing perfect is accessible to man. Hence
nothing which Mephistopheles could give him would satisfy Faust's
striving for the perfect realization of his powers.

1688 Mephistopheles, as Faust has said, fails to understand that anyone
could regard these sensual satisfactions with contempt. He knows
that their enjoyment is exhausting and he seeks to suggest, as the
best thing he can offer, the luxurious indolent repose of idle 'retirement' as an ultimate delight. This is the one thing Faust is sure
he will never wish to enjoy.

1698 **die Wette** Faust wagers his life that Mephistopheles cannot persuade him to give up his striving. One of the essential qualities
of the human spirit is its drive to higher things, its aspiration toward
perfection. Faust knows that if this drive is lost, all is lost. Faust's
wager is by no means identical with the bargain proposed by Mephistopheles (1656–1659), although if Faust loses, he expects to become
Mephistopheles' servant (1710–1711). — When Faust says "Die
Wette biet' ich . . .," he holds out his right hand toward Mephistopheles, who, with the interjection "Topp!" claps his own right hand
into that of Faust. Thereupon Faust claps his left hand upon the
two right hands thus joined, with the words: "Und Schlag auf
Schlag!" which represent an unusually strong confirmation of the
bargain thus sealed.

1699 The agreement here made is a contract pursuant to the wager.
Mephistopheles is bound to serve Faust until such time as Faust
concedes his wager to be lost. If that time comes, then Faust is
bound to be the captive of Mephistopheles. The form of Faust's
admission of defeat is to be the expression of satisfaction with a
condition which he would wish to have continue (see line 11 582).
It is quite possible for Faust to enjoy the services of Mephistopheles
without surrendering to him.

1705 **Uhr . . . Zeiger** Various explanations of the falling of the pointer
have been suggested. If the *Zeiger* is part of the *Uhr* here mentioned, it would seem likely that the clock in question was a water
clock. These clocks had a single pointer which rose along a scale,
usually for a period of twenty-four hours. At the end of this rise,
the mechanism dropped the hand to the bottom of the scale and the
rise began again. If at any time the lifting pressure of the water in
the clock failed, the pointer at once fell back to zero.

1707 **wir** Mephistopheles, the party of the first part in the contract.

1710 **wie ich beharre** 'as I am living now,' or 'no matter how persistently
I strive,' or 'as soon as I cease to strive.' The interpretation hinges
on the meaning assigned to *beharre:* 'persist' or 'stagnate.' *beharren*
usually means 'to persist.' The meaning 'to stagnate,' although

not documented elsewhere, is required for the usual interpretation of this passage. — In the word *Knecht* some critics see an ironical echo of line 299.

1712 **Doktorschmaus** The doctoral banquet is the normal sequel to the successful passing of the final oral examination for the doctor's degree. Mephistopheles knows somehow (1582) that one is scheduled for this evening. — We know that Goethe once planned to include a doctoral examination scene in his FAUST. He subsequently gave up that idea, and aside from this reference we have only a draft of his plans plus a small fragment of the planned disputation.

1714 **um Lebens oder Sterbens willen** 'just in case something should happen to you.' A formula used to ask for a written contract without the discourteous implication that the other person's oral word alone was not enough.

1718 The contract entered into is to be binding throughout Faust's entire life. He regards his oral promise as adequate. But the thought of this kind of permanence suggests the basic impermanence of a world in which all things flow (Heraclitus); see lines 1720–1721.

1722–1725 **Wahn** The curious notion of fidelity to one's pledged word. This fidelity is the basis of all social peace and it is a source of great satisfaction to know that one has always kept faith.

1726–1729 These lines reflect the experience that a written and sealed contract very often is the cause of much distress, since the written word loses the benefit of the full level of presupposition which goes with the spoken word. It becomes rigid, or dead, and thus the instrument of parchment, with wax seal, rather than the will of the contracting parties, dominates the execution of the provisions set down.

1731 Faust has no fear of such a contract. He offers a document, engraved with a stylus in bronze, cut with a chisel in marble, or inscribed with a pen upon parchment or paper. He seems to be just a bit violent in his contempt as he makes this offer; see Mephistopheles' reaction, lines 1734–1735.

1737 **Blut** The use of blood of contracting parties to bind a serious bargain is attested as far back as records go. This feature is a part of the Faust story in all the forms known to us before Goethe.

1739 **Fratze** 'If this will satisfy you completely, then I will not balk at such tomfoolery.' Faust, a scholar and a man of reason, regards this use of blood to bind a contract as nonsense. Mephistopheles insists upon the use of blood, because he knows the strength of popular belief in the efficacy of a signature in blood, and he expects this popular superstition to help constrain Faust to abide by the terms of his contract. — Goethe here follows the tradition of the Faustbuch.

1741 **Bündnis** Faust has bound himself (1701) to surrender to Mephistopheles if he ever reaches the point where he is willing to cease striving because he has become satisfied. Evidently he could not resist Mephistopheles' authority, if he ever became subject to it by the terms of this contract. When he accepts Faust's wager (1698), Mephistopheles binds himself to serve Faust (1704) until he can persuade Faust to give up his striving. The contract is not that proposed by Mephistopheles in lines 1656–1659.

1744 Here there is an abrupt transition from the Faust whose character Goethe depicts in the completed poem to the Faust of the old legend and of the URFAUST. Faust says here that his aspiration to associate with the major world-spirits overreached his capacities (compare line 500) and that he is at best capable of converse only with lesser spirits, with whom Mephistopheles has identified himself (1641). The Earth Spirit had scorned him (512–513): he confronts a blank wall in his quest for nature's secrets. He has lost the directing line for his thinking and is sick of his studies.

1750 The difference between Faust's action here and his decision to drink the poison cup (735–736) so that he might escape to another sphere of activity can be attributed to the fact that Faust now has at his disposal the arts of Mephistopheles. Since in the past his contemplative life has brought him no adequate reward, he will now turn to the active life. From the uses of reason he will turn to the uses of the senses. He invites Mephistopheles to produce his full program of miracles, in their inscrutable magic form. He will not try to penetrate their outward guise to learn their inner reality, but will allow them free play on his senses. The point at which the older conception of Faust fuses with the newer and final conception is the *purpose* which is attributed to this attitude of Faust. Originally, Faust's major purpose was escape. Now, he desires most of all to experience to the full the joys and sorrows of the human heart.

1758 **miteinander wechseln, wie es kann** There are two problems here: what is the antecedent of *es;* what dependent infinitive is to be supplied with *kann?* We should expect either (1) *Da mögen denn Schmerz und Genuß, Gelingen und Verdruß miteinander wechseln, wie sie können;* or (2) *Da mag denn Schmerz und Genuß, Gelingen und Verdruß eins mit dem andern wechseln, wie es kann.*

Probably what is actually in the text is to be regarded as a telescoping of these two constructions. In that case, the implied dependent infinitive is *wechseln:* 'Let the pleasant and the painful alternate to the limits of the possible' or 'as may well be possible.' — If *es* refers to *das Wechseln* (suggested in the verb *wechseln*), then the missing infinitive should be something like *geschehen, vorkommen, sein.* — In either case, we should expect *wie es nur kann* 'as much as it can' or *wie es wohl kann* 'as it quite possibly may.' Perhaps the occurrence of *nur* in line 1759 led Goethe to omit it here.

1764 **mir** 'I tell you.' See note to line 320.

1766 **dem schmerzlichsten Genuß** Like *verliebtem Haß, erquickendem Verdruß,* an oxymoron, a figure of speech which brings together two apparently contradictory notions in order to challenge the reader to reconcile them. The essence of *Taumel* is excess, and the excess of any positive emotion easily results in its negative counterpart.

1774 **zu ihrem Selbst** Faust wishes to expand his own being until this comprises the whole of humanity. Such expansion of the self to the proportions of the whole of humanity seems to bring with it an end in disaster, when humanity itself (*sie* 1775) crashes against some unyielding obstacle and is ruined (*zerscheitern*).

1779 **Sauerteig** Humanity, human life on earth, is compared with bread containing an indigestible mass of fermented dough. It is as difficult for any man to know all of human life as it is for anyone to digest a lump of fermented dough.

1780 Infinite light can be endured only by a divine being. Mephistopheles and his group (*uns*) have no light, while human beings like Faust must have light and darkness alternately, and so must lack complete power to apprehend everything all the time.

1785-1802 Mephistopheles replies with irony to Faust's insistence upon the impossible. There is only one little thing, he says, that might keep Faust from achieving his purpose: there may not be time enough at Faust's disposal for him to learn all he wishes to know. Perhaps a poet might help Faust in this undertaking. Poets can create imaginary characters whom they endow with every virtue; possibly one of them might so endow Faust. These noble qualities in real life as a rule are mutually exclusive. The climactic contradiction suggested is that of instinctively falling in love according to plan (1800).

1790 **den Herrn** The poet.

1792 **Ehrenscheitel** 'revered head.' The word is conceivably applicable to the Faust of the scene *Vor dem Tor*, but if the reference is to the effect of the future action of this poet, then *Ehrenscheitel* is a short cut for *auf Euren Scheitel zu Eurer Ehre häufen*, 'to pile upon your head, thereby to honor you.'

1796 **des Nordens** This form is peculiar, if it means what it appears to mean in contrast with *des Italieners*. *Der Norden, des Nordens* normally means the geographical region 'north,' while *der Norde*, which is used elsewhere by Goethe to mean the inhabitant of these northern regions, should have as its genitive *des Norden*, and this is sometimes printed here.

1801 This gentleman is the creation of the poet, made of all the ingredients just named. He would indeed be Mr. Microcosm, since he would comprise within himself an epitome of the universe of human experience.

1804 **der Menschheit Krone** The goal of Faust's strivings is the perfect realization of human potentialities, to become the perfect human being and thus to comprise all humanity within himself. This is equivalent to becoming "like God." The belief in the perfectibility of the human individual is an important part of Goethe's thought. A notable example is his novel WILHELM MEISTER, which follows the development of the hero from apprenticeship to mastership.

1807 **Perücke** Probably the *Staatsperücke* or *Allonge*, which was most luxurious in its baroque exuberance about 1700.

1808 **Socken** Probably to be taken in the sense of 'shoes.' Goethe uses the word again in line 5546, where it is clearly the German word for the flatsoled, heelless footwear of wool, which was somewhat like what we should today call "loafers." — **ellenhohe** refers to the height or length of these *Socken*, and presumably the wealthier the man, the longer his *Socken*, within natural limits. The intent of the two lines 1807-1808 is clear enough: 'No matter how big a wig you put on; no matter how high your shoes, you are what you are.' Many commentators take this *Socken* to be the 'sock' of ancient comedy. Some even believe that Goethe misused the form here instead of *Kothurnen (cothurni)* 'buskins,' which the actors in ancient tragedy wore. These were built up with very thick soles and high heels. It is impossible to believe that Goethe did not know the difference between *soccus* and *cothurnus*, and it is not likely that he had either in mind here.

1816–1817 Mephistopheles recognizes in Faust's despair nothing of its real causes, but sees only the despair itself. Hence he says, in effect, 'Well, good sir, your way of looking at things is that of everyone else, but we have a chance to fix things up, if we get at it before you become quite inaccessible to the joys of life.'

1820 Mephistopheles somewhat drastically points out that a man is more than his physical body. His enjoyments are also a part of him. — Goethe has given no indication of the precise syllables represented by the dashes of line 1821. According to the standards of his day, in any event, the word was vulgar or indecent.

1825 **die meine** Instead of the normal form *die meinen*, in order to rime with *Beine*. A plural *die meine* was permissible in the language of the sixteenth century, but exceptional in that of the eighteenth, although the form without *−n* is regularly used in the Frankfurt dialect.

1828 **Sinnen** The contemplative life, which Mephistopheles cannot comprehend.

1829 **grad mit in die Welt** An imperative verbal idea may be supplied. It is implied in *frisch*, and we may translate: 'Come right along with me into the world.' It has been suggested that *mit* may stand for *mitten*, in which case *grad mit* would mean 'directly into the midst of.'

1835 Mephistopheles regards Faust's study as a place of torture and his occupation as a teacher of the young a frightful bore for one so gifted as Faust. It is a life for someone with embonpoint and without distracting ambitions and driving force, for someone who thrives on the easy life of repetitious rehearsings of things already known — straw from which the grain has been threshed (1839).

1841 Compare here lines 590–593.

1847 The spirit of negation (338–339, 1338) in the garb of the professor presents an incongruity which could be highly amusing, because professors are people who are supposed to be dedicated to the active search for truth.

1851–1867 This soliloquy of Mephistopheles reflects rather the poet's early than his final conception of the Faust problem. In terms of earlier plans, the Mephistopheles who speaks here was a servant of the Earth Spirit, and this Faust is the Faust of the first monologue (354–385). Mephistopheles is pleased to see Faust renounce reason and science and place his reliance in works of magic and in the help of spirits like himself. Faust's incontinent drive to achieve the satisfaction of his great urge for transcendent knowledge will lead him, as Mephistopheles sees things, to disillusionment and ruin. Hence Mephistopheles refers to this drive as Faust's *Lügengeist*. Efforts to reconcile these lines in detail with the features of the later Faust are more likely to confuse than to clarify the issue. For example, it is not necessary, and probably not permissible, to identify the *übereiltes Streben* of line 1858 with the *Gärung* of line 302, for lines 300–307 were not written until 1797 or 1798, while the monologue of Mephistopheles, lines 1851–1867, was printed in 1790.

1862   The figures are from the bird catcher's trade. The bird is caught in the "lime." It struggles, but the more it flaps and jerks (*zappeln*), the sooner it becomes exhausted and the more firmly it becomes entangled in the glue, until finally it is seized with cramps (*starren*) and sticks fast firmly and helplessly (*kleben*).

1863   **Unersättlichkeit**   Dative. Food and drink for his insatiable appetite for experience and knowledge shall dangle before him, but he shall never partake of them.

1868   The scene between Mephistopheles and the Student is one of the oldest parts of FAUST. It underwent drastic revision between the URFAUST and the finished FAUST, Part I. This revision changed the scene from a mere satirical burlesque to a dramatically acceptable interlude after the climax of the scene at line 1867. The *Schülerszene* remains episodic, but it is interesting and pertinent because of the parallels which suggest themselves between this youngster and Faust. We shall meet this fellow again at line 6689, as a *Baccalaureus*.

1873   Mephistopheles' first lie to the student.

1879   **hieraußen**   This student when at home would refer to the city in which this university is located as *draußen im Reich*. When he gets there he says he is *hieraußen* (*im Reiche*). This points to the eighteenth century use of the term *Reich* to designate Upper Germany, or even more narrowly the western regions along the Rhine and Main rivers and exclusive of Bavaria and Austria. Probably this student comes from some province in central or northern Germany, whereas the university is located '*im Reich*,' in one or the other of the senses indicated. This student is a boy from a good home, who is away from home for the first time and who takes his mission very seriously.

1881–1887   The halls of learning are not a natural environment. Culture and nature are in many particulars at odds with each other. Too much culture to the exclusion of nature is distressing.

1897   **Fakultät**   See note to line 354. In this discussion the fields of Law, Theology, Medicine are mentioned as possible fields of specialization after preliminary courses in logic and metaphysics.

1898–1901   This youth voices the same ideal of knowledge as that which possesses Faust, but he is made of much less stern stuff, as is shown by 1905–1907.

1908   **der Zeit**   Genitive object of *gebrauchen*, instead of the more usual accusative, as in line 235.

1911   **Collegium Logicum**   *Collegium* is used here in the German sense of *Kolleg*, 'course.' The course in logic was the chief occupation of students in their first semester, even in Goethe's day, and he wrote of this part of his experience in Leipzig [DICHTUNG UND WAHRHEIT, Book VI.]: "Meine Kollegia besuchte ich anfangs emsig und treulich . . . In der Logik kam es mir wunderlich vor, daß ich diejenigen Geistesoperationen, die ich von Jugend auf mit der größten Bequemlichkeit verrichtet, so auseinander zerren, vereinzeln und gleichsam zerstören sollte, um den rechten Gebrauch derselben einzusehen."

1913 **spanische Stiefeln** Instruments of torture used in the Spanish inquisition and designed to squeeze the calves of the victim's legs within iron boot-shafts which could be contracted by means of wedges or screws.

1924 **Tritt** The normal hand-operated loom has two foot-bars or treadles by which the operator lowers and raises the heddles. These guide the longitudinal threads of the warp. When one treadle is up the other is down. Each movement of a treadle raises or lowers half of the total number of longitudinal threads on the loom. The shuttles carry the cross threads of the weft, each of which is ultimately held in place by the alternately raised and lowered threads of the warp. The weft is settled neatly into place by the reed and packed tight by a blow (*Schlag*) of the batten.

1928–1935 The philosopher's ability to analyze a process does not enable him to create a masterpiece.

1929 The first stress is on the third syllable of this line. The second stress falls on *Euch*, or in the pause after *Euch*. The third and fourth stresses fall on *müßt'* and *sein*, respectively.

1930 In our own day logicians speak rather of A, B, C, D than of *das Erste, das Zweite*, and so on. These appear here to be terms of a conjunctive conditional syllogism, perhaps of what was once called a "destructive dilemma."

1936–1941 The phraseology of these lines rests either upon the lectures or on the book, INSTITUTIONES CHEMIAE, 1763, of Professor J. R. Spielmann, who was one of Goethe's teachers in Strassburg in 1770–1771. The chemical study of organic life involves extracting and identifying the components of the living body, but this can only be accomplished by driving out the apparently non-material bond (the spirit) which unites and animates these parts. This bond disappears under analytic procedure and without it no synthesis of the parts to form a living organism is possible.

1940 **Encheiresin naturae** The process of nature by which substances are united into a living organism. The term *encheiresis* is frequent in the chemical literature of the eighteenth century, but the term *encheiresis naturae* is not. Chemists had no *encheiresis* which would permit them to do what nature did in every living organism. By giving a name, 'nature's *encheiresis*,' to something which they could not describe or use, but which is an essential component of that whole they were seeking to explain by their science, chemists put themselves into the ridiculous position of having to concede that they understood everything but the indispensable essence of it all.

1944–1945 **reduzieren, klassifizieren** Two logical procedures: reduction of propositions to their basic terms, and the classification of observed data according to a limited number of characteristic features.

1946 **alle** An uninflected, invariable form, equivalent to *all*.

1949 Metaphysics is that part of philosophic speculation which seeks to transcend experience and to understand the ultimate or the first principles of existence.

1955 **der . . . Ordnung** Genitive object of *wahrnehmen*. Modern usage requires an accusative object.

1956 **habt Ihr** 'you will have,' for such is the prescribed course.

1957 **drinnen** In the lecture hall.

1959 The paragraphs are those of the textbook, which served as the basis for the lectures of each day. Despite the fact that the lecturer is likely to say nothing that is not in the book, the student is advised to be exceedingly industrious in taking notes.

1972 **Gesetz' und Rechte** = *leges et jura* Laws enacted by a legislature (*leges*), and laws which have grown up out of custom and court decisions (*jura*). — Goethe was a student of law at Strassburg, graduating in 1771.

1975 **von Ort zu Ort** As the laws of Rome have become the basis of the laws of Germany, and indeed of all western civilization.

1977 By the changes which come with the lapse of years, and by the transfer of laws from the environment out of which they grew to an environment in which they make little or no sense, the grandson who inherits these laws is made to suffer grave inequities.

1978 The natural law of justice to the individual which inheres in his innate human rights.

1982 The freshman appears to believe that Mephistopheles is professor of theology. He believes him to be Faust, who, at any rate, was qualified in that field (356).

1983 When Goethe (in 1829) was supervising the preparation of a performance of this scene, he directed that a considerable pause be made after line 1982 and before this speech. Then he had his Mephistopheles speak with some show of malice and irony.

1986 **verborgenes Gift** Theology is the science of religion and the pursuit of this science by a young scholar may be damaging (*Gift*) or healing (*Arzenei*): damaging, if it leads him away from religion to heresy; healing, if it helps him to find true religious faith. But the theological doctrines which lead to heresy are not easily distinguished a priori from those which lead to the true faith. Peace of mind comes most readily to those who learn only one doctrine, for a conflict of basic teachings is incompatible with the ideal of a unique truth.

1990–1996 **Worte** A Mephistophelian aspersion of merely verbal learning, which is too strong even for our freshman, who thinks that words must mean something. This Mephistopheles admits, but he adds that frequently, when thinking becomes vague and nebulous, the mere symbols of meanings are bandied about without regard to their appropriateness. The use of *Pforte* in line 1991 is probably an ironic allusion to the "gate that leadeth unto life." Matthew 7.14.

2000 **Jota** 'iota.' The expression is based on Matthew 5.18: "Till heaven and earth pass away, one jot or one tittle shall in no wise pass away from the law till all things be accomplished." There may be an allusion here also to the bitter conflict between the Arian and Athanasian Christians at the Council of Nicaea (325 A.D.), where the debate hinged upon the presence or absence of an iota in the Greek word which was to be used to define the nature of Christ: *"homoousios,"* the form without the iota, means 'of the same nature'; *"homoiousios"* means 'of similar nature.' The Athanasians, who introduced the word without the iota, were victorious and their form of the creed has become the orthodox one for the Eastern and Roman communions and for the majority of the Reformed churches. Hence, what Mephistopheles says cannot be done may appear actually to have been done at Nicaea and some critics therefore regard these lines as ironical.

2003   The boy has asked or has been told about philosophy, law, and theology. Medicine is the last of the four faculties and he wishes to be advised about it also.

2005   **Jahr**   The uninflected form after a numeral instead of the plural form *Jahre*, which is now required. In FAUST, Goethe uses this monosyllabic form six times after numerals. He uses the normal plural form *Jahre* seven times, but only once (2342) after a numeral.

2009   This aside warns us that what Mephistopheles now says will be in a quite different vein from that of his previous, not wholly flippant comments. He proposes to speak now as the Devil would speak, if he had got into the professor whose role Mephistopheles has been playing. Nevertheless, some of the things he says have very high practical value (2016–2018, 2021–2022).

2012   **die groß' und kleine Welt**   The world of organic life (courses in biology and botany) and the world of man (courses in human anatomy and physiology).

2026   **Punkte**   Mephistopheles means that the source of most female ills, real or imagined, is the reproductive function of the female body.

2029   **Titel**   The *Doktortitel*, or M.D. degree.

2030   **viel**   The older uninflected form, now normally *viele*.

2031   The meaning of this line is defined in lines 2033–2036. The word *Siebensachen* means 'things,' usually trifling things, which belong to a person, and then by metaphor it is used to refer to the physical charms of the fair sex.

2042   'To plumb the depths of your wisdom by listening (to you).'

2045   Students of the eighteenth century usually carried an album in which they collected autographs and appropriate comments from people of importance with whom they became acquainted.

2048   The Latin version of the end of Genesis 3.5, except that *Deus* has been substituted for *dii*. These are the words the serpent spoke to Eve in the Garden of Eden, advising the first lady to go ahead and eat of the forbidden fruit, saying: "Ye shall not surely die; for God knoweth that in the day ye eat thereof, then your eyes shall be opened and ye shall be as God (or as Gods), knowing good and evil."

2049–2050   These lines are sometimes scanned as hexameters but may better be taken as somewhat irregular Alexandrines. — The meaning is: 'Go ahead and become like God, and you will surely sooner or later thereby get into a state of anxiety.'

2052   The antithesis here is not that of microcosm to macrocosm nor yet
that of line 2012, but rather the practical distinction between the
world of the little man and the world of the great, the burgher and
the courtier. The trip on which they are about to embark is compared with an academic course (*Cursum*); but in this one, loafing
will bring advantages (*Nutzen*), and this course will not cost anything. *Durchschmarutzen* means to enjoy as a parasite, without
paying tuition or contributing to the support of the enterprise.

2065   Travel by magic cloak is standard procedure in the Faust legend.

2069   **Feuerluft** Usually taken to allude to the balloon flights of the
brothers Montgolfier (first on August 27, 1783), who lifted their
balloon with heated air. In the same year, J. A. C. Charles flew a
balloon filled with hydrogen. Goethe is known to have been interested in the flights of the Montgolfiers, and it is not probable
that he would have referred to hydrogen as *Feuerluft;* hence it is
unlikely that this line refers to the flight made by Charles.

2070   **behend** 'expeditiously.'

7. AUERBACHS KELLER IN LEIPZIG

Auerbach's Keller, in Auerbach's Hof in Leipzig, was a restaurant
and wine room in which Goethe frequently sat with friends while he
was a student in Leipzig (1765–1768). It has long been associated
with the Faust legend and has mural paintings of scenes from the
Faust story, painted about 1625.

This scene in all its essentials was part of the URFAUST (1775?). It
was revised in the direction of greater politeness and less realism of
diction when the prose of the URFAUST was replaced by the verse of
the FRAGMENT (1790). Also, the magician's tricks with the wine,
which were performed by Faust in the first version, are performed by
Mephistopheles in the FRAGMENT and all subsequent editions.

The scene is a very successful and amusing genre picture of one
phase of German student life. Its function in the economy of the
Faust play is slight. We have to assume that our Faust, the renowned
University teacher and physician, was familiar with such scenes as
are here depicted. Hence this visit in Auerbach's Keller cannot be a
new experience for him. Neither should we charge Mephistopheles
with being so stupid as to suppose that this sort of thing would captivate or divert Faust. Faust speaks only twice during the scene, once
to greet the assemblage politely, and once to say that he would like
to leave. The scene is therefore an episode and an interlude between
Faust's decision to try Mephistopheles' plan and the real embarkation
upon that journey through the little and the great world as promised
in line 2052. The scene begins late in the course of the night's revelry,
when things have become dull and some new incitement is needed to
stimulate the weary drinkers.

SD 2073 **Frosch** A student nickname for a new freshman (*Fuchs*). So also the name *Brander* suggests *Brandfuchs*, a student in his second semester; and *Altmayer* suggests *alter Herr*, a student of advanced standing. Hence it is presumed that this is a party of students. Although the name *Siebel* has no connotations similar to those of the other names, its bearer must be supposed to belong to the same social group. A mixture of town and gown in such a party is unthinkable.

2078 **Sauerei** May mean either 'swinishness' or 'obscenity' — in either case 'dirtiness.' There is possibly a play on this word in these lines, in that Brander may mean by *Sauerei* a dirty story, while Frosch turns the word to the meaning 'swinishness.'

2079 **Doppelt Schwein** (You are) 'doubly a swine'; once for the *Dummheit*, once for the *Sauerei*.

2082 **Runda** Often the first word of a refrain to be sung by all, while one of the group has to empty his glass at a single draught.

2090 The Holy Roman Empire in Goethe's day was a frequent target for satire because of its lack of unity and because of the disparity between its pomp and its lack of real power. Brander, in lines 2093–2096, is not just indifferent to world affairs; he is aware that the Emperor and his Chancellor are in no enviable position.

2098 Students in the 17th and 18th centuries often amused themselves in drinking bouts by choosing one of their number to be "Pope." The criterion for elevation to this high eminence was the capacity to consume beer. The person chosen was seated on a chair on a table. If he could still talk, he was obliged to answer (in Latin) the questions which other members of the company addressed to him, beginning with the formula: "O lector lectorum, dic mihi . . ." He also was supposed to drink to the health of everyone present until he became incapable of doing so any more. Or, in another version of the game, the "Pope" had to sing a Latin song of twelve stanzas draining a measure of beer after each stanza. The name *Papst* is also given to a mixed drink composed of the finest ingredients, and the preparation of this potion — *einen Papst machen* — is sometimes referred to as *einen Papst wählen*. Just which of these rites Goethe had in mind is not clear.

Some editors suggest that lines 2099–2100 are an obscene allusion to the legend of Pope Joanna and to the procedure of the college of cardinals in subsequent elections to assure themselves that the candidate was not a woman. This view ignores the student custom of choosing a "Pope" as just described, according to which the critical *Qualität* was not masculinity but *Trinkfähigkeit*.

2101 This line is the exact duplicate of the first line of an old folk song of the mid-seventeenth century, and the next line is very much like the last line of many folk songs.

2103 Siebel takes this song to be addressed to a particular person with whom his own affairs of the heart have not been particularly fortunate.

2111 **Kobold** An unpleasant, unlovely, torturing goblin, an imp, a son of Satan.

2112 **Kreuzweg** According to general popular superstition, the inter-
section of two roads is a favorite meeting place of evil spirits.

2113 **Blocksberg** The popular name of the *Brocken*, in the Harz Mountains. This is a high, flat-topped summit of bare rocks where on
Walpurgis Night (the night between April 30 and May 1) witches
are said to disport themselves in the company of all manner of
evil spirits. Some of these took on the form of goats and galloped
up and down the mountain-side.

2118 **die Fenster eingeschmissen** By way of taking revenge for the
failure of this damsel to open her window to him in response to his
amorous attentions.

2122 **nach Standsgebühr** 'as is due them according to their station'
(as lovers).

2123 **zur** 'as a toast to,' or 'to put us all into the spirit of' (a fine, jovial
evening).

2124 **vom neusten Schnitt** This statement that the song about to be
offered is strictly up to date (it is a coarse satire of love) need not
be taken to mean that Goethe intended this song to be like any particular song or songs of the mid-sixteenth century. However, the
mention of Dr. Luther, the use of the auxiliary *tät* (2145) and of the
old form *genung* (2139) give the song an archaic flavor.

2129 The usual pictures of Dr. Martin Luther show him to be exceedingly
well-fed.

2138 **tät** The old preterite indicative form for the first and third persons
singular, later replaced by *tat*, by analogy to the plural form *taten*.
tät schnaufen (2145) is vernacular for *schnaufte*, with *tät* serving as
an auxiliary verb. In this use the plural form is commonly *täten*,
by analogy to *tät*, as in line 2781.

2139 **genung** A middle German form of *genug* used by Hans Sachs,
Gryphius, and Goethe, but in FAUST only in Part I, and only in
rime (five times). The usual form in FAUST is *genug* (fifty times).

2151–2152 Siebel, who is quite as *platt* as the rest, thinks that poisoning
rats is a stupid business which should not interest anyone, and the
cruel exuberance of his fellows moves him to compassion for the victim: Siebel is already a bit maudlin.

2154 **Schmerbauch** Siebel is meant.

2172 **ein klein Paris** Paris was the center and zenith of style and refinement for European society. Leipzig in Goethe's day prided itself
upon its approach to Parisian manners, social refinement, and
gallantry.

2174 **Bei einem vollen Glase** When they have drunk one full glass with
the party.

2176 The idiom is French: *tirer les vers du nez*, and is an ironic sample of
the elegance so hotly emulated in Leipzig.

2179 **Marktschreier** 'advertising agents.' Leipzig has long been the
chief German city of fairs. Anyone who appeared "foreign" there
was likely to be taken for a person connected with the exhibition and
the trade in furs or manufactured articles, for which these fairs
were held.

2184 **hinkt** Mephistopheles has one human foot and one horse's hoof, which makes his gait uneven. His *Pferdefuß* is mentioned a number of times, for instance at 2490 and 4065 in Part I.

2188 **verwöhnt** Because of his expressed contempt for the locally obtainable vintages.

2189 **Rippach** A village southwest of Leipzig, and last post station on the route Naumburg-Leipzig. The people of Leipzig in Goethe's day spoke of Rippach as the home of yokels. *Herr Hans von Rippach* is a variant of a widely used Leipzig name for a country bumpkin of uncouth manners. Mephistopheles turns the insult back upon Frosch by calling him and his companions cousins of this yokel (2193).

2205 Since there is no other reference to this trip to Spain, this appears to be one of Mephistopheles' superfluous falsehoods. The Faust of the Chapbook was widely traveled.

2210 'I think a flea is a fine kind of a fellow.'

2211 This song, set to music by M. P. Moussorgski (1879), is a popular concert piece for baritone or bass singers.

2214 **Sohn** In the dialect of Frankfurt am Main the vowel of this word is nasalized and the final –*n* is more or less inaudible. Therefore in that dialect *Sohn* is an endurable, if not attractive, rime with *Floh*.

2222 **die Hosen** 'The hose' (or trousers) of a Spanish cavalier were skintight from hip to toe, and absolute freedom from wrinkles was the ideal of the wearer and his tailor.

2225 **Bänder** Perhaps horizontally around the puffed sleeves, perhaps embroidered ribbons used on the margins of the coat, possibly to be connected with the decorations mentioned in lines 2226–2228.

2226–2228 **Kreuz, Stern** 'decorations.' The highest class decoration is the *Großkreuz*, worn on a broad ribbon running over the left shoulder and down to the right hip, together with a jeweled star (*Stern*) on the left breast.

2230 **Herrn** A plural form, instead of the dissyllabic *Herren*.

2237 **wir** The people who sing the song, or those for whom it is sung.

2246 See line 2186.

2251 Siebel undertakes to mollify the proprietor if he protests.

2255 Since a full mouth makes fine distinctions of taste impossible, this remark brands its maker as a man of no discrimination.

2256 **vom Rheine** Altmayer suspects that the newcomers come from the Rhine, where the finest wines reputedly are grown, and that perhaps they are even wine merchants.

2268 **Champagner** A French wine, from the one-time province Champagne, with its capital at Troyes.

2269 **moussierend** The characteristic quality of champagne, bubbling.

2276 **Tokayer** A golden yellow sweet wine from the region around the town of Tokay, in northern Hungary.

2284 The first lines sound like a children's rime. The incantation begins with statements of facts and proceeds to nonsense.

2293–2294 These lines suggest the bestiality which Mephistopheles wishes to show Faust (2297–2298). They are to be understood also as the refrain of a drinking song, well known to these carousers.

2295 A sarcastic observation made to Faust and referring apparently to some discussion of freedom which the two have had.

2304 **Er** See note to line 548.

2307 Here and in line 2538 *Hokuspokus* is neuter. The noun is now regularly masculine.

2308 **Weinfaß** An allusion to Siebel's corpulence; see 2154.

2313 Another incantation to delude the senses of the party.

2330 An allusion to a different Faust episode, which was depicted on one of the murals in Auerbach's Keller.

2332 **Mein!** Comparable with the English interjection: "My!" from which something like "Goodness," "Lord," or "God" has been left off.

2336 **Nun sag' mir eins** 'now just let someone tell me . . .' *eins = einer = irgend jemand.*

8. Hexenküche

In this scene witchery is afoot, for the Faust we have come to know has to be made over into the very different Faust of the Gretchen tragedy which follows. The hocus-pocus and the magic potion which make Faust a young and amorous fellow would be completely incredible in any other story. Indeed, except for the rare skill with which it is managed, it would be intolerable here.

No witch's kitchen is complete without a cauldron. The various figures which appear in the steam from this one may be thought of as scorpions, salamanders, and the like. The *Meerkatzen* are monkeys with long tails, who have been given by the Devil to his old sweetheart, the witch, to be her servants. In medieval folklore and art they are often used as symbols of sexual incontinence and lust.

2338 **genesen** The malady from which Faust hopes to recover is described in lines 2055–2060. He cannot enjoy his journey through the world until he is relieved of his reticence and of the burden of his years.

2342 This mention of thirty years makes the Faust of the *Studierzimmer* scenes a man of about fifty.

2345 The hocus-pocus of this witch's kitchen revolts Faust by its irrational nonsense. He suggests that some product of nature or of man's noble intelligence would have a better chance to make him young again than this witchcraft.

2349 **Buch** Not in the book of magic, but in some other book.

2353–2359 This advice is, in sum, to live the life of nature, the simple life with no intellectual effort to expand one's environment. An old couple who have lived this life appear in Part II, Act V, in the persons of Philemon and Baucis.

2361 **auf achtzig Jahr** 'until you are eighty years old.'

2369 Brewing this potion takes a great deal of time, indeed much too much time and patience to suit Mephistopheles. — The Devil is a noted builder of bridges, by means of which he reaches souls he seeks to capture. Many natural bridges and wild arrays of rugged rocks are called *Teufelsbrücke*. See line 10 121.

2376   sie = *die Hexe.*

2381–2383   The lady of the house is out for dinner.

2385   Typical nonsense. They cease to toast their toes when the mistress returns.

2392   The essence of a beggar's soup is that it is copious, has no meat, and is easy to digest.

2393   **Publikum**   Since this word suggests an audience rather than a group of customers (*Kundschaft*), it is inferred that Goethe intended these two lines as a satirical quip directed against the taste of the great bulk of the public of his day for shallow, "meatless" literature of entertainment (*Unterhaltungsliteratur*).

2394–2399   The papa-ape finds himself distraught by the lack of funds (*schlecht ist's bestellt*), and thinks that if he could win some money by gambling he might be normal again (*bei Sinnen*).

2401   **Lotto**   While traveling in Italy (1786–1788), Goethe was impressed by the ruinous effects of the state-supported numbers lottery, which was called in Italian *lotto*.

2402–2415   Attempts of commentators to find deep meaning in nonsense of this kind amused Goethe no little. Line 2410 is probably best taken as a parenthetical exclamation by the ape, as he leaps aside to escape the rolling ball. Having done so, however, he goes to get the sieve, which has nothing whatever to do with the sphere. Another interpretation takes line 2410 to be a statement made by the sphere itself.

2419–2421   **Sieb**   Popular belief has it that if you look at a thief through a sieve and say his name, the sieve will turn in your hands.

2427   **Wedel**   Something bushy, to be waved back and forth; a fly-brush, a feather duster, a fan. This one has a considerable handle with which Mephistopheles breaks glasses and pots (SD 2475).

2428   **in** = *in'n*, from *in den*. A contraction not unusual in Goethe's early works, especially in GÖTZ VON BERLICHINGEN.

2429–2430   What Faust sees is the image of an unidentified beautiful woman, lying on a couch, presumably like the Giorgione or the Titian *Venus*. Because of lines 2601–2604 and 6495–6497 it is often inferred that this was an image of Helen of Troy, but this inference does not have to be drawn. It has also been suggested that the lady was Cressida, and that the scene shows the influence of Shakespeare's TROILUS AND CRESSIDA, particularly of the scene in Pandarus' orchard (III, 2).

2442   **"Bravo!"**   A somewhat brash version of Genesis 1.31: "And God saw everything that he had made, and, behold, it was very good."

SD 2448   While Faust fixes his eyes upon the image of feminine beauty which he sees in the mirror and becomes progressively obsessed with its erotic suggestion until he is driven to propose flight from the scene, Mephistopheles lolls in an armchair, waving a *Wedel*, which he says might well be his scepter, if he had a crown to go with it. He encourages Faust to look his fill at the image, and meanwhile he listens to the young apes who sing their rime about a broken crown. There is no immediately evident connection between this crown and the talk about it and the purposes of this scene. Hence critics have looked for a hidden meaning at this point.

2450–2452 Damaged crowns are commonly restored by the sweat and blood of the subjects thereof. Although it is often held that these lines refer to the French crown and the French Revolution of July 1789, it is clear that this scene was composed in February 1788 in Rome, and it is relatively certain that these lines were written then and not interpolated later.

2453–2455 For no good reason, the little apes now pose as poets, and what they say is a satire on the rimesters who, if by some happy chance they achieve a good rime, pretend that there is a meaning behind their words. Mephistopheles concedes that as poets they are, in any event, honest in thus describing their methods (2464).

2483 Anacoluthon: *Was hält mich ab,* [*daß ich nicht zuschlage*] plus [*wenn du mich nun nicht erkennst,*] *so schlage ich zu.*

2484 **Katzengeister** The *Meerkatzen,* the apes.

2485 See lines 1536–1539. As a badge of their eminence the leading actors of traveling theater troupes used to wear a red waistcoat, called a *Permissionsweste;* and they behaved much as Mephistopheles is behaving, if they thought they dared do so.

2491 **Raben** The two ravens are usually associated with the Germanic god, Wotan (Odin), whom they served as messengers. Here Goethe associates them with Mephistopheles, as he does again at lines 10 664 and 10 717.

2495 **beleckt** 'covers with a thin surface coating or veneer'; *alle Welt* is the object.

2498 The conception of the Devil as a creature with horns, a tail ending in a dart, and vulture-like claws for hands, seems to be peculiar to Northern European mythology, and to rest perhaps on Revelation 12.9, where the devil is called, "the great dragon and the old serpent, he that is called the Devil and Satan."

2500 **bei Leuten** If the Devil is to appear among people (and if he is to be a possible figure in a serious drama) he must be stripped of these wholly nonhuman attributes.

2502 **falsche Waden** Pads worn to simulate large muscles of the lower leg. They can be seen in many of the paintings of the Brueghels.

2504 **Junker Satan** (also 1535), and *Junker Voland* (4023). Mephistopheles does not object so much to the name *Junker* as to the name *Satan.* He prefers to be called (2510) *Herr Baron.*

2507 'The name of Satan and the belief in a Satan have become part of fabulous lore in which men no longer seriously believe.'

SD 2513 The 'indecent gesture' poses a problem for the actor. Goethe taught one actor here to face the witch, with his back to the audience, to raise one leg high, and to slap his thigh as he did so. What gesture Goethe had in mind when he wrote the scene is another matter. There is a problem of the same sort at 3291, and another at lines 5778–5794 in Part II.

2518 **schafft** This use of the verb *schaffen* in the sense of *befehlen* is dialectal and old. Dialectal and old also is the neuter gender of *Saft*, implied by the reference *das älteste* (2520). Standard German has now only *der Saft*, which is Goethe's form in all other unambiguous occurrences in FAUST.

2538 This hocus-pocus with a big book is not unlike the conjuration of the Earth Spirit by Faust himself, SD 481.

2540 The *Hexen-Einmaleins* is sheer nonsense, but with unction. There is a vast body of critical comment on these lines.

2553 **dünken** Used with the accusative more often than with the dative in FAUST. The ratio is approximately three accusative forms to one dative.

2555 **das ganze Buch** This is the book of the witch, SD 2540.

2556 **manche Zeit** The use of *manche*, rather than *viel*, expresses the repetition of the waste of time as well as the quantity of time wasted: 'I have often wasted a great deal of time over it.'

2561 A reference to the numerical difficulty of the doctrine of the Holy Trinity, which Goethe found it impossible to resolve. See Eckermann's report of his conversation of January 4, 1824:

"Ich glaubte an Gott und die Natur und an den Sieg des Edlen über das Schlechte, aber das war den frommen Seelen nicht genug: ich sollte auch glauben, daß Drei Eins sei und Eins Drei. Das aber widerstrebte dem Wahrheitsgefühl meiner Seele; auch sah ich nicht ein, daß mir damit auch nur im mindesten wäre geholfen gewesen."

2564 **den Narrn** A monosyllable for the dative plural *Narren*, people who spread error rather than truth. It is too much trouble to bother to try to stop them. The crowd is against such an effort.

2568 **Wissenschaft** 'The things known,' *das Wissen*, 'knowledge, wisdom.' What the witch says about it is, as Faust observes (2573), nonsense. But it is the kind of nonsense which is particularly seductive to the gullible or the intellectually lazy.

2577 **Sibylle** A general name for a divinely inspired prophetess. It comes from the name of the Cumaean Sibyl of Virgil.

2581 **vielen Graden** The many degrees in the *Bierfehde* or *Bierskandal*. These were drinking bouts, regulated by various *Bierkomments* in the various university communities. They recognized six or seven "degrees" of "insults." A *"Doktor"* was usually a three-glass insult. Or, this may mean that Faust is many times over a D. C. n. e. b., that is, *Doctor Cerevisiae, nunc est bibendum*, the degree "Doctor of Beer, now let us drink." This degree was won in drinking examinations, where the capacity to take on the liquid was the quality which won "promotion."

SD 2582 **sie** = *die Schale*.

2590 **Walpurgis** Walpurgis Night, the night of April 30 to May 1. Then all witches convene on the *Blocksberg* (the Brocken) and receive their due rewards for services rendered the Devil; see note to line 2113. — The name is that of an English nun, Walpurga, who died February 25, 779, as abbess of the Bavarian convent Heidenheim. She became a Saint and her day is May 1. — **darfst** Used here in the

sense of 'have to,' 'need to,' as is frequently the case when it is used
with a restrictive *nur, kaum,* or *nicht.*

2591 **Lied** A song printed on a single sheet of paper and prepared for
public distribution. This song was presumably lewd.

9. Strasse

With this scene we enter upon the Gretchen tragedy and the central
problem of the earliest Faust of Goethe. In the ultimate composition of the poem this became an episode, rather than the central
problem. Indeed, four scenes which were not part of the Urfaust
are now included within the compass of the Gretchen tragedy. These
are the scenes: *Wald und Höhle, Nacht, Walpurgisnacht,* and *Walpurgisnachtstraum.*

The scenes which portray the tragedy of the deserted sweetheart
do not stem from the old Faust story. They embody rather the revolt
of eighteenth-century individualism against the pedantically harsh
treatment of the unfortunate victims of nature's strongest impulse.
The catastrophe of the deserted Gretchen is the inevitable resolution
of this conflict between nature and a human society which does not
dare to permit the free sway of impulses and which has to exact expiation for the transgression of its laws, whether this transgression results
from crass lewdness or from yielding to the impulses of purest love.

The desertion of the sweetheart, rather than the socially acceptable
justification through wedlock, is the result of a second natural impulse,
the drive for individual freedom. To a man of any human dignity,
this act of desertion brings the feeling of guilt and the need to perform
expiation.

2605 **Fräulein** This form of address in Goethe's day was proper only to
persons of the nobility. Commoners were addressed as *Jungfrau*
(3018) or *Jungfer.*

2606 **Ihr** Dative of *Sie,* used like *Er* as a pronoun of the second person.
See note to line 548.

2611 **sitt- und tugendreich** The hyphen should indicate either *sittreich*
or *sittenreich.* Goethe used *sittenreich* at least once in another context; *sittreich* does not occur elsewhere. The usual word is *wohl-
gesittet.*

2619 **Dirne** Originally without pejorative connotation, this word even
before Goethe's day had fallen from good usage except when applied to a girl from the country, *Bauerndirne.* The romantic poets
tried to reinstate this old word in its earlier pleasant flavor. Nevertheless, perhaps because of *schaffen,* this line sounds a bit coarse
and brutal, and line 2627 is indubitably so. See also line 3174.

2627 **Jahr** For *Jahre;* see note to line 2005.

2628 **Hans Liederlich** *Hans* is used with an adjective or noun, to
describe a person who appears to be the incarnation of the quality

named. This usage was once widespread. English remnants are Jack Frost, Jack Sprat, Jack-an-apes (*Hans Aff*), jack-ass (*Hans Eselein*). German forms similar to *Hans Liederlich* are *Hans Nimmersatt, Hans Ohnesorge, Hans-im-Glück*.

2630 **dünkelt ihm** The subject is an impersonal *es:* 'in his conceit he imagines . . .'

2633 **Magister Lobesan** 'Worthy Master.' *Lobesan* (or *lobesam*) was sometimes used after titles, e.g. *ein König lobesam* 'a worthy king.' It is here used ironically. The connotation is that of a dogmatic academician, who lays down the law to his listeners.

2634 **Gesetz** Faust understands line 2632 to concern the legal impediment to the fulfillment of his desires. Mephistopheles has merely indicated that some things are beyond his powers to procure (2626), and indeed that some things may even be impossible for Faust.

2638 This threat to dissolve their agreement at midnight reflects the oldest conception of the relationship between Faust and Mephistopheles, but it is also quite in keeping with the wager of lines 1699–1706.

2639 **gehn und stehen** A fixed riming phrase which means 'be done.' — **mag** Here used in its older meaning 'can.'

2645 **Franzos** The French novel of amatory adventure led to the use of *ein Franzos* as a symbol for a roué or rake.

2652 **welsche Geschicht'** Refers to the lubricious Renaissance love romances from France or Italy.

2654 **Schimpf** Here in its older meaning of 'jest,' hence a synonym for *Spaß*.

2674 Mephistopheles' use of the foreign words *reüssieren* and *revidieren* contributes to the impression of sophistication and lubricity he makes here and contrasts with the hot impetuosity of the newly enamored Faust. To complete the French atmosphere, the line is an Alexandrine.

2676 Buried treasure is generally thought to be in the Devil's care.

10. ABEND

The function of this scene is to make vivid the basic antagonism between Margarete's simple purity of heart and the baseness of the threat to her peace. Neither Faust's heedless passion nor Mephistopheles' lewd sensuality is compatible with the cleanliness of this room and its occupant.

The atmosphere of the room has its effect upon Faust. His passion is, for the moment, sublimated in a romantic analysis of the objects around him, until he finally realizes the incongruity of his present undertaking with his former standards of conduct (2720). Mephistopheles intervenes before this turn of thought can become effective in a decision which might disrupt his plans.

2683 **keck** Namely in lines 2605–2606.

2694 **Kerker** A clear indication that this lover would regard permanent residence here as imprisonment. — Some critics see in the use of this word a grimly ironic anticipation of the final scene of the Gretchen tragedy (Scene 27).

2706 After the floor has been duly scrubbed, sand is strewn upon it, and fastidious housewives arrange the sand in ornamental patterns, or, at any rate, in undulating lines.

2708 **Hütte** Throughout his works Goethe employs the *Hütte* as a symbol of peace, happiness, and contentment — an ideal state of life, which often becomes the target of the destructive impulses of self-assertion, self-expansion, and desire for power. See lines 3353 and 11 304–11 315 for other instances.

2711 With *bildetest* supply a subject *du*.

2712 The angelic quality of this girl is innate; after her birth, nature has merely developed it. The process is restated in lines 2715–2716.

2714 **den Busen** An accusative absolute.

2715 **Weben** The 'weaving' is probably best understood in the sense of *webe* (503) or of *webt* as this occurs in Luther's translation of Genesis 1.21: "Gott schuf allerlei Tier, das da lebt und webt." In this usage, the noun *Weben* means 'the free movement of a living being.'

2717–2720 Faust recognizes the despicable nature of the intention which brought him here. A conflict seems about to arise within him. But his senses and his lust are too strong, though some change has come over him. The forthright urge to animal indulgence has changed, with the dissolution of his emotions, into a dream of love.

2732 **woanders** He has 'found' it, never mind where.

2736 **eine andere** Mephistopheles says he put jewels into this box to enable Faust (*Euch*) to win a different sort of lady. In the URFAUST this line reads: *Um eine Fürstin zu gewinnen.* When he changed *Fürstin* to *andere*, Goethe, for some reason, wished to remove this reference to a lady of noble rank, but he left the essential situation unchanged. The contents of this casket will assuredly astonish so simple and ingenuous a girl as Gretchen.

2737 The game is the same and the person involved is not important.

2738 **soll ich?** The hesitancy is in the face of the decision whether to seduce or not to seduce this maiden. Mephistopheles, as is frequently the case, fails to understand Faust's motive for hesitation and thinks in terms of his own patterns of behavior.

2740 **Eurer Lüsternheit** 'Your Greediness,' a title like 'Your Highness.'

2744 Gestures of extreme exertion, mental and physical.

2751 The subjects of the lecture Faust seems about to deliver.

2753 The Devil, Mephistopheles, has left an ominous, oppressive atmosphere behind him.

2759 A ballad which has often been set to music, notably by Liszt, Schumann, Gounod, and Berlioz. The melody most frequently heard, however, is that by Zelter (1821). — It is a song about the faithful lover, which the workings of Margarete's subconscious mind have brought to focus.

2761 **Buhle** The emotional value of this word is usually unpleasant or pejorative, either mildly, as in the case of a paramour, or more violently, when used of persons on a lower social level.

2775 **Zecher** The king is so called, because he is at the moment drinking at a gay banquet. It is not necessary to believe that he was a habitual heavy drinker.

2781 **täten . . . sinken** This use of the auxiliary past-tense form of *tät* or *täten* with an infinitive in place of a simple past-tense form is a characteristic feature of the style of the folk song. See note to line 2138.

2786–2787 These lines indicate that Gretchen's family was moderately well-to-do, so that upon occasion the mother could lend money to persons who needed ready cash. It is not likely that Gretchen's mother should be thought of as a professional pawnbroker.

2800 'But people pay no attention to those qualities.' Beauty and youth are not enough; one must be really wealthy in order to attract a fine suitor.

11. SPAZIERGANG

The word *Spaziergang*, which replaced an earlier *Allee* ('tree-lined avenue') at the head of this scene, means 'Promenade,' a place suitable for strolling, perhaps outside the city, perhaps on its walls.

The function of the scene is threefold. It retards the progress of the main action of the Gretchen adventure; it introduces Gretchen's mother as an opposing force in that conflict; and it removes the last uncertainty as to Faust's scruples (2730, 2738), or his determination to have this girl (2857).

2805 **Elemente** A very frequent oath in the literature of Goethe's time. We do not know its origin, but it may be noted that *Element* rimes with *Sakrament* and may be a substitute for this word. If it is one of the four elements, it is fire.

2807 **Was hast?** 'What's the matter? What ails you?'

2808 **So kein Gesicht sah ich** = *So ein Gesicht sah ich nie.*

2812 Irony.

2814 **Pfaff** In this context *Pfaff* has a strongly pejorative connotation of contempt and disgust; compare note to line 367.

2817 **gar einen feinen** = *einen gar feinen.*

2819 **Möbel** Used here in the older meaning of *fahrende Habe*, 'piece of personal property,' 'goods and chattels.'

2823–2824 **ungerechtes Gut** Reflects Proverbs 10.2 "Unrecht Gut hilft nicht," or as the popular version has it: "Unrecht Gut gedeiht nicht."

2828 **geschenkter Gaul** The proverb says: "*Equi donati dentes non inspiciuntur*," or "Einem geschenkten Gaul sieht man nicht ins Maul." 'One doesn't look a gift horse in the mouth.'

2835 Reflects several verses of the second chapter of Revelation, which promise various rewards "to him that overcometh." (Verses 7, 11, 17, and 26), or Chapter 21.7: "He that overcometh shall inherit these things."

2838 **übergessen** The participle of the compound *überessen*.

2843 The subject of *strich . . . ein* is the priest.

2849 **Gretchen** Faust always uses this form of the girl's name. In the stage directions of scenes 9, 10, 12 (except at line 3006), 14, 15, 18, and 27 Goethe writes her name *Margarete*. In scenes 17, 19, 20, 21, 22 he writes it *Gretchen*. No consistent correlation between the use of these two forms of the name and any factor, such as date of composition or dominant emotional tone, has been established.

2851 Faust brought her the jewels, and Gretchen thinks of Faust. Whether or not she suspects him of bringing them is not indicated, but she could hardly fail to make the connection.

2857 **mach** 'Bestir yourself! Do something!'

2859 **Teufel** Has been construed as an expletive, a vocative, or a predicate nominative. *Brei* is thick porridge, which flows sluggishly, like molasses in January. Hence either: 'Confound it, don't be slow about it!' or 'You devil, don't be slow about it!' or 'Be a devil, but just don't be slow about this!'

2861 Faust has asserted his authority with some vehemence and Mephistopheles replies, as a servant would reply, with "gnädiger Herr." If there is irony in his voice it is not sufficient to stop Faust in his departure.

2863 **Euch** Includes each member of the audience among those who are being imposed on by this extravagant lover.

12. Der Nachbarin Haus

The function of this scene is to prepare for the tryst between Faust and Margarete. It is difficult to imagine how Mephistopheles could have arranged a more favorable site for the love affair he is promoting than he finds ready-made in the house and garden of Gretchen's older friend and neighbor, Marthe.

2868 **Stroh** = 'bed' (by metonymy). In olden days it was customary in Germany to fill mattresses with straw. Goethe probably intended an allusion here to the noun *Strohwitwe*, a woman whose husband has gone on a long journey or remains away from home for a long time. The word should not be understood to imply poverty.

2869 **tät** See note to line 2138.

2872 The death certificate would make it possible for Marthe to take another husband.

2873 **Gretelchen** A double diminutive, with somewhat saccharine connotation.

2879 **Sie** See note to line 548.

2880 **tät** Serves equally well as a subjunctive past in these auxiliary forms; hence *tät's tragen* 'would carry.'

Notes

2883 **Gassen** An old dative singular form.

2884 **mit** Instead of *damit*.

2889 **gibt's** 'there will be.'

2890 The dative with *sehen läßt* is an old construction with *lassen*, which perhaps was suggested by a synonymous *zeigt*, and accepted because it was not wholly obsolete in Goethe's day. Perhaps also the choice was influenced by the French idiom *faire voir à quelqu'un*.

SD 2896 **Vorhängel** Most old European houses had some kind of arrangement which permitted those inside to see who was at the door before they unlocked it. In this case it is a peep-window with a curtain.

2897 **Bin so frei** The standard reply in accepting a favor offered by a superior, here the request to enter: 'If you don't mind, I'll come right in.'

2902 Mephistopheles pretends to think Margarete a fine lady, because he finds her adorned with a precious necklace and pearl earrings.

2904 **nach Mittage** Here we follow the text of the URFAUST and the edition of 1790. The editions from 1808 onward print *Nachmittage*, which must be construed as an adverb, and should not be capitalized.

2806 **Fräulein** See note to line 2605.

2911 The use of *Sie hat* and *bringt Er* (2913) as second person forms is formal or 'polite' speech for these people. See note to line 548. — **scharf** 'keen.'

2921–2922 Tragic irony: this is precisely what happens to her.

2923 Mephistopheles is not wholly conventional here. The first half of his statement is nearly universal. Proverbs 14.13: "Even in laughter the heart is sorrowful and the end of mirth is heaviness," or Chaucer in the "Nun's Priest's Tale" (line 4395): "For evere the latter ende of joye is wo." What is unusual is the second half of the sentence. He evidently knows that Marthe is not one to pine for a long time over the death of a husband; and, certainly, constancy in Marthe would fit poorly with Mephistopheles' schemes.

2926 The basilica of St. Anthony in Padua is one of the finest structures of its kind. The tomb of the saint is in a splendidly decorated chapel in the basilica, which would be a quite incongruous resting place for the remains of the errant Schwerdtlein.

2927–2928 *an einer Stätte wohlgeweiht zum ewig kühlen Ruhebette* would be the more usual order.

2931 Three hundred masses at the rate of one each weekday, but none on Sundays or holidays, would require practically a whole year. Masses for the dead were usually said at the funeral service and on the third, seventh, and thirtieth days after a person's death, and then on the anniversary of his passing. Three hundred masses in such a sequence would require nearly three centuries.

2943–2950 This brief but important exchange with Margarete is managed while Marthe turns away to quiet her weeping.

2946 **Galan** A high-sounding foreign word (from Spain) for the native *Buhle*.

2948 The *lieb Ding* is the *Galan*, whom Mephistopheles is recommending to Margarete.

2954 **hätte** The subjunctive softens the assertion of Schwerdtlein's turpitude and gives it a cautious and polite tone.

2968 **aller Treu', aller Lieb'** Genitives, objects of *vergessen*, now regularly with the accusative, as in lines 3333, 4114.

2970 **Euch** The so-called ethical dative, indicating the person according to whose desire something is done. See note to line 320.

2974 Naval warfare between Turkish and Christian ships was incessant well down into the eighteenth century. Each party plundered the ships of the other whenever it could do so.

2981 **Ein schönes Fräulein** Here a euphemism for streetwalker. The form of the word *Napel*, instead of the German *Neapel*, suggests the French *mal de Naples*. This was one of the euphemisms used for venereal disease, particularly syphilis. Probably this was the lasting gift the lady gave Mr. Schwerdtlein.

2992 **mein erster** Hints that she is ready to entertain the idea of finding *einen zweiten*.

2998 Marriage with Schwerdtlein was a possible arrangement, provided he overlooked about the same amount and kind of transgression on the lady's part.

3005 **Wort** The conditional promise of 3001–3002.

3007 This aside is an astonishing lapse from the cynicism characteristic of Mephistopheles. It is probably primarily the expression of the attitude of strong sympathy for Gretchen which the poet wished to create in his audience. Even a devil is moved to compassion.

3009 **Zeugnis** Marthe wishes some legally valid evidence that her husband is dead, so that she can publish the fact of his death in the local paper, thereby making her status as a widow legally clear. In the absence of a proper death certificate the facts can be established by the testimony of witnesses in court (3016).

3013 The theory was that if at least two witnesses testified to the same effect, their testimony must be true.

3020 **Fräuleins** A plural in *–s* like *Mädels, Jungens;* here the indirect object of *erweist*.

3024 **der Herrn** Genitive plural, predicate to *warten*.

13. STRASSE

This little scene exhibits the state of Faust's emotions, and furnishes motivation for the scene which follows.

3028 Goethe changed the reading of this line from *Nachbars Marthen* in the FRAGMENT of 1790 to *Nachbar' Marthen* in the edition of 1808 and it has remained in that form. The URFAUST had *Nachbaar Marthen*. Neither *Nachbar Marthen* nor *Nachbars Marthen*, that is, *des Nachbars Marthen*, would occasion comment. The use of an apostrophe to indicate the omission of *–s* is odd. Perhaps the two words should be written as one; for compounds like *Nachbarfriedel*,

Nachbarliese are well known, and Goethe may have so intended his *Nachbar Marthen.*

3030 **Kuppler- und Zigeunerwesen** Gypsy women practiced the arts of clairvoyance and divination to predict the future of the love affairs of the young people of the community. From this it is a short step to the business of a procurer. A case in point is found in the *Alte* of lines 872–883.

3031 **was** = *etwas.*

3037 **Sancta Simplicitas** Latin, 'Holy Innocence!' An exclamation said to have been uttered by John Hus when he saw an old woman throw a fagot into the fire to feed the flames by which he was being burned to death in the year 1415.

3040 **Da wärt Ihr's nun!** 'There you are!' or 'Isn't that just like you!'

3050 **Sophiste** The essence of sophistry is the fallaciousness of the sophist's reasoning. The fallacy here is the argument (*secundum quid*) from the proposition that Faust as professor of theology has stated as true many things which he did not know to be true, to the conclusion that he could with equal propriety testify falsely concerning Schwerdtlein's death.

3051–3054 The meaning is: 'Yes, you might call me a liar and a sophist with some justification, if I did not know that very soon you yourself will be just as much a liar and a sophist in your relationship with this girl.'

3057 The incomplete sentence implies the idea: (*wird*) *die Rede sein,* 'there will be talk.'

3059–3066 A good example of the style of Storm and Stress.

3069 If a person is determined to come out on top of an argument all he has to have is a tongue. If his determination and his lungs hold out, he will eventually emerge victorious.

3072 Faust concedes that he means to deceive and betray Gretchen. He says he is being forced to this action by his inability to resist the compelling force of his impulses. It is the poet's task to make this appear credible.

14. GARTEN

This scene and the next display the first tryst between the two lovers. The chief function of the scenes is to demonstrate the purity of the girl and the genuineness of her attraction to Faust. The contrasts between Gretchen and Marthe and between Faust and Mephistopheles, as the pairs pass alternately before us, are used to emphasize the differences between nature at work and the Devil at play.

When the scene opens, the visit of Faust and Mephistopheles is well along in its course. We have been spared the sight of Faust's perjury concerning Marthe's husband. Also the rather difficult business of Gretchen's first meeting with the dashing gallant, who has twice sent her jewels with obvious intent, has been skipped; and Faust and

Gretchen have reached a comfortable stage in their conversation when we first see them.

3081 **Inkommodiert** A distinguished foreign word to fit a distinguished guest of a higher social level.

3091 **kömmt** The only occurrence in FAUST of this archaic form of the third person singular present indicative of *kommen*.

3094 **weiten** An archaic adverbial form; see note to line 532.

3112 **spat** An old adverbial form beside *spät*, now no longer in use. It occurs in FAUST only in conjunction with *früh* (4958, 11 416) or for the sake of a rime (11 339).

3118 **vor der Stadt** 'just outside the city.' In the older towns with walls the burghers had their gardens outside the limits of these fortifications.

3122 **liebe** Like English 'blessed,' used to indicate a mildly unpleasant connotation.

3146 **wie heut so morgen** 'tomorrow the same as today.'

3147 'Under these circumstances one isn't always fresh and lively, full of courage.'

3153 **nichts** Equivalent to *niemand*.

3155–3156 The proverb says: "Eigner Herd ist Goldes wert," and the virtuous wife is praised in Proverbs 31.10: "Wem ein tugendsam Weib beschert ist, die ist viel edler denn die köstlichsten Perlen." 'To the man who has one, a virtuous wife is more precious than the choicest pearls.' The Devil is citing scripture for his purpose, which at the moment is evasion.

3174 **Dirne** The word is chosen to reflect what Gretchen thought Faust thought she was, at their first encounter.

3176 **hier** In her heart. — **begonnte** An old weak past-tense form of *beginnen*, regularly used by Goethe in his youth but not in the second part of FAUST.

3179 **Was soll das?** 'What is that meant to be?' The answer: *Es soll nur ein Spiel.* 'Only a game is intended. I'm just going to play a little game.'

3198 **niemand nichts** Double negation is frequent in natural, colloquial speech, but has been frowned upon in careful prose by those who accept the heresy that two negatives make an affirmative. Goethe used these double negative forms at times in his most dignified prose. They often give added emphasis or intensity to the utterance, as here.

3204 **der Lauf der Welt** Alludes to the second chapter of Ephesians, which deals with the evils of unredeemed life, with its governing lusts of the flesh and anger, prior to the coming of Christ. The meaning here is simply: 'That is the way things go in this (wicked) world.'

15. EIN GARTENHÄUSCHEN

The scene is the interior of the summer house in the garden. The action is so brief that it is commonly staged as a part of the preceding scene.

3211–3216 There is nothing in the garden scene which would justify these words of Margarete, for up to this point Faust has said almost nothing, while listening to a great deal.

16. Wald und Höhle

In the URFAUST only a small part of this scene (lines 3342–3369) existed, and these lines occurred after the monologue of Valentin, where they followed directly after line 3659. In the FRAGMENT of 1790 this scene was created as it appears now: Faust's monologue (3217–3250) and his dialogue with Mephistopheles (3251–3341) were put first; to them the lines of the URFAUST (present lines 3342–3369) were added, and then finally lines 3370–3373 were added. The scene was then put between *Am Brunnen* and *Zwinger.*

In the FRAGMENT, therefore, what is said about Faust and Gretchen is said after Faust has seduced the girl. In the present sequence of scenes, these things are said before Gretchen's fall, and some of them do not fit the new situation. In the FRAGMENT, however, the whole tone of Faust's monologue was incongruous with the situation in which Faust was supposed to be. Hence Goethe, in 1808, with deep insight into the essential values of this monologue, moved the scene to its present position. He did not revise the text to fit his changed conception of the *Erdgeist* and of Mephistopheles. We cannot reconcile in detail all of the relationships which appear here with the premises set up by the final plan of FAUST, Part I. The fact that Goethe allowed these discrepancies to remain is evidence that he did not regard them as vitally important to the effect he sought to produce, provided the text was read, as he wished it to be read, by readers who would take these lines at their face value, understanding them on the basis of the text as it now stands, without trying to search out the history of composition behind this scene.

By putting these lines in their present position after the scene in the Summer House, Goethe produced a symmetrical structure by giving two soul-revealing scenes of self-examination, one devoted to Faust (*Wald und Höhle*) and the other to Gretchen (*Gretchens Stube*), which might be thought of as occurring simultaneously, rather than one after the other, as the exigencies of the theater dictate.

As to the scene itself, we have to think of Faust in a forest glade, to which he has withdrawn to think. The landscape is not gloomy, but it is wild, rocky, mountainous, and, for a lazy fellow like Mephistopheles, arduous and dank. There is a grotto into which Faust could withdraw and before which he stands.

The opening soliloquy of this scene has two parts. The first is a paean of triumphant bliss. Faust is as nearly completely happy in the realization of his intellectual powers as a human being is likely to be. The second part of the soliloquy, however, is the antithesis to this bliss. Faust is reminded of his limitations once more, and particularly of his debasing association with Mephistopheles.

In the dialogue which follows, Mephistopheles brings all his cunning to bear upon the problem of getting Faust out of this mood and back to his amorous adventure with Gretchen, which has not yet reached its culmination. He first reproaches Faust for what he thinks is a return to morbid, solitary speculation about the universe. This once had led Faust to the brink of suicide and will again exhaust and ruin him, if he persists in it. Then Mephistopheles ridicules the incongruity between this great intellectual ambition (as he conceives Faust to feel it) and Faust's overpowering sexual drive, which has been aroused in the Witch's Kitchen and by Gretchen. And then Mephistopheles turns to sheer sensuous incitement, until Faust has been whipped into a frenzy of emotion.

3217–3239 Faust's thanksgiving for the granting of all his prayers. The items granted are referred to one by one: (1) knowledge of the world about him, (2) knowledge of himself, (3) the peace of contemplative living.

3223 **ihre** Nature's.

3225 **die Reihe der Lebendigen** The series of phyla of animate creatures, from the single-cell protozoa through the invertebrates to the mollusca, thence to the vertebrates, from the fishes to man (in the order: pisces, amphibia, reptilia, aves, mammalia).

3231 'The hill reverberates upon its (*der Riesenfichte*) fall with the dull and hollow sound of thunder.'

3232–3239 When the storm interrupts his contemplation of the world of nature outside himself, his thoughts are turned inward upon his own being. And when the clear moon rising above him stimulates his imagination, this brings before his inner eye shadowy figures from the past. The desire for these experiences was expressed in lines 392–397.

3240–3250 The relation between Faust and Mephistopheles is laid before the spirit to whom Faust speaks. Calmly the case is put, and but for the interruption, some solution would certainly have been prayed for.

3241 **zu** 'along with' the bliss of this all-embracing insight into the works of creation.

3243 Mephistopheles is meant.

3245 **erniedrigt** Mephistopheles has introduced Faust to the juvenile doings in *Auerbachs Keller*, to the revolting irrationality of the *Hexenküche*, and has lately enticed him into perjury as to Schwerdtlein's alleged death and burial in Padua.

3248 **Bild** The symbol of sexual attraction; see lines 2599–2600.

3249–3250 **Genuß** As the scene now stands, before the seduction of Gretchen, these lines must be read in a general sense, expressing the turmoil of a striving human spirit which cannot be satisfied with mere enjoyment of any sort.

3254 **Neuen** A weak form instead of the usual strong form *Neuem*, chosen here for the sake of rime. — Mephistopheles is trying to get his program (of lines 1860–1864) started again.

3256 The implication is that Faust also has his bad days, when he is much less at peace with himself. One such bad day is revealed in lines 1544–1571.

3258 **darfst . . . nicht** 'You really have no grounds' (for complaining).

3268 **Kribskrabs der Imagination** The frustration and confusion of the Faust of lines 354–736. Mephistopheles had indeed induced Faust to turn his back on this kind of "nonsense" *auf Zeiten lang* 'for quite some time.'

3271 Mephistopheles claims that if he had not appeared Faust would have 'left this world.' The only plan for suicide which we know Faust to have entertained is that of the Easter night of lines 686– 736. Mephistopheles knows about this (see lines 1579–1580), but he had nothing at all to do with preventing its fulfillment. More- over, when Goethe added these lines 3266–3277, neither lines 720– 736 nor lines 1579–1580 were in the text of the Faust play. Yet we can accept it as quite probable that Faust's earlier confusion and feeling of frustration would have led him to attempt suicide if there had been no change in his way of life. It is easier for us to understand this than it was for the readers of the FRAGMENT, for we have seen Faust once (720–736) on the brink of suicide, and again (1570–1571) in a proper mood for it.

3274–3277 Faust has apparently been drinking from springs and small streams and eating water cress and similar delicacies. This is ab- horrent to Mephistopheles, who implies that only toads, very despicable beasties, do this. He can imagine a Ph.D. doing some- thing of this kind, but not a proper human being. — The reason for Mephistopheles' antipathy to Faust's communion with nature becomes clear from a letter which Goethe wrote to Herder, August 9, 1776. He said: "Ich führe mein Leben in Klüften, Höhlen, Wäldern, in Teichen, unter Wasserfällen, bei den Unterirdischen, und weide mich aus in Gottes Welt." This also throws light on lines 3278– 3281, for such retirement into nature was a normal procedure for Goethe.

3278–3279 Goethe reveals how invigorating this kind of experience was for him in the letter of May 10, 1771 at the beginning of his novel: DIE LEIDEN DES JUNGEN WERTHERS (1774).

3282–3292 In these lines Mephistopheles satirizes the overweening desire for knowledge of the Faust of the *Erdgeist* scene, and the Faust of lines 1770–1775. He thinks (3277) that Faust's withdrawal into the forest and cave shows a return of this intellectual ambition. — Lines 614–622 provide parallels to the substance of lines 3283– 3290. Yet Mephistopheles clothes his satire in erotic imagery cal- culated, even as brutally sardonic overtones, to incite the passion of Faust and to prepare for more overt appeals to his lust.

3287 The allusion is to the first chapter of Genesis, which tells of God's work of creation.

3291–3292 'And then to bring this lofty intuitive insight to a close — I dare not say how.' The gesture of SD 3292 presumably indicates copulation.

3293 will . . . behagen 'You find that difficult to accept.'

3294 Bitterly ironical.

3298 vorzulügen The allusion is to Faust's conviction that he can intuitively or rationally know everything (3220–3234) and penetrate the central secrets of the universe (3285–3287). The *Vergnügen* of line 3297 is the same as that of line 3282.

3300 abgetrieben 'worn out' by the days in the forest (3272–3277), as Mephistopheles thinks of them. According to another view, *abgetrieben* is used in the nautical sense, 'drifted off course.' — The shift of pronouns of address reflects a shift in attitude from distant politeness (*Euch, Ihr*), to irritated contempt (*Ihm, Er*), to cajoling intimacy (*du*).

3303 dadrinne = *dadrinnen*, with a gesture pointing toward the town: 'in yonder.'

3307–3310 The metaphor is that of a spring torrent in a mountain brook. Faust's wooing is compared with the torrent of a mountain stream swollen with melted snow. Such torrents last but a short while, after which the brook becomes a shallow stream.

3318 A well-known folksong begins:

> "Wenn ich ein Vöglein wär'
> und auch zwei Flügel hätt',
> flög' ich zu dir . . ."

3324 Schlange The serpent, according to Genesis 3, was the first and a very successful tempter of human beings.

3325 Gelt 'I'll wager (that I capture you),' (in the sense of lines 312–314). This remark indicates Mephistopheles' satisfaction with the effect of his suggestions upon his intended victim. Since the words are spoken to no one in particular, the expression: 'I'll wager,' is not a proposal, but an expression of confidence.

3326 Hebe dich The phrase is reminiscent of Christ's words to the Devil, Matthew 4.10, which Luther rendered: "Heb dich weg von mir, Satan!" There is an analogy between the temptation of Christ in the wilderness and Mephistopheles' incitement of Faust in this scene.

3329 halbverrückten Sinnen Having once put his desire away, Faust protests against its being brought again to his senses, distraught by the conflict between his conscience and his lust.

3334 The 'Body of the Lord' is either the image of Christ on the Crucifix or the bread of the Holy Sacrament.

3335 indes While Faust is not with her.

3337 Zwillingspaar A direct allusion to the Song of Songs 4.5, which Luther rendered: "Deine zwei Brüste sind wie zwei junge Rehzwillinge, die unter den Rosen weiden."

3339 Bub' = *Buben*. This kind of contraction in pairs of words joined by *und* is frequent in FAUST.

3339–3341 A scurrilous interpretation of Genesis 1.27–28: "And God created man in his own image, in the image of God created he him; male and female created he them. And God blessed them; and God said to them: 'Be fruitful, and multiply, and replenish the earth, and subdue it' . . ." — **Beruf** Alludes to *Kuppler* (3338) and *Gelegenheit machen* means *kuppeln* 'act as procurer.' — Faust has called Mephistopheles a pander; Mephistopheles maintains that God recognized this as the noblest calling and practiced it Himself by bringing Adam and Eve together.

3349 **Unmensch** 'brute." In contrast to the composed and purposeful *Mensch* 'human being' he ought to be.

3350–3360 These lines symbolize the ruin brought about by irresistible natural forces.

3352 **mit kindlich dumpfen Sinnen** 'childlike, with senses half-aroused.'

3353 **Hüttchen** See note to line 2708.

3362 In the present sequence of scenes the reference must be to the conflict within himself and within the girl's heart, whether or not to yield to their passion.

3369 **er** The man with the *Köpfchen*, or with the *Kopf*, which is implied in *das Köpfchen*. Goethe changed *es* of the URFAUST to *er* in this line in the FRAGMENT of 1790.

3372–3373 Since a devil has nothing for which to hope, despair on his part is a silly waste of time and a complete lack of realism.

17. GRETCHENS STUBE

Since this scene was composed with no reference to the content of the scene *Wald und Höhle*, which now precedes it, there are several difficulties of reference in the text as it is now constituted.

Gretchen's distress is not at all based on the belief that Faust has deserted her (3330–3331), though lines 3315–3319 fit her condition well enough. She is in love and this alone robs her of her peace.

The scene is a necessary antecedent and motivation to the discussion of religion in Marthe's garden. Also, without this scene *Am Spinnrade* we could not understand Gretchen's acceptance of the sleeping potion for her mother.

SD 3374 **Gretchen am Spinnrade** The women of Goethe's day, both of peasant and of small town circles, were likely to spend any leisure moments they could find at their spinning wheels.

3378 **Wo** Any place where he is not with me.

3390 **Nach ihm** 'Hoping to see him.'

3392 **nach ihm** 'hoping to meet him.' Lines 3390–3393 stress Gretchen's longing for Faust; whether she stands looking from her window, or goes out to do her errands (3145), always she longs for him.

18. MARTHENS GARTEN

Having shown us the emotional state of the two young people, the poet brings them together again in the garden. Here, as in the first

Garden Scene (3073–3204), we are plunged into the middle of a conversation during one of a number of such meetings between the lovers in this convenient trysting spot.

The function of this scene is to exhibit the conquest of Gretchen by Faust (3502–3520) and to provide the motivation which makes tragedy inescapable in this case (3511).

3414　**Heinrich** The Faust of the legend before Goethe was *Johann*. In order to exclude the vulgar associations connected with the name *Johann Faustus*, particularly in the puppet plays, Goethe selected a different given name. The reasons for his choice of the name *Heinrich* are not certainly known.

3415　**wie hast du's mit . . .** 'just how *do* you feel about . . . ?'

3422　**auf dich könnte** = *über dich vermöchte* 'had any influence on you'

3428　**Magst . . . fragen** 'Ask, if you wish . . .'

3429–3430　**Spott über den Frager** Because the answer of theologians and philosophers is in terms of names (3457), which mock the real seeker after truth and conceal the true divinity rather than reveal it.

3432　The declaration of faith which Faust here gives is usually viewed as the most eloquent expression of Goethe's pantheistic belief in God. Insofar as the utterance is pantheistic, it is most like Spinoza's pantheistic philosophy. In the main, however, it is the expression of the impatience of the men of the Storm and Stress with the inadequacy of mere names, and of the intuitive belief in love as the central principle of the universe.

3447　'Does not the divinity, all these things — you and I, the sky above, and the earth below, life — crowd in upon your senses and your feelings, forever mysteriously visible in the invisible close beside you?'

3451　**so groß es ist** 'to its full capacity.'

3456–3458　'Feeling is the all-important thing; a name is noise and smoke, which beclouds the glowing light of heaven.' In sum, the mere confession by His name: *Ich glaube an Gott*, may well enough be completely empty. But the person whose heart is full of God's all-pervasive spirit cannot help but confess his faith in that spirit.

3460　The priest, too, tells her that God is a mysterious presence and that He is present in all things — that God is love, and that she must love God.

3463　**unter dem himmlischen Tage** 'wherever the light of heaven shines.'

3470　**der** Has demonstrative force, 'that.'

3475　**widrig** Here probably in its older meaning: 'hostile.'

3480　**dem** Demonstrative 'that.'

3481　**Schelm** Here with its older unpleasant meaning: 'scoundrel,' 'wretch.' In line 2515 (*Hexe* to Mephistopheles) and in line 3205 (Faust to Margarete) the word is used playfully, hence with a pleasant meaning, such as attaches to 'rogue' or 'rascal' in some uses.

3488　The double negative gives added emphasis. See note to line 3198.

3490　**mag** = *vermag* 'he is (not) able.'

3492 **hingegeben warm** 'warm in my surrender.'

3494 Faust recognizes and appreciates this girl's intuitive perception of evil.

3496 **wo . . . nur** 'wherever.'

3498 'I just couldn't pray at all.'

3501 'This is just a case of natural antipathy,' the opposite of a "natural affinity."

3505–3506 In order to understand the character of this girl, it is necessary to understand the customs of her country and her day. It was not at all unusual for a respectable girl to admit her suitor to her bed before wedlock. Gretchen's fault is that she, with her *kindlich dumpfen Sinnen*, fails to make a clear distinction between a lover and a suitor, although she is at times aware of the reality of the case, and although she knows that her mother would not regard Faust as a proper person to be her companion. Church and society placed severe penalties on young women who were deserted by their lovers. See the scene *Am Brunnen*, 3544–3586.

3511 One may assume that this situation has been foreseen by Faust. Gretchen's mother ultimately dies from taking this sleeping draught. Some see in this merely the result of Gretchen's anxiety and fear of being apprehended by her mother, a fear which led her to give to her mother an overdose of the potion. Others see in this the evil treachery of Mephistopheles, who gives Faust a slow-working, deadly poison in the guise of a harmless sleeping draught, and thereby places the onus of murder on Faust if Gretchen's mother dies. A similar act of treachery towards Faust is the act of Mephistopheles in destroying Philemon and Baucis in Part II.

3512 **in ihren Trank** Supply *gegossen*.

3523 **wurden** The so-called plural of majesty, used in particularly formal speech to lofty personages; hence *Ihnen* in the next line.

3527 Girls, says Mephistopheles, believe that wholly orthodox religious belief on the part of a husband-to-be is a good omen for their future ability to control the man of the house.

3531–3532 'Which in her sight is absolutely the only way to salvation.'

3534 **übersinnlicher sinnlicher** Two attributes of this suitor which alternately dominate him: at one time he is above all sensuous motives, at another he is all amorous desire. In sum, he is befuddled. — The trope which puts two contradictory attributes together in this way is called oxymoron; see note to line 1766.

3536 Plato said (*Protagoras*, 320, c/d = § 30) that the Gods had made all mortal creatures out of earth and fire. Faust alleges that the dirtiest of dirt must be a constituent part of Mephistopheles.

19. Am Brunnen

The function of this scene is to reveal the fact of Faust's betrayal of Gretchen. The time of the action is some days or weeks after her seduction and before her condition becomes known.

The village well was the usual place for neighborly gossip among young women. Beside the *Brunnen* was the *Brunnensäule*, where notices of social disgrace were usually published. In Tyrol, and elsewhere also, the hair of a girl who had associated with soldiers or with men from other regions was cut off and nailed to the *Brunnensäule*.

3544 **Bärbelchen** Diminutive of *Barbara*, the name of one of the four great virgin saints of the third century: Agnes, Barbara, Catharine, and Margaret.

3546 **Sibylle** A woman's name, presumably that of a neighbor.

3548 **Es stinkt** 'Something is rotten.'

3560 **Gekos' und Geschleck'** Both words have a strong connotation of vulgarity.

3561 **Blümchen** The symbol of maidenhood.

3569 **Sünderhemdchen** The law required a girl found guilty of fornication to appear in public in the church, dressed in a sinner's smock, or shift, and to confess the transgression and receive a public reprimand (*deprecatio publica in templo*). Fear of this ordeal led many unwed mothers to kill their illegitimate offspring in an attempt to conceal their guilt. The situation was quite serious in Goethe's day, and he had a hand in the abolition of this public expiation in the churches of Weimar by a decree of May 15, 1786.

3572 **anderwärts** In another district the young man would not be made to suffer for his wrongdoing, as he would if he remained on the scene.

3575 **Kränzel** A young woman who bore an illegitimate child was forbidden to appear before the altar for her wedding wearing a bridal wreath, and candles before the altar could not be lighted. If she appeared with a bridal wreath it was snatched from her head and torn up by her neighbors.

3576 **Häckerling** 'Chopped straw, or sawdust, will be scattered before her door.' Indeed, a trail of chopped straw was often made from the girl's door to that of her lover.

3579 **andrer** Genitive plural of the pronoun: 'other people's.'

3580 **der Zunge** Dative, 'for my tongue to say.'

3581 **schwärzt's** = *ich schwärzte es* 'I made it blacker.'

20. ZWINGER

Like the preceding and the following scenes this is a brief picture which reveals Gretchen's soul as her suffering progresses. Several weeks must be assumed to have elapsed. There is no single English word which translates *Zwinger*. This is the narrow space between the town wall and the nearest houses. There is a niche in the town wall of this scene, where a shrine with an image of the Holy Virgin at the cross has been set up.

3587–3588 **neige: Schmerzenreiche** Strictly speaking, this is a case of assonance rather than a pure rime. However, Goethe pronounced intervocalic *-g-* without voice and as a spirant, like the *ch* of *mache* or *reiche*. See Introduction, p. 144 f.

3590–3592   These lines refer to the image of the Holy Virgin at the foot of the Cross of Christ. — Some medieval paintings of the Mater Dolorosa depict the Holy Virgin with a sword piercing her heart.

3599–3600   **banget, zittert, verlanget** Best taken as intransitives, and *was* as equivalent to *wie*.

3605–3606   The moment she is left alone, she begins to weep.

3608   Outside her windows she keeps potted plants. From these she has picked the bouquet which she has placed in the vases on the shrine.

21. NACHT. STRASSE VOR GRETCHENS TÜRE

Gretchen's brother has learned of his sister's disgrace. He is lying in wait for her lover, to avenge her betrayal. The dramatic function of this scene is to break off the Gretchen affair by forcing Faust to flee from her town. It also adds one more murder to the guilt of the two lovers.

3621   **mag** Implies the plausibility of such an occurrence, hence: 'Where, as is quite to be expected, many a man speaks boastfully.'

3623   **gepriesen** Supply *haben*.

3624   **Mit vollem Glas** 'With a toast' (to the lady). — **verschwemmt** Supply *haben*.

3625   Valentin did not participate; he was an observer of these boastful harangues.

3633   Like our own: "Hold a candle to," the idiom "das Wasser reichen" implies a worthiness to serve another person. The same idea is seen in Mark 1.7: "The latchet of whose shoes I am not worthy to stoop down and unloose."

3637   **stumm** Because they could not produce anything to surpass the praise of Gretchen.

3638   'It is enough to make one . . .'

3648   **er** The betrayer of Valentin's sister.

3650   **Sakristei** The vestry is usually located immediately adjacent to the choir of the church and not far from the main altar. Conceivably — though it is certainly not usually the case — the altar lamp, which is kept lighted day and night, might cast some light from a window of the vestry. It is to be thought of here as a weak shaft of flickering light coming from below upward and casting no light upon the street below the window.

3654–3655   Faust is depressed; Mephistopheles is gleeful. — **sieht's** = *sieht's aus* 'things look.'

3656   Villagers and farmers usually kept a ladder handy to permit them quickly to reach their roofs to extinguish fires which might be set by sparks. Cats used these ladders to reach the thatched roofs which were choice hunting and trysting places for feline society.

3658   **tugendlich** To feel 'virtuous' is to feel that one is doing what one should do: that is, that one is *tüchtig*. This is a comfortable feeling, and the comfort is really what Mephistopheles means to express: 'I'm quite satisfied with myself.'

3661   **Walpurgisnacht** The night of April 30 to May 1; see note to line 2590. — **übermorgen** in line 3662 indicates that this scene occurs on the night of April 28.

3664–3665 According to popular superstition, a buried treasure is revealed to a spirit seer by a phosphorescent glow above its resting place. This one is being elevated to the surface by mysterious unnatural powers. Such a treasure is said to "bloom" (*der Schatz blüht*). This one is a kettle full of silver coins with the Lion of Bohemia embossed on them.

3673   Pearls are associated in popular superstition with tears.

3679   **Kunststück** Not merely the song that is to be heard, but the cynical trick of using a truly moral song for the accomplishment of quite immoral purposes.

3682–3697 This song has many points of similarity with the Schlegel translation of Ophelia's song in HAMLET IV, 5. The borrowings were cheerfully conceded by Goethe in a conversation with Eckermann, January 18, 1825: "So singt mein Mephistopheles ein Lied von Shakespeare, und warum sollte er das nicht?"

3684   **Kathrinchen** Catharine was the name of one of the four virgin saints; see note to line 3544.

3693   **Dinger** This form of the plural is often used to refer to small helpless human beings, or to inexperienced young girls, as here.

3698   **Element** See note to line 2805.

3699   **Rattenfänger** Either an allusion to the Pied Piper of Hameln or a reminiscence of Shakespeare's ROMEO AND JULIET III, 1, where Mercutio calls Tybalt a rat-catcher. Some suggest that both Shakespeare and the Pied Piper are reflected here.

3703   Supply a verb of motion: *Nun soll es . . . gehen.* 'Now we proceed . . .'

3704   **gewichen** Like *zugestoßen* (3707), a past participle used in a command. This usage is most frequent in short sharp commands or warnings.

3711   **zahm** 'no longer dangerous.'

3714–3715 **Polizei : Blutbann** With the former, which deals with crimes other than murder, Mephistopheles can deal. With the latter, which deals with matters of life and death, he cannot. The most likely reason would appear to be that this court requires imperial sanction and the Emperor is looked on as the instrument of God. Mephistopheles says he has no means of controlling decrees arrived at in the Emperor's name or in his behalf.

3720   By calling Valentin 'Your mother's son,' rather than 'Your brother,' the crowd indicates its abhorrence of the fallen Gretchen. Stage directors usually make the crowd show their revulsion by turning away from Gretchen.

3731   **sei** Probably best taken as imperative, second person, with *'s* = *eine Hure* as predicate.

3732   **Was soll mir das?** 'Such words to me?' or 'What's all this going to come to?'

3737   **mehre** An inflected form of *mehr*. In older German this word was occasionally inflected when used as a pronoun, but it is now invariable: *mehr*.

3740–3744 These lines prefigure the birth and destruction of Gretchen's child.

3752 **Leichen** An old dative singular form in *–n*, like *Erden* (1374); see also 3763.

3754 **soll** Expresses the will of the speaker.

3756 Valentin lists a few of the penalties his sister is to suffer, all of them in accordance with the laws and customs of the time. Young women of ill repute were forbidden by local or church law to wear golden jewelry, to participate in church services, or to wear fine clothes in public places.

3757 **Altar** This word occurs twice in Part I of Faust and has the stress on the first syllable (3757, 3778). In Part II it occurs three times and has the stress on the second syllable (4788, 9433, 10 959).

3760 **Jammerecken** An archaic accusative singular.

3765 **Lästrung** The blasphemy is implied in his cursing Gretchen despite the possibility that God forgives her (3762–3763).

3766 Supply *kommen*: 'If I could only get . . .'

3767 This is a direct accusation of Marthe's complicity in Gretchen's fall.

3769 **reiche Maß** This is the only feminine form of this noun in Faust. The other forms are either clearly or presumably neuter.

3772 **der Ehre** Genitive singular with *lossprechen*.

22. Dom

Originally this was the last of three short scenes revealing in consecutive pictures the growing anguish of the desperate girl. The insertion of the Valentin scene between the second and the third of these scenes (between *Zwinger* and *Dom*) interrupted the continuity which these scenes had in the Urfaust, where the sequence was unbroken.

As the scene was first planned, Gretchen is in the cathedral to attend the funeral services of her mother, who has been killed by the sleeping potion given her by her daughter. Gretchen's disgrace was not yet a matter of public knowledge.

After the introduction of the Valentin scene, it is impossible to explain the presence of Gretchen in the cathedral except on the grounds that the authorities have not yet acted on what must, after lines 3726–3763, be regarded as a notorious situation. On the whole, it is more satisfactory simply to concede that there are in Faust, as we have it, certain irreconcilable discrepancies, due principally to Goethe's only partially carrying out a late intention to lighten the weight of guilt on Gretchen by making it appear that she had sinned but once. (See lines 12 065–12 068.)

The evil spirit of this scene is Gretchen's own consciousness of sin, her bad conscience, personified as a demon, probably analogous to the evil spirit of Jehovah (I Samuel 16.14), who plagued Saul.

3779 **Büchelchen** Her prayerbook, handed down from generation to generation and hence well-worn.

3788 **Pein** In purgatory, because she died unshriven in her sleep and without benefit of extreme unction. According to Roman Catholic belief, the souls of persons who die in the grace and love of God expiate in purgatory such sins as do not merit eternal damnation.

3795 **Gedanken** Genitive plural with *los*. Modern usage requires the accusative, as at line 2509.

3797 **wider mich** 'in spite of all I can do.'

3798 This famous Latin hymn (a sequence) is often incorporated in masses for the dead. Its author is unknown, and its attribution to Thomas of Celano (ca. 1250) is uncertain. The hymn can be found with a German translation in Karl Simrock's LAUDA SION, 2nd ed., Stuttgart, 1863, p. 333, or Friedrich Wolters, HYMNEN UND SEQUENZEN, 2nd ed., Berlin, 1922, pp. 136–138. Goethe quotes directly from the first, sixth, and seventh of the seventeen stanzas, and alludes to the content of the third and fourth. The first two lines go: 'Day of wrath — that day will change the world into cinders.'

3800 **Grimm** The wrath of the Day of Judgment (*dies irae*).

3801 The trumpet of I Corinthians 15.52: ". . . at the last trump: for the trumpet shall sound, and the dead shall be raised incorruptible . . ." In the hymn:

> "Tuba mirum spargens sonum
> per sepulcra regionum
> coget omnes ante thronum."

'The war-trumpet, casting its astonishing sound
through the sepulchres of the lands,
summons everyone (to appear) before the throne (of God).'

3803–3807 Gretchen's Evil Spirit tells her that instead of being raised up incorruptible to dwell forever with God, as St. Paul promised the Corinthians and the Thessalonians, she will rise from her grave to suffer the torments of flaming Hell. Even such peace as her heart will meanwhile find in the grave is described as a 'peace of ashes,' *Aschenruh*.

3811 'As if the song would break my heart.'

3813 'For when the judge shall hold court,
whatever is hidden will appear publicly;
nothing will remain unavenged.'

3821 **Verbirg dich!** This imperative form is best taken ironically: "Hide yourself, indeed!" The more direct utterance from the *Böser Geist* would be a question: *Verbirgst du dich?* 'Do you think you can hide?' The URFAUST has: *Verbirgst du dich! Blieben verborgen dein Sünd' und Schand'!* These are exclamatory questions with ironic tone. — Gretchen's Evil Spirit is telling her what she has thought to herself all the while as the answer to her perplexed query: "What can I do?"

3822 **bleibt** A singular verb with a compound subject (*Sünd' und Schande*) which is thought of as a single unit.

3825 'What then am I, wretched one, to say?
What patron am I then to implore,
when scarcely the just man is secure?'

3829 **Verklärte** Transfigured souls (see I Corinthians 15.49–54), who have risen from their graves (see I Thessalonians 4.16–17). These turn away from the sinful soul.

3834 This *Fläschchen* contained smelling salts. — In the days when women fainted frequently, most of them carried a little bottle containing an aromatic preparation of carbonate of ammonia, usually with some perfume added, the vapor from which they inhaled when they felt faint.

23. WALPURGISNACHT

The *Walpurgisnacht* scene, plus the *Walpurgisnachtstraum*, plus a third scene, planned but never written, were to have presented Faust's adventures between the slaying of Valentin and Faust's unsuccessful attempt to rescue Gretchen from prison. Since the third scene was not written, the subtitle *Intermezzo* does not fit the *Walpurgisnachtstraum* too well.

Dramatically these scenes are important; theatrically they are well-nigh impossible. Mephistopheles, in his campaign to win Faust's soul, has snatched him from his intellectual pursuits, has transformed him into a young man, has involved him in a tragic love-affair and in two murders; but he has never been able to stifle the essential nobility of Faust's soul completely. In his love for Gretchen there was something more than mere bestiality and lust, something still of the true God-given urge of love. To drag Faust still lower, Mephistopheles now takes him to this witches' holiday on the Brocken, where he can bring to bear the strongest of his wiles to captivate Faust's soul.

The scene is geographically accurate. Schierke and Elend are two little towns on the slopes of the mountain, whose summit is called the Brocken. Schierke is at the southern foot of the mountain, 650 meters above sea level. Elend (508 meters above sea level) is a bit farther south and somewhat lower than Schierke. The top of the Brocken is 1142 meters above sea level. The two usual footpaths from Schierke to the top of the mountain are respectively 7 and 9.2 kilometers long, requiring a walk of two or two and a half hours. A shorter path of 6 kilometers takes about two hours.

One has to imagine a constant change of scenery as the action moves along until we reach line 4117. Since the festivities are to begin at midnight, the time of the beginning of this scene is perhaps 9:30 or 10 P.M.

3835 Standard transportation for witches and sorcerers calls for either a broomstick or a male goat.

3841 **hinzuschleichen** 'to stroll at a comfortable pace.'

3845 **Frühling** It is the night of April 30, a little more than a year from the time of the monologue in Faust's study with which Part I begins.

3849 Since Mephistopheles is eternal, he feels no seasonal changes with the passage of time. He is also lazy and vexed at the labors of this climb. He would prefer to ride to his destination; hence he feels *winterlich*.

3851 **die unvollkommne Scheibe** Probably a gibbous moon, with the bright part greater than a semicircle and less than a circle. A gibbous moon can rise only after sundown. The later it rises the less of its surface is visible and the more it has waned. We hear that this one is rising late, with its light diffused to a reddish glow by the dense lower air through which its rays must travel from the horizon to the observer, thus giving just the right kind of light for the ghostly scene which is to come. Goethe was an unusually keen observer of nature and this kind of minute accuracy is not unusual in his writings.

3855 Since the usual occupation of an *Irrlicht* (*ignis fatuus*) is to lead travelers astray and to their destruction, these creatures are thought of as servants of the Devil.

3857 **fodern** Instead of *fordern;* used only here and at 11 314 in FAUST. Although *fodern* was the newer of the two forms, it was used chiefly in poetry in Goethe's day and has not survived.

3861 **leichtes Naturell** A pun: *leicht* in the sense of 'irresponsible' and in the sense of 'airy.' The *ignis fatuus* is a gaseous phenomenon, not a solid body.

3862–3863 With impatient irony Mephistopheles compares the normal zigzag course of the *Irrlicht* with normal human conduct. Human behavior is as devious and unsteady as the will-o'-the-wisp's course.

3870 From here on the problem of staging this scene is almost insoluble. A revolving stage and a backdrop of moving pictures help, but the result is much less satisfactory than a reader's imagination.

3871–3911 Goethe did not indicate the distribution of the roles for this colloquy in song. It is clear that the third stanza belongs to Faust, the fourth to Mephistopheles. The fifth should probably be assigned to Faust and the second to the *Irrlicht*. Whether Faust or Mephistopheles sings the first stanza is problematical. The most satisfactory arrangement is to assign it to Faust.

3876 **Seh'** For *ich sehe.*

3880 There are two great blocks of rock between Schierke and Elend, called the *Schnarcherklippen*. One of them is said to contain a large natural magnet. The name is said to have been given them because a strong wind blowing over the rocks produces sounds similar to the sound of snoring.

3885 Voices of those divine days when love's dear lament, songs, the rustling of a brook, still found his heart full of hope and full of love, — a state of which Faust speaks in elegiac tone as of something gone but not forgotten. This personal past suggests to him the comparison of the echo with the memory of ancient days.

3886 'What things we hope for! What things we love!'

3889 **Uhu! Schuhu!** Mephistopheles imitates the cry of the night-owl. Both of these words are current as names of this bird.

3890 These are all birds which are usually quiet at night.

3893 This line is troublesome, since one could attribute the fat bellies to salamanders, but certainly not the long legs. Probably one has to think of lizard-like creatures (*Molche*) which are still not lizards, or at any rate not normal ones — possibly overgrown toads crossed with fire-salamanders.

3898 **Masern** These are large erratic growths on trees, particularly on oak trees. Here the protuberances from the tree trunks are said to seem to be living creatures thrusting out arms like the tentacles of an octopus to seize the passing traveler.

3908 **drehen** Used intransitively instead of *sich drehen*.

3916–3931 Mammon, the ninth prince of Hell, the demon of earthly riches, puts on a show for his lord and master, with special illumination of the deep abyss in which his treasure house of gold is hid.

3919 **er** = *der Schein*.

3921 **Dunst und Flor** Hendiadys, 'the veil of vapor, the hazy veil.'

3923 **sie** = *die Glut*.

3935 **die ungestümen Gäste** The boisterous witches and sorcerers en route to their revel on the mountain top. They ride on the wings of the gale.

3939 **sie** = *die Windsbraut*.

3943–3944 **Säulen** The trunks of great trees are thought of as the columns which support eternally-verdant palaces.

3955 **Zaubergesang** The song of the witches, which follows.

3959 **obenauf** 'uppermost,' 'in first place.' Hence, 'Herr Urian is sitting (or will sit) in first place,' or 'be in command.' But *oben auf*, as the text is printed in the editions published under Goethe's supervision, may be taken to mean: 'Herr Urian will mount (his throne) up there' (to preside over the revels and bestow his rewards). The first interpretation is probably now the usual one.

3961 A coarse line usually disguised in this way, as Goethe himself caused it to be printed.

3962 **Baubo** Demeter's lewd nurse, — a classic figure astray in a Teutonic-romantic revel.

3964 **Ehre** St. Paul's Epistle to the Romans, 13.7: "Render . . . honor to whom honor (is due)."

3965 **angeführt** A participle for an imperative: 'Let Frau Baubo come forward (*vor*) and let her lead (us) on.'

3966 This line appears to have a double meaning. Baubo is mounted on a *Mutterschwein*, and she is herself a swine, and a mother also. The story has it that she is so evil because her daughter was stolen from her.

3968 **Ilsenstein** Now called *Ilsestein* (near Ilsenburg), a granite block which towers 150 meters above the surrounding valley floor. Ilsenburg is on the edge of the Harz, northeast of the Brocken.

3972 **sie** The same incontinent hag who has just been invited to go to hell because of her great hurry (3970–3971).

3976 The pitchforks and brooms, on which the crowding witches ride, inflict injury on those who are jammed into them by the throng.

3977 This is a very dense crowd. An unborn child is crushed and its mother squeezed until she bursts, like a rubber balloon.

3980 **des Bösen** The Devil's.

3986 **Felsensee** This place name, unlike the others in this scene, has not been identified with any real lake or town in the Harz.

3986–4015 Take these speeches at face value as satirical hocus-pocus. None of the proposed explanations or interpretations of these lines has been generally accepted. Still further impish playfulness on the part of Goethe is evidenced in these voices from above and from below. A half-witch evidently isn't a whole witch: she cannot catch up with the crowd, and she can't stand it at home.

4008 **Salbe** = *Hexensalbe* A magic unction which, being spread on a broomstick and on the person, permits the witch to fly.

4010 A trough with a sail for aerial navigation.

4015 **Hexenheit** A parody of the then current fashion of making new words with *–heit*, such as *Griechheit* for *Griechentum, Deutschheit* for *Deutschtum.*

4023 **Junker Voland** The Devil was called *vâlant* in the twelfth and thirteenth centuries; this name has become *Voland.* We do not know its origin.

4030 The contradictory nature of Mephistopheles' proposal is ironically stated (4032–4033). They have come to the mountain for the very party from which they are now withdrawing.

4035 The club is composed of a general, a minister of state, a parvenu, and an author. These persons are joined together by their common annoyance with things as they are and their preference for the 'good old days.' See note to lines 4076–4091.

4036–4040 **Kleinen** In this little world (4045) there are things and people to see, flames and gay revelers. Faust, however, wishes to push on to the summit where he may find answers to some of his questions about the nature of things.

4039 **zu dem Bösen** 'To the throne of Satan,' where, according to Goethe's earlier plan, the Devil was to discourse cynically with goats, male and female.

4045 An allusion perhaps to the creation of little cliques in the society of eighteenth-century courts.

4050 Mephistopheles is annoyed by any music but his own, but especially by such as implies the harmonious endeavors of a number of people. — These people are probably playing horns of some kind.

4054 By introducing Faust into this circle, Mephistopheles will put him under renewed obligation of gratitude.

4058 Faust and Mephistopheles have entered a cavern filled with picnicking, dancing, carousing witches in various groups. The sad little club of oldsters is also here.

4064 **Knieband** An allusion to the Order of the Garter, the highest distinction of this kind in Great Britain.

4065 **Pferdefuß** The Devil's hoof; see note to 2184.

4069 So many of these persons are intimately acquainted with him.

4071 This line has to do with the relation of Faust and Mephistopheles to the witches at their dancing. First, however, they overhear the club of discontented old men.

4076–4091 The general has been retired, by popular demand. The minister, once all-important in the public eye, laments the passing of the old generation. The parvenu would have liked to preserve the status quo, in which he had worked his way to the top by shrewd but dishonest maneuvers. The author finds no admiring readers but plenty of young hostile critics for his works of moderate and wise content. — In sum, we have a group of caricatures of the reactionaries of Goethe's day.

4089 **mäßig** A pun: 'moderate and moderately.'

SD 4092 Mephistopheles parodies these old and gloomy gentlemen.

4094 When the wine cask has been almost completely emptied, the dregs begin to be drawn out with the wine, making it cloudy. When a glass of such wine has been almost drained, the sediment at the bottom is disturbed and runs out with the rest. Hence *auf der Neige* (4095), applied to the world as well as to a glass of wine, means 'about finished,' 'down to the dregs.'

SD 4096 **Trödelhexe** Every fair and folk festival has booths in which all sorts of things are offered for sale. The items specifically offered here reflect and suggest the Valentin-Gretchen outrages of the pair who pass by.

4110–4113 Mephistopheles does not approve these suggestions of the past. He needs something new to lure Faust to his doom.

4114–4115 Faust, meanwhile, has been pushed about by the throng until he hardly knows which way he is going. He thoroughly approves this great fair.

4119 **Lilith** Rabbinical tradition teaches that the woman created with man (Genesis 1.27) was Lilith, but that she proved unsatisfactory and that therefore another woman, Eve, was subsequently created from one of Adam's ribs (Genesis 2.21–22). Lilith was reputed to have become a spirit, who specializes in seducing men and in injuring little children. At Isaiah 34.14 Luther translated the Hebrew word *"lilith"* by 'der Kobold,' 'the goblin.' The American revised version of the year 1901 translates it 'the night-monster.'*

4121 **einzig** She is otherwise unadorned.

4124 **zwei** Two witches: they have been dancing wildly. A new round is about to begin. Faust and Mephistopheles join in the dance.

---

* The Revised Standard Version of 1952 translates *lilith* as 'the night hag.'

Die Alte may well be the witch from the *Hexenküche* (2590 ff.). In one sketch of this scene she is tagged: "*Hexe aus der Küche.*"

4126 **Das** Probably best taken to refer to the wild goings-on.

4130 The allusion is to the witch's breasts.

4132 **ihr** 'all you men.'

4138 The dashes here and in the witch's reply represent some sort of abysmal indecency which Goethe chose not to print. — At this point Faust has sunk as low into sheer sensual lust as he can well go. The question is: will he stay there?

SD 4144 **Proktophantasmist** Derived from Greek *prōktós,* 'buttocks.' See note to line 4161. — The first of a considerable number of personal caricatures aimed at Goethe's contemporaries. This one is directed at Friedrich Nicolai (1773–1811), a Berlin publisher and writer, who satirized Goethe's novel, DIE LEIDEN DES JUNGEN WERTHERS (1774), in a parody which he called DIE FREUDEN DES JUNGEN WERTHERS. The rationalist Nicolai was opposed to the uncontrolled or excessive play of emotions which marked the works of Storm and Stress.

4150 **schätzen** The allusion is to the critical activity of Nicolai.

4155 **Mühle** The place where he produces his own literary works and those of others of his kind — his publishing house, where these things are 'ground out' in great quantities. One very extensive publication of this house was the *Allgemeine deutsche Bibliothek* (1765–1806).

4157 **begrüßen** 'ask politely for it as a favor.'

4160 **Regel** These are the geniuses who heed no rules of composition or of aesthetics.

4161 **Tegel** A little town near Berlin. The story is that Nicolai, the great enemy of supernatural spirits in literature, in 1791 himself suffered hallucinations and saw visions. To relieve him thereof, leeches were applied to his posterior, and with some success (hence *Proktophantasmist*). In 1799 he discussed this ghost business in an essay which he called "*Beispiel einer Erscheinung mehrerer Phantasmen.*" Here he included the report of a ghostly visitation in the home of a Mr. Schulz in Tegel.

4166–4167 An intentional pun. Nicolai revolted not only against the despotism of *Geister* ('ghosts') but, according to this thrust, against the supremacy of other peoples' *Geist* ('intelligence'). See line 4175. His own intelligence isn't able to force these leading spirits through standardized drills. There may even be a suggestion of *exorzisieren* ('exorcise') in *exerzieren*.

4169 **Reise** An allusion to the very dull and very long (twelve large volumes) BESCHREIBUNG EINER REISE DURCH DEUTSCHLAND UND DIE SCHWEIZ IM JAHRE 1781, which Nicolai published in the thirteen years from 1783 to 1796. Nicolai is again referred to as the 'Traveler' at lines 4267 and 4319. He says here that he will at least take home with him this trip to the Brocken, presumably to add it to the REISE.

4170 **vor meinem letzten Schritt** 'before my death.'

4171 **bezwingen** He hopes to overcome the devils by means of leeches, applied as indicated; he hopes to overcome the poets through his literary attacks on their works.

4172 **Pfütze** The source of the leeches.

SD 4176 Something has given Faust pause in his sensuous revels.

4179 The significance of the red mouse is mysterious, but the effect of its appearance is revulsion. After all, the lady is a witch. Mephistopheles points out that it wasn't a real (gray) mouse anyway (4181).

4184–4205 The illusion by which Faust here sees the figure of Gretchen is a clairvoyant dream in which Faust's knowledge of the girl's condition lets him see, as it were in a vision, her future fate: her arrest (4186), her death (4195) by the executioner's axe (4203–4205). In the revels on the Brocken Mephistopheles has produced the most powerfully sensuous diversions at his command. His object is to beguile Faust and perhaps to win his wager at once. To succeed he needs first of all to erase from Faust's mind the memory of Gretchen's pure love for him and of Faust's love for this girl. That Faust should see in this phantom on the Blocksberg the form of Gretchen is precisely opposite to Mephistopheles' plans. He hastens to assure Faust that it is not Gretchen but sheer hocus-pocus; the figure is a witch. Nevertheless Faust is not diverted from thoughts of Gretchen, and his last words in the Walpurgis Night presage with tragic irony the discovery he is about to make about Gretchen — a discovery which drives him to furious reproaches against Mephistopheles (in the scene *Trüber Tag*) and to a futile attempt to liberate Gretchen from prison.

4194 The Gorgon Medusa, a terrible monster in Greek mythology, who was laying waste the country of Polydectes. This monster had once been a very beautiful maiden whose chief glory was her hair. But Minerva, who found the girl's beauty troublesome, transformed the curls of her hair into hissing serpents and made her so horrible to look upon that any living thing which did so was turned into stone.

4207 The most noted of the dead who are thus able to walk about with their heads severed from their bodies is probably Bertrand de Born, described in Dante's Inferno. Another is Anne Boleyn.

4208 Perseus was sent out by Polydectes to attempt to destroy the Medusa. He skillfully used his shining shield as a mirror, so that he might approach the monster without looking at her. When he found her, either asleep or in prayer — one is not certain which — he chopped off her head. The image of the Medusa's head was embossed on the shield of Minerva (Pallas Athena).

4209 Faust is still fascinated by this vision which looks to him like Gretchen and which Mephistopheles calls a delusion (*Wahn*). The Devil's purpose is ill suited by a return of Faust's thoughts to the kind of love represented by his experience with Gretchen.

4211 **Prater** An intentionally anachronistic reference to a famous sylvan park in Vienna, with great open-air cafés. It was dedicated to the public in 1766. Mephistopheles is thinking of something like the *Volksprater* or *Wurstelprater* (from *Hanswurst*), with merry-go-rounds, swings, grottoes, puppet theaters, shooting galleries and refreshment booths.

SD 4214 **Servibilis** A name created by Goethe for the dilettante manager of a dilettante theater. The word means apparently 'the one eager to serve.' Just which of Goethe's acquaintances is here satirized we do not know, and he would interest us little if he could be identified.

4217 **Dilettant** After the death of Schiller in 1805, Goethe took a hand in the direction of the court theater in Weimar. He had a great deal of difficulty with people who had no liking for the great works of the theater, but who demanded something new and something flashy. — The essential mark of the dilettante is his delight in a smattering of knowledge and his lack of powers of concentration and of the ability to do hard work.

4220 **mich dilettiert's** An expression coined by Goethe on the model of Italian *mi diletta* 'it delights me.'

4221–4222 Dilettantism belongs with the creatures of the Devil and their hocus-pocus.

24. Walpurgisnachtstraum

The title of this scene is a direct allusion to Shakespeare's play 'A Midsummer-Night's Dream. The names Oberon, Titania, and Puck are directly from Shakespeare's play. The fairy story of this drama had been used by Wieland in his Oberon; and an operetta, by one of the Wranitzky brothers, dealing with the reconciliation of Oberon and Titania, had been produced in Weimar under Goethe's direction in 1796.

This celebration of the golden wedding of Oberon and Titania was intended originally as a separate little entertainment, bringing together a continuation of the satirical criticism of the contemporary scene which Goethe and Schiller had begun in the *Xenien* (1796–1797). Indeed, some of these stanzas were offered for publication in Schiller's *Musenalmanach* (Summer, 1797). That is to say, in its original conception much of the content of this scene had nothing at all to do with Faust.

As the *Walpurgisnacht* scenes were first sketched, the *Walpurgisnachtstraum* was to have come between two other scenes as an entr'acte entertainment. As it now stands, it is not, properly speaking, an intermezzo in that series, although it may be taken as an interlude in the sequence of scenes in which Faust participates.

The scene belongs in the category of the romantic *Märchendrama*. The director of the play, the leader of the orchestra, the audience, all intervene in the progress of the dialogue. There is no plot and nothing happens. The characters step forward one by one and tell who they are and what they represent, or one of them marches past while some of the others make remarks about him. In the main, each character is a caricature of some contemporary figure in whom we now have very little interest.

Notes

Various types of literary figures and critics are satirized 4255–4290; then individual critics 4295–4330; representatives of various schools of philosophy 4343–4362; finally, types of politicians 4367–4390.

4224 **Mieding** Johann Martin Mieding, the court theater's master carpenter and scene builder in Weimar, whose title was *Hofebenist und Theatermeister*. He died in 1782 and was immortalized by Goethe's poem *Auf Miedings Tod*. *Miedings Söhne* are therefore the successors of Mieding, or the carpenter's crew, who have but little to do for this performance, since the scenery is very simple.

4229–4230 The reconciliation of Oberon and Titania, rather than the fifty years, is the real cause for jubilation. This royal pair long quarreled over Titania's boy attendant, stolen from an Indian potentate, and the alleged too great promiscuity of the king. Finally, by magic means, Titania is made to see the error of her ways and peace is restored.

4235 **Puck** Robin Goodfellow, the jester of King Oberon. He leads the dance of the comic figures.

4239 **Ariel** An airy spirit, whose name is taken from Shakespeare's THE TEMPEST. He leads the nobler figures of this ballet-like scene.

4241 The heavenly song of noble poetry attracts the beautiful souls (*die Schönen*) as well as many caricatures thereof (*Fratzen*).

4247–4250 Titania repeats Oberon's advice.

4251–4254 The first group enters. The Orchestra, all playing (*tutti*) very loudly (*fortissimo*) to accompany the procession, also steps up and identifies itself and its members. What follows is playful fantasy.

SD 4255 **Solo** The soap bubble speaks alone and says he is the bagpipe. At least the two have this in common: each is full of wind.

4259 Just who was meant to be caricatured here and how this caricature is to be understood is not clear. The elements of this person's creation are quite incongruous, but if too unnatural for nature, they suffice for his poem. It is also not clear whether this *Geist* speaks thus about himself or whether, while he is taking form, someone else speaks about him. Anything can happen here.

4263–4266 No plausible interpretation of this pair has been found. They appear to be poets whose "flights" of fancy are but hops, whose enthusiasms outrun their powers.

4267–4270 This traveler is Nicolai, who disliked phantoms, but was troubled by them. See notes to SD 4144 and to 4161, 4169.

4271 This orthodox person, who judges everything from the standpoint of Christian theology, finds that Oberon is a devil, despite his lack of appropriate claws and tail. As the reference to Schiller's *Die Götter Griechenlands* reveals, Goethe aimed this shaft at Count Friedrich Leopold von Stolberg, who had found blasphemy in Schiller's poem.

4275 The idea is that the northern artist needs to go to Italy to learn how to give his materials that classic form which will transform them from mere sketches into an artistic whole.

4279–4282 This purist is an academician of the old, stiff, narrow-minded, pedantic school. What this purist sees on the Brocken is the precise opposite of what he can approve. Hence he characterizes the behavior of these naked witches as *ludern*.

4282 The allusion in *gepudert* is to the hair or wig which was customarily very heavily powdered. Even so, two properly powdered persons have succeeded in getting into this bad company. Who they are no one knows.

4283–4290 The purist gets an answer to his allusion from one of the party of witches, and she in turn gets a nasty wish from one of the elderly dames to whom she alludes. One may surmise that the young witch may represent erotic frankness for its own sake while the matron may represent prudery in art or letters.

4291–4294 The orchestra again, this time reproved by the director. They have been looking at the young witch to the detriment of their playing. Some indeed have left their places for a more immediate inspection of the lady. Now comes the second group of persons.

4295–4302 The weather vane points with the wind, has no opinion of its own. This one reacts first to the point of view of the young witch. This is a good party. Then he reacts to the opposed point of view and concedes that these are all creatures of Hell, or he'll be damned. There are a number of candidates for the distinction of being immortalized in this character, but no identification is certain.

4303 The *Xenien* are the satirical epigrams published by Goethe and Schiller in the *Musenalmanach* of 1797. These brief stanzas had dealt very severely with most of the contemporary literary products in Germany.

4307 August von Hennings, publisher of a literary journal called *Genius der Zeit*, had attacked Schiller's *Horen* (1795–1797) and his *Musenalmanach für 1797*. — **sie** = the *Xenien*, those insects!

4311–4314 Musaget The name of a collection of poems published by Hennings. The name means 'Leader of the Muses' and was applied by the Greeks to Apollo in that capacity. It seems, however, that this person is better fitted to lead witches than muses.

4315 Ci-devant Genius der Zeit In 1800 Hennings changed the name of his journal *Genius der Zeit* to *Genius des neunzehnten Jahrhunderts*, and so Goethe pokes fun at the new name by calling it 'Erstwhile Genius of the Age.' This one invites all to join him and foresees for them all plenty of room on the broad top of the German mountain of muses. (Parnassus was a mountain in Greece sacred to Apollo and the nine muses.) The implication of the broad top is that there is no high standard of exclusion in the choice of candidates for artistic eminence in Germany.

4319–4322 It is not clear who speaks these lines. The best guess is that two speakers are involved, each commenting on the figure of the traveler (Nicolai) which passes near by. Nicolai was a very active enemy of the Jesuit order in Germany.

4323 The crane is Johann Kaspar Lavater (1741–1801), a pious religious poet (4325) and an "expert in physiognomy." Goethe at one time was a very close friend of this man, but later turned away from him. There is no doubt about this identification, as Goethe himself con-

firmed it in conversation with Eckermann (February 17, 1829).
— To fish in troubled waters is to seek advantage from the agitation
and difficulties of others. This trait of character is thus imputed to
Lavater by Goethe and qualifies the author of 100 CHRISTLICHE
LIEDER (1776) for a place among these devils.

4327–4330 This *Weltkind* is Goethe himself. A youthful occasional lyric
poem, *Zwischen Lavater und Basedow* (1774), by Goethe concludes:

"Und wie nach Emmaus, weiter ging's
   mit Geist- und Feuerschritten,
Prophete rechts, Prophete links,
   das Weltkind in der Mitten."

Here too, as in FAUST, Goethe is the Weltkind, between Lavater,
the theologian, and Basedow, the educator. The latter failed to
find a place in FAUST, although one was planned for him.

4331 Transition to the third group of persons. This dancer hears a
monotonous drumming and thinks it is the bitterns drumming in
unison in the swamp. The dancing master (4335) sees the next
group advancing.

SD 4339 **Fiedler** This word appeared in all of the editions published
under Goethe's supervision as *Fideler*. The whole group of lines
(4335–4342) was first put into the text in the edition of 1828. There
has been a great deal of discussion about the name without an indis-
putable conclusion having been reached. We choose the form
Fiedler as the more appropriate to the meaning of the lines. The
fiddler belongs with the dancer and the dancing master, all of whom
comment on the approach of the philosophers.

4339 **sich** Here, as in 4340, the reciprocal pronoun 'one another' rather
than the reflexive.

4341–4342 Alluding to the power of Orpheus with his lyre to quiet the
animosities of savage beasts. Orpheus was the son of Apollo and
the muse, Calliope. He was one of the Argonauts. — **Bestjen**,
with two syllables, rather than *Bestien* with three. One of Goethe's
manuscripts has the form *Bestjen*, and we have retained it to suggest
the pronunciation required by the rime with *Restchen*.

4343–4346 The dogmatist argues (4345–4346) that since there are devils,
the Devil must have a real existence. One characteristic of a dogmatic philosopher is his unconditional belief in the correlation of his
thinking with reality. If he can by thinking arrive at *"der Teufel,"*
then *"der Teufel"* must correspond to reality.

4347 The idealist, in the philosophical sense, regards himself, his own ego,
as the creator of everything he experiences. All existence to him is
merely the representation of his own mind. This one thinks that if
all of the wild goings-on on the Brocken are products of his own
mind, then he must be crazy.

4351 The realist (this one seems to be a naive rather than a critical realist)
accepts as real all objects of his perception. These are so manifold
and so insane this evening that he is befuddled by what his senses
tell him.

4355 The supernaturalist believes in reality transcending our powers to
perceive. He believes in "supernatural" events, and in the divine

revelations thereof. He feels himself able, on the evidence of the demoniac existence he observes, to conclude that there must be good spirits, even though he hasn't seen any.

4359 The skeptic regards all perception as delusive and denies the possibility of arriving at any generally valid truth. This skeptic compares his fellow philosophers with seekers after buried treasure (see note to 3664–3665). Such a negative spirit belongs with the devils on the Brocken and knows it.

4363 The orchestra is out of hand again, this time because of the incompetence of the dilettantes and the negligence of the professional musicians among them. A brief transition to the fourth group of persons.

4367 This group of adept political opportunists call themselves *Sans Souci*, 'Without a care.' They have no principles to bother them. They get along — if not one way, then another.

4371 These clumsy fellows are the so-called *Hofschranzen*, hangers-on at court and bootlickers generally. Unlike the skilled ones, when the administration changes these fellows are helpless and suffer the consequences of their previous favor-seeking.

4375 The will-o'-the-wisps are the parvenus, newly made in the confusion of political upheaval, who fall at once into the dance as resplendent courtiers.

4379 The shooting star may represent those gentry of ephemeral fame, who disappear from the public eye as suddenly as they have appeared. Just why this one is lying askew in the grass is not apparent, except that this indicates that he is on the way out.

4383 The massive ones are the proletarian and lower middle classes, whose rise in European politics so distressed the aristocrats. Even as ghosts they trample everything under foot with their ponderous bulk. They are out of place here, where everything should be light and airy. Hence Puck reproaches them.

4391 Ariel leads all the participants in this scene upward to the rose-covered hill, where, according to Wieland's *Oberon*, the castle of the fairy king is located.

4395 The orchestra playing its softest brings this intermezzo to an end. This cannot reasonably be the end of the *Walpurgisnacht* revels, for the two adventurers, Faust and Mephistopheles, had not yet reached the top of the mountain and the main ceremonies of the night have not yet taken place. We have therefore to recognize a lacuna between the *Walpurgisnachtstraum* and the next scene, *Trüber Tag*.

25. Trüber Tag.

This is one of the oldest scenes in the Faust poem. It was part of the Urfaust which young Goethe read to his circle of friends at the court of Weimar. It made a deep impression upon them because of the consuming rage of Goethe as he read Faust's attack on Mephistopheles. It is the only scene in the play which has remained in its original prose form. Goethe planned to put it into verse, as he did the prison scene, but it is clear that the elemental passion of Faust here could not be confined to a strict metrical form.

The scene is in harmony with the emotional state of the principal character: dark, lowering clouds in a late evening sky. Why Faust is in an open field is not explained, except that he had to flee from Gretchen's city to escape arrest for the murder of Valentin and that after every great emotional experience he seeks solitude in nature. To be sure, the entire *Walpurgisnacht* episode has been introduced between this scene and its original presuppositions. Yet if we assume that Faust has just been through the wildest of nights on the Brocken it will not appear unreasonable to find him the next evening in a different place.

Faust has somehow learned of the disasters which have befallen Gretchen: she fled from her home, or was driven from it, and wandered about the countryside in misery. She has been captured by officers of the law and is now in prison. Goethe once planned to have this information given Faust in the third Walpurgis Night scene. As things stand, we are plunged immediately into the midst of Faust's tirade against Mephistopheles, and indeed against himself as well. The dramatic function of the scene is to show Faust's return to his nobler self and his determination to risk everything in an attempt to alleviate the suffering he has caused.

TT 2 **lange** The time factor is ambiguous. Presumably Faust fled from Gretchen's neighborhood immediately after the murder of Valentin. Two days intervened between the murder and the *Walpurgisnacht*, but the interval between that and the time of *Trüber Tag* is not indicated.

TT 4 **Bis dahin** (*ist es gekommen!*)

TT 5 **Steh nur** Mephistopheles is trying to walk away from his master.

TT 9 **Bösen Geistern** Such as the one of the cathedral scene; see the introductory note to Scene 22, *Dom*.

TT 15 **Hundsgestalt** When these lines were written, there was as yet no poodle in the scene *Vor dem Tor*, who transformed himself into Mephistopheles. Hence this appeal to the Earth Spirit (the *unendlicher Geist*) to change this lowest form of life (*Wurm*) into a dog has to be understood more generally and not as a specific reference to earlier motivation in the poem as it now stands. Any demon or evil spirit, which for one reason or another had to serve a human being, quite commonly appeared in the form of a dog. Mephistopheles is here said to have so appeared with Faust on many an evening walk. Indeed, it was the favorite form of this spirit. Such a Mephistopheles, of course, is a creature of the Earth Spirit and not the fallen angel of the Prologue in Heaven.

TT 24–26 Faust speaks from the premise that vicarious expiation of sin is just, and he may be assumed still to believe that guilt can be expiated in the sight of God. He cannot understand why the deep misery of the first girl to suffer as Gretchen is suffering should not have expiated the guilt of all other such transgressors in the eyes of God.

TT 31–32 A reference to Faust's necromancy with Nostradamus' book (420). This devil classifies himself as a subordinate spirit of the realm of the *Erdgeist*.

TT 32–33 People who wish to fly should be secure against attacks of dizziness: people who associate with demons should be secure against attacks of conscience.

TT 36–40 The Earth Spirit seems to have attached Mephistopheles to Faust with a bond like that of a forged iron fetter.

TT 44–45 Gretchen has been found guilty of the murder of her infant child. Mephistopheles cannot control the decrees of the court which deals with murder, because the decrees of that court are given "in God's name." See also note to lines 3714–3715.

TT 47 **Donner** An allusion to the god, Jupiter, who hurled thunder-bolts at those who displeased him.

TT 53 **Blutschuld** By the murder of Valentin, blood-guilt has been put upon the city or state, which is obliged then by law to remove this blood-guilt by bringing the murderer to his due punishment.

TT 55 **rächende Geister** Analogous to the Furies of ancient Greece.

TT 64 **Zauberpferde** These are a new means of transportation. Usually the magic cloak suffices (2065).

26. Nacht. Offen Feld

The time, presumably, is in the night following *Trüber Tag*. As Faust and Mephistopheles approach their destination they look down and see a group of figures in an open field.

4399 **Rabenstein** The ravens' stone is a block or platform of masonry built beneath a gallows, or used as a platform for the decapitation of convicted criminals. Hence the word often means a place of execution.

4403 The reference is to the gestures of these figures. Mephistopheles says they are witches and most commentators seem to believe him. Others hold that these are favorable spirits preparing to receive Gretchen's soul when she is executed.

27. Kerker

The scene shows Faust first outside the prison, and then in the cell in which Gretchen is chained. The function of the scene is to present the denouement of the Gretchen tragedy and the end of one phase of the Faust drama.

4405 **Schauer** Faust is once more accessible to the sentiment of com-passion and love for humankind.

4408 **Verbrechen** Not the murder of her child, but its ultimate cause: her yielding to Faust's urgings of love and to her own natural, and hence good, impulses, in the belief that anything so good and anything so lovely as this love must also be right (3585–3586).

4411   **Fort** 'Forward.'

4412–4420 This song, sung by Gretchen, somewhat as the distraught Ophelia sings in HAMLET (IV, 5), demonstrates the pathological condition of Gretchen's mind. The text of the song suggests the song of the bird in the *Märchen von dem Machandelbaum* (Grimm):

> Meine Mutter, die mich umbracht'!
> Mein Vater, der mich aß! —
> Meine Schwester, die Marlenichen,
> sucht alle meine Gebeine,
> bind't sie in ein seidenes Tuch,
> legt sie unter den Machandelbaum.
> Kiwitt, kiwitt! Was für ein schöner Vogel bin ich!

4423   **Sie** As Gretchen thinks, the servants of the executioner, come to take her to be beheaded. She does not recognize Faust until line 4470, and even then only dully.

4436   **Kranz** = *Mädchenkranz, Jungfernkranz* Every bride hoped to appear before the altar for her wedding wearing a bridal wreath to signify her maidenhood. Gretchen's wreath here may be taken as the symbol of the maidenhood she had lost; see 3561 and 3575.

4443   A hallucination. Her child is dead.

4449–4450 'There is an old tale that ends with a girl's killing her own child. Who bids them apply that tale to me?'

4460   There is a popular belief that a sleepwalker will promptly wake up upon hearing his given name spoken. Faust arouses Gretchen from her distraught condition by calling out her name.

4475   Even before she can take a step to escape, Gretchen is overcome by the sweet memories of a happy past. This is a demonstration of the insuperable power of her love impulse.

4493   Faust is no longer driven by his overpowering love for Gretchen but by his sense of guilt and his sense of duty to expiate this guilt. There is no fire of love on his lips now, and Gretchen infers at once that someone has come between them.

4512–4517 Another hallucination. She thinks Faust's hand is wet with the blood of her brother — that he is still there in the street, sword in hand, after slaying Valentin.

4520–4528 In her imagination the tragic events are all brought together in time, so that the burial of all the victims is to be attended to in the morning.

4532   She feels unable to revive this love as it once was.

4538–4541 Gretchen has prepared herself to die in the first hours of the dawn. She cannot accept a change in this idea. She will go with Faust, if to do so is to go to death with him, but not otherwise.

4545   **Sie** The representatives of state and church, the officers of the law.

4551   Another hallucination. Gretchen thinks she is leading Faust to the rescue of the child she had drowned.

4557   **die Planke** 'the board fence.'

4565　Now Gretchen's mind turns to the death of her mother and the condition in which she found her on the morning after she had given her the sleeping potion.

4567　Gretchen thinks she feels something (*es*) seize her by the hair of her head. Such a hallucination is the result of her anticipation of this sensation as a part of her coming execution. The line is parenthetical and probably derived chiefly from the exigencies of rime; yet the very disjuncture of the imagery suits the mental state of distraction here depicted.

4583　For the explanation of the *Kranz*, see note to 4436.

4590　**Glocke**　The *Armesünderglocke* tolls while the condemned is being led to the place of execution. — The rod is broken above the head of the condemned as a symbol of the death decree of the court. Before each execution, the court decree which orders it is read. Then either the judge or his representative breaks a small white wand.

4593–4594　An allusion to the fact that every witness of an execution by the axe so far identifies himself with the victim as to feel, momentarily at least, that the knife is falling on his own neck.

4595　She thinks the blow has fallen, so that she hears nothing.

4597　**Auf!**　'Up and away!'

4599　These horses will disappear into thin air with the first ray of the dawn or the first crowing of the cock.

4603　**heiligen**　Because she has resigned herself to God's judgment and this has brought her here, she calls the place sacred. Then too, any prison is an asylum against pursuers bent on doing harm to a fugitive or prisoner.

4606　Mephistopheles is desperate. He threatens to leave Faust to suffer arrest and execution along with Gretchen, because he cannot himself submit to arrest by human hands.

4609　An allusion to Psalm 34.7: "The angel of Jehovah encampeth round about them that fear him, and delivereth them."

4610　Gretchen's terror of her lover results from her determination to follow God's judgment and her conviction that Faust is not included therein. The conviction crystallizes when she sees Mephistopheles with Faust (see lines 3470–3500).

SD 4611　**Stimme, von oben**　This voice of God is part of the traditional folk-drama of Faust, and Goethe uses it effectively to balance the verdict of Mephistopheles. Gretchen is not to be thought of as condemned to Hell: she has cast herself on God's mercy.

4612　Mephistopheles drags the dazed Faust away, but Gretchen's voice still reaches him. It is the voice of love which will not pass away.

FAUST II

Act I

The first part of FAUST was not composed in acts; it is a series of scenes. The second part was ultimately arranged in five acts by Goethe, who in 1826–1832 was evidently thinking in terms of the production of his play in the theater. Lines 4613–6036, the greater part of the first act, were printed in 1828 in the twelfth volume of the edition of Goethe's works known as the *Ausgabe letzter Hand*. Part of this material was written much earlier.

The structure of this first act is essentially one of two parts — (1) the Emperor's lack of funds, (2) the Emperor's demand for entertainment. Faust and Mephistopheles appear as adventurers at the Emperor's court. They find him in financial straits and they solve his troubles by persuading him to issue paper currency against the security of gold as yet unrecovered from the earth. They also provide the climax for an elaborate Shrovetide masque, in which the whole court takes part. The two adventurers are retained at court, and Faust agrees to produce the shades of Helena and Paris for the entertainment of the Emperor.

Here Faust collides with Mephistopheles' alleged lack of authority over the shades of antiquity. Nevertheless Mephistopheles provides Faust with a key to these mysteries of the other world and sends him off to the realm of the "Mothers," from whom he is to get power to produce Helena.

Having brought the shade of Helena to the Emperor's court, Faust is enamored of her beauty, attempts to rescue her from Paris, lays hands upon the "shade," whereupon the whole vision dissolves in an explosion. Mephistopheles carries Faust off unconscious and takes him back once more to the study in which we first met him.

There is no dramatic motivation of the appearance of Faust and Mephistopheles at the Emperor's court, beyond the fact that as adventurers they might well hope for amusement and profit there. However, Goethe's purpose is clear enough in the light of the Faust legend. All forms of the legend which Goethe knew contain a scene in which Faust and Mephistopheles appear before the Emperor and perform spectacular feats of conjuring. Most important for Goethe was the scene in which the shade of Helena was produced for the delectation of the court.

The connection of the sojourn at the imperial court with the action of Part I of FAUST is tenuous and unstated. The bridge between the two parts is our first scene, in which a weary, restless Faust is refreshed by a night of sleep in a pleasant place on a mountain meadow.

28. ANMUTIGE GEGEND

The scene depicted is reminiscent of Goethe's journey to Lucerne, Switzerland, in 1797, and Faust's monologue (4679–4727) was probably composed as early as 1798, in the winter after the poet's Swiss visit. The scenic detail best fits the region around St. Gotthard.

The *Dämmerung* is the evening twilight. Faust, perhaps shortly after his harrowing experience in Gretchen's prison cell, tosses restlessly on his flowery couch, surrounded by a hovering host of kindly spirits, led by Ariel, the airy fay of Shakespeare's THE TEMPEST. This is presumably the same Ariel who appears (4239, 4391) in the *Walpurgisnachtstraum*, where he leads many spirits with his song. We have to think of Faust as recovering, under the ministrations of these spirits, from a complete collapse after Gretchen's death.

4613 **Frühlingsregen** In the spring the lovely rain of blossoms falls equally upon all; the green wealth of growing grain shows itself to all men. So too the elves give their aid to everyone who requires it. The passage suggests Matthew 5.45 'For he maketh his sun to rise on the evil and the good and sendeth rain on the just and the unjust.'

4617 **Geistergröße** Subject of *eilet*. After the two if-clauses, the verb might be expected to precede its subject. — The elves hasten to aid the unfortunate man, and they do so because of their quality of spiritual greatness. The additional implication of 4617 is that it is astonishing to find such greatness in such little creatures. The form *Geistergröße* is unique, and is understood to represent *Geistesgröße von Geistern* [Grimm, *DWb.*].

4620 **sie** Accusative, either singular with the antecedent *Geistergröße*, or plural with the antecedent *Elfen*. — **Unglücksmann** Faust, the man of misfortune. Perhaps intended both actively and passively: the one who suffers and the one who brings misfortune.

4621–4633 These lines are spoken, not sung. Ariel interrupts his song to speak to the circle of spirits hovering over Faust.

4624 The reference is to Faust's sense of guilt in the tragedy of Gretchen.

4625 **Graus** The horror of the scene in the prison cell.

4626 An allusion to the four watches of the night, each of three hours duration, according to Roman usage.

4627 Each watch has its own song; see 4634–4665.

4629 **Lethe** A river which flowed close by the Elysian fields. It was known as the river of oblivion. Souls which drank from its waters forgot their past experiences. By the bathing of Faust's body in dew from Lethe, Goethe probably meant to suggest the relaxation of muscular tensions characteristic of the paroxysm through which Faust is passing.

4632　**Elfen** 'elves.' There were at least two, possibly three kinds of elves. Certainly there were light elves and dark elves, and perhaps also brown elves (Scotch "brownies"). The light elves lived among the gods, the dark elves among the dead in the nether world. The dark elves are identified with the dwarfs. All elves are irresistibly moved by the song and the dance. There are many sources of information about the dark elves and their harmful doings among men. We know very little, however, about the behavior of the light elves, and Goethe's statement that it is the finest duty of these elves to restore the unhappy sleeper to health appears to rest on no well-known tradition.

4633　**dem heiligen Licht** The fact that these eives regard the light of day as sacred may put them in the category of the light elves.

SD 4634　The following four stanzas are sung by the spirits which hover over Faust as he lies upon the greensward. The stage direction indicates a rather complicated operatic arrangement of the parts, so that at times we have a solo or a duet, while at other times all voices participate. In the first manuscript (now lost), each stanza is said to have had a musical direction: Sérénade (evening song), Notturno (night song), Mattutino (morning song), and Reveille (call to awake).

4637　**die Dämmerung** This is the song of the first watch of the night, eventide, which brings with it (*senkt*) sweet fragrances and enshrouding mists.

4638　**lispelt** With *wiegt, schließt* in the following lines, may best be taken like *senkt*, as predicates of *die Dämmerung*. Some commentators take them as imperatives.

4641　The day is thought of as a lighted citadel, the gates of which the evening swings shut before the eyes of the weary wayfarer.

4642　These pictures are not static. The view shifts and time passes. The second stanza describes the second three-hour vigil of the night. First the great stars and then the more remote faint stars shine and are reflected in the lake. Then the full splendor of the moon dominates the scene.

4643　The stars are proverbially chaste, and hence holy. *heilig*, here an adverb, implies something like 'in chaste holiness.' — With *schließt* supply the impersonal subject *es*, 'One star joins another.'

4647　**klarer Nacht** An adverbial genitive of place, 'in the clear night,' analogous to the idiom: *des Weges gehen* 'proceed on one's way.'

4650　**Stunden** The 'hours' of Faust's past life are extinguished from his memory. The sufferings and the joys of his past are gone; the dew of Lethe has done its work.

4652　The elves address Faust, putting into his mind the idea that he will recover, that he can look forward confidently to the new day, and that if he did open his eyes he would see the landscape unfolding before him out of the departing night. This is the third watch.

4654 Again a changing scene. The hills loom up out of the darkness and as the light increases bushes appear on the hills, providing shade in which to rest.

4656 Growing grain as it passes from green to golden has a stage at which it appears to be silvery. The time at which this happens varies with the climate and with the kind of grain. The range indicated would be from late May to early July.

4658 **Wunsch um Wünsche** 'one wish after another.'

4660 **umfangen** 'embraced' by the sleep which holds him.

4661 By implication the awakening Faust is compared with a newly hatched bird emerging from its shell, or a butterfly emerging from the chrysalis. This is to be a new Faust.

4662 **erdreisten** 'make bold' to attack life's problems. What Goethe here hints at is more fully stated in WILHELM MEISTERS WANDER-JAHRE (*Maximen und Reflexionen*, 594): ,,Ein jeder Mensch sieht die fertige und geregelte, gebildete, vollkommene Welt doch nur als ein Element an, woraus er sich eine besondere, ihm angemessene Welt zu erschaffen bemüht ist. Tüchtige Menschen ergreifen sie ohne Bedenken und suchen damit, wie es gehen will, zu gebaren, andere zaudern an ihr herum, einige zweifeln sogar an ihrem Dasein."

4663 **wenn** = *wenn auch*, 'even if.'

4665 **versteht und rasch ergreift** Since no object is given, something like *alles* may be understood: 'the noble man who understands everything and quickly makes it his own.'

SD 4665 "The dawn comes up like thunder." At dawn Helios (or, as Goethe has it in line 4670, Phoebus-Apollo) drove the four-horse chariot of the sun up out of the eastern ocean with a tremendous clatter. See also lines 243–246.

4666 **die Horen** The Hours, Seasons, guardians of the gates of heaven. They harness the horses for the sun-chariot each morning. Goethe appears to make them participate in the uproar of the dawn.

4667 **tönend** See line 243 and the note.

4669 **Felsentore** Evidently the gates of heaven, more commonly thought of as being composed of clouds. Homer has them make a loud noise when they open (ILIAD VIII, 393).

4670 **Phöbus** Apollo, the charioteer of the sun.

4674 The ear of the elf is confounded by the completely inordinate uproar and is not able to listen to it.

4675 The elves are bidden to withdraw lest the too great noise of the sun destroy their hearing.

4679–4727 The metrical form of this monologue is known as the *terza rima* (in German, *Terzine*). This is an Italian form best exemplified in Dante's DIVINE COMEDY. The essence of it is the interlocking riming of groups of three lines: aba bcb cdc ded . . . yzy z.

4680 **Dämmerung** The twilight of the dawn.

4681 One more night has passed without the earth's having dissolved into chaos.

4682 The freshness of the earth at dawn is compared with the refreshed new vigor of an awakened sleeper.

4683 **Lust** Used metaphorically for things which excite Faust's delight. Increasingly, as the dawn becomes day, the earth reveals to Faust reasons for rejoicing.

4684 **regst und rührst** Taken together mean 'inspire, arouse.'

4685 **zum höchsten Dasein** 'to the perfection of existence.'

4688 This is an alpine landscape, with clouds of mist hanging along the sides of deep valleys until the sun rises high enough to dissipate them. The first rays of the rising sun light up the summits, but as the sun rises higher its rays fall into the deeper valleys.

4690 **entsprossen** The past participle, with which *sind* should be understood, by analogy to *ist ergossen* above.

4695 **Hinaufgeschaut!** Faust speaks to himself. An imperative participle; see note to line 3704.

4697 **des ewigen Lichts** Genitive with *genießen*, as in lines 7267, 11349, instead of the accusative, as in lines 1416, 1822, 3221, 4198, 5161.

4699 **grüngesenkt** = *grün in Grün gesenkt.* These meadows, themselves green, seem to be sunk into the green of the pines and fir trees around them. The observer watches the effect of the sunrise upon the scene before him. First the mighty summits of the mountains catch the new light. Next the light falls upon the green meadows of the high mountain pastures giving them (as the rays of the rising sun strike them) new brilliance and clarity of delineation. Some interpreters take *grüngesenkt* to be a combination of the green of the meadows with the lowering of the line of vision of the observer (*gesenkt*) 'meadows green as the lowered eye observes them.'

4701 **stufenweis** Step by step the rays of the rising sun fall lower on the sides of the mountains and set them out in new clarity to the view of the onlooker.

4702 **Sie** The sun.

4704–4714 The experience of the spectator watching the sunrise is compared with the experience of a man watching for the fulfillment of his highest wish. As the sun has burst forth with blinding brilliance from the infinite reaches of space, so, out of the eternal depths revealed by the opening of the gates of fulfillment, a flame bursts forth, far in excess of that the watcher expected, and unbearable to his eyes. Instead of lighting his torch of life at this source of light, the watcher is engulfed in a sea of flames.

The comparison is continued in the metaphor of the last lines of the passage. As the watcher turns his eyes from the blinding light of the sun to the earth still veiled in the mists of morning, so the man who aspires to transcendent experiences turns from them to the satisfied immediacy of earliest youth which seeks no transcendent knowledge of the universe, but desires only to learn of the world at hand.

4706 The way to the fulfillment of this ardent hope passes through a great portal, the gates of which are widely opened.

4711–4712 **die . . . umwinden** Some plural noun has to be supplied as the antecedent of *die*: something like *die Flammen*. The observer cannot be sure whether it is the flames of love or the flames of hatred, or the flames of both love and hatred, which engulf him:

these elemental forces produce alternately pain and joy (4712). The order of the nouns *Liebe : Haß, Schmerz : Freuden* produces a trope called "chiasmus."

4715 This attitude of Faust contrasts sharply with that of the earlier Faust (lines 1074–1075) who wished for wings so that he might always follow the sun on its course.

4720 **Schaum an Schäume** This may be construed as an absolute phrase, equivalent to a prepositional phrase like the phrase *in tausend . . . Strömen* of the preceding clause: 'roaring high in the air, foam upon foam.' According to another interpretation, *sausend* is construed as a transitive verb with the object *Schaum an Schäume*, and the whole then means: 'sending up with a roar foam upon foam.'

4725–4727 Human endeavor is symbolized by the rainbow: human life is like the colorful reflection of the light of the sun from myriad drops of water cast up into its rays. The individual drops are cast into the light, reflect the rays of the sun for a moment, and then disappear. The sun and the rainbow remain. As we observe human life, therefore, we are urged to remember that what we see is reflected light, not light directly from the source, and that the permanence which human life appears to have implies the continuous casting up of individual human lives into the light which they reflect. It is probably correct to equate light with truth in the metaphor. We know the truth only indirectly from its reflection in the lives of men. The reference is to philosophic truth, not to specific facts. — The long soliloquy (4679–4727) ends, as it began, with a reference to *das Leben*.

Kaiserliche Pfalz

In this 'Imperial Palace,' Goethe provided an intentionally vague setting for the following six scenes, which make up the main body of the first act. The whole is conceived as a satire of a ruler who had every possible capacity for losing his kingdom (see Eckermann's report of October 1, 1827). The imperial conditions satirized are roughly parallel to those which existed in the time of Maximilian I, "The Last Knight," who ruled over the Holy Roman Empire from 1493 to 1519.

The Faust tradition brings Faust to the imperial court to display his powers as a conjurer and magician. One of Faust's best tricks was to produce phantoms of great personages of the past. Goethe, by causing Faust to produce the phantom of Helen of Troy, provided the initial impulse for the Helena episode of Act III.

Goethe originally planned to explain the appearance of Faust at the imperial court in a scene in which Mephistopheles was to persuade the Faust of *Anmutige Gegend* that such an adventure would be amusing. This explanatory scene was never fully worked out, and Goethe dropped it entirely from the text when he printed the first act of Part II in 1828. There is now no clear indication of the relation of this scene in time to the scene which precedes it. It would appear from the reference to mummery in lines 4765–4769 that this convocation of the peers of the realm takes place in the pre-Lenten period of Carnival. The reference to Ash Wednesday (5058) makes this inference seem secure. This period is usually in February or early March. On the other hand, the stage directions for the scene *Anmutige Gegend* call for green turf with spring flowers, and line 4613 indicates 'blossom time,' which in these regions is rather May than February. One is well advised not to concern oneself too seriously with problems of time and place in this part of FAUST.

29. SAAL DES THRONES

SD 4728 **Staatsrat** At the annual Reichstag, convened before the Emperor, all court officials, from the highest rank (*Staatsrat*) to the lowest (*Hofgesinde*), have been assembled to hear the Emperor's address on the state of the nation. — **Astrolog** One of the two most trusted advisors of this ruler. The other, and more important one, is the Fool. Astrology, as a means of predicting the future, was taken seriously by many important people in the sixteenth and seventeenth centuries. A well-known case in point is that of the great general Albrecht von Wallenstein (1583–1634), who in his later years took few decisive steps without the approval of his astrologer. Rudolf II of Hapsburg (ruled 1567–1612) relied similarly on his astrologer, the great scientist Johannes Kepler.

4728 The standard formula for royal address to the immediate vassals of the court was: "Liebe Getreue!" These are princes of the realm. The Emperor does not go on with his address when he notices the absence of his fool.

4730 **Den Weisen** The astrologer, on the Emperor's right. The place of the court fool, on the Emperor's left, is vacant.

4734 **Fettgewicht** Metonymy for 'very fat person,' say, 'tub of fat.' Gluttony and alcoholism are two manifestations of the moral decay of this court. The Fool exemplifies notable excess in both.

4735 **tot oder trunken** There is a third possibility not mentioned in FAUST: Mephistopheles may have removed this fool for a time. Goethe, in his account of this scene to Eckermann, October 1, 1827, says that this fool was "schnell beseitigt" by Mephistopheles.

4743–4750 Theoretically there should be a single answer to all of these riddles and that answer should be "folly" or "court fool." Another possible answer is "money." The linking of apparently irreconcilable opposites in these questions is effective in its combination of bafflement and evident intent.

4753 **Sache dieser Herrn** His chancellor, his general, his treasurer, his marshal have come to ask him hard questions which he finds it as difficult to answer as riddles. He invites the fool rather to solve these problems than to propose riddles of his own.

4755 **ging weit ins Weite** Probably a euphemism for *ist tot*.

4757–4760 This protestation of the crowd has to be thought of as individual complaints from the group, each speaker uttering a half-line, as indicated by the dashes. It is not intended to be spoken in chorus.

4758 **Wie kam er ein?** A reference to the fact that the halberds of the guards (4741) failed to keep him out.

4763 The astrologer has approved the calling of this meeting.

4767 The Emperor has prepared a carnival, patterned after the well-known carnival of Rome. His primary interest in life is to amuse himself with exotic and lavish festivities. He dislikes being hindered by matters of state, 'when we plan to have a carnival masquerade at which we shall all wear costumes and masks.'

4771 What has happened (*geschehen*) is the convocation of the council; what the Emperor wishes to get on with (*getan*) is the actual deliberations of this group of officials.

SD 4772 **Kanzler** The Archbishop of Mainz, one of the electoral princes, was by imperial law the Chancellor of the Empire.

4772–4808 The Chancellor complains that the machinery of the law has completely broken down in the empire. — The reference to a halo suggests the sanctity of the Emperor's person as "King by divine right."

4781 One evil, by over-prolific self-reproduction, becomes many evils.

4782 **Wer** 'Whoever.'

4784 **Mißgestalt** Metonymy for a person or a thing having a misshapen form. Here the reference is to officers of law and order who are caricatures of what they should be and who hold sway in a situation which is a caricature of law and order.

4785–4786 These two clauses also depend upon *wo* (4784). 'Where a caricature of law prevails by law, and where a whole world of topsy-turvy perversity is evolved.'

4787 **Der . . . der** 'this one . . . that one.'

4794 'the growing tumult of revolt.'

4795–4800 The guilty perversely boast of their crimes, while the innocent, who seek to protect themselves in this topsy-turvy world, are pronounced guilty. In this way society (*alle Welt*) is on the point of breaking up into its individual components, and right (*was sich gebührt*) is on the point of being destroyed.

4801 **Sinn** The sense of justice (4775).

4803 **ein wohlgesinnter Mann** The *Richter* of 4805.

4807 **schwarz** 'I have not painted this picture with bright colors. Indeed, I have used very dark colors. Yet I should prefer to hide this picture with a still denser veil of obscurity.' The chancellor suggests that this is not a thing one likes to look at and that he would not bring the matter up at all except that the Emperor's very throne is endangered by this lawlessness (4811). — **zög' ich . . . vor** 'would draw over' (and thus conceal).

SD 4812 **Heermeister** 'Minister of war.' Apparently Goethe's invention: imperial law provided for no such officer.

4812–4830 The minister of war complains about the disintegration of his army. The conditions are much like those of the period of the robber barons during the reign of Maximilian I (1493–1519). The burghers fortified their towns and the barons reinforced their castles high on inaccessible rocky heights. This speech could well enough have been made at the Reichstag in Mainz (1517).

4818 **halten . . . fest** The rebellious *Bürger* and *Ritter* keep their fighting forces intact for their own use, instead of sending off their quota of troops — with the necessary supplies — to the Emperor for the common good.

4823 **Verbiete wer . . .** 'Let anyone forbid . . .' = 'If anyone should forbid . . .'

4824 The conclusion of the implied condition ('if anyone should . . .') is put into the indicative to increase the sense of the certainty of its occurrence.

4825 **sie** These mercenary soldiers.

4829 **Könige** In line 4831 they are called 'allies.' — **draußen** means beyond the boundaries of the Emperor's rule. — There were a number of kingdoms more or less closely associated with the Empire as vassal states or allies. Theoretically, all Europe was subject to the Emperor; but Holland, Spain, France, Bohemia, Sicily, Naples, all at one time or another refused to cooperate.

SD 4831 **Schatzmeister** Also an office not specifically authorized by imperial law.

4833 **Röhrenwasser** was proverbially unreliable. 'Piped water' was the usual comparison when something hoped for failed to arrive.

4834–4851 The situation is that of the tax collector at the time of the disintegration of the old feudal system. The old nobility, ruined by the crusades and other wars, had to give up their homes to new owners (4836), who owed no feudal homage to the Emperor. In the feudal bargain between Emperor and vassal, land was given the latter in return for certain rights to income which should be paid the Emperor's treasury. The Emperor could, if properly pressed, be persuaded to relinquish these rights. Act IV gives a good illustration of the technique of persuasion.

4841 **wie sie heißen** 'whatever their names may be.' — **Parteien** Such as the Ghibellines (*Waiblingen*) and the Guelfs (*Welfen*); see line 4845. The Ghibellines were Swabian Hohenstaufens of the twelfth century and later; the Guelfs were Bavarians and Saxons. Frederick Barbarossa and Henry the Lion were distinguished representatives respectively of the two parties. Philip of Swabia and Otto IV were later opponents in this strife. The use of these names is an anachronism, for at the time otherwise indicated by our context (the early sixteenth century) these parties were entirely unimportant in imperial affairs.

4843–4844 'It is immaterial whether these parties are against us or for us; in either case they have become indifferent and without energy.'

4846 **auszuruhn** Armed conflicts between these factions exhausted their current resources of men and money, and periods of recuperation were necessary.

4850 The metaphor of scratching and scraping applied to the laborious gathering together of small means.

SD 4852 **Marschalk** The old form of the title of the first officer of the court, the *Hofmarschall*. Under imperial law this office was held by the Elector of Saxony. Usually the Marshal's duties were confined to the supervision of the Emperor's stables, the hunt, and other forms of entertainment in the imperial household. The kitchen, wine-cellars, banquets — hospitality in general — came under the super-vision of the steward (*Truchseß*).

4859 **Deputate** The income of the Emperor was in the form of "rents" or revenue assessments, part paid in money and part in kind. He collected these "rents" from the princes of the realm, who were his vassals. These princes in turn collected their incomes from the vassals who administered the farms of their countries. A goodly portion of this revenue was in the form of natural produce. These payments in kind were the *Deputate*, and they were the most reliable part of the prince's income.

4863 **Berg'** = *Weinberge*.

4865 **der edlen Herrn** Perhaps with some of the irony that attaches to V.I.P. (Very Important Personage). The Marshal includes the present company in this reference.

4866 **Lager** The reserve stock of the city Ratskeller.

4868 The wine is wasted by the greediness of these carousers who try to drink it out of the largest possible containers instead of drinking with moderation from honest wine glasses.

4870 The moneylender will not allow the state to get out of his clutches. He insists upon being paid each year by a new loan against future income so large that it leaves no margin for improvement of the in-come-producing property.

4872 These loans are thought of as feeding upon and consuming in advance (the income of) year after year.

4875 **vorgegessen Brot** Bread eaten before it is paid for.

4876 The grim humor of a harassed, incompetent monarch.

4877–4882 Mephistopheles flatteringly professes to see no distress in all this splendor and asks a rhetorical question: 'Was there ever lack of confidence where there was firm rule and ready power to destroy any opposition, where intelligent good will and lively and varied activity were at hand?'

4879 **gebeut** Poetic third person singular present indicative of *gebieten*.

4893–4894 **Bergesadern : Mauergründen, gemünzt : ungemünzt** A chias-mus; see note to line 4711. — Coins are deposited in the corner-stones of walls, and otherwise hidden in their foundations.

4896 **Natur- und Geisteskraft** The power which belongs to a gifted man by virtue of his nature and his intelligence, or by virtue of his innate intelligence (hendiadys).

4897–4916 The Chancellor thinks Mephistopheles is putting Nature and Spirit, or Mind, in the place of God. He calls this atheistic and dangerous to the state. — The Chancellor's speech is in a medieval three-part lyric form: two *Stollen* and an *Abgesang*. Lines 4897–4902 and 4903–4908 are parallel in rime and even (to a very con-siderable extent) in syntax and rhetoric. Lines 4909–4916 are the *Abgesang*; longer than either of the two *Stollen* but shorter than both.

The *Abgesang* has a slight break in rime-pattern and meaning-pattern at the midpoint.

4900 To the Chancellor as an orthodox Christian, man is by nature sinful and unclean, and if spirits get into him they are *Lügengeister*, leading him astray from the true faith. This would result in doubt as to the teaching of the church, and of this the Chancellor strongly disapproves.

4903 **Uns nicht so!** Ellipsis, in effect equivalent to *Zu uns darf man nicht so sprechen.* — **Kaisers** Instead of *des Kaisers.* Goethe in his later years was very likely to omit the definite article. This trait at times amounts to a mannerism.

4904–4908 The two social classes, or estates, are the clergy (*Heiligen*) and the knights (*Ritter*). They confront (*stehen*) every storm which threatens the Empire and take as their due recompense the churches and the secular territories of the several states.

4909–4910 **Dem Pöbelsinn . . .** 'Out of the mob-mentality of confused minds there springs . . .'

4911 **die Ketzer** The Chancellor is calling names. People who advocate what Mephistopheles has suggested are 'heretics and witch-masters.'

4915 The reference of *ihr* is uncertain. The best guess is that the Chancellor addresses the whole court (*diese hohen Kreise* 4914), saying that if they allow Mephistopheles to bring in these heretics and sorcerers, they will be putting their faith in a depraved heart — that of the fool, Mephistopheles.

4924 The Emperor speaks to the Chancellor.

4931 The period of the migrations of peoples (*Völkerwanderung*), the fourth to the sixth centuries of the Christian era.

4940 According to ancient law, all treasures which lie deeper in the earth than a plow runs belong to the Emperor. These laws are recorded in various places, most interestingly in the *Sachsenspiegel* (about 1222) and the *Schwabenspiegel* (after 1250).

4949 According to the astrological lore of the time, the universe was composed of nine or ten hollow, concentric, transparent spheres around the earth. Closest to the earth was the sphere of the Moon, and thence outward the spheres were subject to Mercury, Venus, the Sun, Mars, Jupiter, and Saturn. Enclosing these seven spheres was the eighth, the sphere of the fixed stars, and beyond that the crystalline heaven, and enclosing this the *Primum Mobile*, which got its motion from God and transmitted it to the other spheres. Some versions identify the *Primum Mobile* with the crystalline heaven and thus have nine, rather than ten, spheres. Outside this finite universe was the abode of God, infinite and motionless. The spheres were all in motion and each of the planets moved within its own (moving) sphere. Hence a human observer on the stationary, central earth saw different parts of the several spheres in different relationships with each other, according to the period of their motion. The sphere of the fixed stars was divided arbitrarily into twelve regions, each of thirty degrees, and each characterized by a definite constellation, called a sign of the zodiac, and referred to by astrologers as a 'house' (*domus*).

Each of the planets except the Sun and the Moon (Sun and Moon were considered planets in this astrology) had two such houses, one for the day and one for the night. The Sun and the Moon had only one house each. Horoscopes were based upon observations of the position of the planets in the sky relative to their houses and to the houses of other planets at the moment for which the prediction was to be made. Every hour of the day was believed to be ruled over by one of the planets, and its influence was thought to be beneficial or harmful according to the nature of the house in which it happened to be at that hour. Every house, or constellation of the zodiac, represented a different feature of human life: Aries — life, Taurus — riches, Gemini — brothers, Cancer — parents, Leo — children, Virgo — health, Libra — marriage, Scorpio — death, Sagittarius — religion, Capricornus — dignities, Aquarius — friends, Pisces — enemies.

Of the planets, Mars and Saturn were considered to be definitely hostile to human affairs; the Sun, Venus, and Jupiter were considered to be favorable to man. The Moon and Mercury were considered fickle or merely supporting the influence of any other planet with which they appeared "in conjunction." Hence a properly schooled astrologer, by observing the relative positions of the heavenly bodies in their spheres at the hour for which the horoscope was to be made, would predict probable good or evil outcome for any life or any enterprise.

SD 4955 **bläst ein** 'prompts.' See line 6400, the promptings of the devil.

4955–4970 Purposeful mystification, with many expressions of double meaning — astrological and everyday usage in confusion.

4958 Venus can appear only as Morning Star or as Evening Star in close proximity to the sun. — **spat** is an archaic form beside *spät;* see note to line 3112.

4963 **Metall** Each planet was equated with a certain metal. Thus the Moon was silver, Mercury = quicksilver, Venus = copper, the Sun = gold, Mars = iron, Jupiter = tin, and Saturn = lead.

4969 Mephistopheles, speaking through this astrologer, puts in a reference to a 'very learned man,' because he wishes to establish a pretext for introducing Faust to the Emperor.

4971 **doppelt** Both the alchemistic astrological intention and the everyday meaning of the astrologer's words are apprehended by the Emperor, he thinks, but he can come to no decision. Also, the Emperor hears both Mephistopheles and the astrologer speak these words; see SD 4955.

4973 **Gedroschener Spaß** A joke from which all the substance has been threshed.

4974 **Kalenderei** 'astrological nonsense.' The hocus-pocus of almanac-making and interpretation was the major business of the astrologer. — **Chymisterei** Alchemy, which sought to make gold out of baser metals.

4976 **er** The 'learned man' of 4969–4970.

4979 **Alraune** The plant, mandrake. Superstition teaches that this plant, when it grows beneath a gallows, takes on the form of a human being. If it is forcibly pulled up, it emits a loud shriek which is fatal to anyone who hears it. Yet it is very useful, because a person who has such a plant — duly pulled up from beneath a gallows, washed in red wine, and wrapped in red cloth — can do many miraculous things.

4980   A black dog is the approved agency through which a mandrake can be obtained. One ties the plant securely to the black dog, carefully stops one's ears with wax, as a protection against hearing the fearful shriek, and then induces the dog to pull up the plant by enticing him away from the spot with meat. For additional protection, a loud blast is blown on a horn when the mandrake comes out of the ground.

4981–4984   After all, everyone experiences the itching foot or the stumbling step which indicates something buried underfoot. Why make fun of these supernatural manifestations, or call them witchcraft? — There was formerly a widespread belief in the ability of certain persons to use the divining rod with accuracy, or of others to sense subterranean deposits of metal or of water by some "magnetic" effect upon their bodies.

4992   **Da liegt der Spielmann** (*begraben*) 'That's the lucky spot.' A proverbial saying used when one stumbles.

4993–4996   The symptoms of the crowd are induced by Mephistopheles' powers of suggestion.

5006   An aside by Mephistopheles; supply *ich* as the subject of *wüßte*.

5011   Wall saltpeter, calcium nitrate, is formed by exudation on old mortar. The nitrogen in it is moderately useful as fertilizer and the salt was once widely used as a medicine. Occasionally, when a peasant broke down a wall where this exudation had occurred, he found a hidden treasure (see line 4893).

5013   **kümmerlicher** It is rather the farmer than his hand that is miserable.

5020   **sich** Dative of interest or advantage. See note to line 320.

5026   Popular belief has it that the tartar deposited from old wine upon the inside of the cask becomes solid enough to contain the wine, even after the staves have rotted away.

5036   Proverbially, all cows are black and all cats are gray at night.

5041   Aaron made a golden calf out of the earrings of his people (Exodus 32.4); here this allusion is hyperbolically extended to mean 'untold riches.'

5044   **die Geliebte** Mephistopheles probably refers to the Emperor's mistress, rather than to the Empress.

SD 5048   **wie oben** As at SD 4955, Mephistopheles 'prompts.' The Astrologer, Mephistopheles' mouthpiece, speaks with irony: this treasure hunt is serious business, not to be undertaken until the carnival spirit has passed. Due penance (5051) must be done, in order to earn the lower (riches) by means of the upper (religious fervor). Miracles require strengthened faith.

5049   **Freudenspiel** The pre-Lenten carnival; see lines 4765–4769.

5056   See line 766: "Das Wunder ist des Glaubens liebstes Kind."

5063–5064 'If these people had the stone of the wise men (which provides riches, power, and long life), the stone would be without a wise master who knew how to use it properly. They fail to see that success is causally connected with hard work and merit.'

30. WEITLÄUFIGER SAAL

This carnival masquerade probably takes place on Shrove Tuesday (Mardi gras). It is not to be thought of as a consistent allegorical representation of some important general idea, but rather to be taken at face value as a masque. It is put together after the fashion of the Italian Carnivals. In the dramatic economy of FAUST, the masque serves to depict the levity of this court and to introduce Faust into this milieu.

The masque is well organized. First we have groups of real characters: gardener girls, gardeners, a mother and her daughter, fishermen, fowlers, woodcutters, clowns, parasites, an intoxicated man, and at least one poet. These figures dispose themselves on the stage and form the frame within which the following "acts" are produced. They are joined by a second group of figures who come from Greek mythology: the Graces, the Fates, and the Furies. The mythological figures are followed by allegorical ones: Fear, Hope, Prudence, and a quite remarkable fiction, Zoilo-Thersites.

We are thus prepared for the two major groups of the masque: (1) Plutus-Faust, representing wealth, with his charioteer, Poetry, and his footman, Mephistopheles-Avarice, (2) Pan-Emperor, with his retinue of fauns, satyrs, gnomes, giants, and nymphs.

5065–5066 The master of ceremonies warns everyone not to expect a German *Fastnachtsspiel*, at which robust and inelegant dances by devils and clowns will be performed, or an allegorical representation of the Dance of Death will be staged. The Dance of Death was a macabre dance by skeletons, with Death playing the pipe or the fiddle for their clattering gyrations.

5071 **gewonnen** Until 1493 each newly elected emperor was obliged to journey to Rome to receive the formal blessing of the Pope (*an heiligen Sohlen*) and kiss the Pope's slipper (*der Pantoffelkuß*).

5079–5080 Disguised as a fool, the man of sense acts as wisely as he can under the circumstances.

5083 **zudringlich** 'crowding eagerly.'

5084 **unverdrossen** 'Don't feel abashed' in your caperings; the whole world is foolish, in the last analysis.

SD 5088 The first group in the procession is disguised as Florentine flower girls. They sing to the accompaniment of a lutelike instrument called a *Mandoline*. The modern development of this instrument is the Italian mandolin, with five double courses of strings which are plucked with a plectrum. The older instrument had four or five courses of single strings and was much more like the modern Spanish guitar. See SD 5177.

5091 folgten They were attracted to this German court by its splendor.

5096–5099 Their flowers are artificial flowers which blossom all year. That they wear such flowers in their hair is a thing of which to be proud, as they see it.

5100–5107 In the making of these artificial flowers, a proper symmetrical arrangement (*ihr Recht*) was given to all sorts of colored pieces cut out of paper. Some readers see in these lines a compliment paid by Goethe to his wife, Christiane Vulpius, who, before her union with the poet, earned her living by making artificial flowers. — The goal of art is beauty and the essential quality of woman is closely related thereto.

5109 Häupten An old dative plural form, without the plural ending *–er*. This form still survives in a few set phrases. — The girls from Florence are thought of as carrying baskets of flowers on their heads and on their arms.

5114 zu umdrängen 'to be surrounded.'

5116–5119 The gardener girls address the others on the stage; they invite offers to purchase their wares (*feilschet*), but admonish against haggling over prices (*Markten*). Each of the flowers is to address the company, as it offers itself for sale, and to say in a few well-chosen words what its excellent qualities are, so a would-be purchaser may know what he is bidding for. First comes the olive branch with olives — that is, a girl duly dressed up to represent an olive branch, or at any rate presenting one and speaking for it. — Another interpretation takes *feilschet = feil bieten* and holds that the chorus of gardener girls is addressing itself.

5122 The antecedent of *'s* is to be supplied from the context, something like 'invidious conflict' (from *beneid'* and *Widerstreit*), which is contrary to the peaceful nature of the olive branch.

5123 Olive culture is the mainstay of the economic life of the Italian provinces. These girls are from Florence.

SD 5128 Ährenkranz A wreath made up of the ripe heads of wheat, barley, rye, or millet.

5128 Ceres A sister of Juno, Pluto, Neptune, and Jupiter, also known as Demeter. She was the goddess of sowing and reaping, of harvest festivals, and of agriculture in general.

5130 Those gifts of Ceres which, to the person using them, are the most highly desired of benefits.

5135 Mode It was a new fashion in the last quarter of the eighteenth century in Weimar to wear artificial flowers, either imported from Italy or made nearer home. See note to lines 5100–5107 above.

5137 Theophrastus of Lesbos (about 372–287 B.C.), pupil of Aristotle and himself a great peripatetic philosopher. Most of his many works are lost, but two concerning plants are preserved and he has therefore sometimes been called the father of botany. The implication is that not even the greatest botanist would venture a name for this artificial bouquet.

5139 mancher Dative singular feminine: the sales appeal is to the ladies.

5144 The rosebuds challenge these artificial flowers. — **Phantasien** The abstract for the concrete = *Phantasiesträuße* (SD 5132, SD 5136).

5155–5157 'What we promise, what we grant, — that dominates, in the realm of flowers, eye, mind, and heart, all together.'

5156 Flora, the goddess of flowers.

SD 5158 **Theorben** An arch-lute with fourteen to sixteen strings, half of which were bass courses tuned in a relatively low range of pitch.

5160 Fruits, as distinct from artificial flowers, offer no deception. They are enjoyed when tasted, not merely when looked at.

5162 **bräunliche Gesichter** Gardeners with sun-bronzed faces. — Another interpretation takes *bräunliche Gesichter* as accusative, object of *bieten*, and thus understands the nouns *Kirschen*, *Pfirschen*, and *Königspflaumen* as subjects of *bieten*.

5168–5169 The contrast is between romantic aesthetic pleasures on the one hand and pragmatic practical enjoyments on the other.

5170 The gardeners now address the flower girls and join them.

SD 5177 **stufenweis** In the arbors in which these wares are displayed there are terracelike sets of steps, on which the baskets and bouquets may be tastefully arrayed. — The girls' chorus first appeared at line 5088 singing to the accompaniment of *Mandolinen*. Now the 'mandolins' seem to have been replaced by *Gitarren*.

SD 5178 **Mutter und Tochter** Solo parts with very earthy content are set between two groups of fanciful romantic mummers. — The mother has tried to catch the eye of a desirable suitor for her daughter by putting her on display, much as the flower girls have displayed their artificial blooms. Now, the mother advises more drastic means to catch a husband, somewhat in the sense that the gardeners have recommended the enjoyment of their wares.

5194 **Pfänderspiel** Any kind of a game in which the penalty for a mistake or failure is a kiss, or several kisses. — **Dritter Mann** A variety of drop-the-handkerchief. A number of pairs of players form a circle, leaving some space between each two pairs, and having one member of each pair directly in front of the other. Two players are outside of this circle; one, who is armed with a knotted handkerchief, pursues the other, who at his pleasure enters the circle and stands before one of the pairs. The player on the outside thus becomes the 'third man' in that 'pair' and must flee at once or be hit with the handkerchief, in which event he becomes the pursuer of the player who has hit him.

5196 **Narren** Carnival activities conduce to amorous adventures and foolish actions. This irresponsible mother advises her daughter to seize the opportunity to obligate some man to marry her.

SD 5198 The scene may be thought of as a ballet, and the 'most pleasant dialogues' are in pantomime. This dainty play is interrupted by the clumsy groups which next appear.

5203 **tragen** They carry the logs they have cut.

5220 The *pulcinelli* traditionally wore tall conical "dunce's caps," and gaily colored, loose-fitting clown suits of light, flimsy material.

5223 Take the verb *sind*, by implication from 5217, with this *wir*.

5228 **anzukrähen** An allusion to the basic meaning of *pulcinella*, which is derived from *pulcino* 'chicken.'

5229 **auf** 'in response to.'

SD 5237 **Parasiten** In the political sense. — Fawning, greedy parasites were stock figures in ancient comedy.

5244 **Doppelblasen** Possibly an allusion to the Epistle of James 3.10: "Out of the same mouth cometh forth blessing and cursing," but more probably the proverbial "kalt und warm aus einem Munde blasen," which goes back to one of Aesop's fables and means 'to appear both to favor and to oppose a thing.' These parasites flatter the woodcutters, for, without wood, there would be no fires at which to cook for their greedy maws.

5266 **sie** Presumably refers to *frische Lust* and *heitre Lieder*. Others take *sie* to refer to the companions of this Drunken Man.

5269 **Du** Addressed to one of his audience.

5271–5272 His lady cried out in dismay at his carnival costume and turned up her nose at it.

5274 **Maskenstock** Literally, a dummy: a wooden form for the making or the display of a costume, like *Haubenstock, Perückenstock.* — The lady meant that the speaker was "wooden" and "lifeless," perhaps even "brainless."

5293 **Span** Perhaps 'a tub.'

SD 5295 This stage direction suggests Goethe's intention, not fulfilled, to amplify this scene. It is, however, the sort of thing a competent theater director could manage without further text.

In the sketches which Goethe made for this scene there are two groups of lines which appear to be correlated with the words *Naturdichter* and *Hof- und Rittersänger*. The first he called *Natur und Liebe*, and these would seem to be appropriate also to the *zärtliche Poeten*. The second he called *Ruhm und Leidenschaft*, which might be associated with the enthusiasts. It appears probable that Goethe was not satirizing major figures in eighteenth and early nineteenth century German letters, but rather the "à la mode" poets of lesser stature who were in the public eye in 1827 or 1828.

5295 The Satirist, viewing the windy rivalry of the poets of SD 5295, ironically proposes to write something which no one at all would wish to hear.

SD 5298 This stage direction, like that at line 5295, puts something of a burden on the director. Probably it, too, indicates an intention on Goethe's part to amplify the scene at this point.

Poets of the Night and Grave are the exponents of horror, such as E. T. A. Hoffmann, in his *Nachtstücke* (1817) or in the *Bergwerke zu Falun*. Goethe's remarks to Eckermann, March 14, 1830, throw some light on what was here in his mind. In his discussion of the revolution then going on in French literature he said: "So wollten auch die Franzosen bei ihrer jetzigen literarischen Umwälzung anfänglich nichts weiter als eine freiere Form; aber dabei bleiben sie jetzt nicht stehen, sondern sie verwerfen neben der Form auch den bisherigen Inhalt. Die Darstellung edler Gesinnungen und Taten fängt man an für langweilig zu erklären, und man versuch sich in Behandlung von allerlei Verruchtheiten. An die Stelle des schönen Inhalts griechischer Mythologie treten Teufel, Hexen und Vampire, und die erhabenen Helden der Vorzeit müssen Gaunern und Galeerensklaven Platz machen. Dergleichen ist pikant! Das wirkt!'' The Vampire, therefore, is the symbol of this ghastly, ghoulish vogue in literature. Greek mythology, on the other hand, was in Goethe's mind the antithesis of this poetry of horror, and hence Goethe summoned certain figures from Greek mythology to appear at this point.

SD 5299 The Graces were goddesses presiding over the banquet, the dance, and polite social intercourse in general. There were three of them: Euphrosyne, Aglaia, and Thalia. Instead of Thalia, Goethe used the name Hegemone, which he got from the mythological lexicon of Hederich, his usual source for this kind of information. [Benjamin Hederich, GRÜNDLICHES MYTHOLOGISCHES LEXIKON; see Volume I, p. 325]. We have then, Aglaia, the resplendent one; Hegemone, the leader; Euphrosyne, the joyous one.

5299–5304 Goethe here follows Hederich. The first grace bestows the favor, the second receives it, and the third requites the favor with gratitude.

SD 5305 **die Parzen** The Fates, whose function it was to spin the thread of human destiny and to cut it off as they saw fit. Hence they are equipped with flax, a reel, and a pair of shears. Goethe's assignment of the spinning to Atropos and the shears to Klotho reverses the usual arrangement. This is a special concession to the gaiety of the occasion. The one whose duty normally is to cut the thread of life has been asked to spin it.

5309 **euch** Addressed to the revelers of the carnival.

5315 **Grenzen** Here in the unusual sense of 'limitations.' The word *Grenze* is usually applied either to a boundary in space or metaphorically to a limit as if in space, e.g., *die Grenzen der menschlichen Kraft,* 'limits beyond which human strength does not go.'

5316 **möchte** 'might possibly.'

5320 **unsrer Alten** Refers to Atropos.

5321 **Zerrt** Like *schleppt* (5324), a present tense form. The tense normally to be expected after *war . . . erbaut* is past, as in *irrte* (5326). — The accusation is that Atropos had prolonged the life of the most useless creatures and had sent the most promising young people to their graves too early.

5327 **heute** This being a day of festivity, Klotho has put away the shears, lest she inadvertently cut off some life and thus spoil the party.

5333 **verständig** Supply *bin.*

5335 **Weife** A reel for winding up the thread which has been spun. Each length of thread represents a human life.

5343 **zählen, messen** Either intransitives, equivalent to *zählen sich, messen sich* with the subjects *Stunden* and *Jahre* respectively, or infinitives, to be understood with a governing verb such as *muß ich* (Lachesis) and with the objects *Stunden* and *Jahre.* Either: 'Hours are counted off, years are measured,' or '(I must) count off hours, measure off years.'

5344 der Weber The Supreme Weaver, at his pleasure, takes a skein from the reel to weave this thread into the pattern of human life as he sees fit.

5349 The Furies were attendants of the Queen of Hades, Proserpine, who had a dual nature. When Proserpine is Goddess of Spring, dear to men, she brings with her on her annual visit to earth a cornucopia replete with flowers. When she is Goddess of Death, enthroned beside Pluto in Hades, she sends the Furies out on their cruel missions and is the enemy of youth, life, and hope. Some of this dual nature has been transferred to the Furies, who here, for the special occasion of this carnival, are endowed with unusual attractiveness.

5352 schlangenhaft The heads of the Furies are wreathed in serpents. They look like doves, but they are as dangerous as serpents. — **Tauben** is the subject of *verletzen*.

5355 They do not claim to be angels; they confess their evil nature.

SD 5357 All three Furies incited an unpunished evildoer to the frenzies of remorse. But each also had a special function: Alecto instigated suspicion, hatred, jealousy, and war; Megaera incited to envy; Tisiphone drove her victims to vengeance.

5357 Was hilft es euch? 'This warning by the Herald will avail you nothing.'

5362 sie The *Liebeschätzchen* of **5359**.

5366 Freund Her fiancé.

5372 Stunden The astronomical hours which determine the horoscope of each person. They differ because each horoscope is taken for the moment of the individual's birth. See note to line 4949. — Megaera finds her task of creating trouble easy, because people are different, or unequal, both as to natural endowments and as to their fortunes.

5375 vom höchsten Glück To be construed with *sich (weg)sehnte*, meaning approximately: 'No one has firmly in his embrace the one he most has desired who would not, turning from this highest bliss to which he is becoming accustomed, long foolishly for another which he desires even more ardently.'

5376 This line summarizes the preceding two lines in a metaphor. He flees from the sun (the woman who loves him), and seeks to make warm the freezing coldness (of some other lady, who appears to him more desirable).

5378 Asmodi Asmodeus, the evil spirit of anger and lust who foments discord between husband and wife. He is a figure of Jewish demonology, where he is King of the Demons, having Lilith as his Queen.

5382 dem Verräter The traitor who is faithless to vows of love is to die by poison or by the dagger.

5384 hat durchdrungen The present perfect, used as a very vivid future: 'will run you through' (as a sword runs through its victim).

5386 Gischt Apparently a play of words, based on the hackneyed phrase *Gift und Galle* 'bitterness.'

5388 **er** The 'traitor' of line 5382. — **beging** Prose would be: *wie er es auch begangen hat* (or *hätte*) 'Regardless of the circumstances under which he committed this (betrayal),' or 'As surely as he did it, just so surely will he pay for it.'

5390 Tisiphone's "cause" is vengeance. She addresses her appeal to the rocks, because they are unfeeling and relentless. They give her the reply she seeks: the echo of her complaint. This confirms her in her purpose: *Rache.*

5392 **wechselt** 'He who is inconstant in his love . . .'

5394 **euresgleichen** This is addressed to all and sundry — the participants in the masque and the others on the stage.

5397 **Schlangenrüssel** This beast is a richly and gaily decorated elephant (Power) guided by a beautiful damsel (Prudence) seated upon its neck. On its back it bears a towering structure in which another lady stands, most resplendent in her beauty (Victory).

5403 The two ladies in chains are Fear and Hope, who speak at 5407 and 5423. The words of each are equally misleading.

5412 **Verdacht** The suspicion that they are hostile to her.

5415 She picks out one individual among the revelers, a former friend.

5418 This amounts to a stage direction for the individual thus "discovered."

5419–5420 Fear would gladly take any route of escape out into the world, but is deterred by the threat of her destruction, which she sees beyond the boundaries of this masque. So she is held gripped between the fog of uncertainty and the terror from beyond.

5438 **wir** Hope and the ladies of the masque, whom she is trying to persuade to follow her.

5440 **irgendwo** 'If we just look about hopefully, we must find the best, the highest good, somewhere. There's no need to do more than hope.'

SD 5441 **Klugheit** Prudence holds Fear and Hope captive, while from her perch on the elephant's neck she points to Winged Victory standing in the battlements of a tower which has been built on the back of the pachyderm.

5444 **Ihr** The people of the crowd, and hence all mankind.

5445 **Den Kolossen** An unusual weak singular accusative form. This noun is regularly strong.

5453 **Glorie** A synonym of *Glanz* 'splendor, radiance.'

SD 5457 **Zoilo-Thersites** A hybrid creature — a combination of Zoilus, the bitter, envious, unjust, carping critic of Homer, and Thersites, the ugliest and most scurrilous of the Greeks before Troy. Probably Goethe intended this character to wear a mask with two faces, one in front and one behind. At any rate, Mephistopheles is responsible for the introduction of this unpleasant person into the midst of the festivities — if indeed he is not himself the wearer of this mask.

5466 Prose order would be: *bringt es mich sogleich in Harnisch.*

5467–5470 This noisome churl is happy only when he can turn everything upside down.

5472 **Meisterstreich** Reminiscent, perhaps, of the blow Ulysses gave
Thersites (ILIAD 2, 265). But now something quite uncanny occurs.
The doubly masked dwarfish figure becomes a mere shapeless mass
which behaves like a great egg, out of which an adder and a bat
emerge. — **frommen Stabes** The staff is 'pious' because it is a
badge of its bearer's authority, for which respect is demanded.

5494 **Seit** The conjunction, equivalent to *da.*

5499 **wanke, weiche** Indicatives, with the subject *ich* understood.

5504–5505 If what Zoilo-Thersites did aroused suspicion, that was nothing
compared with the commotion stirred up in the background.

5511 What the Herald sees is a chariot drawn through the crowd by four
snorting winged dragons, which is somehow able to come roaring
along in the midst of the people without forcing any of them to
move. The Herald can't understand this, but we see that it is some
more of Mephistopheles' magic.

SD 5521 **Knabe Wagenlenker** The personification of Poetry, as we
know from Goethe's remarks to Eckermann, December 20, 1829,
and from lines 5573–5574.

5525 **Räume** The imperial palace.

5542 **Wort** The answer to the riddle.

5546 **Socken** 'shoes.' See note to line 1808.

5551 **lehrten** Unreal subjunctive: 'would teach' the ABC of love.

5559 Greater than his happiness in his possessions. *Besitz und Glück* is
hendiadys for an unrecorded compound *Besitzes-Glück.*

5562 **beschreibt sich nicht** 'cannot be described.'

5563–5566 A verb, *beschreiben sich* (or *lassen sich beschreiben*), may
be inferred from line 5562. One cannot adequately describe dignity; but the face, the mouth, the cheeks, and the rich comfort of
this person's flowing raiment can be described.

5568 The Herald's business requires that he recognize a king when he
sees one.

5569 **Plutus** An allegorical personification of wealth, not Pluto, the
King of Hades.

5578–5579 Poetry gives life and beauty to the festivities of wealth. It
adds spiritual exaltation to the material comforts wealth can give. —
One needs to remember that even in Goethe's day many poets depended upon the patronage of princes for their livings.

5588 **Flämmchen** The spark of inspiration; see lines 5630–5639.

5592 **Kleinode** The sentence is elliptical: 'he flips jewels (round about
him) as (one sees such things only) in a dream.'

5595 **was einer . . . griffe** 'No matter what one may have seized.' —
griffe is a past subjunctive form, with past time value, as in earlier
German. Another interpretation takes *griffe* as equivalent to *greife,*
the present subjunctive, used concessively, and substituted for the
sake of the rime.

5596 **des** = *dafür, davon.*

5598–5599 The glittering pearls (of poetry) turn into crawling bugs in
the hands of the many (*die liebe Menge* = *hoi polloi*).

5607 **der Schale Wesen** The inner nature of this outer appearance, with the added implication that in this case *Wesen* and *Schale* are inseparable, as Goethe elsewhere said: "Natur hat weder Kern noch Schale." — Logically, one should expect *Wesen zu ergründen* to be the subject of *sind* (5608), but this has taken its plural number from its predicate *Hofgeschäfte*.

5616–5621 The association between Poetry and Wealth is not a new one. Poetry has always engaged in the glorification of its wealthy patrons.

5617 **Palme** The palm is the usual token of military or political victory, as the laurel (5620) is the token of victory in a poetic competition.

5623 Genesis 2.23. The man from whose rib Jehovah has just created woman looks upon this creation and says: "This is now bone of my bones and flesh of my flesh." *Geist von meinem Geiste* may be an allusion to this biblical verse.

5627 **grünen Zweig** Of laurel; see note to 5617.

5629 A paraphrase of the words of the Voice from Heaven acknowledging Jesus as Son, during the baptism of Jesus and just before Jesus was sent into the wilderness by the Spirit; see Luke 3.22, Mark 1.11, Matthew 3.17, John 1.32–34.

5630–5639 A little of the divine afflatus of poetry is vouchsafed to everyone, but many fail to recognize it before it burns out. Only a few momentarily show that they possess it. — Darting flames on the head of a figure were used as symbols of "spirit" by Christian artists, probably on the basis of Acts 2.3–4: "And there appeared unto them cloven tongues like as of fire, and it sat upon each of them. And they were all filled with the Holy Ghost, and began to speak with other tongues, as the Spirit gave them utterance."

5642 The clown squatting on the chariot of Plutus is Mephistopheles, who personifies Avarice.

5645 One of the women has pinched (or thought of pinching) him, but he is so skinny there is no meat beneath his hide.

5648 **die Frau** Every woman, as lady of her own house.

5653 **Laster** Covetousness or greed (*Avaritia*) is second on the list of the seven deadly sins in the view of the medieval church.

5654–5665 The fiction is that the women of this court and time had ceased to be careful with money. Hence *Avaritia*, a feminine noun, has changed gender (5665) and become *der Geiz*, a masculine noun, to symbolize the fact that it is now the husbands who have become miserly.

5666 **der Drache** The Devil, here in the mask of Covetousness. 'Let the old dragon be stingy with his own kind! It is all a hoax anyway!'

5668 **Er** The skinny fellow, Covetousness.

5671 **Marterholz** The skinny figure of *der Geiz* is compared with a wooden cross or rack used for torture, or with one of the wooden crucifixes so often set up beside the roads in Roman Catholic countries.

5684–5688 Quite miraculous, since these dragon steeds presumably have no hands.

5686 **Gold und Geiz** The gold is inside; Covetousness is sitting upon the box.

5689–5696 Plutus refers to the material world, represented by the chest of gold, as an all-too-burdensome weight upon the chariot of Poetry. Poetry's place is not amidst the confusion of everyday life but on the high summits of solitary clarity. These words recall those of the *Dichter*, lines 59–66.

5697 **Abgesandten** An ambassador from the material world to the new world he is to create, in which only the good and the beautiful are accepted. These two worlds are thought of as mutually exclusive; men must choose between them (5702).

5705–5706 The act of creating poetry forces the poet to divulge his secret thoughts: poetry is self-revelation by the poet.

5712 **goldnem Blute** Liquid gold which threatens to engulf and to melt the crowns and jewels, which at first appear on the surface of this bubbling mass.

5713 **zunächst** 'next to' (the bubbling gold).

5718 **gemünzte Rollen** A metaphor for rolls of minted coins, *Geldrollen*. This hot, bubbling mass miraculously does not immediately burn the wrappings of these rolls of coins. Ducats, themselves gold coins, hop out of the chest as if they were just being minted.

5721 **alle mein Begehr** *Begehr* is neuter, *alle* is an invariable, uninflected form of the adjective. Similar uses occur at 1946, *Mir wird von alle dem so dumm*, and at 9849, *alle den Kämpfenden*.

5725 The speakers alternate throughout this section, 5715–5726. The last group proposes to take possession of the chest itself. The preceding group had picked up ducats.

5727 The Herald protests in surprise this unscheduled intervention of the crowd. He sputters: "*Was soll's? Ihr Toren!*" 'What's the meaning of this? You fools!' *Soll mir das?* may be taken either as repetition = *Was soll mir das bedeuten?* or as equivalent to "*Soll mir das geschehen?*" 'Is this going to happen to me?' 'Is this party, for the orderliness of which I am responsible, going to get completely out of hand?'

5734 **soll** 'Is, in your sight.'

5735 **soll** 'Of what use (is truth to you)?'

5736 **Zipfeln** These belong to the *Wahn*, the delusion, which stands for the thing causing the delusion: 'You seize a stupid sham by every tag and end.'

5741 **Sud und Glut** Hendiadys for *siedende Glut* 'boiling fire' (of the treasure chest, 5716). See also *Glut und Sud* (5925).

SD 5748 The following lines are to be managed, like lines 5715–5726, as a series of outcries from various members of the group of bystanders, this time in sequence, as Plutus makes his round forcing back the crowd with the Herald's glowing staff.

5762 The invisible band is a magic circle now quickly drawn around the chest. Included in the area within this circle are only Plutus, *der Geiz*, and the Herald.

5792   This lewd *Geiz* has made a phallus out of the pliable gold. — **übelfertig** 'skilled in evil.'

5797   It is not probable that this is true, for this rascal, the *Geiz*, is in fact
Mephistopheles, who must be supposed to know about all of this
hocus-pocus.

5800   **Gesetz** The authority of the Herald might restrain the *Geiz*, but
the hubbub to come will certainly put a stop to this lewd behavior.

5801–5806 **das wilde Heer** 'Wild,' because it knows no discipline. —
These lines are spoken by the arriving vassals of the great god Pan,
who describe their own procession, instead of letting it be described
by the Herald. A similar device is used at 5816, 5819, 5829, 5864.
The first to appear are fauns, satyrs, gnomes, giants, and nymphs.

5804   Pan was the son of Mercury and a wood-nymph, or dryad. He
was the god of the woods and fields and the protector of shepherds
and flocks. He was noted as the inventor of the syrinx, or shepherd's pipe, which he played like a virtuoso. This Pan seems, however, to be the late Greek god, who ruled over all nature, his name
having become confused with the Greek pronominal word meaning
'all' (cf. *Pan-Hellenic*).

5805   **was keiner weiß** The "Wild Army" says that it knows something
which none of the others present knows. This is that the Emperor
is disguised in the mask of Pan. Plutus knows this too; see line 5809.

5810   **schuldig** 'as duty requires.'

5815   This line is addressed to the bystanders and masqueraders outside
the circle.

5816   One would expect: *Wir kommen, wir treten*, since these singers are a
part of the retinue of Pan (5801). However, they address the on-
lookers as *geputztes Volk* and then report their own arrival as though
they were the Herald.

5819   Fauns were sportive minor deities of Roman mythology, named
after Faunus, the grandson of Saturn. They are usually represented
as having the ears and legs of a goat.

5829   Satyrs were morphologically peculiar forest deities of Greek mythology. Like the Roman fauns (see note 5819) they sometimes appear
with snub noses, luxuriant beards, goats' ears, and horses' tails.
At other times they look like handsome young men except for
sprouting horns. In Roman poetry a satyr is likely to be described
as having the legs of a goat.

5831   **ihm** *(dem Satyr) sollen sie (Fuß und Bein) mager sein.*

5834   **Freiheitsluft** This contrast of freedom on the mountain tops with
confinement in the valleys was used effectively by both Goethe and
Schiller as a symbol of the contrast of *Natur* with *Kultur*. It is not
unlikely that Goethe here remembered Schiller's lines:

> Auf den Bergen ist Freiheit! Der Hauch der Grüfte
> steigt nicht hinauf in die reinen Lüfte;
> die Welt ist vollkommen überall,
> wo der Mensch nicht hinkommt mit seiner Qual.

[*Die Braut von Messina*, 2585–2588]

SD 5840   The gnomes belong to Germanic rather than to classic mythology. These appear to be *Schrate, Wald- und Bergschrate,* little elflike spirits who specialize in mining operations. Hence they carry little lanterns and their clothing is moss-stained.

5841   The *Bergschrate* do not dance in pairs, as the fauns and satyrs did.

5845   **Leuchtameisen**   Creatures of the poet's imagination. They are what ants would be if they had the ability to show a flashing light like that of the beetles we call fireflies or lightning-bugs.

5848   **Gütchen**   Helpful, friendly little house sprites or goblins, like our brownies.

5851   **Adern**   Veins of precious minerals in the rocks.

5853   **Glückauf!**   The standard greeting to a miner about to descend into a mine; also a general greeting, used whenever miners meet.

5859   This general murder is war.

5860   **die drei Gebot'**   An allusion to Exodus 20.1–17. The three here referred to are: 'Thou shalt not kill' (5859), 'Thou shalt not steal' (5857), and 'Thou shalt not commit adultery' (5857).

5864   The giants are describing themselves in the third person. These particular giants are also creatures of Germanic mythology. A similar giant figure, complete with uprooted pine or fir tree in hand, can be seen on the coats of arms of numerous North German noble families.

5865   The highest mountain in the Harz is the Brocken, the scene of the *Walpurgisnacht* of Part I (Scene 23). These hills lie about 45 miles south and a little east of the city of Hanover, and 135 miles northeast of Frankfurt-am-Main.

5871   The giants proclaim themselves a better bodyguard than the Vatican guards of the Pope in Rome.

SD 5872   There were several classes of nymphs. Pan's partners in the dance here are Dryads, tree-nymphs. There were also the Oreads, nymphs of mountains and caves, and the Naiads, water-nymphs.

5873–5875   Pan is falsely interpreted to mean 'all' by a confusion of two Greek words: *pân,* and a very common pronoun and prefix *pan* (neuter singular of *pas*), meaning 'all' or 'wholly.' His name, *pân,* properly means 'the shepherd,' the protector of grazing animals. — Goethe was aware of this error but assumed that it would not trouble his readers. See also note to line 5804.

5876   The nymphs call upon each other to surround the great Pan.

5884   The noonday silence which comes over nature used to be observed with the remark: "The great Pan is asleep."

5885   **regt**   Moved from the beginning to the end of its clause for the sake of the "rime," which is an assonance, rather than a pure rime. Assonance is not unusual in this part of FAUST. See Volume I, p. 143.

5888   No one dares disturb Pan's slumber.

5893   **wo ein noch aus**   'Which way to turn.'

5894–5895   Pan may cause a 'panic' (*der panische Schrecken*); see lines 10 780–10 782.

5896   Paul's Epistle to the Romans 13.7: 'Render . . . honor to whom honor is due.'

SD 5898   The gnomes are miners. Having discovered gold, they send a deputation to their ruler to announce this fact, as is required by law.

5898   **Gute** The vein of gold.

5900   The divining rod was supposed to have the magic power to indicate the location of any treasure which its operator wished to find. These rods, called "dowsers," are still widely used in the search for promising locations for wells.

5907   **Quelle** A rivulet of pure gold and even an abundance of gold coins (5717–5718) have been discovered running from the chest which has been unloaded from the chariot of Plutus. This is the *Feuerquelle* of line 5921.

5914   **im hohen Sinne** 'serenely.'

5917   Plutus (Faust) knows what turn the hocus-pocus is to take. The Herald proceeds to describe it, 5920–5969.

5921–5925   A gaping abyss (*Schlund : Mund*) opens up, from which fire intermittently flames forth.

5925   **Glut und Sud** Like *Sud und Glut* (5741), hendiadys for 'boiling fire.'

5929   **Wesen** 'goings on': the fiery manifestations.

5931   Pan loses part of his disguise, is almost, but not quite, unmasked.

5935   The beard falls into the fire, is ignited, and then flies back to its place, where it sets fire to the rest of Pan's costume.

5940   **es = man** The crowd.

5948   The Herald foresees the news report of the day which is to come. That report will say that the Emperor, having participated in the masque in the guise of the great god Pan, was severely burned in a great fire which took place, and is (5951) suffering great agony.

5954   **sie = die Schar** (5953). The young courtiers of the Emperor's retinue. The Herald censures their bad judgment in persuading the Emperor to put on a highly flammable costume for which even pine twigs (5955) were used.

5970   **genug** Enough of horror to convince this Emperor that Faust (Plutus) is a very powerful fellow, whom he would do well to retain in his service. Any time evil spirits threaten trouble, Faust, the great magician, will deal with them (5985–5986).

5972   Again using the Herald's staff, Plutus restores order by calling down mists and fog to engulf the flames.

5983   **Wetterleuchten** As the flames are quelled by steam clouds, they flare up occasionally, producing an effect like that of heat-lightning.

31. LUSTGARTEN

This scene takes place on the morning following the masque. Its function is to bring Faust into a position of prominence in the Imperial Court. He becomes a great figure in the great world (2052), and thus lays the basis for his further enterprises as a feudal lord and land-holder.

5987 **Flammengaukelspiel** Described in lines 5920–5969. This is the first indication given in the text that Faust was Plutus.

5990 Since the Emperor (Pan) had entered (5920) the magic circle drawn by Plutus-Faust (5762), he had enjoyed the proceedings without fear (5926–5927). He had felt as though he were lord of the nether world (Pluto; see note to line 5569), amidst all the fire and flames of Faust's "show." His vision of the vast subterranean vault and the homage of great crowds of people was an illusion.

5991 **Aus** 'Appearing out of,' 'showing itself in the midst of.' — **Nacht und Kohlen** Hendiadys, like *Sud und Glut* (5741) 'coal (black) night.'

5995 The dome of the *Gewölbe* (5994).

5996 **ward, verlor** The dome was not stable, it formed and broke up intermittently.

5997 **gewundner Feuersäulen** 'twisted columns of fire.' One may think of long rows of twisted columns such as the four which support the baldachin over the main altar in St. Peter's in Rome.

6001 **ein' und andern** 'one and another,' 'various people.'

6002 According to popular superstition, salamanders are unharmed by flames.

6003 **Element** Mephistopheles speaks here in terms of the philosophy of Paracelsus (1493–1541). The Emperor may be thought of as a contemporary of Paracelsus. See also Part I, lines 1273 ff., where fire, water, air, and earth are cited. Just as the Emperor had fancied himself the center of homage in a realm of fire (5990–6002), so he will find himself the ruler of the realm of water, if he throws himself into the sea (6006). Mephistopheles paints a very flattering picture.

6008 **Rund** A charmed circle (or sphere) within which the Emperor is secure. This repeats the motif of the circle of 5747.

6009–6010 The choice of colors here is not arbitrary, but carefully considered and in accord with Goethe's FARBENLEHRE, *Didaktischer Teil*, § 164.

6014 The very walls of this submarine palace are alive with the denizens of the deep which dart back and forth in great hosts with the speed of an arrow. They, like the sea monsters, would be attracted by the resplendence of a submarine imperial court, at which they may look but which they are forbidden to enter. — Goethe was here imaginatively describing the wonders of the deep which, up to his time, no human being had seen.

6022 **Nereiden** Nereids, the fifty daughters of Nereus, god of the sea. Best known of this host of beauties were Panope, Galatea, Thetis, and Amphitrite. We encounter these charming creatures as a chorus in the Classical Walpurgis Night, and Galatea even speaks a few lines there.

6025 **spätern** One of the manuscript notes penciled in Goethe's own hand has *alten* instead of *spätern*, and there seems to be no doubt that the adjective was intended to refer to the older, more experienced Nereids.

6026   Peleus, one of the Argonauts, and a grandson of Jupiter, married Thetis, daughter of Nereus. From this union sprang Achilles, the great hero of the Trojan War. Mephistopheles suggests that Thetis will see in the Emperor a second Peleus and by espousing him endow him with a throne on Mount Olympus, the home of the Greek Gods of Heaven. In this way the Emperor could achieve immortality.

6028   **luft'gen**   The third element, the air.

6030   **Erde**   The fourth element.

6032   The tales of "A Thousand and One Nights," a very ancient collection of oriental fairy tales, anecdotes, and beast fables, generally known in English as the "Arabian Nights," in German as "Tausend und eine Nacht." These tales are alleged to have been told by Scheherazade to the Emperor of the Indies.

6035   **eure**   The Emperor feels himself superior to the everyday world, is frequently strongly displeased by it. Hence 'your' world — 'you can have it, I don't want it.'

6039   **als**   'Such as.'

6047   **Lanzknecht**   An early sixteenth-century popular version of *Landsknecht*, a mercenary soldier in the Imperial army.

6048   **haben's gut**   They are prosperous from the openhanded spending of the soldiery.

6057–6062   This is the warranty under which this paper was to circulate as money. It lacks the essential "promise to pay" of a responsible agency, but says only that steps are being taken to make available the buried treasure of the empire as replacement (*Ersatz*) for the paper. — The interest of the public of Goethe's day in this kind of scheme was keener than our own. John Law introduced paper money into the economy of France in 1716–1718. Louis XV, by putting such paper currency into circulation without regard to its redeemability in hard money or goods, caused the whole fiscal structure of the French state to collapse (1721) and cast great discredit upon the system. In 1789, during the French Revolution, the French Government resorted to printed money (Assignats), which within four years was worth only one third its face value. Many small German principalities tried similar experiments in the late eighteenth century. Prussian *Tresorscheine* were selling at prices beyond their real value in December 1829, and the matter was discussed by Goethe and his son (Eckermann, December 27, 1829).

6068   This portion of the doings of the night of the masque is first reported here. According to these lines one should infer that the Chancellor and the Treasurer were members of the Deputation of Gnomes (5898–5913). However, the whole business of the paper money, its preparation, its circulation, has been accomplished by magical means, and this alleged signature has been obtained, or falsified, in the same way.

6072   **Tausendkünstler**   Clever fellows who can do all sorts of handwork with great skill. Also used in the sense of *Schwarzkünstler*, 'magician,' but here equivalent to *Bastler*, or *Boßler*, 'artisans skilled in many kinds of light handwork.'

Notes

6074 **Reihe** Series of notes in all denominations, as indicated.

6081–6082 **überzählig** = *zu groß an Zahl* 'having an unnecessarily numerous membership.' One does not need all of the letters of the alphabet to 'read' the 'sign' of the Emperor on this paper money. This *Zeichen* may be thought of as the usual intricate imperial monogram, which was a rectangular figure of three lines of three letters each, vertically and horizontally, and representing, if the Emperor's name is Frederick, the words, "Signum domini Frederici Romanorum imperatoris invictissimi."

6086 **Flüchtigen** The new imperial notes, once issued, changed hands rapidly. The Proverbs of Solomon have it (23.5): "For riches certainly make themselves wings, like an eagle that flieth toward heaven."

6090 Since the tradespeople required payment as usual in hard cash, these paper notes were first taken to the money brokers for exchange. The money brokers charged a fee for their service in the form of a discount taken from the face value of the notes when they bought them and gave hard money in payment for the balance.

6091 **Schenken** = *Schenkwirt* 'retailer of wines and beer.'

6095–6096 **sprudelt's, kocht's, brät's** 'There is a bubbling, a boiling, a roasting going on.' One would expect also *klappert's*, but the traditional text is *klappert*. Hence one may supply the impersonal *man*, 'people are banging plates about.'

6098 **die Schönste** A lady of pleasure, in search of a paying guest.

6108 **Gürtel** He will lighten his money belt by exchanging metal coins for these paper notes.

6111 **erstarrt** Faust is thinking of the veins of gold in the igneous and metamorphic rocks of the mountains. This gold has solidified from a molten state. Mephistopheles, on the other hand (4931–4938), was thinking in terms of buried treasures of money and jewelry. Faust's fiscal idea is sound and honest: Mephistopheles' is fraudulent.

6121 The necessity for haggling in the exchange of hard money arises from the variations in the purity of the metal, in the coinage of the many different European countries involved, and also from the fact that all gold or silver coins had to be weighed before one knew how much they were really worth.

6125 The buried treasure of ancient peoples will be sold at auction, presumably for hard money, although Mephistopheles passes over this vital point lightly. With the proceeds of this sale, at any rate, the paper money will be redeemed and the people who go to the trouble of presenting it for redemption will be made to appear silly.

6133 Faust and Mephistopheles are appointed custodians of the buried treasure of the land.

6137 **Meister** On the one hand Faust and Mephistopheles, masters of buried treasure and so representatives of *die Unterwelt*, and on the other hand the Treasurer, master of the imperial exchequer, the representative of the upper world.

6144 **er** Each man in turn.

6151–6154 The Emperor observes that an increase of means does not change the nature of these subordinates or fire them with zeal for new adventure. They have never been free men and do not know what the prospect of unlimited possibilities can mean. Since the Emperor also remains what he has always been, some critics see an ironical intent in these lines.

6155 This is the fool who was carried off insensible; see line 4734.

6159 **fallen** The Emperor is throwing bank notes to his old fool.

6161 **wären** The fool is reading the face of the bank note: 'It would appear from what it says here that I have 5000 crowns!'

6170 **gestrengen Herrn** Landed gentry were addressed by their servants and other lesser folk as "*gestrenger Herr.*" Mephistopheles says he would be interested in seeing this fool as a landowner on his own estate, with all those possessions about which he has inquired (6167–6169).

32. FINSTERE GALERIE

Faust has led Mephistopheles away from the Great Hall of the palace into a dimly lighted gallery nearby, in order to explain to him privately their next undertaking in the realm of magic.

6177–6182 Faust rejects Mephistopheles' suggestion that they enjoy the fun which might be had from playing tricks on the courtiers and their ladies. He says that Mephistopheles has long since worn out such sources of amusement (*an den Sohlen abgetragen*), and that Mephistopheles is merely trying to avoid the issue. Faust is now being pressed for action in an adventure which Mephistopheles pretends not to wish to undertake. — **Hin- und Widergehn** Just where Mephistopheles has been flitting back and forth is not made clear; he has evidently been evading Faust.

6184 Paris, son of King Priam of Troy, while a visitor in the home of the Greek king of Sparta, Menelaus, made love to the latter's wife, Helena, and carried her off to his home in Troy. Helena, the daughter of Jupiter and Leda, was the fairest of her sex among mortals. Paris was the shepherd-prince, young, handsome, and popular.

6195 **greifst in** 'you are invading.'

6199 **Hexen-Fexen, Gespenst-Gespinsten** Tautological compounds, 'witch-witches,' 'ghost-ghosts,' hence: 'With witchy witches and ghostly ghosts.'

6200 As the antithesis of the beauty of Helen and Paris we have these dwarfs with great goiters. According to folklore a person with a goiter is the impish offspring of a union of the Devil with a witch. Mephistopheles concedes that the kind of ladies he can produce would not be accepted in the role of ancient beauties like Helen of Troy.

6205 **Vater** Suggests an allusion to John 8.44, where the Devil is called: 'a liar, and the father thereof.'

6209 The contrast between the northern, medieval, Christian world and the southern, ancient, pagan world is emphasized.

6216 **Die Mütter** These goddesses are an invention of Goethe, based on remarks of Plutarch (*Life of Marcellus*, Ch. 20; *Concerning the*

Decline of Oracles, Ch. 13 and Ch. 22). To Eckermann's persistent inquiry concerning the philosophical meaning of these figures Goethe's only answer was to repeat line 6217. Poetically, the scene is a very interesting attempt to render perceptible to the senses a supersensuous conception, lying outside the frames of time and place. The interpreter of these lines is well-advised to stick to the text.

6220   Mephistopheles won't (or can't) go: Faust will have to make the trip, if he insists on going through with the project. Hence: *magst* 'may, if you like.' After all, it was Faust who promised to produce these images of Helena and Paris. — **schürfen** From the technical vocabulary of miners; implies searching or prospecting underground.

6228   Faust is unimpressed by Mephistopheles' cryptic speech. He has long since learned rightly to evaluate the hocus-pocus of the Witch's Kitchen.

6231   Faust is reminded of those days long ago when, as Professor of Theology, he felt himself more and more thrust into a vacuum. If he said what he believed to be true, his opponents' contradictions were doubly noisy: he even had to flee into the woods to avoid unpleasant treatment at their hands, and finally, to avoid complete isolation, he was obliged to take up with the Devil. This reminiscence does not correspond in detail with the experiences of Faust set forth in Part I.

6249–6250   **Mystagogen: Neophyten** These words allude to the interpreters of the religious mysteries of the early Christian church and to the new converts to this faith. — **erster** 'foremost.'

6251   **umgekehrt** The *Mystagog* was supposed to clear up mysteries and make complex things appear simple. This one intensifies the mystery and makes simple things appear complex. The mystagogs used mysterious but concrete images for their purposes; Mephistopheles has promised Faust the complete absence of anything he can see, or feel, or otherwise perceive.

6252   **so . . . als** = *sowohl . . . als auch.*

6253   **jene Katze** The cat (Raton) of the old fable (La Fontaine, Book 9, No. 17), who lets the monkey (Bertrand) persuade it to pull hot chestnuts out of the fire for him.

6256   Faust recognizes the complete antithesis between his search for truth and the thinking of Mephistopheles. — **deinem Nichts** 'what you call nothing.'

6259   **Schlüssel** The significant fact is that Mephistopheles has this key, which, like a divining rod, will lead its bearer to the timeless, trackless void where *die Mütter* dwell.

6272   **Schaudern** The most hopeful faculty of humankind is its capacity to apprehend intuitively what it cannot put into words, and to stand in awe of it. Goethe spoke of this kind of awe as the highest achievement of man (to Eckermann, February 18, 1829: ". . . und wenn ihn das Urphänomen in Erstaunen setzt, so sei er zufrieden."). The essential quality of the Urphänomen is its lack of limits (*das Grenzenlose*), and its inaccessibility to study. We know it only by its effects, not directly.

6273–6274 **ihm . . . er** Refer to *der Mensch*, which is implicit in
Menschheit. — However much life in this world may tend to make
this feeling of awe prohibitively expensive, still, being seized with
it, man feels deeply the import of the tremendous unknown.

6277 **in . . . Reiche** 'into the detached realms of images.' — **losgebundne**
= Latin *absoluta* 'detached from all relationships.' — The home of
the Mothers, where phantoms without substance reside. The Ms.
and early editions have *Räume* instead of *Reiche*, which has been
accepted by all modern editors. These 'spaces' or 'realms' cannot
be defined as a place or determined as to time (line 6214). Apparently, the phantoms of all creation are assembled here. Faust is
in search of the phantom of Helena, not yet in search of Helena
herself. That comes later.

6283 **Dreifuß** An allusion to the tripod (stool) on which the oracle of
Apollo at Delphi sat. The tripod of the Mothers glows with a fire
and has a bowl upon it, from which incense vapors arise (6424).

6288 The never-ending amusement of intelligence, whether divine or
human, is the creation of a form, something substantial to match
an insubstantial thought.

6289 **aller Kreatur** 'of all creation.'

6296 **sie** = *die Mütter*.

6298 Paris and Helena are meant.

6302 **Weihrauchsnebel** Presumably, mists of incense arising from the
bowl on the glowing tripod (6424), if treated with proper magical
techniques, may be transformed into visible shapes — for example,
into gods and goddesses. In any event, the phantoms which later
appear are subsequently dissolved in vapors (SD 6563).

6305 The evident poetic purpose of this line is to emphasize the mysterious
hazards of the enterprise upon which Faust has embarked. Mephistopheles' unconcern about his contract with Faust increases the
effect of this mystery.

33. Hell erleuchtete Säle

This scene is an interlude in the interest of realism. Faust's journey
must be made to appear difficult, and the poet can best do this indirectly by insisting that it takes time to accomplish.

6310 The Emperor has promised his guests a special treat: Faust and
Mephistopheles are to produce the spirits of Helen of Troy and her
lover, Paris. If the show fails to materialize, the Emperor will be
made to look ridiculous and thus disgraced. — This situation is
typical of the traditional Faust of the Faust Books.

6313 **laboriert** Mephistopheles lies to the Marshal when he says that
his companion is locked up in seclusion in his laboratory working
on this project. He has sent him off to the abode of the Mothers.

6315 Since buried treasures are the conventional lucky find, the idiom
for finding and recovering any treasure has become: "einen Schatz
heben."

6319 Members of the court are moving about in the thronged halls before the beginning of the spectacle, conversing with one another. A lady approaches Mephistopheles, who, as far as she knows, is a magician.

6327 **er** = *der Mond* To be inferred from *Mondlicht.*

6332 Prose order would be: *selbst zum Gruß beweg' ich mich ungeschickt.*

6333 The *Fußtritt* was a legally recognized symbol of the authority of the one who gave it over the person to whom it was given. The bridegroom stepped on the foot of the bride immediately after the completion of the marriage ceremony to show that he was now master of this woman. A feudal lord, especially a bishop in his capacity as secular ruler, set his right foot upon the right foot of a vassal to show his sovereignty. The brunette appears to confuse *Fußtritt* with *Füßeln*, the caressing play of lovers' feet under a table (6342).

6336 An allusion to the homeopathic theory of medicine, which Goethe regarded as fraudulent.

6345–6346 **er, ihr, mir** The eternal triangle of one man and two women.

6357 Superstition has it that a piece of a hangman's rope or a fragment from the ashes of a fire which has burned someone at the stake has great magic powers.

6358 **wir** The fire by which witches and heretics were burned at the stake was supposed to be tended by devils, to see to it that every fragment of the person and of the embers was consumed. Of course, these devils often had the outward appearance of religious fanatics.

34. RITTERSAAL

The dramatic purpose of this scene is to bring Faust into direct contact with the ideal of feminine beauty, the phantom of Helena, and thus to inspire him to a new all-consuming quest.

6378 This is to be a spirit-show, hence spontaneous and unrehearsed. The Herald cannot announce the play, its actors, and its portent, as is his custom with ordinary performances here. He can merely describe the audience to the audience and invite the show to begin. The Emperor sits in front, facing what appears to be the wall, where on ancient tapestries, like gobelins, he can see depicted the glorious deeds of battle of ancient heroes in the great days of the empire — perhaps the deeds of Frederick Barbarossa, or others of the Hohenstaufen emperors. Or perhaps the scenes were more ancient conflicts, such as the Siege of Troy, or the Wars of Alexander the Great.

6386 **drängen sich** 'are crowded.' People have crowded into their seats to watch the show.

SD 6391 The Astrologer is at the right hand of the Emperor, as usual (SD 4728), and speaks for him, echoing the Herald's signal to begin, and describing the opening of the curtains of the theater. He is also to be master of ceremonies, and therefore mounts the stage.

6394 The tapestries are rolled up as if they were being consumed in a great fire.

6397 **zu erhellen** Dependent upon *scheint* (6396).

SD 6399 The *Souffleurloch* is a recess below the level and in the center of the front margin of the stage, usually hidden from the audience by a low hood. Here the prompter sits with his book in easy view of the players, whom he directs and prompts as necessary.

6405 The columns are compared with Atlas, who supported the vault of heaven on his shoulders. The temple is evidently a Doric structure.

6409–6410 **wär', wüßt', sollte** 'So that's what they mean by antique. I shouldn't know what to say in praise of it. It ought to be called unwieldy and overweighted.'

6412 This architect is praising the characteristic features of the Gothic (northern, medieval) style. *Schmalpfeiler . . . strebend* appears to refer to the delicately arched buttresses (*Strebepfeiler*) which, together with the pointed arch, are the marks of Gothic as compared with Romanesque style of architecture. The Greek Doric temple displeases him. What Winckelmann, the great German critic of ancient art, would call "die edle Einfalt und die stille Größe" of this Greek structure appears rude and awkward to the Architect.

6416–6418 The Astrologer asks that reason be held captive by magic words and fancy allowed free play.

6420 An adaptation of the saying: "Credo, quia impossibile," 'I believe, because it is impossible,' which is a misquotation from Tertullian's *De carne christi*, Ch. 5, where this Carthaginian foe of heretics, gnostics, and philosophers in general had defiantly said concerning God's fatherhood of Christ: "Credo, quia absurdum," 'I believe it, because it is silly,' and concerning Christ's resurrection: "Certum est, quia impossibile est." 'It is certain, because it is impossible.'

6423–6424 **Dreifuß, Schale** The tripod is the support upon which the *Schale* — a shallow bowl — rests.

6427–6438 Faust's incantation as he prepares to conjure up the shades of Paris and Helena by touching the tripod with his key. In the process he says something about these mysterious Mothers. They have heads about which float active but inanimate images of life, indeed images of everything that ever was. Some of these are assigned by the Mothers to the realm of day, and are caught up by the course of life. That is, the images acquire living form. Others are assigned to the realm of night and these the magician can produce at will for the delectation of his audience. It would appear, then, that Faust has said that some of the past is made accessible to human reason by these Mothers, while other parts of the past are not subject to pragmatic study but are accessible only as phantoms. Some critics understand the distinction made to be essentially the distinction between rational, pragmatic knowledge of the past and the "unconscious, instinctive retention of the past" which some scholars seek in the subconscious and others see in mythology.

6442 **gedehnt** These participles describe a progression of developments. The cloud is elongated, compressed then to spherical form, two parts of it appear interlocked, then divided, and then made a pair. This describes a process of becoming (*ein Werden*), and the pair which finds shape from the cloud is Paris and Helena. They are the persons referred to by the pronoun *sie* in 6444 and 6446. The process is analogous to that of Goethe's lyric poem "Howards Ehren-gedächtnis" (1820–1821), where the changing forms of clouds delight the god who directs them.

6445　At this point soft music begins to play. The phantoms of Paris and Helena move in time with this music in a kind of ballet.

6459　**Schäferknecht** Alludes to the fact that Paris, son of Priam, was indeed a shepherd-prince. With a leopard skin over his shoulder he does not look like a prince to these northern, medieval courtiers.

6466　The Lord Chamberlain is master of decorum at court.

SD 6468, 6470, 6472　**Derselbe** = *der Kämmerer.*

6471　Paris was asleep on Mount Ida when three goddesses, Juno, Venus, and Minerva, came to ask him to be the judge of their respective claims to the golden apple of Eris (Discord).

6477　Ambrosia, usually the food, as nectar was the drink, of the Greek gods. Sometimes poets have referred to it as a perfume or unguent. Homer (ILIAD 14, 170) has Hera (Juno) use ambrosia as a bathing oil to cleanse her body before anointing it with 'purer oil' when she sets forth on a venture of amorous conquest. The old lady of our passage pretends to more wisdom than she has, though the same notion that youth exhales a fragrance of its own reappears at 9046.

6479　'So that's the lady! She wouldn't excite me at all!'

6483　**Feuerzungen** An allusion to Acts 2.3–4: "And there appeared to them cloven tongues, like as of fire, and it sat upon each of them. And they were all filled with the Holy Ghost and began to speak with other tongues, as the Spirit gave them utterance." Our line represents an interrupted or elliptic utterance: 'And had I tongues as of fire, I could not describe this beauty.'

6487　The appearance of this phantom of Helena provides a new driving force in Faust's career and a new motivation for the poem. Part I dealt in the main with the problem of Faust in the bourgeois world, with his love for and desertion of Gretchen as its principal manifestation. Here he is established in imperial favor and could operate to his heart's content in the greater world of national and international affairs. However, he is carried away by this image of Helena, and is destined to devote himself to the effort to acquire possession of the reality of which this image is the reflection.

6492–6497　The world for the first time appears to Faust as desirable and substantial. He hopes he may die (6493) if he ever turns from this ideal beauty which is revealed to him in the shade of Helena. He recalls another deep experience of beauty — the figure he saw in the mirror in the Witch's Kitchen (2429–2440) — but he feels that this was but a pale adumbration of the beauty of woman, as he now sees this beauty in Helena.

6502　**zu klein** This criticism of Helena is similar to the reaction of many observers to the Venus de' Medici, an ancient statue, copied after the original of Praxiteles. This Venus has an unusually small head.

6509　Endymion was a shepherd youth who was so surpassing fair that the goddess of the moon repeatedly visited him. When her love was discovered, Jupiter gave Endymion the choice between death, in whatever form he might prefer, and perpetual youth coupled with perpetual sleep. Endymion chose the latter alternative, and in his slumber he is still watched over lovingly by the goddess of the moon.

6510 **Derselbe** = *der Poet* of line 6508.

6528–6530 A scurrilous allusion to Helena's hectic love-life. As a mere child she was abducted by Theseus (see note to 6530). After being much sought after by many suitors, she was duly given in marriage to Menelaus. She deserted him to run away with Paris, whom she married in Troy. Upon his death she married his brother, Deiphobus (see note to 9054). After the fall of Troy she returned to Menelaus.

6530 A malicious allusion to the fact that Theseus had stolen Helena from her home in Sparta when she was quite young. She was quickly rescued by her brothers, Castor and Pollux.

SD 6533 **Gelahrter** An old form of *Gelehrter*, used with irony to characterize the pedant. *Hochgelahrter* is used without irony in line 984 and marks the speaker, the old peasant, as an old man. In line 4969 Mephistopheles, speaking through the Astrologer, uses the adjective *hochgelahrte*. Elsewhere Mephistopheles uses the modern form; see 1325, 4917, 6590, 6638, 6644.

6537 An allusion to the ILIAD, Book 3, 156–158, where the Old Men of Troy say:

Tadelt nicht die Troer und hellumschienten Achaier,
die um ein solches Weib so lang' ausharren im Elend!
Einer unsterblichen Göttin fürwahr gleicht jene von Ansehn!

[Translation by Voß]

Small blame is it that Trojans and well-greaved Achaians
should for such a woman long-time suffer hardships;
marvellously like is she to the immortal goddesses to look upon.

[Translation by Chapman]

6555 **Doppelreich** The twofold realm of the real and the ideal, which a spirit may here construct for itself. Essentially, this would be achieved by giving substantial reality to an ideal of beauty, such as the shade of Helena. — **sie** = Helena, who was once remote and now is near at hand.

6557 **doppelt** Once because he had brought her forth from the shades of the Mothers; and once because, as he now intends to do, he will rescue her from Paris, who appears to be carrying her off.

Act II

The basic problem which confronted the poet at this point in the development of his play was that of bringing together in a world of reality his hero, Faust, and Helena, the archetype and symbol of classic beauty. Faust has conjured up the shade of Helena and has been so captivated by this apparition of grace that he will stake his life upon the quest for the reality this shade represents. Helena must return to life upon earth and Faust must bring this about. To accomplish this, he must go to the realm of Persephone (Proserpine) and obtain from her the permission for Helena's return from death to life.

This is an undertaking which transcends the powers of Mephistopheles. He is a stranger in the world of the spirits of classic antiquity and hence unable to lead Faust in this adventure. For this task of leadership Goethe invented Homunculus, a non-corporeal spirit in a glass bottle. This much discussed figure represents pure spirit unhampered by finite form, yet as such imperfect, since the complete *homo sapiens* must have body as well as spirit. The private problem of Homunculus is precisely how to acquire this body. To be sure, when he does so he will no longer be Homunculus, but something else, which may evolve into a man.

When Mephistopheles asks him to look at the unconscious Faust, Homunculus at once discerns Faust's crucial ambition and the way the problem must be attacked, if Faust is to live. The party of three — Homunculus, Mephistopheles, and Faust — sets out for Greece, where each is to work his way through the Classical Walpurgis Night into the classic world of ancient Hellas.

Having alighted upon the soil of Greece, Faust swiftly revives and each of the trio sets out on his own quest. The remainder of Act II therefore has three threads of action, as we observe (1) how Homunculus finally finds his destiny by plunging into the sea to begin corporeal life there, (2) how Faust is led to Manto, who promises to guide him to the throne of Persephone, as she once guided Orpheus, and (3) how Mephistopheles prepares himself for the adventure in classic Greece by acquiring an appropriately repulsive classic shape from the daughters of Phorkys.

The first two scenes constitute the transition from the German world of the Emperor's court and Faust's study to the Classical Walpurgis Night, which is itself the transition to the central action of the entire second part of FAUST, the Helena Episode.

35. HOCHGEWÖLBTES, ENGES GOTISCHES ZIMMER

After the explosive conclusion of the spirit-play at the Emperor's palace, Faust, in a condition of total insensibility, has been carried back to his old study and laid on his bed by Mephistopheles. He has been away from his starting place long enough for the new student, who interviewed Mephistopheles, believing him to be Faust (1867–2048), to become a Baccalaureus, that is, to receive his first degree. This has required certainly not less than three or four years. He is still a student, since the Bachelor's degree merely marked the half-way stage in his seven or eight years' course toward the Magister, which was a degree entitling its holder to teach others.

6567 **schwergelöstem** = *schwer zu lösendem* 'difficult to loosen.'

6572 A reference to the stained glass windows of the study (line 401).

6577 A reference to lines 1737–1740.

6582 **Pelz** The *Pelzrock* of line 1846.

6584 The *Schüler* of lines 1867–2048.

6588 **Dozent** = *Hochschullehrer* 'professor.'

6590 **'s** 'it,' the air of infallibility.

SD 6592 **Farfarellen** Used by Goethe in the sense of a small moth. The Italian *farfarello* is the name of a demon in Dante's *Inferno*, while the Italian word for the moth in question is *farfalletta*.

6593 **Patron** Mephistopheles called himself (1516–1517) 'Lord of rats and mice, of flies, frogs, bedbugs, and lice,' and is probably to be regarded as lord of all vermin.

6600–6603 Moths in a fur coat are well hidden, but the Devil in a human heart is even more difficult to find.

6605 **säe** The present subjunctive third person singular, used as an optative: 'let one sow.'

6609 Take *euch* with both verbs: *Eilt euch, ihr Liebchen, euch zu verstecken.*

6615 **Grillen** Here in the double sense of 'insects' and 'whims.' Mephistopheles immediately acts on a whim.

6617 **Prinzipal** There is something of a double meaning in this word also. First, it means 'director,' and in Goethe's day was often applied to the director of a traveling troupe of actors. Mephistopheles is about to take the leading role in a theatrical performance. The other meaning of *Prinzipal* is 'boss' or 'head man' in a business house.

SD 6619 A bit of Mephistophelian mischief, to arouse the inanimate halls of learning. These were usually far from being the luxurious structures of our own times. The buildings were rickety, unheated, and often without glass in the windows. Chairs in the lecture halls were a rarity; straw was strewn on the floors, and the students often sat on the floor. Despite the relative luxury of Faust's study, this building is a rambling, dilapidated structure with a long dark corridor.

6624 **das Estrich** *Estrich* is normally a masculine noun. The only other occurrence in Faust, at line 4891, could be either masculine or neuter.

6633 This *Famulus* has been assigned to his duties by Wagner (now Professor Wagner), and he is terrified by the tumultuous appearance of a person whom he must believe to be the great Doctor Faust, returned as mysteriously as he had disappeared (6660).

6634 **Nikodemus** The choice of the name should indicate the character of the person. The Nicodemus of the Gospel of John (3.1) was a Pharisee and a member of the Sanhedrin; he was a good man, a seeker after truth, but a literal-minded conservative.

6635 **Hochwürdiger Herr** 'Right Reverend Father.' The famulus addresses Mephistopheles as he would address a member of the clergy.

— **Oremus!** Latin, 'let us pray.' This, like the making of the sign of the cross, is a defense against evil spirits.

6637 **Student** A member of the university who has not yet attained a degree.

6638 **Bemooster Herr** A blend of the terms *bemoostes Haupt* and *alter Herr*, which are used to designate a student who has been in the university a comparatively long time. Occasionally an indolent student, or one lacking in decisiveness, remains for years at a university without standing his examinations for a degree.

6643 In the later development of the Faust story Wagner was made the famous successor of Faust. The *Wagnerbücher* appeared in a number of editions from 1593 onward, the most interesting one in 1714 in Berlin.

6644 **jetzt** Since Doctor Faust has withdrawn from the academic world.

6650 St. Peter (Matthew 16.19) was given the keys of the Kingdom of Heaven. Wagner also has the knowledge, that is, the keys to unlock the mysteries of the material and of the spiritual world.

6655 **erfand** Here in the older sense, like English 'find out,' meaning 'discovered.'

6667 **Sternenstunde** The astrological notion that the conjunction of the planets brings bliss or destruction to men. (See note to line 4949.) Nicodemus is afraid the stars are not propitiously arranged with reference to Faust's deserted study, which seems to him to have been burst open by an earthquake.

6670 **kamt** = *wäret . . . gekommen.*

6678–6682 Dr. Wagner is engaged in a laboratory experiment involving the use of a charcoal fire. He is intent upon its outcome and eagerly seeks (*lechzt*) every moment he can find to devote to it. He has, therefore, ordered his famulus not to disturb him (6673).

6686 **dort hinten** 'off yonder'; see 6711.

6687 **den Neusten** He belongs to the most recent group of graduates, at the half-way point in the curriculum.

6688 **erdreusten** 'Be brazenly audacious,' a middle-German variant of *erdreisten*. It connotes an amused tolerance of the expected bombast.

SD 6689 In the person of this Bachelor of Arts, who is the neophyte of lines 1868–2048, Goethe personifies the presumptuous egotism of youth, which believes without doubt that the world was created for its immediate personal benefit, and that the world is in dire need of its genius. See the conversation with Eckermann, December 6, 1829.

6692 **der Lebendige** We young students, who have some life in us.

6694 This life of the scholar, for which he was supposed to be fitting himself, appeared to him a living death.

6699 **verwegen wie nicht einer** 'I'll take as many chances as anyone else.' He has been attracted to the scene by the thunderous, earthquake-like upheaval which resulted when Mephistopheles rang the old bell. But he thinks he has ventured far enough into these ruins.

6707 **Bücherkrusten** Metonymy for 'books.' The 'crust' is the heavy pigskin binding characteristic of medieval books.

6721 As the Baccalaureus addresses the supposed Professor, he shifts from lively four-beat lines to five-beat iambic lines with *abba* rime, as if to speak in sonnet form. Yet he completes no more than three lines before he reverts to his former easy *Knittelvers*. — **Lethes trübe Fluten** 'the murky waters of forgetfulness'; see note to line 4629.

6724 **Ruten** The liberal use of the rod to drive home the lesson was still recognized in medieval universities as proper to the discipline of the younger pupils. The brutal application of this discipline occasionally resulted in the death of a student.

6729 **Raupe** 'larva' (caterpillar). The larva, the chrysalis (pupa), and the butterfly are the three stages in the metamorphosis of this insect. Mephistopheles, by using this metaphor, continues the theme of lines 6604–6615.

6731 **Lockenkopf** Probably the boy's own long curly locks, in which he first appeared at the university. This type of hairdress and the lace collar would mark him as a member of a well-to-do family. It is not likely that as a 'freshman' he would appear in the *Allonge*, or *Staatsperücke*, which was a powdered wig with long flowing locks. Lace collar and *Allonge* were worn by members of the court, clergy, and professional classes in the early eighteenth century.

6733 **Zopf** The wig commonly associated with pedantry and narrow-mindedness, while the *Schwedenkopf* (6734) was a close-cropped style of haircut, which succeeded the powdered wig in Europe. In Weimar, many of the young men of high position shifted from *Zopf* to *Schwedenkopf* about 1780. The style is said to have its name from the fact that the Swedes first gave it general vogue. Conventionally, the *Allonge* symbolizes dignified reserve, the *Zopf* symbolizes pedantry, and the *Schwedenkopf* revolutionary disrespect of convention.

6736 **absolut** A word with double meaning (see 6739). So too is *kommt*, which may be taken either as indicative or as imperative. If one takes *kommt* as imperative, then *absolut* means devoid of hair, and Mephistopheles is merely warning the young man not to carry his radicalism so far as to shave off all his hair. It is likely, however, that a more profound irony is intended. Mephistopheles says in effect: 'You, a person for whom everything is "absolute" and who look to be resolute and substantial, still are a vagrant. You cannot go home, either physically or in your thinking.' In philosophy the absolute is the antithesis of the relative and is characterized by having no dependence upon anything else. The philosophy of the absolute believes in knowledge a priori, that is, in knowledge independent of experience (6758). Fichte found the absolute in the *ego;* others tried to define it differently, notably Schelling and Hegel. Fichte's absolutism was popular in some circles in Jena from 1790 onward and it is probable that Goethe was poking fun particularly at Fichte's followers.

6737 **Mein alter Herr** An expression of benevolent condescension.

6738 **erneuter Zeiten** Times made new by a changing order.

6745 **gelben Schnäbeln** = *Gelbschnäbeln* Young birds before they are able to fly = callow youths.

6750 **Schelm** 'scoundrel.' The Baccalaureus is not quite willing to go all the way with Mephistopheles and refer to his teacher as a dolt and numskull. And he means 'scoundrel' only in the sense of one who trifles with the truth in the interests of comfort and piety.

6758–6761 An utterance typical of brash, keen-minded young scholars with a new set of names for familiar things. They reject all past scholarly work as useless — not worth learning about. This particular chap appears to have no patience with the empiricist point of view, which teaches that experience is the best source of knowledge.

6767–6768 These lines recall the words of Faust (604–605).

6771 The young man seeks to make a virtue, truthfulness, out of a typical German shortcoming, bluntness of speech and lack of conciliatory skill. Of Germans, Mme de Staël said (1810): "Les allemands, à quelques exceptions près, sont peu capables de réussir dans tout ce qui exige de l'adresse et de l'habileté . . . Ils ne savent pas traiter avec les hommes." Goethe said of them (1813): "Deutsche haben keinen Geschmack, weil sie keinen Euphemismus haben und zu derb sind."

SD 6772 **Rollstuhle** a chair on casters, or a wheel chair.

6774 **zur schlecht'sten Frist** 'To gain a most miserable delay in one's passing from the scene.'

6782 **die halbe Welt gewonnen** To be taken in the sense of a conquest of ideas, rather than in a military sense. The half-informed young men of the period from 1810 to 1830 were caught up in the tremendous lift of German idealistic philosophy, which culminated in the system of Hegel. These lines need not be understood to express contempt of Hegelianism, which was and is the most comprehensive and complete synthesis ever attempted by the human mind, nor yet of the great Fichte, but rather of those bumptious disciples of Fichte, Schelling, and Hegel, who with youthful energy and lack of wisdom were disturbing the academic scene at this time.

6787–6788 This idea has been entertained by young men under thirty from time immemorial. Schopenhauer at the age of thirty wrote to Goethe (July 23, 1818) expressing his approval of the less drastic notion of the French littérateur, Helvetius, that a man has had all the ideas he ever will have by the time he is thirty, or at most thirty-five.

6790 Mephistopheles said of himself (lines 1342–1344) that destruction was his proper element.

6791 A perversion of Fichte's doctrine that the universe is the manifestation of pure will, the symbol of the moral idea, which is the real *Ding-an-sich*, or the real absolute. This youngster mistakes his own will for this absolute, universal, pure will.

6794 This sentiment was several times described by Goethe. So to Eckermann, December 6, 1829: "Auch glaubt jeder in seiner Jugend, daß die Welt eigentlich erst mit ihm angefangen, und daß alles eigentlich um seinetwillen da sei." Also in an epigram (*Sprichwörtlich*, 1810–1812):

> Das junge Volk, es bildet sich ein,
> sein Tauftag sollte der Schöpfungstag sein. *(cont.)*

This attitude of our young Baccalaureus may be explained also as resulting from the misapprehension of Fichte's doctrine of the moral will. It seems that this young man has gone even farther than Mephistopheles' motto in his album (line 2048) had indicated. He has not only made himself acquainted with good and evil, he has made himself the creator.

6802 These 'narrow-minded ideas' are perhaps those of the empirical doctrine of materialism, in something like the sharp form given it by the French physician and philosopher Cabanis (1757–1808): "Intellectual and moral phenomena are, like all others, necessary consequences of the properties of matter and the laws which govern beings." Perhaps these lines refer more generally to the revolt of the romanticists against the more pragmatic among the rationalists, when young men went about shouting: "*Krieg den Philistern!*" ('Philistines' in this use means 'literal-minded people' whose interests are material and commonplace.)

6804 **innerliches Licht** = *lumen naturale:* a well-known philosophical and theological term for reason, logical thought as opposed to intuition.

6807 **Original** This seems to be the starting point of the use of the term *Original* for a person *sui generis,* 'derived from no other source and hence unique in his qualities.' — Decidedly ironical, in view of lines 6808–6810.

6811–6814 **diesem** With this young bachelor of arts. These lines are addressed to the audience, and indeed to an audience of older, experienced persons. — Mephistopheles echoes, benevolently or sardonically, the same confidence that the Lord expressed about Faust, in lines 310–311.

6813 **Most** Fruit juice in the process of fermentation. The word is a widely used metaphor for impetuous, effervescent youth. When the process of fermentation is completed, the result is a wine.

6814 **'e Wein** = *einen Wein* A dialectal form, giving these two lines something of the air of a popular proverb.

36. Laboratorium

The scene is an elaborate alchemist's workshop, where all manner of extensive physical and chemical experiments could be undertaken. The center of all operations was the oven and forge-fire where ingredients were heated. The alchemists, as philosopher-scientists, believed that they could imitate in their laboratories the processes of nature and produce there any of nature's products. They were usually most interested in producing gold and the legendary "philosopher's stone." They were also very active in their attempts to produce living organisms by chemical and physical means, and here the abiogenesis of a human being was a primary interest. — Goethe's treatment of these matters is based primarily upon the works of Theophrastus Paracelsus (1493–1541), especially the *De generationibus rerum naturalium.*

Notes

The relationship of this scene to the preceding one in time is not wholly clear.

6819   **die Glocke** Either the bell of the nearby church (see SD line 737) which tells Wagner that the hour has come when, according to his computations, his experiment should come to fruition, or (less likely) the bell of SD 6619.

6823   **Finsternisse** Either the plural form in lieu of the singular, as in line 10 758, or plural, 'dark places.' It is probably to be taken as equivalent to *das Dunkel* (6827) and to refer to the darkness within the phial.

6824   The phial is a laboratory flask. This one contains the results of a long process of chemical treatment or mechanical mixing from which Wagner hopes to produce a living organism.

6826   The quality of the carbuncle essential to this comparison is its deep, rich red color, like ruby or garnet.

6829   The implication of earlier failures is clear. This gives a foundation for Dr. Wagner's reputation for zeal and persistence.

6831   Mephistopheles' greeting is a most unusual use of the interjection *Willkommen* by the person who is arriving. The word here appears to be equivalent to the French "*Salut!*" or the South German "*Grüß Gott!*" In the following line *willkommen* is the adjective, in an elliptical utterance meaning: 'You are welcome with the star of this hour.'

6832   **Stern der Stunde** Every hour of the day is presided over by one of the seven planets. Each day gets its name from the name of the planet which rules its first hour (midnight to 1 A.M.). Thus Saturday (Saturni dies) is so called because Saturn rules its first hour. Thereafter each hour is ruled in turn by one of the seven planets: Saturn, Jupiter, Mars, Sol, Venus, Mercury, Luna. Hence Saturn would rule the 1st, 8th, 15th, and 22nd hour of Saturday. The 23rd hour would be ruled over by Jupiter, and the 24th by Mars, so that the first hour of Sunday would be ruled by Sol, the sun.

    Just what Wagner means by his reply to Mephistopheles' greeting is not clear, but we may take it that his 'Welcome' is addressed equally to Mephistopheles and to the ruling planet of the hour which has just taken over at the tolling of the bell.

6840–6844   What is here adumbrated is the process of natural reproduction of living organisms. That the analysis does not correspond step by step with the process as modern embryology understands it, is not surprising. Essentially, Wagner says that he and his kind can now dispense with natural means of reproduction, and need no longer hold in honor the hitherto indispensable procedure of zoological reproduction. — **Der zarte Punkt** may be the germ cell, **die holde Kraft** the life principle, or vital force, which was held to distinguish living organisms from inorganic compounds (see *organisieren : kristallisieren*, 6859–6860). Others understand *der zarte Punkt* to mean the ovum and *die holde Kraft* to be the sperm. — **sich selbst zu zeichnen** 'to draw, to make an image of, to reproduce itself.'

6858   **verständig zu probieren** 'To analyse and test with our intelligence.' Mephistopheles ridiculed this procedure in lines 1936–1941.

6859 **sie** = *die Natur.*

6864 No one knows exactly what Goethe meant by crystallized human
beings. The best guess appears to be that he meant human beings
who behaved like mere chemical compounds, lacking the vital
principal of organic life, — that is, *"verkalkt," "versteinert"* 'petrified
old fossils.' — Another possibility is that *kristallisiertes* means
'enclosed in a crystal, or bottle' and thus refers to a *"spiritus
familiaris"* or personal protecting and guiding spirit. The nature
of these familiar spirits is discussed at some length in Widmann's
FAUSTS LEBEN as revised by Nicolaus Pfitzer (1674).

6868–6870 **des Zufalls lachen** 'We will eliminate accident or chance
in the creation of humankind, and a thinker will then be able to
produce a brain which can think.'

6872 **also** Since the contents of the flask have developed according to
his plans and expectations, the process has now come to the point
where Wagner believes it must be on the verge of completion.

6874 **Männlein** A homunculus. We have here an interesting conflict
between Goethe's conception of his Homunculus as an incorporeal
spirit seeking a body and the necessity of describing the contents of
the flask. Strictly speaking, this *Männlein* can have no *Gestalt*, but
he has to have one if he is to be seen by Wagner.

The alchemists persistently tried to produce a living human being
by chemical and mechanical processes. Wagner's experiment has
been very much like that of Paracelsus (*De generationibus rerum
naturalium*) according to whom male sperm cells, if made to putrefy
for forty days in a sealed flask, will develop into something like a
human being alive in the bottle, but quite transparent, without a
body. This "something" is then to be treated daily with the life
element of human blood and kept at body temperature for forty
weeks, whereupon it will have developed into a replica of a human
child, only much smaller. This can then be reared to maturity like
any other infant. Wagner's Homunculus is preternaturally mature:
he speaks the day he is "born."

6879 **Väterchen** 'daddy.' Homunculus salutes Wagner as his 'parent.'
The emotional tone of the diminutive *Väterchen* is uncertain: some
take it as an affectionate greeting, others as a precocious imperti-
nence tinged with condescension.

6883 Probably a reflection of the thought of Goethe's Maxims from his
posthumous papers: *Über Natur und Wissenschaft.* "Die Natur füllt
mit ihrer grenzenlosen Produktivität alle Räume . . . Alles, was
entsteht, sucht sich Raum und will Dauer; deswegen verdrängt es
ein anderes vom Platz und verkürzt seine Dauer."

6885 Homunculus recognizes Mephistopheles as a near relative. Mephistopheles returns the compliment. Goethe explained this to Eckermann (December 16, 1829): ". . . for such spirits as Homunculus,
which have not yet been obscured and limited by becoming completely human, were counted as demons, and for this reason there is a
sort of relationship between them." Two things characterize
Homunculus: first, his imperative drive to activity (6888), and second, his quest for a "material" form.

6886 **Im rechten Augenblick** Without the help of Mephistopheles, Wagner's experiment would have failed as it often had before (6829). Mephistopheles needs the help of Homunculus in the furtherance of his efforts to revive Faust. Homunculus, to this extent the creature of Mephistopheles, recognizes his indebtedness.

6888 **dieweil** 'inasmuch as,' an older usage equivalent to *weil*. Similar to English: 'As long as I'm here . . .'

6892 **alt und jung** 'Everyone,' hence a singular verb, *bestürmt*.

6894–6896 Wagner is bedeviled by the problem of the dualism of body and soul. How can body and soul be so firmly united as to appear to be inseparable and yet manage to make each other so much trouble? — Goethe never accepted this dualism.

6899 **hierüber** The reference is either to the conflict between body and soul, which perplexes Wagner (6894–6896), or to the conflict between man and woman, which Mephistopheles suggests is a preferable object of concern. The answer to either or to both questions raised is in the nature of affinity and repulsion as these qualities are manifest in "love."

6903 **Bedeutend!** 'remarkable!' Homunculus, the incorporeal spirit, is able to see at once the content of Faust's mind, a dream of Leda and the Swan; and this appears to him to be an important clue to Faust's problem. — Jupiter in the form of a swan wooed and loved Leda, a descendant of Endymion. Offspring of this union were a son, Pollux, and a daughter, Helen of Troy. Leda's children by Tyndareus were Castor and Clytemnestra.

6907 Endymion, the ancestor of Leda, was the father of Aetolus, founder of one of the great families of the older Heroes. There is, according to the usual legend, no god in the ancestry of Leda, though apparently some stories regard Endymion as the son of Zeus.

6924 **jung geworden** = *geboren*. The allusion is to the fact that the ancients had no devils in their mythology, only gods who behaved very much like men, exerting both good and evil influence on human destiny. The myth of the Devil, as we know it, is essentially medieval. — **Nebelalter** The Middle Ages, when the Church of Rome and the feudal system clashed in Germany, and the affairs of state were chaotically confused; when human conduct was dominated by terrors and authoritarian despotism which precluded the spirit of enjoyment of earth's beauty and free inquiry into nature's mysteries.

6927 **Düstern** The northern, medieval, 'romantic' world is contrasted with the southern, ancient, 'classic' world in the terms 'obscure: clear.' — This line breaks the rime pattern, since it stands alone, having no line joined to it by rime. The poet is usually charged with an inadvertence here, and some critics have volunteered to supply the "missing" line.

6929 **schnörkelhaftest** An absolute superlative, and a Latinism, meaning 'extremely ornate.' The uninflected form is a rarity, though not without precedent in archaic German.

6930 **dieser** The sleeping or unconscious Faust.

6937–6938 Homunculus seeks for each his proper milieu. For the warrior the proper element is battle; for the maiden it is the dance. So for Faust the proper element is the Classical Walpurgis Night. Since Walpurgis Night is a gathering of northern, 'romantic' demons, a 'classical' Walpurgis Night is a contradiction in terms, but this is Goethe's name for an analogous convention of the ghosts of classic antiquity.

6942–6943 Elliptical, "telegraphic style": 'This is the best thing which could possibly happen. It will bring him to his proper environment.'

6946–6947 Just as Mephistopheles has no understanding of or patience with the classical, so Homunculus has no understanding of or patience with the romantic.

6949 **antikische** 'antique.' In the double meaning of 'interested in the ancient world' and 'aged.'

6950–6951 **Nordwestlich** 'In the northwest,' primarily Germany and England, where the romantic spirit and the Gothic style prevail, compared with *südöstlich* 'to the southeast,' primarily Sparta and Arcadia, where the classic spirit and the Greek style will be found.

6952 **Peneios** The Greek form of the name Peneus, a river in Thessaly, which flows from the slopes of Mt. Pindus through the valley of Tempe, between Mt. Olympus and Mt. Ossa, into the Aegean Sea on the northeast coast of Greece.

6955 **Pharsalus** The Latin form of the name of the Greek city Pharsalos, which, according to Goethe's sources, had two sections: Old Pharsalos and New Pharsalos. The city is on the river Apidanos in Thessaly and is particularly remembered for the great battle fought on the nearby fields between Caesar and Pompey, August 9, 48 B.C. At this point, Homunculus sounds a little like a tourist guide.

6957 Caesar, Pompey, and Crassus were all tyrants, perpetuating themselves in public office by force and fraud. Pompey became a dictator in 52 B.C. after the death of Crassus. Shortly after this he collided in civil war with his erstwhile co-tyrant, Caesar. The decisive battle between the two was fought in 48 B.C. on the Pharsalian fields. Pompey was defeated and soon afterwards murdered, when he tried to land in Egypt.

6961 **Asmodeus** A demon of strife and destruction; see note to line 5378. He is here credited with inspiring the tyrants of the world to anger and mutual destruction. From time immemorial, slaves have revolted against tyrants and fought for the rights of liberty; yet, looked at closely, neither party is really free.

6970–6971 Confronted with the problem of reviving Faust's interest in life, and thus his capacity for being caught by the Devil, Mephistopheles realizes the futility of a lot of hocus-pocus, such as he produced during the *Walpurgisnacht* on the Brocken. He knows that nothing but Helen of Troy can satisfy Faust; and he — being a northern, romantic, and medieval creature, and having no powers over the spirits of the ancient world — is embarrassed by this new demand of Faust's striving spirit. Hence he belittles the Greeks.

6977 Witches of Thessaly, very powerful in sorcery, entice men into their power and transform them into dumb beasts. Apuleius calls them *lamiae* and we shall meet them later as *Lamien* (7235, 7692–7800). The implication of their great sexual attraction is clear.

6989–6994 Homunculus advises Wagner to search through his old manuscripts, and then to collect the elements which will produce a living organism, and to put these together with care. It is not so difficult to learn what these elements are as how they go together. Perfection for the product, however, is not to be had from the manuscripts, but requires search by Homunculus. He has to find *das Tüpfchen*, the last item required to perfect the construction.

7003–7004 These lines emphasize the fact that Homunculus is a creature of Mephistopheles; but, as Eckermann said to Goethe (December 16, 1829), they have deeper implications also. To this Goethe replied: "Ich dächte, man hätte eine Weile daran zu zehren. Ein Vater, der sechs Söhne hat, ist verloren, er mag sich stellen wie er will. Auch Könige und Minister, die viele Personen zu großen Stellen gebracht haben, mögen aus ihrer Erfahrung sich etwas dabei denken können." No creative act is without its effect upon the person responsible for it. Very often such a creator becomes dependent upon his creatures, whether these are his own flesh and blood or whether they are political or administrative subordinates.

KLASSISCHE WALPURGISNACHT

The function of the Classical Walpurgis Night in the dramatic economy of the play is threefold: the restoration of Faust to active life by the implementation of his quest for Helena, the furnishing of an outward form to Mephistopheles, in which he may with propriety appear on the classic scene in Greece, and the final disposal of Homunculus, who has served his dramatic purpose when he deposits the two northerners on the fields of Pharsalus, where they enter the world of classic mythology.

It must be observed, however, that there is a difference between the dramatic purpose of Homunculus and his poetic raison d'être. Goethe did not have to invent Homunculus in order to get Faust to Greece. He invented Homunculus in order to give poetic expression to an idea. Concerning the nature of this idea, "higher criticism" of FAUST has entertained a number of different notions. A simple interpretation is that Homunculus represents the idea that both body and spirit are essential to human life, and that the "Tüpfchen auf das *i*" which makes the union of body and spirit perfect is Love. Another interpretation sees in Homunculus the symbolization of the poet's idea of the origin of life on earth. Homunculus is said to begin life as an animalcule (class: *Infusoria*). He is then said to be related to Helena as one end of the history of evolution is related to the other, for in Helena this higher criticism sees the ultimate product of nature's self-perfection: the beautiful human being, *der schöne Mensch*. What this beautiful human being symbolizes is still another problem for the critics. — Quite apart from any simple symbolism, the presence of Homunculus in addition to Faust and Mephistopheles makes possible a significant enrichment of the points of view from which the reader contemplates the Classical Walpurgis Night. Beside the unfolding of potentialities of personality in Faust and the compulsive self-degradation of Mephistopheles' form and motives, the reader can share with Homunculus the maturing of curiosity to clarity, and an irrevocable decision.

The fiction upon which the Classical Walpurgis Night rests is this: each year on the eve of the anniversary of the great battle of Pharsalus (August 9, 48 B.C.) the ghosts of the participants return to the scene of their great adventure. In this battle Caesar defeated Pompeius Magnus and thereby laid the foundation of a unified Roman Empire which was to dominate most of the then known world. However, this second act of FAUST is not concerned with these characters from ancient history; neither Caesar, nor Pompey, nor any of their armies appears here. Goethe used this fiction only to provide the ghostly milieu in which he presents a great variety of figures from ancient mythological lore, together with the spirits of two Greek philosophers, whose debate concerning the aquatic or the volcanic origin of the earth's crust provides a variation of one significant theme of this act: the origin, evolution, and maintenance of organic life in the physical universe.

The events of this act take place in Thessaly, a region noted in ancient lore for the magic practices of witches and spirits. The scene of action shifts several times up and down the course of the river Peneios. The upper regions are rocky and barren; the lower reaches of the river valley are rather fertile than lush. Goethe did not go to the trouble of adjusting his conceptions of these regions to the facts of geography.

37. Pharsalische Felder

This preliminary scene introduces the three travelers — Homunculus, Mephistopheles, and Faust — to the terrain where each is to prosecute his own search alone.

SD 7005 **Erichtho** A Thessalian enchantress and prophetess. At the request of Pompey's son, she summoned up the shade of a soldier to foretell the outcome of the impending battle (Lucan, Pharsalia 6, 413 ff.). According to Ovid and Lucan, she was an extremely hideous and repulsive creature.

7005 **dieser Nacht** The anniversary of the night before the great battle between Caesar and Pompey, August 9, 48 B.C. Erichtho calls this a *Schauderfest*, 'a weird festival' because it commemorates the never-ceasing conflict of tyrants and the resulting destruction of liberty and glorification of violence.

The following lines are in the metrical pattern most often found in the dialogue of classic Greek drama, the so-called iambic trimeter. This is a six-beat iambic line which Goethe uses here and elsewhere because of its associations with antiquity. The Greek verse was subdivided into three dipodies (units of two beats each). In general, the German trimeter shows no such dipodies, but is simply a six-beat iambic line which differs from the Alexandrine principally in the location of the caesura. In the trimeter, the caesura is either after the fifth (as in 7007) or after the seventh syllable (as in 7010), whereas in the Alexandrine the caesura is regularly after the sixth syllable (as in 10 849 ff.). For further analysis of this meter see Volume I, Introduction, p. 140.

Goethe's criticism of the trimeter (to Eckermann, October 21, 1823) as the verse of tragedy deserves to be quoted: "Der sechsfüßige Iambus wäre freilich am würdigsten, allein er ist für uns Deutsche zu lang; wir sind wegen der mangelnden Beiwörter gewöhnlich schon mit fünf Füßen fertig." Hence it is not surprising that the poet here soon turns to other verse forms in this part of FAUST. Indeed, the Classical Walpurgis Night is replete with examples of Goethe's great skill in the use of metrical forms.

7006   **tret'** . . . **einher** 'come,' with the added notion of dignified and stately bearing.

7007   The allusion is to Ovid's HEROIDES (15, 139) and Lucan's PHARSALIA (4, 507), where Erichtho is described as 'fury-like' and 'repulsive.'

7010   The tents of the two armies appear to fill the fields (see 7033). — Something like 70,000 men fought in the battle of Pharsalus. According to the fiction of this scene, their shades appear on this field every year on the night of the eighth to the ninth of August.

7014   The violent usurper of power is acceptable to no one. There may be an allusion here to Caius Julius Caesar, who, on March 15, 44 B.C., was murdered by a group of republican aristocrats. Goethe said of this: "Wie wenig selbst die besseren (Römer) begriffen, was Regieren heißt, sieht man an der abgeschmacktesten Tat, die jemals begangen worden, — an der Ermordung Cäsars."

7018–7020   The civil war between Pompey and Caesar was a fight between a dictator and a general who was being deprived of his powers by this dictator. The senate and the aristocracy supported Pompey, Caesar was supported by the advocates of democratic rule. Upon his return to Rome after defeating Pompey at Pharsalus (48 B.C.), Caesar was made dictator for one year, but subsequent events prolonged his dictatorship until his assassination in 44 B.C. Not much liberty was destroyed by these wars, for not much liberty existed before they began.

7022   **Magnus** Pompey. Lucan reports that here, on the eve of his last great battle, Pompey dreamed of his youthful triumphs in Rome.

7023   **Zünglein** The pointer of a balance, which moves back and forth past the point of equilibrium. Great issues are thought of as being decided by weighing the two causes in a balance.

7031–7033 The moon is a gibbous moon, as was the moon at the beginning of the Walpurgis Night of Part I (lines 3851–3853). As it rises, the illusion of the tents upon the fields disappears and the color of the fires changes from red to blue. Blue light is associated in popular lore with the presence of ghosts. Erichtho, a ghost surrounded by ghosts, sees the fires turn blue upon the approach of Faust, the living man. — According to Goethe's FARBENLEHRE, a fire appears red against a dark background, but blue against a bright background.

7034 Meteor Homunculus, luminous in his bottle. The 'corporeal ball' is Mephistopheles and Faust, wrapped in the magic cloak (6983–6986).

7036 Erichtho does not wish to increase her evil repute among men. Yet if she met any living beings she would involuntarily do them harm. Therefore she decides, after due consideration, to avoid such a meeting.

7040 Schwebe The subject *ich* is omitted, as frequently happens in this part of the poem.

7041 Flamm' = *Flammen*. This is usually printed *Flamm-*, implying a compound such as *Flammengrauen* or *Flammgrauen*. We translate the line: 'over the flames and the terrifying horrors.'

7044 das alte Fenster The window of his own abode at home. Mephistopheles says he sees quite hideous ghosts, just as he would at home, if he looked out into the wild goings-on of the North. Supernatural beings — gods, angels, devils — are thought of as having a house and looking out of its windows at the events on earth.

7048 eine Lange Erichtho, who is leaving the scene before the visitors arrive.

7051 sah The subject is *sie, die Lange*.

7056 Faust revives immediately when he touches the soil of Greece. He inquires at once where Helena is.

7057 Supply '*ist es*' from the '*s* of line 7056.

7062 an meinem Teil An unusual use of this phrase, which normally means *meinerseits, was mich betrifft* 'for my part,' but which here seems to mean 'on my behalf, in my own interests.' — Mephistopheles is asserting an independent interest in this journey, which is explained by lines 6979–6983.

SD 7069 Ab This stage direction is not in the manuscripts. It is probably best to assume that Goethe intended both Homunculus and Mephistopheles to leave — probably in different directions — at this point, since Faust is at once described as "*allein.*" Yet Mephistopheles may merely have retired to the depths of the scene without completely leaving the stage. At line 7080 Mephistopheles comes forward *umherspürend*, and at line 7181 Faust comes back *herantretend*. The latter has been searching through the area (*durchforsch' ich ernst*, 7079), while the former has been roaming (*durchschweife*, 7080). — The uncertainty occasioned by the inadequate stage directions here and at 7495 has led some editors to insert a new scene heading "*Am obern Peneios*" after Faust leaves the stage at 7079.

7070 The verse form here is a five-beat iambic line, with masculine or feminine cadence. Its scheme may be marked: x´/x´/x´/x´/x´ :x. Lines 7070–7075 have masculine cadence, lines 7076–7079 have feminine cadence. See Volume I, Introduction, pp. 139–140.

7071 Helena was not born in Thessaly, but, at any rate, Thessaly is in Greece.

7072 **Welle** The river Peneios.

7077 **Antäus** The giant whom Hercules slew. He was the son of Poseidon and Gaea (Neptune and Mother Earth). Antaeus was a wrestler, whose strength was invincible so long as he remained in contact with his mother, Earth. Hercules finally had to lift him off his feet and strangle him in mid-air.

7078 **find' ich** = *indem ich finde*. 'Since I find here the strangest things, I will investigate . . .'

7081 **entfremdet** Mephistopheles feels that he is in a land quite foreign to his nature and experience. — The following lines are a satire directed against prudishness in the display of art. The Devil is of the same mind as the museum trustees of Goethe's day, who used anything from a fig leaf to tin coats to conceal the nakedness of which Mephistopheles complains. Mephistopheles can use the lewd and the lascivious in his business, but the nudity of these ancient figures is frank and devoid of prurience.

7083 **Sphinxe . . . Greife** Fabulous animal monsters. The Sphinx of Thebes, whom these creatures appear to resemble, had the upper body of a woman and the lower body of a lion. She proposed a riddle to the Thebans and killed all who could not guess it. When Oedipus solved her riddle, the Sphinx killed herself. — Griffons, also, were composite monsters: part eagle, part lion, part wolf. Their special function was the guarding of treasures.

7087 **das Antike** The antique, classic style.

7094–7098 The griffons take the position of those etymologists who believed in the onomatopoetic theory of the origin of words, according to which each word originally imitated by its sounds the sounds made by the thing which it designated. Mephistopheles explodes the theory in line 7099. Of course, the words of line 7096 are derivatives, each with a long history behind it. Their present forms do not reveal their primary meanings, to say nothing of their origins. None of them has anything to do with the noun *Greif*.

7097 'Having by their etymologies the same feeling-tone.'

7103 **Greifenden** By another bad etymology, the griffons associate their own name with the verb *greifen*.

SD 7104 Ancient sources (Herodotus and Pliny) mention gigantic ants, like marmots or foxes in size, which bring forth from the earth particles of gold which they collect and store in caverns. The griffons were the traditional guardians of such treasure.

7106 The Arimasps were a race of one-eyed monsters, who lived in northern Scythia and carried on a feud with the griffons, from whom they stole (or attempted to steal) the treasures which the griffons guarded. This time, according to the report of the ants, the Arimasps have been successful.

7109   The Arimasps confront the griffons and the ants boldly, since this is a night of truce, when no warfare is allowed; and by the time the truce is ended, they expect to have squandered the stolen treasure.

7114–7115   The Sphinx is explaining to Mephistopheles how it is that he thinks he understands these spirits so completely. Mephistopheles himself is furnishing the material to give substance to their spirit-sounds.

7116   **bis**   'Until such time as we know you better, we should like to know your name, at least.'

7118   The British have been the world's most avid sight-seers, and other Europeans have on occasion sneered at their devotion to this form of amusement.

7122   **Bühnenspiel**   The reference is perhaps to Ben Jonson's play, THE DEVIL IS AN ASS, where Vice calls itself *Vetus Iniquitas*, or 'Old Iniquity.' It should be said, however, that in none of the old English morality plays is the Devil identified with this figure of vice. The two figures frequently appear in the same play but they have distinct identities.

7127   **beschnittner Mond**   The waning moon. Mephistopheles looks up, observes the shooting stars and the waning moon, neither of which phenomena interests him at all.

7129   **Löwenfelle**   See note to line 7083.

7130   Mephistopheles would be wasting his time if he concerned himself with the business of guessing what the stars might be saying, when he had such an expert author of riddles at hand (see note to line 7083). He much prefers the riddles she will propose.

7131   A charade is a syllable riddle: a riddle in which the word is to be guessed from clues, written or acted out, for each of its syllables and then for the whole word. An interesting collection of modern charades was published in 1929 by Dean L. B. R. Briggs, with the title: THE SPHINX GARRULOUS. This specimen was printed on the jacket of that book:

> To smell my first is thought delicious;
> to smell my second is thought suspicious;
> reft of his home and place to swim in,
> my whole enfolds luxurious women.

(The answer is: "muskrat.") — Mephistopheles himself proposed a simple riddle, not a charade, at 4743–4750.

7132   The Devil is an enigmatic creature, "ein Teil von jener Kraft, die stets das Böse will und stets das Gute schafft" (1335–1336).

7134–7137   The answer to this riddle is: "the spirit of evil." (Compare lines 338–343 and 1338–1384.)

7135–7136   *Dem frommen Mann ein Plastron, dem bösen Mann ein Kumpan.*

7138   **Den**   Mephistopheles.

7140   The griffons have been annoyed by the presence of the intruder Mephistopheles and have snarled at him. His own claws, he says, are as dangerous as those of the griffons.

7144   With *tust* supply *du*, as the subject.

Notes

SD 7152   By their sweet singing the sirens lured seafarers to their death. They are represented as part woman, part bird of prey. They balance themselves in the branches of the poplar trees which stand on the banks of the river. — **präludieren** may refer either to preliminary vocal exercises or to preliminary tootlings on flutes, before their song begins. The inference that the sirens have flutes rests on SD 8034 and is not a necessary one, since *flötend* can describe vocal warblings as well as instrumental notes.

7153   We have printed here an emendation of the usual text (*Des Pappelstromes*). This is Goethe's own manuscript change (H. C41) to *der Stromespappeln* 'the poplars of the river.'

7155   The Sphinx warns Mephistopheles that the very best of heroes have been conquered by these sirens. The best stories, however, are those which tell how great men escaped the lures of these singers. Ulysses, for example, at the prompting of Circe, stopped the ears of his crew with wax so that they could not hear the sirens, and then had himself bound firmly to the mast of his vessel, lest he cast himself into the sea when the sirens sang. Indeed, when his ship passed near these sweet singers, Ulysses was so ravished by the song that he struggled and begged to be released, but his crew bound him the tighter and thus all escaped the enchantresses.

7156   The sirens sing to the newcomer, Mephistopheles, hoping to entice him away from the Sphinx, whom they describe as an ugly supernatural being.

7166–7171   The sirens appear to propose a truce between themselves and the Sphinxes in order properly to entertain their 'welcome guest.'

7174–7177   The reference is probably to ornate, coloratura singing and the romantic or baroque ornamentation of the melodic line.

7182   Faust finds satisfaction in the grand and vigorous forms he sees even in these hideous ancient creatures.

7184   **Blick** = *Anblick*, 'spectacle.'

7185   Oedipus solved the riddle of the Sphinx of Thebes, who thereupon cast herself down from her rocky perch and was killed; see note to line 7083.

7186   Ulysses had himself bound to the mast of his ship, yet struggled to free himself; see note to line 7155.

7187–7188   Ants were the traditional collectors and griffons the traditional defenders of treasure; see note to SD 7104.

7191   Faust's intensity of purpose in his quest for Helena makes him tolerant of repulsive ugliness such as he once shunned and cursed (*Hexenküche*, 2337–2340, 2387).

7197   **reichen . . . hinauf**   'We don't come down that far in time, since Hercules killed the very last of our race long before her (Helena's) days.' This feature appears to have been invented by Goethe. Hercules slew many kinds of terrible creatures, but we know no ancient account of his having killed a sphinx.

7198   **letztesten**   A double superlative, since *letzte* is superlative like English 'last'; hence 'the very last ones.'

7199   Chiron, a centaur, instructed by Apollo and Diana in hunting, medicine, music, and the art of prophecy. The centaurs had the body of a horse, with a human head and upper torso, where the horse's head should be. Chiron was the tutor of the youthful Achilles, and a contemporary of Helen of Troy. Goethe once referred to him as an "Urhofmeister," a 'tutor par excellence.'

7201 **wenn er dir steht** 'if he stops and answers you.'

7202 **'s = es** To persuade Chiron to pause. 'You should not fail to achieve this.' Or, perhaps, 'You shouldn't miss (a visit with us).'

7203–7208 The sirens are lying. Ulysses never stopped to visit with them and they have no information about Helena to confide.

7210 Extreme ellipsis for *Statt daß du dich binden ließest, wie sich Ulyß (mit hänfnen Banden) binden ließ.*

7219 **Alcides** Another name for Hercules, one of whose "Labors" was the destruction of the monstrous birds of the valley of Stymphalus. These creatures had iron beaks and talons; they killed and devoured many of the inhabitants of the land.

7224 **Stammverwandte** These creatures of ancient mythologic lore were all composites of two or more kinds of animals. The stymphalids, even with vultures' beaks and goose feet, hardly qualify as sufficiently grotesque composites, since both vultures and geese are birds.

7225 The predominance of sibilants in this line is a playful suggestion of the hissing hydra heads.

7227 The Lernaean Hydra was a water serpent which ravaged the country of Argos. It had nine heads, the middle one being immortal. Hercules knocked off the heads with his club, but in the place of each one thus disposed of two new heads appeared. Finally, he burned away all the heads but the middle one, which he buried under a rock.

7235 **Lamien** The Lamiae were ghosts with an appetite for human flesh and blood. To satisfy this taste they assumed various shapes in order to entice their victims into their embrace. — **lustfeine Dirnen** = *feine Lustdirnen* with *fein* in the sense of *raffiniert*, 'very crafty, accomplished prostitutes.'

7237 **Satyrvolk** See note to line 5829.

7238 **Bocksfuß** This is the trope pars pro toto for Satyr. Mephistopheles has no *Bocksfuß*, but his *Pferdefuß* is an acceptable substitute. The Sphinx means to say: 'Why don't you try?'

7242 **in tausend Jahre** 'for thousands of years.'

7243–7244 'If you pay close attention to our situation you will see that we define the months and the years.' In ancient times the summer solstice occurred when the sun was between Leo and Virgo, the fifth and the sixth signs (constellations) of the zodiac. The Sphinx of Gizeh, near Cairo, is said to have been built with careful reference to astronomical calculations. Our Sphinxes are from Egypt, and have the upper body of a woman (virgo) and the lower body of a lion (leo); see note to 7083.

7246 **zu der Völker Hochgericht** is parallel to *vor den Pyramiden.* It may be translated: 'Watching the high doom of nations.' The Sphinxes look on impassively as the decrees of the gods are carried out. They see the floods of the Nile, war and peace, without showing any emotion.

38. [AM UNTERN PENEIOS]

The stage direction of the chief manuscript at this place does not indicate a change of scene. It simply gives the persons *Peneus und Nymphen*. The scene heading "Am untern Peneios" was introduced by Erich Schmidt and most editors retain it.

In the course of this scene Faust is transported by Chiron to the lower reaches of the river, in the Vale of Tempe, north of Mt. Ossa and near the northwestern bay of the Aegean Sea. The river itself is a speaking person in this scene; indeed, it speaks first.

SD 7249 **Gewässern** River gods, allegorical figures, like Peneios himself, and representing presumably the tributaries of Peneios. The song of the Nymphs (7263–7270) reminds one of Goethe's ballads, *Der Fischer* (1778?) and *Erlkönig* (1782).

7253 Peneios has been awakened from his sleep; he invokes his reeds and the leafy branches nearby to lull him to sleep again, so that he may return to his dreams that have been interrupted. What has aroused him is an earth tremor (*Zittern*), a forerunner of an earthquake, and the atmospheric disturbance that accompanies the tremor (*Wittern*).

7271–7276 Faust observes to himself that he is no longer dreaming. He sees now with waking eyes the scene of which he had dreamed, while lying on the couch of his study (6903–6920).

7273 **mein Auge schickt** A curiously recondite, but correct way of saying 'my eye sees'! The image is on the retina, and the perception of space relationships between the eye and the object seen is a part of the interpretation of the sensory stimulation of the retina.

7294 Queen of the nymphs is Leda (see note to line 6903), mother of Helen of Troy. The event described is the same as that seen by Faust in his dream (6903–6920).

7301 This is Jupiter in the form of a swan.

7305 **Welle . . . wellend** 'Himself a wave tossing upon waves.'

7311 Their proper office was to attend their queen at all times lest any act of indecorum or indiscretion occur.

7316 The horse's hoofs belong to the centaur Chiron; see note to line 7199.

7317–7318 The meaning of these lines is not clear. One guess is that the nymphs know that these horse's hoofs belong to Chiron and expect to be disturbed by him. They wish they knew who had so promptly brought him news of this special night of their revelry. Another interpretation takes *dieser Nacht* as an adverbial genitive of time and *zugebracht* as the equivalent of *zubringt:* 'Would that I knew who on this night is swiftly bringing news (to us)!'

7322 The Sphinxes have told Faust (7199 and 7212) that Chiron could help him find Helena. The problem is to find Chiron, and to persuade him to pause in his restless galloping about through the night. Now it seems that a friendly fate is bringing Faust his chance to do just this.

7329   Philyra, according to Goethe's source, was the mother of Chiron. His father was Saturn. For most of this lore Goethe consulted Hederich, Gründliches Mythologisches Lexikon.

7333   The problem of staging the ensuing ride of Faust on Chiron's back is a difficult one. Goethe gave no indication of a change of scene, but it is clear that between 7333 and 7469 they have crossed the river from the pool of Leda and the Swan to the temple of the sleeping Manto, before which the two emerge from the river to interview the prophetess.

7337   **Pädagog** Chiron was the teacher of Hercules, Aesculapius, Jason, and Achilles, as well as of many other Grecian princes in their boyhood. He was noted for his wide range of information in matters of science and history.

7338–7340   'This heroic people, the Argonauts, and all the other figures who built the world of mythology, which poets later took as their own.' — The Argonauts were a group of fifty heroes organized and led by Jason in his quest of the Golden Fleece. Castor, Pollux, Orpheus, Hercules, Theseus, and Nestor were prominent among these bold youngsters.

7342   Pallas-Athena (Minerva) and Telemachus, son of Ulysses, went to the isle of Calypso, to try to free Ulysses from the wiles of this enchantress. The goddess assumed for this journey the shape of Mentor, son of Anchialos. Mentor was the teacher to whom Ulysses had entrusted the education of Telemachus, when he had set out for the war before the walls of Troy. The expedition reached the isle of Calypso, but there young Telemachus was also caught in the alluring wiles of this charmer. Finally, when no other means of escape is discoverable, Pallas-Mentor and Telemachus leap from a cliff into the sea and swim to a nearby boat in which they manage to get away. They are foiled, however, in their attempt to rescue Ulysses, and the instructions of Pallas-Mentor were of no avail.

7343   **sie** The young people, whom one has tried to direct and educate, behave all too often as though they had had no teacher.

7345   Chiron had been instructed by Apollo in the art of healing. He was in turn the teacher of Aesculapius, son of Apollo and the Thessalian princess Coronis. Aesculapius became the most renowned physician of antiquity.

7369   **Dioskuren** Castor and Pollux, half-brothers, sons of Leda. Castor was the son of Tyndareus, King of Sparta; Pollux was the son of Jupiter, and a full brother of Helen of Troy.

7372   **Boreaden** Zetes and Calais, sons of Boreas (the North Wind) and the nymph Orithyia. They were winged warriors who proved particularly effective in the fight of the Argonauts against the Harpies.

7374   **Jason** Son of Aeson, of whose throne he was unjustly deprived. He was incited by the usurper of this throne to set out in quest of the Golden Fleece, it being supposed that he would perish in this expedition. He organized the Argonauts and set out, to return finally with his mission accomplished. — **Frauen angenehm** Perhaps an allusion to Jason's adventures with Medea and Creüsa.

7375   **Orpheus** The sweet singer, son of Apollo and the muse Calliope. His crucial contribution to the success of the Argonautic expedition was his outsinging the sirens, so that the ship was brought safely past their shores.

7377 **Lynkeus** The lynx-eyed pilot of the ship Argos, who could see through earth, sea, and sky. Goethe uses this name for the Tower Watchman of Act III (9218 ff.) and again in Act V (11 143 ff.).

7381 Hercules, son of Jupiter and Alcmene, and the greatest of the older heroes. When Juno drove him to insanity, he slew his own children. To expiate this bloodshed he was made subject to the will of his cousin Eurystheus, who imposed upon him a series of desperate undertakings, the Labors of Hercules. Chiron thinks of Hercules as the perfect man.

7383 **Phöbus** Apollo, God of the sun.

7384 **Ares** Mars, God of war. — **Hermes** Mercury, Herald of Jupiter.

7389 **Bruder** Eurystheus was a cousin, not a brother, of Hercules.

7390 **den . . . Fraun** The plural is puzzling, since the servitude alluded to is usually thought to be the three years Hercules spent as the slave of Queen Omphale.

7391 **Gäa** Mother Earth.

7392 **Hebe** Daughter of Juno and wife of the immortal Hercules, after the mortal part of him had been consumed in his funeral pyre and the immortal element raised to Heaven by Jupiter.

7394 **sie** Sculptors who try to create images of Hercules. Neither poets nor sculptors can do justice to this subject.

7396 **so herrlich** No artist has ever depicted Hercules so splendidly as you (Chiron) have just done.

7403–7404 **Die Schöne** = *die Schönheit.* Beauty is its own excuse for being: that is, beauty is highly delightful (*selig*) to itself, since beauty presupposes the free satisfaction of the requirements of its subject — *Freiheit in der Erscheinung* (Schiller). Grace, on the other hand — *Schönheit in der Bewegung,* as Schiller defined it — has an irresistible charm which attracts all sensitive observers and leads beyond mere contemplation to active devotion. "Beauty" and "Grace" were frequently discussed by Goethe and Schiller, as their letters show. — Chiron has no patience with mere beauty, as he has no patience with quiet contemplation in any form (7332, 7479–7480).

7406 This story of Helena's ride on Chiron's back is an invention by Goethe.

7411 **verlier' ich mich** 'I am beside myself.'

7414 **gewähren** is appropriate rather to the request of 7411 than to the question of 7413. The sentence is a condensed reply to Faust's request and question. A full form would be: *Die Bitte läßt sich leicht gewähren, und die Frage läßt sich leicht beantworten.* Chiron's narration will answer Faust's question.

7415–7420 **Dioskuren** Castor and Pollux (see note to line 7369), who rescued their sister Helena from Theseus. Theseus had carried Helena off to Attica and held her captive in the castle of Aphidnus (see lines 8848–8852). She was a mere child (see note to line 6530) when this abduction occurred. The story of the pursuit (7417–7424) is Goethe's invention.

7417 diese Theseus and his band.

7420 Eleusis Site of the mysteries of Ceres. Next to Athens it was the
most important town of Attica, on the shore of the bay of Eleusis,
opposite and north of the island of Salamis.

7426 Philologists, who concern themselves with the literature and the
language of a people, or an age, have taught Faust something they
have inferred from the poets: namely, that Helena was but ten years
old at this time. Chiron, who knows the agelessness of mythological
ladies, finds fault with the attempt to say at all how old Helena was
on this or any other occasion. The philologists by so doing have
brought ridiculous anomalies into their interpretations, such as the
notion that a fifty-year-old Theseus should abduct a ten-year-old
child — or was she only seven years old, as some mythologists had
suggested? All of this, says Chiron, is nonsense, but it is to be expected, if one pedantically tries to reduce mythological narratives
to logical chronology. Pierre Bayle (1647–1706) calculated (on the
assumption that all of the legends about Helen of Troy were true)
that she must have been at least sixty, and probably even more than
a hundred years old at the time she was abducted by Paris.

7435 According to Hederich (see Volume I, p. 325), Helena, after her
death, was said to have married Achilles, who had long since been
slain by Paris at Troy, but who was dwelling posthumously on the
island of Leuce. For Leuce Goethe substituted Pherae, which he
seems to have thought to be an island or a castle (*auf*), but which
was a town in Thessaly, near the home of Achilles. One of the gate-
ways to Hades was believed to be near Pherae. — The son of the
union of Helena and Achilles was called Euphorion.

7437 gegen das Geschick Fate had prevented the marriage of Achilles
and Helena in their lifetime. Achilles, along with numerous other
illustrious heroes, had been a suitor of Helena before her marriage
to Menelaus. — The simplest way to deal with the construction of
this line is to supply the subject *er* = Achilles, and the auxiliary *hat*.
Hence: *Errungen hat er Liebe* . . .

7438 sehnsüchtigster Gewalt Appears to mean *durch die Gewalt der
allergrößten Sehnsucht*. The phrase is then an adverbial genitive
construction, conveying the source or means by which the action is
to take place, but it is also explanatory of the expectation in *sollt'*
and hence is set off from the verb by commas.

7442 heut Faust saw the phantom of Helena at the Emperor's court
(6479–6563). He is unaware of the passage of time since the explosion (6563), but believes it to have been but a brief sleep from which
he has just awakened (7056). There is no evidence in the text to
show that he is not right in this belief.

7447 verrückt Chiron, from the standpoint of a mythological figure,
regards Faust's ambition as nonsense. His desire to call to life this
ancient heroic queen appears to Chiron impossible of fulfillment,
unreasonable, and hence requiring correction (7458, 7487).

7451 Aesculapius, son of Apollo, pupil of Chiron, and the world's most
famous physician. That Manto, otherwise known (Hederich) as a
Greek soothsayer, was a daughter of Aesculapius is an invention of
Goethe. Here (7453–7454), as at lines 7351–7352, Goethe casts

rather bitter aspersions upon the practitioners of medicine in his own time. Compare also lines 1050–1055, 2011–2036.

7455 **Sibyllengilde** Soothsayers. The great Sibyl of Cumae, who prophesied encouragingly to Aeneas (AENEID 6, 95), has given her name to the whole class of prophetesses.

7459–7460 **mein Sinn ist mächtig** 'my senses rule me,' 'I am *compos mentis*, not out of my senses.' Faust regards any attempt to annul his striving — now directed toward the winning of Helena — as base. If he were to submit to the proposed "cure," he would be like other men and no longer Faust.

7461 **Quelle** Manto is referred to as a source of healing.

7465–7468 **trotzten** 'met in battle,' 'bade each other defiance.' The allusion is to the battle of Pydna (168 B.C.) between Perseus, King of Macedonia, and the Romans under Aemilius Paulus, in the latter years of the ascendency of the Roman Republic and before the decay of republicanism set in. The defeat at Pydna marks the overthrow of the Greek world by the growing Roman state. The Greek, Chiron, mourns the fall of the Greek king and deplores the triumph of the Romans, who (to him) represent the common man, the *Bürger*. — Actually, Pydna is some thirty miles north of the mouth of the river Peneios, and also north of Mt. Olympus.

7467 **das größte Reich ... verliert** The Kingdom of Macedonia, which under Alexander the Great (366–323 B.C.) extended as far as India and the Egyptian desert. It came to an end at Pydna (168 B.C.) and was dissolved into four independent republics under the protection of Rome. — Line 7467 is not syntactically connected with anything in this sentence.

7470 The temple of Apollo, presided over by Manto. Though we have no stage direction to that effect, we must assume the temple to be visible at line 7470 on the high shore, and then that the action is within the temple at line 7471.

7477 The implication is that his coming is as certain as the existence of Manto's temple.

7482 **verrufene** Chiron, the rational, sensible tutor of great heroes, is repelled by this irrational hocus-pocus of the Walpurgisnacht.

7487 'He is worthy more than others of healing by the arts of Aesculapius.'

7488 Manto recognizes Faust's desire to be impossible of fulfillment, but she is pleased by it and promises him (7489) pleasures from it. In "Kunst und Altertum" Goethe once said: "In der Idee leben heißt das Unmögliche behandeln, als wenn es möglich wäre."

7490 Persephone, or Proserpine, was the daughter of Ceres and Jupiter. She became Queen of Hades, and wife of Pluto. She has the dual role of goddess of spring and goddess of death. — Goethe once wrote a monodrama "Proserpina," which he then used as the main part of the fourth act of his play, TRIUMPH DER EMPFINDSAMKEIT (1777). The figure interested him and he once contemplated writing a scene for FAUST in which Manto should plead Faust's cause before the throne of the Queen of Hades.

7491 The living could communicate with the ghosts of Hades only through certain oracles of the dead, located in cavernous holes or great chasms, dangerous marshes, and the like. Here Proserpine herself is alleged to be hidden in a cave at the foot of Mt. Olympus for the purpose of such interviews. These places came to be regarded as entrances to the nether world.

7493 Orpheus, the most famous of sweet singers, son of Apollo and the muse Calliope, lost his bride Eurydice by snakebite. He descended with his lyre to the throne of Pluto and Proserpine and by his song moved them to restore Eurydice to him. They agreed to permit her to return to life on condition that he should not look at her until they should have reached the upper air. When they were almost free, the condition was violated: Orpheus looked upon her and she had to return to Hades. — Manto takes credit here for arranging Orpheus' admittance to the lower regions.

39. Am obern Peneios

Faust and Chiron have arrived at the temple of Manto, which is near the mouth of the river. The sirens who now speak, however, are still where we left them on the Pharsalian fields. The problem of stage management for the scene between Faust and Chiron was not solved by Goethe in the manuscript directions he gave. In one of the manuscripts of Scene 39, however, Goethe wrote in his own hand: "(wie zuvor)" where we have printed it, after the name of the speaker, *Sirenen*. Other editors have attached these two words to the scene heading, and read: *Am obern Peneios wie zuvor;* they then insert a scene heading before line 7080.

7498 **dem Volk** It is not at all clear for whose benefit these sirens are singing — presumably, however, for any non-sirens present. This might comprise the sphinxes, griffons, ants, pygmies, dactyls, and cranes who next appear, but particularly the sphinxes (see 7161–7171), or it may refer to Seismos and his party of Vulcanists.

7500 **Führen** The past subjunctive of *fahren*, 'if we should go.' — **mit hellem Heere** Analogous to *zu hellen Haufen* (10 737) 'with a goodly, numerous group.'

7501 The river Peneios flows into a bay of the Aegean Sea on the northeast coast of Greece near the Macedonian border.

7509 **Gäste** It is not clear to whom this is addressed. Possibly these guests are the theater audience, who are thus invited to go with the sirens to a gay party in the sea.

7510 'The merry festival in the sea.'

7511 **blinkend** Belongs logically with *Zitterwellen*, and is thus a part of the adverbial clause after *wo*. Hence there is no comma before *wo*, as the rules might seem to require. This is a stylistic trick, found in Latin and Greek authors, called prolepsis, or more generally, hyperbaton.

7513 Where the moon's light is reflected from the sea's surface.

Notes

SD 7519 Seismos is the personification of the earthquake and appears here as a primeval giant pushing his way up from the interior of the earth to its surface.

7530 As Seismos pushes his way upward, a large mound rises on the earth's surface. The Sphinxes call this mound a 'dome.'

7533 Seismos is here credited with raising the island of Delos (one of the smaller Cyclades) from the Aegean Sea. Usually this island is said to have been a floating, unstable island until Jupiter anchored it to the bottom of the sea in order that Latona might there give birth to their twin children, Diana and Apollo.

7538 Atlas stood in the far west, bearing upon his shoulders the vault of heaven. He was the son of one of the Titans, condemned to this chore when the Titans were defeated by their ancient enemies, the Gods, under Jupiter.

7542–7547 The violent upheaval of the valley floor is witnessed and described by the Sphinxes. They see the initial breaking through of the surface (7539–7543), and the terrific and untiring exertion of Seismos, as he lifts a great mass of rock (7546) on his shoulders (7538) until he himself has emerged head, shoulders, and chest from the earth (7547). The Sphinxes, having taken their positions ages ago, are certain that this new disturbance will not proceed so far as to affect them. — **trägt** A subject may be inferred from the context. Seismos is meant.

7559 Seismos, in company with Titans, and probably himself to be considered one, was disporting himself in the presence of the first ancestors. — According to Hesiod's Theogony, Chaos preceded all else in the universe. Gaea, or Mother Earth, came into being next after Chaos. From Chaos emerged Erebus, the mysterious darkness that is under the earth, and Night, which dwells in the regions of the sunset. Erebus and Night were wedded and from them sprang Light and Day. Gaea, or Mother Earth, was wedded ultimately to Uranus, the personification of Heaven, and from this union sprang (1) the Titans, (2) the hundred-handed monsters, and (3) the Cyclopes. Ultimately two of the Titans, Cronus and his sister-wife Rhea, produced the gods, who thereupon engaged in warfare with the majority of the Titans, whom they overcame and sent to Tartarus as captives. Hence *die höchsten Ahnen* would appear to be Chaos, Erebus and Night, Mother Earth and Uranus, of whom two are here named: Chaos and Night.

7561 Pelion and Ossa are mountains in northeastern Greece not far from Mt. Olympus. The Titans, or the Giants, are said to have tried to scale the heights of Heaven by piling Ossa on Olympus and then Pelion on Ossa. Goethe seems to have invented the ball game of 7561, as well as the piling of Pelion and Ossa on Mt. Parnassus, which is geographically remote from the rest of the places in this scene.

7564 Parnassus is a mountain in Phocis, in north central Greece, on the slopes of which, at Delphi, the famous oracle of Apollo held forth. Apollo was, among other things, the patron of music and poetry. The muses, nine in number, were daughters of Jupiter and Mnemosyne (Memory); they presided over song and assisted the memory.

— **Doppelmütze** Mount Parnassus has two summits, Tithorea and Lycorea.

7566 **hält** 'detains.'

7569 **Sessel** Jupiter's throne was on Mount Olympus.

7573 **Bewohner** All forms of plant and animal life (see 7578).

7575 **Emporgebürgte** A neologism by Goethe, meaning *"burgartig emporgebaute"* 'raised up like a lofty castle.' The Sphinxes are observing the last stages of the creation of a mountain. Rocks are still being added to the pile.

7580 **ein Sphinx** Masculine, although these figures are consistently treated as females (7195). This usage was current German practice in Goethe's time and probably stems from the French *le sphinx*. Present-day German usage distinguishes between *die Sphinx*, whom Oedipus outwitted, and *der Sphinx*, one of the Egyptian figures such as the Sphinx of Gizeh.

7585 **Imsen** See note to SD 7104. The griffons see new treasures of gold in the newly made mountain and dispatch the ants to gather it in.

7586 **ihn** = *den Schatz* The ants are exhorted by their chorus to bring the treasure to the surface as quickly as it has been lifted from the interior of the earth by Seismos, to whom they refer as a plurality of giants.

7602 **Herein** The busy ants are returning with their loads of gold.

SD 7606 **Pygmäen** The pygmies of Greek legend (ILIAD 3, 6) lived on the shores of the river Oceanus and fought an annual war with the cranes, when these great birds returned from their southern migration. Goethe has given the pygmies the attributes of the dwarfs of Germanic lore.

7607 These mountains are sudden creations and just as suddenly, out of nowhere, these mountain-dwelling dwarfs have come.

SD 7622 **Daktyle** The dactyls were, according to Greek legend, a race of metalworkers, who lived on Mt. Ida. Goethe makes them into very tiny creatures, analogous to the *Däumlinge*, or thumb-long dwarfs of northern German lore. The word *Daktyl* is from the Greek word meaning 'finger.'

7625 The subject of *finden* is to be supplied from *die Kleinsten* (7624) who are the dactyls. — *die Kleinen* (7623) are the pygmies. — Anaxagoras is reported to have said: "Nor is there a least of what is small, but there is always a smaller; for it cannot be that what is should cease to be by being cut. But there is also always something greater than what is great, and it is equal to the small in number, and, compared with itself, each thing is both great and small." It is known that Goethe (ca. 1813) was interested in Leibnitz' monadology and in the controversy as to the claims of Leibnitz and Newton to the prior discovery of the differential calculus.

7629 Optative: 'Let agility make up for the lack of strength.'

7635 **rührig im Schwalle** = *im rührigen Schwalle*, 'in busy throng.'

7642 **heimliche Flammen** Covered flames inside the earth-covered pile of wood, which is not consumed but burnt to charcoal for the smelters.

SD 7644 This is the generalissimo of the pygmies, whose army is to be prepared for war with the cranes. They attack the herons in order to provide ornaments, heron feathers (aigrettes), for their helmets.

7653 **mit Helm und Schmuck** = *mit geschmücktem Helm.*

7654–7659 The ants and dactyls are held in serfdom by the pygmies. They agree to be docile till the proper moment for revolt appears.

SD 7660 Ibycus was a Greek poet, who, as the story goes, was attacked and murdered at Corinth. As he died, he called upon a passing flight of cranes to avenge his death. These cranes did indeed participate in the detection of the criminals, since one of the murderers later in the amphitheater at Corinth was heard to exclaim as he saw cranes flying overhead: "Behold, the cranes of Ibycus!" The pair was thereupon arrested and confessed to the crime. (See Schiller's ballad, *Die Kraniche des Ibykus.*)

7660–7667 The cranes witness the pygmies' attack on the herons.

7666 **mißgestaltete Begierde** = *begierige Mißgestaltete* 'greedy monsters,' 'a monstrous incarnation of greed.'

7669 In some of the pictorial representations of pygmies, on vases and walls, they are shown with bowed legs and big bellies.

7671 Cranes in their migratory flight form a wedge-shaped close-knit group similar to that of ducks or wild geese. Here (SD 7675) they set out in all directions to assemble their forces. They begin their attack on the pygmies at line 7884.

7680–7682 The allusions are to *Ilsenstein* (3968), *Heinrichshöhe*, the *Schnarcher* (3880), and *Elend* (SD 3835), all place names in the neighborhood of the Brocken in the Harz Mountains.

7683 The mountains and rocks of the Brocken are established; no convulsions attendant upon the making of new mountains shake the earth there. To be sure, this new one is hardly high enough to be called a mountain (7688), but still it and its origin constitute a spooky experience (7691, *Abenteuer*).

7693 **Chor** Of the Lamiae; see note to 7235.

7704 The allusion is to Mephistopheles' *Pferdefuß.*

7710–7711 **Mannsen, Hansen** Contemptuous names for stupid males, with whom Mephistopheles in his disgust identifies himself. Men have been made fools of by women from Adam on down: it is their lot.

7714 **das Volk** Women in general, and these Lamiae in particular. Mephistopheles knows that feminine beauty is often illusory.

SD 7732 **Empuse** The spirit Empusa is supposed to have two feet, one of which is of iron, or, according to some versions, is an ass's foot (7737). The creature is capable of changing herself into all sorts of shapes (7745), such as that of a plant (like Alraune), a cow, a snake, a fly, a beautiful woman. Here she associates herself with the Lamiae (7733). — Empusa is a fitting Mephistophelian counterpart to Proteus; see Note to line 8152 and Volume I, p. 95.

7732   **eine solche**   The antecedent is the neuter *Frauenzimmer* (7730) and the feminine form *eine* is due to the meaning of the antecedent rather than to its grammatical form (gender).   This is called *Fügung nach dem Sinn* 'agreement according to sense.'

7742   The book which tells the story of diabolical creatures on this earth is an old book with many pages.

7747   The ass's head on Empusa seems to be Goethe's invention.

7751   Mephistopheles is loath to class himself as an *Eselskopf*, even though he may be 'cousin' to Empusa and the Lamiae.

7756   **Mühmchen**   The Lamiae.

7759   **Metamorphosen**   See lines 7716–7717.

7763   **Geleier**   Lines 7756–7759.   The taunt (7764) drives Mephistopheles to take direct action (7766).   He proceeds to lay hands on one after another of the Lamiae.

7774   Lacerta is a genus of small lizards, with which Goethe compared the lithe little streetwalkers of Venice (in his *Venetian Epigrams*). Here he is thinking of real lizards, into one of which the little Lamia has changed. — **Lazerte** for *eine Lazerte.*

7777   "Thyrsus" is the Greek-Latin word for the staff entwined with ivy and surmounted by a pine cone, which the Maenads waved in the air as they attended Bacchus (Dionysus) at the Bacchanalian feasts.

7783   Orientals are here alleged to favor women of embonpoint to the extent of paying high prices for them.

7788–7789   These lines are elliptical: 'Fly (or hover) around his head in irregular, awe-inspiring circles, on silent wings, like bats!'

7795   These Lamiae have just performed a masquerade.   Every masquerade is a play, confusing the senses with a mixture of reality and unreality.

7802   **Graus**   Either 'a thing arousing terror' or 'a wild confusion of rocks,' probably the latter in this passage.

7807–7808   Mephistopheles, who is certainly no novice at hocus-pocus, is astonished that in a single night these antique sorcerers could raise up such a mountain as this one.   Now that he is laboriously trying to cross it, he seems to have more respect for it than at 7688.

SD 7811   Oreas, a mountain nymph who speaks from the natural rocks nearby, to say that her mountain is an original, not a Johnny-come-lately, like this recent upheaval.

7813   **Verehre**   Either imperative, or indicative with the subject *ich* to be supplied.   Probably best taken as imperative; see 7821.

7814   The Pindus range of moderately high mountains lies on the curving western border of Thessaly in northwestern Greece.

7816   **Pompejus**   Gnaeus Pompeius Magnus, the triumvir and foe of Caesar at Pharsalus; see note to 7018–7020.

7817–7818   This mountain is mere hocus-pocus, and like all work of spirits, will disappear with the coming of day.

7846   **neue**   New 'ghosts,' hypothetical entities, with which philosophers are said to operate.

7847   Mephistopheles says in effect, "progress toward understanding comes from trial and error." God said (317) "Error accompanies striving to progress." Mephistopheles' doctrine could be reconciled with Darwinian theories of selection and survival, and in any event does not seem to be a typical Mephistophelian, ironical remark. Indeed, it suggests the motto Goethe gave the first part of his autobiography: 'The man who has not been flayed, has not been educated.'

SD 7851   Anaxagoras (ca. 500–430 B.C.), friend of Pericles and teacher of Euripides, was the first philosopher to propose the idea of the supersensible. His incorporeal "mind," however, was not integrated into his theories of the cosmos, although he did regard this mind as the initial force which first imparted to matter a circular motion, separating air (the source of water, earth, stone, and whatever is cold, dark, and dense) from the "ether" (the source of whatever is warm, light, and rare). This "ether" must not be confused with ethyl oxide.

    Thales (ca. 620–546 B.C.), the first philosopher of Greece, said by Herodotus to be of Phoenician descent, contemporary of Croesus and Solon, and one of the Seven Wise Men. According to Aristotle, Thales taught that water is the source of all things.

    Goethe makes the spirits of these two ancient men antagonists in an argument in which he satirized the contemporary debate between Vulcanists (or Plutonists), who believed that the earth got its form from sudden and violent fiery upheavals, and the Neptunists, who believed that the earth emerged from the water by slow, non-violent processes. This conflict of opinion, in the light of our present knowledge of geology, now seems quite incomprehensible, but it was an animated quarrel in Goethe's day.

    In these two characters Goethe personifies two basic forms of human behavior. Anaxagoras appears as a fanatic, an activist, and a revolutionary, impatient and intolerant in his argument, violent as the fiery upheavals he represents. Thales, on the other hand, is a patient, tolerant observer, moderate, experienced, a realist to whom the existence of things is of greater importance than theories about their origin. He represents slow consistent evolution. Anaxagoras can be taken in by the hocus-pocus of the demoniac spirits of the night: Thales is not deluded thereby. Hence Homunculus attaches himself to Thales rather than to Anaxagoras, who gives him bad advice (7880).

7852   **weiteres** Anything more than the sight of this mountain which has just been pushed up by Seismos.

7853–7854   Perhaps Thales is replying, in metaphors, to the accusation of obstinacy just made by Anaxagoras. Perhaps what he says is a continuation of what he may be assumed to have been maintaining so stubbornly as to provoke the accusation. In any event, the statement of line 7854 is, on its face, not true, and Goethe's intention is therefore obscure.

7855   'As a result of the action of fiery vapor this mountain was created and now exists.'

7859–7864   This sharpens the principal issue between the two schools of thought: the belief of the Vulcanists in cataclysmic, sudden changes as the creative force in nature, and the belief by the Neptunists in slow processes extending over great periods of time, without violence at any point.

7864 **im Großen** 'on a mighty scale.'

7865 **war's!** = *war es Gewalt!*

7866 **äolischer** The allusion is to Aeolus, king of the winds. He dwelt on the island of Aeolia with his six sons and six daughters. Here he lived a life of riotous carousal. He kept the winds penned up in a cavern and from time to time released them, sometimes on orders from his superiors, sometimes at his own pleasure. *Äolisch* means then 'like the pent-up winds of Aeolus,' and *äolische Dünste* amounts to 'vapors entrapped underground.'

7869 Thales' point is that this mountain is an isolated event, not part of a process on which one could build a theory of the cosmos.

7873 **Myrmidonen** A collective name for the pygmies, ants, dactyls, and other tiny living creatures (see note to SD 7622). The word occurs in ancient sources as the name of a tribe of southern Thessaly under the command of Achilles in the siege of Troy, but the name was wrongly associated with the Greek word 'myrmex,' which means 'ant,' and Goethe uses it in that meaning.

7875 **Däumerlinge** Now usually *Däumlinge;* see note to SD 7622.

SD 7877 In some of the stage directions, the use of a definite article with *Homunculus* makes that word seem to be a common rather than a proper noun. Forms with the article appear in SD 7877, SD 8238, SD 8245. Forms without the article, where *Homunculus* appears to be a proper noun, occur in 7828, SD 8082, SD 8231, 8469.

7880 Anaxagoras, speaking about these 'active little things,' turns to Homunculus and with a bit of whimsical humor proposes to make him king of these myrmidons. But Homunculus isn't sure that would be a good thing; and Thales advises against it, for general reasons (7882–7883), and also on practical grounds, since things are going badly for the pygmies (7884–7899).

7884 The cranes have assembled their forces (see 7670–7675), and are descending upon the pygmies to avenge the wanton slaughter of the herons. The herons are frequently confused with the cranes, though the two species are zoologically distinct. Neither the heron nor the crane has talons or claws such as those of the birds of prey.

7897 **Reiherstrahl** Occurs only in this line. *Strahl* might be expected to mean 'arrow' and some commentators take this to mean 'arrow winged with heron feathers.' However, the clear purpose of the pygmies in their assault on the herons was (7652–7653) to obtain heron feathers with which to adorn their helmets. Therefore, the word is probably best taken to mean the "bush" of heron feathers on each pygmy's helmet, perhaps only a single feather on each helmet.

7900 Anaxagoras approved the action of the subterranean spirits, because by creating this mountain they gave evidence to support his cosmological contentions in his debate with Thales.

7905 According to Goethe's source (Hederich), Hecate was the name given the moon in Hades, Diana was its name on earth, and Luna its name in Heaven. Indeed, the moon is said to have three forms (7903). Horace (Carmina III, 22, 3–4) refers to Diana as the three-named and three-formed goddess. Diana and Hecate were more or less confused by ancient writers, since they had many attributes in common.

7908   Anaxagoras appeals to the powers above, specifically to the moon, to provide darkness to protect his people, the pygmies and their allies. He wants an eclipse of the moon and he wants it to occur without magic. This is a reference to the report that Anaxagoras sought to explain eclipses as due to natural causes rather than as "acts of God."

7914   Coincident with his prayer to the goddess a meteor falls from heaven. Anaxagoras takes this meteor to be the throne of the moon-goddess, and sees in its approach the confirmation of the report that Thessalian witches have by incantation conjured the moon down from the sky.

7924   **Schild** = *Runde* (7918) The blazing disc of the falling meteor, which Anaxagoras believes to be the throne of Luna.

7928   Supply here *werfe ich mich* from SD 7929. Anaxagoras prostrates himself before the throne of Luna, which he believes to be coming down from the sky.

7939   **der Fels** The meteor which hit the top of the mountain has changed the shape of the summit and crushed the pygmies and the cranes (7941).

7946   Thales, who hasn't experienced at all (7932–7935) the same things Anaxagoras and Homunculus report, is unimpressed. It's all imagination, anyway, to him, this Vulcanism.

7947   **Brut** The pygmies.

7954–7955   In the odor of resin there is some suggestion of pitch, and this, next to the hell-smell of sulphur, appeals to the devil of fire and brimstone. — The manuscript here reads: "Zunächst der Schwefel . . ." which is an unfinished sentence, the full meaning of which cannot be inferred from the context. Hence we have followed other editors in emending the text by setting *dem* for *der*.

SD 7959   **Dryas** A tree spirit, or dryad, associated with the oak tree. She suggests that tourists should not always make invidious comparisons of what they see with what they have at home. She is a spirit of the same type as *Oreas* (SD 7811).

7959   **sei** Concessive: 'you may be clever enough in your own way at home,' or imperative: 'in your own land be clever and environment-integrated (*einheimisch*).'

7967   **Phorkyaden** Also called "Graeae." Three daughters of Phorcys and Ceto, gray-haired and ancient witches with one eye and one tooth among them, which they used in turn. They were sisters of the gorgons, the sirens, and the six-headed monster, Scylla.

7972   **Alraune** See note to line 4979. Here Mephistopheles refers to the hideous human form assumed by the mandrake. The *Alraune* was probably the ugliest creature in Mephistopheles' demonology.

7973 The hideousness of the Graeae is compared with the hideousness of sin, specifically the deadly sins, presumably: pride, covetousness, lust, wrath, gluttony, envy, and sloth.

SD 7982 **Phorkyade** The manuscript has an abbreviated form of this name which has been variously interpreted as Phorkyas, Phorkyade, or Phorkyaden. It cannot be determined with certainty whether Goethe intended these lines to be spoken by one of the Graeae, as at line 8018, or whether two of them were to speak. The names of these three monsters are said to be Pephredo, Enyo, and Chresis (or Deino). They kept their one eye, when not in use, in a special little box; and any one of them could affix it to her head, if she wished to bother to see what was going on.

7984 Mephistopheles is engaged in flattery. One need not believe anything he says.

7989 Ops is the Roman goddess of sowing and harvest and the wife of Saturn. Rhea was one of the Titans, wife of Cronus and mother of Vesta, Ceres, Juno, Pluto, Neptune, and Jupiter. Sometimes these two goddesses were identified with one another in the confusion of later, imperfect traditions.

7990–7991 Faust called Mephistopheles the son of Chaos (1384), as well as a son of Hell (1397). Neither designation has to be considered as evidence of Mephistopheles' genealogy. At 8027 Mephistopheles calls himself the son of Chaos and he is presumably lying — at least, the Graeae are skeptical about it, when they say that they themselves are beyond doubt the daughters of Chaos. Here (7990) Goethe appears to regard the Graeae as sisters of Chaos and of the Fates. According to Hesiod, the Fates are daughters of the night.

7991 Mephistopheles says he saw the Fates recently, he isn't sure just when. He is himself timeless, as are the Graeae. The remark need not be taken to refer to the figures of the masque in Act I (5305–5344), but it is sometimes so understood.

7996 **sagt!** Imperative, addressed to the Graeae.

7999 More flattery. Mephistopheles pronounces the Phorkyads more worthy of the sculptor's art than the three highest goddesses of antiquity: Juno, sister and wife of Jupiter, Minerva (Pallas-Athena), the virgin goddess who sprang from the brain of Jupiter, fully armed for war, and Venus, goddess of love and beauty. Beneath this flattering remark one may suspect an allusion to Lessing's remarks on the repulsive in art (LAOKOON XXV).

8006–8007 These lines are usually understood to refer to the great activity of sculptors (and painters) in Berlin in 1830, when these lines were written. Many marble or bronze statues of military heroes were being erected in the parks and on the streets of Berlin at that time.

8015 **mythologisch** After the fashion of mythology (which combines Ops and Rhea, for example), Mephistopheles, who is looking for a 'shape' in which he may properly appear in Sparta, proposes that one of the Graeae lend him hers for a short time. In the meanwhile the three sisters could get along with two 'shapes.'

8022–8025 Mephistopheles looks like a one-eyed, one-toothed daughter of Phorcys if he closes one of his own eyes and appears always in profile, with just one of his two canine teeth (tusks) showing.

8029 **Hermaphroditen** 'hermaphrodite.' A condition normal for the earthworm; but, for a human being, abnormal and usually accompanied by impotence and sterility.

8030 **Drei** 'trio.' When the numeral is used as a noun to denote a group of three, rather than three individuals, it is singular and usually neuter, as here.

8031 The Phorkyads, since Mephistopheles has become one of them, have their own eye and the one eye of Mephistopheles, as indicated in lines 8022–8023. Hence they have two eyes, and, in the same way, two teeth.

40. FELSBUCHTEN DES ÄGÄISCHEN MEERS

In place of the hideous Phorkyads, the grotesque battling between cranes and pygmies, and the disgusting Lamiae, we have here the glory of beauty, personified in Galatea. The demons of Fire are replaced now by the spirits of Water. The moon is arrested in its course at the zenith, thus symbolizing the halting of time, timelessness, as the proper condition for the ensuing festival in which the origin of life is to be celebrated and Homunculus is to find his way out of his bottle.

The keynote of the entire scene is the reconciliation of opposites: destructive and preserving deities (sirens and Cabiri) are joined in the same enterprise; worshippers of the sun (Telchines) are invited into the service of the moon; a goddess of beauty (Galatea) is hailed as the embodiment of human grace and divine immortality. In the medium of timelessness, this concluding scene of the Classical Walpurgis Night symbolizes the creative process of art, the synthesis of the elements of nature with the spirit through Love.

8035 **dich** The moon, Luna; see note to line 7914.

8038–8039 This is equivalent to "*auf der Zitterwogen mildeblitzendes Glanzgewimmel.*" 'Look down calmly from the arch of your night upon the gently sparkling tumult of brilliance of the lightly rippling waves.'

SD 8044 The Nereids are daughters of Nereus (the Old Man of the Sea) and the nymph Doris. The Tritons appear to be later multiplications of Triton, son of Neptune and Amphitrite. They are represented here as sea beasts. Hederich says they had the torso of a man, yet with sea celery for hair and scales instead of skin. Their lower bodies were those of dolphins plus feet like those of a horse.

8046 **Volk** The object of the imperative *ruft*.

8047 The storm may be thought of as the result of the atmospheric commotion caused by the earthquake (SD 7502) and the upheaval of Seismos.

8054 **eure** The sirens'; they are the spirits of this bay.

8057 **Dämonen** 'Spirits.' The word is used here with pleasant rather than with unpleasant connotations.

8063 **mehr als Fische** The sirens demand that the Nereids and Tritons show themselves to be more than mere unmotivated fishes. They agree to do so, and announce that they have planned to contribute importantly to the festivities.

8071 Samothrace is a small island in the northeastern reaches of the Aegean Sea. Its shores are rocky and steep, and it lacks a good harbor.

8074 **Kabiren** Oriental deities, whose cult was centered in Samothrace. Not much is known about them, but they have been much discussed. According to various authorities there were two, three, four, seven, or eight Cabiri. In Goethe's time there was a very considerable and windy debate about them, which led the poet here to satirize the theories of some of the disputants, notably those of Creuzer, the antiquary, and of Schelling, the philosopher.

8081 These sirens, like all spirit phenomena, must disappear with the coming of the dawn.

8082 **Nereus** Son of Pontus (the deep sea) and Mother Earth. Nereus is usually portrayed as the benevolent and wise Old Man of the Sea, noted for his ability to foretell the future and for his devotion to fair play and truth. Here Thales calls him peevish and hard to please.

8089 **dafür** = *davor.*

8093 **Glas und Flamme** For Homunculus equivalent to "flesh and blood," his life.

8096–8097 Reminiscent of Faust at the outset of the play; see lines 410–517.

8107 **harten** 'stubborn,' unmoved by the advice.

8108 **So oft auch ... sich gescholten** 'However often (the deed) has proved to be its own grim accuser ...' That is, whenever the event has proved the idea of the deed to have been wrong and deserving of censure.

8109 **Volk** = *Menschenvolk.*

8110 **Paris** See note to line 6184.

8111 **fremdes Weib** 'the wife of another,' or 'a woman from a foreign land.'

8113 Nereus foretold the fall of Troy.

8116 **festgebannt** This event has been fixed forever in the rhythms of the poets, particularly in the ILIAD of Homer and in Vergil's AENEID.

8121 The eagles of the Pindus Mountains (see note to line 7814) are depicted as scavengers on the battlefields before Troy, something like two hundred and fifty miles away. Hence some commentators understand these 'eagles' to be the Greek warriors, who finally won the victory at Troy.

8122–8123 Ulysses, after the fall of Troy, was led by the gods on very adventurous wanderings in his attempt to return home. — Circe dwelt on the isle of Aeaea. She was a powerful sorceress, who could turn men into lions, tigers, swine, or other beasts. She used her ability as a sweet singer to entice her victims into her power. She trapped part of Ulysses' party, but he, by bold attack, then forced her to release them. According to the legend, it was Mercury, not

Nereus, who warned Ulysses of the dangers of Circe's charms. —
The Cyclopes dwelt on an island off the east coast of lower Italy.
They were of gigantic size and had but one eye each. One Cyclops
trapped Ulysses and his men in a cave, but the hero finally escaped
by a ruse, though not without the loss of a number of his ship's company.

8124   Ulysses' 'hesitation' appears to be his seven-year dalliance with
Calypso, on whose island he was cast up from a raft (*vielgeschaukelt*,
8126), after the loss of his whole crew due to their irresponsible vio-
lation of his command not to touch the cattle of the Sun.

8127   **gastlich Ufer**   The land of the Phaeacians, who received Ulysses
hospitably and finally arranged his return to his home. Notably
Nausicaä, the daughter of the king, received him well.

8137   **Doriden**   Another name for the Nereids (see note to SD 8044),
since their mother was the nymph Doris, daughter of Oceanus. —
Later on (8383–8385) the daughters of Nereus and Doris are divided
into two groups: the Nereids and the Dorids; see note to lines
8379–8390.

8138   **Olymp**   The home of the gods. — **euer Boden**   The Earth, the
home of men.

8144   **Muschelwagen**   A seagoing chariot made of a large mussel shell,
usually associated with Galatea, the fairest of the daughters of
Nereus and Doris. Goethe makes Galatea the successor of the Cyp-
rian Venus, who is here said to have turned away from her relatives
of the sea. — This is a reflex of a twofold myth of the origin of Venus.
According to the younger tradition (Hesiod), Venus-Aphrodite was
born of the foam of the sea. She was carried in the sea by the west
wind and surf to the island of Cyprus, where she ruled by the power
of grace and beauty.

8146   **Kypris**   Venus.

8147   **Paphos**   A city on the island of Cyprus, the principal scene of the
cult of Venus.

8149   **Wagenthron**   The *Muschelwagen* of line 8144.

8152   Proteus was an attendant of Neptune and, according to some sources,
a son of Neptune. Like Nereus, he was an old man of the sea, but
his special gift was that of changing his shape at will.

8156   **steht er euch**   'if he stops and answers you.'

8160   **von weiten** = *von weitem*   An archaic phrase form; see note to
line 532.

8162–8163   **Als wie** = *wie wenn*   'as if.' — **anzögen** = *herangezogen kämen*
'came sailing up.'

8170   Chelone was the name of a nymph whom Hermes (Mercury) transformed into a tortoise, the Greek word for which is *chelônê*. This in
German is *Schildkröte*, from which Goethe formed *Riesenschilde*. —
The Nereids and Tritons are carrying the Cabiri from Samothrace
(8064–8077) in or on a giant tortoise shell, identical with or similar
to that of Chelone.

8171   **ein streng Gebilde** = *die (drei) Kabiren*. The collective *Gebilde*
(like *Gebirge*) makes a unit of the mythological construction Cabiri,
'an austere group.'

8172 **Götter** Cabiri; see note to line 8074. — Schelling (ÜBER DIE
GOTTHEITEN VON SAMOTHRACE, 1815) had argued that the four
Cabiri were not equals, but constituted an ascending series, with
Kadmilos the most powerful. Subsequently the Cabiri are increased
in Schelling's treatise to seven, and finally to eight "personalities."
Indeed, Kadmilos is said by some to be the fusion of an original
trinity of Cabiri. Creuzer operated with seven, and then with eight
Cabiri. Goethe is making sport of his contemporaries Creuzer and
Schelling for this kind of mythological argument (8194–8205). —
Pronoun subjects must be supplied: (*es*) *sind* (8172); (*ihr*) *müßt*
(8173).

8174–8177 The Cabiri were said by Herodotus (III, 37) to have been very
small in size, like pygmies, and Greek writers usually refer to them
as "mighty gods." They rescue the shipwrecked — thus often
robbing the sirens of their victims. The sirens concede the greater
power of the peace-loving Cabiri (8182–8185).

8182 **euch** The Cabiri.

8190–8193 The Nereids and Tritons have reported a disagreement
among the Cabiri (8186–8189). The sirens advise against taking
sides; they pray to all gods (8206–8209). They advise respect for
propitious gods and fear of harmful ones. — **Ehrt . . . fürchtet**
Either imperatives or indicatives: either 'honor all mercy, fear all
harm' or 'if you honor all mercy, (you must) fear all harm' (since
by expressing gratitude to one god you may provoke another to a
hostile act against you).

8198 **west** An unusual third person singular present indicative of *wesen;*
here 'lives and has his being,' or simply 'is.' — **der achte** This was
Schelling's theoretical 'overlord' over the other seven.

8202–8205 In his interpretation of the Cabiri, Schelling operated extensively with the term "potential existence," that is, an existence not
yet real. Each of his seven Cabiri represented a different stage of
development toward the perfect being, and each reflected the stage
before it and anticipated the stage which followed, thus forming a
progressive series. The final stage of perfection is possible but as
yet unachieved. None has finished the course of development —
each yearns and hungers for the perfection unattainable for him.

8215 The Golden Fleece of the ram sent by Mercury for the escape of the
children of Nephele. The girl, Helle, and the boy, Phryxus, were
put on the ram, which then set out to the east through the air. The
girl fell off into a body of water which has since been known as the
Hellespont. The boy arrived safely in Colchis, on the east shores of
the Black Sea at the foot of the Caucasus mountains. Here the
ram was sacrificed to Jupiter and its fleece placed in a consecrated
grove guarded by an ever-wakeful dragon. Jason was sent after
this fleece by his uncle, Pelios, who hoped thereby to dispose of
his nephew, the rightful heir to the throne of Aeson. The winning
of the Golden Fleece by Jason became the greatest glory of the long
adventurous journey of the Argonauts.

8215–8216 **sie** The Argonauts. They brought back the Golden Fleece;
but that, say the sirens, is nothing compared with the achievement
of the Nereids and Tritons, who have brought back the Cabiri.

SD 8217 A baroque, operatic repetition in the form of a chorus of all voices.

8220 The allusion is to the pictorial representations of the Cabiri as clay jugs or pots with human heads. Homunculus sees only the clay jugs.

8221 **die Weisen** Alludes to people like Creuzer and Schelling, who had debated these problems in print.

8224 The intrinsic value of the things these people seek is entirely subordinate in their minds to the antiquity of these things. An old, rusty iron coin is more highly valued than a modern silver one.

SD 8227 **bauchrednerisch** In ancient times ventriloquism was sometimes used as a form of divination.

8233 **gestaltet** 'having taken on a form.' Proteus could assume any form he wished. This time he is a tortoise (SD 8237). — **stockt** 'is concealed for the moment.'

8240 **auf menschlich beiden Füßen** 'on your two feet in human form.' Proteus was a lesser Greek god, and most of the Greek divinities were anthropomorphous.

8242 **wer** 'if anyone.'

8250 **greiflich Tüchtighaften** Goethe coined a number of words in *-haft* (*regelhaft* 9022, *doppelhaft* 8872, *zweighaft* 9541, *wogenhaft* 10 046), in which *-haft* means essentially 'having.' This one is less readily susceptible of such analysis, but what seems to be intended is: 'having the suitability (*Tüchtigkeit*),' that is, 'being suitable' to be grasped or touched (*greiflich*). In the context, however, *greiflich Tüchtighaften* may be taken together to mean simply 'substantiality.'

8258 **so wie er anlangt** Homunculus seeks a place where he may acquire physical form. Proteus is to direct him there. Hence *anlangt* probably refers to this place: 'in whichever form (or as soon as) he arrives at his destination.' Others take *anlangt* to mean 'achieves existence.' The bisexual quality of Homunculus (8256) will facilitate matters, since he can assume either male or female form as circumstances may require.

8260–8264 The allusion is to the evolution of all forms of life from the minute organisms of the primordial seas. The fact that Proteus prescribes this course need not be taken to be related to the debate between Anaxagoras and Thales, although the suggested procedure is in line with Thales' doctrine and is applauded by him (8321–8326).

8268 **behäglicher** Comparative, now usually *behaglicher*. Goethe uses the positive degree *behaglich* six times in Faust, but at 10 157 he wrote *behäglich*. Some editors change that form to *behaglich*.

8271 **Zug** See SD 8275.

8274 **Geisterschritt** The 'walking' of Proteus, Homunculus, and Thales to a point of vantage from which they can view the procession of Telchines. Homunculus is made to see this action from the point of view of a spectator and to find it remarkable on three counts: that Proteus, a god, Thales, a man, and Homunculus, a spirit, should be walking together as a trinity — god, man, spirit — to find a physical form for the spirit.

SD 8275 The Telchines were the original inhabitants of the island of Rhodes in the southeastern part of the Aegean Sea, northeast of Crete. They were reputed to be sons of the sea, and particularly distinguished as workers in bronze and iron. They are credited with the construction of the Colossus of Rhodes, a bronze statue of great size representing Helios, the Sun god, who is therefore thought to have been their national deity. They are also sometimes said to be the forgers of Neptune's trident, a three-pronged spear, with which this god of the sea could shatter rocks, summon or subdue storms, and rock the shores of earth. — **Hippokampen** Mythological sea horses with horses' hoofs on their forelegs and a fish's tail for the back half of their bodies.

8277 **der Donnrer** Jupiter, whose thunderbolts subdued his opponents and kept his enemies at a distance.

8281 **was** Generalizing pronoun, 'whoever and whatever.' The auxiliary *hat* is to be supplied with *gerungen*.

8283 **weshalb** Because it possesses power to incite and to calm the stormy seas, Neptune has given his trident to the Telchines to insure calm weather for this night's festival.

8285 Helios, god of the sun, is said to be the national deity of the Telchines, whom the sirens hail.

8287–8288 The hour is 'astir' with homage to the moon. The sirens welcome the Telchines, who are worshippers of the sun, and invite them to join this celebration, dedicated to the moon.

8289 **Bogen** The vault of the sky, referred to as an arc.

8290 Luna, or Diana, was the sister of Apollo, god of the sun.

8291 Rhodes, the island, for the people of the island, by synecdoche.

8293 From the beginning to the end of his journey through the sky, the sun sends his radiance down upon this favored island.

8297–8298 Rhodes is noted for a delightful climate with cloudless skies. Any cloud which formed, the Telchines say, was quickly dissipated by a ray from the sun and a little breeze.

8299 The reference is to the many statues of Helios, large and small, which the Telchines made. They boast of their priority in this field of art. The most famous product of their skill was said to have been the Colossus of Rhodes.

8302 The Greeks were the first people in the Western World to represent their gods in human, rather than in monstrous form. To be sure, their statues were several times life-size, but they adhered to the form of the human body.

8303 **du** Homunculus.

8306 **Das** 'Those people,' the Telchines.

8311 **sie** The bronze statues of gods made by the Telchines of Rhodes. The Colossus is said to have been destroyed by an earthquake and subsequently broken up and sold for old metal. At any rate it has never been found.

SD 8317 **verwandelt sich** Proteus changes himself into a dolphin.

8319–8320 The situation parallels, externally at least, that of Faust and Chiron (7333–7470).

8321–8326   Thales speaks to Homunculus, advising him to permit himself to pass through all of the evolutionary stages in the development of man, that is, to repeat in his ontogeny the phylogeny of humankind.

8327   **geistig** 'as a spirit.'

8330   **Orden** The reference is to the progression in the orders of biological forms from unicellular protoplasms to the end-form in man. Proteus warns Homunculus that his strivings for a higher order of life will lead him into troubles and that once he has become a human being his doom is sealed. Proteus thinks that man's estate is hopeless, perhaps because it is not possible for a human to proceed beyond it, although enlightened human beings are aware of the imperfections of this estate and inclined to strive for the unattainable perfection they conceive.

8333–8338   **Nachdem** = *Je nachdem.* — Thales has the practical answer to the problem of human life and the solution to which Faust will eventually come. Proteus concedes that in the case of a man like Thales, who amounts to something in his own day, the answer may be valid.

8341   **Tauben** Doves were symbols of chaste love. They were sacred to Venus (Aphrodite).

8343   **Paphos** See note to line 8147. The doves of Venus are here represented as the escort of Galatea, daughter of Nereus (see note to line 8144).

8347   **Nennte** = *es würde* (or *könnte*) *nennen* Conditional, or potential.

8353   **Wunderflugs** Qualifies *begleiten* and refers to the behavior of the doves.

8356–8358   **dem wackern Mann** Either the *nächtiger Wandrer* of line 8347, or any upright man. — **Neste** A metaphor for heart. — **ein Heiliges** A god, or a myth about one. — Thales says that he approves what is pleasant to good men, the earnest belief in something sacred, as opposed to the rationalistic explanation of everything as a mere physical phenomenon (8347–8348).

SD 8359   Goethe's conception of these creatures seems to rest on Pliny (NATURAL HISTORY 28, 3, 30): "The Psylli and Marsi, and they who on the island of Cyprus are called Ophiogenes." Ophiogenes is taken to mean 'snake-born.' Vergil (AENEID 7, 750–755) credits Umbro, the priest of the Marsi, with the ability to heal snakebite by wand and holy words. The Marsi lived in Italy. Lucan (PHARSALIA, 9) says that the Psylli were magic healers and snake charmers who lived in Libya. Goethe makes these two groups members of the retinue of Galatea, probably because he thought they came from Cyprus. Specifically (8365), he makes them the custodians of Venus' chariot, here used by Galatea. Hence they appear as sea spirits, mounted on sea beasts.

8365   **Cypriens** 'Of Venus.'

8368   **Geschlechte** The race of men who have taken over these regions when the gods and the giants withdrew.

8369   **Tochter** Galatea, daughter of Nereus.

8371–8372   **Adler** Stands for the Romans, *Leuen* for the Venetians, *Kreuz* for the Christians, and *Mond* for the Mohammedans, principally the

Turks. Each of these peoples, at one time or another, controlled the island of Cyprus. The sea spirits pay no attention to these political changes, but keep their ancient ways in the caves of the island, underground.

8379–8390 The dance of the daughters of Nereus is described by the sirens. The daughters who take after their father in vigor and size are here called Nereids; those who are more delicate, like their mother Doris, are called Dorids. Galatea is the one most like her mother and here the one celebrated by all the others.

8388 **würdiger Unsterblichkeit** Like *lockender Anmutigkeit* (8390), a predicate genitive indicating a quality belonging to the subject. Galatea is 'of worthy immortality,' that is, she is immortal as is her due, and she is 'of attractive grace.'

8392 The 'flowery garland of youth' are the young men whom the Dorids have rescued from the sea, their prospective husbands.

8406 The Dorids would like to have and to hold forever the youths whom they have rescued from the sea. Nereus cannot grant eternal life, or permanent youth, to these human beings. However, he does permit the Dorids to keep their 'catch,' and advises each to fashion her youthful partner into a mature man and husband. There can be no permanence to their relationship and their love will wear itself out in time. — According to another view, *bildet euch* (8409) is to be taken as equivalent to *bildet euch ein* 'imagine.'

8411 **was** Only Zeus can grant immortality.

8425 Galatea is borne rapidly past the spot where her father, Nereus, together with Proteus, Thales, and Homunculus, is watching her approach. She calls upon her steeds to halt, but they bear her swiftly onward. The climax of this Water Festival is the passing of beauty and perfection in the person of Galatea. But it is for a moment only and cannot be made to endure.

8426 **sie** The daughters of Nereus, Galatea's retinue.

8431 The separation for the whole year, until the next Classical Walpurgis Night.

8435 We return now to the Neptunist.

8445 Nereus is still watching Galatea and his other daughters as they return to their sacred city, Paphos.

8463 See SD 7068. The glass in which Homunculus is enclosed gives off both light and sound. Proteus finds the sound here in the sea much more impressive than in the air.

8465 **offengebaren** A bold neologism for *offenbaren*.

8469 Homunculus is moved (*verführt*) by Proteus' promise (8461–8463) and by Galatea's perfection and beauty to throw himself at the foot of her throne in the hope that there he may begin life with her in the sea. His glass breaks and his light suffuses the waters round about. Thales foresees trouble for Homunculus.

8474 **feuriges Wunder** The luminous Homunculus, whose refulgence may find a quasi-rationalization in the phenomenon of phosphorescence due to the animalculae in sea water. The possible causes of this phenomenon were much discussed in 1830 while Goethe was working on this scene.

8479 **Eros** Love, who, according to the poet Hesiod, started life on earth by creating creatures male and female out of matter and then bringing them together with natural affinities.

8482 The conclusion of this vast flight of poetic fancy is the reconciliation and joint praise of the two traditional opposites, Water and Fire.

SD 8484 **All-Alle** All together, the whole ensemble, in a grand finale.

8486 In the celebration of all four of the constituent elements of the world there is the hint of a synthesis of all in the creation of the cosmos.

ACT III

In 1827, four years or more before Goethe completed the second part of FAUST, as we know it, he published this third act in the fourth volume of the Cotta edition of his collected works, known from its title page as the *Vollständige Ausgabe letzter Hand.* He called it there: HELENA, KLASSISCH-ROMANTISCHE PHANTASMAGORIE. ZWISCHENSPIEL ZU FAUST. A year later (1828) in the twelfth volume of this *Ausgabe letzter Hand* Goethe printed what is now essentially Act I of the second part (lines 4613–6036) under the title: FAUST. ZWEYTER THEIL. To this text was appended the note (*Ist fortzusetzen*). At this time Goethe did not give his readers a clear indication of the relation of this first act of FAUST II to the previously published HELENA. As it stands now, Act III, the Helena episode, is in what should be the center of dramatic interest. It represents essentially the repetition in a quite different sphere of the experience of Faust in his love for Gretchen. Through this experience with Helena, Faust's spirit is to be made "gereinigt und frisch, nach dem Höchsten strebend," as Goethe put it in the sketch he once intended to include in the eighteenth book of DICHTUNG UND WAHRHEIT.

Dramatically, the Helena episode is difficult, because it lacks a basis of reality. Faust, in so far as he is important, is a human being. Helena is a phantom, the shade of a famous character in the great legend of ancient Greece. Her very existence in our play is fragile and illusive. Since she can hardly be said to "be," she is almost of necessity taken to "stand for something." Two possibilities of interpretation then arise: either Faust, the man, experiences something symbolized by Helena, the beautiful woman *par excellence;* or Faust is taken as "standing for something," which is brought into marital union with that "something" for which Helena stands. On these points one encounters very different and very strong opinions among commentators and critics. In such cases the beginning of wisdom is the admonition: "Read the text!"

41. Vor dem Palaste des Menelas zu Sparta

SD 8488   Sparta, the principal city of Laconica, the most southern of the ancient Greek kingdoms, was the capital city of King Menelaus, Helena's husband. Goethe uses Menelas, the French (and Doric) form of the name Menelaus, probably because it was more manageable in his verse.

    The assumption here is that Helena is just returning from Troy, where she had been "liberated" after many years of fighting between the Greeks (who sought to restore her to her husband, Menelaus) and the Trojans (who sought to preserve her for her lover, Paris). She brings back a retinue of Trojan women as her attendants. These women are now prisoners of the Greeks. Their leader is Panthalis. The name Panthalis is mentioned in ancient sources as belonging to a female companion of Helena.

8488   The metrical form of the non-lyric portions of this scene is Goethe's version of the classic trimeter. (See Volume I, Introduction, p. 140, and the note to line 7005.) Goethe also often uses extra syllables in the unstressed portions of the metrical unit, in order to avoid monotony. The lines here are not rimed. One peculiarity which needs special notice is that the last beat of the line often falls on a syllable which we should regard as unstressed, but which could have secondary emphasis in Goethe's diction. Thus the last syllable of *Helena, regsamem, Menelas, schwesterlich, entgegenleuchtete, verhängnisvoll, phrygische* carries the beat of the last measure and must be read with somewhat greater stress than the syllable next preceding it.

8491   **phrygischen Blachgefild**   The plains of Troy (Ilium) in Phrygia.

8493   **Euros**   The east wind. Troy lies northeast of Sparta across the Aegean Sea.

8494   **Dort unten**   At the seacoast. Sparta lay on the river Eurotas some twenty miles upstream from its mouth, where the returning Greeks came ashore from their ships.

8497   Tyndareus was the mortal husband of Leda, who bore him a son, Castor, and a daughter, Clytemnestra. Leda also bore to Jupiter (see note to line 6903) a son, Pollux, and a daughter, Helena.

8498   **Pallas' Hügel**   A hill sacred to Minerva (Pallas-Athena). This goddess presided over the useful and ornamental arts. Her chosen seat was Athens. Tyndareus built his palace near the slope of a hill. It is probable that this was *Pallas' Hügel* — that is, a local hill dedicated to Minerva, and having upon its summit a temple sacred to her. The return of Tyndareus, referred to by *wiederkehrend*, was his return from Aetolia, presumably when he married Leda and brought her to his home in Sparta. Some commentators understand *von Pallas' Hügel* to restrict *wiederkehrend* and take this to mean that Tyndareus had been in Athens and returned thence to Sparta.

8504   **erwählt**   Helena had been sought by many princely suitors, all of whom, at the suggestion of Ulysses, had taken an oath to sustain the choice and defend it if necessary. Tyndareus selected Menelaus. When she fled with Paris to Troy and thus precipitated the Trojan

War, it was chiefly her former suitors who carried out the great military expedition of the Greeks.

8508   Helena prays that all of her immediate past — her life at Troy with Paris and the tremendous conflict of the Trojan War, which brought death to so many great heroes and destruction to so much splendor — might be shut out of her life from this point forward. She wishes to put these dire doings wholly behind her and begin life anew.

8511   The temple of Venus was on the large island of Cythera, south of the Laconican Gulf and about 100 miles from Sparta. One version of the story of Helena and Paris says that the son of Priam first landed on the island of Cythera and that Helena went there out of curiosity to see this famous protégé of Venus. Paris then proceeded to carry her off to his Trojan home in Phrygia. — **heiliger Pflicht gemäß** 'to worship as was my duty.'

8518–8523   This is the strophe of a tripartite choral ode; the antistrophe is sung at lines 8560–8567 and the epode at lines 8591–8603. — The structure of the ancient (Pindaric) ode comprises (1) the strophe, or 'turn,' a set of verses sung or said by one part of the chorus, (2) the antistrophe, or 'counter-turn,' a set of verses in the same form as the strophe, sung or said by the other part of the chorus, and (3) the epode, or 'after-song,' a set of verses to be sung or said by the whole chorus. The epode is not identical in form with the strophes, but is usually longer than either and shorter than both together.

8523   **Schöne** = *Schönheit.*

8533   **Begleiter** In apposition to *Ruf und Schicksal* and an object of *bestimmen* (8531).

8535   **im hohlen Schiffe** Below, in the body of the ship, where the cabin was located.

8537   **gegen mir** = *mir gegenüber.*

8538   The river Eurotas empties into the bay of Laconica about twenty miles south of Sparta (see note to line 8494).

8539   **hinangefahren** An absolute participle, after the manner of Latin or Greek absolute constructions: 'But now, when, having sailed up the deep roadstead along the shore of the bay of the Eurotas, the prow of the leading vessel had scarcely touched the shore, he said . . .'

8549   **Betrete** An imperative by analogy to the weak verbs, instead of the normal *betritt.*

8564   **fordre sie auf** The jewels are personified and challenged to compete with Helena for the crown of greatest beauty.

8570   The instruments for a sacrificial offering: tripods for the burning of incense, vessels for the washing of the priest's hands, or perhaps for the catching of the blood of the victim. Other dishes contain wine, barley meal, and the like, to be put on portions of the animal which are to be burned on the altar. — **das flache Rund** (8573) The *patera*, the plate or libation saucer, in which blood of the victim was carried around among the celebrants. — As Goethe tells the story, Helena was abducted from the isle of Cythera when about to perform a similar act of sacrifice.

8578 **geb' ich heim** = *geb' ich anheim* 'I entrust.' The manuscripts are not satisfactory at this point and some editors print *hin*, instead of *heim*.

8580 **zeichnet** = *bezeichnet*, with a shift to the present tense for greater intensity of feeling. — **der Ordnende** Menelaus, Helena's meticulously orderly husband; recall *nach der Ordnung* in lines 8541, 8555, 8569.

8583 **heimgestellt** = *anheimgestellt* 'Placed in the hands of (the Gods).'

8596 **auch verkündet** 'Even when it is prophesied for us.'

8601–8603 With *schauen* supply *wir nicht* (from line 8599): 'Do we not look upon the dazzling sun of the heaven and upon the most beautiful thing on earth, you, gracious toward us fortunate ones?'

8604–8606 **geziemt** It is her duty to enter the palace which once more stands before her eyes, incredibly, after she has long been absent from it, has often longed for it, and frivolously almost lost it forever by going off with Paris. This palace had been her childhood home.

8621 **Götter** Presumably Zeus (Jupiter, Helena's father), Poseidon (Neptune), and Tyche (Fortuna).

8647 Zeus (Jupiter) was indeed Helena's father, and Homer usually refers to Helena in this way.

8653 **die Stygischen** Those powers who dwell beyond the river Styx, in the lower world; hence, the powers of Hades.

8656 **(gern) . . . scheiden mag** 'Am moved to leave.' — This line is an Alexandrine.

8657–8658 **sollt ihr** = *ihr sollt*.

8676 **welch** = *irgend welches* 'Some.'

8687 **das Wunder** 'The strange, monstrous woman' (*Weib* 8676).

8697 The chorus speaks in the first person singular, as though it were an individual. — This choral song is usually considered to consist of two strophes (or a double strophe), 8697–8701, 8702–8706; two antistrophes (or a double antistrophe), 8707–8712, 8713–8718, an epode, 8719–8727, and then two new strophes, 8728–8735, 8736–8743, followed by two antistrophes, 8744–8748, 8749–8753.

8711 **Sturmes Wehen** The violent air currents produced by the fire serve to spread the conflagration.

8735 **Graien** See note to line 7967.

8741 **er** Phoebus, the sun.

8746 **Augenschmerz** The sensation of pain in the eye, which is aroused in lovers of beauty by that which is reprehensible and 'everlasting-wretched.'

8747 **das Ewig-Unselige** Should mean 'that which is eternal and wretched,' just as *das Ewig-Weibliche* (12 110) means 'the eternal-feminine.'

8754 **Alt ist das Wort** 'Old' from our point of view. For example, in Juvenal (about 65 A.D.–128 A.D.): "Rare indeed is the friendly union of beauty of form and chaste modesty." (10th Satire, line 297.)

8772 The Maenads were female attendants of Bacchus. In the Bacchanalian revels they danced and sang, waving aloft the Thyrsus, a staff entwined with ivy and having a pine cone on top. See note to line 7777.

8779 Zuhauf euch sehend 'As I see you in a crowd . . .' — *sehend* qualifies *mir*.

8792 der Nächste In Leviticus 19.18 (cited in Luke 10.27) the Hebrew Law required: "Du sollst deinen Nächsten lieben wie dich selbst." A German proverb has it that: "Jeder ist sich selbst der Nächste." 'Everyone looks out for his own interests first.'

8808–8809 As the beauty of a swan is to the dubious beauty of geese, so is Helena's beauty when compared with that of her retinue. Helena is later referred to as *die Schwanerzeugte* (line 9108); see note to line 6903.

SD 8812 The chorus consists of the leader and twelve '*Choretiden*.' It is divided into two halves which stand on opposite sides of the stage, one headed by the chorus leader, the other standing behind Helena. Phorkyas is between the two groups. Here members of the half chorus led by the *Chorführerin* step forward singly and speak. The dialogue takes the form of the alternate exchange of single lines (stichomythy), which is characteristic of lively dialogue in the classic Greek drama.

8812 Erebus The mysterious darkness that is under the earth, which, when wedded to Night, became the father of Light and Day. The girl implies that Phorkyas is the offspring of darkness and night.

8813 Scylla Daughter of Phorcys and Ceto, and hence sister of the Graeae. She was transformed by Circe into a six-headed monster hideously compounded of serpents and barking dogs. 'Cousins of Scylla' thus is an opprobrious name given this chorus by Phorkyas.

8814 This may be a reference to oriental heraldry, in which monsters are frequently shown leaping or climbing upon trees.

8815 Orkus Helena and her retinue (the chorus) have indeed just come from Hades.

8817 Tiresias Aged blind soothsayer of ancient Thebes.

8818 Orion Son of Neptune. He was killed by Diana, and then transformed into a constellation and set in the sky. The point is that Phorkyas must be very old if her great-great-grandchild was the nurse of Orion, whose death was prehistoric.

8819 The Harpies were grandchildren of Pontus (the sea) and Gaea (the earth). They were foul creatures with the heads of fair maidens, but with the bodies, wings, and claws of birds. Their faces were pale from hunger. They befouled whatever they touched.

8820 was Used in place of the missing dative form of the interrogative pronoun.

8821 Phorkyas chides the chorus with being vampires. In Slavic folklore, vampires are corpses which rise during the night from their graves to suck the blood of sleepers. The vampire is thus nourished and kept alive, while its victims pine away and die.

8825 The riddle has two components. (1) How can these chorus members appear here? They are, as Phorkyas knows, phantoms from the underworld. (2) What is Phorkyas doing here? She (or he) is also far from her proper place. — **hebt sich auf = läßt sich aufheben** 'Can be canceled out,' in the mathematical sense that one factor is equal to another opposed to it in the equation. Both parties are demonic spirits.

8829 **unterschworner** Inwardly poisoned and yet glossed over with the outward appearance of healthiness, 'festering beneath the surface.' This line refers to the evils of dissension among (or between groups of) subordinates, each one of whom is loyal to the master, but whose mutual and reciprocal hostilities are as pernicious as though disloyalty were at work.

8833 **den Selbstverirrten** The master's order should be followed by swift obedience, as automatically as an echo follows his words. But when the master's orders are willfully unheeded, he finds himself engulfed in the noisy confusion of his own and other peoples' wills. He becomes unsure of himself (*an sich selbst irre*), and his reproaches are in vain.

8835 The horrors mentioned by Phorkyas and the members of the chorus bring to Helena's mind the terrifying figures she herself has seen, and remind her that she has come from Orcus and perhaps belongs there rather than on earth.

8838 Helena is confused. She has indeed just emerged from Hades and found herself on the scene of her youthful adventures, the memories of which flood her mind. She isn't sure the whole thing isn't a delusion; perhaps even her life was a dream.

8840 **jener Städteverwüstenden** Genitive plural. Helena was at once the dream and the terror of the Greek heroes who destroyed Troy. The line is cast in the style of Homer.

8848 **Theseus** See note to line 6530. Theseus is sometimes called a second Hercules. He was one of five mortals to go down to Hades to the throne of Pluto and return to live on earth. Indeed, he owed his safe return from the realm of the dead to Hercules, who released him from an enchanted rock where Pluto had put him.

8851 **Aphidnus' Burg** A fortified town in Attica, where, according to Hederich, Aphidnus, a good friend of Theseus, was to care for the young Helena. Castor and Pollux soon liberated their sister (see notes to lines 7369 and 7415).

8853 **Heldenschar** Construed with *umworben*, is probably in the genitive, instead of the usual expression of agency by *von* plus the dative. However, one cannot prove that this form is not dative, rather than genitive, because the locution is exceptional and has no known parallel. If construed as a dative, it may be explained as an imitation of the Greek or Latin dative of the agent: 'wooed by an elite band of heroes.' — Another possibility is to construe *Heldenschar* with *standst du* rather than with *umworben*. In that event the form has to be taken as a dative in the unusual sense of 'presented to, before.'

8855 **Patroklus** Bosom friend of Achilles, here called his 'image.' Achilles was the son of Peleus, and hence was called *Pelides*, or *der Pelide*.

8858 Tyndareus, foster father of Helena, was king of the city-state Lacedaemon, or Sparta, as it is more often called. He gave his daughter Helena and his royal power to Menelaus.

8860 **Kretas Erbe** Menelaus is said by Hederich to have gone to Crete in order to see to it that he got his share of the estate of his maternal grandfather, Creteus, who had died there. He became involved in a long struggle for his rights and hence was away from home for a long time. During his absence, Paris is said (8861) to have come to Sparta.

8864–8865 This fiction of Mephistopheles-Phorkyas — that Menelaus had brought her back from Crete a captive slave and installed her as stewardess when he found his home deserted by his wife — is intended as part of the progressive shift by which the world's most beautiful woman comes ultimately to put her trust in the world's most hideous creature.

8868 **Die** Plural, 'those things' referred to in line 8867.

8872 According to a later version of the Helena story, on which Euripides based his play, Mercury carried off the real Helena to Egypt, while Paris, with the aid of Venus, managed to abduct and carry off to Troy only the phantom of Helena.

8876 Another late legend tells that the King of Hades restored Helena and Achilles to earth as phantoms, putting them on the island of Leuce in the Black Sea. There a child, Euphorion, was born to their ghostly union (see note to line 7435). Achilles is said to have been one of the early suitors of Helena, before her marriage to Menelaus.

8880 **die Worte** = *Idol . . . Idol.*

8882 The chorus speaks to Phorkyas in an ode, the structure of which here is: the pro-ode (8882–8886), strophe (8887–8894), antistrophe (8895–8902), and epode (8903–8908).

8889–8890 The three-headed dog is Cerberus, who lies at the gate of Hades. He welcomes those spirits who seek to enter, but is hostile to any who attempt to depart from Pluto's realm.

8898 **denn** 'than.' Archaic usage, where *als* is now usual.

8900 **mit** 'along with, together with.'

8907 **Gestalt aller Gestalten** This use of the genitive is analogous to that of the phrase *Lied der Lieder*, 'Song of Songs'; 'the best of all . . .'

8909 The verse form here is the trochaic tetrameter, another of the Greek forms found in the dialogue of ancient tragedy. It is used without rime. The tetrameter is, in theory, an eight-beat line comprising four dipodies of two beats each, the last measure being catalectic (having no unstressed syllable). A dipody is a unit of two measures or feet. It is often impossible to identify these dipodies in German tetrameters. The caesura should appear after the eighth syllable. We find here the same irregularity as to the number of unstressed syllables in the arsis that we met in the case of iambic trimeter (see note to line 8488 and Volume I, Introduction, p. 141). — Phorkyas addresses Helena metaphorically as the sun. The clouds are the clouds of Helena's fainting spell, from which she has just recovered.

8913–8914 Helena, at the command of Menelaus, has come up from the seacoast to make arrangements for her husband's sacrifice to the gods. She has met with unexpected nervous strain in her encounter with Phorkyas, has fainted (SD 8881), and now feels weak and exhausted. At the challenge of Phorkyas (8909) Helena steps forward, saying: 'Although I come forth with faltering step from the solitary desolation which enveloped me in my fainting spell, I should like to rest again . . .' *Tret' ich* . . . and *pflegt' ich* . . . may be taken respectively as the subordinate and the principal verbs of the sentence, the first clause of which is rather "concessive" than "conditional." According to another view *Tret' ich* . . . and *pflegt' ich* . . . are correlative, with poetic inversion, and mean: 'With faltering step I come forth . . .; I should be glad to rest again . . .'

8917–8918 **Stehst du nun** 'Now you stand' The inversion is poetic and does not mean 'if': *da* need not be translated.

8924 Phorkyas foretells the death of Helena as a sacrificial victim on the altar of the house. Her attendants, however, who must die with their mistress, will be unceremoniously hanged from the rafters, like thrushes caught in a bird-catcher's net. The idea stems from the ODYSSEY, 22, 462–467. They will not be given the 'pure death of the sword' but will be strangled like the perverse servants in Ulysses' household.

8930 Phorkyas calls the members of the chorus 'ghosts,' which indeed they are. They are here in daylight by virtue of the special dispensation of Persephone, who has permitted this reappearance of Helena and her union with Faust. Faust's mission to Persephone (7490–7494) has been successful.

8932 All human beings are said to be 'ghosts,' even as these women of the chorus are ghosts. Sophocles makes Ulysses say: 'For now I feel all we who live are but an empty show and idle pageant of a shadowy dream.' (AJAX, 125–126.)

8934 **bittet oder rettet** 'Will save by prayers of intercession or by direct help' from the inevitable end (*Schluß* = death).

8936 **ans Werk!** Phorkyas turns to the business of preparing for the sacrifice of Helena and the coincident death of the members of the chorus.

SD 8937 In spite of Mephistopheles' alleged lack of power in the realm of classic antiquity, he (as Phorkyas) appears now to be operating as usual with various useful spirits under his command. — This portion of the act has many of the features of a ballet.

8937 **Ungetüm** One rotund dwarf is thus addressed for all. These are hostile and destructive creatures (*schaden* 8938).

8939 **goldgehörnten** 'with horns of gold,' like the one described in Exodus (30.1–3).

8940 **Silberrand** The silver binding around the edge of the top of the portable altar.

8945 **eingewickelt** Burials in ancient Greece were commonly made without coffins, the body being wrapped in a cloth or rug, as here indicated, and laid in a cave or under a pile of rocks.

8949 **Mir deucht** = *Mir deucht es gut* 'it seems advisable to me.'

8951 Faced with the prospect of death, the leader of the chorus, speaking for her girls, appeals for help to the same Phorkyas whom they but lately reviled as hideous. Indeed, the chorus, 8957–8961 and throughout this act, is quite avidly concerned with its self-preservation. The members of the chorus are spirits who have been given a renewed existence on earth as phantoms, and they are now greatly afraid of having to go back to dull, monotonous Hades.

8955 **Zugaben** 'Appendages.' A *Zugabe* is something or someone 'thrown in' to complete a deal, a sort of bonus or extra, that goes along with a bargain 'to boot.' There is considerable contempt for the Chorus in Phorkyas' remark.

8957 **Parzen** The Fates. The allusion here is probably to Atropos, although Klotho had the shears during the masque of Act I. See note to SD 5305. — **Sibylle** A general name for a divinely inspired prophetess. See note to line 2577.

8958 **Tag** Life.

8962 **diese** The members of the chorus, Trojan slaves. Helena feels no fear, only pain and sorrow, because of her husband's alleged intention to kill her (see lines 9052–9053).

8969 **Rhea** See note to line 7989.

8978 **Richte** 'Line.' Apparently a unique use of this word, meaning either the structure of his doorway and the place where it is (D. Sanders), or the line or limit of his threshold (M. Heyne, in Grimm's Deutsches Wörterbuch). — **heilig** Because the house inside the threshold was protected by Zeus.

8982 **wohlbekannte** What Phorkyas has just said amounts to the proverbial: "Bleibe im Lande und nähre dich redlich!" Psalm 37.3.

8983 **Verdrießliches** Vexatious thoughts of her failure to remain at home and attend to her husband's house (8978–8979).

8985–8989 This is the account of Phorkyas, the pretended Cretan stewardess left in charge of the house by Menelaus. According to the usual interpretation, the siege of Troy lasted for ten years at the beginning of the twelfth century B.C. After the fall of Troy Menelaus and his wife Helena set out for home in a ship. They were buffeted about the Mediterranean for a long time, landing in Cyprus, Phoenicia, and Egypt, before they finally arrived in Sparta. We do not know just how many years this journey required. Phorkyas puts it at nearly ten years (line 9004).

8994 **Talgebirg** Beyond Sparta to the north, on the border between Laconica and Arcadia.

8996 **Taygetos** Four syllables, with stress on the second: Ta-y'-ge-tos. This is a range of mountains west of Sparta and running approximately north and south, making part of the boundary between Laconica and Messenia.

9000 **aus kimmerischer Nacht** The Cimmerians were a mythical people, described by Homer as living in a land of mist and darkness. Goethe fuses legendary events of the twelfth century B.C. with historical events of the thirteenth century A.D., when Franconian knights on the fourth crusade set up a kingdom in the Peloponnesus, which endured for a century and a half, until 1346. These are the peoples called barbarians by the Greeks in line 9013.

9007–9009 The lord of this castle has raided the royal palace of Menelaus at Sparta while the king was away fighting before the walls of Troy. —**konnt' er** = *hätte er können.*

9015 menschenfresserisch Particularly the conduct of Achilles toward Hector (ILIAD 22, 346–347):

> Daß doch Zorn und Wut mich erbitterte, roh zu verschlingen
> dein zerschnittenes Fleisch, für das Unheil, das du mir brachtest!

9016 acht' . . . vertraut' Ambiguous forms: either indicatives: 'I respect his greatness, and have entrusted myself to him,' or conditional subjunctives: *(achtete . . . vertraute)*: 'I should count on his loftiness of mind and trust my fate to him,' or indicative and subjunctive: 'I respect his magnanimity, and (if I were in your predicament) I should entrust my fate to him.'

9018–9021 The allusion is to the rude masonry of the earliest inhabitants of Greece, in which huge stones were piled up *(aufgewälzt)* without the use of mortar, to form rude walls for buildings. The Cyclopes had gigantic strength and were therefore thought to have piled up these incredible structures, which are found especially in the cities of Tiryns and Mycenae, the home of Menelaus.

9026–9030 A description of a medieval castle such as the Franconian crusaders would construct; see 6929.

9030 Wappen Heraldry, with its coats of arms, is a medieval invention, unknown to the ancient Greeks but resembling in a way the devices which they caused to be wrought upon their shields. — **Ajax** A Greek hero before the walls of Troy, second only to Achilles in warlike strength. He was supposed not to be very intelligent, however.

9032 The Seven against Thebes were the younger heroes Polynices, Adrastus, Tydeus, Parthenopaeus, Capaneus, Hippomedon, and Amphiaraus. Their exploits were celebrated by Aeschylus.

9038 seinen When Goethe changed line 9037 from its older form: *Und solch Gebild führt hier ein jeder Heldensohn* to its present reading, he failed to change *seinen* in 9038 to *ihren,* as is required by the new antecedent *Heldenschar.*

9045 Blond northern boys should attract these Trojan damsels, who were, it is to be supposed, Mediterranean types.

9047–9048 Helena is annoyed on two counts. She dislikes reference to Paris, and she dislikes this straying from the purpose of the tale to excite the desires of her servants. She wants to know what Phorkyas has to propose.

9049 sagst = *wenn du sagst.*

9054 Deiphobus, the bravest brother of Hector, and brother also of Paris. According to later legends, Deiphobus is said to have taken Helena as his wife after Paris died. During the sack of Troy, Menelaus overcame Deiphobus and dismembered him by degrees (AENEID VI, 494–497).

9060 jenes willen 'On his account.' Reference is to Deiphobus.

9061 der 'He who.'

9062 lieber 'Rather' (than share possession of it).

SD 9063 Since Menelaus participates in this action only in the mind of Helena and of her retinue, and since there is no question of his having been released from Hades to wander about here in Sparta once more, these trumpets can only be understood to be part of Mephistopheles-Phorkyas' magic, designed to persuade Helena to go to Faust's castle.

9068 **Herr und König** Menelaus, who, according to Phorkyas' story, has appointed her stewardess here.

9069 **ihren Tod** Helena's death.

9075 **Das andre** Antithetical to *das Nächste*, which is Helena's decision to go to the castle of the strange lord and again forsake her home and husband, Menelaus. Just what is meant by *Das andre* is not clear: perhaps the consequences of her act. What comes next, at any rate, and what Helena may well have had in mind, is her union with this "foreigner" in the stone castle.

9078 Again a choral ode, with pro-ode, strophe, antistrophe, and epode, ending at line 9121. See note to line 8882.

9081 **abermals** The first time was behind the protecting walls of "the topless towers of Ilium."

9084 **Schütze sie** 'May it (the wall) protect . . .'

9087 **List** A reference to the Trojan horse and the attendant trickery.

SD 9088 **nach Belieben** 'At the pleasure (of the stage manager).' — Lines 9088–9121 accompany the change in scene and describe it as it is accomplished behind a veil of mist, which "arises from the river Eurotas." Lines 9113–9121 allude directly to the shifting scene.

9102 The allusion is to the belief that the swan sings when it is about to die.

9108 The allusion is to Helena, daughter of Leda and Jupiter, who appeared in this love affair as a swan.

9117 Hermes-Mercury was assigned the task of conducting souls of the dead to the realm of darkness. For this office, Hermes had a golden wand twined with snakes and surmounted by wings. The chorus knows this figure, because he had led their souls to Hades once before (9118).

9122–9123 At this point the mists vanish and the new scene is revealed. It is a remarkable mist, in that its dispelling is not accompanied by sunlight, as is usually the case. The chorus and Helena now find themselves surrounded by unfamiliar walls.

42. Innerer Burghof

Helena and her retinue have been persuaded to follow (9074) Mephistopheles-Phorkyas to the castle of Faust, which is to be thought of as one of those Franconian structures which the participants in the fourth crusade erected in the Peloponnesus and which are still discernible as ruins there. The transition from the world of antiquity to the world of Faust has been accomplished, but this is still a world of fantastic structures, not altogether real. Indeed, the transition from one world to the other has been managed so as to preserve the illusion of complete unity of place. Our dramatic characters have been indeed surrounded (9123) by Faust's castle, without really leaving the soil of Sparta.

It is probable that what Goethe called the second part of the HELENA begins with this scene, rather than with scene 43; *Arkadien*, though this is not certain. Definite stage directions calling for musical accompaniment cover only lines 9679–9938. Goethe intended this second portion of the HELENA to be treated as an opera. He called it "die opernartige romantische Hälfte," and said about its casting (to Eckermann, January 29, 1827): "Der erste Teil erfordert die ersten Künstler der Tragödie, sowie nachher im Teile der Oper die Rollen mit den ersten Sängern und Sängerinnen besetzt werden müssen. Die Rolle der Helena kann nicht von einer, sondern sie muß von zwei großen Künstlerinnen gespielt werden; denn es ist ein seltner Fall, daß eine Sängerin zugleich als tragische Künstlerin von hinlänglicher Bedeutung ist." The author's further remarks about his intentions here deserve to be quoted: "Es steckt ein ganzes Altertum darin," sagte ich [Eckermann]. "Ja," sagte Goethe, "die Philologen werden daran zu tun finden . . . Aber doch ist alles sinnlich und wird, auf dem Theater gedacht, jedem gut in die Augen fallen. Und mehr habe ich nicht gewollt. Wenn es nur so ist, daß die Menge der Zuschauer Freude an der Erscheinung hat, dem Eingeweihten wird zugleich der höhere Sinn nicht entgehen, wie es ja auch bei der 'Zauberflöte' und anderen Dingen der Fall ist."

This "higher meaning" is clearly enough embodied in the union of the romantic with the classic, both in the persons of Faust and Helena and in the forms of their utterances, which commingle classic with romantic verse patterns and other stylistic devices. Faust, the romantic, northern man, achieves his highest spiritual perfection when he achieves union with the beauty of classical antiquity. At the end of this experience, his life is no longer a frenetic quest for something mystically outside and beyond himself, which he requires for his self-realization, but this striving has become a purposeful, active drive toward a practical goal.

9135   Helena, who does not know the name of this mysterious person who has guided her thus far, addresses Phorkyas with the generic name *Pythonissa*, which means 'Prophetess, wonder-worker.' The word *Pythonissa* is used by Praetorius, by Paracelsus, and in the Latin literature of witchcraft which Goethe had read extensively. The form is medieval Latin.

9136   **der düstern Burg** Genitive, separated from the noun it modifies (*Gewölben*) by the imperative *tritt hervor*.

9142   **Bild** Pythonissa = Phorkyas.

9146   The allusion is to the striking contrast between the architectural unity of ancient Grecian palaces and the agglomeration of parts in the medieval castle, which is a unit only because it is surrounded by a wall.

9155   Pages, marching in formation, had never previously been seen by this chorus. The pages are blond, fair-skinned, rosy-cheeked Teutonic boys.

9156   **erscheinen** A plural verb because of the plurality of persons involved in '*Volk.*' This lack of grammatical agreement is usual only when the verb precedes its subject.

9163   Thus Satan (Milton, PARADISE LOST X, 564–567) and his brood were deceived by the fair fruit of the tree beside the lake of Sodom.

> . . . They, fondly thinking to allay
> their appetite with gust, instead of fruit
> chewed bitter ashes, which the offended taste
> with spattering noise rejected . . .

It is not clear what previous experience of the chorus is here alluded to, but it is evident that they suspect that these attractive boys may be mere phantoms — like themselves.

9176   **eingeladen** Invited by someone not named, but perhaps to be thought of as a herald or master of ceremonies who is directing the arrangements. The chorus itself is next invited to take places in orderly ranks on the steps leading to the throne. The whole will produce a tableau.

9180   **Würdig** A predicate adjective: 'let it gratefully be pronounced worthy.'

SD 9182   The essential features of the court dress here ascribed to Faust are the crownlike headdress and the rich, full-length robe, ornamented with broad bands of gold embroidery, set with jewels and perhaps trimmed with fur.

9182–9187   If the qualities apparent in this man are his own and not just a pretense, the passing prank of some god, he is indeed a very distinguished personage.

9192   The chorus leader has spoken in trimeter. Faust speaks in blank verse. A modern is thus opposed to an ancient verse form.

9193   **statt ehrfurchtsvollem Willkomm** In FAUST, *statt* is usually construed with a following genitive, as in line 9192. Other unambiguous datives with *statt* occur at lines 8643 and 9104. There are twelve unambiguous genitives with *statt*, nine of them in Part II.

9194   **solchen** = *diesen*, as in line 8797.

9195   **entwand** *Entwinden* means to 'wrest from,' hence 'violently to deprive.' By failing in his duty, the watchman has deprived Faust of the opportunity to meet the lady at the door, as was his duty and privilege.

SD 9218   **Lynkeus** The name of the hero who served the Argonauts as lookout and watchman (see line 7377 and the note). He was famous for his sharpness of sight. — Goethe uses the name here and in Act V for a watchman, but there is no necessary connection between the Lynceus of Act III and the Lynceus of Act V, and neither need be considered identical with the hero of the Argonauts. The name is almost a stock name for a keen-eyed watchman. It is derived from the same source as 'lynx,' which is a proverbially keen-sighted animal.

9221 **Frauen** Archaic dative singular. — Lynceus is speaking in stanzas with rime, a modern, not a classical verse form.

9222 **des Morgens Wonne** = *die Sonne.*

9225 For the geography, see 8995. Helena approaches Faust's castle from the south.

9231 **auf höchstem Baum** 'In the top of the tree,' like the Latin: summa in arbore.

9234 Lynceus had difficulty in seeing through the clouds of mist in which Mephistopheles-Phorkyas effected the transfer of Helena to Faust's castle, or of Faust's castle to Sparta. He could not even find the battlements or towers of his own master's castle.

9239 **an** An adverbial prefix with *sog: ansaugen* where *einsaugen* would be a more usual verb.

9240–9242 **blendet, blendete** 'As the beauty of Helena now blinds all, so it then blinded me, and I forgot my duty.'

9243 **Horn** Lynceus was bound by his oath of office to blow his horn whenever anyone of importance approached his master's castle.

9250–9252 **Raubend** As in the case of Theseus. — **verführend** As in the case of Paris. — **fechtend** In the Trojan War. — **entrückend** In her tortuous journey home (8989). —Demigods of Helena's past were Theseus and Achilles. Heroes were Menelaus and Paris. Of the gods, the one most concerned with Helena was Hermes-Mercury. The demoniac spirits have not been identified, although usually Phorkyas is named as one of them.

9254–9255 **Einfach** In her simple form, as she was abducted by Theseus and subsequently carried off by Paris. — **doppelt** In a second form (lines 8872–8873), when she was simultaneously in Troy and in Egypt. — **dreifach** In the form in which she has just returned to Sparta, there to cause new turmoil by her flight; and now, fourthly, she brings distress to poor Lynceus.

9257 **Gottbetörten** A god is concealed (or revealed) in beauty, and anyone under the spell of beauty is deluded by a god.

9259–9263 Faust refers to Helena's beauty as to a sure-shooting archer whose arrows (the darts of love) have first wounded Lynceus (*jenen,* 9261) and now wound Faust, and soon will wound all his retainers.

9274 Lynceus refers to himself as *der Reiche.* He accounts for his wealth in lines 9301–9306.

9280 His vision does not penetrate the beauty of this throne with its present occupant, whereas normally he could see through clouds and mountains with no difficulty at all.

9281–9296 The allusion is to the Migration of Peoples (375–568 A.D.), when great hosts of Germanic invaders overran the Roman states of the Western Empire.

9285–9288 There were a hundred men to take the place of anyone slain. Even a thousand killed was a loss no one noticed.

Notes

9307–9308 We take *der* of 9306 to be demonstrative = *dieser:* 'this jewel.' As Lynceus picks it up he says it is the most splendid of his loot. 'Now,' says Lynceus, 'only this emerald is worthy to adorn your breast.'

9309 **zwischen Ohr und Mund** The pearl pendant is to hang down from the Queen's diadem, over her cheek.

9310 **Tropfenei** A pearl shaped like a teardrop. — The first strophe of Goethe's "Buch der Parabeln" in the WESTÖSTLICHER DIWAN tells how a raindrop, falling into the sea, was changed into a pearl.

9317–9318 'However many chests I now bring, I still have many more.'

9319 This use of *erlaube* is unusual. One would expect *dulde:* 'Permit me to remain among your entourage.'

9324 **Gestalt** See line 8907. Another reference of this kind occurs in line 9352.

9326 **lose** In antithesis to *fest:* 'Now that I loosen my grasp upon it.'

9329–9332 No possessions are worth anything to Lynceus without the favor of his new queen.

9337–9345 Faust orders the erection and decoration of a resplendent rococo palace with paintings of unheard-of splendor: vaulted ceilings spotted with starlike jewels — paradise-like settings of artificial figures. Before Helena, as she walks, carpet upon carpet is to be unrolled; and on every hand such brilliance as only a God can endure is to meet her eye.

9338 **ungesehnen** 'Never before seen.'

9347 **gespielt** To do this is mere play for Lynceus.

9349 **Übermut** Has no pejorative meaning here, but means 'high spirits,' or 'proud glory.' Similarly in line 9410 *übermütiges* means 'proud, as they have a right to be.'

9359 Prose would be: *Erst laß die treue Widmung, die ich dir knieend bringe, dir gefallen, hohe Frau!* Faust dedicates himself to Helena, as a vassal to a queen.

9363 The realm in which Helena is queen is the realm of beauty. Since beauty conquers all, as has just been demonstrated, this kingdom has no limits.

9367 **die Rede** The words of Lynceus, last at 9346–9355, are rimed verses. These astonish Helena, in whose antique world rime was not used.

9380 Helena has asked (9377) to be taught how to speak in rimes. Faust teaches her by so shaping his sentences that each time the only appropriate completion involves a word which rimes with one he has just spoken. The process is described in the "Buch Suleika" of the WESTÖSTLICHER DIWAN:

> Behramgur, sagt man, hat den Reim erfunden.
> Er sprach entzückt aus reiner Seele Drang;
> Dilaram schnell, die Freundin seiner Stunden,
> erwiderte mit gleichem Wort und Klang.

9390–9392 See note to lines 8985–8989 for the story.

9396–9400 **Hirten ... Faunen** Datives, indicating the persons to whom women like these Trojan captives give themselves with equal alacrity.

9401 **sie** Faust and Helena.

9407 The object of *versagt* is *Offenbarsein* (9410). Their Majesties do not deny themselves proud public display before the eyes of the people.

9411–9412 **fern** and **nah,** like **verlebt** and **neu** (9415), reflect consciousness on the part of Helena that she belongs to two worlds, one remote and past, the other new and immediate. — The playful manipulation of end rimes (lines 9377–9384) is resumed, with the added feature of internal rimes: *fern : gern.* This continues through line 9418.

9416 Helena is not fully able to understand herself or what is happening to her. But her instinct of love moves her to devote herself with complete sincerity to this unknown Faust, as indeed she had given herself with complete sincerity to Menelaus, and again to the once equally unknown Paris.

9419–9434 Phorkyas can only intend by this package of falsehoods to work upon the emotions of Helena and thus to persuade her through fear to yield completely to Faust's love (see note to SD 9063). In this, Phorkyas is as blind to the real nature of Helena as Mephistopheles is blind to the real nature of Faust. Indeed, Phorkyas in her lack of patience with the dalliance of these two sensitive souls is as blind and as brutal as the Mephistopheles of the Gretchen episode. — Phorkyas' use of rime in this tirade is a satire of the riming efforts of Faust and Helena, 9411–9418.

9430 **Deiphobus** See note to line 9054.

9432 **die leichte Ware** The women of the chorus, who are to dangle from the rafters; see lines 8927–8929.

9433 **dieser** Helena.

SD 9441 These explosions come from Faust's army, which is preparing to defend the castle against an imaginary Menelaus. They do so at the behest, presumably, of Mephistopheles-Phorkyas. — Gunpowder was first used in Europe about 1350 A.D., and its use here is a part of the general commingling of medieval and ancient elements in this portion of the FAUST play. — It is impossible to say with certainty whether Faust himself believes in the fiction of Menelaus' threatened approach to his castle, or whether he is a party to the deception of Helena on this score.

9446 **angehaltnem stillen** The two adjectives are not coordinate, or each would have the ending *–em*: 'with a silent fury, which is restrained.'

9448–9451 The commander-in-chief is recognizing his army units as they appear before him. They are "present or accounted for." The North is represented by the Franks (9470), the Saxons (9471), and the Normans (Vikings) (9472). Perhaps the *Germanen* (9466) belong here too. The East is represented by the Goths (9469). — These Germanic tribes all participated in the conflicts of the Migration of Peoples and wrecked many of the older states of Europe, as they fought their way one after another to new homes or to ultimate extinction.

9450 **Strahl** The radiance of their polished armor seems to surround them (*umwittert*) with lightninglike brilliance.

9454 **Pylos** Principal harbor of the western shores of Messenia, once the home of Nestor. In the Trojan War Nestor was the oldest of the Grecian chiefs and looked to by all for advice. — The landing described here is appropriate rather to the fourth crusade (in the years 1202–1204) than to the Migration of Peoples, to which lines 9451–9453 best apply.

9459 **dem Meer** = *an das Meer* or *zu dem Meere.*

9460 See line 8857, where Menelaus is called *der kühne Seedurchstreicher.*

9462–9465 At the request of the Queen of Sparta, the leaders of the army are to become dukes in this land. They are to conquer mountain and valley, give it to their queen, and receive it back from her as her vassals to hold in fee. It is understood that this queen is also the queen of their own king.

9466 **Germane** Seems to be used here as the name of a Germanic tribe coordinate with such names as Goth, Frank, and Saxon. — *Corinth*, like Sparta, was a city-state; it was the principal city of Argolis. *Achaia* was a province west of Corinth, *Elis* a province west and south of Achaia. *Messene* was the province to the south, where they had landed at Pylos. *Argolis* is the province in the northeast of the Peloponnesus, in which Corinth is situated. — This disposition of fiefs and defensive assignments covers all of the Peloponnesus below the gulf of Corinth except Laconica, the province in which Sparta is located, and Arcadia, which is surrounded by the others named.

9472 Normans were Scandinavian vikings.

9477 In 1204 Norman, French, and Venetian knights built a stronghold at Mistra, near Sparta. Faust's castle, as it is here described, is usually associated with this structure at Mistra.

9478 **All-einzeln** may be construed with *sie* (*Sparta* 9476 or *Königin* 9477) 'the single, sole sovereign,' or with *euch* (9478) 'each and every one (of you).'

9493 **sich verband** He, being himself so valiant, judiciously made such alliances that the bravest and the strongest obey him.

9500 **sie** Helena.

9503 **die** Accusative plural, referring to the chorus.

9508 **sie** The leaders of the armies, with their troops.

9510–9513 These troops are to protect the peninsula which is (almost) surrounded by water and which is the last outlier of the Macedonian mountain range (the Pindus Mountains). This region is connected with the mainland only by the narrow isthmus of Corinth. Goethe's word *Nichtinsel* for *Halbinsel* emphasizes the almost completely insular coastline of the Peloponnesus.

9514 **vor aller Länder Sonnen** Means simply *vor allen Ländern.* The land which early looked upon Helena (9517) is Sparta.

9519 Jupiter, in the guise of a swan, visited Leda and begot Helena; so it is here assumed that the child emerged, chicklike, from a shell, in a nest among the whispering reeds of the Eurotas river. — The entire course of this river lies within the province of Laconica.

9520 **Geschwister** Castor and Clytemnestra were half-brother and half-sister of Helena; Pollux was Helena's full brother.

9521 **das Licht der Augen** 'the ability to see.' The infant Helena was such a brilliant phenomenon that the members of her family were dazzled by their first sight of her.

9522–9525 Faust asks Helena to stay in her native land, and begs her to give that country preference before all others of the earth, though these too now belong to her. — Although geographically it is Sparta to which these lines must refer, it is clear that poetically Goethe is beginning here to describe an ideal Arcadia — a mythical land of timeless happiness and perfection, where death is unknown.

9526–9529 Whenever at least a few rays of the sun can fall past the jagged summit of these mountains onto the main ridge, then vegetation will show green and goats will find their portion to eat. — These mountains are never completely barren, as are the mountains of the north.

9534 'Separately, cautiously, with measured step the horned cattle walk.'

9536 **den sämtlichen** 'for them all.'

9538 **Pan** See note to line 5804. Pan was regularly attended by the wood-nymphs who are called Dryads. The Oreads were the nymphs of the mountains and rocky caves. The nymphs are called *Lebensnymphen* here, perhaps because they were thought of as personifications of the forces that give animation to nature.

9552 **unsterblich** 'immortal,' because each perpetuates himself in his offspring, who remain in the ancestral abode.

9556–9557 In Arcadia men by their nature grow to perfection; they do not have to strive to achieve it. In this natural perfection men are indistinguishable from gods.

9558 **zugestaltet** 'made like in form, to dwell with.' — Jupiter punished Apollo for shooting arrows at the Cyclopes by making him live as a mortal for one year. Apollo became a shepherd in Thessaly, serving King Admetus. Upon another occasion, Apollo was made to herd cattle on Mt. Ida for King Laomedon.

9560–9561 The world of men and the world of gods commingle in free nature. Here things are what, by their nature, they should be without impairment (*rein*). — Faust exhorts Helena to forget the past events of her life and to remember her divine origin. The first world is probably to be thought of as that world in which the gods associated intimately with men, before the growing sinfulness and arrogance of men drove the immortals out of man's world. This may quite simply be called the world of nature.

9569 **Arkadien** Arcadia is the central province of the Peloponnesus, north of Laconica and Sparta. It has become the symbol for a place of rustic simplicity and untroubled quiet.

9570–9573 These lines anticipate the shift of scene from Sparta to Arcadia.

43. [ARKADIEN]

The function of this scene is to portray the union of Faust and Helena and its immediate consequences. The place of action is shifted northward from Faust's magic castle to the hills of Arcadia. There is an indeterminate interval of time between the end of the preceding scene and the beginning of this one.

This is the climax of Faust's search for sensuous beauty. This union is also the climax of artistic development, as Goethe wished to portray it.

Faust, the representative of the drive and strength of the northern, romantic spirit, is united with Helena, the representative of the sensuous beauty of classic antiquity. Their child is Euphorion, a genius of the highest aspirations and finest sensitivities, capable of attaining supreme artistic inspirations but not able to restrain himself from attempting the impossible, and thus becoming a victim finally of his own fine qualities.

The scene heading *Arkadien* is not found in the text as printed in Goethe's lifetime, nor is it in the manuscripts. It has been added by various editors, and we have retained it.

9578 **Bärtigen** As frequently happens in Greek comedy, this line is addressed to the audience. The Greek audience was composed wholly of grown men.

9582 These long, eight-beat lines are in the German form of the trochaic tetrameter, with the caesura normally after the eighth syllable. See note to line 8909.

9588 **Frauen** Singular, as also in line 9599.

9592 Phorkyas, behaving as a wise old woman should, gathers herbs, pretending to prepare medicines and ointments, but really just being discreet in her attendance upon the lovers.

9598 **auf einmal** The passage of time in the developments of these events is simply not indicated: it is not important, since Helena, as well as what she represents, is timeless. Her child is godlike, rather than human, a phantom grandchild of Jupiter (Zeus). The birth of Euphorion is a supernatural birth, and the rapidity of his development lies quite outside the natural limits of time. — This birth has been compared to the process of poetic creation, which some critics believe this scene to represent.

9603 **Genius** 'Genius' in this use, is the spirit of virility or masculine energy of an individual man with whom it is born and with whom it dies. The Romans worshipped the genius of the head of the house. By extension, the genius of the family becomes the genius of the town (*genius loci*). Sometimes ancient art depicted a genius as a near-human creature with wings.

9608 The impulse to attempt free flight symbolizes the impulse to transcend the limitations placed upon the human spirit by the finite, material existence which conditions the human being. Euphorion has no wings (9603), although he is the representative of the highest spiritual capacities of man. In his impulse to fly, Euphorion is a true son of Faust (see lines 1074, 1090 ff., 1116 ff.). In so far as Euphorion is thought of here as the spirit of poetry, the restrictions placed upon his free flight may be taken to reflect the aesthetic conviction that poetry may not with impunity depart from the firm foundation of reality.

9611 **Antäus** See note to line 7077.

9613 The metrical pattern of this line crosses the usual intonational and syntactic pattern of this kind of sentence. Metrically, there should be no stress on *so* and there should be a pause after it (caesura); syntactically, *so* should be separately stressed, not linked with *wie*. In the *Ausgabe letzter Hand* (1828) this line is printed without internal punctuation. Most editors have set a comma after *umher;* at least one has pointed the line to match the metrical pattern: . . . *und umher so, wie ein Ball* . . . It has also been suggested that the line be pointed: . . . *und umher — so, wie ein Ball* . . . In this conflict between the metrical and the logical pattern some critics see *Lautmalerei:* the suggestion of abrupt reboundings by the verse, to match the leaping of Euphorion.

9620 Apollo (Phoebus) provided music for the daily feasts of the Olympian gods by playing upon his lyre, while the muses sang to his playing.

9621 **Überhang** 'Overhang.' The edge of a cliff which projects beyond the vertical wall which supports it.

9623–9624 An aureole, or halo, is seen about the head of the boy.

9625 **Knabe** Nominative. — The boy gives evidence that he will become in the future the master of all things beautiful. He is the symbol of poetic art, as Goethe said to Eckermann (December 20, 1829): "Der Euphorion ist kein menschliches, sondern nur ein allegorisches Wesen. Es ist in ihm die Poesie personifiziert, die an keine Zeit, an keinen Ort und an keine Person gebunden ist."

9630 **Kretas Erzeugte** The chorus behaves as if it believes Phorkyas' story (lines 8864–8865) and her claim that she is a native of Crete.

9633 The Ionia of ancient times was a district on the west coast of Asia Minor. The home of the Ionians in Greece was especially the provinces of Attica, southern Boeotia and Euboea. The Ionians were the perfecters of Greek epic poetry, and the Homeric poems are preserved in an Ionian dialect, with some Aeolic forms, chiefly in proper names. Hence the legends of Ionia here referred to are the stories of Homer's ILIAD and ODYSSEY. — Hellas was originally the name of a little town and state in Thessaly, but became the collective name for all the states of Greece. The legends of Hellas, therefore, would include all Greek legends, and particularly those not found in Homer.

9644 **sang** The subject is *liebliche Lüge.* — **Sohn der Maja** Hermes (Mercury), whose birth and supernatural development is compared with that of Euphorion. Goethe follows Hederich's description of Mercury's babyhood quite closely.

9645 **zierlich . . . kräftig** As written, these words must be construed as adverbs, limiting *geborenen;* from the standpoint of meaning, they should be adjectives, *zierlichen . . . kräftigen*, qualifying *Säugling.*

9650 Their unreasonable expectation was that this infant should remain even briefly wrapped in swaddling clothes.

9655 **Schale** Like the integument of the chrysalis or pupa, which contains the insect in its torpid stage of development from larva (caterpillar) to imago (butterfly). The *Puppenzwang* of 9658 is imposed by this *Schale*.

9663   Mercury was the patron of gamblers and the god of chance, and he was himself at times a trickster and a thief.

9674   An unreal condition, brought up into the present time, as the other verbs here are historical present forms.

9678   **Gürtel** A magic band worn by Venus upon or around her breast. It had the power to create love-longing at the will of its wearer. According to the ILIAD (Book 14, 215), it was embroidered, presumably with magic-working symbols. It was rather a talisman than a girdle, as we understand that word.

9679–9686   Phorkyas sounds like Mephistopheles when she wants to hear nothing of the old Greek gods, and she sounds like Faust when she prescribes the proper conditions of poetic effectiveness. See lines 534–545 and 7175–7177.

9689   **genesen** Saved from death at the hands of Menelaus, as they believe. — The chorus is so carried away by the form of this scene that it too begins to phrase its song in rime.

SD 9695   Euphorion is the offspring of the union of Faust and Helena. The name is that of the child of Achilles and Helena in their union after death on the island of Leuce (see note to line 8876). The name apparently means "the agile one, the light one." The role of Euphorion is an exacting one, since it requires distinction of performance, both as a singer and as a dancer. It is usually taken by a woman, sometimes by two women.

9700   **sie** Redundant repetition of the subject *Liebe*.

9705   **so** Through their love and through their child, Euphorion.

9707   **Wohlgefallen** Reminiscent of Luke 3.22: "Du bist mein lieber Sohn, an dem ich Wohlgefallen habe." (See line 5629.) 'In the gentle radiance of the boy there is concentrated upon this pair the pleasurable satisfaction, the bliss of many years.'

9721–9722   Any disaster to this boy would destroy his parents' happiness. His excessive urge to fly aloft threatens this, and his father pleads for moderation. See also lines 9609–9611.

9731   **kränke** The subjunctive of implied indirect discourse after the imperative *denke!* Euphorion gives his parents pain by insisting that they release him. They ask him to think of their pain and also to think of the fact that he will destroy the trinity they have achieved if he insists upon leaving them.

9742   **Plan** 'Glade.' Euphorion's parents beseech him to adorn the glade in rustic placid quiet. They would like above all else to "freeze" this moment of joy into an everlasting tableau of beauty.

9745   **Leichter** Probably the comparative of *leicht*, 'very lightly.'

9767–9772   Euphorion proposes a new game to the girls. They are to pretend they are does from nearby. The whole party is in the outdoors of a mountain glen. He will be the hunter, they the hunted, and he wants no easy chase.

9774   **behende** The girls ask Euphorion not to hurry too much. They would like to prolong this delightful game.

9800 **In dieser Hülle** 'Within me.' The girl symbolizes Love, which the
spirit of poetry thinks he can snatch by physical force. Love,
however, is not subject to physical constraint.

9804 **im Gedränge** 'in a tight place,' 'cornered.'

SD 9808 Stage managers of Goethe's time, like modern magicians, delighted in play with fire. Here the girl is enveloped in flames.
Much of this fire falls upon the clothing of Euphorion, as the girl
is lifted aloft to dangle above him and to disappear from view.

9821 **muß** The compulsion lies in his own nature, the essential quality
of which is the inability to be satisfied with its achievements. In
this respect Euphorion's spirit is Faustian.

9824 **Insel** It looks like an island, but it is only almost (Latin *paene*) an
island = peninsula (see note to lines 9510–9513). This peninsula is
called the Peloponnesus, a Greek word which does indeed mean the
island of Pelops. — Pelops was the son of King Tantalus and the
father of Atreus. Thus he was the grandfather of Menelaus. —
Arcadia, where this scene is laid, is the central region of the Peloponnesus.

9826 The Peloponnesus is linked to the earth (the continent) by the
isthmus of Corinth, bound to the sea by all the rest of its perimeter.

9830 **Reben in Zeilen** Grapes cultivated in orderly rows in a vineyard,
as distinct from wild grapes which grow on the higher uncultivated
slopes of the hills.

9832 It is probable that Goethe meant *Apfelgold* to indicate 'oranges'
(*pomum aurantium*) rather than 'golden apples.'

9835 At this point the shift in Goethe's conception of Euphorion becomes
evident. After he had planned this scene and written a great deal
of it, the death of Lord Byron (1788–1824) moved him to transform
his Euphorion into a memorial to this young British poet, whose
poetry he so greatly admired. Some measure of his interest may be
seen in the fact that Byron was the subject of thirty-four discussions
in Goethe's conversations with Eckermann, while Shakespeare was
the subject of twenty-eight, Diderot of five, Dante of three, and
Corneille of two. The poetry of Byron's later period particularly
attracted Goethe, and all Europe was impressed by the manner of
his death.

After leaving England in 1816, Byron lived in Switzerland and in
Italy, where he took an active interest in the revolutionary movement of the Carbonari, then going on in Italy. In 1823 the Greeks
rose in rebellion against their Turkish rulers, and Byron volunteered
to fight in their war. He went from Genoa to Greece in July 1823,
landed on the island of Cephalonia and thence went to the seaport
town of Missolonghi. Here the rebels were encamped in the lowlands north of the Gulf of Patras. In 1824 Byron was appointed
commander of the Greek forces for an expedition against Lepanto,
but he was seized with a fever and died after a brief illness. His
heart is buried in Missolonghi, where a statue marks the spot.

Euphorion passes with miraculous rapidity through the stages
of infantile delight in vocal expression and muscular movement
(9598–9613), childish pleasure in costumes and toys (9617–9624),
satisfaction in skilled muscular coordination (9625–9628), boyish

gratification in adults' reactions to his charming remarks (9679–9698), teen-age enjoyment of independence in act and motion (9711–9728), adolescent excitement in the first discoveries of sex (9745–9810), youthful *Wanderlust* (9811–9834), the young man's aspiration to achieve fame for himself, through the swift accomplishment of military marvels in the cause of idealism (9835–9876). Later (9897–9902), there is a hint of the final stage of Euphorion's brief symbolic life: the dedication to intellectual and artistic striving which is the lot of the mature man of genius. — Euphorion perishes at the beginning of this phase; the Faust of the opening monologue (354 ff.) was revealed to us in a moment of middle-aged frustration, when he had seemingly exhausted the possibilities of the intellectual approach to achievement. In a sense, Euphorion's career supplies a foreshortened summary of Faust's development before the opening of the play.

Here, at line 9835, Euphorion is at the stage where sex, adventure, idealistic self-sacrifice in war, and poetic endeavor are components of his aspirations. Thus depicted, Euphorion is an irresistible analogy to Lord Byron as Goethe envisaged his young British contemporary.

9843–9850 This passage is difficult, primarily because of line 9847, where the first word has been variously transmitted as *den*, *dem*, and *mit*. It seems probable that Goethe intended the form to be *den*, as we print it, and if so, *den Sinn* is in apposition to *Gewinn* (9850). We have to take *den Kämpfenden* (9849) as antecedent of *welche* (9843). Matters are still further complicated by *alle* (9849) which can only be the invariable, uninflected form of this word, where a dative plural would be the usual form. The subject of the optative *bring'* is *es*, which means the free expenditure of patriotic blood by the Greeks in the revolution against the Turks, but there is no grammatical antecedent for *es* in this context. — Thus the whole speech appears to mean: 'To those whom this land brought forth from one danger into another, — being free, of unlimited courage, and prodigal in the expenditure of their own blood, — may this (their warlike action) bring to (Greeks and) all fighters the profit and advantage of a sacred purpose which cannot be subdued.'

9861 **Amazonen** A race or nation of female warriors, usually said to have lived in Asia Minor. They were enemies of the ancient Greeks.

9866 'Distant and thus (as it continues to rise toward Heaven) more distant still.' The figure of Euphorion moves farther and farther away as the watching chorus sings.

9873 **getan** In the pregnant sense: 'done something important, achieved great things, done great deeds.'

9897 **Flügelpaar** Euphorion imagines himself to have the power to do what he so strongly wills to do. He is deceiving himself when he thinks he has wings, as the following stage direction shows.

9901 **Ikarus** Son of Daedalus, a skillful engineer. Minos of Crete imprisoned them both. Daedalus built two pairs of wings, one for his son and one for himself, to permit them to escape from their prison. However, after they were well on their way, the boy, with an excess of exuberance in his new-found capacity for flight, soared too high;

the heat of the sun melted the wax which held his wings in place, and he fell to his death.

SD 9902   The well-known figure is that of Lord Byron. The aureole is the halo of light (see 9623–9624) which surrounded Euphorion. The aureole was the symbol of great intellectual and spiritual powers.

9907–9938   This choral song is an ode to Lord Byron. Its artistic justification as part of this scene is the spiritual affinity between Lord Byron, as Goethe conceived his character, and Euphorion. Goethe spoke of this to Eckermann (July 5, 1827): "Mich soll nur wundern," sagte Goethe lachend, "was die deutschen Kritiker dazu sagen werden; ob sie werden Freiheit und Kühnheit genug haben, darüber hinweg zu kommen. Den Franzosen wird der Verstand im Wege sein, und sie werden nicht bedenken, daß die Phantasie ihre eigenen Gesetze hat, denen der Verstand nicht beikommen kann und soll. Wenn durch die Phantasie nicht Dinge entständen, die für den Verstand ewig problematisch bleiben, so wäre überhaupt zu der Phantasie nicht viel. Dies ist es, wodurch sich die Poesie von der Prosa unterscheidet . . ." — What this choral ode says is said equally of Lord Byron and of all poets as poets. It is both specific and general in its import.

9924   **ins willenlose Netz**   The allusion is to Byron's collision with the social canons of Britain in his time. This network of social propriety is spoken of as being without will. It did not itself willingly contribute to Byron's trouble; in other words, Byron was at fault. His young manhood was spent in dissipation. His wife, who married him in 1815, left him immediately after the birth of their first and only child, and society drove Byron out of England in 1816.

9927   **das höchste Sinnen**   Byron's resolve to devote himself to the lofty cause of Greek independence.

9932   **der**   The antecedent is *Frage:* 'the question from which.' When confronted with this question, fate hides herself away in a disguise.

9935   **erfrischet**   'renew'   Like *steht* this is imperative, addressed by the chorus to itself and to all the audience as well.

9937   **sie**   Poets like Euphorion-Byron.

9939   Helena reverts to a classic meter, this time iambic trimeter. See note to line 8488 and Volume I, Introduction, p. 140.

9940   This line occasioned Goethe great difficulty. The manuscripts show eleven different versions, the last having been decided upon only minutes before the completed copy was sent to the printer. The basic trouble was that the syntax required a plural verb and the meter required a final stressed syllable. — Incidentally, the word *Schönheit* (spoken by Helena) is the last occurrence of this word in Faust, if we except the compound *Seelenschönheit* (referring to Gretchen) at 10 064.

9941   'The bond which ties me to life, as well as the bond which links me to your love, is torn asunder' (by the death of Euphorion).

9944   **Persephoneia**   Proserpine, the queen of the nether world.

SD 9945   The content of lines 9945–9953 has seemed to many readers quite incongruous with the character of Phorkyas-Mephistopheles. The lines would come more naturally from the Chorus, and one editor (Fiedler) has changed the stage direction from *Phorkyas* to *Chor*.

9950–9953 The external garments of Helena are taken to symbolize the outward form of classical poetry. Even this outward form has the power to lift Faust far above all things trivial and mean.

SD 9955 The cast-off trappings of Euphorion are the *exuviae* of the spirit of poetry, the outer symbols of the poetic craft. Mephistopheles-Phorkyas can pass these out in such a way as to create envy and strife among groups or schools of professional poets. This is therefore construed to be a satirical thrust at imitators of great poets, not solely at the imitators of Byron.

9962 Zauber The spell under which Phorkyas had placed them all.

9963 The reference to Phorkyas as a Thessalian hag is not genealogical evidence, but merely brands her as a very potent evil witch.

9964 Geklimpers The allusion is to the instrumental music and perhaps also to the rimed verses which have been heard through most of the just completed operatic portion of this act (9679–9938).

9966 Hinab zum Hades! It was the duty and an honor for servants to follow their master or mistress in death. These servants, particularly, belong in Hades, because they had come from there when Faust brought Helena to the upper world.

9969 The throne of Pluto and Persephoneia (Proserpine).

9975 Asphodelos-Wiesen The meads of asphodel were barren or at best sparsely covered with hopelessly dormant bushes and the pale-flowered weeds called asphodel. These resemble daffodils. — It was on this mead that the souls of the dead were wont to stroll.

9979 Fledermausgleich An allusion to the ODYSSEY (24, 5–9), where the souls follow Hermes like bats, fluttering or making shrill noises in a dark cave.

9981–9984 Panthalis consigns these anonymous ladies of the chorus to their original elements. — Goethe had the quite serious conviction that a man's chance for personal immortality depended upon his achievement of something notable in this life (*Verdienst*) and upon his steadfastness and fidelity of character (*Treue*). (Letter to Knebel, Dec. 3, 1781, and conversation with Eckermann, Sept. 1, 1829). Goethe believed in immortality in the sense that: "If I actively strive throughout my life, then Nature is obligated to assign to me another form of existence, whenever my present one becomes insufficient for my spirit." (To Eckermann, Feb. 4, 1829.) He expected to labor and to strive until "the world-spirit shall summon us to return to the ethereal realms" of a new life, where new activities await us, and he hoped never to cease to be a part in the operation of the universe. He did not believe in a heaven where the body is resurrected from the grave, or in a hell where departed souls remain forever without change. (See letter to C. F. Zelter, March 19, 1827.)

9985 Zurückgegeben The women of the chorus do not have to return to the darkness of Hades, whence they but lately came with Helena. They are now spirits, natural spirits, or spirits of nature.

9992–9998 These ladies have become the spirits of trees, or trees with spirits. They are therefore Dryads.

9997 The two reflexives (*sich*) have to be taken with *versammeln* in 9996; *drängend* is used intransitively here, as in 8703 and 10 457.

9999–10 004 The members of the second group of the chorus have become mountain spirits and have taken up their abode at the foot of a rocky cliff whence they send back echoes of every sound they hear. These we may call Oreads.

10 000 One would expect *schmiegen wir uns an.* — The waves are sound waves.

10 002 **furchtbarer Stimme** Dative, like *jedem Laute*, dependent upon *lauschen: Wir lauschen jedem Laute, (sei es) Vogelsängen, Röhrigflöten, sei es Pans furchtbarer Stimme.*

10 005–10 010 The third group has become a brook or the water spirits in a brook. These may be called Naiads.

10 009 The cypress trees mark the location of the house with the garden.

10 011 The fourth group becomes spirits of the vineyard. They watch the always uncertain success of the winegrower's efforts toward a successful crop and a good vintage. The most indispensable factor is good sunlight in quantity. This song develops into a Bacchanalian hymn to the wine harvest. — These four groups of "Spirits" may be associated further with the four elements — earth, air, water, fire — and the little scene then may be said to represent the resolution of organic forms (the women of the chorus) into "Nature," or into the elements. The parallel is not a close one, but some critics have associated these lines with Goethe's two poems, *Die Metamorphose der Pflanzen* (1798) and *Metamorphose der Tiere* (1806/1810).

10 017 **der Weichling** Bacchus, as a young boy, was said to have been of delicate appearance. He was usually also very easygoing and inclined to be sleepy-eyed.

10 029 **widerlich zerquetscht** 'Crushed into a repulsive mass.'

10 031 The mysteries of Dionysos were the rites proper to the worship of Bacchus. These are in part described here.

10 032 Satyrs with goat's feet were regular members of Bacchus' retinue. Their cloven hoofs are mentioned in 10 034.

10 033 Silenus was the potbellied, erstwhile tutor of the infant Bacchus. He commonly rode about on a long-eared ass.

SD 10 038 Goethe apparently never wrote any formal commentary for his Phorkyas at this point. In stage productions the 'commentary' is usually a gesture signifying: "I did it; what do you think of it?" — Mephistopheles-Phorkyas has dissolved the Greek adventure of Faust — his quest for the ultimately beautiful — into a hymn of Dionysian revelry; and this magnificent scene ends in much the same state as did the scene in Auerbach's Keller. Here as there, the final note is *das Gemeine,* and is in sharp contrast with Faust's aspirations.

Act IV

Concerning this fourth act, which was the last part of the whole poem to be written, Goethe said to Eckermann (February 13, 1831): "Ich werde nun diese ganze Lücke, von der Helena bis zum fertigen fünften Akt, durcherfinden und in einem ausführlichen Schema niederschreiben, damit ich sodann mit völligem Behagen und Sicherheit ausführen und an den Stellen arbeiten kann, die mich zunächst anmuten. Dieser Akt bekommt wieder einen ganz eigenen Charakter, sodaß er, wie eine für sich bestehende kleine Welt, das Übrige nicht berührt und nur durch einen leisen Bezug zu dem Vorhergehenden und Folgenden sich dem Ganzen anschließt."

As finally written, Act IV links the Emperor of Act I with Faust's last ambitious scheme of action in Act V. The colonization of new land, wrested from the sea by feats of engineering skill, can only be undertaken with the Emperor's permission. To gain this permission, Faust and Mephistopheles save the Emperor from the party which is seeking to overthrow his power. This major action of Act IV is preceded by a transitional scene.

44. Hochgebirg

Faust is returning from Greece to Germany. He has been transported by the cloud which developed out of Helena's robes (SD 9954). The trip has required a number of days (10 042), during which Mephistopheles has followed along on the ground, using seven-league boots to try to keep pace with Faust's flight. No special 'high mountains' have to be identified here; but presumably this *Hochgebirg* would lie in the Austrian or Tyrolean Alps, north and west of Faust's Greek point of departure.

The effect of Faust's Grecian sojourn is reflected in the verse form in which he speaks, the trimeter. With the arrival of Mephistopheles, however, the lines go over into the rimed Faust verse (or *Knittelvers*) and rimed five-beat iambic lines. Toward the end of the act there is a further shift to the Alexandrine.

10 044 **geballtem** These are cumulus clouds.

10 050 **Junonen, Ledan, Helenen** Datives with *ähnlich*. The series represents a progressive development of the definition of this shape and its recognition by Faust. Juno was the sister and wife of Jupiter; Leda, the mother of Helena. Of Juno Faust has only vague conceptions, of Leda he has dreamed, with Helena he has lived.

10 052 Stratus clouds appear with the cumulus clouds.

10 053 **in Osten** Like *nach Osten* (10 044), *von Osten* (9281), without the article. The form *im Osten* (7620) is more in accord with modern usage.

10 054 **Sinn** The 'meaning' of his brief union with Helena.

10 057 The *es*, while it does not refer directly to the *Nebelstreif* above, does refer to a similar configuration of clouds forming themselves into images from Faust's memories. — The cloud formations here are cirrus clouds.

10 059 The allusions here are to his first love, Gretchen. — **als** 'in the form of.'

10 061 **Aurorens Liebe** Aurora was the rosy-fingered goddess of the morn. Faust's first love of Gretchen is thus symbolized. — The subject of *bezeichnet* is the same shifting cloud formation referred to by *es* in 10 057. *Leichten Schwung* is also the object of *bezeichnet*, as is *Blick* in 10 062.

10 063 **überglänzte** Subjunctive past, in an implied unreal condition. 'If one held fast this first moment of awareness of pure love, this would outshine every treasure.'

10 064 **steigert sich** 'becomes increasingly perfect.'

10 066 This amounts to an evaluation of the relative worth of pure and unselfish human love and of the artistic quest for perfect beauty: Margarete versus Helena. The former attracts the best qualities of Faust's being.

SD 10 067 Seven-league boots belong to northern legend; and Mephistopheles, who arrives in them, first speaks in the northern *Knittelvers* of four beats, but soon shifts to rimed five-beat iambic lines.

10 067 **endlich** Used here in an older meaning: 'vigorously, quickly.'

10 069–10 070 Mephistopheles, who is physically lazy, finds fault with the rocky mountain summit on which Faust has alighted, although he recognizes it as having once been a part of the abyss of Hell. Goethe reverts momentarily to the Vulcanist theories earlier represented by Anaxagoras and Seismos, and has them satirized by Mephistopheles. The cosmography upon which Mephistopheles bases his remarks is that of the early Church Fathers, as formulated by the Jesuit archaeologist Athanasius Kircher (1601–1680).

10 075 **warum** The reason was the revolt of Lucifer, who with his followers tried by force to seize control of affairs in Heaven, and who was on that account

> hurled headlong flaming from th' ethereal sky,
> with hideous ruin and combustion down
> to bottomless perdition . . .
>
> [Milton, PARADISE LOST, I, 45–47.]

What Goethe intended to imply by the parenthetical clause — *ich weiß auch wohl, warum* — cannot be said with certainty. In any event, Mephistopheles concedes the necessity of the expulsion and he may mean to indicate that the rebellion was so powerful, and the rebels so implacable, that they could not be dealt with in any other way.

Notes

10 087   **Zipfel**   The idiom: *etwas beim rechten Zipfel fassen* 'to tackle a thing in the right way,' seems to underlie this use of *an einem andern Zipfel haben*, which would thus mean: 'to manage things differently.' The devils who blew up their prison have escaped in this volcanic upheaval.

10 089   **Sie**   The Vulcanists or Plutonists, whose doctrines Goethe satirized.

10 092   The devils, among whom Mephistopheles reckons himself, now reign with complete freedom of movement and are no longer confined in the bottomless pit. This is a secret open to all, but not revealed to the peoples of earth until quite late in their history. The reference to Ephesians 6.12 is to the admonition of Paul to his followers in Ephesus: "Put on the whole armor of God, that ye may be able to stand against the wiles of the devil . . . Against principalities, against the powers, against the world rulers of this darkness, against the spiritual hosts of wickedness in the heavenly places," or as Luther put it: "Mit den bösen Geistern unter dem Himmel." In terms of Goethe's days, this may be taken as a satirical reference to Satanic evil in the high places of state and church.

10 095   For Faust, these mountains are the awe-inspiring, mysterious manifestations of nature's creative mastery, which he accepts with reverence, and into the secrets of which he is not disposed to inquire.

10 097   **sich in sich selbst**   Out of its own materials, the form arising from the organization of substances present in primeval chaos.

10 098   **rein**   Without the intervention of forces not her own.

10 102   **gemildet** = *gemildert* 'made gentle.' By diminishing the elevation gradually, nature has made the hill fuse into the valley. Other forms like *gemildet* are *verlängt* (10 147) and *kraftbegeistet* (10 216).

10 104   **Strudeleien**   Those eruptive, uncontrolled forces to which the Plutonists ascribe the form of the earth's surface.

10 106   **der** = *derjenige, der*   Mephistopheles now speaks as though he had adopted the views of the Vulcanists of Goethe's time. Faust, in lines 10 122–10 123, speaks as Goethe might speak of these views.

10 109   **Moloch**   The name comes from Leviticus 18.21. He was the national god of the Ammonites, the consuming, destroying, and yet purifying fire. Klopstock, in his *Messias*, made Moloch a vassal of Satan, a giant spirit who piled mountain upon mountain to make himself a fortress from which the sounds of thunder come as he labors. Goethe gave him a hammer, like that of Thor. The great erratic blocks of rock are explained as "chips," so to speak, which flew from mountains under Moloch's hammer blows.

10 116–10 121   The common people see in these unusual rock formations the work of supernatural forces; and since these were obviously violent, terrifying forces, people name these rocks "Devil's Rock," "Devil's Bridge" and so on. — Probably the best known of many *Teufelsbrücken* is the one near St. Gotthard's pass, between Göschenen and Andermatt.

10 120   By speaking of the *Wandrer* as *"mein,"* Mephistopheles expresses his approval of these common people, who call rocks by his name.

10 125   Mephistopheles insists upon his own explanation. His honor is at stake, he says, since he was an eyewitness, and the rejection of his testimony would make him out a liar.

10 127   **Zeichen**   The huge erratic blocks of line 10 110.

10 129   **unsrer**   Mephistopheles speaks as though he were the "ruler of this world" (John 12.31).

10 131   The first eleven verses of the fourth chapter of Matthew deal with the temptation of Christ by the Devil, and it is particularly verses 8 and 9 which seem more or less pertinent here. "Again the devil taketh him unto an exceeding high mountain, and showeth him all the kingdoms of the world and the glory of them; and he said unto him: All these things will I give thee, if thou wilt fall down and worship me."

10 135–10 136   Faust asks Mephistopheles to guess what has attracted him; and Mephistopheles, as usual, reasons from his own inclinations. Mephistopheles, if he were to follow his own bent, would hunt up a metropolitan city.

10 137   **Bürger-Nahrungs-Graus**   Has been taken in two ways, because *Graus* can mean either 'a heap of rubble' or 'a horror.' When *Graus* is taken to mean 'a horror,' *Nahrung* then becomes 'nourishment,' and the whole a synonym for a repulsive public market. Since this is specifically mentioned in 10 139, it seems unlikely that what Mephistopheles calls a *'beschränkten Markt'* could two lines earlier have been called *Bürger-Nahrungs-Graus.* Hence it appears more reasonable to take the compound of 10 137 to mean the complex of buildings at the center of an old city, where men busy themselves at their jobs to earn a living. — The market place is usually at or near the center of this business section. Until the time of Napoleon, German cities were mainly confined within the limits of their medieval walls. Hence most of them have an unusually crowded central district near the market place. This was true, for example, of Frankfurt, Nürnberg, Strassburg, München, Köln, and Heidelberg. In other cities, such as Leipzig, Dresden, and Mannheim, energetic city planning in the later eighteenth century had eliminated these congested areas and replaced them with wide squares and avenues. About 1800 many cities, particularly in western and southwestern Germany, began to expand beyond their old city walls.

10 142   **du**   Mephistopheles is speaking rather of and to himself than to Faust. Or, one may take *findest du = findet man.*

10 148–10 151   Outside the city gates, the gay young bloods disport themselves in light carriages with fast horses and in general there is great activity of merrymakers. Mephistopheles thinks he (and Faust) would enjoy all this. — **Hin- und Widerrutschen** The rapid movement back and forth of fine carriages, as well as the constant going and coming of pedestrians (*Hin- und Widerlaufen*).

10 159   Faust sounds like a disillusioned benevolent despot, whose subjects, despite all his benign care, would rather not be subjects. The more people learn, the more inclined they are to object to

authority over them. This is a view toward which Goethe, as he grew older, was increasingly inclined.

10 160 A reflection of the extravagances of Louis XIV and his successor, the regent Philip, Duke of Orleans, who set an example of the most shameless fiscal excesses. In Germany, similar arrogant display of princely extravagance is to be seen in Schönbrunn, Sans Souci, Nymphenburg, and many castles and parks with French names, such as Solitude, Favorite, Monrepos.

10 161 **Schloß zur Lust** = *Lustschloß* A country seat designed for royal recreation and amusement.

10 163 **umbestellt** Of such geometrically arranged "French Gardens," the Wilhelmshöhe (near Kassel) was particularly famous in Goethe's time.

10 168 **steigt es** The water of one of the fountains shoots up in the center, while numerous smaller jets play in a circle around it.

10 171 Many European princes of the eighteenth century built "garden houses" and park palaces for their mistresses.

10 173 **geselliger Einsamkeit** 'sociable solitude.' An oxymoron, meaning isolation from all else save the company one desires.

10 176 Sardanapalus is sometimes identified with Ashur-bani-pal, Emperor of Assyria 668–626 B.C. Lord Byron dedicated his tragedy SARDANAPALUS as follows: "To the illustrious Goethe, a stranger presumes to offer the homage of a literary vassal to his liege lord, the first of existing writers, who has created the literature of his own country, and illustrated that of Europe. The unworthy production which the author ventures to inscribe to him is entitled, Sardanapalus." Byron's Sardanapalus is an effeminate voluptuary, but not an ignoble man. — The term 'modern' is used to point the contrast between Mephistopheles' lewdness and the healthy, sensuous delight of antiquity.

10 177 **strebtest** Mephistopheles refers to Faust's flight through the air with which he was unable to keep pace (SD 10 067).

10 179–10 180 There is a play here on the word *mondsüchtig*, 'moonstruck.' *Sucht* is identical with the *Streben* alluded to in line 10 177.

10 188 This is the central thought in Goethe's philosophy. See note to line 9981–9984.

10 189–10 191 If Faust achieves power and possessions, then, says Mephistopheles, there will be poets who, by their portrayal of Faust's successes, will induce others of a later day to emulate Faust in this 'folly.'

10 192 Mephistopheles, "der Geist des Widerspruchs, der stets verneint," cannot view with sympathy or approval the positive, constructive striving of a man like Faust. He regards Faust's desire for great deeds for their own sake as silly (line 10 191). Faust tells him here, as he had told him before (1675–1677), that he, Mephistopheles, has no comprehension of human aspirations.

10 202 Faust feels that the sea, by intruding upon the low-lying shore, has violated the rights of this shore, and he resolves to put a stop to this usurpation. Faust compares his vexation with the distress

and anger which assail a free spirit when confronted by an act of haughty presumption (*Übermut*). A free spirit cherishes all rights and hates all violations of rights. These lines reveal a more mature attitude toward the rights of others than the opening monologue of Part I.

10 210 Mephistopheles here proves that, for him, tides are tides and that he does not at all comprehend Faust or understand Faust's motives.

10 212 **Sie** = *die Woge* (10 207).

10 215 **widerlich** Because it is *wüst*.

10 219 This waste of energy is the antithesis of intelligent management, and this is what challenges Faust now.

10 223–10 226 The waters steal around every bit of higher land and pour off through every depression. This suggests to Faust that dike and drain are the instruments with which to achieve this conquest.

10 228 **dir** Faust. — **erlange** Imperative: 'acquire for yourself the precious delight.'

10 239 **Fauste** The Latin form for the vocative case of *Faust* suggests the meaning of the Latin adjective *faustus* 'fortunate, lucky,' as a *double entendre* in Mephistopheles' exhortation.

10 259 **Genießen** Here, as in 10 251, the antithesis of *regieren* or *herrschen*. The idea is that the ruler must be a solitary man, whereas the enjoyment of anything requires the companionship of equals: the two things are antithetical.

10 260 **Er** The Emperor, who need not be further identified. — In Germany, the kind of anarchy here described was most violent in the years 1256–1273.

10 268 **Vor den Toren** Outside the city gates the traveling merchants had no protection except their own arms.

10 280 **wählen** 'choose' (a new emperor).

10 281 **den neuen Kaiser** Object of *laßt*, understood from line 10 280. The two infinitives *beseelen* and *vermählen* depend upon this *laßt*: 'Let the new Emperor give new spirit to the empire.'

10 284 **Fried' und Gerechtigkeit** An allusion to Psalm 85.10: "Righteousness and peace will kiss each other."

10 285 **Pfaffen** The princes of the Church. — The Archbishops of Mainz, of Trier, and of Cologne were among the seven electors to whom the election of the emperor was entrusted by the Golden Bull of 1356. In practice, these elections became struggles of power politics, in which the three clerical electors often held the balance of power. In this instance they have given their support to the counter-emperor.

10 294 The idea is that if the Emperor is saved this once, the result will be the same as if he were saved a thousand times: that is, he will be saved permanently.

10 302–10 303 'Make yourself more secure in your grand plans by considering your ultimate purpose.' By keeping his own goal in mind, Faust can now make more certain the achievement of the great things he plans.

10 305   Goethe wrote eleven lines in which the Chancellor pronounced
and the Emperor confirmed the bestowal of a fief upon Faust.
The lines were not included in the final form of the poem.   They
are:

> DER KANZLER *liest:*
>
> Sodann ist auch vor unserm Thron erschienen
> Faustus, mit Recht der Glückliche genannt,
> denn ihm gelingt, wozu er sich ermannt,
> schon längst bestrebsam, uns zu dienen,
> schon längst als klug und tüchtig uns bekannt.
>
> Auch heut am Tage glückt's ihm, hohe Kräfte,
> wie sie der Berg verschließt, hervorzurufen,
> erleichternd uns die blutigen Geschäfte.
> Er trete näher den geweihten Stufen!
> Den Ehrenschlag empfang' er!
>
> *Faust kniet.*
>
> KAISER
> > > Nimm ihn hin!
> Duld ihn von keinem andern!

10 314   **Feldmarschall** = *Obergeneral* (10 310)   Faust.

10 315–10 316   In the antithesis between *Kriegsunrat* and *Kriegsrat*, the
incongruity resides in the two meanings of *-rat* represented.   One
of these terms is by no means the mere negative of the other, as
is the case with *Unsinn : Sinn*.   The English antithesis between
counsel and council, — war's ill counsel, and council of war, —
lacks the sharpness of the German contrast between *Unrat* and
Rat. — One has to supply *habe ich* with *formiert*.

10 320   **Bergvolk** = *Berggeister* 'trolls.'

10 321–10 322   **Peter Squenz**   The German form of Shakespeare's Peter
Quince (A MIDSUMMER-NIGHT'S DREAM), the hero of the ABSURDA
COMICA ODER HERR PETER SQUENTZ, SCHIMPFF-SPIEL of Andreas
Gryphius.   Peter Squenz was the manager and director of the play
within the play, and indeed the one person without whom it could
not have taken place, hence the *Quintessenz* (Latin *quinta essentia*),
the 'fifth essence' of the play. — The ancient Greeks recognized four
elements (fire, air, water, and earth).   The Pythagoreans added a
fifth element and called it "ether," the fifth essence.   The alchemists sometimes considered alcohol the fifth essence.

SD 10 323   In 2 Samuel 23.8–11 three mighty men of Israel are named
and described; they are David's chief reliance in his wars with the
Philistines.   The names *Raubebald* and *Eilebeute* occur in the German translation of Isaiah 8.1 and 3, where they are prescribed
by the Lord as the names which must be given to a son of Isaiah.

10 327   The reference is to the predilection for medieval subjects which
began in German literature in 1796 and culminated in the works
of Richard Wagner (1813–1883).

10 331–10 344   These allegorical figures represent the evolution of the
predator: *Raufebold*, the youth, who fights for the sake of fighting;

Habebald, the mature realist, whose chief motive is acquisitive; *Haltefest*, the old man, who tries to keep what he has got hold of. Their weapons are increasingly numerous and their clothing increasingly scant as their age increases.

45. Auf dem Vorgebirg

The dramatic function of this scene is to portray the assistance which Faust gives to the Emperor in overcoming his foes. This aid, although unasked and accepted with misgivings because of its evident supernatural features, puts the Emperor under the obligation of gratitude to Faust.

10 348   **uns glückt die Wahl**   The General hopes that 'the choice will prove favorable for us.'

10 360   **den Phalanx**   The battle line of the heavy infantry in contrast to that of the light infantry or that of the cavalry. — Goethe treats *Phalanx* here, as in 10 519, 10 530, 10 646, as a masculine noun, but at 10 595 as a feminine, which is the Greek gender of the noun and now the required gender in German.

10 363   **Quadrat**   The square formation of the massed infantry. This one appears to be a solid rather than a hollow square.

10 364   **auf große Tat**   Men by the thousands in this square are aglow with eagerness to achieve a great victory.

10 368   **Doppelzahl**   An army thus disposed can deal with an enemy twice its size.

10 375   These false kin are the Emperor's vassals, who in the florid chancellery style of those days would address him in their letters as brother, uncle, cousin, and the like, regardless of whether or not they were in fact blood relatives of the ruler.

10 380   This revolt is described in lines 10 277–10 290.

10 383   The information sought by this "spy" was not information about the activities of the enemy, but rather whether or not certain vassals would remain loyal.

10 391–10 392   Elliptical. These vassal princes have done nothing on behalf of the Emperor. Their excuse is that they have been having troubles suppressing rebellions in their own domains.

10 395–10 396   The Emperor speaks to these absent subjects, who have failed to come to his aid, and reminds them that if they close out their accounts with him (*voll* = *geschlossen*), the destruction of their neighbor's house will surely bring destruction to their own. — **Hausbrand**   An allusion to the lines of Horace (Epistulae, I, 10, 84–85) "For it is your business when your neighbor's wall is aflame; and flames neglected usually gain strength." — **soll** Connotes the constraint of the force of circumstances: 'must in the nature of the case.'

10 399   He was pleased because he thought he was going to be able to report the great confusion of the enemy. Then the new leader appeared.

10 407–10 410   The Emperor has set out on this campaign as a soldier to
put down an uprising in his empire. Now his very right to the
name of Emperor is challenged, and his campaign has acquired a
larger purpose. He has a personal adversary in the person of the
Pretender.

10 412   Speaking of past festivities at his court, the Emperor says that
he himself had been the only one to feel any lack of anything; he
had found no opportunity to expose himself to danger. Instead
of the dangerous tournaments his fathers fought, his knights in-
sisted upon his playing the harmless and quite safe game of tilting
at the ring.

10 417   **besiegelt** 'Stamped with the seal of independence.'

10 418   **dort** At the masque; see lines 5934–5969.

10 422   **versäumt** 'Has been neglected.'

SD 10 422   Here the stage business requires some additional dialogue or
pantomime to make clear the intent of the poet to an audience
which has no text of the play before it.

10 423   **ungescholten** 'Without reproach.' The predicate of an incom-
pletely expressed clause after *hoffen*, perhaps *ungescholten zu sein*.

10 424   **Vorsicht** = *Voraussicht* 'ability to foresee.' This refers to the
'vision' of the Necromancer of Norcia (10 450–10 452).

10 425   **Bergvolk** 'Mountain dwellers,' 'trolls,' skilled in geognosy. They
have withdrawn from the flat country to avoid the advance of city
culture and have learned to discern mineral deposits in the mountains from outward signs in the rocks. — **simuliert** Taken by
Goethe from popular speech in the sense of 'rack their brains,
ponder,' instead of the now current sense 'pretend, feign.'

10 426   **studiert** 'well versed in.'

10 430   An allusion to the belief that all minerals in the earth's crust
originally occurred in gaseous form before becoming solids.

10 432–10 436   These mountain people are said to create crystals and
engage in crystal gazing. — The passage suggests the extensive
fairy-tale literature produced in Goethe's time by Novalis, E. T. A.
Hoffmann, and Henrik Steffens. This kind of tale was prompted
by the activities and early fame of the Mining Institute at Freiberg
(Saxony). Goethe was closely associated with A. G. Werner,
director of that Institute.

10 439   The Necromancer of Norcia is an invention of Goethe. — There
was an Italian necromancer, by the name of Cecco, who was burned
at the stake in Florence in 1327. Norcia is the name of a town in
the Sabine hills of the Apennines. This region in the Middle Ages
had the same kind of reputation as did Thessaly in antiquity; it
was regarded as the home of black magic. The fiction here is that
this particular necromancer had been condemned by the church to
die by burning at the stake, and was to have been executed on the
day on which our Emperor was crowned in Rome. The newly
crowned Emperor pardoned the necromancer and since that day
the latter has been devoted to the Emperor's cause.
Furthermore, this necromancer is a fiction of Faust, who intends
thereby to disarm the Emperor's natural reluctance to accept help

from supernatural sources other than God. The Emperor can believe that the Necromancer wishes to repay an old debt and does not have to regard this promised magic as the wiles of the Devil.

10 461 zur Morgenstunde Help which comes on the morning of a day of decisive action is help in time to be useful. — **bedenklich** 'critically,' 'precariously,' because the issue is still in doubt, or because the hour is 'ruled over' by an unfavorable planet, perhaps Mars.

10 463 lenket The Emperor asks Faust to defer the drawing of his sword until the issue between himself and the Pretender to his crown can be settled in single combat.

10 467 Selbst ist der Mann! A soldier's remark. Help is welcome, but a man who would be Emperor must be able to stand on his own feet and rely upon himself. The line suggests, and may have been intended to suggest, Schiller's *Reiterlied:*

> Im Felde, da ist der Mann noch was wert,
> da wird das Herz noch gewogen,
> da tritt kein anderer für ihn ein,
> auf sich selber steht er da ganz allein.

10 469 Sei das Gespenst Optative: 'Let that ghost be . . . thrust.' The ghost is the *Gegenkaiser*, the rival Emperor.

10 472 eigner The Emperor's own (hand).

10 475 The purpose of the special adornments on the Emperor's helmet is to permit his followers to identify him and to rally round to defend him when he is in danger.

10 476–10 477 Haupt Used here in two senses: first, physically, the Emperor's head, and then, metaphorically, the head of the nation. — **die Glieder** The vassals of the Emperor.

10 484 The sword first parries the stroke of the opponent and then gives back stroke for stroke.

10 488 The allusion is biblical, Psalm 110.1, where God, speaking to David, said: "Setze dich zu meiner Rechten, bis ich deine Feinde zum Schemel deiner Füße lege."

10 491 Meldung The Emperor's challenge to his opponent to fight out the issue in single combat.

10 497 What has happened — the rejection of the Emperor's challenge — has happened as his most loyal supporters would have wished. In this way the Emperor will not be subjected to personal danger.

10 499 brünstig 'Burning with ardor' (for the battle).

10 507 Faust assigns *Raufebold*, the young warrior, to the right wing for the attack with other young soldiers.

10 523 Faust sends *Habebald*, the mature, well-armed warrior, to join the deliberately slow advance of the center of the battle line. He is accompanied by a female camp follower, *Eilebeute*, whose name seems to come from Luther's version of Isaiah 8.1 and 3.

10 541 To the left flank, which has to hold its ground, Faust sends *Haltefest*, whose age and heavy weapons lend themselves to this task.

10 546 Strahlblitz Either 'lightning flash' or 'flashing arrow.'

Notes

SD 10 554   To the knowing ones among the audience, those who recognize his hocus-pocus, Mephistopheles gives an explanation of what they seem to see. Just why Mephistopheles takes no cognizance of the Emperor or his party and they take none of him is not made clear, nor is it clear, in view of SD 10 344, why he enters here 'from above.'

10 556   **Waffensäle**   The aristocracy of the late eighteenth and early nineteenth centuries pursued the collection of medieval armor as a fad. These suits of armor were set up around the walls of great halls in their castles. Mephistopheles has now looted these halls to provide the outward shapes of his ghostly army.

10 561   **darein geputzt**   Many a ghost has decorated himself by getting into one of these suits of armor, and by so doing has renovated the Middle Ages, as a tailor renovates a coat.

10 568   **frischer Lüftchen**   Genitive plural, object of *harrten*.

SD 10 570   **merkliche Schwankung**   Another stage direction which implies a further development of the dialogue not explicitly indicated by the poet. Goethe may have intended to insert here a few lines of *Teichoskopie* (description or report by an observer on the wall), a device often used in the classic drama, by means of which this notable wavering in the enemy's line should be reported.

10 582   *Raufebold*, a supernatural being, fights with as many arms as he needs, here a dozen.

10 584–10 592   Faust explains what the Emperor saw by suggesting that it was a kind of mirage, the "fata morgana," which is seen especially in the Strait of Messina.

10 592   **bricht**   'Breaks through' and thus becomes visible.

10 596   The flames are St. Elmo's fire, an electrical discharge often seen around the tips of ships' masts. These flames were regarded in ancient superstition as the spirits of Castor and Pollux (10 600), who were the special protectors of sailors at sea.

10 600   **Dioskuren**   Here the reference is to the twin stars of the constellation Gemini. According to one legend, Jupiter rewarded the brotherly fidelity of Castor and Pollux by placing them among the stars as the Gemini, the Twins. See notes to lines 7369 and 7415.

10 606   The *Meister* is the Necromancer of Norcia. His was the white beard (10 615) which escaped the flames by the order of the new Emperor (see note to line 10 439). Mephistopheles arrived on the scene 'from above' at line 10 546 and was not present when Faust told the Emperor (10 439) that the Necromancer of Norcia had sent him and his three mighty men to aid the Emperor. Goethe does not indicate how Mephistopheles knows — as he clearly does know — the purport of those lines spoken by Faust to the Emperor.

10 617   **ihre**   A plural reference to the clergymen included by the collective noun *Klerus* (10 616).

10 624–10 625   This fight between the griffon and the eagle symbolizes the attack of the rival Emperor upon the real Emperor. Indeed, the eagle and the griffon may be the heraldic emblems in the coats of arms of the Emperor and his rival, respectively. — **im Himmel-**

hohen An unusual noun, *das Himmelhohe*, from the adjective *himmelhoch:* 'in the very high air.'

10 636 **Löwenschweif** The griffon is usually depicted in heraldry with the head and wings of an eagle and the body (and tail) of a lion.

10 652 *Nichts Herrlicheres ist (je) ersonnen (worden).*

10 656–10 658 The defenders of the higher positions on this pass should have been throwing rocks down on the attackers who advance from lower positions on the hillsides.

10 664 Mephistopheles has two ravens which are his most trusted messengers. The ravens are usually associated with Wotan (Odin). The witch in the *Hexenküche* (2491) inquired about these ravens. *Rabenbotschaft, Rabenpost* (10 678) often connote 'bad news' and there may be a double meaning intended here.

10 677–10 678 Another effort by Faust to explain this hocus-pocus by analogy to natural and known phenomena. He is concerned lest the Emperor discern the satanic nature of this assistance and reject it. Perhaps there is also a suggestion of the 'dove of peace' in this contrast.

10 680 The Emperor had already pointed to weakness in the defense of the pass (10 654–10 661).

10 689 'Have patience and keep your cunning for the ultimate, final crisis.'

10 701 **Kunden** The reference is to Mephistopheles.

10 705 This action of the Emperor is something less than honorable. He is unwilling to accept responsibility for Mephistopheles' magic by giving him the recognized symbol of authority. Nevertheless he tells him to go ahead and do what he can.

10 708 **Uns andern** 'To us who are of a different sort.' Mephistopheles could not use a marshal's baton surmounted by a cross, since, as the Devil of the Christian religion, he is the antithetical enemy of the cross of Christ. See Volume I, p. 147, 4: Land Strase.

10 712 **die Undinen** The ravens are to ask the water spirits, who dwell in the great mountain lake, to send an illusion of a flood of water to confuse the Emperor's enemies.

10 714–10 715 Another jibe at deceitful feminine wiles, as at 7715. These water nymphs can produce the appearance of a thing without producing its essence.

10 717 **Den Wasserfräulein** Dative plural, object of *geschmeichelt haben.*

10 722 **jener** Genitive plural, refers to the enemy.

10 742 **Meister** Presumably the Necromancer of Norcia. — Some take this to refer to Satan and hold that Mephistopheles at this point is pretending not to be Satan.

10 745 **Gezwergvolk** The dwarfs are traditionally masters of mining and metallurgy.

10 749 **im hohen Sinne** What this means hinges upon the interpretation of *man* here and in 10 755. Mephistopheles clearly is thinking of the effect of his hocus-pocus on people, not on goblins nor yet on himself. We take *man* therefore to mean 'they' and to refer to the Emperor and his party who are to be impressed by these fire-

works. Whether this 'they' may include the enemy is not clear and not important. Hence *im hohen Sinne* probably refers first of all to the Emperor 'in his . . . exalted mind.' If the whole imperial group is included, then 'in their . . . exalted minds'; and the command is to the ravens: 'Go get some fire such as these people imagine fire to be.'

10 769 The ghost-filled suits of armor engage in the combat.

10 772 **als** In their roles of Guelf or Ghibelline (see note to line 4841).

10 774 **wöhnlich** The only use of this word in FAUST, probably best taken to mean 'persistent,' but thought by some to mean 'at home.' Others take it to mean 'as usual,' since it was substituted in the manuscript for *gewöhnlich.*

10 779 **den allerletzten Graus** 'The final, horrible outcome.'

SD 10 782 The shift in the music indicates the end of combat and the celebration of victory.

46. DES GEGENKAISERS ZELT

The victory has been won. Now we see first minor looters and then the Emperor and his retinue, who receive their rewards for loyalty. — The main dramatic reason for this scene is to disclose that the Emperor bestows upon Faust the title to the strip of seacoast, where Faust wishes to undertake his great reclamation project.

10 784 **Rabe** Normally the first scavenger to reach the battlefield is the raven, who feeds upon the flesh of the fallen warriors.

10 796 **ihn** The opponent, whoever it may be.

10 800 **nehm** A weak imperative instead of *nimm.*

SD 10 817 **unsres Kaisers** The poet identifies his audience and himself with the Emperor's party.

10 817 **heiligen** The place is sacred because it contains the throne and presumably the trappings of the Emperor, which his rival had wrongfully appropriated.

10 827 *Habebald* accuses the bodyguards of the Emperor of being just as much robbers as he. The difference is only that the guards call their plundering the collection of a war levy from the conquered people.

10 846 **summt's . . . saust's . . . zischt'** Past tense forms: *summte es, sauste es, zischte.* Presumably the *'s* which belongs with *zischt'* was omitted because of the accumulation of sibilants it would entail. But see note to lines 6095–6096.

SD 10 849 The subject, *Kaiser mit vier Fürsten,* would regularly require a singular verb: *tritt auf.* The plural verb results from "agreement according to sense" (*Fügung nach dem Sinn*).

10 849 The Emperor, like the bodyguards, has been discussing the mysterious doings of the day's battle. — From this line onward to the end of the act (11 042) Goethe uses rimed Alexandrines, iambic verses of six beats each with the caesura after the sixth syllable;

this monotonous and somewhat wooden form well suits the pompous and unenlightened action of the Emperor. Now that the victory has been won, he sets about to restore and even aggravate the very conditions which had made the conflict inevitable.

10 850 **im flachen Feld** The battle began in the mountains, but the enemy has been so completely overcome that his troops are dispersed on the open fields of the lowlands.

10 851 **verräterischer Schatz** = *der Schatz des Verräters.*

10 854 These embassies of the nations do not arrive on the stage, but it is to be supposed that they bring felicitations and renewed pledges of loyalty to the Emperor after his victory. — **Abgesandten** The weak form instead of *Abgesandte* because of the rime with *Trabanten.*

10 858 **uns** Best taken as a dative, representing the party in whose interest and to whose advantage the fighting was done. That is: 'When all is said and done, we alone did the fighting for our side.' — The Emperor is trying to interpret the supernatural events of the day in terms of more or less credible natural events. He is also, rather without warrant, taking credit for deeds of valor he has not done.

10 866 Luther's version of *Te deum laudamus*, a hymn ascribed to St. Ambrose.

10 867–10 868 In his desire to praise God, the Emperor thinks he needs to look into his own heart and follow its dictates of gratitude. As a young prince, he had not often done so. Years have taught him to use such an opportunity as he now has. — **das** = *was.*

10 876 **Erzmarschall** In bestowing these offices, the Emperor is following closely the stipulations of the Golden Bull of Charles IV, 1356. By this decree, the Elector of Saxony was made *Erzmarschall*, the Margrave of Brandenburg became *Erzkämmerer*, the Count of the Palatinate became *Erztruchseß*, and the King of Bohemia became *Erzschenk.* — The Marshal was originally overseer of the Emperor's stables and armory. The Chamberlain was palace inspector and director of personnel. The Steward had charge of the kitchen and of the serving of meals. The Cupbearer was responsible for the supply of wines and beer.

10 881 The Lord High Marshal thinks of his ceremonial duties. When, after a victorious war, the Emperor celebrates the victory at a banquet, the Marshal will bear this sword (10 876) in the ceremonies as prescribed by court etiquette.

10 893–10 894 The same celebration of victory that finds the Marshal, sword in hand, escorting the Emperor will find the Lord High Chamberlain also serving the Emperor. He will supervise the holding of the golden basin over which the Emperor washes his hands in water which a page pours from a pitcher. During these ablutions, the Chamberlain will also hold for the Emperor the Imperial rings, which are worn at such high functions (10 895).

10 901 As officer in charge of the kitchen, the Steward (or "dapifer," as a *Truchseß* is sometimes called) is to prepare the choicest of viands according to season.

10 906–10 907   There seems to be an illogical step here in the Lord High
Steward's flattery. He knows his duty is to provide the royal
table with every exotic viand and each before its common season,
although the Emperor has just expressed his preference for domestic foods in their proper season.

10 921   A Venetian glass goblet was supposed to have magic power to
reveal the presence of any poison which might be in the wine and
to draw out of the wine its power to intoxicate the drinker.

10 922   One may understand *der Wein* as the subject of *berauschet*, by
abstraction from *des Weins Geschmack*.

10 928   **Schrift** Decrees by the Emperor had to be put into formal documents (*Urkunden*); this was done in the Imperial Chancellery.
Such documents were 'signed' in the twelfth and thirteenth centuries by intricate monograms prepared by the Chancellery and
made valid by a pen-stroke (*Zug,* 10 966) drawn by the Emperor
in some characteristic way. See note to lines 6081–6082.

SD 10 931   The Archbishop of Mainz was made Arch-Chancellor by the
Golden Bull. His two ecclesiastical colleagues, the Archbishop
of Cologne and the Archbishop of Trier, do not appear in this
scene. (See notes to 10 285 and 10 876.)

10 936   **Fünfzahl** All five of these imperial officers, exclusive of the Emperor. They are referred to as *sie* in 10 937.

10 955–10 956   When he thinks of his long line of exalted ancestors, he is
reminded that he too lives under the constant threat of death, due
to his mortal nature.

10 957   **seinerzeit** 'When it is time for it.'

10 960   **was** The choice of an Emperor is meant.

10 979   The Archbishop in his capacity as a cleric speaks to the Emperor
as a father might speak to a son. In his capacity as Chancellor his
attitude has been different.

10 986   **Strahl** The *Bannstrahl* of excommunication.

10 987   **zur höchsten Zeit** 'At the great festival.'

10 988   **Zauberer** The Necromancer of Norcia, whose liberation was the
first act of the then newly crowned Emperor (see lines 10 439 and
10 615).

10 991   'Be penitent and give.'

10 996   **zu heiligem Bemühn** For the erection of a cathedral, to further
the holy endeavors of the church.

11 004   **Grenze** The boundary of the lands to be ceded to the church in
expiation of his sin.

11 007   The bishop sees, in his mind's eye, the rapid construction of a
cathedral. First the choir, with the altar, is built; then the cross-
shape of the church becomes clear as the transept is added, and
finally the nave is built.

11 020   **Schluß und Formalität** Hendiadys for 'the formal conclusion'
or 'the final formality' of the transaction.

11 024   **Zinsen** 'rents' payable either in money or in kind.

11 035 This is the sole reference to the bestowal of land upon Faust,
which was, after all, the basic purpose of this act (see note to
line 10 305).

11 036 **diesen** The seashore, not Faust. This threat of a papal ban
upon the land which it is Faust's ambition to wrest from the sea
is a threat to the success of the undertaking, when he comes to
colonize the new area.

Act V

47. Offene Gegend

The scene is in the country near the sea, with only a few trees near a
little house with a small garden, where shrubs and flowers grow under
cultivation. There are sand dunes along the old shoreline; from one
of these there is an unobstructed view toward the sea. — The function
of this scene is primarily to create a mood. This mood contrasts
sharply with that of the following scene. The contrast in mood is
reflected in the metrical form. We find *abab* quatrains throughout this
scene and into Scene 48, where the contrast is found in the couplets
and short, choppy lines of Mephistopheles and the three ruffians.
Faust himself speaks now in *abab* quatrains and now in couplets,
reflecting his changing moods. The cadences of the quatrains are
alternately feminine (*a*) and masculine (*b*) whereas in the couplets the
cadences are predominantly masculine.

11 045 **ich soll** 'it is my good fortune to.'

11 050 The rime *barg : warf* is impure, and is an example of assonance.

11 051 The traveler has found the linden trees and the cottage which
marked the scene of his rescue. He would like to thank once more
the people who took care of him, but they were so old at that time
that he scarcely believes they can have lived to greet him now.

SD 11 059 **Baucis** The wife of Philemon, the peasant. — The names
and much of the milieu and character of this pair correspond to the
Philemon and Baucis of ancient Greek mythology. This ancient
Greek pair took into their humble cottage in Phrygia two unknown
travelers and sheltered them. The gods rewarded the hospitable
old people by granting them a twofold wish: that they be priests
of the temple of Jupiter, and that one and the same hour might
take them both from this life.

11 069 **Philemon** The stress is on the second syllable of this name.

11 070 **Schatz** Presumably the property of this stranger, which Philemon
salvaged from the wreckage of his ship.

11 071–11 072 The beacon fire and the bell of the little church served to
warn seafarers of the nearness of the shore. — These two lines are
'absolutes'; that is, nothing in them is grammatically associated
with anything else in the utterance. One must suppose some connection such as: "I still remember the flames of your quickly built

fire, and the silver tone of your little bell. (They were) the solution, entrusted to you, of the horrible adventure I underwent."

11 075 **hervor** Out into the open, where the lindens do not obstruct his view.

11 083 **Das** Includes the meaning of the relative pronoun: *das, was Euch mißgehandelt hat, seht Ihr als Garten behandelt.* — The separable form *mißgehandelt* is unusual and probably to be charged to the demands of the rhythm here.

11 087 **Älter** 'rather old,' standing for a fuller explanation such as: *Da ich schon älter war,* or *Älter, wie ich es schon war.*

11 089–11 090 The failing of Philemon's strength occurs at the same time as the disappearance of the waters of the sea.

11 096 **Wald** The presence of a forest here may indicate the passing of many years since the beginning of this reclamation project. Gardens, meadows, villages can be established quickly; a forest requires time, unless it is a supernatural forest fabricated by Mephistopheles (see line 11 114).

11 103–11 104 **in der Weite erst** 'Only in the far distance' (can you see).

11 116 **ihm** Faust, to whom the Emperor had conveyed this portion of the seacoast.

11 127 **Menschenopfer** Baucis asserts that human victims were sacrificed in order to further this project. She is thinking probably of sacrifices to appease evil spirits, of the walling up of a living man in the masonry of a building, or the use of human blood in the mixing of mortar. How far her testimony is to be credited in assessing Faust's acts is another matter. She is, after all, an old woman who likes to talk (11 110).

11 131 **Gottlos** Because he would destroy their chapel as well as their home.

11 134 **soll man** 'We are expected to.' It appears from the domineering manner of their new neighbor, Faust, that he expects the old couple to submit to his demands.

48. PALAST

The scene now shifts to the great palace of Faust, built on land reclaimed from the sea. A large ship canal leads from this castle down to the sea. According to Goethe's remark to Eckermann (June 6, 1831), Faust is exactly one hundred years old. Another lynx-eyed watchman, also called Lynceus, appears here (see note to line 9218). The two watchmen are different persons, both named Lynceus.

11 148 **bereit** Since this ship is sailing (11 163), its masts are presumably carrying sail and hence *bereit,* in the sense that they are in a condition to serve the purpose for which they exist. If the ship were not under sail, but being towed up the canal, then the masts, having been cleared of sail, might be ready to receive lines of signal flags and bunting, which would be hoisted when the ship is dressed for its arrival in port. Goethe's intent here is not wholly clear.

11 150 **zur höchsten Zeit** 'at the great festival.' — **Glück** Some see in this a play on the Latin meaning of the name *Faustus* 'the fortunate one.' See note to 10 239.

11 156 **rein** 'free from blemish.'

11 160 Faust is completely unable to tolerate anyone's authority but his own. He could not rest in the shade of the old linden trees of Philemon and Baucis, because their shade would not belong solely to himself. — **fremdem** Some editions follow a manuscript which reads *fremden.*

11 162 Faust behaves like a petulant, impatient old man, who, upon being crossed by a comparatively insignificant hindrance to his plans, wishes he could run away from everything.

11 165 **sein behender Lauf** Metonymy for *das Schiff in seinem behenden Lauf.* 'How the ship, as it skims along, towers with boxes, chests, bales!'

SD 11 167 **Chorus** The three mighty men, speaking in unison.

11 169 **Glückan!** Like *Glückauf!,* a formula of greeting, presumably among sailors, to mean 'Hello,' or 'Greetings.' This is the only occurrence of *Glückan!* of which we have any record.

11 175 **Was große Dinge** = *Was für große Dinge* 'What great things!'

11 178 **Besinnen** 'Reflection, consideration, stopping to think.'

11 185 The form of this line forces a comparison with line 6992 and emphasizes the difference between this pirate (Mephistopheles) and the philosopher (Homunculus).

11 186 **müßte** An unreal condition is implied: 'I should have to be quite ignorant of maritime matters, if I were to infer . . .'

11 188 An incidental jibe by Mephistopheles at the doctrine of the Holy Trinity.

11 193–11 194 Faust's facial expression shows his revulsion at this account of the piracy of Mephistopheles and his crew. — **widerlich** 'nauseated.'

11 201–11 204 These three mighty men demand that all booty be shared equally. What they have already taken in the course of their piracy was merely to keep them interested.

11 217 There has been a good deal of speculation as to the meaning of these 'gay birds.' Perhaps Mephistopheles means the rest of the fleet with colors flying. Perhaps this is a sarcastic allusion to the ribbons of decorations to be awarded for meritorious service. Possibly Mephistopheles refers to the ladies of easy virtue who will rally round the returning sailors, or possibly he means the sailors themselves.

11 225 **sprich** Mephistopheles asks Faust to acknowledge that he now can reach round the world from his own palace. The great work is done and the planner ought to be satisfied. Mephistopheles hopes Faust may even admit that he is content at last; this admission would free Mephistopheles from his obligation to service and Faust would have lost the wager, according to their contract (1699–1706).

11 228 **Bretterhaus** A temporary hut made of boards.

11 234 **'s** = *das Hier.*

11 241 **wenig** The uninflected form, where one should expect *wenigen.*

11 242 **Weltbesitz** = *Hochbesitz* (11 156) 'realm.'

11 262 **Geklingel** Mephistopheles hates the bell, because it represents the church, which concerns itself with every aspect and every event of men's lives. The classic exposition of the relation of the bell to the life of man is Schiller's *Lied von der Glocke*, which every German schoolboy used to memorize.

11 266 **vom ersten Bad** A scurrilous reference to baptism.

11 268 **verschollner Traum** The church and its followers appear to Mephistopheles to regard any portion of life which occurs without the accompaniment of the church's blessing and control (represented by the notes of the bell) as a meaningless, quickly forgotten dream.

11 269 The obstinacy of Baucis, particularly.

11 274 Faust's whole project has involved moving people to new places of residence. Mephistopheles sees no reason why Philemon and Baucis should not be moved also, even though they are unwilling. It is indeed an act of violence (11 280), but their new home will soon reconcile them to the loss of the old place.

11 285 A pun on the two meanings of the syllable *flott* in *Flottenfest*, 'festival of the fleet,' and *flottes Fest*, 'a gay, unrestrained celebration.'

11 287 Naboth's vineyard was coveted by Ahab, King of Samaria (I Kings 21). Ahab offered Naboth a large sum of money or a much better vineyard in exchange, but Naboth declined. Thereupon Ahab became nervously upset and could not eat. Ahab's wife, Jezebel, then plotted the ruin of Naboth, causing him to be falsely accused of treason, convicted, and executed. Ahab had to bear the responsibility for this evil deed.

49. TIEFE NACHT

11 290 **geschworen** Bound by oath to the duties of tower watchman.

11 297 It may be that in his use of *Zier* in this line Goethe intended to suggest the double meaning of the Greek word *kosmos*, which means both 'order' and 'ornament.' (Cf. *cosmic; cosmetic.*)

SD 11 303 **Pause** This marks the end of Lynceus' hymn in praise of the power of sight. Lines 11 304–11 335 are spoken, not sung; but following the long pause after line 11 335, Lynceus begins to sing again.

11 309 **Doppelnacht** It is night, and the shade of the linden grove makes the darkness doubly deep.

11 321 **schwarze Moosgestelle** Standing out black amidst the red flames of the moss-covered cottage of Philemon and Baucis is the framework or skeleton of their home.

11 337 **mit Jahrhunderten** That which in the past had commended itself to the eyes of men is gone, along with the centuries through which

it had delighted them. These words are sung by Lynceus to a dirgelike melody.

11 339   **spat**   The now obsolete adverbial form beside *spät* (see note to line 3112). — The report of the tower watchman has come too late to permit Faust to make any attempt to rescue the old people.

11 341   **ungeduld'ge Tat**   The burning of the property of the old couple. Faust calls this an impatient act, but it is not clear who he thinks has been impatient.

11 342   **sei**   Concessive: 'even though the linden grove is destroyed.'

11 373   **es** = *das Fluchen,* Faust's curse.

11 374   **Wort**   The inevitably-to-be-expected word of dismissal and disapproval which comes eventually to persons who permit themselves to serve as instruments in the hands of ruthless despots. — The chorus of the three mighty men says that the man who serves such masters should do so willingly, ready, if he proves to be reliable, to risk his possessions and even his life without reluctance.

50. Mitternacht

Four ghostly figures approach Faust's palace door, oblivious of Faust himself, who observes them from the balcony. They are allegorical representations of four great tormentors of the human soul — for our interest here is in the heart and mind of Faust, not in his appetites — Want, Debt, Distress, and Care. Of these only Care can gain access to Faust's palace. No Want, no Debt, no Distress can trouble him, for he is a very rich man. The figure of *Schuld* is subject to a different interpretation from that just given (= Debt). Many regard this as a representation of a 'sense of guilt' or 'remorse.' However, 'a sense of guilt' is a proper component of Care and has in fact (line 11 238) entered Faust's heart.

SD 11 398   **im Palast**   No change of scene was described at line 11 384, but there must be a setting which provides space for the Four Gray Women outside Faust's palace, or his apartment in the palace, and which also permits us to see Faust in the palace. This can be managed in several ways, most simply with a drop curtain, before which lines 11 384–11 397 are spoken, and which is raised to reveal Faust in his palace.

11 403–11 407   Here Faust confronts his last major problem. Magic, supernatural aids, whether by incantation or through Mephistopheles, have provided him everything he has asked, but he remains bound by his obligation to these forces which have helped him. Concretely, he is obliged to deal with Mephistopheles and the three mighty men very soon, to provide them their great celebration. Spiritually, he is not a free man, so long as he depends upon supernatural, extra-human forces to gain his ends. Spiritual independence in the face of an unknown and perhaps hostile world is the basic condition of any worth-while living. It is on this point that the critics of our day refer to modern man as "Faustian";

our science and technology seem to have put us into something like the position in which Faust here finds himself. The problem is by no means a new one.

11 408 sonst Before he turned to magic, and before he allied himself with Mephistopheles.

11 409 verfluchte The curse referred to is that of lines 1583–1606.

11 410–11 418 Dealings with the supernatural forces of darkness make a man hypersensitive to creatures of his imagination. For example, when he returns happy from a day outdoors, in the Spring perhaps, he hears a bird (a raven) croak, and at once he has a foreboding of evil. Superstitions hem him in day and night. Everything that happens is ominous for him and so he becomes self-conscious and solitary.

11 419 Die Pforte Perhaps the door of the upstairs room to which Faust has returned from the balcony.

11 423 Faust, in accordance with his wish (11 404) to be free from the black art, resolutely cautions himself not to use his powers in this instance.

11 425–11 426 What this ghostly 'Care' has to say can be said with the inner voice, directly to the heart, without the intermediation of the ear or of the spoken word. 'Care' appears in many different forms and in every place, on land and on the sea.

11 429 ängstlicher = *Angst einflößender* 'terrifying.'

11 434 jed = *jedes.* — **bei den Haaren** 'eagerly, as if it were a piece of good fortune.' See note to line 228.

11 442–11 452 drüben The 'beyond' to which Faust once (702–719) sought entrance. Here he deprecates the too great devotion of men's thinking to this beyond, which cannot be discerned by human eyes, and to the fiction that beyond the clouds there are men such as are on earth. It is better, says Faust, for men to look closely at the world about them.

This doctrine does not deny the existence of a *Jenseits;* but it deprecates the too great preoccupation of men's minds with the unknowable. Faust's conviction is that men should seek to know this world in which we live, to go through life continually progressing in this knowledge and never satisfied with what they know.

11 457–11 458 Even though he has all his physical (*äußern*) senses, the man possessed by Care sees no light; he is filled with darkness, day and night.

11 469 Litanei The feminine rimes of Care's lines (11 453–11 466 and 11 471–11 486) produce a rhythmic flow which we must think of as being chanted monotonously, so as to suggest the monotonous rendition of the formal prayers and responses (which repeat the prayers) characteristic of the litany of some church services. The hypnotic effect of the lines, regardless of their intellectual content, tends to delude even *den klügsten Mann*, says Faust (11 470).

11 481–11 486 These lines depict the final stages of the degradation of man through Care. When his will is wholly destroyed, when he ceases to struggle, he is finished.

11 487 **Gespenster** These 'spectres' may include with Care the others
who came with her but did not gain admission to Faust's palace,
namely Want, Debt, and Distress. These are deterrent and confusing forces quite different from the *Dämonen* (11 491), which
are positive forces driving men to do good or evil, as the case may
be. Goethe believed that everyone has his own *Dämon*, the innate
strength and bent of nature (*Eigenheit*) which more than any other
factor determines the course of his life. (Cf. Goethe's poem of
1817, *Urworte. Orphisch* I.)

11 492 **das geistig-strenge Band** The tie which binds us to these dae-
monic driving forces. This is a bond of the spirit and it is relentless in its severity. The *Dämon* is an inborn personality trait.

11 497–11 498 If her words are to be construed strictly, Care here ex-
cludes Faust from the class 'human beings.' However, Goethe
certainly meant that Faust was an exceptional human being,
rather than that he was not human. Even so, the kind of blindness
that can be ascribed to most men throughout their lives is not the
kind of blindness which befalls Faust now, when Care breathes her
blinding breath upon the old man alone in his palace.

51. GROSSER VORHOF DES PALASTS

11 512 **Lemuren** Goethe stressed this word on the second syllable. The
Latin form is *lemures*, with the accent on the first syllable. — The
Lemurs of antiquity were minor evil spirits, who flitted about,
mere skin and bones, distressing good people without any particular reason or purpose. They were represented on a bas-relief
found in a grave near Cumae in southern Italy, which Goethe
discussed in an essay: "Der Tänzerin Grab" (1812). As he depicts them here, they are not skeletons such as one sees in the
"Dance of Death," but they suggest these macabre figures.

11 516 **halb** The Lemurs are not intellectual giants, but they seem to
remember having half-heard someone talk about Faust's reclamation project. Possibly Faust himself had once addressed the
assembled workmen who were to carry out the project, and these
Lemurs would then have been part of Faust's audience.

11 523 **künstlerisch** No civil engineer is needed for the job in hand.
The Lemurs had come equipped with stakes and chain (11 519–
11 520).

11 527 **unsre Väter** Mephistopheles identifies himself momentarily
with the Lemurs, who are spoken of as the shriveled figures of dead
human beings.

11 531–11 538 **Wie jung ich war** = *Als ich jung war* This song of the
Lemurs appears to have been suggested by the gravedigger's song
in HAMLET (V, 1). The first two lines in each stanza are indeed
free adaptations of Shakespeare, or of his source, a poem by Lord
Vaux, which is included in Percy's RELIQUES OF ANCIENT ENGLISH
POETRY (1765). Goethe almost certainly knew both versions.

11 544–11 550 Mephistopheles defiantly tells the audience that the
devilish destruction of orderliness and of constructive evolution
is built into the nature of the physical universe. Whatever "life"

and "mind" can achieve, Mephistopheles says, will ultimately be undone, bit by bit, by the operation of inexorable natural laws: the modern reader may be reminded of the second law of thermodynamics and entropy.

11 545 **Dämmen, Buhnen** 'dams, levees.' The dam is usually of earth, the levee faced with boards, woven branches, or stones.

11 563–11 564 These lines define *das Höchsterrungene*, 'the greatest achievement.' The 'many millions' need not be thought of as all dwelling at one time on this land, but may represent rather the countless generations of descendants of the present new settlers.

11 567 **Hügel** The man-made dike which protects the land from the sea.

11 571 **es** No antecedent is expressed. One may think of *das Wasser = die Flut* (11 570), which nibbles at the dikes, trying to find a point at which it can force its way through.

11 575–11 576 Faust is no longer satisfied with the ambition he voiced at 10 187 for power and possessions, but has achieved the point of view of the servant of mankind. Security and possessions, of themselves, are not good for people, and Faust reiterates even more forcefully the thought of lines 682–685. His greatest satisfaction would come from establishing a state of such free men as would fulfill his ideal of daily winning liberty by effort. Only that man wins freedom who, along with the others with whom he is living, successfully defends his existence against the daily threatening forces of his environment. It is in this eternal activity that the good life is found. Hence, *der Herr* (340–343) provides the constant irritant of evil to drive men onward.

11 577 **umrungen** = *umringt* 'surrounded by.'

11 582 This word-for-word repetition of line 1700 is not a fulfillment of the terms of Faust's bargain with Mephistopheles. Faust merely says that he might feel this way if he achieved his goal. The anticipation of the achievement of this great result fills him with the highest joy he has yet known.

11 585 **Vorgefühl** Faust has not achieved 'his highest moment,' nor is he looking back upon it. He is looking forward to the possibility of attaining this high satisfaction. He sees the vision of freedom through human effort, without the help of supernatural forces.

11 589 **leeren** Mephistopheles can see nothing in the life of this hundred-year-old man which would make time of any use to him.

11 594 **Der Zeiger fällt** See lines 1703–1706 and note to line 1705. — **Es ist vollbracht** An allusion to the words of Christ on the cross, John 19.30.

11 597 For Mephistopheles there is no difference between 'not-being' and 'being past.' He finds that since all creation in this world ends in death or destruction, the procedure is senseless. He would prefer a world in which time and space are irrelevant, although he has to accept this world as it is and operate in it.

11 600 **zu lesen** = *zu lernen* 'What can be learned from that?'

52. Grablegung

11 604–11 611 This song of the Lemurs is reminiscent of the third stanza of the gravedigger's song in Hamlet (V, 1), but the resemblance is slight. The solo Lemur may be thought of as the one who has lain flat on the ground to be measured for the grave (11 525) and who now criticizes the labors of his fellows. Faust's body is lying on the ground nearby (SD 11 586, 11 612). The reply of the chorus seems to be directed at the first Lemur. All of the Lemurs are spirits of evil-doers and ne'er-do-wells, for whom a burlap shroud would be appropriate. Indeed, they may even be wearing such shrouds as they dig. — **Es** The empty grave is compared with a house which has been stripped of its furnishings. — These lines are usually understood to mean that man's earthly possessions are borrowed, not owned, and that the lenders (creditors) have claimed their property at the end of the short term of the loan. More generally, the lines have been understood to emphasize the transitory nature of all human affairs in the face of the powers of destruction and disintegration. Goethe deprecated this kind of pessimism. He says specifically: "Ich bedaure die Menschen, welche von der Vergänglichkeit der Dinge viel Wesens machen und sich in Betrachtung irdischer Nichtigkeit verlieren. Sind wir ja eben deshalb da, um das Vergängliche unvergänglich zu machen; das kann ja nur dadurch geschehen, wenn man beides zu schätzen weiß" (Maximen und Reflexionen, No. 155).

11 613 Titel The document of lines 1736–1737.

11 614–11 615 These lines are a jibe at a proposal by contemporaries of Goethe to effect the cure of persons "possessed of evil spirits." This plan rested on the rationalistic postulate that the Devil could claim only such persons as believed in him, since for others the Devil did not exist.

11 616–11 617 Both the old way and the new way cause Mephistopheles trouble. The old way is described in lines 11 623–11 625. When the victim died the soul left his body with his last breath. That is, it emerged from his mouth or nose and was easily caught there by the waiting devil. But to sit beside a dying person, waiting for this to occur, gives offense. The new way is one which makes things very difficult indeed for devils. They are not received kindly. The soul now no longer leaves the body at a definite time, but only when the elements of which the body is composed break up and force the unifying principle, the soul, to depart. It can never be predicted when, or how, or where it will escape, since the fact of death is no longer as easy to ascertain as it once seemed to be. Sometimes the apparently dead have been revived.

SD 11 636 flügelmännische 'like those of a fugleman,' a soldier placed before a regiment or company at drill to indicate by arm signals the maneuvers and the cadence for the troops. There is no indication anywhere that Mephistopheles is to be thought of as a winged figure.

11 639 den Höllenrachen The jaws of hell were standard equipment on the stages of the Passion Plays and an essential item in the old Faust stories and puppet plays. The reference to the many jaws of hell, in line 11 640, is probably to be taken as a jibe at Sweden-borg's Arcana coelestia ('celestial mysteries'), where one is told that "there are innumerable hells, each distinct according to the kinds of evils and deceits." It is suggested that the trend is toward less insistence upon differentiations of this sort.

11 644   The gaping maw of hell, like that of a great dragon, has tusks. Inside it Mephistopheles sees and describes for us a part of the infernal scene.

11 647   **die Flammenstadt**   The fiery city of the underworld god Dis, described in Dante's *Inferno* 8, 69–75.

11 654   **Ihr**   The devils with straight horns and those with curved horns, who have set up the jaws of hell as instructed. Mephistopheles says it is a good thing to frighten sinners with such displays, because they normally do not believe in such things and so are inaccessible to the Devil, who can only influence them if they believe in him. (See note to lines 11 614–11 615.)

11 659   **lauert**   Mephistopheles is posting his forces. The fat devils are to watch the lower part of Faust's body. The sign of decomposition, and hence of the impending departure of Faust's soul, is phosphorescence of the putrefying flesh.

11 660   **Psyche**   From the Greek word *psyche*, which meant primarily 'breath of life, vital force, life,' and thence 'soul.' Sometimes the psyche is visualized as a butterfly.

11 661   A warning to the devils not to tear the wings from this Psyche, lest it become a hideous worm.

11 662–11 663   Perhaps this 'mark' of Mephistopheles and the fiery tornado are allusions to the "mark of the beast" (Revelation 14.9; 16.2; 19.20) and the "lake of fire that burneth with brimstone" (Revelation 19.20).

11 667   **akkurat**   Accurate knowledge of the precise seat of the soul is not available and in Goethe's day this problem was frequently discussed.

11 669   **es**   'What I have said.'

11 670–11 671   The long-horned devils are instructed to comb the air above Faust's body, so that they may catch his soul if it takes flight.

11 675   **Genie**   Here in the sense of *Genius, Geist* 'spirit.'

SD 11 676   **Glorie von oben**   'emanation of great light from the opened Heaven.'

11 676   **Gesandte**   A translation of Greek *angeloi* 'angels.' The song is sung by members of the Heavenly Host to each other.

11 679   **vergeben**   An infinitive to express purpose, parallel to *beleben*, and like it, dependent upon the imperative *Folget!* 'Follow, oh fellow angels, in effortless flight, to forgive sinners and bring life to the dead (dust); make friendly traces for all natures in the hovering movement of our slow-moving procession.' They are asked to move in such a way that all natures will feel impelled to follow them.

11 685 **Geklimper** 'jingling.' Bad performance of instrumental or vocal music.

11 686 **Tag** The light from the aureole and nimbus which emanate from the angels.

11 687 **bübisch-mädchenhaft** As this qualifies *Gestümper* it means 'adolescent, immature.' The angelic music of the Heavenly Host, with its integral relationships of melody and harmony, is intolerable to the ears of the *Geist, der stets verneint*. Some see in *bübisch-mädchenhaft* a reference to the belief that angels are sexless.

11 689–11 692 These lines appear to refer to the use of choirs of eunuchs in the services of worship of the Roman church. Another interpretation sees in them a reference to the persecutions of the saints. Still another interpretation regards *das Schändlichste* as the crucifixion of Christ.

11 695 **Waffen** As Mephistopheles sees it, the means of winning a soul are essentially the same, whether they be used by angel or by devil. These means, therefore, are probably promises of bliss and reward, which Mephistopheles knows to be hypocritical on the part of devils and which he regards as hypocritical when made by angels.

11 697 The loss of Faust's soul would be an everlasting disgrace to the devils, for Mephistopheles would have to stand in the presence of God and confess his failure (327–329).

11 699 The angels have obtained these roses from penitent women in Heaven. The roses are symbols of Divine Love and they also contain an essence of this love which emanates from the opening rosebuds (11 702–11 704) and overpowers the devils.

11 703 **zweigleinbeflügelte (Rosen)** Roses which float on the 'wings' of the leaves attached to their stems.

11 706 **Frühling** Subject of *entsprieße:* 'May Spring burst into bud.'

11 708 **Paradiese** The plural form, by metonymy meaning 'blessed joys of all kinds.'

11 715 **das** The snowfall of roses.

11 722 **schwebt's** The snowfall of roses, which has been changed to a sea of sharp clear flames, is approaching.

11 730 This line appears to mean: *wie es das Herz wünscht,* 'to the heart's desire.'

11 731–11 734 These lines have been variously interpreted. The simplest solution appears to be had by taking a verb for this clause from what has just been said, and reading: *Die wahren Worte bereiten im klaren Äther ewigen Scharen überall Tag.* 'The words of truth prepare everywhere in the clear ethereal spaces the light of day for eternal hosts.' Or, if *Klaren* is a noun, as it is sometimes understood to be, then: 'in the clear spaces of Heaven, in the Ether.'

11 739 **Gesegn'** Used ironically: 'may the hot bath agree with you and do you good.'

11 741 Mephistopheles singles out one individual rose for his attentions and addresses it with: "*Du.*"

11 745–11 752 This angelic chorus is not yet visible. Their song comes down from above. Therefore *herein* (11 752) means 'into Heaven,

where we are.' Probably *euch* and *ihr* refer to the retreating devils, who have just left the scene heels over head. 'You can't have Faust's soul, for it does not belong to you; and you can't tolerate love, spread by the falling roses (11 728), since it distresses your hearts.' Then more generally: 'Whenever there is an attempt at violence against us, we must be valiant. Love leads only the loving into Heaven.'

11 747 **euch das Innere** 'your innermost being.'

11 754 **Element** The symptoms cited in line 11 753 point to love as the diabolical force in question, but in the case of Mephistopheles love is perverted sexual longing only. He understands now how scorned lovers feel when they gape at their haughty sweethearts.

11 759 **Auch mir** (*geschieht es so*) 'I too — of all people! — am put into the position of the scorned lover.'

11 760 **mit ihr** = *mit jener Seite.*

11 765–11 766 If Mephistopheles can be beguiled in this way, he cannot call anyone else a fool for becoming the dupe of love.

11 770 Lucifer (Isaiah 14.12) was the name of the angel who fell, or was cast down, from Heaven. The implication seems to be that others of his family may have remained among the angels.

11 775 See line 3655 for the same metaphor. A verbal base for the clause can be had from lines 11 773: *Es ist mir* . . .

11 776 A verb for this clause can be taken from 11 771: *mit jedem Blick seid ihr* . . .

11 782 **ihr** The angels, who are called *Jungen* 'boys' (11 763) and *Kinder* 'children' (11 769). They are really accomplished seducers, since their charms are equally effective upon male and female, as a perverted Mephistopheles sees things. Mephistopheles is so inflamed with lust that he scarcely feels the burning roses with which he has been pelted by these angels.

11 801–11 802 **Klarheit** According to one view, the flaming roses of Divine Love are bidden to return to the light of Heaven. According to another view, the flames of love are bidden to apply themselves (*wendet euch*) to the service of clarity, so that truth (= clarity) may heal those who condemn themselves.

11 803 **die** Demonstrative and relative combined, 'those who,' object of *heile.*

11 809 The allusion is to Job 2.7: "So Satan went forth from the presence of Jehovah and smote Job with sore boils from the sole of his feet unto his crown."

11 810 **der ganze Kerl** 'all over me.' 'Boil after boil, like Job, all over me, so that I shudder at myself; and yet at the same time I triumph when I quite see through the whole business and put my trust in myself and my family tree.'

11 812 **Stamm** May be taken to be equivalent to *Abstammung* 'descent,' or it may be equivalent to *Geschlecht* 'tribe, kin.'

11 816 **euch** The angels, after whom he so recently lusted.

11 818 **Wen** 'Whomever' and 'him who.' Specific reference to the soul of Faust is certainly included in this general relative pronoun.

11 823 **gereinigt** Since the air had been cleansed of the exhalations of the devils, who were driven off at line 11 738, the spirit of Faust can live (breathe).

11 832 Goethe once thought of a scene in Heaven in which Satan would appeal the judgment of the Lord concerning his contract. Some critics believe these lines are a reflex of that unfulfilled intention. Yet Mephistopheles judges himself. He has lost any right he might have had to Faust's soul by his own mismanagement (11 836).

11 837 **Aufwand** The trouble and expenditure of resources which Mephistopheles has had to make in his attempt to 'satisfy' Faust. Mephistopheles, the spirit of negation, never learns to understand the affirmative, positive drive of Faust, which makes it possible for divine grace to save him from the fate Mephistopheles prepared for him (see lines 11 934–11 941).

53. BERGSCHLUCHTEN

This scene begins on a mountainside cut with ravines, perhaps suggested to Goethe by what he had read of Montserrat, near Barcelona. From a Benedictine monastery on Montserrat individual monks withdrew to solitary cells, where they lived in complete isolation, often inaccessible except by means of ladders or of bridges thrown across otherwise impassable ravines. It is also possible that Goethe was here recalling etchings based upon the fresco "Anchorites in the Thebaid" in the Campo Santo in Pisa. These depicted early Christian hermits in the desert of the Nile country around Thebes. Attempts have also been made to relate the details of this scene with descriptions of Heaven in the writings of Swedenborg.

At the summit of the mountain dwells Doctor Marianus (11 989), from whose lofty cell the interior of Heaven is visible. The *Anachoreten*, anchorites, were hermits, saints of the first centuries of the Christian era, who dwelt in the wilderness and by denying the flesh sought to achieve a mystic union with God. Here they are hermit monks like those of Montserrat. — This whole scene is operatic in its conception and effect.

SD 11 844 **Chor** A chorus of anchorites, which might well be much larger than a group composed only of those who are subsequently named. The stage director has a problem with this antiphonal echo, but very impressive effects can be achieved.

11 850 **Löwen** Isaiah 65.25 says: "The wolf and the lamb shall feed together and the lion shall eat straw like the ox." (Similarly: Isaiah 11.6–9.) This is to take place in the new heavens and the new earth which are there prophesied. A graphic representation of the lion with the saint is Dürer's etching of St. Jerome in his study. — The lions, symbols of warlike ferocity, honor this sacred retreat made holy by divine love and the love of God in the hearts of the anchorites.

Notes

SD 11 854   We have here the first of four "fathers," *patres*, each with a particular attribute. *Pater ecstaticus*, the ecstatic father, is able to float in the air, because he has so far put away the flesh that it no longer weighs him down to earth. — The fathers of the Roman church bore such names. St. Anthony, Johann Ruysbroek, Father Dionysius, all were called "*ecstaticus.*" In his account of his Italian Journey (under date of May 26, 1787, Naples) Goethe recorded the story of Philippus Neri, who was a singularly ecstatic cleric with "the highest gifts of religious enthusiasm; the gift of involuntary prayer, of profound wordless adoration, the gift of tears, of ecstasy, and finally even the gift of rising from the ground and hovering above it, which is regarded by all as the ultimate." The figure interested Goethe so much that he later added quite an essay about this saintly man. — The four fathers of this scene are located on different levels according to their relative perfection in divine knowledge. This feature of the scene may have been derived from the writings of Emanuel Swedenborg (1688–1772).

11 862   **das Nichtige**   His material body, which he wishes would dissolve into nothingness.

11 864   **glänze**   Optative, like *verflüchtige*, expressing purpose.

SD 11 866   **profundus**   The profound, the mystic, a name applied to Bernard of Clairvaux (Saint Bernard, 1091–1153).

11 874   **Ist**   Supply the subject *es* 'there is.'

11 882   As subject of *sind* one may supply *es*, meaning the lightning, the rain, the wind, and the waterfall.

11 885–11 887   The body is spoken of as the prison of the spirit; it sets confining limits to the soul by its senses, which hurt, as tight-fitting chains hurt a captive.

SD 11 890   **Pater seraphicus**   A name given St. Francis of Assisi (1182–1226), founder of the Franciscan order of monks. He sees a host of angel boys which looks like a rosy cloud at dawn, as it hovers among the tops of the fir trees.

11 892   **Innern**   The reference is to *Morgenwölkchen*, 11 890.

SD 11 894   The blessed boys are children who have died unbaptized, immediately after birth. They have committed no sin. Yet, as sons of Adam, they are tainted with the sin of their human origin. Hence they are young spirits who have to hover between Heaven and earth until they become mature enough to enter Heaven. — The immediate source of the ideas represented by these boys and by subsequent groups in this scene is the ARCANA COELESTIA of Swedenborg.

11 898   **Mitternachts-Geborne**   An allusion to the popular belief that a child born at midnight is not likely to survive long.

11 901   **Gewinn**   These children, who die immediately after their birth, eventually arrive in Heaven to delight the angels. This they achieve only after an educative process which extends through several stages of increasing perfection.

11 902   This clause is the predicate of *fühlt* in 11 903. One may understand *ist* with *zugegen*. The 'loving one' is the *Pater seraphicus* himself.

11 906　The boys are invited to enter the body of the seraphic father and to look at the things of this earth through his eyes, since their own eyes are unacquainted with earthly scenes. This idea comes from Swedenborg and appears occasionally in Goethe's letters from 1781 to 1824.

11 929　**drein** Either *in den Ringverein,* or *in das Sich-regen.*

11 932　**den** God. See Matthew 5.8: "Blessed are the pure in heart; for they shall see God."

11 934–11 941　In a conversation with Eckermann, June 6, 1831, Goethe is reported to have said: "In diesen Versen ist der Schlüssel zu Fausts Rettung enthalten: in Faust selber eine immer höhere und reinere Tätigkeit bis ans Ende, und von oben die ihm zu Hülfe kommende ewige Liebe. Es steht dieses mit unserer religiösen Vorstellung durchaus in Harmonie, nach welcher wir nicht bloß durch eigene Kraft selig werden, sondern durch die hinzukommende göttliche Gnade." — In the main manuscript of this scene there are penciled quotation marks before 11 936 and at the end of 11 937 which may have been inserted by Goethe himself. Many editions print the lines with these quotation marks, though clearly nothing in Faust is being quoted.

11 938　**teilgenommen** 'taken an interest in,' 'showed concern for.'

SD 11 942　The angels who soar in the upper reaches of the atmosphere bearing Faust's soul to Heaven are divided into two choruses. One is the chorus of the younger angels, who have been the shock troops in the fight against Mephistopheles and his cohorts. The other is the chorus of the more perfect angels, who appear to be actually carrying the immortal remains of Faust. They complain at 11 954–11 957 that this task is unpleasant, and the younger angels suggest (11 978–11 980) that Faust's soul be turned over to the 'blessed boys' who have obeyed *Pater seraphicus* and risen to this higher circle.

11 956　**Asbest** Typically resistant to the typical cleanser, fire. This earthly remnant would be unclean from an angelic point of view, even if it had passed through fire and flame.

11 958–11 965　When a strong spirit has appropriated the physical elements which give it form and temporal identity, not even an angel (the highest created being) can separate the intimate unified duality of spirit and physical elements; this can be separated only by God, through his eternal love.

11 967　The use of the singular pronoun *ich* by the whole chorus of younger angels is irregular and disturbing. Perhaps one should add the stage direction *Solo,* in order to get a logically acceptable form. Or perhaps one may think of the younger angels as so much of a unity that they may all together speak of themselves as "*ich.*"

11 978　**er** Faust or Faust's immortal parts are turned over to the 'blessed boys,' so that he may in due course enter with them into Heaven, when he shall have been freed of his last earthly imperfection.

11 979　**Vollgewinn** Dative with *zu,* to be repeated from line 11 978.

11 984　**Unterpfand** 'A pledge' from the angels that the boys too shall enter into Heaven along with Faust.

11 985 Flocken If this has to do with the chrysalis (11 982) it probably means little tufts of cotton-like fibres, which would be plucked from the cocoon as the boys free Faust's soul from its case.

SD 11 989 Doctor Marianus The fourth anchorite, and the one among them especially devoted to the worship of the Virgin Mary. Goethe first called this one *Pater Marianus*, but changed the title to *Doctor,* without important significance, but still to mark some difference between Marianus and the others. These strive for purification; Doctor Marianus longs for the revelation of the mystery of Maria (12 000). His cell is on the highest level and from it he can look directly into Heaven. This hymn of Doctor Marianus has been very effectively set to music by Robert Schumann. — The adjective *reinlichsten* suggests degrees of cleanliness (or purity?) in the abodes of the preceding hermits and rests, probably, upon the observation of Wilhelm von Humboldt concerning the hermits on Montserrat (near Barcelona). Humboldt was impressed by the cleanliness of these hermit-cells.

12 001–12 004 Brust Either the object of both *beweget* and *entgegenträget:* 'Approve the force (*was*) which moves the heart of man seriously and tenderly, and which with the holy joy of love bears that heart to you,' or the subject of *entgegenträget:* 'Approve the feelings (*was*) which the heart of man, being seriously and tenderly moved, and with the sacred joy of love, offers you.' In this case the phrase *ernst und zart beweget* is parenthetical and should be enclosed in commas.

12 009–12 012 The apostrophes to the Virgin are ecstatic adorations, not statements; hence there is no verb.

SD 12 032 Mater gloriosa The Virgin in Glory, the counterpart of the *Mater dolorosa* of SD 3587.

SD 12 037 Magna peccatrix The sinful woman, who in the house of Simon, the Pharisee, bathed Christ's feet with her tears, anointed them with precious ointment from an alabaster cruse, and then wiped his feet with the hair of her head. — **St. Lucae** = *sancti Lucae* (Latin genitive singular forms) 'of St. Luke.' The reference is to Luke 7.37–50.

12 040 Simon, the Pharisee, when Jesus received the ministrations of the sinful woman, remarked that if Jesus were really a prophet he would have known what sort of vile person he was permitting to touch him.

SD 12 045 The woman of Samaria (John 4.7–30), whom Jesus met at Jacob's well and asked for a drink of water from her pail, was living with her sixth "husband," who was not really her wedded husband. Whatever the writer of the Gospel may have believed this woman to represent, Goethe presents her as a representative of feminine frailty and sinful abandon.

12 045 Bronn This was Jacob's well. Jacob was the son of Isaac and the grandson of Abraham.

SD 12 053 Maria Aegyptiaca (Acta Sanctorum) The 'Acts of the Saints' is a collection of legends about the saints and martyrs of the Christian church. It was begun in the seventeenth century and continued until 1875, when the work had reached sixty-three volumes. According to the story there, this 'Mary of Egypt' led a life of sensual abandon for seventeen years. Finally, when she tried on a festival day to enter the church in Jerusalem, an invisible hand stopped her. She repented her sin, prayed to the Virgin, and was miraculously picked up and set down in the church. There she heard a voice which commanded her to go out into the desert beyond the river Jordan to find peace. This she did, living a life of penance in the desert for forty-eight years. When she came to die, she wrote in the sand a request to the Monk Socinius that her body be buried and that he pray for her soul. The reason for her presence here is that she, like the great sinner of Luke 7 and the Samaritan woman of John 4, was a sinful woman of carnal lusts.

12 053 **Orte** The place where Christ's body was buried.

12 065 The three famous sinners pray for the soul of Gretchen, who appears here as a penitent woman.

12 069 This prayer bears a strong outward resemblance to the prayer addressed to the Virgin by Gretchen in the *Zwinger* (3587–3619). Its joyful content contrasts sharply with the agony of the earlier petition.

12 076 The boys come bringing the immortal portion of Faust. In his spiritual body, he is much larger than they, and the boys hope he will repay in kind their careful attention. Indeed, they hope that he will make this requital by teaching them what he has learned.

12 090–12 091 'See how the fresh vigor of youth is evident under the ethereal robe he now wears.'

SD 12 104 **mysticus** Goethe first called this a *Chorus in excelsis*, 'a chorus on high.' Later he substituted the present title. The change relates the heading more closely to the content of the lines, for here the mystery of Heaven is suggested.

12 105 **Gleichnis** An image, an allegory, giving no direct access to truth, but permitting man to learn about it.

12 107 **Ereignis** What remains unrealized on earth, because of the insufficiency and inadequacy of all earthly endeavor, reaches its fulfillment in Heaven, in an event which is the realization of the soul's striving.

12 110 **das Ewig-Weibliche** 'Eternal Love' leads man upward. This final chorus says that human life is an allegory. In the everlasting realm where the *Chorus mysticus* dwells, all the inadequacies of human strivings disappear, and the realization of the soul's desires is achieved. Here the inexpressible perfection of man is attained. Through all human endeavor, the leading, guiding force is Love, which appears to man in its embodiment in woman, but which is the everlasting driving force, and, in the end, 'saves' the man who strives without ceasing.

VOCABULARY

It is the purpose of this vocabulary to replace a German-English dictionary for the student who is reading *Faust*. Every word in the text and the stage directions was given an English translation or interpretation. In cases where widely different English translations were required, line numbers have been given, or entire phrases translated, where this practice appeared helpful. For example, tief is glossed as follows: "deep, heavy (*sleep*); remote, hidden (9975); low (11866); im tiefsten Grunde, utterly, completely (9374)." Since it is the purpose of this vocabulary to help American students understand *Faust*, and since *Faust* is what it is, the choice has occasionally been made against a prudish and in favor of an explicit rendering of certain items.

Morphological information is given after the head-word. For nouns, if a given noun appears in the plural in *Faust*, the nominative plural ending is indicated, as follows: "das **Märchen**, —; die **Maske**, -n; das **Maß**, -e"; but no plural is indicated for "**Matrone, Mauerloch, Maul, Mäuschen**," which do not occur in the plural in *Faust*. If a verb occurs in the preterit or past participle forms it will have a morphological indication (*wk*) for weak verbs, or the appropriate vowels for strong verbs, as follows: "**meinen** (*wk*); **mitbringen**, a, a (*wk, irreg*); **mitnehmen** (i), a, o"; but no indication is given for "**mitgehen, mitspielen, sich modeln, murren**," which occur only in the present tense forms. When a strong verb occurs only in the present tense, but in the second or third person singular with mutated vowel, that vowel is indicated, as follows: "**nachgeben** (i); **nachhalten** (ä)."

Some supplementary interpretation has been included in the items with mythological and geographical entries. Examples are: "**lernäisch** Lernaean (*a swamp near Argos*); **lernäische Schlange** Hydra; **Luzifer** Lucifer (*Satan before his fall*); **Lynkeus** Lynceus (*sharp-eyed pilot of the Argonauts*); Faust's watchman; **Pharsalus** Pharsalus (*scene of battle, 48 BC, between Caesar and Pompey*); **phrygisch** Phrygian, of Phrygia (*country in Asia Minor*)."

A

a! tara lara da! [*warming-up exercise for the voice*] do: mi: sol: do

aalgleich like an eel

der **Aar** eagle

das **Aas** carcass, carrion

ab downward, off; exit, exeunt; leave(s) the stage

abbrauchen (*wk*) wear off

das **ABC** the ABC, alphabet

der **Abend** evening

der **Abendhimmel** evening sky

das **Abendrot** evening glow

die **Abendsonneglut** glow of the evening sun

der **Abendstrahl** beam (radiance) of evening

der **Abendwind** evening breeze

das **Abenteuer** adventure, exploit

aber but; however; again (8451)

der **Aberglaube,** **-n** superstition

abermals again, once more

abertausend yet another thousand, yet more thousands

der **Aberwitz** imbecility, mental confusion

abestürzen plunge, fall

abfahren leave

abfallen fall off, drop off

abfertigen (*wk*) dispatch

sich **abfinden** make arrangements, get along

abgehen, i, a happen, proceed; go down; go off, leave the stage

der **Abgemagerte** the emaciated one (= Avarice)

der **Abgesandte, -n** ambassador, envoy

abgeschmackt in bad taste, insipid, absurd

sich **abgewöhnen** (*wk*) give up

der **Abglanz** reflection, reflected splendor

abgleiten slide down, slip down

der **Abgrund** precipice, abyss

abhalten (ä) restrain, keep away

abhängen (**von**) depend (upon)

abhängig (**von**) dependent (upon)

sich **abhärmen** pine away, languish

abkehren (*wk*) turn away

sich **abkehren** (*wk*) turn one's back, desert

ablecken lick

ablegen (*wk*) bear (witness)

ablenken turn aside, divert, parry (10484)

ablocken (*wk*) lure from

ablösen detach

abmachen (*wk*) settle, arrange

abmähen (*wk*) mow down

abmessen (i), a, e measure off; **abgemessen** with measured step (9534)

abnehmen (i) decrease, wane; take away (10344)

Abram Abraham

abraten (ä), ie, a dissuade, advise against

abriechen, o, o detect through the sense of smell

abringen, a, u wrest from

abründen (*wk*) round off

der **Abscheu** aversion

abscheulich horrible, loathsome

abschlagen (ä), u, a strike off, cut off

abschläglich in part payment

abschneiden, i, i cut off

abschütteln shake off

abschweben float down, soar down

abschweifen digress, change the subject

abschwellen: auf und ab schwellen (6009–6010) rise and fall, expand and contract

abseits aside, to the audience

absenden *see* der **Abgesandte**

absolut absolute

absondern (*wk*) separate, withdraw

abspazieren (*wk*) stroll away, stroll down

abspiegeln reflect

abspinnen, a, o spin off, reel off

abspringen, a, u jump off

abstecken (*wk*) mark off, set (a goal)

absteigen descend

abstreifen (*wk*) strip off, lay aside the attributes of

abstürzen plunge down

absurd absurd, irrational

abteilen divide

abtragen (ä), u, a wear out

abtreiben, ie, ie jade, drive to the point of exhaustion

abtun, a, a finish, finish off

abwallen surge down

abwärts downward

abwaschen wash off

abwechselnd alternately, in turn, antiphonally

sich **abwenden, a, a** (*wk, irreg*) turn away

abwischen wipe dry

abzehren (*wk*) emaciate, waste away

abziehen divert; drain off

abzupfen pluck off

abzwacken (*wk*) take by fraud

abzwingen extort

ach ah, alas, oh; cry of "ach!" (2024)

Achaia Achaia (*Greece, district in the northern part of the Peloponnesus*)

Achill Achilles (*Greek hero*)

achselzuckend shrugging the shoulders

acht: in acht nehmen observe, keep an eye on; **sich in acht nehmen** take care, be careful (not to); **acht geben** heed, pay attention, be careful; **außer acht lassen** neglect, ignore

die **Acht** eight

achte eighth

achten (*wk*) consider, esteem; have respect for

achtzig eighty

das **Ächzen** groaning

der **Acker** field, farmland

ackern cultivate, plow

Adam Adam

ade! good-bye

der **Adel** nobility

der **Adept, –en** expert (alchemist)

die **Ader, –n** vein

der **Adler, —** eagle

der **Affe, –n** ape, monkey; fool

affenjung very young, inexperienced; **affenjunges Blut** very young and inexperienced creature

Ägäisch Aegean (*sea east of Greece*)

Agathe Agatha

Aglaia Aglaia (*the Grace of festive brilliance*)

Ägypten Egypt

ah! ah!

aha! aha!

der **Ahn, –en** ancestor

ähneln (**ähnlet = ähnelt** 5079) liken, cause to resemble

ahnen (*wk*) have an idea, suspect, be aware of, have a presentiment of

der **Ahnherr** ancestor, founder of a family

der **Ahnherrntag, –e** ancient day, time of our ancestors

ähnlich like, similar, similar to

die **Ahnung** anticipation

der **Ahnungsdrang** intuitive impulse

ahnungsvoll sinister, ominous, foreboding; intuitive; with awed intuition

der **Ahorn** maple

der **Ährenkranz** wreath of ears of grain

Ajax Ajax (*Greek hero*)

akademisch academic

der **Akkord, –e** chord

akkurat exacting, accurate

der **Akt, –e** act

albern silly

Alcides Alcides, Hercules

Alekto Alecto (*one of the Furies*)

all(e) all, every, universal; **all und all** each and every one

All-Alle all together

allbereits already

allbewegend all-moving

allbezwingend all-subduing

die **Allegorie, –n** allegory

allegorisch allegorical

allein(e) lone, solitary, alone; solus; only, however

all-einzeln exclusively, quite alone, as sole (sovereign)

allemal: ein für allemal once and for all, under all circumstances

allemsig very industrious

allenfalls at all events, in any case

allerbeste best of all

allerderbste most sturdy and uncouth

allerdings of course, just so

allergrößte largest of all

der **Allerhalter** Preserver of the universe

allerhöchste highest, supreme, All-highest

allerklarste clearest of all

allerklügste most judicious, most wise

allerlei all kinds of

allerletzt last of all, very last

allerliebste dearest, kindest, best loved

allerliebst-gesellig having the most pleasant company

allermeist most of all

das **Allermindeste** very smallest thing

allerneuste most recent, very latest

allerorten everywhere

allerreichste richest of all

allerreifste ripest of all

allerschlimmste worst of all

allerschönste loveliest of all, finest of all

allerseitig universal, on all sides

allerseits on all sides, everywhere

allerstillste very quietest

allertiefste very deepest

allerwegs under all circumstances

allerweit'ste broadest

allesamt one and all, in toto

allgemein general, universal

der Allgesang chorus

allgewaltig all-powerful

allhier here, right here

allieblichste loveliest of all

allmächtig almighty, omnipotent

allseits on all sides

der Allumfasser Encompasser of the universe

allunverändert wholly unchanged

der Allverein universal oneness

allwärts in all directions

allwißbegierig desirous of knowing everything

allwissend omniscient

allzu too, all too

allzudeutlich all too plainly

allzugewohnt all too accustomed

allzugleich all too quickly

allzugroß excessive

allzuherb all too bitter

allzulästig all too annoying

allzuleicht all too easy

allzulüstern all too greedy

allzumal all at once, all together

allzusammen all together, one and all

allzuschändlich unbearably shameful

allzuschön all too handsome

allzutoll all too mad

allzuviele excessive

allzuweit all too far

die Alpe mountain pasturage (4699)

Alpen Alps (5070)

das Alpenfeld Alpine field, meadow

das Alphabet alphabet

der Alraun, –e mandrake (*plant thought to have magical properties*)

als as, when; as if; like; than; but, except (3697)

alsbald immediately

alsdann then, forthwith

also so, accordingly, therefore, thus

alsobald immediately, thereupon

alsofort at once

alt old, ancient; old one, Old Man (350)

der Altan, –e balcony

der Altar altar

das Alter age, old age

das Altertum antiquity, ancient times

altklug knowing

Altmeyer Altmeyer

alt-thessalisch of ancient Thessaly (*in northern Greece*)

altväterisch ancestral, ancient, primitive

altvergraben long buried

altverwahrt long guarded, long locked-up

der **Alt-Wald,** ⸚er primeval forest

altwürdig venerable

am = an dem

die **Amazone, –n** Amazon

die **Ambrosia** ambrosia (*food of the Greek gods*)

die **Ameise, –n** ant

der **Ameis-Wimmelhaufen, —** swarming anthill

die **Amme** nurse

amortisieren (*wk*) redeem

das **Amt** office, duty; mass (3776); **hier schweigt mein Amt** I need not speak officially, in my official capacity (6451)

amtsgemäß in accordance with one's office

amüsieren entertain, divert

an at, by, along, near, up to, on, with, in; to (2855)

der **Anachoret, –en** anchorite, hermit

die **Anarchie** anarchy, lawlessness

Anaxagoras Anaxagoras (*Greek philosopher*)

anbauen (*wk*) cultivate

der **Anbeginn** beginning

anbeginnen begin, make a start

anbetend worshipping, adoring

die **Anbetung** adoration

anbieten, o, o offer

anbinden: kurz angebunden brusque, snappish

der **Anblick** sight, view

anblicken (*wk*) look at, view

anblinken gleam (before one's eyes)

anbrechen (i) fall (*night*)

die **Andacht** reverence, worship

andächtig reverent

das **Andachtsbild** image in a shrine

ander other, different, else; next (11126, 11464)

andermal other time

ändern change, alter

anders otherwise, differently, else

anderwärts elsewhere

sich **andrängen** force itself upon, attach itself to

Andreas Andrew

andringen, a, u press forward

aneignen appropriate, assimilate

aneinander against one another

anerkennen, a, a (*wk, irreg*) recognize, appreciate, acknowledge

anfächeln fan

anfachen (*wk*) kindle, fan into flame

der **Anfall** inheritance

anfallen (ä) attack

der **Anfang** beginning; **anfangs** in the beginning

anfangen (ä), **i, a** begin, undertake, do

anfassen (*wk*) take hold of, seize, grasp

anfechten (i), **o, o** oppose, attack

anfrischen (*wk*) refresh, reinvigorate

anführen (*wk*) lead on; cheat; bring forward; direct

anfüllen (*wk*) fill up, occupy

das **Angedenken** memento, keepsake

angehen, i, a concern; be practicable; make advances to (8817)

angehören belong

die **Angejahrte**, –n mature one, grown-up, middle-aged woman (6362)

die **Angel** fishing pole

angenehm pleasant, acceptable, attractive

der **Anger** green place, lawn, meadow

das **Angesicht** face, countenance; **auf das Angesicht** flat on one's face

angestrengt striving with great exertion

anglühen (*wk*) heat to a glow

der **Angriff** attack

angrinsen grin at

angrünen (*wk*) grow green

die **Angst**, ⁔e terror, anxiety

ängsten distress

der **Ängstesprung** anguished leap

ängstlich uneasy, worried, timid, over-scrupulous

ängstlich-labyrinthisch torturously roundabout

angstumschlungen closely surrounded by worries

anhaben get a hold on

anhalten (ä), ie, a restrain, check

anhauchen breathe upon

anhäufen accumulate, pile up

sich **anhäufen** accumulate

anheimgeben entrust, place in one's keeping

anhören listen to

anhüpfen (*wk*) skip up to

anketten (*wk*) attach, chain together

anklagen make complaints

anklammern cling to, clutch

der **Anklang** harmonious echo

anklingen, **a**, **u** clink, touch glasses

anklopfen (*wk*) knock at the door

anknüpfen (*wk*) attach

ankommen, **a**, **o** depend; require; arrive

ankrähen crow at, screech at

ankünden announce

ankündigen (*wk*) announce

anlangen arrive

der **Anlaß** occasion

anlegen (*wk*) put on

sich **anlehnen** make contact (with something)

anlernen (*wk*) learn, acquire by training

anlocken (*wk*) attract, entice

sich **anmaßen** arrogate to oneself

anmaßlich presumptuous

anmästen fatten; **sich ein Ränzlein anmästen** grow a paunch by overeating

anmessen (i), a, e take measurements (for clothes); suit, adapt for

die **Anmut** grace, charm

anmutig graceful, agreeable, pleasant

die **Anmutigkeit** gracefulness, agreeableness

annehmen (i), a, o accept

sich **annehmen** (i), a, o take an interest in

die **Anordnung** preparation, instruction, arrangement

sich **anpaaren** join so as to form couples

anpacken seize

anpochen (*wk*) knock

anrauchen (*wk*) smoke to a brown color, smudge

anregen stir up

anriechen discover by smelling

anrufen call upon, invoke

ans = an das

ansagen say on, speak on; tell, announce (8666, 8965)

ansaugen, o, o drink in

anschaffen (*wk*) procure

anschauen (*wk*) look at, contemplate

sich anschicken prepare to do something, set to work

anschießen come shooting up (toward one)

sich anschließen join, attach oneself

anschmausen feast on, eat with satisfaction

anschmiegen press close to, nestle up to

sich anschmiegen press close to, nestle up to

anschnauzen snort at

anschreiten stride on, stride forward

anschüren (*wk*) stir up

anschwimmen come swimming

ansehen (ie), a, e look at, look upon, regard

sich ansiedeln (*wk*) settle

ansprechen (i) speak to

der Anspruch claim

ansprühen (*wk*) scatter sparks upon, ignite by a spark

der Anstand propriety, modest behavior; bearing (9184)

anständig with propriety, suitable, decorous; with honor, with due dignity

anständig-nackt suitably nude, decently naked

anstatt instead of

anstecken (*wk*) infect, taint

anstehen be suitable for, become

anstellen (*wk*) appoint, assign to a task

anstimmen strike up (a song)

anstoßen (ö), ie, o push against, nudge; clink (glasses); give offense (11616)

anstrahlen (*wk*) beam upon, cause to glow

anstreifen (*wk*) touch in passing

sich anstrengen (*wk*) exert oneself

antasten infringe upon

Antäus Antaeus (*a giant*)

der Anteil interest

antik classical, belonging to Greek and Roman antiquity

antikisch classical, of antiquity

die Antipathie antipathy

die Antizipation, –en advance against future income

das Antlitz countenance

Antonius Anthony

antragen offer

antrauen (*wk*) betroth, engage

antreiben, ie, ie urge on, impel

antreten advance

antun, a, a dress, put on (clothes); bewitch, cast a spell upon

die Antwort answer

antworten answer

anvertrauen (*wk*) entrust

der Anverwandte, –n relative, kin

anwandeln come over

anweiben (*wk*) give in marriage, marry

anweisen, ie, ie assign, force to depend upon

anzeigen indicate, point out

anziehen, o, o attract, summon; draw on, draw tight; dress

äolisch Aeolian, pertaining to Aeolis (*Greek-colonized Asia Minor*)

die Äolsharfe, –n Aeolian harp

Äonen eons, immeasurable ages

apart specially reserved

der Apfel, ⸚ apple

der Apfelbaum apple tree

das Äpfelchen, — little apple

das Apfelgold gold of apples; golden apples, oranges (*pomum aurantium*)

Aphidnus Aphidnus (*friend of Theseus*)

Apoll Apollo (*god of light, wisdom, poetry*)

der Apparat, –e apparatus, piece of apparatus

der Appetit appetite

appetitlich appetizing, attractive

applaudieren applaud

die Arbeit work

der Arbeiter, — workman

der Architekt architect

Ares Ares, Mars (*god of war*)

arg bad

ärgern make angry, annoy

die Arglist craftiness

Argolis Argolis (*district in Peloponnesus*)

der Argonaut, –en Argonaut (*Greek hero, sailor on the ship Argo, quester for the Golden Fleece*)

der Argonautenkreis band of Argonauts

Ariel Ariel

Arimaspen Arimasps (*a people of Scythia, having but one eye each*)

das Arimaspen-Volk race of Arimasps

Arkadien Arcadia (*unspoiled rural region in central Peloponnesus*)

arkadisch Arcadian

der Arm, –e arm

arm poor

armausbreitend spreading out the arms

der Ärmel sleeve

ärmlich wretched, miserable

die Armschiene, –n armlet (*piece of armor for the arm*)

armselig miserable

die Armut poverty

ärschlings tail first

die Art kind, sort, type; manner, style, way

artig well-behaved, pleasing

die Arzenei medicine

der Arzt, ⸚e physician

der Asbest asbestos

die Asche ash, ashes

das Aschenhäufchen little pile of ashes

der Aschenhaufen heap of ashes

die Aschenruh peace of death (ashes, dust)

Aschermittwoch Ash Wednesday (*first day of Lent*)

asketisch ascetic

asklepisch Aesculapian, medical

Äskulap Aesculapius (*god of medicine*)

Asmodeus Asmodeus (*a demon*)

die Asphodelos-Wiese, –n meadow of asphodel (*daffodils*)

assoziieren associate

der **Ast**, ⁻e bough, branch
der **Astrolog** astrologer
der **Atem** breath
atemholend catching breath
die **Atemkraft** power of breath-
ing
der **Atheist**, –en atheist
der **Äther** sky, ethereal realm,
upper air
das **Ätherblau** ethereal blue
ätherisch ethereal
Atlas Atlas (*giant who held up
the vault of heaven*)
atmen (*wk*) breathe
die **Atmosphäre** atmosphere, air
atmosphärisch through the atmosphere
Atropos Atropos (*the Fate who
cuts the thread of life*)
Attika Attica (*district of Greece
including Athens*)
die **Attitüde** pose, attitude
au! ow! ouch!
auch also, too, likewise; even;
either; (**was, wer, wenn . . .**)
-ever
die **Aue**, –n meadow
Auerbach Auerbach (*owner of a
wine cellar in Leipsic*)
auf on, upon; in response to;
in, at, to, for, up, up to; **auf
und ab** up and down, back
and forth; **auf!** get up!
der **Aufbau** construction, building up
aufbauen (*wk*) build up
aufbeben rise trembling
aufbewahren (*wk*) preserve, keep
aufbinden fasten up, tie up
sich **aufblähen** blow itself up,
expand
aufblicken glance up, look up

aufblühen bloom, come into
flower
aufbrechen (i), a, o depart
aufdämmern dawn, grow light
sich **aufdringen**, a, u intrude
upon, force oneself upon
aufeinander at one another
der **Aufenthalt** place to stay,
abode
auferbauen (*wk*) edify, raise
(into man's estate)
auferlegen (*wk*) place under
someone's control, assign to
someone as a responsibility
auferstanden resurrected
die **Auferstehung** resurrection
auffahren jump up, start up
auffallen stand out, attract attention, be conspicuous
auffassen catch, pick up
auffinden, a, u discover
aufflammen burst into flame
auffliegen, o, o fly off, take wing
auffordern summon, invite, challenge
auffressen (i), a, e devour, en-
gorge
auffüttern (*wk*) feed (by hand)
aufgeben (i) set, pose (a riddle)
aufgehen, i, a be opened; rise,
go up
aufhalten (ä), ie, a detain, delay
aufhäufen (*wk*) heap up, accumulate
aufheben, o/u, o suspend, re-
peal; cancel; lift up; lay away
aufhören cease, stop
aufjauchzen shout for joy
aufkeimen (*wk*) bud
aufklären (*wk*) establish enlightenment
aufklettern scramble upward

aufladen (ä), **u, a** impose upon, charge with

auflauern lie in wait for

sich **auflösen** dissolve, fall apart, melt

aufmachen open

aufmerken notice, pay heed to

aufmerksam attentive; paying attention to; becoming aware (4461)

aufnehmen (i), **a, o** receive, accept

aufpacken (*wk*) pack up, take away

aufpassen (*wk*) pay attention, be on guard

aufpolstern (*wk*) pad, cushion

aufputzen (*wk*) deck out, dress up, adjust (*another's*) finery

aufquellen well up

aufraffen pick up, snatch up

aufregen (*wk*) excite, arouse

aufreiben, ie, ie wear out, exhaust

aufreißen tear open

sich **aufreißen** get up quickly

aufreizen stir up, provoke to action

sich **aufrichten** rise, straighten up

aufrichtig candid, honest

aufrufen summon

der **Aufruhr** tumult, uproar

aufs = auf das

aufschaffen, u, a revive (to further torture)

aufschallen sound up, peal out

aufschauen look, look up

aufschäumen surge foaming

aufscheuchen (*wk*) scare off, startle, frighten

aufschimmern begin to gleam

aufschlagen (ä), **u, a** open; set up

aufschließen unlock

aufschrecken startle

aufschweben float up, soar up; **auf- und abschweben** soar up and down

aufschwellen (i) distend, swell, expand

sich **aufschwingen** soar, take wing

der **Aufseher** overseer, inspector

aufsetzen (*wk*) put on

aufsieden boil up

aufsitzen, a, e sit up, mount, mount one's throne

aufspringen jump up; fly open

aufstehen, a, a get up, arise, stand up, be open for business (6088)

aufsteigen mount, ascend, rise

aufstellen (*wk*) set up, arrange, erect

aufstemmen (*wk*) prop up; **den Ellenbogen aufgestemmt** leaning on one's elbow

aufstreichen, i, i spread on

aufstutzen (*wk*) renovate (*as a tailor does*)

aufsuchen seek out, look up

auftappen come stalking up

auftauchen emerge above the surface

der **Auftrag** assignment, task

auftragen (ä), **u, a** ask to convey, set as a task or errand

auftreten (i), **a, e** appear, come forward

sich **auftun, a, a** open up

sich **auftürmen** (*wk*) tower up, tower

aufwachen wake up

aufwallen surge up

aufwälzen (wk) roll together

der Aufwand effort, expenditure of energy

aufwärmen (wk) warm

aufwarten wait for; beg (dog)

aufwärts upward

aufwirbeln (wk) whirl up

aufzehren consume

aufziehen, o, o bring up, raise; proceed along (8543–8544)

aufzieren (wk) adorn, dress up

das Auge, –n eye

äugeln make eyes, ogle

der Augenblick, –e moment, instant

das Augenblickchen fleeting instant

der Augenblitz sharpness of vision

Augenbrauen eyebrows

der Augenschmerz pain in the eyes

der Augenstrahl sharpness of vision

die Augentäuschung optical illusion

die Aureole aureole, halo

Aurora Aurora (goddess of dawn)

aus out of, from, because of, for

ausbauen build, build to completion

ausbieten offer for sale

ausbilden (wk) form, bring to perfection

ausbitten request urgently

ausblasen blow out

ausbleiben fail to appear

ausbreiten (wk) spread out, extend

ausbrennen, a, a (wk, irreg) gut by fire; burn out, go out

ausdauern hold out against, outlast

ausdenken, a, a think out

ausdrücken express

auseinanderfahren separate, scatter

auserlesen made to order, selected

ausersehen (ie), a, e select, set aside

ausfahren (ä), u, a depart, set out

ausfinden, a, u discover

die Ausforderung challenge, defiance

ausführen execute, carry out

ausführlich in detail

ausfüllen fill out

der Ausgang way out, exit

ausgaukeln (wk) go fluttering to its end, finish its butterfly-like career

ausgehen, i, a start

das Ausgesprochene what has been said

ausgleichen reconcile, settle; make up for (8919)

aushalten (ä) endure

sich aushelfen resort to

aushöhlen (wk) hollow out

auskitten repair with cement or putty

ausklauben pick out with the fingers

auslachen laugh at, ridicule

ausleeren empty completely

auspichen (wk) cover or coat with pitch; ausgepicht case-hardened

auspusten blow out

ausraufen tear out

ausräumen (wk) clear, clean out

ausrecken (*wk*) stretch out

ausreiben, ie, ie rub (the sleep from one's eyes)

ausruhen rest

ausrupfen pluck out

ausschicken (*wk*) send out

den Ausschlag geben decide the issue, turn the scale

ausschließen keep out, exclude

ausschlürfen sip to the end

ausschmücken (*wk*) decorate, adorn

ausschneiden cut out

ausschreiten traverse

aussehen (ie), a, e seem, appear

außen out, outside

außer beyond, aside from, except

äußere outer, external

sich aussetzen expose oneself to

die Aussicht prospect, view

aussinnen, a, o think out, think up

ausspannen (*wk*) stretch out

ausspenden dispense

aussprechen (i), a, o speak out, express, utter

ausspüren (*wk*) trace, trail, track down

aussteigen disembark, leave (the ship)

ausstreuen (*wk*) scatter about, sow seeds

aussuchen (*wk*) choose, select

austeilen distribute, give

austrinken, a, u drain, drink

ausüben practice, exercise, exert

auswachsen (ä), u, a grow up

der Ausweg way out, issue

ausweichen retreat, withdraw

ausweinen (*wk*) cry one's heart out

auszeichnen distinguish, set apart

ausziehen, o, o pull out, extract; march out (7645)

sich ausziehen undress

auszieren (*wk*) ornament, decorate

der Auszug essence, extract

der Autor author

Avaritia Avarice

B

der Baccalaureus bachelor of arts

Bacchus Bacchus (*god of wine*)

der Bach, ⸚e brook, torrent

das Bächlein, — brooklet

die Backe, -n cheek

backenrot red-cheeked

der Backenstreich slap on the cheek

der Bäcker baker

die Bäckertür, -en bakery door

das Bad bath, bathing place

baden bathe

die Bahn, -en pathway, course, orbit, way

bahnen (*wk*) break a path

die Bahre bier

bald soon, nearly; bald ... bald now ... now

baldig early

der Balken beam, rafter

der Balkon balcony

der Ball dance

der Ball, -e (*dat. pl.*) Ballen ball, globe, sphere

der Ballen, — bale

sich ballen (*wk*) clench (fist); coagulate, fold into globular shape (*cloud*)

der **Balsam** balm
der **Balsamduft** gentle fragrance
der **Balsamsaft** balm-bringing juice
bammeln dangle
das **Band, –e** bond, tie
das **Band, ‿er** ribbon
bändigen (*wk*) restrain, subdue
bang uneasy, nervous, fearful, anxious
bangen be disquieted, be disturbed
bänglich uneasy, fearful
die **Bank, ‿e** bench
der **Bann** excommunication
bannen (*wk*) banish; confine, force into and restrain in (a place)
der **Bannerherr** banneret, knight with rank just below that of baron
bar pure (9327)
der **Barbar, –en** barbarian
das **Bärbelchen** Barbara, "Babs"
barmherzig merciful
der **Baron** baron
barsch rude, impolite
der **Bart** beard; key bit, key web (671)
der **Bärtige, –n** bearded man
baß further, rather, downright
der **Baß** bass
die **Baubo** Baubo
der **Bauch, ‿e** belly
bauchrednerisch as a ventriloquist
Baucis Baucis
bauen (*wk*) build
der **Bauer, –n** farmer
die **Bauernarbeit** farm work
die **Baulichkeit** edifice

der **Baum, ‿e** tree
das **Bäumchen** sapling
die **Baumwolle** cotton
die **Baute** building
beängsten (*wk*) worry
beängstigen worry
beben (*wk*) tremble, quake
beblümt covered with flowers
bebräunt browned
bebuscht filled with bushes
der **Becher** goblet, chalice
das **Becken, —** basin; (small) cymbal
der **Bedacht** deliberation
bedächtig prudent, deliberate
bedauern pity
die **Bede** tribute
bedecken cover
bedenken, a, a (*wk, irreg*) consider, reflect, bear in mind
bedenklich delicate, difficult, suspicious, requiring thought, doubtful
bedeuten signify, mean
bedeutend important, significant, meaningful
die **Bedeutung** significance, meaning
bedeutungsvoll full of significance
bedienen serve (10677)
sich **bedienen** make use, avail oneself, take advantage
der **Beding** condition, stipulation
sich **bedingen** derive its nature, be conditioned
mit **Bedingnis** with the stipulation
die **Bedingung** condition
bedrängen afflict, oppress
bedränglich afflicting, grieving
die **Bedrängnis** distress, affliction

bedrohlich threatening

bedürfen (a), **u, u** (*irreg*) need, require, be in need of

bedürftig in need, needy

die **Beere,** –**n** berry

das **Beeren-Füllhorn** cornucopia full of berries

befangen (ä), **i, a** implicate, ensnare, imprison (3818); **befangen machen** trouble, confuse, perplex (2824)

sich **befangen** (ä), **i, a** occupy oneself with (319)

sich **befassen** occupy oneself

sich **befehden** (*wk*) engage in feuds

der **Befehl,** –**e** command, order

befehlen (ie), **a, o** command, order; commend, entrust

befestigen establish, fortify

befeuchten moisten, dampen

sich **befinden** be getting along

befitticht equipped with wings

beflaumt covered with down

sich **befleißen, i, i** apply oneself to the study or practice

beflügeln (*wk*) lend wings to

beflügelt winged

befördern advance, promote, further

befragen question

befreien (*wk*) free, set free, liberate, exempt

befrieden appease, pacify, soothe

befriedigen satisfy

die **Befriedigung** satisfaction, contentment

begabt gifted, talented, endowed

sich **begeben** (i) betake oneself; occur (9582)

die **Begebenheit** event, occurrence

das **Begebnis** happening

begegnen (*wk*) meet, encounter; treat; occur, happen

begehen, i, a commit, perform, carry out

das **Begehr** desire

begehren (*wk*) request, wish, desire, hanker after, crave, long for, covet

begeistern fill with enthusiasm, inspire

die **Begier** craving, appetite

die **Begierde,** –**n** eager desire, lust

begierig eager, hungry

begierlich greedy, covetous

beginnen, a (begonnte 3176), **o** begin, undertake; do (1383); be active

begleiten accompany, escort

der **Begleiter,** — attendant, companion

beglücken (*wk*) bless, bring happiness to, make happy

begnadigen pardon, show mercy to

sich **begnügen** (*wk*) be content

begraben (ä), **u, a** bury

das **Begräbnis** burial

begreifen comprehend, understand

der **Begriff,** –**e** idea, notion, comprehension; **im Begriffe sein** be about to (11145)

begriffen engaged (5298)

sich **begrünen** become green

begrüßen (*wk*) hail, greet, welcome; apply (to someone) for permission (4157)

begüten (*wk*) pacify, soothe

behagen suit, fit, give pleasure to, please

sich **behagen** enjoy oneself; **sich behagen lassen** take pleasure in, enjoy

das **Behagen** enjoyment, delight

behaglich comfortable, easy

behalten (ä) keep, retain; **recht behalten** be right, win an argument

das **Behälter** receptacle

behandeln (*wk*) handle, treat, manipulate

behängt covered, hung

beharren remain unchanged

der **Behelf** resort, expedient

behemdet clothed in a shirt or slip

behend agile, adroit, skillful, nimble

behendig agile

die **Behendigkeit** agility

beherrschen rule, govern

der **Beherrscher** ruler

beherzt bold, emboldened

behüte! forbid!

bei in connection with, with, by, at the house of, near, in case of, during

die **Beichte** confession

beide both, two

beidrängen press, crowd

der **Beifall** applause

beihakeln pull in with grappling irons

beikommen get at

das **Beil** hatchet, executioner's axe

beilegen add, place beside

beim = bei dem

das **Bein**, –e leg; bone (4417)

beinah(e) almost

beinstellen trip

beipressen press into service

beisammen together

das **Beisein** life together

beiseit(e) aside, to one side

das **Beispiel** example; **zum Beispiel nur** merely for the sake of example

beißen bite

der **Beistand** support, helper

beistehen, a, a assist, help

beizeiten (beizeit 4277) betimes, in time

beizend strong, stinging

beiziehen transport hither

bejahen affirm, agree

bejahrt aged

bejammern bewail, mourn

bekämpfen combat, subdue

bekannt known, well-known, familiar

bekehren convert, dissuade

bekennen admit, acknowledge, confess

das **Bekenntnis** acknowledgment, confession

sich **beklagen** complain

beklommen depressed

beknurren growl at

bekommen, a, o get; agree with; **Lust bekommen** think one would like to

bekräftigen (*wk*) confirm

die **Bekräftigung** confirmation

bekränzt wearing a wreath

bekriegen make war against

beladen laden, loaded down

sich **beladen** (ä), **u, a** burden oneself, assume a burden

belasten (*wk*) encumber, burden

beleben (*wk*) animate, enliven, give life to, bring to life

belecken lick

belehren (*wk*) instruct, advise, teach, set aright

beleuchten illumine, light up

die **Beleuchtung** lighting, illumination

belieben (*wk*) please, seem desirable

das **Belieben** pleasure, desire, will; **nach Belieben** at will, ad libitum

beliebig to one's liking, as one likes, at one's pleasure

bellen bark

beloben commend, laud

belohnen reward

belügen, o, o lie to

sich **belustigen** enjoy, take pleasure in

sich **bemächtigen** take possession

bemeistern master

bemerken (*wk*) observe, notice; indicate (9679)

bemerkenswert worth noticing

bemodert moldy

bemoost moss-covered, venerable; **bemooster Herr** "patriarch" (*student who has delayed his final examination beyond the normal semester*)

bemühen (*wk*) trouble

sich **bemühen** (*wk*) exert oneself

das **Bemühen** exertion, effort

benagen gnaw at

benedeien (*wk*) bless

benehmen (i), a, o take away, withhold from

beneiden envy

beneidenswert enviable

benennen classify

benutzen use, make use of

bepflanzt planted

beprägen (*wk*) seal

bequem convenient, opportune, comfortable; easygoing, easily pleased (6935)

sich **bequemen** adapt oneself, conform, submit, lower oneself

bequemlichstens most comfortably

sich **beraten** deliberate, make plans

berauben rob

beräuchern purify by burning incense

berauschen intoxicate

berechnen calculate

das **Bereich** sphere of activity

bereit ready, available, in readiness

bereiten (*wk*) prepare, make ready, contrive

bereits already

die **Bereitung** preparation

bereuen (*wk*) regret, feel remorse for

der **Berg**, –e hill, mountain

der **Berg** deads, rock containing no ore (7601)

der **Bergast** mountain spur

bergen (i), a, o conceal; save, protect

die **Bergesader**, –n vein of ore

die **Bergeshöhe**, –n mountain height

die **Bergeshöhle** mountain cave

das **Berggebäu** mountain structure

bergig hilly

das **Bergregal** royalty from mines

die **Bergschlucht**, –en ravine, gorge

der **Bergsee** mountain lake

das **Bergvolk** mountain people

berichtigen (*wk*) settle

bersten burst

der **Beruf** activity, function, calling

berufen, ie, u summon, invoke, call for

die **Berufung** appeal (from a legal decision)

beruhigen (*wk*) make peaceful, content, quiet, pacify

sich **berühmen** boast

berühmt famous, celebrated

berühren touch

berußt grimy, soot-covered

besänftigen (*wk*) soothe, assuage, calm

beschäftigen (*wk*) keep busy, occupy

beschämen (*wk*) shame, make ashamed, disconcert

beschauen examine

bescheiden modest, sober, discreet, moderate

bescheiden, ie, ie allot, assign

die **Bescheidenheit** modesty

bescheinen, ie, ie shine upon

beschenken give a present to

bescheren (*wk*) bestow

beschimpfen insult, call names

beschlagen well-versed, expert

beschleunen speed up, hasten

beschleunigen accelerate, hurry up

beschließen resolve, determine, decide

der **Beschluß** prescription, dictate (8878); end, termination (9140)

beschnitten cut, pared down

beschränken (*wk*) confine, limit, narrow; **beschränkt** weak-minded

beschreiben, ie, ie describe; cover with writing (1726)

beschuldigt accused

beschützen protect, guard

beschwatzen wheedle, persuade

beschwätzen discuss at length

beschweren bother

sich **beschweren** complain

beschwerlich inconvenient

beschwichtigen (*wk*) appease, soothe

beschwören, o, o conjure; take an oath upon (9243)

die **Beschwörungsgebärde, –n** conjurer's gesture

beseelen (*wk*) animate, inspire

besehen (**ie**), **a, e** look over, scrutinize

der **Besen** broom

der **Besenstiel** broomstick

besetzen occupy

besiegeln (*wk*) seal, confirm by sealing

besiegen (*wk*) conquer, overcome, defeat, capture (10683)

sich **besinnen** reflect, think over

das **Besinnen** thought, pondering

der **Besitz** possession(s), property

besitzen, a, e possess; call one's own

der **Besitzer** owner

besitzlos without lawful owner

das **Besitztum** possession(s)

besondere peculiar, strange; particular, special

besonders especially, particularly

sich **bespiegeln** (*wk*) be reflected

besprechen discuss; conjure

sich **besprechen** converse, confer

besprengen purify by sprinkling

besser better

bessern improve

der **Bestand** permanence, stability

beständig continual, constant, steadfast

bestärken strengthen, confirm

bestätigen (*wk*) confirm, establish

die **Bestätigung** confirmation

bestatten (*wk*) bury

beste best, dearest

der **Bestecher** briber

bestehen, a, a pass (a test)

besteigen, ie, ie mount, ascend

bestellen (*wk*) arrange, order; appoint

die **Bestellung** management

die **Bestialität** swinishness

die **Bestie**, −n wild beast, "beastie"

bestimmen (*wk*) destine, allot (8531)

bestimmt definite, explicit

bestrafen punish

das **Bestreben** exertion, effort

bestürmen besiege, assail

bestürzt thrown into confusion, dismayed

der **Besuch** visit; company, visitor (2902)

besuchen visit

die **Besudelung** sullying

betätigen (*wk*) bring about

sich **betätigen** (*wk*) be active, participate actively

betauen (*wk*) bedew

beteiligt involved, implicated

beten (*wk*) pray, offer a prayer

die **Bethe** tribute

betören (*wk*) delude, fool, make a fool of, bedazzle, seduce

betrachten see, consider, study, look at

die **Betrachtung** meditation, study

sich **betragen** (ä), u, a conduct oneself

das **Betragen** behavior, conduct

betrauern (*wk*) be in mourning for

betreffen (i), a, o surprise; **was ...betrifft** so far as ... is concerned

betreten (i), a, e tread, set foot on; enter

betrüben (*wk*) grieve, afflict, cause sorrow

der **Betrug** fraud, humbug

betrügen, o, o deceive, cheat, trick, delude

betrunken drunken

das **Bett**, −en bed; channel

bettelarm very poor

betteln beg

die **Bettelsuppe**, −n weak thin soup

betten (*wk*) put to bed, lay to rest

der **Bettler**, — beggar

der **Bettvorhang** bed curtain

betupfen (*wk*) touch lightly

beugen bend; **den Sinn beugen** yield, give oneself up

sich **beugen** (*wk*) bend, bow

die **Beugung** bending, bowing

die **Beule** boil

sich **beurlauben** (*wk*) take one's leave

die **Beute** booty, loot, plunder; victim (11318)

der **Beutel** money bag, money pouch

der **Beuteschatz** treasure gained by plundering

das **Beuteteil** share of the loot

bevorstehen be in store for, be imminent

bewaffnet armed, in armor

der **Bewaffnete**, **–n** armed man

bewahren (*wk*) preserve, guard

bewähren (*wk*) test, try

sich **bewähren** (*wk*) prove true, prove trustworthy

bewegen (*wk*) move, stir, set in motion, excite, agitate

sich **bewegen** (*wk*) move, be stirred

die **Bewegung**, **–en** movement, motion

beweinen mourn the loss of, weep for

der **Beweis** proof

beweisen, ie, ie show, prove, display

bewitzeln sneer at, display wit in finding fault with

bewohnen (*wk*) inhabit

der **Bewohner**, **—** inhabitant

bewundern (*wk*) admire

die **Bewunderung** admiration, astonishment

der **Bewundrer**, **—** admirer

bewußt known; **sich bewußt** conscious, aware; **sich selbst bewußt** confident

bezahlen pay for, pay

bezähmen curb, moderate

bezeichnen (*wk*) show, designate

bezeugen make a declaration

der **Bezirk**, **–e** region

bezirken limit, circumscribe

bezüglich referring (to)

bezwingen bring under control

sich **bezwingen** restrain oneself

bieder trusty, stalwart

sich **biegen** bend

das **Bier** beer

bieten (ie/eu), o, o offer, bid, make an offer

das **Bild**, **–er** image, picture, portrait, representation, symbol

bilden (*wk*) form, constitute, fashion, shape; cultivate, educate

sich **bilden** assume form

der **Bildner**, **—** artist, sculptor

die **Bildnerei**, **–en** pictorial representation

das **Bildnis** likeness, image

die **Bildung** process of formation, formation

das **Billett** ticket

billigen approve, sanction

Bim ding, first note of a bell

das **Bim-Baum-Bimmel** dingdong

die **Binde**, **–n** bandage, band, ribbon

binden, a, u bind, put under constraint

sich **binden**, a, u put oneself under obligations

der **Binnenraum** interior

die **Birke**, **–n** birch

bis until, up to, as far as, to the point of, all the way to; by (*future time*, 7110)

der **Bischof** bishop

bisher up until now, formerly, previously

der **Biß** bite

ein **bißchen** a little, a bit, a little bit, rather, somewhat

der **Bissen** morsel

die **Bitte** request, petition

bitten, a, e ask, ask for, entreat; beg; **bitte** please bitter bitter

das **Blachgefild** open level country

sich **blähen** (*wk*) be puffed up, swell, show off

blank gleaming, shiny, polished

die **Blase** bubble

blasen (ä), ie, a blow

blaß pale

das **Blatt,** ⁻er leaf, sheet of paper; petal (3179)

das **Blättchen,** — little sheet of paper, scrap of paper, metal foil

blättern turn the pages in

blau blue

blechklappernd rattling tin

bleiben, ie, ie stay, remain, continue to be, endure, persist, always will be; **übrig bleiben** be left over, survive; **hängen bleiben** be caught, fail to work out; **stehen bleiben** stop; **sich der Nächste bleiben** look after one's own interests first (8792)

bleich pale, pallid

bleichen grow pale, be bleached

das **Bleigewicht** lead weight

bleischwer heavy as lead

blenden (*wk*) dazzle, bedazzle

blendend-weiß dazzling-white

die **Blendkraft,** ⁻e delusively dazzling power

das **Blendwerk,** -e work of specious deception

der **Blick,** -e view, vision, spectacle, sight; glance, look; insight (2288); gleam (11008, 11378)

blicken glance, look

blickschnell (= blitzschnell) swift as a lightning flash

blind blind

blinken gleam, sparkle

blinzeln blink

blinzen blink

der **Blitz,** -e flash, lightning flash; (*a mild oath*, 828)

blitzartig like lightning

blitzen flash, lighten

das **Blitzesknattern** crackling of lightning

der **Blitzeswink** lightning-like movement

der **Blocksberg** Blocksberg (*summit of the Harz, the Brocken Mountain*)

blöde bashful, shy

die **Blondine** blonde woman

bloß openly (3746); bare (4046); **der Sünde bloß** vulnerable because of my own transgression (3584)

die **Blöße** bare space, clearing in a forest

bloßgeben expose, lay bare

blühen blossom, bloom, flourish

das **Blümchen** flower (*of maidenhood*, 3561)

die **Blume,** -n flower

die **Blümelei,** -en posy, wretched flower

der **Blumenflor** display of flowers

die **Blumenkrone,** -n corolla (*a flower's petals*)

der **Blumenkrug,** ⁻e vase, flower jar

blumenreich rich in flowers

blumenstreifig braided or edged with flowers

das **Blumenwort** flower's word

blumig flowery

das **Blut** blood, spirits, temperament; lineage; precious fluid

(5712); **junges Blut** young creature

der **Blutbann** criminal court

die **Blüte, -n** blossom, flower

der **Blutegel, —** leech

bluten bleed

der **Blütentag** flourishing time

blutgeschrieben written in blood

blutig bloody

blutig-trüb blood-clouded, bloodshot

die **Blutschuld** blood guilt

der **Blutstuhl** executioner's block

der **Bock** he-goat

der **Bocksfuß** goat foot; satyr

der **Boden** ground, soil; floor

das **Bögelchen, —** little arch

der **Bogen, —** bow, arch; rainbow (4722)

der **Bogenstrahl** arched waterfall

bohren (*wk*) bore, bore a hole

der **Bohrer** gimlet, auger

der **Bootsmann** boatman

Boreaden Boreades (*two of the Argonauts*)

borgen (*wk*) lend, give credit

die **Börse** purse

borstig bristly

bös bad, evil, wicked, harsh, unkind; angry

bösartig malevolent

der **Bote, -n** messenger

die **Botschaft** message, tidings

der **Bovist** puffball

der **Brand** fire, conflagration

Brander Brander

die **Brandung** surf, breakers

braten (ä) roast

der **Braten, —** roast

der **Brauch** custom, usage

brauchen (*wk*) use, make use of; need, require

brauen (*wk*) brew, cook up

braun brown; die **Braune** brunette woman

bräunen turn brown

bräunlich brownish, brunette

brausen (*wk*) rage, roar

die **Braut, ⁀e** fiancée

das **Brautgemach** bridal chamber

der **Bräutigam** bridegroom

die **Bräutigamsgestalt** form of a bridegroom

brav good, decent, upright, well-behaved, honest, fine, valiant

bravo! bravo!

brechen (i), a, o break, pluck off (flower); break through

der **Brei** porridge, mush

breit broad, wide, spread-out; breadth (1814); watery (2392)

die **Breite** breadth, width; **Länge und Breite** dimensions (extension) in space

breiten broaden, spread

brennen, a, a (*wk, irreg*) burn, blaze, be on fire

das **Brett, -er** board

das **Bretterhaus** house of boards; theater

das **Brevier** breviary, book of prayers

das **Brimborium** elaborate nonsense

bringen, a, a (*wk, irreg*) bring, make progress (573); (**um**) deprive of (4497)

der **Brite, -n** Briton

der **Brocken** Brocken Mountain

das **Brockenstückchen** adventurous episode, as on the Brocken (**Walpurgisnacht**)

der **Broden** vapor, foul air

der **Bronn(en)** well, source

das **Bröselein** tiny crumb

das **Brot** bread

die **Brücke** bridge

der **Bruder**, ⸚ brother

brüderlich fraternal

die **Brudersphäre**, –n brother sphere

der **Brüllgesang** bellowing song

brummen rumble

der **Brunnen** fountain

brünstig ardent

die **Brust**, ⸚e bosom, breast, chest, heart; **aus voller Brust** (333), **mit offner Brust** (2082) with a loud voice

sich **brüsten** (*wk*) give oneself airs

brusterweiternd causing the heart to swell

das **Brüstlein**, — little breast

die **Brut** spawn, brood

brutal brutal

der **Bube**, –n boy

die **Bubenschar** troop of boys

bübisch-mädchenhaft characteristic of adolescent boys and girls

das **Buch**, ⸚er book

das **Büchelchen** prayer book

der **Bücherhauf** accumulation of books

die **Bücherkruste**, –n book crust

die **Büchse**, –n box, jar

buchstabieren spell

die **Bucht**, –en bay; garden alcove (5175)

das **Buchtgestad** shore of the bay

sich **bücken** (*wk*) bow down, bend over

die **Bude** temporary shack

das **Büfett** sideboard

das **Büffelhorn**, ⸚er buffalo horn

der **Bügel** loop; bridle (*mech.*)

die **Buhle** sweetheart, paramour

der **Buhle**, –n lover, sweetheart

buhlen make love to

die **Buhlerin** courtesan, hussy

die **Buhne**, –n diversion dam

die **Bühne**, –n stage

das **Bühnenspiel** stage play

der **Bund** covenant; league, alliance

das **Bund** bunch, bundle

das **Bündel** bundle

das **Bündnis** covenant, compact

der **Bundsgenoß**, –genossen confederate

bunt motley, having various colors, gay, vivid, stained, bright-colored (6572); variegated (11166)

die **Burg**, –en castle, citadel; **feste Burg** stronghold, mighty fortress

Burgdorf Burgdorf

der **Burgemeister** mayor

der **Bürger** citizen

das **Bürgermädchen**, — girl of middle-class family

der **Bürger-Nahrungs-Graus** rubble heap of bourgeois occupation, hideous anthill of burghers earning their daily bread

Bürgersleute townspeople

der **Burghof** castle courtyard

der **Bursch**, –e, der **Bursche**, –n young man, youth, young fellow

der **Busch**, ⸚e bush, underbrush

sich **buschen** be covered with bushes

buschig bushy

der **Busen** bosom, breast; heart; mind

die **Buße** penance
büßen expiate, atone (for), suffer for
der **Büßer** penitent
die **Büßerin, –nen** penitent
die **Büste** bust
die **Butter** butter

C

[See also **K** and **Z**]

Cäsar Caesar
Ceres Ceres (*goddess of crops, especially small grains*)
der **Champagner** champagne
das **Chaos** chaos
der **Charakter** character
Chelone Chelone, turtle, tortoise; (*Greek nymph changed into a tortoise*)
die **Chemie** chemistry
der **Cherub** cherub
Chiron Chiron (*centaur, teacher of many heroes*)
das **Chor** [der Chor 7693] **–e** choir, chorus
das **Chor** church choir loft, gallery (11008)
die **Choretide, –n** female member of the chorus
die **Chorführerin** leader of the chorus
der **Chorgesang** choral singing
der **Chorus** chorus
Christ Christ
der **Christ, –en** Christian
der **Christ, der heilige Christ** Christmas present (2699)
die **Christenheit** Christendom
das **Christentum** Christian faith
die **Chrysalide** chrysalis
die **Chymisterei** alchemy

Ci-devant Genius der Zeit former "Genius der Zeit" (*a journal*)
cimmerisch *see* **kimmerisch**
Circe Circe (*a sorceress*)
der **Cupido** desire, lust
der **Cursus** [*acc.* **Cursum**] course of lessons
Cypern Cyprus (*island*)
Cypria Cypria (*Aphrodite, Venus*)
Cythera Cythera (*island*)

D

da [*conj*] when, since
da [*adv*] then, there, here, in that respect, in such a case, under those circumstances
dabei present, with that, participating, in that connection, at the same time
das **Dach, –er** roof
dadrinne at home (yonder in the city)
dadurch thereby, in that way
dafür in return for that, to make up for that, instead, for it, for that
dagegen in return for that, on the other hand; against it (11723)
daherbrausen come roaring along
daherkommen, a, o come up, come along
dahier here
dahin to there, to that place, into that place, whither (458), gone (11724)
dahinaus out there
dahinein into which

dahinfließen melt away

dahinschreiten stride off, proceed

dahinsinken, a, u sink away

dahinten back there, behind it

dahinterstecken be behind it

dahinziehen go along

der Daktyl, -e Dactyl (*mythological ironworker*)

daliegen lie there

damals at that time, then

die Dame, -n lady

damit [*conj*] so that

damit [*adv*] with that, with it, with them; by that; thereby; with which (3671, 10895)

der Damm, ⸚e dam, dike

der Dämmer half-light

dämmern grow faint, grow dim (light)

der Dämmerschein dusk

die Dämm(e)rung twilight; dim light of early dawn (4680)

der Dämon, -en daemon, guardian divinity

der Dampf vapor

dampfen emit vapor, steam

dämpfen (*wk*) extinguish (5980); subdue (9847); muffle (11402)

danach about that

daneben next to it, alongside; moreover, also (11029)

der Dank thanks, gratitude

dankbar thankful, grateful

die Dankbarkeit gratitude

danken (*wk*) thank, give thanks, be grateful for

dann then, at that time, thereafter; dann und wann now and then (5588)

daran on it, from that fact, to it, of that, because of that, about it

darauf thereupon, in addition, on that

daraus out of it

darbringen, a, a (*wk, irreg*) offer, present

darein in there

dareinscheinen shine into a place

darnach for that, about that, afterwards, later, about it

darneben beside, next, next to it

darnieder down, down there

darüber: darüber gehen surpass it in value

darum for that reason, about that, concerning that

darunter among them

das the, that, that one, it; which

das Dasein existence; plane of existence

daselbst there, on the spot

daß that; bis daß until

dastehen, a, a stand there

die Daube, -n barrel stave

die Dauerbarkeit steady perseverance, hardihood, sticking qualities

dauerhaft lasting, permanent

dauern (*wk*) make one feel sorry for (297)

dauern (*wk*) last, endure; take (time)

der Dauerstern fixed star

der Däumerling, -e Tom Thumb, dwarf, fingerling

davon of that, about that, from that; away (Trüber Tag 66, 5485)

davonflattern flutter away

sich davonhalten keep away from it

davonkommen escape (the consequences); get off (too easily 7790)

davonlaufen (äu), ie, au run away

davonschleichen creep away, sneak off

davonziehen march away

davor before it; at the idea of it (9162)

dazu for that, to that, to do that; in addition

dazwischen in between, mingled with it

die **Decke** ceiling; cover (7543)

decken (wk) cover; set (11079)

das **Deckenband** ceiling framework, ceiling support

die **Definition, –en** definition

der **Degen** sword

dehnen (wk) stretch, extend

sich **dehnen** (wk) stretch out, extend

dein your, yours, of you

deinesgleichen your kind, the like(s) of you

um **deinetwillen** for your sake

Deiphobus Deiphobus (brother of Paris)

deklamieren recite, declaim

Delos Delos (island)

der **Delphin, –e** dolphin

die **Demut** humility

demütig humble

denken, a, a (wk, irreg) think, intend, plan, imagine, realize (1965)

der **Denker** thinker

denn [conj] for, because (justifying previous remark)

denn [adv] in that case, then (implying uncertainty as to reply); than (8898)

dennoch yet, nonetheless

das **Deputat, –e** payment in produce or goods

die **Deputation** deputation

der the, that, that one, he, it; who, which

derb crude, sturdy, vigorous

dergleichen the like, something similar, like that, something like that, anything like that

derselbe the same, that very one

derweil meanwhile

deshalb for that reason, because of that, that's why

desto the (8226); all the (8257, 8617, 10330)

deuten (wk) interpret; point, foretell

deutlich clearly, well

die **Deutlichkeit** distinctness

deutsch German

das **Diadem** diadem

der **Dialog, –e** dialogue

Diana Diana

dicht thick; dense, opaque, impenetrable; close (11847)

die **Dichtart** genre, type of poetry

dichten write poetry

sich **dichten** imagine, invent

der **Dichter, —** poet, creative literary artist

die **Dichterhöhe** poetic eminence

dicht(e)risch of a poet

dichtgedrängt closely crowded

dichtgewebt closely woven

dick fat, thick

der **Dickteufel, —** fat devil

die the, that, that one, those, she, her, it, they, them; who, whom, which

der **Dieb, –e** thief

das **Diebsgelüst** desire to steal, kleptomania

das **Diebsgeschmeiß** thief, low thieving rabble

dienen serve, be of service

der **Diener,** — servant

die **Dienerin,** –nen servant, serving maid

die **Dienerschaft** servants, household staff

der **Dienst** service, good turn; **zu Diensten stehen** be required as service; be ready for service

dienstbar serviceable

dienstlich of service, useful

das **Dienstmädchen** servant, housemaid

dies this, this latter, the latter

diesmal this time

dieweil the while, during the time that

diktieren (*wk*) dictate

der **Dilettant,** –en dilettante, amateur

dilettieren delight

das **Ding,** –e/–er thing, creature, matter; **guter Dinge** in good spirits (6145); **es geht nicht mit rechten Dingen zu** there's something wrong about this, things like this don't happen by proper means

Dionysos Dionysus (*god of wine and orgies*)

Dioskuren Dioscuri; Gemini (*Castor and Pollux*)

der **Diplomat** diplomat

direkt direct, right

der **Direktor** director

die **Dirne,** –n wench, girl

der **Diskurs** discussion

distilliert distilled

doch though, after all, yet, still, in spite of that, however

der **Dogmatiker** dogmatist

der **Doktor,** –en doctor

der **Doktorschmaus** doctoral banquet

das **Dokument** document

der **Dolch** dagger

dolorosa suffering, sorrowful

der **Dom** cathedral, dome (5995)

die **Dommel,** –n bittern

der **Donner,** — thunder, thunderbolt

der **Donnergang** thunderous movement

der **Donnerkeil,** –e thunderbolt

donnern thunder

der **Donnerschlag** thunderclap

das **Donnerwort** thunderous word

der **Donnrer** thunderer, Zeus

das **Doppelblasen** blowing both ways

das **Doppel-Flügelpaar** double pair of wings

der **Doppelgewinn** double gain, gain both ways

doppelhaft twofold, having a duplicate

die **Doppelmütze** cap with two peaks

doppeln (*wk*) double

die **Doppelnacht** double night

das **Doppelreich** double realm

der **Doppelschritt** quick step, double time

doppelsinnig ambiguous, having a double meaning

doppelt double, doubly, on two counts

die **Doppelzahl** double the number, twice as many

die **Doppelzwerggestalt** dwarfish figure of double aspect

das **Dorf** village

Doriden Dorides (*nymphs*)

der **Dorn** thorn

dorren become dry

dörren (*wk*) dry, wither

dort there, at that place

dorten there

dorther that place, from that place, thence

dorthin there, to that place, thither

dortwohin there, into that place

der **Dozent** lecturer, tutor

der **Drache, –n** dragon

das **Drama** drama, theatrical performance

dran at that, at that task, doing that, of that, in that, to that, on that; off (2508, 3149); **dran kommen** take one's turn

der **Drang** impulse, stress, pressure; throng

drängen (*wk*) urge; squeeze; crowd together, throng, press, press together; **gedrängt** crowding upon one another (186); closely packed (3904)

sich **drängen** (*wk*) press, crowd

dräuen (= **drohen**) threaten

drauf in addition, to that, on it, to it; thereupon, forthwith

drauß outside

draußen outside, out there

drechseln bandy, exchange

der **Dreck** filth

drehen turn, twirl

sich **drehen** rotate, whirl, turn around

drei three

dreieinig triune, constituting a trinity

dreifach threefold, triple; as a trio (7966)

der **Dreifuß** tripod

das **Dreigetüm** trinity of monsters

dreihundert three hundred

dreiköpfig three-headed

dreimal three times, thrice

drein in it, into it; at it; on (6914)

die **Dreinamig-Dreigestaltete** (goddess) with three names and three forms

dreinsehen (ie) look on, gaze at it; have an expression on one's face (2748, 3486); look, present an appearance

dreißig thirty

dreist daring; dictatorial, overbearing (847)

der **Dreizack** trident

dreschen (i), o, o thrash

dressieren (*wk*) drill, train

die **Dressur** training

drin therein, within, inside

dringen, a, u press, force a way, penetrate, urge

drinne inside, in there

drinnen inside, in there

dritte third

zum **drittenmal** for the third time

drob about it

droben up there, on high

drohen (*wk*) threaten, menace

drohend-mächtig menacing and mighty

dröhnen (*wk*) resound, crash, creak

die **Drossel, –n** thrush

drüben over there

der Druck pressure, oppression

drücken (wk) press, oppress, squeeze, clasp

der Drudenfuß witch's foot, pentagram, five-pointed star

drum so, therefore, for it (2678, 2915, 4517); of it (4497)

drunten down there, below

Dryas dryad, tree spirit

du you (thou); du und du on intimate terms

ducken yield, conform, submit

sich ducken stoop, humble oneself; duck, dodge

der Dudelsack bagpipe

die Duenna duenna (elderly lady employed as chaperone)

der Duft, ⁻e haze; fragrance; vapor

duften (wk) give off fragrance; be fragrant with

duftig fragrant

der Dukaten, — ducat, a coin

dulden stand for, suffer

dumm stupid, awkward, stupefied

die Dummheit bit of nonsense

dumpf musty; muffled, rumbling; moist; dull; still scarcely aroused (3352)

dumpf-hohl with a dull and hollow sound

dumpfig musty

die Düne, –n dune, sandhill

düngen manure

das Dunkel darkness

dunkel obscure, unclear, dark, gloomy

dunkelgräulich dark gray

dunkel-hell faintly bright, in a dim light

dünkeln flatter oneself, conceitedly imagine

dünken (wk) conceitedly imagine (615, 7772, 8563)

dünken, eu, eu (irreg, impers) seem

der Dunst, ⁻e haze, vapor; uncertainty (5422)

dunstig misty, smoky

der Dunstkreis misty murky atmosphere, realm of mist; aura of fragrance; region filled by sweet fragrance

durch through, by means of, throughout, thoroughly

durchaus complete, thoroughly, quite; throughout (9679)

durchbrausen roar through

durchbrechen (i), a, o break through

sich durchbrennen, a, a (wk, irreg) burn intensely (feeding upon itself)

durchbringen, a, a (wk, irreg) spend, use up wastefully

durchdringen, a, u push through, pierce; penetrate, pervade, fill with a sense of; take form, come through (from imagination to expression 71)

durchdröhnen resound throughout

durcheinander in confusion

durchflattern flutter through

durchforschen investigate thoroughly

durchführen carry through

der Durchgang passageway

durchgleiten glide through

durchglühen (wk) inspire, inflame

durchgrübeln moodily reflect

upon, spend much time thinking about

durchkämpfen (*wk*) fight out

durchklingen sound through, chime through

Durchlauchtigster Your Most Serene Highness

durchleben (*wk*) live through, experience

durchmachen (*wk*) go through, undergo, experience

der **Durchmarsch** marching through

durchproben try out

durchrasen (*wk*) race through, furiously rush through

durchs = durch das

durchschauen see through, understand thoroughly

durchschauern cause to quiver, send a shiver through

durchschmarutzen loaf through

durchschweifen ramble through

durchschwimmen, a, o swim through, swim across

durchsehen (ie), a, e look through (2419); look over, inspect thoroughly (8569)

durchsichtig transparent

durchstechen (i), a, o stab

durchstudieren study thoroughly

durchstürmen (*wk*) rush through, live stormily

durchtanzen (*wk*) wear out by dancing

durchtragen (ä), u, a carry through

durchwandern traverse, wander through

durchweben weave through

durchwettern strike (*lightning*)

durchwühlen stir to the depths, burrow through

dürfen (a), **u, u** (*irreg*) be allowed to, may, can, dare; **nicht dürfen** must not; **du darfst nur** you need only (2590); **es durfte kaum** it needed scarcely (3139)

dürr dry, barren, dried-up

der **Dürrteufel, —** skinny devil

der **Durst** thirst

der **Dust** dust

düster gloomy, dismal, dark, mournful

das **Dutzend** dozen

E

e' (= **einen**) a (6814)

ebben ebb

eben even, flat; neither more nor less than, precisely, just, exactly, simply; just now, right away; when all is said and done; the point is that

das **Ebenbild** image

ebenbürtig of equal birth, of equal rank with; **mit...ebenbürtig** the peer of...

die **Ebene, –n** plain, flat country

ebenfalls likewise, too

das **Ebenholz** ebony

ebenso just as, equally

das **Echo** echo

echoen echo

echt genuine, real, authentic, true

die **Ecke, –n** corner

der **Eckzahn, ⸗e** eyetooth, tusk

ecstaticus ecstatic

edel noble, precious; vital

(11813); high-born, aristo-
cratic

die **Edelfrau** noblewoman

das **Edelgestein** jewels

der **Edelstein**, -e jewel, gem

edel-stumm nobly silent, awe-
inspiring and mysterious

der **Effekt** effect

der **Egoist** egoist

eh! eh; **eh nun** that's all right

die **Ehe** marriage

ehe before

ehegestern the day before
yesterday

ehelich marital

ehemals once, formerly

eher sooner, more easily, rather

ehern bronze, brass, brazen

der **Ehherr** husband

ehrbar honorable

die **Ehre**, -n honor, glory, good
reputation, credit; **in allen
Ehren** with all due respect;
zu Ehren kommen gain glory;
euch zu Ehren in your honor

ehren honor, respect, revere

der **Ehrenbesitz** honorable possession

ehrenhaft honorable

der **Ehrenkranz** wreath

der **Ehrenmann** man of honor;
dunkler Ehrenmann an honest
man of solitary habit

der **Ehrenpunkt** point of honor

der **Ehrenscheitel** revered head

der **Ehrentitel** title of honor

ehrenvoll sacred, creditable,
honorable, venerable; reflecting credit, respectable

ehrenwürdig worthy of honor

ehrerbietig respectful, deferen-
tial

die **Ehrfurcht** awe, awed respect

ehrfurchtsvoll reverent, awed

ehrlos brazen, shameless

ehrwürdig sacred, worshipful,
venerable

das **Ei** egg

ei! well! why! ay! indeed!
but . . . !

die **Eiche**, -n oak

die **Eichenkraft** strength of an
oak

der **Eichenkranz** wreath of oak
leaves

der **Eifer** zeal

eifern (*wk*) work zealously

die **Eifersucht** jealousy

eigen own, very own, of one's
own; special, particular, peculiar; **auf eigne Hand** on one's
own responsibility

die **Eigenschaft** quality, property,
nature

der **Eigensinn** obstinacy

eigensinnig capricious, self-
willed, obstinate

eigentlich really, actually,
strictly speaking; proper, true

das **Eigentum** property

eigenwillig self-willed

eignen convey, grant (11021)

sich eignen be suitable for;
come to pass, occur (11417)

die **Eile** haste

Eilebeute Speed-the-booty

eilen hurry, hurry up, hasten

sich eilen hurry, hasten

das **Eilgebot** urgent order

eilig quick, speedy, hurried

das **Eiligtun** ostentatious haste

der **Eimer**, — bucket, pail, vessel

ein a, an; one

ein in; **aus und ein** in and out

einander one another, each other

sich einbilden (wk) imagine, flatter oneself; be vain

einblasen (ä) prompt; whisper

die Einbläserei, -en insinuation, prompting

einblicken (wk) peek into, look into

eindämmen (wk) dam in

eindringen, a, u force one's way in

einen (wk) unite, bring together

einerlei all the same, all one

das Einerlei monotony, question of no importance; dull routine

einfach simple

einfallen (ä) occur to, come into one's mind

die Einfalt artless simplicity

einfalten (wk) wrap clothes about, muffle in clothes

einfassen surround, round up; capture

sich einfinden make one's appearance

einführen introduce

eingeboren innate, inborn; born

eingehen, i, a enter, go in; come in (4860)

das Eingeweide entrails, "innards"

eingreifen strike (pluck) a chord

einhalten stop

einheimisch native, homebred

einherlaufen walk forth

einherschweben soar along

einherstolpern (wk) stumble along

einherstolzieren strut along

einhertreten make an entrance

einige several, some, any

die Einigkeit harmonious union

der Einklang accord, harmony

einklemmen confine, restrict

einkommen, a, o come in

einladen (ä), u, a invite

einlassen (ä) let in, admit

sich einlassen (ä) meddle, entangle oneself, get mixed up with

einleiten (wk) usher in, introduce

sich einlügen gain favor by lying

einmal once, one time, some time; even, after all; auf einmal all at once; nicht einmal not even; ein für allemal once and for all (2656); noch einmal again; laßt einmal just wait

sich einmischen intervene

einnehmen capture, occupy

die Einöde wilderness, desert place

einrammeln (wk) ram in, cram in

einräumen put away

einrosten (wk) grow rusty, become unsusceptible through age

einrufen, ie, u call, summon

einsacken (wk) bag, gather in

einsam alone, solitary, lonely

die Einsamkeit, -en solitude, loneliness; lonely place

einschärfen impress upon

einschießen invade, shoot in, rush in (water)

einschlafen (ä) go to sleep, fall asleep

sich einschleichen, i, i sneak in, steal in

einschließen, o, o lock in

einschlingen swallow, gulp down

einschlurfen sip

einschmeißen, i, i break, smash in

einschmelzen (i), o, o melt down

einschneien snow under

einschnüren (*wk*) lace in, strap in

sich einschränken restrain oneself, be economical

einschwärzen (*wk*) smuggle in

einsehen (ie) perceive, see, get the point

die Einsicht insight, discernment

einsiedlerisch-beschränkt hermitlike and narrow

einsingen, a, u sing to sleep

einsperren (*wk*) imprison

einst at one time, once, once long ago

einstecken sheathe

sich einstellen put in an appearance

einstimmen, mit einstimmen agree, be unanimous

einstreichen, i, i pocket

einstudieren (*wk*) learn by rote

einstürzen fall in, collapse

einswerden (i), a/u, o become one, be made one

einteufeln (*wk*) initiate into the ways of the devil

eintreten (i) enter

eintrippeln skip in, come skipping in

der Eintritt entrance

einverleiben (*wk*) incorporate; einverleibt sein be a part of, become incarnate in

sich einverleiben (*wk*) become a member of

einweihen initiate, consecrate

einwickeln (*wk*) envelop, wrap up

einwirken affect

einwurzeln (*wk*) root

einzahnig one-toothed

einzeln separate, isolated, single

einziehen, o, o enter, march in

einzig unique, single, only, alone, one and only

das Eis ice

das Eisen iron, fetters, weapons

die Eisenkiste, –n iron chest

eisern iron

das Eisgebirg, –e ice-covered mountain range

eitel vain, useless, mere

die Eitelkeit vanity

ekel disgusting, loathsome

ekeln disgust, nauseate

elastisch elastic, sinewy

der Elefant elephant

das Elefantenkalb, ⸚er elephant calf

das Element, –e element; beim Element! (*a mild oath*)

elend wretched, miserable

das Elend misery

Elend Elend (*a village*)

Eleusis Eleusis (*city, scene of mysteries and festivals*)

der Elf, –en elf, fairy

Elis Elis (*city, district in Peloponnesus*)

der Ellenbogen elbow

ellenhoch an ell high (*ell = two to three feet*)

elterlich parental, with parental pride

Eltern parents

empfahn = empfangen

der Empfang reception

empfangen (ä), i, a receive, welcome; conceive (634)

empfänglich susceptible; der Flammen empfänglich easily ignited (8576)

empfehlen (ie), a, o commend, entrust (9469); recommend (11617)

sich empfehlen (ie), a, o present itself; take one's leave politely (2048)

empfinden, a, u feel, experience, perceive

die Empfindung feeling

die Emphase emphasis

emporbürgen (wk) build up

sich empören (wk) rise, revolt

emporflammen flame up

emporheben, o, o lift, raise

sich emporheben, o, o rise

emporputzen put on display

emporschieben, o, o push upward

emporschwanken (wk) rise billowing

emporschwellen (i), o, o rise swelling

emporsteigen rise, mount, climb

emporstreben strive upward

emportragen carry upward

emportreiben, ie, ie force upward

emporzüngeln (wk) lick upward

Empuse Empusa (a cannibalistic goblin)

emsig eager, busy, industrious

Encheiresis [acc. -in] process

das Ende, -n end, direction, death; am Ende after all, possibly, finally

enden end, finish

endigen finish, be through

endlich finally, at last; quickly, vigorously (10067)

das Endurteil, -e final judgment

Endymion Endymion (youth loved by the moon goddess)

eng narrow, tight, small, restricted; es wird ihr eng she begins to feel oppressed

die Enge narrowness, restriction

der Engel, — angel

die Engelslippe, -n angels' lip

der Engelsschatz beloved, my sweet angel

englisch angelic

der Enkel grandson, descendant, latecomer in world history

ennuyieren bore

entatmen expire, breathe one's last

entbehren (wk) do without

entbieten offer, present

entbinden, a, u deliver, set free

entdecken (wk) discover; reveal

die Ente, -n duck

enteilen hasten from

entfachen (wk) fan (into flame)

entfalten (wk) unfold, reveal

sich entfalten (wk) unfold, evolve

entfernen (wk) remove, let go, separate

sich entfernen (wk) move away, leave

entfernt remote, far-off; separated, apart

entfesseln unchain

entflammen (wk) catch fire

entfliegen, o, o escape by flying

entfliehen, o, o desert, run away, escape

entfremden (wk) estrange, become alien

entführen (wk) abduct, carry off

entgegen in preparation for (4631)

entgegenblühen (*wk*) bloom, blossom at one's coming

entgegenfletschen grin at, bare one's teeth at

entgegenfliegen fly toward

entgegenheulen howl at

entgegenleuchten (*wk*) shine, be radiant toward

entgegenragen stand out against

entgegenschlagen (ä), u, a strike against

entgegensetzen oppose

entgegenspringen leap toward

entgegenstehen confront, oppose

sich entgegenstellen oppose, stand in the way of

entgegentragen (ä) bear as an offering

entgegnen offer objection; make a reply; go toward (7721)

entgehen escape

entglänzen emerge radiant

entgleiten slip (*from an insecure footing*)

enthauchen breathe out, be spoken, be exhaled from

enthüllen (*wk*) reveal

der Enthusiast, –en enthusiast, fanatic

sich entkleiden undress

sich entladen (ä), u, a unburden oneself, relieve oneself

entlang along

entlassen (ä), ie, a release, dismiss

entnerven unnerve, enfeeble

entquellen spring forth from, issue from (8444)

entquellen (i) gush forth from, pour out from (11645)

sich entraffen disentangle oneself from

entreißen, i, i snatch from, rescue from (999)

entrichten (*wk*) pay (debt)

entrinnen, a, o escape, run away from

entrollen (*wk*) unroll, unfurl

entrücken (*wk*) carry off, carry away, enrapture; isolate

entrüstet angry, enraged

entsagen renounce

entschieden decidedly, certainly; resolutely

entschlafen (ä), ie, a become dormant

sich entschlagen dismiss from one's thoughts

sich entschließen, o, o resolve, make up one's mind

entschlossen resolute

die Entschlossenheit determination

entschlüpfen slip from one's grasp, escape

der Entschluß, –schlüsse resolution, decision

entschmeicheln lure away by flattery

entschuldigen excuse; sich entschuldigen lassen decline an invitation

entschweben float away

entschwinden, a, u vanish from

entseelt lifeless

entsenden, a, a (*wk, irreg*) send off

das Entsetzen horror

entsetzen (*wk*) depose, dismiss from office (6844)

entsetzlich horrible

entsiegeln (*wk*) unseal, open

entsprießen, o, o be born, spring from

entspringen, a, u originate; run away from (1529)

entstehen, a, a come into existence, arise, assume reality, gain real form

entsteigen emerge from

sich entsündigen clear oneself of sin, make atonement

entwachsen (ä), u, a outgrow

entweichen, i, i vanish, slip away

entweihen (*wk*) desecrate

entwenden (*wk*) steal, embezzle

sich entwickeln develop, unfold

entwinden: mir die Pflicht entwinden make me neglect my duty (9195)

sich entwinden, a, u unfold from

sich entwirken (*wk*) work itself out

entwischen (*wk*) elude, slip away from

entwohnt unaccustomed, once known but now unfamiliar

entwöhnt = entwohnt

entziehen, o, o withdraw; deprive, withhold (11615)

entzücken (*wk*) delight, enchant, overjoy

sich entzücken (*wk*) be delighted

entzückt enraptured

die Entzückung rapture

entzünden (*wk*) set ablaze, inflame

sich entzünden (*wk*) catch fire

entzwei in two, broken apart

entzweibrechen (i) break in two

sich entzweien (*wk*) quarrel; disunite

entzweiplatzen burst in two, explode

entzweischlagen smash in two

der Epilog epilogue

er he, it; Er you

eratmen pant

sich eräugnen occur, take place, happen

erbangen feel fear, be frightened

sich erbarmen pity, have pity, have mercy

erbärmlich pitiable

erbauen (*wk*) edify; erect (10932)

der Erbe heir

das Erbe heritage

erbeben tremble, shake

erben inherit

erbeten ask for and receive

erbeuten capture, take as booty

die Erbin heiress

erbitten, a, e ask for and receive, get by asking (6224)

erbittern (*wk*) embitter, turn sour

erblich hereditary

erblicken (*wk*) see, catch sight of, perceive

erblinden (*wk*) become blind

erblitzen flash forth (*lightning*)

erblüht blooming, full-blossomed

sich erbosen get angry

erbötig ready, at one's disposal

sich erbrüsten show off

das Erbteil inheritance

der Erdball terrestrial globe

das Erdbeben earthquake

die Erde earth, world, earthly life; ground, soil

das Erdebeben earthquake

das Erdeleben earthly existence

das Erdenband earthly bond

die **Erdenbreite** breadth of the earth

das **Erdenglück** happiness on earth

der **Erdenkreis** earth, entire earth, globe (10181, 11441)

der **Erdenrest** earthly remnant, earthly residue

das **Erdenrund** earth, globe

der **Erdensohn,** ⸚e son of earth, earthling

die **Erdensonne** sun of this world

der **Erdentag** day on earth, earthly life

der **Erdestoß** earthquake shock

der **Erdetag,** –e day on earth, life

das **Erdetreiben** doings on dry land

erde-verwandt related to the soil

der **Erdeweg,** –e earthly path

erdgebeugt bowed to earth

der **Erdgeborene,** –n earthborn, mortal

der **Erdgeist** Earth spirit

erdgemäß appropriate to the earth

der **Erdkreis** world, section of the world (9524)

sich **erdreisten** (*wk*) be bold, dare, consider oneself equal to

sich **erdreusten** = sich **erdreisten** become brazenly bold

erdrücken suppress, crush

erdulden (*wk*) endure, suffer

die **Erd-weite** expanse of earth

Erebus Erebus (*a place of darkness between Earth and Hades*)

das **Ereignis** event, happening; reality

ererben (*wk*) inherit

erfahren (ä), u, a find out, learn, experience, hear (about)

die **Erfahrung** experience

die **Erfahrungsfülle** fullness of experience

das **Erfahrungswesen** empiricism; world of experience

erfassen get hold of; understand

erfinden, a, u find, discover; invent, contrive

erflehen (*wk*) pray for and receive, entreat

erfolgen (*wk*) follow, come as a reward (11508)

erfragen discover, learn, find out by asking; question (9147)

erfreuen (*wk*) please, give pleasure, delight

sich **erfreuen** rejoice, find pleasure

erfrieren, o, o freeze, freeze to death

erfrischen (*wk*) refresh, delight; cool (9539)

erfüllen (*wk*) fill, fill up; fulfill, perform

die **Erfüllungspforte,** –n portal of fulfillment

sich **ergeben** (i), a, e devote oneself to; submit to, surrender, acquiesce in

die **Ergebenheit** submissive devotion

ergehen, i, a happen, turn out

ergießen, o, o pour

sich **ergießen,** o, o pour out, break forth

erglänzen gleam, sparkle, shine forth

erglühen begin to glow

ergötzen (*wk*) delight, give pleasure

sich **ergötzen** (*wk*) be gratified, be delighted

das **Ergötzen** pleasure, gratification

ergraut turned gray

ergreifen, i, i lay hold of, seize, grasp; affect, stir deeply (6274)

sich **ergreifen, i, i** be linked (9561)

ergrimmt angry

ergründen fathom; penetrate, see through

erhaben [*adj*] sublime, exalted, noble

erhalten (ä), ie, a preserve, uphold; maintain

sich **erhalten** (ä), ie, a preserve oneself, maintain oneself

erhaschen snatch, catch

erheben, o, o elevate, raise

sich **erheben**, o, o arise, rise

erheitern (*wk*) cheer, enliven, brighten

erhellen illuminate

sich **erhellen** be lighted, become bright

erhöhen (*wk*) elevate, heighten, exalt

sich **erhöhen** (*wk*) be heightened

erholen (*wk*) rest

sich **erholen** (*wk*) recover

erhören (*wk*) heed; **erhört sein** have one's prayer answered

Erichtho Erichtho (*a Thessalian witch*)

erinnern remind

sich **erinnern** remember

die **Erinnerung**, –en memory, remembrance, recollection

erjagen chase down, pursue and capture

erkennen, a, a (*wk, irreg*) recognize, perceive, understand

erklären explain, expound; declare

die **Erklärung** explanation

erklingen, a, u sound, resound

sich **erlaben** revive, be refreshed

erlangen (*wk*) obtain, attain

sich **erlängen** grow in length

erlassen allow, grant

erlauben (*wk*) allow, permit, grant

die **Erlaubnis** permission

erleben (*wk*) experience, live to see

erledigen (*wk*) take care of

erleichtern lighten

erlesen (*pp*) selected, picked out

erleuchten (*wk*) illumine, light up

erliegen, a, e succumb to

erlöschen (i) be extinguished, die down, fail

erlösen redeem

sich **erlösen** set oneself free

ermangeln lack

sich **ermannen** (*wk*) screw up one's courage

ermorden murder

ermüden (*wk*) tire out, wear out; grow tired (11272)

ermuntern encourage

ernähren feed, nourish

sich **ernähren** feed on, feed oneself

ernennen appoint

erneuen (*wk*) renew, resume

erniedern reduce to humble terms

erniedrigen degrade

der **Ernst** a matter of serious importance, seriousness; **im Ernste** seriously

ernst earnest, grave, serious, stern

ernsthaft serious, solemn

ernstlich earnest, intent

die **Ernte** harvest; gains

ernten harvest

der **Erntetag** harvest day

erobern (*wk*) win in battle, conquer

eröffnen open, reveal, clear the way for

sich **eröffnen** open up, become open

erörtern (*wk*) discuss fully

Eros Eros, love

erpflegen foster, preserve with care

erproben (*wk*) prove, test, try

sich **erproben** try one's strength, prove one's strength

erquicken (*wk*) refresh, exhilarate

erquicklich comforting, edifying

die **Erquickung** refreshment; quenching of thirst

der **Erquickungstrank** refreshing drink

erraten (ä) guess, surmise

erregen agitate, stir up

erreichbar attainable, within reach

erreichen (*wk*) attain, reach; overtake, befall (6698, 7323)

errichten (*wk*) erect

erringen, a, u win, struggle through to

der **Ersatz** compensation, equivalent

ersaufen drown

ersäufen (*wk*) drown, inundate; drench

erschaffen, u, a create, produce; bring about

erschallen, o, o resound

erscheinen, ie, ie appear

das **Erscheinen** appearance

die **Erscheinung** appearance, apparition, phenomenon

erschlaffen (*wk*) slacken

erschlagen (ä), u, a kill, slay

erschleichen stealthily come upon

erschließen, o, o open, unlock

erschranzen (*wk*) wheedle

erschrecken (*wk*) frighten, terrify

erschrecken be frightened (11081)

erschrecklich terrifying

erschüttern (*wk*) shake, convulse, move

erschwellen (i), o, o swell up

sich **ersehen** (ie), a, e select, choose

ersehnen (*wk*) long for

ersetzen make up for

ersinnen, a, o devise, plan, think out

erspähen spy out, find and look at

ersprießen spring up from, come out of

erspulen earn by spinning

erst first, foremost; at first; not until, only, only now, not before now; **erst recht** now more than ever; **erst noch** just now, only lately; **wenn ... erst** as soon as, once

erstarkt strengthened

erstarren (*wk*) stiffen, solidify, congeal, become numb

erstaunen (*wk*) wonder, be astonished, astonish

das **Erstaunen** astonishment

erstaunenswürdig marvelous

erstehen, a, a arise, rise up, come into being

ersteigen, ie, ie climb

erstemal first time

ersterben (i) die

ersticken (*wk*) smother, stifle

erstlich in the first place

erstreben strive for

sich **erstrecken** (*wk*) extend

sich **erstreiten, i, i** obtain by fighting

ertönen sound out, resound

ertöten (*wk*) kill

ertragen (ä), u, a endure

ertränken (*wk*) drown

erwachen (*wk*) awake, waken

erwachsen (ä), u, a grow; result from

erwägen, o, o consider, ponder

erwählen (*wk*) elect, select

erwähnen mention

erwarmen become warm, make warm (5376)

erwärmen (*wk*) warm

erwarten expect, wait for, await, wait to see (5589)

die **Erwartung** anticipation

erweichen (*wk*) soften

erweisen, ie, ie show

sich **erweisen, ie, ie** prove oneself

erweitern (*wk*) enlarge

sich **erweitern** (*wk*) expand

erwerben (i), a, o obtain, acquire

erwidern render in return, reply, return

sich **erwühlen** be violently stirred up

erwünscht wished for, welcome

das **Erz** brass, bronze

erzählen tell about, tell

der **Erzbischof-Erzkanzler** Archbishop Lord High Chancellor

erzeigen reveal, display, demonstrate

das **Erzeigen** manner (9387)

der **Erzengel,** — archangel

erzeugen (*wk*) beget, produce, bear

das **Erzeugnis, –se** product

das **Erzgetön, –e** clanging sound of brass instruments

erziehen, o, o bring up, educate, rear

der **Erzkämmerer** Lord High Chamberlain

der **Erzkanzler** Lord High Chancellor

der **Erzmarschall** Lord High Marshal (*chief manager of the royal household*)

der **Erzschenk(e)** Lord High Cupbearer

der **Erztruchseß** Lord High Steward

erzwingen, a, u force, extort

es it, someone, people; there

der **Eselsfuß** donkey's foot

der **Eselskopf** stupid person

das **Eselsköpfchen** donkey's head (*mask, a form assumed*)

essen (i), a, e (gessen) eat

das **Essen** food, eating

die **Essenz, –en** essence

der **Estrich** stone floor

etwa by any chance, perhaps

etwas something, anything; **so etwas** anything like that

etymologisch etymological

euer your, yours, of you

die **Eule, –n** owl

Euphorion Euphorion

Euphrosyne Euphrosyne (*the Grace of joy*)

euresgleichen the like(s) of you, your ilk, your kind

eurige your

das **Europa** Europe

Euros Euros (*east wind*)

Eurotas Eurotas (*a river*)

ewig eternal, forever, everlasting

die **Ewigkeit, –en** eternity

das **Ewig-Leere** eternal emptiness

das **Ewig-Unselige** the eternal wretched

das **Ewig-Weibliche** eternal feminine, supremely womanly quality, love (12110)

exerzieren exercise, practice

exeunt leave the stage

die **Explosion, –en** explosion

Exuvien exuviae, castoff skin or covering, discarded outer trappings

F

f——t [3961, farzt? furzt?]

die **Fabel, –n** fable, fairy tale

das **Fabelbuch** storybook

fabelhaft fabled, fabulous

fabeln (*wk*) talk wildly, be delirious

das **Fabelreich** realm of fable

der **Fabler** storyteller

das **Fach, ⸗er** pigeonhole

die **Fackel, –n** torch

der **Fackelschein** torchlight

der **Faden, ⸗** thread, chain of thought

fadenweis threadlike

der **Fahnenfetzen, ——** rag of a flag

fahren (ä), u, a travel, wander, go; dip (2474); **fahren lassen** let go

die **Fahrt** journey, trip

das **Fahrzeug** vehicle, ship

die **Fakultät** faculty; course

der **Fall, ⸗e** fall; case, event

fallen (ä), ie, a fall

fällen fell, chop down (5201); **Urteil fällen** pass judgment

falsch wrong, false

fälschen (*wk*) forge

die **Falte, –n** wrinkle; **keine Falten werfen** fit perfectly

falten fold

das **Faltenhemd** shirt with pleats or gathers

das **Faltenkleid** skirt with pleats or gathers

faltig wrinkled

der **Famulus** famulus (*professor's assistant*)

der **Fang** catch, booty

fangen (ä), i, a catch, imprison, capture; **der/die Gefangene** prisoner, captive

die **Farbe, –n** color

färben (*wk*) color, dye

der **Farbenglanz** colored splendor

das **Farbenspiel** opalescence

das **Farbgestein** colored gem

farbig colored

die **Farfarelle, –n** moth

farzen fart

faseln drivel, talk nonsense

das **Faß, Fässer** barrel, cask

das **Fäßchen** keg

fassen (*wk*) lay hold on, take hold of; take, seize, grasp; understand, encompass; contain; **kurz fassen** express briefly; **Mut fassen** take heart; **ein Herz fassen** take heart; **Fuß fassen** gain a foothold; **einen Plan fassen** conceive a plan

sich **fassen** (*wk*) compose oneself

die **Fassung** composure, calm frame of mind

fast almost

das **Fasten** fasting

die **Fastenpredigt** Lenten sermon preaching penitence and abstention

faul foul, stagnant

das **Faulbett** bed of ease

faulen decay, rot

der **Faun, –en** faun

faunenartig faunlike

die **Faunenschar** troop of fauns

Faust Faust, Faustus

die **Faust** fist; **mit eigner Faust** with (my) own hand (10472)

fechten (i), **o, o** fight, fence

die **Feder** pen

der **Federzug, ⸚e** stroke of the pen

das **Fegefeuer** purgatory; fire from purgatory

fegen sweep

die **Fehde** feud, conflict

der **Fehl** mistake, flaw

fehlen (*wk*) be a lack (of), be lacking, be needed; go astray, be wrong

der **Fehler, —** mistake

feierlich solemn

feiern celebrate

die **Feierstunde** glad hour, hour of celebration

der **Feiertag, –e** holiday

die **Feige, –n** fig

feil for sale

feilschen bargain; offer for sale (5116)

feiltragen (**ä**)**, u, a** risk; be ready to sell

fein fine, delicate, artful, deft, refined

der **Feind, –e** enemy, foe

die **Feindeskraft, ⸚e** hostile force

das **Feindeszelt, –e** enemy's tent

feindlich hostile, as an enemy

die **Feindschaft** enmity

feindselig hostile

feist fat, greasy

das **Feld, –er** field

die **Feldersaat** field crop

der **Feldmarschall** field marshal

das **Fell** skin, hide

der **Fels, –en** rock, rocky cliff

felsauf up the rock

die **Felsbucht, –en** rocky bay

der **Felschirurg, –en** rock surgeon

felsenab down the cliff

der **Felsenabgrund** rocky precipice

die **Felsenbreite** rock-strewn expanse

das **Felsengedräng, –e** crowd of rocks; confined rocky space

der **Felsengipfel, —** rocky summit

der **Felsengrund** rocky valley

die **Felsenhöhe** rocky height

die **Felsenhöhle, –n** rocky cave

die **Felsenlast** weight of rock

die **Felsennase, –n** cliff nose

das **Felsennest** rocky nest, crag castle

der **Felsenrand** brink of rock cliffs

das **Felsenriff** rocky reef, ledge

die **Felsenritze, –n** rocky crevice

der **Felsenschlund** rocky gorge

die **Felsenschrift** writing (= *evidence*) of rocks

der **Felsensee** lake surrounded by cliffs

die **Felsenspalte, –n** crack in the rocks

der **Felsensteig, –e** rocky path

die **Felsensteile** steep rocky slope

die **Felsenstelle** rocky place

das **Felsentor, –e** door of rock

die **Felsentreppe, –n** rock stairway

die **Felsenwand, ⸚e** cliff wall

das **Felsgebirg** rocky mountain range

das **Felsgefecht** mountain battle

der **Felsweg** mountain road

das **Fenster, —** window

fern far, far-off, remote, distant

die **Ferne** distance

das **Fernglas** telescope

sich **fernhalten (ä)** stay away from

die **Ferse** heel

fertig finished, completely developed; ready

die **Fessel, –n** fetter

fesseln captivate; enchain

fest firm, solid, tight; **feste Burg** stronghold, mighty fortress

das **Fest, –e** festival, holiday, feast

festbannen (*wk*) hold fast, hold in a magic spell

die **Feste** prison, fortress

der **Festesdrang** festive throng

der **Festgebrauch** festive usage

festgemäß fitting for a holiday or festivity

festhalten (ä), ie, a hold fast, keep

festkrallen clutch firmly (with talons)

festlich solemn; festive

die **Festlichkeit** festivity

das **Festvergnügen** festive pleasure

fett fat, rich

das **Fett** lard

der **Fettbauch-Krummbein-Schelm, –e** potbellied bowlegged scoundrel

die **Fette** fatness

das **Fettgewicht** tub of fat

feucht moist, damp

die **Feuchte** moisture

feuchten moisten

das **Feuer, —** fire

die **Feuerbacke, –n** fiery cheek

feuerblasen blow on a fire

das **Feuerchen, —** little fire

der **Feuerdunst** fiery vapor

der **Feuerfunke, –n** fiery spark

die **Feuerglut, –en** fiery glow

die **Feuerleiter, –n** fire ladder

die **Feuerluft** (fiery) heated air

das **Feuermeer** sea of fire

die **Feuerpein** burning pain

die **Feuerquelle** fiery fountain

das **Feuerreich** realm of fire

die **Feuersäule, –n** pillar of fire

der **Feuerschein** fiery radiance

der **Feuerschlund** fiery abyss, crater

feuerspeiend spitting fire

der **Feuerstrom** fiery current, stream of fire

der **Feuerstrudel** fiery eddy

feuerumleuchtet lighted up by fire on all sides

der **Feuerwagen** fiery chariot

der **Feuerwirbelsturm** fiery tornado

die **Feuerzunge, -n** fiery tongue; power of eloquence

feurig fiery, ardent

die **Fichte** fir

die **Fichtenhöhe, -n** fir-covered height

der **Fichtenstamm** fir trunk

das **Fieber** fever

fieberhaft feverish

die **Fieberwut** fury of fever

die **Fiedel** fiddle

der **Fiedelbogen** fiddlestick, bow

fiedeln fiddle

fiedern (*wk*) adorn with feathers

der **Fiedler** fiddler

finden, a, u find, discover; consider, think

sich finden, a, u be found; find the way (for oneself); **sich finden in** reconcile oneself to; **zum besten finden** find most advantageous (7618)

der **Finger, —** finger

die **Fingerspitze** finger tip

der **Fingerzeig** hint

finster dark, gloomy, dim

die **Finsternis, -nisse** darkness, shadow

der **Firlefanz, -e** buffoon, ridiculous fellow

der **Fisch, -e** fish

der **Fischbach** fish-filled brook

fischen fish

der **Fischer, —** fisherman

fischreich abounding in fish

der **Fittich, -e** wing, pinion

der **Fittig, -e** = **Fittich**

flach flat, level; vapid

die **Fläche, -n** surface, plain

der **Flachs** flax

das **Flackerleben** flickering life

flackern flare up

das **Flämmchen, —** little flame

die **Flamme, -n** flame

flammen flame, blaze

die **Flammenbildung** thing of fire

das **Flammenfeuer** (open) fire

das **Flammengaukelspiel** illusion involving flames

die **Flammenglut** flaming white heat

die **Flammenqual, -en** fiery torment

die **Flammenstadt** city of flames (= *hell*)

das **Flammenübermaß** excess of flames

flämmern flicker

die **Flanke** flank, wing

das **Fläschchen** small bottle, bottle of smelling salts (3834)

die **Flasche** bottle

das **Flatterhaar, -e** fluttering hair, loosely hanging hair

flattern flutter

der **Flaum** down

der **Flaus** rough cloth, old garment

flechten (i), o, o entwine, twist together, wreathe; braid, plait

der **Fleck, -en** spot, blemish

die **Fledermaus, ⸚e** bat

fledermausgleich batlike

der **Fledermaus-Vampir, -e** batlike vampire

der **Flederwisch** feather duster (= *rapier*)

die **Flegelei** ill-bred conduct

flehen implore, beseech, pray

das **Fleisch** flesh

die **Fleischbank, ⸚e** butcher's stall

der **Fleischer** butcher

der **Fleiß** diligence, industry

flicken (*wk*) patch
die Fliege, –n fly
fliegen, o, o fly
der Fliegengott god of flies, Beelzebub
die Fliegenschnauze fly snout
fliehen, o, o flee, flee from, take flight
fließen, o, o flow
flimmern (*wk*) glimmer, glitter
flink brisk, lively
der Flitter, — tinsel
die Flitterschau tinsel display
die Flocke, –n flake, dross
der Floh flea
der Flor bloom, blossoming time, flower; abundant flowering
der Flor veil
Flora Flora (*goddess of vegetation*)
die Florentinerin, –nen Florentine woman
flöten play the flute; warble in flutelike tones
flott gay, merry
die Flotte fleet
das Flottenfest festival for the fleet
der Fluch curse, a curse
fluchen curse
die Flucht flight, retreat
flüchten (*wk*) flee, escape
flüchtig fugitive, fleeing, flying
flüchtig-leise momentary and quiet
der Flüchtling fugitive
der Flug flight; swarm
der Flügel, — wing, part of a folding door, wing of an army
das Flügelchen, — little wing
das Flügelflatterschlagen fluttering beating of wings
flügelmännisch like a man with wings, wing flapping (?); like a file leader (?)
flügeln (*wk*) wing, adorn with wings
flügeloffen wide open (*double door*)
das Flügelpaar pair of wings
der Flügelschlag beat of wings
die Flur, –en landscape; plain
der Fluß, Flüsse river; flood; current (255)
flüstern whisper
das Flüsterzittern whispering trembling
die Flut, –en flood, waters; fluid, flowing flood (733)
flutend at high tide, at flood
der Flutstrom flood tide
fodern (*wk*) ask, require
die Folge order, line (6369); train, following (7733)
folgen (*wk*) follow
der Folger successor
folgerecht logical, of the right sort to follow
die Folgezeit time to come, future age
förderlich useful
fordern demand
fördern (*wk*) promote, advance, be of use, expedite; go forward, make progress; Will's fördern? Are you getting anywhere?
fördersamst first of all, with greatest effect, most profitably
die Form, –en form
die Formalität formality
formen (*wk*) form, shape
formieren (*wk*) form, mold, model
förmlich formal

formlos shapeless

forschen investigate

fort away, gone, go away; continuously; **immer fort** always

fortan from now on, henceforth;
und so fortan also in the future

sich **fortbegeben** betake oneself
off, depart

fortblühen keep on blooming

fortbuhlen continue to make love

fortdrängen (*wk*) press on

forteilen hurry off, hasten away

sich **forterben** be inherited, be
passed on

fortfahren (**ä**) continue

fortfliegen fly away

fortgehen, i, a go on, go away,
continue

forthelfen (**i**) help along

fortklingen continue to sound

fortkriechen creep away

fortlassen let go, release

fortliebeln keep on billing and
cooing, continue dalliance

sich **fortmachen** take oneself off

fortnehmen take away

fortpochen (*wk*) continue to
knock

fortrasen move or flow on furiously

fortreisen travel on

fortreißen, i, i snatch along,
carry

fortschicken send away

fortschreiten stride on, stride
away

fortschwärmen roam on, continue to ramble

fortsegeln sail ahead, sail on

fortsetzen (*wk*) continue, further, advance

fortstreben strive to get away

fortstudieren continue to study

fortstürmen (*wk*) storm on, push
the attack

fortstürzen rush forth

forttanzen (*wk*) continue dancing

forttollen (*wk*) continue to frolic,
keep romping

forttönen sound on

forttragen (**ä**), **u, a** carry away

fortträumen dream on

forttreiben expel, drive away;
es forttreiben continue to behave (7343)

Fortuna Fortuna (*goddess of
chance*)

fortwachen (*wk*) stay awake

fortwerfen (**i**) throw away

fortziehen take away; draw on

die **Frage, –n** question, question
at issue

fragen (*wk*) ask, inquire; **es
fragt sich** the question is
(6967)

der **Frager** questioner

frank free; **frank und frei** unrestrained

der **Franke, –n** Frank

der **Franze** Frenchman (2272)

der **Franzos** Frenchman

die **Fratze, –n** spectre, ugly face;
nonsense (1739)

das **Fratzengeisterspiel** silly or
grotesque spectral play

fratzenhaft grotesque, ugly

die **Frau, –en** woman, wife, lady;
Mrs.

das **Frauenbild, –er** woman's
image; female creature

das **Frauenglied, –er** woman's
limb

die **Frauenschönheit** feminine
beauty

das **Frauenzimmer,** — woman, female

das **Fräulein,** –s young lady

das **Fraungebild** image of a woman, feminine shape

das **Fraungeleit** escorting a lady, taking a lady under one's protection

frech insolent, shameless, bold, impudent

die **Frechheit** boldness

frei free, released, uninhibited; **frei geben (Wahl)** give liberty (of choice); **frei stellen** give free choice

freibewegt freely moving

das **Freie** out of doors, open, clear

der **Freier** suitor

freigeboren freeborn

das **Freigeschenk,** –e freewill offering, voluntary gift

die **Freiheit** freedom, liberty

die **Freiheitsluft** air of freedom

das **Freiheitsrecht,** –e right of liberty

freiherzig generous, openhearted

freilassen set free, release

freilich to be sure; I admit; certainly

freisprechen (i), a, o absolve from

freistehen be open to free choice

freistellen give a free choice

fremd foreign, not one's own, someone else's, not properly belonging, unfamiliar, strange

die **Fremde** foreign lands

der **Fremde** stranger, foreigner

die **Fresse** mouth (*vulgar usage; therefore:* beezer, kisser, puss, trap)

fressen (i) eat, devour

die **Freude,** –n joy, delight, pleasure

das **Freudebeben** joyous trembling

das **Freudenfest** joyous festival

das **Freudenspiel** joyous sport

der **Freudentag** day of rejoicing

freudig joyous

freudumgeben surrounded by joy

freuen (*wk*) please, give pleasure, make happy

sich **freuen** (*wk*) rejoice, be happy, be glad, enjoy oneself

der **Freund,** –e friend, lover

freundlich friendly, kind, cheerful; of friends

die **Freundschaft** friendship

der **Frevel** evil deed, sin and crime

frevel wicked; wanton, mischievous; worthless (5603)

frevelhaft wicked, sinful and criminal, blasphemous

freveln blaspheme, be wicked

das **Frevelwort** blasphemy, wicked word

freventlich wicked, evil, morally irresponsible, outrageous

der **Friede** peace; **in Frieden** undisturbed

der **Friedenstag** day of peace, time of peace

der **Friedensweiher** peaceful pond

das **Friedenszeichen** symbol of peace

die **Friedenszeit,** –en time of peace

friedlich peaceful

frisch fresh, vigorous, healthy, brisk; recent

die **Frische** coolness, cool place

die **Frist** period of grace, period of time

froh happy, joyous

fröhlich happy, merry, gay

die **Fröhlichkeit** gaiety, joyousness

frohmütig cheerful, jolly

fromm devout, pious; gentle, good

frömmelnd pious, sanctimonious

frommen be good for, be advantageous, do good

frönen labor, drudge

der **Frosch**, ⁼e frog; Freshman

der **Froschlaich** frog spawn

der **Frost** frost

die **Frucht**, ⁼e fruit

fruchtbar fertile, fruitful

die **Fruchtbarkeit** fertility (*of imagination and invention* 6033)

fruchtbegabt blessed with fertile crops

früh early

der **Frühling** spring

die **Frühlingsblüte**, –n spring blossom

die **Frühlingsfeier** rite of spring

der **Frühlingsregen** spring shower (*of blossoms* 4613)

der **Fuchs** fox; university student in his first semester

die **Fuge**, –n joint, joining

fügen (*wk*) fit together, fit into place; make to coincide (9968)

sich **fügen** happen; fit together

fühlen (*wk*) feel

sich **fühlen** (*wk*) feel, feel oneself

die **Fuhre**, –n task of transporting; trucking and hauling (11031)

führen (*wk*) lead, lead along; handle, wield, manage; conduct, bear, carry, bring; take; **das Leben führen** live, spend one's life

die **Fülle** abundance, profusion, fullness

füllen (*wk*) fill, fill up

sich **füllen** (*wk*) swell, expand, fill oneself

der **Fund** find, discovery

fünf five

fünfhundert five hundred

fünftausend five thousand

fünfte fifth

die **Fünfzahl** number five, Five, council of five

funfzig (= **fünfzig**) fifty

das **Fünkchen** little spark

der **Funke**, –n spark

funkeln sparkle

der **Funkenblick**, –e (= **Funkenblitz**) flash of sparks

der **Funkenwurm**, ⁼er glowworm

für for, for the sake of; in return for, instead of; **für sich** for oneself, to oneself, aside; **Mann für Mann** every one, man by man; **Rechnung für Rechnung** every bill, bill by bill; **Nacht für Nacht** night after night; **Stufe für Stufe** step after step, one on each step (*stairs*, 9178)

die **Furche** furrow

die **Furcht** fear

furchtbar awful, fearful

fürchten fear, be afraid of

sich **fürchten** be afraid

fürchterlich frightful

furchtsam timid, easily frightened

die **Furie**, –n Fury (*Erinys, avenging spirit*)

fürliebnehmen put up with what one finds

fürs = **für das**

der **Fürst**, –en prince, ruler

das **Fürstenhaus** ruler's house

fürstenreich rich as a prince

die **Fürstin**, –nen princess, mistress

fürstlich princely

fürwahr forsooth, indeed

furzen fart

der **Fuß**, ⸗e foot; footing, base (7491); **Fuß fassen** get a foothold

füßeln play with the feet, "play footie"

der **Fußtritt** tread, kick

das **Futteral** case

füttern feed

G

Gäa Gaea (*earth goddess*)

die **Gabe**, –n gift, talent

die **Gabel** fork, pitchfork

Gabriel Gabriel (*an archangel*)

gaffen gape, stare (at)

die **Gage** pay

gähnen yawn

der **Galan** lover, paramour

galant gallant, coquettish; die **Galanten** courtiers (4378)

der **Galatag** festive day

Galatee Galatea (*a sea nymph, a naiad*)

die **Galerie**, –n gallery

die **Galle** gall

der **Gallert-Quark** gelatinous mess

der **Galopp** gallop

der **Gang**, ⸗e course, way; corridor, passageway, path; bearing, gait

gänglich passable, easily traveled

die **Gans**, ⸗e goose

der **Gänsefuß** gooselike foot

ganz whole, entire, complete, total, all; quite, altogether

gänzlich complete

gar quite, absolutely, at all, very; even (360); really

das **Garn** trap, net

garstig foul, nasty, disgusting, ugly

das **Gärtchen** little garden

der **Garten**, ⸗ garden, orchard

das **Gartenhäuschen** garden summerhouse

der **Gärtner**, — gardener

die **Gärtnerin**, –nen (female) gardener

die **Gärung** ferment

das **Gas** gas

das **Gäßchen**, — narrow little street or lane

die **Gasse**, –n (narrow) street

der **Gast**, ⸗e guest, visitor, caller; fellow

der **Gastempfang** reception of guests

gastfreundlich hospitable

gastlich hospitable

das **Gastrecht** hospitality

der **Gatte**, –n husband, spouse

die **Gattin** wife, spouse

der **Gau**, –e province, district

der **Gauch** fool, simpleton; rascal

die **Gaukelei** jugglery; trickery; flitting about

gaukeln deceive by quick movements, juggle, flutter about, dance

der **Gaukeltanz** light flitting dance

das **Gaukelwerk** jugglery; illusion(s)

der **Gaul** horse

der **Gaumen** palate, taste

das **Gebälk,** –e beam, timber

die **Gebärde,** –n gesture

sich **gebärden** behave; act; gesticulate

gebaren conduct oneself

gebären, a, o bear, give birth to; **geboren** born

das **Gebäu** edifice, building

das **Gebäude** building, structure

das **Gebein** skeleton, bones

geben (i), a, e give, present, give as a treat, yield; inflict, produce, cause; **es gibt** there is/ are; goes on; **zum besten geben** exhibit; offer as a treat, offer as a favor; **verloren geben** give up as lost; **acht geben** take care, watch; **frei geben** (**Wahl**) give free (choice); **den Rest geben, das Restchen geben** finish off, do for

sich **geben** (i), a, e surrender; announce oneself, claim to be; work out; **es gibt sich** it does happen

der **Geber** giver, donor

das **Gebet,** –e prayer

das **Gebetbuch** prayer book

das **Gebiet** region

gebieten (ie/eu), o, o command, give orders, order

der **Gebieter** commander, master

die **Gebiet(e)rin** mistress

gebiet(e)risch imperious, peremptory

das **Gebild,** –e image, structure, creature, formation

das **Gebirg,** –e mountain, mountain range

gebirgauf up the mountain side

die **Gebirgsmasse** mountain mass

Gebirgstrümmer broken fragments of mountains

das **Gebirgtal** mountain valley

das **Gebiß** (array of) teeth

das **Geblüt** blood, shed blood

das **Gebot** command, commandment, order

gebrauchen use, make use of

gebrechen (i) be lacking

gebühren (wk) be due, be proper

sich **gebühren** (wk) be fitting, be right and proper

die **Geburt** birth

das **Gebüsch** shrubbery

das **Gedächtnis** memory, recollection

der **Gedanke,** –n thought, idea, notion; revery

die **Gedankenbahn** course of thought

die **Gedankenfabrik** thought factory

gedankenvoll in deep thought

gedeihen do good, benefit; flourish

gedenken remember, recall; think of, bear in mind

das **Gedicht** poem

das **Gedichtchen** little poem

das **Gedränge** crowd; difficulty; jostling

die **Geduld** patience

geduldig patient

die **Gefahr, –en** danger

gefährdet endangered, running a risk

gefährlich dangerous, hazardous

der **Gefährte** companion

das **Gefäll, –e** tax, due

gefallen (ä), ie, a please, appeal to; **er gefällt mir** I like him

sich gefallen (ä), ie, a take pleasure; be satisfied with oneself; **sich gefallen lassen** put up with, make no objection to

der **Gefallen** favor, kindness; pleasure

gefällig pleasing, agreeable

der **Gefangene, –n** prisoner, captive

die **Gefangene, –n** (female) prisoner, captive

die **Gefangenschaft** imprisonment, captivity

das **Gefäß, –e** vessel, receptacle

das **Gefecht** combat

der **Gefesselte** prisoner in chains

das **Gefieder** plumage

das **Gefild, –e** country; fields

das **Geflügel** birds

der **Geflügelhof** poultry run

geflügelt winged

das **Geflüster** whispering(s)

gefräßig greedy

das **Gefühl, –e** feeling

gefühllos heartless

gegen against, contrary to; compared with (5164, 9018); opposite (8537)

die **Gegend** region

gegeneinander against one another

der **Gegengruß** return greeting

der **Gegenkaiser** counter-emperor, pretender

der **Gegenmann** opponent

die **Gegenseite** opposite side

die **Gegenwart** present; presence

gegenwärtig present

gegenwarts in the presence of

gegenwirkend reacting, counteracting

der **Gegner** opponent

die **Gegnerin** opponent

geharnischt in armor

geheim secret

das **Geheimnis** secret, mystery

geheimnisreich mysterious

geheimnisvoll mysterious

gehen, i, a go, walk; come; happen, proceed, work; go away, depart, escape; **es geht** (one's path, the route) leads; **gehen lassen** forgive; **darüber gehen** exceed it in value; **zugrunde gehen** be destroyed; **gehen und stehen** go along somehow, be; **gehen in** approach, go to the point of (10084)

das **Gehör** hearing; **Gehör geben** lend an ear

gehorchen obey, follow

gehören (wk) belong

sich gehören (wk) be appropriate, be fitting

gehörig appropriate, fitting

gehörnt horned

gehorsam obedient

der **Geier** vulture

der **Geierschnabel** vulture-like beak

der **Geist**, –er spirit, soul; intellect, mind; ghost
das **Geisterchor** chorus of spirits
die **Geisterfülle** intensity of spiritual experience
die **Geistergröße** spiritual greatness
geisterhaft ghostly, supernatural
der **Geisterkreis** circle of spirits
das **Geisterleben** spiritual life
das **Geister-Meisterstück** supernatural masterpiece
die **Geisternacht** ghostly night
das **Geisterreich** spirit realm
geisterreich abounding with spirits
die **Geisterschar**, –en host of ghosts, troop of spirits
der **Geisterschritt** spirits' pace, motion of spirits
die **Geisterstunde**, –n ghostly hour
die **Geisterszene** scene in which spirits appear
der **Geisterton**, ⸚e spirit tone
die **Geisterwelt** world of the spirits, realm of the supernatural
der **Geisterzahn** spirit's fang
der **Geistesdespotismus** intellectual despotism
die **Geistesfreude**, –n intellectual pleasure
die **Geisteskraft** spiritual and intellectual power
das **Geistesohr**, –en spirit ear
der **Geisteszwang** compulsion exerted by spirits, hypnotic spell
geistig spiritual, intellectual
geistig-strenges Band inexorable bond of the spirit

die **Geistkraft** spiritual strength
geistlich ecclesiastical
der **Geiz** avarice, miserliness
geizen be stingy
geizig avaricious
das **Geklimper** tinkling, bad playing
das **Geklingel** ringing of bells
das **Geklirr** clanging
das **Gekos(e)** continual petting
das **Gelächter** laughter, laugh
das **Gelag** revel, drinking bout
gelagert lodged, stationed
gelahrt learned, erudite
gelangen attain, arrive at
gelassen calm, serene, composed
geläufig customary, easy
gelb yellow
das **Geld** money
gelegen convenient, appropriate
die **Gelegenheit**, –en opportunity, occasion
gelegentlich occasionally, when opportunity offers
gelehrt learned, well-read
der **Gelehrte** scholar
das **Geleier** monotonous music; pointless talk
das **Geleit** escort, guide; safe-conduct fee (10947)
geleiten escort, accompany
gelenk supple, pliable
gelind gentle, mild
gelingen, a, u succeed, prosper, turn out well; **es gelingt ihm** he is successful; **von ungefähr gelungen** achieved by a lucky chance (1405)
das **Gelingen** success, outcome
gellen sound piercingly, crash
gelt! don't you think?
gelten (i), a, o be worth some-

thing, be important, be at
issue, have value, pass current,
be in favor; **gelten lassen** accept without dispute

die **Geltung** acceptance

das **Gelüst, –e** longing, lust,
desire

gelüsten (*impers*) hanker for

das **Gelüsten** hankering, craving

das **Gemach, –̈er** room

gemächlich gentle, unhurried

der **Gemahl** husband

gemäß suitable, in accordance
with, appropriate to

das **Gemäuer** masonry, walls

gemein vulgar, common, undistinguished

die **Gemeinde** parish, congregation, community

der **Gemeindrang** common impulse

die **Gemeinschaft** common cause

das **Gemenge** motley crowd,
congeries

die **Gemse, –n** chamois, mountain goat

gemsenartig like a mountain
goat

das **Gemurmel** murmur

das **Gemüte** soul, temperament

gemütlich good-natured, easygoing

genäschig nibbling, stealing food

genau exact, exacting, strict,
close

der **General** general

der **Generalissimus** generalissimo

der **Generalstab** general staff,
high command

genesen, a, e recover, get well
again

das **Genick** neck, nape of the
neck

das **Genie** genius; demoniac
spirit (3540); spirit (11675)

sich **genieren** (*wk*) stand on
ceremony, make any bones
about (11273); **geniert sein**
feel hampered by social conventions (842)

genießen, o, o enjoy, partake,
take one's pleasure (in)

der **Genius** genius; elemental
spirit (9603)

der **Genosse, –n** companion,
comrade

genug enough, sufficient

G(e)nüge tun satisfy; **zur Gnüge
sein** be enough

genügen (*wk*) be enough, suffice

das **Genügen** delight; **ums
Genügen** delightful (1482)

genung = genug

der **Genuß** pleasure, enjoyment

das **Geplauder** chat

das **Geprassel** clattering, clashing

das **Gerät** piece of equipment

geraten (ä), ie, a fall, come; turn
out well (9439, 11607); come
to pass (10183, 11506)

geräumig roomy, spacious

gerecht just

die **Gerechtigkeit** justice

die **Gerechtsame, –n** right, prerogative

das **Gerede** gossip; **ins Gerede
kommen** get talked about

gereichen (*wk*): **zum Schaden
gereichen** cause harm

gereuen cause regret

das **Gericht** court of justice,
judgment

der **Gerichtstag** day of judgment, last day

gering slight, inconsiderable, unimportant

das **Gerippe** skeleton

der **Germane** Teuton

gern like to, gladly, eagerly, willingly

das **Geröll** rubble, scree, rocky debris

der **Geruch** sense of smell

geruhig completely calm

gerührt touched

das **Gerüst**, –e frame

gerüstet armed

gesammelt in a group (4634); in composure (10976)

gesamt all, joint, together, in entirety

Gesandte ambassadors (angels 11676)

der **Gesang**, ⁻e song

das **Gesäufte** heavy drinking

das **Geschäft**, –e business, business transaction, errand

geschäftig busy, energetic, active

das **Geschaukel** rocking, rolling

geschehen (ie/geschicht 11358), a, e take place, happen, befall; **geschehen lassen** not interfere in; **geschehen sein** have happened, be all over

gescheit clever

das **Geschenk**, –e present, gift

die **Geschichte**, –n story

geschichtlich historical

das **Geschick** fate

geschickt skillful

das **Geschlecht**, –er generation; clan; social class; gender, sex; race, species

das **Geschlecke** continual kissing and slobbering

der **Geschmack** taste

das **Geschmeide**, — jewelry, piece of jewelry

geschmeidig flexible, yielding, docile (7659)

das **Geschmuck** adornment

das **Geschnarr** racket

das **Geschöpf**, –e creature

das **Geschöpfchen** little creature

das **Geschrei** outcry, shout

geschunden flayed, skinned

geschwätzig talkative, gossipy

geschwind quick, prompt, speedy, fast

das **Geschwister** sister; **Geschwister** (*pl*) brothers and/or sisters

das **Geschwisterkind** cousin; nephew, niece

geschwisterlich like a sister (8025)

gesegnen bless

der **Gesell**, –en companion, friend, fellow

sich **gesellen** (*wk*) join, associate, ally oneself

gesellig social, in company with others

die **Gesellschaft** society, company

das **Gesetz**, –e law

gesetzlich by legal means

das **Gesicht** sight, power of vision (4067, 5609)

das **Gesicht**, –e vision, apparition (482, 520, 9354, 10589)

das **Gesicht**, –er face; grimace (2074, 3909, 11194); **Gesichter schneiden** make faces

das **Gesinde** household, retinue

gesinnt disposed, inclined

gesittet in a well-bred way

das Gespenst, -er ghost, spectre

gespensterhaft ghostlike, spooky

das Gespenst-Gespinst, -e spooky fabrication

gespenstig spectral, ghostly

gespenstisch spooky

die Gespielin, -nen female play-mate

das Gespinst, -e web, fabric, fabrication

das Gespräch conversation

gessen (= gegessen) eaten

das Gestade, — shore, beach

die Gestalt, -en shape, form, figure; stature

gestalten (wk) form, shape

die Gestaltung formation, shap-ing

das Geständnis confession

der Gestank stench, bad smell

gestehen admit, confess

das Gestein,-e rocks; stone, gem

gestern yesterday

das Gestöhn groaning

das Gesträuche shrubbery

gestreng stern; Gestrenger Herr dread majesty

das Gestümper bungling

gesund healthy, in good health, safe and sound; health-giving, wholesome

gesunden (wk) recover

die Gesundheit good health

das Getändel dalliance

das Getön ringing, sound

das Getöse din, loud noise

das Getränk, -e drink

das Getreibe moving throng, milling crowd

getreu loyal, faithful

getrost confident, with confident assurance, with a comfortable sense of security

getrübt troubled, perturbed

das Getümmel bustle, turmoil

getupft speckled

gewagt venturesome, risky, hazardous

gewahr aware

gewahren (wk) become aware of, perceive

sich gewahren beware, be on guard

gewähren (wk) grant, give, vouchsafe, allow

die Gewalt, -en violence, power, force

gewaltig mighty, powerful, vio-lent; intense (7069)

gewaltsam violent

gewaltsam-innig violently ar-dent

das Gewand, -e/-er garment, raiment

gewandt skilled, apt, clever, nimble; with a bent for

gewärtig expecting, awaiting

das Gewässer, — waters, body of water, stream

das Gewebe web

das Gewehr, -e weapon

das Gewerb business, trade

das Gewerbesband, -e burden-some routine of trade

das Gewicht weight; impor-tance, emphasis, validity; serious meaning (9928)

das Gewimmel swarm, busy crowd

das Gewinde, — festoon, wreath

der Gewinn gain, profit, ad-vantage

gewinnen, a, o win, gain, acquire (spiritual) gain (12063)

der **Gewinst, –e** winnings, gain

gewiß certain, sure, safe, assured; **du bist mir gewiß** I have you, you're in my power

das **Gewissen** conscience

gewissenhaft conscientious

die **Gewißheit** assurance, certainty

das **Gewoge** waves

gewogen well-disposed toward, fond of

sich **gewöhnen** (wk) accustom oneself to, get used to

die **Gewohnheit** habit

gewöhnlich usual, customary

gewohnt accustomed; familiar, usual

gewöhnt accustomed to, habituated to

das **Gewölb(e), —** vaulted ceiling, arch, dome

das **Gewühl** tumult

geziemen be suitable, be meet; become (8647)

das **Gezücht** breed, inferior race

das **Gezwergvolk** dwarf people

Ghibellinen Ghibellines (*political faction, supporting the Hohenstaufen emperor*)

die **Gicht** gout

der **Giebel, —** gable

gierig eager; greedy

gießen, o, o pour out; cast (8307)

das **Gift** poison

der **Gift** poison (1053)

die **Gift** gift (10927)

giftig poisonous; angry

der **Gildneid** guild envy

der **Gipfel, —** summit, peak

der **Gipfelriese, –n** gigantic summit, giant-like pinnacle

der **Gipfelwald** summit forest

girren creak, grate (3945)

der **Gischt** froth; rancor, spleen

der **Glanz** splendor, radiance

glänzen (wk) gleam, glitter, shine

glänzend brilliant; **glänzendreich** resplendently rich

das **Glanzgestein** gleaming gem

das **Glanzgewimmel** lustrous swarm

das **Glas, ⸚er** glass

das **Gläschen** (small) glass

glatt smooth, slippery; level

die **Glatze** bald head

der **Glaube** faith, belief

glauben (wk) believe, have faith; think

die **Glaubenskrücke** crutch of faith

glaubenswert credible, worthy of belief

glaubhaft authentic, credible, true

glaubhaftig believable

der **Gläubige, –n** believer, devout person

der **Gläubiger, —** creditor

gleich like, similar, same, equal; even, uniform

gleich [adv] immediately, right away, at once, now, right (2317)

gleichen, i, i resemble, be equal to, match (9819)

gleicherweise similar, in similar vein, in like manner

gleichfalls likewise, also

gleichgültig unconcerned, indifferent

der **Gleichmut** calm, equanimity

Gleichnis

das **Gleichnis** symbol
gleisnerisch hypocritical
gleißen glitter, shine
das **Glied, -er** limb, member
das **Gliederchen, —** little limb
glimmern gleam faintly
glitzern glisten, glitter
der **Glitzertand** glittering trifles, tinsel
das **Glöckchen** little bell
die **Glocke, -n** bell; cup (5148)
der **Glockenklang** chimes
der **Glockenruf** call of a bell
der **Glockenschlag** stroke of the bell
der **Glockenton** sound of a bell
das **Glöcklein** little bell
die **Glorie** halo; aureola and nimbus (*emanation of light from very holy persons or spirits*)
gloriosa in glory
das **Glück** fortune, happiness, success, good luck
Glückan Greetings! Hail!
Glückauf Hail! Good luck!
glücken (*wk*) turn out well, be a success
glücklich happy, fortunate, successful
glückselig favored by fortune, lucky
Glückzu! Good luck!
glühen glow, burn
glühend intense, ardent
die **Glut, -en** intense heat, glow, fire
glutend glowing
die **Gnade, -n** grace, mercy, favor; Grace (287)
die **Gnadenpforte** gate to paradise; the "strait gate" that

"leadeth unto life" (Matt. 7:14)
gnadenreich merciful
gnädig merciful, gracious; **gnädiger Herr** Sir; der **Gnädigste** His Majesty
der **Gnom, -en** gnome, diminutive subterranean being
gnug = genug
Gnüge = Genüge
gnügt = genügt
das **Gold** gold
gold gold-colored
goldbeschuppt having gold scales
golden golden; precious, lovely
golden-golden golden (roll) of gold
die **Goldespforte, -n** gateway to gold, source of money
goldgehörnt with golden horns
goldgelockt golden-haired
goldgesäumt with a gold hem or border
das **Goldgewicht** heavy gold
goldgewirkt gold-embroidered
goldlockig golden-haired
der **Goldschmuck** gold jewelry
der **Goldtopf** pot of gold
goldverbrämt gold-braided
gönnen (*wk*) bestow upon, vouchsafe, grant gladly, permit; **nicht gönnen** begrudge
der **Gönner, —** patron, benefactor
der **Gote** Goth
gotisch Gothic
der **Gott, ⸗er** God, god; **um Gottes willen** for nothing, out of sheer benevolence (1652)
die **Gottähnlichkeit** likeness to God
gottbeglückt blessed by the gods

gottbetört made mad by the gods

der Götterausspruch oracle

das **Götterbild,** –er divinely beautiful form; being in God's image (2716); statue of a god (8310)

die Göttergewalt divine might

göttergleich godlike, divine

die Göttergunst divine favor

die Götterhand godlike hand

die Götterhöhe superior power of the gods

das Götterleben life fit for the gods

die Götterlust divine pleasure

der **Göttersohn,** ⸗e son of God (*angel*)

der **Götterstamm** divine family (*origin*)

die Götterwonne divine bliss

die Gotteslust joy in God

gottgegeben god-given

die Gottheit divinity, deity

die **Göttin,** –nen goddess

göttlich divine

göttlich-heldenhaft divine and heroic, of gods and heroes

gottlos irreligious, godless, impious

der Gottverhaßte one hated by God

gottverklärt divinely transfigured

das **Grab,** ⸗er grave, tomb

das Gräbchen little ditch

der **Grabdichter,** — poet of the tomb

der **Graben,** ⸗ ditch

graben (ä), u, a dig

die Grablegung burial

der **Grad,** –e degree; **ein Mann von vielen Graden** no beginner

grad(e) straight, right, right away; precisely, exactly, just; **das Grade** that which is straight

gradehin without standing on ceremony (3174)

gradgeführt laid out in a straight line

Graien Graiae (*three sisters, born with gray hair, having one eye, one tooth among them*)

der Gram grief

grämlich sullen

grämlig = grämlich

grandios grandiose, magnificent

das Gras grass

der **Grasaffe** young fool (*who cavorts on the green*); kittenish young person

das **Gräschen,** — little blade of grass

graß monstrous, horrible, hideous

gräßlich terrible, monstrous

gratulieren congratulate

grau gray, colorless

der **Graubart,** ⸗e graybeard

grauen grow gray (*at dawn* 4579)

grauen cause one to feel horror or dread or terror; **es graut mir** I am filled with terror

das **Grauen** dread, shuddering (8034, 11916), horror

grauenvoll horrible

graugeboren born with gray hair

der **Graus** terror, terrifying thing; wilderness of rocks (7802)

graus horrible, dreadful

grausam cruel, unfeeling

grausam-blutig cruel and bloody

das **Grausen** dismay, horror

grausenhaft horrible

grauslich dreadful

grautagend dimly-lighted (*as by a gray dawn*)

gravitätisch solemn, grave

Grazien Graces (*Aglaia, Euphrosyne, Thalia or Hegemone*)

das Grei, grei- (*as a syllable, part of the word* Greif)

der Greif, –e griffon, fabulous monster

greifen, i, i grasp, clutch, reach, grab, seize; trespass upon (6195)

greiflich tangible

der Greis, –e old man

grell shrill, piercing

die Grenze, –n limit, boundary, frontier; limitation

grenzenlos unbounded, limitless

grenzunbewußt knowing no boundaries

Gretchen Margaret

Gretel Margaret

Gretelchen Margaret

der Greuel, — abomination

der Greuelschlund horrible throat, abyss of abominations

greuelvoll abominable, atrocious

greulich frightful, horrible

der Grieche, –n Greek

das Griechenland Greece

das Griechenvolk Greek race

griechisch Greek

der Griesgram grumbler; bad humor

griesgram ill-humored

der Grieß gravel

der Griff act of seizing

der Griffel stylus

die Grille, –n whim, melancholy thought; cricket (4253, 4293, 4363)

grillen be capricious

grillenhaft capricious, changeable; strange, queer, fantastic

der Grimm wrath (*of God* 3800); rage (*of the witch* 2481; *of the Devil* 4458)

grimm fierce

grimmen rage

grimmig fierce, furious, wrathful

das Grinsen grin

grob rude, uncivil; unrefined (5207)

groß large, big, great, tall, grand, huge, important; **groß tun** swagger, boast, give oneself airs

großartig in the grand manner

die Größe greatness; height (8689)

die Großheit greatness

die Großmut generosity

großmütig generous, magnanimous

die Grotte, –n grotto

die Grube pit

grübeln reason subtly

die Gruft, ⸚e cavity; grave, vault

das Grün green

grün green

der Grund, ⸚e ground, foundation, soil; bottom, valley; background (4692); reason (6379); **im Grunde** basically, fundamentally; **auf den Grund** completely, to a conclusion; **von Grund (aus)** thoroughly; **aus dem Grund** completely der **Grundbesitz** ownership of real estate

gründen (*wk*) establish, found, base

die **Grundgewalt** deep strong notes

der **Grundtext** original (text)

die **Grüne** greenness

es **grunelt** there is a fresh smell of growing vegetation

grünen (*wk*) become green; be green (9308)

grüngesenkt embedded in green

grünumgeben surrounded by green(ery)

grünumschränkt bounded by green

die **Gruppe** group; grouping

der **Gruß**, ⸚e salutation, greeting, regards, salute

grüßen (*wk*) salute, greet, give greetings to; **seid uns gegrüßt** accept our greetings (upon arrival); **grüßen lassen** send kind regards

gucken peep, peek

Guelphen Guelphs (*Italian political faction, supporting the pope*)

die **Guitarre**, –n guitar

der **Gulden**, — guilder (*a coin*)

gülden golden

gültig valid

die **Gunst**, –en good will, favor, permission (8241)

günstig favorable, propitious

der **Gürtel** girdle, belt, money belt (6108)

der **Gürtelschmuck** belt clasp, girdle ornament

das **Gut**, ⸚er property, piece of property; blessing (1068);

farm, estate (11136); **höchstes Gut** summum bonum; **Güter** wares

gut good; well; desirable; kind, pleasant; (*with dative*) **gut sein** be fond of, love; be well disposed toward (3478)

das **Gütchen**, — good elf, brownie (5848)

das **Gütchen** little estate (11276)

die **Güte** kindness, goodness

gütig amiable

die **Gütigkeit** amiability

gütlich friendly, amicable

H

H— — [1821, **Hint(e)rer?** **Hintern? Hoden?**]

ha! ha!

das **Haar**, –e hair

ein **Haarbreit** a hair's breadth

Habebald Get-quick

haben (*wk, irreg*) have, own, possess; **zum besten haben** make a fool of

die **Habichtskralle**, –n hawk-like talon

die **Hacke** hoe, mattock

hacken hoe, grub

der **Häckerling** chopped straw

der **Hader** quarrel, wrangling

Hades Hades (*underground dwelling place of the dead*)

der **Hafen** harbor

hafenein into port

hager haggard

der **Hagestolz** bachelor

der **Häher** jay

der **Hahn** rooster

die **Hahnenfeder** cock feather

der **Haifisch** shark

der **Hain,** –e grove

der **Haken** hook

halb half, semi-; **der halbe Weg** halfway mark; **halb und halb** more or less

halb in the interest of, on the subject of (9147)

das **Halbchor** one half of a divided chorus

halberstorben half-dead

halbgefault half-rotted

halbgeschlossen half-closed

der **Halbgott,** –er demigod (*off-spring of a god and a mortal*)

halbgöttlich like a demigod

die **Halbhexe** half-witch

halblaut half aloud

die **Halbnatur,** –en half-and-half being

halbverklungen half faded away

halbverkohlt charred, half-consumed

halbverrückt half-crazed

halbweg halfway

halbwüchsig half-grown

die **Hälfte** half

die **Halle,** –n public room, great room

der **Hals,** –e neck

das **Halstuch** neckerchief, scarf

halt after all

Haltefest Hold-fast

halten (ä), ie, a hold, hold on to, cling to; restrain, stop; keep, keep house; consider; **halten auf** insist on; **halten für** take to be, consider; **halten von** think of; **Haus halten** set up one's establishment; **Stich halten** pass the test; **an der ist nichts zu halten** that is of

no value any more, that is of no further use (3702)

sich **halten (ä),** ie, a cling to; behave (3370); keep (5150), keep to; compare (5165), maintain oneself; stop

der **Hammer** hammer

die **Hand,** –e hand; **zur Hand** at hand; **auf eigne Hand** on one's own responsibility

der **Händedruck** handshake, pressure

der **Handel** business

Händel (*pl*) quarrels

das **Handeln** bargaining, haggling (5387)

handeln do business (3174), act

sich **handeln (um, von)** be concerned, be involved

das **Händeringen** wringing of hands

handhaben handle

das **Handwerk** trade

das **Handwerksband,** –e burdensome routine of the craft

der **Handwerksbursch,** –e journeyman artisan

der **Handwerksgruß** trade password

der **Handwerksneid** trade envy

hänfen hempen; coarse hempen (cloth, *e.g. burlap,* 11606)

der **Hang,** –e slope, side

hangen (ä), ie, a hang, cling, dangle (5198)

hängen hang to, cling to; **hängen bleiben** persist, remain as residue (5368)

sich **hängen** hang on to, attach oneself to

Hans, –en Jack; **der große Hans** the great gentleman (2727)

Hans Liederlich a dissolute fellow

hänseln (*wk*) make a fool of

der **Hanswurst** Hanswurst, buffoon, clown; Jack Pudding, Merry Andrew

harmlos innocent

harmonisch harmonious

der **Harnisch** armor; **in Harnisch bringen** enrage

sich **harnischen** (*wk*) put on armor

die **Harpye**, **–n** harpy (*malignant and filthy monster, half woman and half bird*)

harren (*wk*) wait

hart hard, severe, tough, rough; close (2623, 3705)

hartnäckig stubborn

der **Harz** Harz Mountains

das **Harzgebirg** Harz Mountains

harzig resinous

haschen (*wk*) catch, seize

der **Hase**, **–n** rabbit, hare

der **Haß** hate, hatred

hassen (*wk*) hate

häßlich hateful, ugly

häßlichen make ugly

die **Häßlichkeit** ugliness

häßlich-wunderbar grotesquely amazing

hastig hasty

das **Häubchen** little cap

der **Hauch** breath

hauchen breathe, exhale, speak softly

der **Haufe**, **–n** crowd; pile, heap (9305, 10737); **zu Haufen in** great numbers; *see* **zuhauf**

häufeln pile up

häufen (*wk*) pile on

sich **häufen** (*wk*) accumulate

häufig in large numbers (3098)

das **Haupt** head; **zu Haupten** about the head (9623); **auf den Häupten** on your heads (5109)

die **Haupt- und Staatsaktion** tragedy of blood (*sensational and moralizing drama of kings and princes*)

die **Hauptmacht** principal strength

der **Hauptmoment** crucial moment

die **Hauptstadt** capital

der **Hauptverdruß** major annoyance

das **Hauptweib** principal woman (*in a chorus of women* 5666)

das **Haus**, **⸚er** house, home; family; twelfth part of the zodiac (4949); **zu Haus** at home; **nach Haus** homeward, home; **Haus halten** set up one's own establishment; **von Haus aus** by one's very nature

der **Hausbewahrer** protector of the home

der **Hausbrand** burning of the house

das **Häuschen** little house

hausen stay, lodge; rage (4827)

die **Hausfrau** lady of the house

der **Hausgenosse**, **–n** one who lives in the same house

das **Hausgesinde** domestic servants, domestic staff

das **Häuslein**, **—** cottage

häuslich belonging to the house; domestic; at home (9474)

das **Hausrecht** authority as head of the house

haußen (= **hier außen**) out here

Haut

die **Haut** skin; **mit heiler Haut** unscathed; **an eigner Haut** oneself, on one's own person

he! hey!

Hebe Hebe (*goddess of youth*)

der **Hebel,** — lever

heben, o, o lift; raise, turn up (5010); recover (6062)

sich **heben, o, o** rise, arise; **hebe dich von hinnen** be gone

Heda! Hey there!

das **Heer, -e** army, host

die **Heereskraft** armed force

der **Heereszug** army on the march

der **Heerführer** general

der **Heermeister** commander of an army group

die **Heerschar, -en** host, legion

heften hold firmly

sich **heften** be fixed, be attached

heftig agitated, violent

Hegemone Hegemone (*one of the Athenian Graces*)

hegen (*wk*) cherish, shelter; contain (989, 10935); entertain, harbor (4901, 8526)

sich **hegen** (*wk*) take shelter, derive sustenance from, put one's faith in (4915)

hehr sublime, august

die **Heide** heath, waste land

der **Heidenriegel,** — heathen bolt or bar

das **Heidenvolk** heathens

das **Heil** welfare, salvation, prosperity; **Heil!** Hail!

heil sound, unscathed

der **Heiland** Savior

heilen (*wk*) cure, heal

heilig holy, sacred, blessed; august; godly (*ironic*) (3040);

der **Heilige** saint; der **Heilig' Geist** the Holy Ghost; der **heilige** Saint

heiligen (*wk*) sanctify, give a blessing

der **Heiligenschein** halo

das **Heiligtum** holy place, sanctuary; godliness, holiness; religion (*Holy Church* 10992)

heilsam healing (760), beneficial (1380)

die **Heilung** cure

die **Heimat** home (*land, region*)

die **Heimfahrt** journey home

heimführen (*as a bride*) marry

heimgeben entrust, place in one's keeping

heimlich secret, mysterious, concealed

heimlich-kätzchenhaft with catlike stealth

heimstellen (*wk*) leave to

heimsuchen (*wk*) punish, persecute

Heinrich Henry

heisa! *cry of festive high spirits*

heischen demand

heiser hoarse

heiß hot, ardent, burning (4106)

heißen, ie, ei be called, have the title of; be supposed to be (409); call, mean; command (2305, 2705); **es heißt** it is said, the conclusion is, someone says, the saying goes (6749, 6962, 7837, 11400); **willkommen heißen** welcome (8496)

heiter serene, calm; cheerful, glad, happy; clear, bright

die **Heiterkeit, -en** cheerfulness, cheerful enjoyment

heitern be cheerful

Hekate Hecate (*goddess of moon, earth, and underworld*)

der **Held, –en** hero

der **Heldenherr** lord of heroes

der **Heldenmann** heroic man, hero

heldenmäßig heroic

der **Heldenmut** heroic courage

die **Heldenschar** band of heroes

der **Heldenstamm** heroic family

die **Heldentat, –en** heroic deed

das **Heldenvolk** race of heroes

die **Heldin** heroine

Helena Helen of Troy

helfen (i), a, o help; do good

der **Helfer** helper

der **Helfershelfer, —** accomplice

Helios Helios (*Apollo, sun god*)

hell bright, clear; cheerful; broad (daylight); **zu hellen Haufen** in large numbers (10737)

Hellas Hellas, Greece

die **Hellebarde, –n** halberd (*long-handled weapon, combined spear and battle-axe*)

sich **hellen** become light

hellenisch Hellenic, Greek

die **Hellung** illumination

der **Helm** helmet

hemmen (*wk*) inhibit, impede, hinder, curb, restrain

der **Hengst, –e** stallion

der **Henker** hangman, executioner; **was Henker!** what the devil!

Hennings Hennings (*editor of "Genius der Zeit," literary adversary of Goethe*)

Hephästos Hephaestus (*Vulcan, god of fire, patron god of blacksmiths*)

her to this place; here; bring! come! **hin und her** to and from; **um ... her** around; **rings um ... her** all around; **von ... her** hither, from as far back as; **wo ... her** from where

herab down, down to here

herabbewegen move downward

herabführen lead down

herabkommen come down

sich **herablassen (ä)** condescend

herabnehmen (i), a, o take down

herabrollen roll down

herabschicken send down

sich **herabsenken** sink down

herabsingen, a, u lure down by singing

herabsinken sink down

herabsteigen, ie, ie climb down, descend

herabstürzen descend with a rush, swoop down

sich **herabstürzen** (*wk*) descend

herabtreten (i) step down

herabwehen drift down

herabziehen, o, o pull down, lure down

Herakles Herakles, Hercules (*demigod of great physical strength*)

heran to, up to, hither; come here! from somewhere else

heranbringen bring here

herandrängen (*wk*) press up close

sich **herandrängen** (*wk*) crowd up close

herandringen push one's way forward

sich **herandrücken** (*wk*) press up close

sich **heranfügen** join, fit into

heranführen lead up to

herangehen, i, a go up to

herankommen (ö 3091), **a, o** come, draw near, approach

herankriechen, o, o come crawling along

herannahen approach

heranraffen (*wk*) collect, gather

heranschleichen creep up stealthily

heranschnauben come up panting

heranschwanken approach swaying

heranschweben soar, come floating toward me / us

heransegeln sail up, sail along

heransenken lower, bring down

heransingen, a, u lure by singing

heransteigen climb up

herantraben (*wk*) trot up

herantragen (ä), **u, a** carry up, bring

herantreten (i) step forward

heranwachen (*wk*) wakefully observe (something) approach

heranwachsen (ä) grow up

sich **heranwagen** dare to approach, risk approaching

heranziehen, o, o draw near; draw, attract (8049)

heranzögern bring to pass through hesitation

herauf up; come up (7811)

heraufdringen, a, u penetrate upward, force a way up

heraufführen (*wk*) lead up

heraufkommen come up

heraufscheinen, ie, ie shine up

sich **heraufschmiegen** come up

heraufsteigen rise, ascend

sich **heraufwälzen** come rolling up

heraus out, come out!

herausblasen bring forth by blowing

herausfahren (ä), **u, a** rush out

herausfallen (ä) fall out

die **Herausforderung** challenge

herausführen lead out, help to escape

herausheben lift out (*of the fire*)

herauskommen, a, o come out of it, survive

heraustreiben expel

heraustreten (i) step out

herauswischen slip out

herausziehen extricate

sich **herausziehen** get out of difficulties (4336)

herb harsh, severe

herbannen (*wk*) conjure up

herbei here; bring here! come here!

herbeiberufen summon (by name)

herbeibringen produce

herbeidringen come pressing up

herbeigeben (i) give here

herbeiholen (*wk*) produce, procure

herbeikommen come up

herbeilaufen (äu) come running

sich **herbeimachen** come close, approach

herbeiraffen (*wk*) collect violently

herbeischaffen produce, get and bring

herbeischleichen sneak up here

herbeischleppen drag up

herbeiziehen move up

herbescheiden, ie, ie summon

herblicken look; **allseits um . . . herblicken** look all around

herbringen, a, a (*wk, irreg*) bring here; **hergebracht** established by tradition

der **Herbst** autumn; harvest (10533)

herbstlich in autumn

der **Herd** hearth

die **Herde, –n** flock, drove, herd

die **Herdesbreite** (entire) width of the hearth

herein come in! enter!

hereindringen force (its) way in

hereinführen lead (in)

hereinkommen, a, o come in, enter, get in

hereinschauen gaze in here

hereinschlüpfen (*wk*) slip in

hereinsinken, a, u sink down

hereinspringen, a, u leap in, come running in

hereintragen carry in

hereintreten (i), a, e enter, step in; set in, come (11015)

sich **hereinwagen** risk entering, dare to enter

herführen (*wk*) bring here

hergeben (i) give (me); hand (it) over

hergrinsen grin at

herkollern roll crazily along

herkommen come here, come from

herkömmlich traditional

Herkules Hercules (*demigod of great physical strength*)

herläuten (*wk*) summon by ringing

herlocken (*wk*) attract, allure

der **Hermaphrodit** hermaphrodite (*individual with characteristics of both sexes*)

hermaphroditisch hermaphroditic

Hermes Hermes (*Mercury, messenger of the gods, patron god of thieves*)

Hermione Hermione (*daughter of Menelaus and Helen*)

hernach later, afterwards

hernehmen (i), a, o take from

herniedertropfen (*wk*) fall drop by drop

sich **herniederwenden** descend, turn downward

die **Heroine, –n** heroine, somewhat more than human woman

heroisch heroic, somewhat more than human

der **Herold, –e** herald, announcer

die **Heroldspflicht, –en** duty of a herald

der **Herr, –en** gentleman, Lord, Sire, sir, master; Mr.; **der Herr** you (*respectful*); **mein Herr** sir

die **Herrin** lady, mistress

herrisch domineering, imperious

herrlich splendid, glorious, lordly

herrlich-hehr magnificent and august

die **Herrlichkeit, –en** magnificence, splendor; splendid thing (2795)

die **Herrschaft** authority, mastery; **Herrschaft führen** be in control

herrschen (*wk*) rule, govern, prevail

der **Herrscher** ruler, commander, sovereign

der **Herrscherherr** sovereign lord

die **Herrscherin** mistress, ruler, queen

das **Herrscherwort**, **–e** command, order

herrufen, ie, u invoke, conjure up

herschaffen procure, produce

herschauen look here

herschießen, o, o shoot (down) here; fly hither

herschiffen (*wk*) come by ship

herschleppen drag up, come dragging

herschwanken sway this way

herschweben come floating this way (8272)

herschwimmen, a, o come floating

hersehen (**ie**) look here, look at this

hersenden (*wk*) dispatch, send here

herstellen produce, establish, restore

herstürmen come boisterously up, approach stormily

hertoben storm along uproariously

hertrotten trot along

herübergehen go across; **herüber und hinüber gehen** go back and forth

herüberkommen come over

herüberschießen fly across

herübersteigen climb across

herum around, all around, around and around

herumfahren (**ä**), **u, a** rush around

herumführen (*wk*) lead around and around

herumgehen, i, a go around and around

sich **herumkehren** turn around

herumquirlen stir around

sich **herumschlagen** contend against

herumschleichen slink about

herumsprengen gallop about

herumspringen leap about

herumspüren sniff around

herumwälzen roll from side to side

herumziehen pull around (after oneself)

herunterfahren (**ä**), **u, a** rush down

herunterholen take down

herunterklimmen climb down

herunterkommen come down

heruntersteigen descend

heruntertreten (**i**) step down

sich **herverlieren** lose oneself in this place, merge oneself into this environment

hervor! come out!

hervorblicken look out, peep forth

hervorbrechen (**i**) break forth, burst out

hervorbringen, a, a (*wk, irreg*) produce, bring forth, give birth to, elicit

sich **hervordrängen** come crowding out

hervordringen crowd forth, emerge from

hervorhupfen (*wk*) hop out

hervorkommen come forth

hervorrollen roll out

hervorrufen call forth, summon, evoke, conjure up

hervorschieben, o, o extrude, thrust forth

hervorschlagen (ä) leap forth (*flames*)

hervorspringen spring forth

hervorsprühen scatter, emit

hervorsteigen mount up

hervortreten (i) step forth, emerge, appear

sich **hervorwagen** dare to come out

herwanken come staggering along

herweben: hin und her weben weave to and fro (503)

herwehen: hin und her wehen float to and fro

herwenden: hin und her wenden turn this way and that

herwuseln: hin und her wuseln swarm to and fro

das **Herz, –en** heart; darling; **von Herzen** heartily; **ein Herz fassen** take courage

herzen (*wk*) fondle, press to one's heart

der **Herzensdrang** heart's desire

der **Herzensstoß** thrust to the heart, mortal blow

herziehen draw near, come up

herzig sweet

herzlich heartily, thoroughly; hearty, of the heart (8428); very, very much

der **Herzog, –e** duke, commander

sich **herzudrängen** crowd up

heucheln play the hypocrite, dissemble, pretend

heulen howl

heut(e) today

heutig present, this (day)

heutzutage these days, nowadays

das **Hexchen, —** witch

die **Hexe, –n** witch

der **Hexenberg** witches' mountain

das **Hexenchor** witches' chorus

das **Hexen-Einmaleins** witches' multiplication table

das **Hexenelement** element (*fire*) fit for witches

der **Hexen-Fex, –e** witch monstrosity

der **Hexenhauf** crowd of witches

der **Hexenhausrat** witch's house-furnishings

das **Hexenheer** host of witches

die **Hexenheit** witchhood

die **Hexenküche** witch's kitchen

der **Hexenmeister, —** sorcerer, wizard

der **Hexenritt** witches' ride

der **Hexensohn** witch's son

die **Hexenzunft** company (guild) of witches

hie here; **hie und da** here and there

hiebei with this, with what has been said

hieher here, hither, to this place; **bis hieher** up until now

hieneben close by

hier here; **von hier aus** from this point; **von hier an** from here on

hierauf upon this, upon this basis

hieraußen out here

hierher hither, here, to this place

hierherblicken look this way

hierhin this way

hierüber concerning this matter

hierunten down here, here below

hieselbst in this very place

hilf- *see* **hülf-**

der **Himmel,** — heaven, heavens, sky

himmelan up to the sky, up to heaven

himmelein into heaven

himmelhoch high as heaven, very high

das **Himmelreich** heaven

das **Himmelsangesicht** lovely face (*of heavenly beauty*)

die **Himmelsenge** heavenly retreat

die **Himmelsfreude** heavenly bliss

die **Himmelsgabe, –n** gift of heaven

der **Himmelsglanz** heavenly radiance

die **Himmelsglut** light (inspiration) from heaven

die **Himmelsklarheit** heavenly clearness

die **Himmelskönigin** queen of heaven

die **Himmelskraft, ⸗e** heavenly power

das **Himmelslicht** heavenly light: (*sun and moon* 235); (*reason* 284); (*sun* 400)

die **Himmelsliebe** divine love

das **Himmelslied, –er** heavenly song

die **Himmelsmanna** manna, bread from heaven

der **Himmelsraum** celestial space, the heavens

der **Himmelstag, –e** heavenly day

der **Himmelston, ⸗e** heavenly tone

himmelsverwandt related to heaven

die **Himmelsweite** expanse of the heavens

das **Himmelszelt** canopy of heaven

himmelwärts heavenward

himmlisch celestial, heavenly

hin there, go there, away, gone; **hin und wieder** back and forth; **hin und her** to and fro; **laßt es hin** let it go; **wo . . . hin?** to what place?

hinab down, downward

hinabbilden (*wk*) form so that it slopes downward

hinabfolgen follow downward

hinabgleiten glide down

hinabrauschen rush down (*like a mountain stream*)

hinabritzen (*wk*) scratch into the surface

hinabschauen look down

hinabsinken sink down

hinabsteigen descend, climb down

hinabstürzen hurl down

hinabzucken move spasmodically down

hinächzen go off groaning

hinan to; up to

hinanfahren (ä), u, a sail up (*to shore* 8539)

hinanhellen grow bright over an increasing area

hinanleuchten glow over an increasing area

hinanschreiten step, walk

hinanschwanken expand waveringly

hinansteigen, ie, ie climb up (to)

sich hinanverbreiten spread up a slope

hinanziehen draw onward

hinauf up, up to

hinaufblicken (wk) look up, glance up

hinaufdringen press onward

hinaufgehen: es geht schnell hinauf the ascent is rapid

hinauflaufen run up

hinaufleuchten light the way upward

hinaufreichen reach, extend to a (later) time

hinaufschauen (wk) look up

hinaufschicken send up

hinaufsehen look up

hinaufsteigen ascend, go up the steps

hinaufstreben try to climb up

sich hinaufversteigen climb unnecessarily high, venture too far

hinaufzüngeln lick upward (flames)

hinaus out, away from in here, out to, go out

sich hinausbegeben (i) betake oneself out

hinausblicken look out

hinausflattern flutter out

hinausfliehen, o, o fly out

hinausführen lead out, liberate

hinausgehen go out

hinauskehren (wk) sweep out

hinauslaufen (äu) turn out, end

hinausschallen resound

hinausschauen look out

hinausschlagen leap out (flames)

hinausspazieren stroll out

hinausweisen, ie, ie show the way, direct

hinauswollen (i) end; wo will's hinaus? what will the upshot be?

hinausziehen enter and walk across the stage (into the countryside)

hinbeten pray

hinbreiten spread out

hinbringen take there

hindern (wk) hinder

das Hindernis, −se obstacle

sich hindrängen yearn to be with

hindurchlassen let through, make way for

hineilen hasten to that place

hinein into that place, into, go into

hineinbeißen, i, i bite into

hineindringen set upon, attack

hineinfallen (ä) fall in

hineinfressen (i) eat into

hineingehen go into

hineingreifen reach into and grasp

hineingucken (wk) peep into

hineinlassen let in, admit

hineinschauen look in

hineinschielen (wk) squint in

hineinschlupfen slip in

hineinstellen put inside

hineintreten enter

hineintun, a, a put in

sich hineinwagen dare to enter, risk entering

hineinwittern penetrate very faintly and tentatively (3919)

hinfahren proceed, travel on, go away, depart

hinfließen flow on

hinführen take there

hingeben (i), a, e surrender

sich **hingeben** (i), a, e surrender

hingegen on the contrary

hingehen go off, go away

hingehören belong (there)

hingelangen arrive at that place, achieve that

hingrinsen grin away, keep on grinning

sich **hinkauern** (wk) crouch, squat

hinken (wk) limp

hinlaufen run; **Hin- und Wiederlaufen** running back and forth

hinlegen (wk) lay away

sich **hinlegen** lie down

hinnehmen (i) take, take and keep

hinnen: von **hinnen** away, away from here

hinraffen (wk) sweep away

sich **hinräkeln** stretch out, loll

hinrauschen rush along

hinreichen suffice, be adequate

hinreihen (wk) line up

hinreißen, i, i carry away

sich **hinrekeln** stretch out, loll

hinrutschen make an excursion

hinschauen look there

hinschleichen creep along

hinschlottern dangle loosely

hinschmelzen (i), o, o melt into a heap

hinschreiten stride along

hinschütten scatter abroad

hinschwanken sway this way; **hin und her schwanken** sway to and fro; **hin und wieder schwanken** sway back and forth

hinschweben float away

hinschweifen stray off

hinschwinden, a, u vanish, pass away

hinsehen (ie) look, look there; consider (112)

sich **hinsehnen** yearn to be away

hinstellen (wk) place before, serve (food)

hinstreben struggle toward, strive to

sich **hinstrecken** (wk) recline, stretch out at full length

hinstreichen glide along to a stop, glide in to a landing

hintappen (wk) grope one's way along

hinten back, back there; **von hinten** from the rear

hintendrauf behind

hintennach afterward

hinter behind

hinterdrein along behind, afterwards

der **Hint(e)re** (also colloq. **Hintern**) behind, rump

der **Hintergrund** background

hinterher afterwards

hinterlassen (ä), ie, a leave behind; leave as legacy (3117, 8553)

hinterm = **hinter dem**

der **Hintermann** person standing behind; **du Hintermann** you back there!

hinterrücks from behind

hintragen (ä) transport, carry along

sich **hintun**, a, a hide away

hinüberblicken look across

hinüberfolgen follow across

hinübergehen: **herüber und**

hinüber gehen go back and forth

hinübernehmen (i), a, o take across

hinüberschießen fly across

hinüberschlafen (ä), ie, a die in sleep

hinüberschwimmen, a, o swim across

hinübertragen carry across

hinunter down

hinuntereilen (wk) hasten downward

hinunterlassen (ä), ie, a allow to go downstairs

hinunterwerfen (i), a, o throw down

sich hinwälzen writhe

hinweben: hin und her weben weave to and fro

hinweg away; be gone (6956)

sich hinwegbannen (wk) go into voluntary exile

hinwegdrängen force away, push out of sight

hinweggehen, i, a go away

hinweggraffen (wk) snatch away

hinwegschwinden, a, u vanish away

hinwegtragen (ä), u, a carry off

hinwegweisen, ie, ie motion away, wave back

hinwehen: hin und her wehen float to and fro

hinwelken (wk) wither away

hinwenden turn, divert; hin und her wenden turn this way and that

sich hinwenden, a/e, a (wk, irreg) turn

hinwiegen (wk) balance, sway

hinwuseln: hin und her wuseln swarm to and fro

hinziehen, o, o extend along (11559); go away, move off (11825)

sich hinzugesellen join a group

hiobsartig Joblike, grievously afflicted

der Hippokamp, -en hippocampus (fabulous monster, part horse, part dolphin)

das Hirn brain

hirnlos brainless

der Hirsch, -e stag

der Hirte, -n shepherd

die Hitze ardor, passion, enthusiasm

hitzig hotheaded

ho! ho!

hoch high, tall; noble, grand, sublime; advanced (age)

die Hochbegrüßung formal and ceremonious greeting

hochbegünstigt highly favored

der Hochbesitz grand possession, realm

im Hochentzücken ecstatic, in ecstasy

das Hochgebirg high mountain country

hochgeehrt highly honored

hochgefeiert highly extolled, enthusiastically celebrated

hochgeheiligt highly consecrated

hochgelahrt very learned, erudite

das Hochgericht decree of a high court

hochgeschätzt highly esteemed

hochgetürmt towering high

hochgeweiht highly sanctified

der Hochgewinn great prize

das **Hochgewölb** high vaulted ceiling

hochgewölbt high vaulted

höchlich lofty

hochmütig haughty, arrogant

der **Hochpalast** royal palace

hochsinnig high-minded

höchstens at most

das **Höchsterrungene** greatest achievement

die **Hochverehrung** reverence, adoration

hochwürdig reverend, respected

die **Hochzeit** wedding

der **Hochzeittag** wedding day

der **Hode, –n** testicle

der **Hof, ⁀e** farm; royal court, walled enclosure; courtyard (9026, 9124, 9597); **Haus und Hof** all one's real property

hoffen (*wk*) hope, hope for; **es läßt sich hoffen** there is reason to hope

hoffentlich I hope

die **Hoffnung** hope

das **Hoffnungsglück** happiness of hope; messenger of spring (905)

das **Hoffnungslicht** gleam of hope

hoffnungsvoll hopeful

das **Hofgedränge** court crowd

das **Hofgeschäft, –e** occupation at court

das **Hofgesinde** court household

die **Hofkleidung** court dress

Hofleute courtiers

höflich courteous; refined (6470)

die **Höflichkeit** courtesy

die **Hofmanier, –en** court manner

der **Hofmann** courtier

der **Hofsänger, —** court singer

die **Höhe, –n** height, high place, elevation, high rank (10311); **in die Höhe** up; **in der Höhe** aloft

die **Hoheit** majesty, supreme power

hohl hollow, empty; **im hohlen Schiff** in the depths of the ship

das **Hohlauge** hollow eye

die **Höhle, –n** cavern, cave, cavity

die **Höhlengruft, ⁀e** cave vault

der **Höhlenraum, ⁀e** cavernous space

die **Höhlung** cavity (of a drinking vessel)

der **Hohn** scorn, mockery; **zum Hohn** in defiance of

höhnen mock

das **Hokuspokus** hocus-pocus

hold lovely, gracious, pleasing, gentle, sweet, favorable (7103)

holdmild graciously assuaging

holen go and get, come and get (4429)

holla! holla

die **Hölle, –n** hell

der **Höllenbrauch** customary usage in hell

die **Höllenbrut** crew from hell

das **Höllenfeuer** hell-fire

die **Höllenflamme** hell-fire

der **Höllenluchs** lynx from hell

die **Höllenpein** agony

der **Höllenpfuhl** bottomless pit of hell

die **Höllenqual** torment of hell

der **Höllenrachen** maw of hell, jaws of hell

der **Höllenschwefel** brimstone, sulphur of hell

die **Höllenstrafe,** –n torment of hell

höllisch infernal

holpern (*wk*) jolt, bump along

das **Holz,** ⸚er wood

hölzern wooden

der **Holzhauer,** — woodcutter

holzverschränkt with intercrossing beams

Homunculus Homunculus

der **Honig** honey

der **Honigtau** honeydew

honorieren honor, pay on demand

horchen listen

der **Horcher,** — listener

horchsam attentive

Horen Horae (*goddesses of order in nature, of the seasons*)

hören (*wk*) hear, listen, listen to

der **Hörer,** — hearer

der **Horizont** horizon

das **Horn,** ⸚er horn

hörnen (*wk*) adorn with horns

das **Hörnerblasen** blowing of horns

der **Hörsaal** lecture hall

der **Hort** hoard, treasure

die **Hose,** –n hose (*tights*)

hu! ugh! (*expression of disgust*)

hübsch pretty, handsome, fine (3117), right, nicely (4073)

hucken load upon someone's back

der **Huf** hoof

die **Hüfte** hip

der **Hügel,** — (small) hill, knoll

das **Hügelchen** hillock

die **Hügelkette** chain of hills

der **Hügelkreis** circle of hills

der **Hügelrand** edge of a hill

der **Hügelraum** hilly area

der **Hügelzug,** ⸚e line of hills

das **Huhn,** ⸚er chicken

die **Huld** favor, kindness

huldigen (*wk*) pay homage

die **Huldigung** homage

huldvoll gracious, benevolent

die **Hülfe** help

hülflos helpless

hülfreich helpful

hülfsbereit helpful

die **Hülle** cover, garment, outer wrapping, covering

hüllen (*wk*) wrap up, cover up, encase

der **Humor** humor, sense of humor, good humor

der **Humpen,** — bumper, tankard, large glass

der **Hund,** –e dog; (*Cerberus* 8890)

der **Hundebrauch** common canine ways or behavior

hundert hundred

hundertfach hundredfold

hundertmal a hundred times

hunderttausend hundred thousand

die **Hundsgestalt** canine form

der **Hunger** hunger

der **Hungerleider,** — sufferer from hunger

der **Hungermann** starved-looking man

hungern go hungry

die **Hungersnot** famine

hupfen hop

hüpfen skip about, gambol, hop, leap with joy

die **Hure** whore

hurtig swift, with furious speed

husten cough

der **Hut** hat; **unter dem Hut** in one's power

die **Hut** guard, protection; keeping (5911); **seid auf eurer Hut** be on your guard (5742)

sich **hüten** be careful not to (351, 9608); watch out, be on guard

das **Hüttchen** little cottage

die **Hütte, –n** hut, cottage

die **Hyäne** hyena

I

das **I** letter I (i 6994)

Ibykus Ibycus (*poet whose murderers were revealed by cranes*)

ich I

der **Idealist** philosophical idealist

das **Idol** illusion, phantom; image

idyllisch idyllic, pastoral

ihm him, it; to him, to it; for him, for it

ihn him, it

ihnen them, to them, for them

ihr you, ye

ihr her, it; to her, to it; for her, for it

ihr her, hers; its, of it; their, theirs

ihrer of them

Ihresgleichen her kind, the like(s) of her; their kind

Ikarus Icarus (*son of Daedalus, perished flying too close to the sun*)

Ilios Ilios, Troy

Ilse Ilse (*mythical nymph of the Ilsenstein*)

der **Ilsenstein** Ilsenstein (*rock in the Harz Mountains*)

im = in dem

die **Imagination** imagination

immer ever, always, still, after all; **immer mehr** more and more

immerfort continually, evermore, again and again

immerhin after all, in spite of all; always

die **Imse, –n** ant

in in, inside, at, into

der **Inbegriff** essence (693); epitome (2439); totality (6499)

inbrünstig ardent, passionate

indem while, as long as, during the time that

indes while; in the meantime; whereas (7480)

indessen while; meanwhile, but meanwhile

ingrimmend spitefully, wrathfully

der **Inhalt** content, substance

inkognito incognito, in disguise

sich **inkommodieren** go to (any) trouble

der **Inkubus** incubus (*evil spirit which descends upon sleeping persons*)

innehalten stop, pause

innen within, inside

inner inner, within, interior of (11312)

das **Innere** inner part(s), interior; heart of the matter; **aus dem Innern** from within; **im Innern** within

innerlich inward

das **Innerste** inmost part(s), inmost being

innig ardent, intimate (9973, 10509); deeply

ins = in das

das **Insekt**, −en insect

die **Insel**, −n island

insgeheim secret, in concealment

inskünftige in the future

insofern in so far as

das **Instrument**, −e instrument; piece of apparatus

interessant interesting

interessiert interested

das **Intermezzo** intermezzo (*light dramatic presentation between the acts of a serious play*)

die **Intuition** intuition

inwendig inside, behind the scenes

Ionia Ionia (*East Greece and Greek Asia Minor*)

das **Iota** iota

irden-schlecht earthen and bad

irdisch earthly, of this world

irgend in any way, at all

irgendein any...at all

irgendwo anywhere, in one way or another (4889), somewhere or other

irre wandering, in perplexity, in confusion; **irre führen** lead astray; **irre schreien** confuse by screaming

irreführen lead astray

irren (*wk*) wander; rove; err, go astray, be mistaken

sich **irren** (*wk*) be misled; lose one's way

die **Irrfahrt** wanderings

der **Irrfunkenblick** (= **Irrfunkenblitz**) flash of wandering sparkles

das **Irrlicht**, −er will-o'-the-wisp

irrlichtelieren move erratically (*like a will-o'-the-wisp*)

der **Irrtum** error, delusion

sich **isolieren** isolate oneself, withdraw

der **Italiener** Italian

italienisch Italian

J

ja yes

ja certainly, indeed, after all; be sure to (1955, 1962); you must admit; (*recognizes or anticipates agreement*)

die **Jacke**, −n jacket

die **Jagd** hunt, chase, hunting preserve

jagen chase after, follow

der **Jäger** hunter

das **Jägerhaus** game keeper's lodge, forester's lodge

jäh precipitous

das **Jahr**, −e year

Jahresläufte vintages

die **Jahreszeit** season

das **Jahrhundert**, −e century

das **Jahrtausend**, −e thousand-year period, millennium

der **Jammer** misery, wretchedness; **es ist ein Jammer** it's a pity, it's too bad

die **Jammerecke** wretched corner; corner of misery

die **Jammerknechtschaft** wretched servitude, imprisonment

jämmerlich lamentable

jammern make one feel sorry, move to pity (4620, 10291); lament (9615, 11340, 11756)

der **Jammertag**, −e day of misery

das **Jammerwort** lamentable utterance

Jason Jason (*leader of the Argonauts*)

jauchzen be jubilant, shout for joy

je ever; the (3748, 3749, 8226); **von je** from the beginning, always; **wie nur je** as has ever been the case

jeder each, every; all; either

jedermann every one, everybody

jederzeit at all times, always

jedesmal each time

jedoch and yet, however

jeglich each and every

jeher: von jeher all along, from the very beginning

jemals ever

jemand someone, somebody, anyone

jener that, those; that particular, those particular; the former; the well-known (6253)

der **Jesuit**, –en Jesuit

jetzo now, at this time, for the present

jetzt now, at present

das **Jota** iota

das **Journal**, –e newspaper

jubeln (*wk*) rejoice, exult, shout in celebration

die **Jubelnacht** night of merrymaking

juchhe! *shout of jollity and high spirits*

juchheisa! *shout of jollity and high spirits*

jucken itch

der **Jude** Jew

judizieren pass judgment, give a criticism

die **Jugend** youth; **von Jugend auf** from youth on

die **Jugendblüte** bloom of youth

der **Jugendbraus** youthful revelry

die **Jugendbrust** youthful breast

jugenderst first of one's youth

der **Jugendflor** youthful bloom; flowery garland of youth

die **Jugendfülle** youthful exuberance

die **Jugendkraft** youthful vigor

jugendlich youthful

die **Jugendnacht** night of one's youth

jugendrein of unsullied youth

der **Jugendtrieb**, –e youthful impulse

das **Jugendwalten** youthful governing

die **Jugendzeit** youth, time when one is or was young

jung young, new, recent, fresh, youthful

der **Junge**, –n boy, young chap

der **Jünger**, — disciple

der **Jungfernsohn** son of a virgin

die **Jungfrau** maiden; the Virgin

der **Junggeselle**, –n bachelor

junghold youthfully gracious

der **Jüngling**, –e youth, young man

der **Jünglingsknabe**, –n youth, adolescent boy

der **Junker** young nobleman, squire

Juno Juno (*goddess, consort of Jupiter*)

Jupiter Jupiter (*chief of the gods, god of thunder*); planet Jupiter (4961)

die **Juristerei** jurisprudence, law

just just, exactly; of all things; really (3115); **es wird mir nicht just** I don't feel at ease

das **Juwel, –en** jewel

juwelen jeweled, begemmed

K

Kabiren Cabiri (*group of deities, worshipped at Samothrace, Lemnos, and Imbros*)

der **Käfer, —** beetle

kahl bald, bare

der **Kahn** boat, vessel

der **Kaiser** emperor

das **Kaiserland, –e** empire, imperial land

kaiserlich imperial, with imperial dignity

die **Kaiserpracht** imperial splendor

die **Kaiserschar, –en** imperial troop

der **Kaiserschatz** imperial treasure

das **Kalb, ⸚er** calf

die **Kalenderei** astrological hocus-pocus, almanac predictions

der **Kalk** lime

kalt cold, indifferent, unfeeling

der **Kamm, ⸚e** comb, crest; cogs (*of a cogwheel* 669)

die **Kammer** room

der **Kämm(e)rer** chamberlain

der **Kampf** battle, contest

kämpfen (*wk*) struggle, contend

sich kämpfen (*wk*) fight one's way

der **Kanal** canal, channel

kannibalisch tremendous (like cannibals)

die **Kante** (sharp) corner, (sharp) edge

die **Kanzlei** chancellery

der **Kanzler** chancellor

das **Kapellchen** little chapel

die **Kapelle** chapel

der **Kapellmeister** bandmaster, orchestra conductor

das **Kapitel** chapter (*of a book* 2350); chapter (*of priests* 10266)

die **Kappe, –n** fool's cap

karessieren caress

der **Karfunkel** carbuncle

karg meager, scanty

das **Karneval** carnival

das **Kartenhaus** house of cards

das **Kartenspiel** card game

die **Karyatide** caryatid (*female figure in stone, supporting roof or arch*)

der **Kaskadensturz** cascading waterfall

die **Kasse, –n** ticket office (54); money chest (4851)

die **Kastanie, –n** chestnut

das **Kästchen, —** little box, jewel casket

der **Kasten, —** box; prompter's box (6501)

Kastor Castor (*one of the Dioscuri*)

der **Kasus** case; occurrence, event

katechisieren (*wk*) catechize

der **Kater** (**Meerkater**) male monkey

das **Katheder** lecture desk, professor's podium

das **Kathrinchen** Katharine, Kitty

die **Katze**, −n cat

der **Katzengeist**, −er cat spirit, feline spook

die **Kätzin** (**Meerkätzin**) female monkey

das **Kätzlein** young (tom)cat

kauen chew

der **Kauf** purchase

kaufen buy

der **Kaufmann** merchant

kaum scarcely, barely, as soon as; **ich bin kaum alleine** the minute I'm alone (3605); (*similarly in* 6007, 6439, 6685, 6958, 8539, 9321, 9585, 9877, 12085, 12086)

der **Kauz**, ⁻e screech owl; peculiar person (3483)

kauzen (*wk*) squat, cower, cringe

der **Kavalier**, −e cavalier

kebsen (*wk*) take as a concubine

keck bold

das **Kegelschieben** bowling

die **Kehle**, −n throat, voice

kehren (*wk*) turn, return

sich kehren (*wk*) turn

das **Kehrichtfaß** trash barrel

der **Keim**, −e germ

kein not any, none, no, not a, neither, no one, nobody

keineswegs by no means, under no circumstances

der **Kelch** goblet, chalice (4788)

der **Keller**, — cellar

die **Kellerei** cellarage, wine cellars

das **Kellernest** nest in a cellar

die **Kellertür(e)** cellar door

die **Kelter**, — wine press

keltern press (*grapes*)

der **Keltrer**, — wine presser

kennen, a, a (*wk, irreg*) know, be acquainted with, recognize; **kennen lernen** become acquainted with

der **Kenner** connoisseur, expert

der **Kennerblick** eye of a connoisseur

die **Kennerin**, −nen connoisseur, expert

der **Kerker** prison, dungeon

der **Kerl** fellow

der **Kern** kernel, heart, essence

der **Kessel**, — kettle, caldron

das **Kesselchen** little kettle

das **Kettchen** little chain (*jewelry*)

die **Kette**, −n chain, connected series (261)

ketten (*wk*) fetter, enchain

der **Kettenkreis**, −e linked circle

der **Kettenschmerz** pain of imprisonment

der **Ketzer**, — heretic

die **Keule**, −n club

keusch chaste, modest

der **Kiebitz** peewit

kielkröpfig with bulging throats

der **Kies** gravel

das **Kiesgewässer** stream with gravel bed

kimmerisch gloomy, Cimmerian; dark; northern

das **Kind**, −er child; girl

das **Kinderspiel**, −e child's play; children's game

die **Kinderwange**, –n childish cheek

der **Kinderzahn** baby tooth, milk tooth

das **Kindeslied**, –er children's song

die **Kindesruh** childlike peace

die **Kindheit** childhood

kindisch childish

kindisch-toll silly, childishly absurd

kindlich childlike

das **Kinn** chin

die **Kirchbuße** penance done publicly in church

die **Kirche**, –n church, Church; religion (3420)

die **Kirchenstelle** church authority

das **Kirchlein** little church

die **Kirsche**, –n cherry

das **Kissen** cushion

das **Kistchen**, — little chest

die **Kiste**, –n chest

kitzeln itch

klaffen gape, yawn

die **Klage** lament

klagen lament, complain; **eine Sache klagen** present a complaint (5390)

der **Kläger**, — complainant, plaintiff

klammern cling, clasp desperately

klang! clank!

der **Klang**, ⸚e sound, ringing

klappen clatter

klappern clatter, rattle

klar clear, unmistakable, pure, bright; **in dem Klaren** in clear waters (4323)

sich **klären** clear, settle

die **Klarheit** clarity, brightness (8392)

klar-vernünftig with clarity and rationality, serenely transparent

klassifizieren classify

klassisch classical

klatschen babble, chatter; **in die Hände klatschen** clap the hands

die **Klaue**, –n hoof; talon, claw

die **Klause** defile, mountain pass

kleben stick, adhere, be attached to

das **Kleid**, –er garment, costume; **Kleider** clothes

kleiden (*wk*) dress, clothe; be appropriate for (2812, 11795)

klein small, little, slight, lesser, petty (1327); **im Kleinen** on a small scale (1361, 8261)

der **Kleingeselle** little fellow

die **Kleinigkeit**, –en trifle

das **Kleinod**, –e jewel, piece of jewelry, treasure

klemmen pinch

sich **klemmen** be oppressed

der **Klerus** clergy

klettern climb, scramble

der **Klettrer**, — mountain climber

klimmen climb

kling! clink; **Kling! Klang!** clink! clank!

klingen, a, u sound, produce musical sounds, clink (5278)

die **Klippe**, –n cliff (3878); rock and reef (7378)

klirren clank, rattle

klopfen knock; **es klopft** there is a knock at the door

Klotho Clotho (*one of the Fates*)

klotzartig stumplike

der Klub club, company

die Kluft, ⸗e cleft, chasm, ravine

klug wise, sensible, clever, intelligent, sagacious, skillful, subtle, judicious

klugerfahren shrewd and experienced

die Klugheit sagacity, intelligence, prudence

der Klump, –en lump, shapeless mass

Klytämnestra Clytemnestra (*wife of Agamemnon, half-sister of Helen*)

der Knabe, –n boy, youth, young fellow; ein braver Knabe a fine young fellow; vom Knaben auf from childhood on (6966)

die Knallkraft explosive force

der Knappe, –n esquire, knight's attendant

knarren creak

knattern crackle

der Knecht, –e servant, slave (1412, 1710, 6963)

knechtisch-heiß: knechtisch-heiße Gruft hot pit of (our) servitude

kneipen pinch, bite

kneten (*wk*) knead, mold

knicken crack (*between finger-nails*); kill off (*fleas*)

das Knie, –e knee; in die Knie to one's knees (6631)

das Knieband garter

knieen kneel

der Kniff, –e trick, stratagem

knirschen crunch, grate

die Knospe bud

knospenentsiegelt released from just-opened buds

der Knoten knot; difficulty

der Knotenstock knotty stick, blackthorn cane

sich knüpfen be tied; develop (4041)

knurren growl

der Kobold imp, hobgoblin, gnome

der Koch, ⸗e cook

kochen cook, do the cooking; boil (5256)

die Köchin cook

der Koffer trunk, box

der Kohl cabbage

die Kohle, –n coal, charcoal

der Kohlenbrenner, — charcoal burner

die Kohlentracht, –en load of coal

kohobieren cohobate, redistill

der Kolben alembic, distilling apparatus (6852)

der Kolben club, cudgel (10516)

der Kollege, –n colleague

kollern roll head over heels

kolonisieren make colonies, displace people to new homes

die Kolonne, –n column

der Koloß colossus

kolossal colossal

der Komet comet

kommandieren command, give orders to

das Kommando command, military order

kommen, a, o come, come away, come about (529); get (2063); ins Gerede kommen get talked about; zu Tage kommen come to light (5034);

ans Licht kommen be born (5178); zum Vortrag kommen lassen permit to speak (5294); ins Gedränge kommen get into difficulties (5591); einem recht kommen suit (5647); zugut kommen benefit (5913); zu Schaden kommen harm (6565); ins reine kommen become clear in one's mind (6899); drauf kommen hit upon that (7124); zu Ehren kommen gain credit (7342); zur Schau kommen be revealed (7396); zum Gewinn kommen be advantageous (10407)

kommentieren comment upon, serve as commentator

der Kömmling arrival, comer

der Komödiant comedian, actor

das Kompliment, –e compliment

komponieren combine, compose, put together

konfus confused, flustered

der König, –e king

die Königin, –nen queen

königlich kingly, royal

das Königreich kingdom, realm, domain

das Königsband, –e royal bond

das Königsgut property fit for a king

das Königshaus royal palace

das Königsmahl royal banquet

der Königsmantel royal cloak

die Königspflaume, –n royal plum

können (a), o, o (irreg) be able to, can, know how to, be possible; etwas auf dich

können be able to exert some influence upon you

die Kontribution contribution, tax, levy

das Konventikel conventicle (*small surreptitious religious gathering*), prayer meeting

das Konzert concert

der Kopf, ″e head

das Köpfchen little head, feeble intellect

das Kopfweh headache

der Korb, ″e basket

das Körbchen little basket

Korinthus Corinth (*a city in central Greece*)

körnig granular; in the form of small hard particles; körniges Eis sleet

der Körper, — body

die Körperkraft physical strength

körperlich physical, bodily

kosen caress, pet

die Kost food, feeding

die Kostbarkeit, –en valuable object

Kosten expenses

kosten (*wk*) cost (481, 5773); involve the destruction of (8093)

kosten taste (5161)

köstlich costly, precious, excellent, exquisite, tasteful

das Kostüm costume

der Kothurn cothurnus, buskin (*boot worn by actors in Greek tragedy*)

krabbeln itch, crawl

krachen crack, crash

der Krächzegruß, croaking greeting

krächzen croak

die Kraft, ⸚e power, force, strength, vigor

kraftbegeistet alive with strength

kräftig strong, powerful, vigorous; ein kräftig Wörtchen an apposite remark

der Kragen collar

krähen crow

krall taloned

das Krallenbein, –e leg equipped with claws

der Kram wares

kramen retail, peddle; rummage about (10818)

der Krämer shopkeeper

die Krämerin, –nen shopkeeper

krampfen: mir krampft es I have a cramp

krampferstarrt cramped, cramp-stiffened

der Kranich, –e crane

die Kranichwolke cloud of cranes

krank sick; der Kranke, –n sick person

kränken grieve; offend

das Krankenhaus hospital; house in which there is sickness (1002?)

die Krankheit disease

der Kranz garland, wreath

das Kränzel bridal garland

kratzen scratch; extract, pull out (6254)

krauen scratch

kraus curly; irregularly shaped, complicated (671)

kräuseln curl, make wavy patterns in (2706); Schnitzel

kräuseln curl up paper spirals (streamers 555)

der Krauskopf curlyhead

die Kreatur, –en creature

der Kreis, –e circle; audience (83); social circle, group; sphere

die Kreisbewegung circling motion

kreisen circle, roam

kreißen give birth, be in labor

Kreta Crete (an island)

die Kreterin Cretan woman

das Kreuz cross; small of the back (10808)

kreuz: kreuz und quer from all sides, in utmost confusion (10262); die Kreuz und Quer zigzag, erratic course (1916, 5847)

kreuzigen (wk) crucify

der Kreuzweg crossroads

kreuzweis crossed

der Kribskrabs hodgepodge

kriechen crawl

der Krieg war

kriegen catch (2196), get (2815, 3574), take (3629); make war (10415)

der Krieger, — warrior, fighter

kriegerzeugt born during wartime

krieg(e)risch military, martial; caused by war

der Kriegsgedanke military design

das Kriegsgeschrei rumor(s) of wars

die Kriegslist stratagem

die Kriegsmusik martial music

der Kriegsrat council of war

der **Kriegstumult** warlike tumult

der **Kriegsunrat** war's ill counsel, war's waste

der **Kristall** crystal (ball), crystal

kristallen crystal

kristallisieren (*wk*) crystallize

die **Kritik** criticism

kritisch critical; as a critic (560)

der **Krittel** petty faultfinding

das **Krönchen,** — coronet

die **Krone, –n** crown; fullest fruition (1804); crown (*monetary unit* 6058, 6161)

krönen (*wk*) crown

der **Krönungstag** coronation day

die **Kröte** toad

der **Krötenbauch** toad's belly

die **Krötenzunge, –n** toad's tongue

die **Krücke** crutch

der **Krug,** ⸚e jug, pitcher, mug; vase

krumm crooked, bent; circuitously (362)

sich **krümmen** (*wk*) wriggle, cringe, writhe

krummeng crooked and narrow

der **Krüppel,** — cripple

die **Kruste** crust

die **Küche** kitchen; cuisine (2529); **die schwarze Küche** alchemist's laboratory

die **Kufe** vat, tub

die **Kugel** ball, globe

kugelrund round as a ball

die **Kuh,** ⸚e cow

kühl cool, refreshingly cool

kühlen (*wk*) cool

sich **kühlen** (*wk*) cool off, become cool

kühn bold, daring

kühn-emsig daring and industrious

die **Kühnheit** daring, audacity

kühnlich bold

die **Kultur** culture

der **Kummer** sorrow

die **Kummerfahrt** sorrowful journey

kümmerlich scanty, paltry, needy, wretched, poor

kümmern concern, worry, make a difference to

sich **kümmern** concern oneself, be concerned about

kummervoll sorrowful

der **Kumpan** companion, associate

kund known; **kund werden** come to light, become known; **kund tun** notify, inform, reveal

der **Kunde** fellow

die **Kunde** news

künden (*wk*) make known, report

kundig knowing, well-informed

die **Kundschaft** reconnoitering, scouting mission

der **Kundschafter,** — scout, spy

künftig future; coming (311); in the future (1668)

künftighin in the future, henceforth

die **Kunst,** ⸚e art, skill, device, trick

kunstgerecht artistically correct

der **Künstler** artist

künstlerisch artistic
künstlich artistic; artificial
(5098, 6884)
das Kunststück masterpiece,
work of art
kuppeln pander, procure
der Kuppler pander, pimp
kupplerisch procuring
das Kupplerwesen business of
procuring
die Kur cure
die Kür choice, power of free
choice
kurieren (wk) cure
kurtesieren (wk) court, pay
court to
kurz short, brief, ephemeral
(5637); in short (1343);
kurz fassen summarize; kurz
und gut in a word; kurz
angebunden brusque, snap-
pish; so kurz such a short
time (4485); auf kurze Zeit
for a little while
kürzen shorten
der Kurzsinn narrow-mindedness
der Kuß, Küsse kiss; divine
benediction (771); Gruß und
Kuß love and kisses
küssen (wk) kiss
die Küste, -n coast, shore
der Kustode, -n custodian,
guardian
Kypris Cypris, Aphrodite

L

laben refresh, delight
das Laboratorium laboratory
laborieren drudge, work in a
laboratory

das Labyrinth, -e labyrinth,
maze
labyrinthisch labyrinthine
der Lächelmund seducing smile
lächeln smile
lachen (wk) laugh; scorn;
beam with glee; be cheerful;
ridicule; smile
der Lacher, — laugher, scoffer
lächerlich ridiculous
Lachesis Lachesis (one of the
Fates)
der Laden shop
laden load, take (upon oneself)
(3765)
laden invite (8503)
die Ladung cargo
der Laffe, -n fop, fool
die Lage position
das Lager bed; store, supply;
wine cellar
lagern (wk) lodge, station
lahm feeble; paralyzed (9351)
Lakedämon Lacedaemon,
Sparta
lallen (wk) speak haltingly
Lamien Lamiae (man-eating
monsters, part beautiful
woman, part snake)
das Lamm lamb
das Lämpchen small lamp
die Lampe, -n lamp
das Lämplein little lamp
das Land, ⁽ʸ⁾er/-e land, country,
district; des Landes in these
parts (2949)
landen (wk) land, disembark
der Landesherr, -n lord, ruler
of a province
die Landesplage public nuisance, national calamity
ländlich rural, rustic

die **Landschaft** landscape

das **Landsgefäll,** –e state tax, provincial tax

lang long, eternal; **die Zeit wird lang** time passes slowly

lang(e) long ago, for a long time, throughout, long since, by far (2648); **lange schon** for quite a while; **lang fragen** deliberate (2283); **auf Zeiten lang** for quite a while (3269)

langbeinig long-legged

die **Länge** length; all the time, day after day; **in die Länge** for any length of time

längelang full-length

langersehnt long yearned for

die **Langeweile** boredom; **Langeweile haben** be bored with, be tired of

langeweilen bore, be bored (9585)

langgedehnt long drawn-out

langgestreckt long stretched-out

länglich longish, notably longer than wide

langsam slowly

langsam-ernst solemn, slow and serious

lang-schön-weißhalsig having a long, beautiful, white (swan-like) neck

längstentbehrt long lacked

die **Lanze,** –n lance, spear

der **Lanzknecht** foot soldier, mercenary soldier

der **Lappen,** — rag

läppisch childish, silly

der **Lärm** racket, noise

lärmen (*wk*) make a noise, work noisily

lärmig noisy

lassen (ä), **ie, a** let, have, make (cause), see to it; leave, leave alone; give up; stop; permit (to be); omit; be becoming (3312)

sich **lassen** (ä), **ie, a** can be (1215)

die **Last** burden, load, weight; bother

lasten weigh heavily

das **Laster** vice, wicked thing to do

lästig burdensome, annoying

die **Lästrung** blasphemy

die **Laterne** lantern

die **Latwerge,** –n electuary (*medicinal powder mixed with honey or syrup*)

lau tepid, mild; lukewarm; still warm (8675)

das **Laub** foliage, leaves

die **Laube,** –n arbor, arcade

der **Laubgang,** ⁻e arcade, covered arborway

lauern wait in ambush, lie in wait, lurk

der **Lauf** course, race; **freien Lauf haben** be free to escape, have a free path (1246)

laufen (äu) run; be on one's feet (3112); walk

die **Laune** mood, whim

launen be whimsical, have moods; be disposed

die **Laus,** ⁻e louse

das **Läuschen,** — little louse

lauschen (*wk*) listen to, listen for; be hidden (10921)

der **Laut,** –e sound

laut loud, aloud; audible

lauten sound, utter

läuten ring (a bell)

lauter nothing but; pure (4955)

laut-heiser loud and hoarse

die Lazerte lacerta, lizard

das Lebechor, ⁻e host of the living

lebelos lifeless, dead

leben (wk) be alive, live, exist

das Leben life, existence; vitality (1107); vitals (1636)

lebendig living, alive, existing; animated; vital; in motion (5335); live (6825); Life (7856); lebendig werden begin to stir (10024)

die Lebensart elegant social poise, social savoir-faire

das Lebenselement, -e vital element

der Lebensfaden thread of life (spun by the Fates)

die Lebensfeuchte life-giving moisture

die Lebensflamme flame of life, vital spark

die Lebensflut, -en tide of life

die Lebensfratze, -n vexation of daily life

das Lebensglück happiness of existence

die Lebensglut glow of life

die Lebenskraft vital energy

der Lebenslauf career, course of life

lebenslustig enjoying life, full of joie de vivre

die Lebensnymphe, -n nymph bringing liveliness

die Lebensregung energy, will to live

die Lebensreihe sequence through life, course of life

der Lebensstrom living flood, swift current

der Lebenstag, -e day of one's life

die Lebenstiefe, -n depth of one's being

die Leber liver

der Lebestrahl, -en life-giving ray

das Lebewohl farewell

lebhaft lively, vivid

leblos lifeless

lechzen be thirsty, be parched

lecken lick

Leda Leda (loved by Jupiter disguised as a swan; mother of Helen and of the Dioscuri)

das Leder leather; leather case (for official documents)

ledern leather, made of leather

leer empty, vacant, void, vain; inane (6232); empty space (6251); useless, ineffective (9439)

leeren (wk) empty

legen (wk) put, lay; set (4941)

sich legen (wk) lie down; turn to (10728)

die Legende, -n legend

die Legion legion, host

das Leh(e)n, — fief, feudal tenure, feudal rights

lehnen (wk) lean; put (6465)

sich lehnen lean

der Lehnsherr liege lord

die Lehre, -n doctrine, discipline, teaching, science; apprenticeship

lehren (wk) teach, tell, relate (2652); gelehrt learned, well-read; der Gelehrte scholar

der Lehrer teacher

der **Leib** body; **dir steckt der Doktor im Leib** you have the doctor in you; **dir an den dürren Leib** lay hands on your skinny carcass; **mir vom Leib schaffen** free me of (2342); **vom Leibe mir!** away! (5646)

das **Leibchen** belly; little body

leibhaftig in person; incarnate, personified

leiblich in person; natural

die **Leibwache** bodyguard

die **Leiche,** –n body, corpse

der **Leichnam** dead body

leicht easy, easily, light, cheerful, gentle, nimble; slight (2582)

leichtfüßig light-footed

leichtsinnig frivolous, indiscreet

das **Leid,** –en sorrow, suffering, grief, pain, misfortune

leid: leid tun make one feel sorry; **ist mir leid** I'm sorry

leiden, i, i suffer, tolerate, stand for; **leiden mögen** like

die **Leidenschaft,** –en passion, ardor

leidenschaftlich passionate

leider unfortunately; alas, I'm sorry to say

leidig miserable, pitiful; disagreeable, cursed

leidlich fairly; sufficient, acceptable

die **Leier** lyre

leiern grind out (music)

der **Leierton** organ-grinder's tune; **der alte Leierton** the same old story

leihen, ie, ie lend

leimen glue together

die **Leimenwand** clay wall

die **Leimrute,** –n lime twig (*to snare birds*)

Leipzig Leipsic

leis(e) gentle, soft, quiet

leisten (*wk*) perform, accomplish; **Verzicht leisten auf** renounce; **Zeugnis leisten** bear witness

leiten lead, direct, conduct

die **Leiter** ladder

die **Leitung** management, direction

Lemuren lemures (*spirits of the wicked dead*)

die **Lende,** –n loin(s)

lenken guide, direct; control, steer, drive (horses)

der **Lenker** driver, charioteer

der **Lenz** springtime

die **Lerche** lark

lernäisch Lernaean (*a swamp near Argos*); **lernäische Schlange** Hydra

lernen (*wk*) learn

lesen (ie), a, e read, interpret

Lethe Lethe (*river of Hades: drinking its water causes forgetfulness*)

letheschenkend offering forgetfulness, granting oblivion

der **Letten** loam, potter's clay

letzen refresh

sich **letzen** enjoy; gloat

letzt last, ultimate

letztemal last time

letztgedehnt farthest extended

der **Leu** lion

die **Leuchtameise,** –n glow ant, phosphorescent ant

die **Leuchte** light, beacon

leuchten gleam, shine bright, shine, glow, beam, sparkle

der **Leuchter** candlestick

leugnen deny

Leute people, persons, folk, public

das **Licht, –er** light, bright hue (2613); light of day (5038); candle (6367); enlightenment (9481); **Licht der Augen** sight, ability to see (9521)

licht light, bright, clear, shining (7924), brilliant (10416)

lichterloh ablaze, aflame

lichtgrün translucent green

der **Lichtschweif** trail of light

lieb dear, beloved, most (loved), treasured (3124); precious (2221); **lieber** rather; **am liebsten** most; **Liebes** dear thing, kindness (2983); **lieb haben** be fond of

das **Liebchen, —** beloved, sweetheart

die **Liebe** love; **zu Liebe** as a favor (3696, 4578)

das **Liebeband** bond of love

liebeln bill and coo, dally

lieben (wk) love; like, like to have; **geliebt** beloved; **die Geliebte, der Geliebte** beloved; **Geliebtes** what is deemed precious (8454); **Liebender** lover

liebend-heilig loving and holy

liebenswert lovable, amiable

liebenswürdig worthy of love, lovable; charming

liebentzündet inflamed with love

lieber rather

ein **Liebes** kindness, good deed

das **Liebesabenteuer** love affair

das **Liebesband** bond of love

der **Liebesbote, –n** messenger of love

das **Liebesbrieflein** billet-doux, little love letter

liebesbrünstig amorously ardent

das **Liebeschätzchen** little sweetheart

das **Liebeselement** proper environment for love

die **Liebesfibel, –n** elementary textbook of love, passion primer

die **Liebesfreude, –n** joy of love

die **Liebesglut** amorous ardor

die **Liebesgunst** favor(s)

der **Liebeshort** safe retreat of love

die **Liebeshuld** favor of love

die **Liebesklage** lover's complaint

Liebesleute (pl) people in love, loving couples

die **Liebeslust** joy of love, amorous delight; amorous desire

das **Liebespaar** pair of lovers

die **Liebespein** torment of love

der **Liebespuk** unnatural amorous infatuation

die **Liebesqual** torment of love

der **Liebestraum** dream (trance) of love

die **Liebeswut** frenzy of love

liebevoll loving, tender, fervent (11876)

liebewonniglich in ardent ecstasy

liebhaben be fond of

liebkosen caress lovingly (rime euphoniously 9371)

lieblich lovely, delightful, graceful, charming, attractive, pleasant, sweet (*in sound* 6871)

lieblich-klug with graceful tact

die Lieblingsbildung favorite shape

die Lieblingsspeise, –n favorite food

die Liebschaft infatuation

das Lied, –er song, poem (779); ein Lied von neustem Schnitt song hit

das Liedchen little tune, ditty

liederlich dissolute

liegen, a, e lie, be contained in (1986); the fault lies (2077); be, rest; be up to (4777); be stored (5023); lie prostrate (8790); liegen lassen leave behind; am Tage liegen be evident (6876)

Lieschen Elizabeth, Betty

die Lilie lily

Lilith Lilith (*Adam's first wife, according to Hebrew lore*)

die Linde, –n linden tree

der Lindenraum area with linden trees

der Lindenwuchs growth of linden trees

lindern (*wk*) soften, calm, allay

die Lindrung alleviation, comfort

linke left; die Linke left wing (*army, stage*); zur Linken on the left

links to the left, left

die Lippe, –n lip

lispeln whisper, murmur plaintively

die List, –en ruse, cunning, trickery, guile

listig sly, crafty, cunning

die Litanei litany

das Lob praise; credit (5205)

loben (*wk*) laud, praise; declare to be to one's liking (4081)

lobenswürdig praiseworthy, laudable

der Lober, — praiser

lobesan praiseworthy; Magister Lobesan Sir Laudable

das Lobeswort word of praise

löblich laudable

das Loch, ⁻er hole; auf dem letzten Loch pfeifen breathe one's last, be at the last gasp

die Locke, –n curl, lock

locken (*wk*) entice, lure, draw, attract, try to attract (3698)

der Lockenkopf curlyhead

das Lockhaar curly hair

lockig curly

das Lockwerk enticement, lure

lodern blaze, flare, be ablaze

die Lohe blazing fire

lohen blaze, flare

der Lohn reward, pay

lohnen reward; pay (8209)

das Lokal meeting place; tavern

der Lorbeer, –n laurel

das Los fate, lot, assignment (9471); prize, lottery ticket (7762)

los rid; loose, free, detached (9326)

losbinden, a, u detach

losbrechen (i), a, o break loose

löschen extinguish, put out (fire)

losdringen, a, u press close up

lösen (wk) dissolve; solve (4040); untie, loosen, unbind

sich losfalten unfold

losgehen go at once

sich losklären stand forth clearly

loslassen let go

loslösen detach, loosen and remove

losmachen (wk) untie

sich losmachen (wk) detach oneself

losreißen, i, i tear away

sich losreißen, i, i tear oneself away, free oneself

sich lossprechen (i), a, o renounce

die Lösung solution; happy ending

das Losungswort watchword

loswerden (i) get rid of

das Lotto numbers lottery

der Löwe, -n lion

das Löwenfell lion skin

der Löwenschweif lion's tail

der Löwentaler, — coin (with the stamp of the Lion of Bohemia)

der Luchs lynx

die Lücke gap, breach

das Luder, — low person, despicable person

ludern (wk) lead a disorderly life

die Luft, ⸗e air; space (3572); breeze; sich Luft machen give vent to one's feelings (Trüber Tag 50); zu allen

Lüften to the uttermost heights of the air

das Lüftchen, — breeze

lüften air, ventilate; lift (11526)

die Lufterscheinung illusion, phantom

der Luftfahrer, — air traveler

luftig airy, aerial

das Lüftlein, — breeze

der Lug lie, deceit

die Lüge falsehood, untruth

lügen, o, o lie

die Lügenfahne, -n false banner

der Lügenfürst prince of lies, Satan

der Lügengeist spirit of deceit

der Lügenschaum, ⸗e false froth, frothy lie

das Lügenspiel illusion, phantasmagoria

der Luginsland lookout tower

der Lügner, — liar

der Lümmel boor, oaf, uncouth fellow

der Lump, -e low fellow, good-for-nothing

der Lumpen rag

lumpen: sich nicht lumpen lassen be unwilling to be called cheap or stingy

der Lumpenhund good-for-nothing dog

das Lumpenpack rabble, riffraff

Luna Luna (moon goddess); silver (in alchemy 4965)

die Lunge, -n lung

lupfen lift

die Lust desire, inclination, pleasure, joy, enjoyment; lust; Lust haben like; Lust bekommen feel the urge lüstern greedy; lascivious

die **Lüsternheit** greediness, lasciviousness

lustfein given to elegant pleasures

der **Lustgarten** garden, pleasure grounds

das **Lustgejauchze** whoop of joy

lustgenießend enjoying a good time

lustig gay, merry, cheerful, lusty; **Lustige Person** comic character, comedian

das **Lustrevier** preserve, pleasure park

Luther Martin Luther

Luzifer Lucifer (*Satan before his fall*)

Lynkeus Lynceus (*sharp-eyed pilot of the Argonauts* 7377); Faust's watchman

die **Lyra** lyre, harp

M

mäandrisch meandering

machen (*wk*) make, do; give, represent, get busy (2857); perform (6546); cause (11026); **Schluß machen** finish; **streitig machen** contest; **sich an . . . machen** start out with, set about . . .; **selig machen** save, bring salvation; **sich Luft machen** give vent to one's feelings; **sich nichts machen aus** not care about; **wie sich 's macht** as it comes; **es . . . recht machen** satisfy . . .; **Anspruch machen** claim; **sich**

groß machen begin to become large (3745)

die **Macht**, ⁀e power, authority, might, force, energy

mächtig forceful, intense, powerful, immense, gigantic, grand, grandiose

die **Madam** madam

das **Mädchen**, — girl, maiden, virgin

das **Mädel**, –s little girl

die **Magd**, ⁀e girl, servant girl

das **Mägdelein**, — little girl

der **Magen** stomach

mager lean, skinny

die **Magerkeit** skinniness

die **Magie** magic, black art

der **Magier** magician, wizard

magisch magic

der **Magister**, — Master of Arts

Magna peccatrix woman who has sinned greatly

der **Magnet** magnet

Magnus the Great (*Pompey*)

mähen (*wk*) mow

das **Mahl** meal, feast, banquet

die **Mähne** mane

mahnen warn, admonish

der **Mai** May

Maja Maia (*mother of Mercury*)

die **Majestät** majesty, Your Majesty, the emperor; royal majesty (10950)

majestätisch majestic, superb

majestätisch-rein majestic in purity

mäkeln criticize, find fault with

der **Makrokosmos** macrocosm

das **Mal**, –e time

malen (*wk*) stain, paint; **wie gemalt** like a (perfect) painting (6509); **gemalte Schei-**

ben stained-glass window-panes

zu malerisch-entzückter Schau (7557) for the rapt gaze of a painter (?); as a picturesque and delightful spectacle (?)

Malta Malta (*Mediterranean island*)

die **Malve, –n** mallow

Mammon Mammon (*worldly riches*); gold (3915)

man one; you; people; man-kind in general; we; some-body; they

mänadisch like maenads (*frenzied nymphs*)

manch many (a)

mancherlei all sorts of, various and sundry

manchmal many times

die **Mandoline, –n** mandolin

der **Mangel, ⁎** want, imperfection, lack, shortage, short-coming

mangeln (*wk*) be lacking to, not have

der **Mann, ⁎er** man; husband; **Mann für Mann** man by man, every one

die **Männerliebe** men's love

die **Männerschlacht** battle that men fight

das **Manneswort** a man's word, pledge, oath

die **Manneswürde** manly dignity

mannigfaltig various, manifold

das **Männlein** little man

männlich masculine, manly, in the prime of life (10335)

mannlustig mad about men

die **Mannschaft** crew

Mannsen fellows, wights, poor fellows

der **Mantel** cloak, coat

das **Mäntelchen** short cloak

die **Mantelschleppe** train of a robe

Manto Manto (*a prophetess*)

die **Mär** information, news (1423); tidings

das **Märchen, —** fairy tale, fable

Margarete Margaret

Margretlein little Margaret; Peggy

Maria Aegyptiaca Mary of Egypt

Marianus Marianus (*especially devoted to the Virgin Mary*)

das **Mark** core, depth; marrow, quick; essential substance

die **Marketenderin** sutler, camp follower

der **Markt** market, public market square

markten bargain, haggle; conclude a bargain

der **Marktschreier, —** mountebank, quack; advertising agent

marktverkauft sold in the market place

der **Marmor** marble

der **Marmorblock** block of marble

Mars Mars (*god of war*)

der **Marschalk** marshal

Marsen Marsi (*Italian tribe*)

das **Marterholz** wooden (torture) cross; skinny person

der **Marterort** place of torture

Marthe Martha

die **Maschine, –n** machine

die **Maser, –n** tree wart

das **Mäskchen** (little) mask, visage; pretty face

die **Maske, –n** mask, disguise

das **Maskenfest, –e** carnival, shrovetide revels

der **Maskenheld** hero of the masquerade

der **Maskenklump** cluster of participants in the masquerade

der **Maskenschwall** confused throng of masqueraders

der **Maskenspaß** masquerade joke

der **Maskenstock, ⁔e** scarecrow

der **Maskenzug, ⁔e** masquerading procession; **holde Maskenzüge** alluring figures on a mask; a succession of charming masked persons

die **Maskerade, –n** masquerade

der **Maskeradenspott** tomfoolery (4267)

das **Maß, –e** measure, degree; discretion (11004); measurement (11524); restraint, limitation (11720); **Maß und Ziel** limit

die **Maß: reiche Maß** in full measure (3769)

die **Masse, –n** mass; crowd, multitude; substance, matter

mäßig moderate, restrained (10913); easy (9717); modest (6640)

mäßigen moderate, restrain

die **Mäßigkeit** temperance, moderation

die **Mäßigung** restraint

massiv massive

der **Mast, –en** mast

mastig ponderous

Mater dolorosa (suffering mother) Virgin sorrowing at the cross

Mater gloriosa (glorious mother) Virgin in glory

die **Matrone** matron

matt feeble

die **Matte, –n** meadow

mattgesungen stale through having been sung too often

die **Mauer, –n** wall

mauerbräunlich brown as weathered masonry

der **Mauergrund, ⁔e** wall foundation

die **Mauerhöhle** hollow place in the wall

das **Mauerloch** cubbyhole, room with bare walls

der **Mauernpfeiler, —** pillar

mauerwärts toward the wall

das **Mauerwerk** masonry

das **Maul** (big) mouth

maulen quarrel

die **Maus, ⁔e** mouse

das **Mäuschen** little mouse

die **Maxime, –n** maxim, principle of conduct

meckern bleat (*like a goat*)

die **Medizin** medicine

Meduse Medusa

das **Meer, –e** sea, ocean

meerab down to sea

der **Meerdrache, –n** sea dragon, sea serpent

das **Meeresfest** ocean festivities

die **Meeresfrau, –en** mermaid

die **Meeresfrische** cool ocean waters

der **Meeresgrund** sea bottom

das **Meergebraus** roaring of the sea

der **Meergott** god of the sea

das **Meerkalb**, ⸗er seal

der **Meerkater** monkey, ape (*male*)

das **Meerkätzchen**, — young monkey, young ape

die **Meerkatze** monkey, ape (*female*)

der **Meerstier**, –e bull seal

der **Meerwidder**, — sea ram

das **Meerwunder**, — sea monster

Megära Megaera (*one of the Furies*)

mehr more

mehren add to (6752)

sich **mehren** multiply, increase, grow

meiden avoid, shun; leave (1244)

meilenfern miles away

mein my, mine, of me; **mein!** by Jove! my God! (2332)

meinen (*wk*) think, believe, mean, expect (2739); **es gut meinen mit** have good intentions toward

meinesgleichen people like me, my equals, my like(s)

meinetwegen on my account, because of me

um **meinetwillen** on my account

die **Meinung** opinion

der **Meißel** (*sculptor's*) chisel

meist most; am **meisten** most, mostly

der **Meister**, — master

meisterlich masterly, clever, like a master

meistern control

der **Meisterstreich** compelling blow

das **Meisterstück** masterpiece

melancholisch melancholy

melden announce, proclaim, tell, report

sich **melden** announce oneself, appear

die **Meldung** proclamation

die **Melodei** melody

die **Melodie**, –n melody

die **Memme** coward

Menelas Menelaus (*husband of Helen*)

die **Menge** mass(es), public, crowd, great quantities (11552); many (2203); abundance (8235)

der **Mensch**, –en man, human being, mortal; person (3471); (*pl*) people, mankind

menschenähnlich resembling human, like a human being

das **Menschenauge**, –n human eye

die **Menschenbrut** human race

der **Menschenfeind**, –e enemy of mankind

die **Menschenflut**, –en flood of people

die **Menschenfrau**, –en human woman

menschenfresserisch cannibalistic

der **Menschengeist** human spirit, human mind

die **Menschengestalt** human form

die **Menschenhand** human hand

das **Menschenleben** human life

die **Menschenliebe** love of
mankind

das **Menschenlos** human
destiny

das **Menschenopfer,** — human
sacrifice; victim (11127)

das **Menschenrecht** rights of
man

die **Menschenseele** human
soul

die **Menschenstimme,** –n human voice

der **Menschenstoff** stuff of
which human beings are
made

das **Menschenvolk** human race,
people

der **Menschenwitz** human ingenuity

die **Menschheit** human nature,
mankind

menschlich human

der **Mentor** mentor, counselor

Mephisto Mephistopheles

Mephistopheles Mephistopheles

merken (*wk*) mark, remember,
notice; observe (9070);
watch for (10238)

merklich noticeable

Merkur Mercury (*messenger
of the gods*)

merkwürdig remarkable

die **Messe,** –n mass (2931,
3425); annual fair (4115)

messen (i) take measurements

sich **messen** (i), a, e to measure
one's strength; be weighed

Messene Messenia (*southwestern district of Peloponnesus*)

das **Messer,** — knife

der **Messerrücken** back of a
knife

das **Metall,** –e metal

metallisch metallic

die **Metamorphose,** –n metamorphosis, transformation

die **Metaphysik**(a) metaphysics

das **Meteor** meteor

die **Meteoren-Schöne** meteoric
beauty

die **Metze** hussy

Michael Michael (*an archangel*)

Mieding Johann Martin Mieding (*stage carpenter at
Weimar court theater*)

der **Mietsoldat** mercenary soldier

der **Mikrokosmus** microcosm

die **Milch** milk

mild mild, suave, soft; delicate, gentle (9544), tender

mildeblitzend gently flashing,
sparkling

milden (*wk*) prepare a gentle
transition for

mildern assuage

sich **mildern** grow less

mildgewogen gently affectionate

militärisch military

die **Million,** –en million, millions of people

minder less

mindern (*wk*) lessen, diminish,
reduce; take away (6752)

im **mindesten** in the least

der **Minister** minister, secre-
tary of state, councillor

mischen (*wk*) mix, mingle

sich **mischen** (*wk*) mingle

die **Mischung** mixture, mixing

miserabel wretched

das **Mißbehagen** discomfort, discontent

mißblickend of evil eye

missen do without, dispense with

die **Missetat** misdeed, crime

die **Missetäterin** evildoer, criminal

mißfallen (ä) displease

das **Mißgeschick** misfortune, disaster

die **Mißgestalt, -en** misshapen form

mißgestaltet misshapen, monstrous

mißglücken (*wk*) miscarry

mißhandeln (*wk*) ill-treat, mistreat, injure; do wrong

mißhören misunderstand, fail to hear correctly

mißraten (ä), **ie, a** fail, turn out poorly

mißredend of evil tongue

der **Mißton, ⁀e** discordant note

der **Mist** rubbish, dirt, manure

mit with, along, at, by, in company of; with it, with them (2884)

mitbringen, a, a (*wk, irreg*) bring along

mitgehen go along

mitgenießen also enjoy, enjoy with someone else

mitkommen come along

mitnehmen (i), **a, o** take along

mitnichten by no means

der **Mitregent** co-regent

Mitschuldigste very guilty accomplices

mitsingen join in singing

der **Mitsinn** sympathetic understanding

mitspielen join in acting

der **Mittag** noon; south (1134); nach **Mittage** (this) afternoon

die **Mitte, -n** middle, center; midst

mitteilen communicate

das **Mittel, —** means; remedy, cure

das **Mittelalter** the Middle Ages

das **Mittelgebirg** mountain range of medium altitude

der **Mittelgipfel** secondary, intermediate peak

die **Mittelluft, ⁀e** middle region of the atmosphere

der **Mittelpunkt** center, central point

der **Mittelste** the one in the middle

die **Mittelwiese** middle meadow

mitten in the middle of, in the midst of; **mitten durch** right through the midst of

mitteninn in the midst

die **Mitternacht** midnight

Mitternachtsgebor(e)ne born at midnight

mittler middle

mitunter now and again

die **Mitwelt** contemporary world

der **Mitwerber, —** rival, competitor

das **Möbel** piece of furniture

die **Mode** fashion, style

sich **modeln** assume form

der **Moder** musty rubbish

das **Moderleben** musty life

modern modern

modisch fashionable, stylish

mögen (a), **o, o** (*wk, irreg*) may, be likely; should like, care to möglich possible, possibly, feasible; wo möglich if possible

der Molch, –e salamander

Moloch Moloch (*Semitic fire deity*)

der Moment moment

der Monat month

monatelang for months at a time

der Mond, –e moon; month

der Mondenglanz radiance of the moon

der Mondenschein moonlight

das Mondgesicht moonlike round face

der Mondhof lunar halo, lunar corona, ring around the moon

das Mondlicht moonlight

der Mondtag, –e lunar day (*24 hrs., 50 min.*)

das Moos moss

das Moosgestelle moss-covered structure

moosig mossy

moralisch moral

der Mord murder

der Mörder, — murderer

mörderisch murderous; enormous

mörderlich terrible

das Mordgeschoß, –schosse murderous missile

das Mordgeschrei outcry of "Murder!"

der Morgen morning; east (1132)

morgen tomorrow; the next day (9292)

der Morgennebelduft haze of the morning mist

das Morgenrot red dawn

morgenrötlich red as the morning sky

morgens in the morning

die Morgensonne morning sun

der Morgenstern cudgel with iron spikes

die Morgenstunde morning hour, early hour

das Morgenwölkchen small cloud at dawn

morsch rotten, decaying

der Most new wine

die Mottenwelt (musty) world of moths, world where moths consume

moussierend effervescent

die Mückennase mosquito bill

müde tired

die Mühe labor, exertion, effort, toil

sich mühen take pains, make efforts, trouble oneself; strive

die Mühle mill

das Mühlrad mill wheel

das Mühmchen, — little cousin

die Muhme (girl) cousin; aunt

das Mühmichen little cousin

Mulier Samaritana woman of Samaria

die Mummenschanz carnival masquerade

mummenschänzlich as masquerade

der Mund mouth; speech (378); gate, opening (717, 5924); testimony (3013); ein voller Mund full lips

mündig of age, adult

munter merry, cheerful, lively, brisk, awake (5888); young

and vigorous (10507); gaily (11144)

die **Münze** coin

münzen (*wk*) coin, mint, make into legal coin

das **Münzregal** royalty from coining privilege

murmeln murmur, mumble

murren grumble, mutter

der **Musaget** leader of the Muses, Apollo

die **Muschel** conch shell

die **Muschelfahrt** journey in a shell

der **Muschelthron** conch shell throne

der **Muschelwagen** conch shell chariot

die **Muse**, –n muse

das **Museum** study(room) of a humanist scholar

die **Musik** music

der **Musikant**, –en musician

müssen (u), u, u (*wk, irreg*) be obliged to, have to, must, ought to, be forced to, be compelled to

müßig idle, lazy

der **Müßiggang** idleness, loafing

das **Muster** paragon, most perfect

das **Musterbild** ideal, paragon

musterhaft exemplary, perfect

mustern muster, review

der **Mut** spirit, boldness, courage, spirit of enterprise (9914); humor; mood, heart; moral courage, assurance; **guten Muts** cheerfully

mutig bold, audacious; cheerful, light-hearted (3147)

die **Mutter**, ⸗ mother; Madonna

das **Mütterchen** little old woman

mütterlich motherly, as mothers do; maternally

das **Mutterschwein** brood sow

der **Mutwille** exuberance of spirits

mutwillig carefree, exuberant, roguish

die **Mütze**, –n cap, beret

der **Myrmidone**, –n myrmidon, "ant-man" (mythical inhabitant of Thessaly)

der **Mystagog**, –en mystagogue (*an interpreter of mysteries*)

das **Mysterium**, **Mysterien** mystery; secret ritualistic ceremony (10031)

mysticus mystical

die **Mythologie** mythology

mythologisch mythological

N

'n (= **einen**) a

der **Nabel** navel

Naboth Naboth (*owner of a vineyard coveted by Ahab*)

nach to, towards, for, in (*direction*), –ward; after; according to; **nach und nach** gradually, little by little; **nach ... zu** toward

nachahmen copy, imitate

der **Nachbar** neighbor

der **Nachbarast**, ⸗e limb from a neighboring tree

die **Nachbarin** neighbor; neighbor's girl

nachbarlich neighborly

die **Nachbarschaft** neighborhood, vicinity
der **Nachbarstamm,** ⸚e trunk
of a neighboring tree
nachbringen make up for, correct an omission
nachdem after, depending upon
the way; **nachdem es kommt**
as the case may be (8333)
das **Nachdenken** reflection
nachdenken reflect, think over
nachdonnern reverberate with
thunder
der **Nachen** small boat, barge
nachfolgen follow after
nachfragen inquire
nachgeben (i) yield, give in
das **Nachgesicht** after-image,
lingering phantom
nachhalten (ä) last, persist
nachher after that, afterwards
nachjagen chase after
der **Nachklang** echo, reminiscence
nachklingen, a, u echo
nachlassen (ä), **ie, a** stop,
relax
nachlaufen run after
der **Nachmittag** afternoon;
nachmittage (this) afternoon
die **Nachricht** tidings, report
nachsehen (ie), **a, e** excuse,
condone
nachsinnen ponder, meditate
on
nachspüren investigate, trace
nächst next, nearest, closest,
most immediate (8668, 9071)
nachstehen be inferior to
nachstellen (wk) set a trap (for)
nächstens very soon, one of
these days

nachstreben (wk) strive after,
strive to equal; strive to
attain (7877)
nachströmen flow along toward
die **Nacht,** ⸚e night, darkness;
Nacht für Nacht night after
night
der **Nachtdichter,** — poet of
the night
die **Nachtgeburt,** -en creature
of the night
nächtig nocturnal, at night,
during the night; dark;
gloomy
die **Nachtigall** nightingale
nächtlich dark, black, dismal;
wrapped in night (sleeping
8712); **nächtlicher Weile** at
night
die **Nachtmütze,** nightcap
nachtragen follow carrying,
carry after
nachtrippeln follow with light,
short, mincing steps
nachts at night, during the
night
die **Nachwelt** posterity
nachziehen pull after; follow
(9900)
der **Nacken,** — neck, nape of
the neck; (hanging down) in
back (10514)
nackt naked, bare
der **Nagel,** ⸚ fingernail
nagelneu brand-new
nagen (wk) gnaw, nibble, eat,
bite
nah near, close (by)
die **Nähe** vicinity, proximity,
neighborhood, foreground;
close quarters; presence
(12062); close by

sich **nahen** (*wk*) approach, draw near

nähen sew

nähern bring together (9700)

sich **nähern** approach, come near

näherrücken approach by a series of jerky movements

nähren feed, provide food for (8998)

sich **nähren** live on, feed, feed oneself; live (10157)

die **Nahrung** nourishment, food, subsistence (11922)

nahverwandt closely related

naiv naïve

der **Name**, –n name, expression, word (3061); reputation (8520)

die **Namensdauer** enduring fame

der **Namenszug** signature

Napel Naples

der **Napf**, –en basin, bowl

der **Narr**, –en fool; jester

das **Närrchen** little fool

der **Narrentanz**, ⸚e dance of fools

die **Narrenteidung** foolish chatter, silly doings

die **Narrenwelt** little world of fools; foolish microcosm

die **Narrheit** folly

närrisch foolish; deranged, mad

naschen (*wk*) peck, nibble, sip secretly, taste (*sweets* 5770); graze, prey on

das **Näschen** little nose

die **Nase** nose; **an der Nase spüren** tell by looking at

das **Naserümpfen** turning up one's nose

naseweis impertinent, forward

nasführen lead by the nose, fool

das **Naß** wetness; wine (5023)

naß wet

die **Nation**, –en nation

die **Natur**, –en nature, temper, disposition

der **Naturdichter**, — poet of nature

das **Naturell** natural disposition

der **Naturfels** natural rock, rock produced by natural processes

naturgemäß in accordance with natural law

die **Naturkraft** natural power

natürlich in a natural manner, natural, naturally

natürlich-nackt naked as in a state of nature

die **Naturschrift** writing (= evidence) of nature

der **Nebel**, — mist, fog, veil, haze

das **Nebelalter** Dark Ages

der **Nebeldunst**, ⸚e misty vapor

der **Nebelflor** misty veil, haze

die **Nebelhülle**, –n misty envelope, enveloping mist

nebeln be wrapped in mist

der **Nebelstreif**, –en streak of mist, wisp of fog

der **Nebelwind** damp wind

neben beside, next to, side by side

das **Nebengemach**, ⸚er side room

necken (*wk*) tease, annoy

die **Neckerei**, –en teasing, bantering

neckisch teasing, mocking

nehmen (i), a, o take, accept, take away, seize (9674); occupy (10297); **in acht nehmen** observe, keep an eye on; **sich in acht nehmen** take care, be careful (not to); **übel nehmen** take amiss; **Platz nehmen** sit down; **zu Sinn nehmen** take under consideration (8065)

neiden envy

neidisch envious

die **Neige** decline; **auf der Neige** drawing to an end, running low, atilt

neigen (*wk*) bend, incline, turn, cause to incline; draw down, persuade to descend (488)

sich **neigen** (*wk*) bow, bend, incline; accept (4804); be about to tip over (6696); be accessible to (9688)

die **Neigung** inclination, fondness, liking, affection

'nein (= **hinein**) go in (11387)

nein no; well! you don't say!

der **Nekromant** necromancer, sorcerer

nennen, a, a (*wk, irreg*) name, call by name, identify, call; bring to mind (15); mention one's name (1871); call by one's name (3432); appoint (10876)

der **Neophyt**, **–en** neophyte, new convert

Neptun(us) Neptune (*god of the sea*)

die **Nereide**, **–n** Nereid (*sea nymph, naiad*)

Nereus Nereus (*a sea god*)

der **Nerv**, **–en** nerve

das **Nest** nest; home (8357)

Nestor Nestor (*aged king of Pylos, noted for wisdom*)

das **Netz**, **–e** net, snare

netzumstrickt ensnared, caught in a net

neu new, anew, fresh, modern, recent, late

neugeboren newborn

neugeschaffen newly created

neugeschliffen recently sharpened

neugeschmückt freshly decorated

die **Neugier** curiosity

neugierig curious, inquisitive, interested to know

neuglühend with renewed ardor

die **Neuigkeit**, **–en** news; novelty (7172)

neulich recently, the other day

die **Neun** nine

nicht not, nor, no, don't you; **nicht doch** certainly not

nichtig of no importance, trivial and transitory

die **Nichtinsel** peninsula

das **Nichts** nothingness

nichts nothing, not anything, no, without any, un-; **mir nichts, dir nichts** without plan, in carefree abandon

nichtswürdig vile, contemptible

nicken (*wk*) nod

nie never, at no time

nieder down; low

niederbleichen pale down

niederdrücken weigh down

niedereilen rush down

niedergehen go down

niederkauern crouch down, cower

niederklettern scramble downwards

niederknieen kneel down

niederlassen (ä), ie, a let down, lay to rest

sich **niederlassen** sit down

niederlegen (*wk*) lay down, deliver; Zeugnis niederlegen make a deposition, attest an oath

sich **niederlegen** lie down

niederrauschen rush down

niederschlagen (ä), u, a cast down, strike down

niederschreiben, ie, ie write down

niederschweben soar down

niedersenken lower

sich **niedersenken** descend, fall

sich **niedersetzen** settle down, sit down

niedersinken drop down exhausted; break down; sink down; descend (7039)

niedersteigen, ie, ie descend

niederstreben strive to descend

niederstreifen brush off and knock down

niederstürzen tumble, fall heavily

niederträchtig base

niedertreten trample down

sich **niederwerfen** (i) throw oneself down

niedlich pretty; nice

niedrig low

die **Niedrigkeit** humility, lowliness

niemals never; at no time

niemand nobody, no one

Nikodemus Nicodemus

das **Nilpferd** hippopotamus

nimmer never, not; könnte nimmer just couldn't (3498)

nimmermehr never again, nevermore

nippen sip

nirgend(s) nowhere

die **Nische**, –n niche

nisten nest, make a nest; take up residence

noch still, yet; even; else, moreover; ever so; in addition to, more; nor

Norcia Norcia (*district noted for magicians*)

der **Norde**, (–ns) Northerner, inhabitant of Northern Europe (1796)

der **Norden** north

nordisch northern, hyperborean

nordwärts northward

nordwestlich northwest

die **Norm**, –en norm, standard

der **Normanne** Norman

Nostradamus Nostradamus (*author of a book of prophecies*)

die **Not** distress, need; emergency; sorrow, care, suffering, misery, trouble, difficulty

nötig necessary, required, indispensable

nötigen force, compel; urgently invite (2428)

notwendig necessary, necessarily

das **Nu** instant

nun now; well …

nunmehr from now on; now (10630)

nur only, merely, simply; nothing but; alone; just; all but die **Nuß, Nüsse** nut

der **Nutz**(en) advantage, gain, benefit

nütze: nichts nütze sein be of no value

nützen use to advantage; be useful, serve; **wie viel es nützt** how useful it is (1965)

nützlich useful

die **Nymphe, –n** nymph

O

o oh, ah, what a

ob whether, if, I wonder if; **als ob** as though; **ob ... ob** whether ... or

ob (= **über**) at, because of (8669)

das **Obdach** shelter

oben above, on high, up, on top, toward the top; heaven; upstairs (11205); earlier; **wie oben** as described earlier

obenan at the top of the list, (ranking) highest

obenauf on top, on the top; **obenauf sitzen** be master, be in command

obenaus up and out

die **Oberbacke, –n** upper cheek

obere upper, superior, higher

der **Oberfeldherr** commander in chief

die **Oberfläche** surface, exterior

der **Obergeneral** commanding general

das **Oberhaupt** chief

Oberon Oberon (*king of the fairies*)

die **Oberwelt** upper world

obgleich although

obige aforementioned

obschon although

obsiegen overcome

das **Obst** fruit

öde bare, barren, desolate, dreary

die **Öde** solitude, desolation, desert

der **Odem** breath

oder or

Ödipus Oedipus (*king of Thebes*)

der **Ofen** stove, fireplace, furnace

offen open, frank, unrestrained, sincere; unlocked

offenbar public; evident

offenbaren (*wk*) reveal, manifest

sich offenbaren (*wk*) reveal oneself, become manifest; become visible (5113)

das **Offenbarsein** manifestation, display

die **Offenbarung** revelation, manifestation

sich offengebaren be revealed, become known

öffentlich in public

öffnen open, unlock; unseal

sich öffnen open; be revealed (3234)

oft often, frequently, many times

öfter(s) frequently, repeatedly, often, more often

der **Oheim** uncle

ohne without, lacking in, devoid of; but for

ohnegleichen unequalled, peerless

in Ohnmacht in a faint

ohnmächtig weak; ineffective; light

das **Ohr, –en** ear; **zu Ohren kommen** come to one's attention

öhrig long-eared

der **Ohrring, –e** earring

das **Öl** oil

der **Olivenzweig** olive branch

der **Olymp** Mt. Olympus (*seat of the gods*)

der **Olympier, —** Olympian, god

das **Opfer** sacrifice, offering, victim (8944)

opfern sacrifice, perform a sacrifice

der **Opfrer** one who performs a sacrifice

Ops Ops, Abundance (*harvest goddess*)

das **Orchester** orchestra

der **Orden, —** order; decoration; genus, order, species (8330)

ordentlich regular

ordnen (*wk*) arrange, regulate, put in order

sich ordnen (*wk*) place oneself, assign oneself

die **Ordnung** order, orderliness, organization, proper sequence

Oreas Oread (*mountain nymph*)

das **Organ, –e** organ

organisieren ließ caused to assume form by organic processes (6859)

die **Orgel** (church) organ

der **Orgelton** sound of organ music

der **Orientale, –n** Oriental

das **Original** queer fellow

Orion Orion (*a hunter*)

Orkus Orcus, Hades (*abode of the dead*)

Orpheus Orpheus (*divine poet and musician*)

der **Ort, –e** place, small city; space (6214); region; spot

Orthodox Orthodox (person)

Ossa Ossa (*a mountain*)

der **Osten** east, Orient

das **Osterfest** Easter holiday, festival

der **Ostertag** Easter Sunday

östlich eastward

die **Otter** adder

der **Ozean** ocean

P

der **Päan** paean (*hymn of triumph and thanksgiving*)

paar a few

das **Paar, –e** pair, couple; **in Paaren** in twos, two and two

paaren (*wk*) pair, form a couple, link

sich paaren (*wk*) pair off, join

das **Pack** rabble

packen seize, lay hands on, get hold of

sich packen be off; **willst du dich packen** be off (11743)

der **Pädagog** pedagogue, instructor

Padua Padua

der **Page** page

der **Pakt** pact, compact

der **Palast, ⁼e** palace

Pallas Pallas Athena (*goddess of wisdom*)

die **Palme** palm (*symbol of victory*)

Pan Pan (*Orphic god of outdoor life and the emotions*)

panisch panic-inducing, panic-induced

Panthalis Panthalis

das **Pantherkätzchen,** — panther cub

pantoffelfüßig with slippers on

pantomimisch by pantomime

der **Papa** papa

Paphos Paphos (*a city on Cyprus*)

das **Papier** paper, document

das **Papiergespenst** paper ghost

die **Pappe** pasteboard

die **Pappel,** –n poplar tree

der **Pappelstrom** poplar-bordered river

der **Pappelzitterzweig,** –e trembling poplar branch

der **Papst** Pope

das **Paradies,** –e paradise

die **Paradieseshelle** radiance of paradise

paradiesisch Eden-like, heavenly

der **Paragraphus,** –i (*acc pl* –os) paragraph (*of law codes*)

paralysieren paralyze

der **Parasit,** –en parasite

parat ready

das **Pärchen** couple in love

parieren parry

das **Paris** Paris (*city*)

Paris Paris (*son of King Priam of Troy, for whom Helen forsook her husband Menelaus*)

der **Parnaß** Parnassus

die **Partei,** –en party

der **Parteihaß** partisan hatred

das **Parterre** pit, occupants of the pit

der **Parvenu** parvenu, upstart

Parzen Parcae (*the Fates*)

der **Paß** pass, mountain defile

passen fit, go well with, agree, be in keeping with; **passen auf** watch for (10238, 11664)

das **Pastetchen,** — small pie, patty

der **Pater** priest, monk, church father

pathetisch with theatrical pathos

das **Pathos** declamatory effort

der **Patient,** –en patient

Patroklus Patroclus (*Greek hero*)

der **Patron** fellow; master, ship's master (owner 11170)

die **Patsche** hand

patschen (*wk*) slap (5940); paddle, splash (7421)

die **Pause,** –n pause, intermission; watch (4626)

das **Pech** pitch

der **Pedant** pedant

die **Pein** misery, difficulty, pain, torture

peinigen (*wk*) torment

peinlich painful

Peleus Peleus (*a king*)

der **Pelide** Achilles (*son of Peleus*)

Pelion Pelion (*a mountain*)

Pelops Pelops (*son of Tantalus*)

der **Pelz** fur, fur garment

Peneios Peneus (*a river; a river god*)

das **Pentagramma** pentagram, five-pointed star

das **Pergamen** parchment manuscript

das **Pergament,** –e parchment manuscript

die **Perle,** –n pearl

das **Perlenband** pearl necklace

perlenreich covered with pearls

der **Perlenschaum** pearly foam

die **Perlenschnur,** ⸚e string of pearls or beads

Persephoneia Persephone (*a nature goddess, abducted by Hades. Latin: Proserpina*)

Perseus Perseus

die **Person,** –en person; human personality (9984, 9986)

persönlich personally; through personality

die **Perücke,** –n wig

die **Pest** plague

Peter Peter

der **Pfad,** –e path, track, trail, course

der **Pfaff,** –en (pompous and arrogant) priest, cleric

die **Pfaffenmiene** priestly expression

die **Pfäfferei** clerical doings

pfäffisch priestly

der **Pfahl,** ⸚e pole, stake

die **Pfalz** (emperor's) palace

das **Pfand** pledge, security, pawn

das **Pfänderspiel** game of forfeits, kissing game

der **Pfarrer** priest, preacher

der **Pfauenschweif** peacock's tail

der **Pfauenwedel** peacock feather fan

pfeifen whistle

der **Pfeil,** –e arrow

pfeilgespitzt as sharp as an arrow

pfeilschnell as swift as an arrow

das **Pferd,** –e horse; **zu Pferd** on horseback

der **Pferdefuß** horse's foot; clubfoot

der **Pferdehuf** horse's hoof

der **Pfiff,** –e trick, trickery, cunning (10689)

der **Pfifferling,** –e a common mushroom; trifle, thing of no value

pfiffig sly, cunning, crafty

die **Pfirsche,** –n peach

der **Pfirsich,** –e peach

die **Pflanze,** –n plant

pflanzen (*wk*) plant

die **Pflege** care, attention

pflegen (*wk*) take care of, care for; be in the habit of; cultivate; indulge in (8914)

die **Pflicht,** –en duty, obligation

pflücken pluck (*e.g. a flower*)

der **Pflug** plow

pflügen plow

die **Pforte,** –n gate, door

der **Pfosten,** — post

die **Pfote,** –n paw

der **Pfropf(en),** — plug, stopper

der **Pfuhl** pool

der **Pfühl,** –e pillow, cushion

pfui fie! shame!

die **Pfuscherei** bungling; slipshod work

die **Pfütze,** –n puddle, mudhole

der **Phalanx** phalanx

die **Phalanx** phalanx

die **Phantasei** fantasy

die **Phantasie,** –n fancy, imagination, fantasy (5144)

der **Phantasiekranz** wreath

made of artificial flowers of imaginative design

der **Phantasiestrauß** bouquet made of artificial flowers of imaginative design

der **Phantast** visionary

phantastisch fantastic

phantastisch-flügelmännisch with fantastic arm flailing (*like a file-leader*)

das **Phantom** phantom, ghost, vision

der **Pharisäerhohn** pharisee's scorn

pharsalisch Pharsalian

Pharsalus Pharsalus (*scene of battle, 48 BC, between Caesar and Pompey*)

Pherä Pherae (*city in Thessaly*)

Philemon Philemon

philisterhaft philistine, narrow-minded

der **Philologe, –n** classical scholar

der **Philosoph, –en** philosopher

die **Philosophie** philosophy

Philyra Philyra (*daughter of Oceanus, mother of Chiron*)

die **Phiole** phial, vial

Phöbus Phoebus, Apollo (*sun god*)

die **Phorkyade, –n** daughter of Phorkys (*monster*)

Phorkyas a daughter of Phorkys (*one of the Phorkyades*)

Phorkys Phorkys (*a sea deity*)

der **Phosphor** phosphorus

die **Phrase, –n** phrase

phrygisch Phrygian, of Phrygia (*country in Asia Minor*)

die **Physik** physics

die **Physiognomie** physiognomy

pianissimo very quietly

piepsen chirp, twitter

die **Pike, –n** pike, spear

Pindus Pindus (*a mountain range in Greece*)

der **Pinienapfel** pine cone

die **Piraterie** piracy

pissen leak, squirt

placken oppress, harass

die **Plackerei** trouble, toil

die **Plage** vexation, bother, worry, nuisance

plagen (*wk*) bother, pester, annoy

sich **plagen** (*wk*) worry, toil

der **Plan** place for dancing in the open, square, glade, plain (10355)

der **Plan** plan, design, scheme

die **Planke** plank

plappern chatter, prattle

das **Plastron** fencer's padded jacket

plätschern splash

platt insipid

die **Platte** tonsure, crown; small plateau (10039)

der **Platz, ⁼e** place, spot, space, room, seat, square; office (6138)

platzen burst, crack, crackle

plaudern chat, prattle

plötzlich sudden

plump coarse, unwieldy, blunt, plump, heavy

der **Plunder** junk, rubbish

plündern (*wk*) plunder

der **Plural** plural

Pluto Pluto (*god of the underworld*)

plutonisch plutonic, infernal

Plutus Plutus (*god of wealth*)

der **Pöbel** rabble, common people

der **Pöbelsinn** mob mentality

pochen knock; brag about; count upon (4831)

Una **Poenitentium** one of the penitents

die **Poesie** poetry, poesy

der **Poet,** –en poet

der **Pokal,** –e (ornate gold or silver) goblet

politisch political

die **Polizei** police

Pollux Pollux (*one of the Dioscuri*)

das **Polster,** — pillow, cushion

poltern bump things about

die **Polypenfaser,** –n tentacle of a polyp (*e.g. octopus, jellyfish*)

Pompejus Gnaeus Pompeius, (106–48 BC)

pomphaft with pomp, stately

der **Port** port

das **Portal,** –e portal, main entrance

die **Posaune,** –n trumpet, trombone

posaunen: es posaunet the brasses blare

der **Posaunenschall** sound of trumpets

Poseidon Poseidon, Neptune (*god of the sea*)

der **Possen,** — trick, prank, hocus-pocus, nonsense

der **Posten** post, station

der **Posto: Posto fassen** take one's position, establish oneself

die **Pracht** splendor, sumptuousness, luxury, glory

das **Prachtgebilde** splendid figure

das **Prachtgefäß,** –e splendid vessel

prächtig gorgeous, splendid, luxurious, superb

prächtig-rein magnificent and pure

prägen (*wk*) impress, coin

pragmatisch pragmatic

prahlen boast, swagger

prallen rebound

präludieren play or sing introductory music

prangen glitter, shine, show off, be resplendent

präparieren (*wk*) prepare

der **Praß** batch, crowd

prasseln (*wk*) rattle, crackle

der **Prater** Prater (*a park in Vienna*)

predigen preach

der **Predigtstuhl** pulpit

der **Preis** price (7783); prize, reward

preisen, ie, ie praise, laud, glorify; sing praises

der **Priester,** — priest, preacher

das **Priesterkleid** priestly garb

die **Priesterschaft** consecration as a priest

der **Prinz** prince

der **Prinzipal** principal, director

die **Probe,** –n trial, test, sample (2253)

probieren test, try, try out

das **Problem,** –e problem

sich **produzieren** produce oneself, exhibit oneself in public

profan profane, secular

das **Profil** profile

profitieren make a profit, profit from

profundus profound

das **Projekt** project, plan

der **Proktophantasmist** buttocks visionary

der **Prolog** prologue

der **Prospekt, -e** scene, setting (*theater*)

das **Proszenium** proscenium, front of stage

Proteus Proteus (*a sea god, versatile in changing his form*)

Proteus-Delphin Proteus in dolphin form

das **Protokoll** minutes, record of proceedings

prudeln bubble

prüfen (*wk*) test, prove

die **Prüfung** test, trial

Prügel (*pl*) fight, beating

der **Prunk** magnificence, splendor

prunken display splendor

Psyche Psyche (*the soul*)

Psyllen Psylli (*Libyan tribe*)

das **Publikum** public, spectators, audience

der **Puck** Puck

der **Pudel** poodle

pudelnärrisch funny as a poodle, very amusing

der **Puder** powder

pudern (*wk*) powder

Pulcinelle Pulcinelli (*clowns*)

der **Puls, -e** pulse, pulsation

das **Pülslein** pulse of a tender hand

das **Pult** desk, reading desk

der **Punkt** point, focus

pünktlich accurate, exact

das **Püppchen** little doll, little darling, baby

die **Puppe, -n** puppet; creature (2390); darling (3476)

der **Puppenstand** chrysalis stage

der **Puppenzwang** constriction of the chrysalis

der **Purist** purist

der **Purpur** crimson

purpurn crimson

purpurrot crimson red

der **Purpursaum** crimson border

pusten puff, blow

der **Püstrich, -e** puffer, snorter

der **Putz** elegant dress; finery; **im Putz** dressed-up

sich **putzen** (*wk*) dress up; adorn, attire, deck oneself out

der **Pygmäe, -n** pygmy, mythological dwarf

Pylos Pylos (*town, home of Nestor; bay*)

die **Pyramide, -n** pyramid

Pythonissa Pythoness (*Pythia, priestess of Apollo*)

Q

das **Quadrat** rectangle, oblong (11528)

die **Qual, -en** torture, torment, agony, pain

quälen (*wk*) torture; coax

sich **quälen** (*wk*) torment oneself, worry, slave, toil; suffer (11362)

die **Qualität, -en** quality, attribute

der **Qualm** thick smoke

qualmen be full of smoke

quammig squashy

quappig wiggly, quivery

der **Quark** trash, mess

die **Quaste,** –n tassel

das **Quecksilber** mercury

der **Quell** source, fountain, spring, well

die **Quelle,** –n fountain, origin, source, well, spring

quellen (i) gush forth, spring, flow, originate, rise, emanate (6445)

das **Quentchen** tiny dram

quer cross, across, sideways (4235); **kreuz und quer** from all sides, in utmost confusion; **die Kreuz und Quer** zigzag, erratic course (1916, 5847)

quetschen (*wk*) squeeze, crush

quillen rise, spring, originate; swell, grow (3791)

die **Quintessenz** quintessence

quirlen swirl around

R

der **Rabatt** rebate, discount

der **Rabe,** –n raven

die **Rabenpost** system of sending messages by ravens

der **Rabenstein** place of execution

die **Rabentraulichkeit** intimacy with ravens

die **Rache** vengeance

der **Rachen,** — maw, jaw; **ihm in den Rachen** down his throat (6018)

rächen avenge

der **Rächer** avenger, executioner

der **Rachesegen** abundant harvest of vengeance

der **Racker,** — young rascal

das **Rad,** ⁼er wheel; **Rad schlagen** turn cartwheels

der **Raffzahn** tusk

ragen stand out, project

das **Ragout** stew, hash, ragout

die **Rammelei** copulation, wantonness

der **Rand** edge, brim, rim; brink (9535)

der **Rang** rank, position; seat of dignity, station

die **Ranke,** –n shoot, vine; branch

das **Ränzlein** paunch

Raphael Raphael (*an archangel*)

rapieren fence with rapiers

rasch quick, brisk, speedy, prompt, rash, youthful and impetuous (3089); swift, in a hurry

rascheln move along quickly (*audibly but invisibly*); scurry

raschgeschäftig quickly busy

der **Rasen** lawn, turf, sod

rasen rage, rave like mad, be delirious, go mad; rush

ein **Rasender** madman

die **Raserei** frenzy, raving, madness

rasseln clatter, rattle

die **Rast** rest, relaxation

rasten rest

rastlos indefatigable, untiring; restless

der **Rat** advice; council; way out (1236); **Rat schaffen** find ways and means (7350); **um Rat fragen** inquire, seek advice (8246)

raten (ä), ie, a advise, give advice, suggest

ratschlagend holding council

das **Rätsel,** — riddle, puzzle, enigma

der **Rätselkram** silly riddles

das **Rätselwort** enigmatic word

die **Ratte,** –n rat

der **Rattenfänger** rat catcher (*Pied Piper*)

der **Rattenzahn** rat's tooth

der **Raub** depredation, looting, robbery, plundering, rape; **für Raub achten** regard as beneath one's dignity

rauben (*wk*) steal, deprive (of), take away

der **Räuber,** — robber, kidnapper (8512, 9489); plunderer (9005, 9006)

die **Räuberfaust** hands or power of kidnappers

raubschiffen (*wk*) sail in pirate fashion

der **Rauch** smoke

rauchen smoke

der **Rauchfang** chimney, flue

das **Rauchloch** smoke vent

rauchwarm warm with fur, fur-warm

der **Raufbold** brawler, bully

Raufebold Fight-hard

raufen fight, scuffle

rauh rough, uncouth, shaggy; chapped (3082); bleak, rugged, hard, unpleasant

der **Raum,** ⁓e space, room, expanse, tract (11563)

das **Raumgelaß,** –gelasse space

die **Räumlichkeit,** –en open space, expanse

raunen (*wk*) whisper

die **Raupe** caterpillar

'raus = heraus

der **Rausch** ecstasy; roar (9964)

rauschen rush, swirl, rustle; roar

das **Rauschen** rush, turmoil (1754)

der **Realist** philosophical realist

die **Rebe,** –n vine

der **Rebell,** –en rebel

rebellisch rebellious, mutinous

der **Rechenpfennig,** –e chip, counter

die **Rechenschaft** accounting

rechnen calculate, count

die **Rechnung** bill, account; **Rechnung für Rechnung** bill by bill, every bill (6041)

das **Recht,** –e law; right, privilege (4839); justice (9481); domain (11093); **mit Recht** rightfully; **Recht tun** do justice; **zu Recht sein** be justly due (11285)

recht right, correct, proper, all right, real, quite, downright, thoroughly; suitable; **recht haben** be right; **es ... recht machen** satisfy; **erst recht** really, more than ever; **mit rechten Dingen** in a proper way, as it should be; **recht behalten** win an argument; **was Recht's** a good deal, something (anything) to be proud of; **zum Rechten** aright; **eben recht kommen** come at just the right time; **recht kommen** be welcome; **die Rechte** the right wing; **nichts Rechtes** nothing of importance; **recht tun** do justice

rechts to the right, on the right

die **Rechtsgelehrsamkeit** jurisprudence, study of law

die **Rede,** –n speech, talk, lecture, words; **davon ist nicht die Rede** that is not the question (1765); **Rede stehen** render an accounting, answer

die **Redekunst** oratory, art of speaking

reden speak, talk

redlich honest, upright

die **Redlichkeit** uprightness, straightforward zeal (1036)

der **Redner** orator

die **Rednerei** oratory

reduzieren reduce, analyze

rege active, alive; enthusiastic (1560); lively, animated, in motion; **rege machen** stir up (8748)

die **Regel** regulation, rule, customary practice (8162)

regelhaft regular

regeln (*wk*) regulate, arrange in orderly fashion

der **Regen** rain

regen (*wk*) set in motion, inspire; move (8993), swell (5720)

sich **regen** (*wk*) move, stir, spring up, come to life, be astir, proceed (6948), be active (8329), spend a little money

der **Regenwurm**, ⸚er earthworm

regieren (*wk*) govern, rule

die **Region**, –en region, part; sphere (11866, 11890)

regnen rain, fall (like rain 2310)

regsam astir; lively

die **Regung** motion; emotion (8428)

das **Reh**, –e deer, doe

reiben rub

das **Reich**, –e empire, kingdom, realm

reich rich, abundant, full; wealthy, opulent; plentiful, heavy, dense (7293); ornamented (9127)

reichen (*wk*) pass, present, hand; extend, give

reichgeschmückt richly adorned (*with Nature's finery*)

reichlich abundant, ample, copious, plentiful, profuse

reichlichstens most abundantly, profusely

der **Reichtum** riches, wealth, opulence (9354), abundance

reif ripe

reifen (*wk*) mature, age, grow to maturity; ripen (10533)

die **Reihe**, –n sequence; line, row, series (6074); rank (10508–9); **der Reihe nach** down the line; **Reih' an Reihe** row after row

der **Reihen** (round) dance

reihen (*wk*) arrange in serried ranks (9156, 10100)

sich **reihen** line up

Reihenwanderer wanderers in serried ranks

reihenweis in rows

der **Reiher**, — heron

der **Reiherstrahl** plume from a heron

reimen make rimes

reimweis in rime

das **Reimwort** riming word

rein pure, clear, clean, free; in full (1416); cleared (8298); neat (10098); unconditional (10389); **rein halten** be a good housekeeper (2686); **die Reinen** pure in heart; **ins reine bringen** clear up; **ins**

reine kommen come to a clear understanding

reingeboren pureborn, developed in natural purity

reinigen (*wk*) purify, cleanse; sweep clean, clear (9472)

reinlich neatly (2705); carefully (6327); clean, pure (11957)

reinlich-hell pure and clear

reinmelodisch unharmonized, having a simple melody, very melodious

die Reinschrift fair copy

das Reis twig

die Reise course, journey, trip

reisen (*wk*) travel, get around (3019)

der Reisende traveler

das Reisig faggots

reißen, i, i pull; tear (split) open (7925); drag (8837); (= **zerreißen**) tear to pieces (3575)

reiten, i, i ride (*on horseback*)

die Reiterei cavalry

der Reiz charm

reizen (*wk*) incite, rouse; fascinate, allure, entice, attract

reizend attractive, enticing, charming

die Religion religion

rennen, a, a (*wk, irreg*) run, rush; **vor einen Felsen rennen** run into a rock (3854)

die Rente, -n revenue, interest, income

das Requiem requiem, mass

resolut resolute

der Respekt respect

respektabel respectable, commanding admiration

respektieren respect

der Rest, -e remainder, remains, rest

das Restchen: das Restchen geben finish off, do for

retten (*wk*) save, rescue

der Retter, — rescuer

der Retterblick face of one who brings salvation

die Rettung rescue, escape

die Reue repentance

der Reuestich pang of regret

reuig repentant, penitent

reüssieren have luck, succeed

der Reuter horseman

revidieren check, inspect

das Revier countryside, area

das Rezept, -e recipe

Rhea Rhea (*Cybele, spouse of Cronus, mother of Olympic gods*)

der Rhein Rhine

der Rheinwein Rhine wine

Rhodus Rhodes (*island sacred to Phoebus Apollo, Helios*)

rhythmisch rhythmical

die Richte (straight) line

richten (*wk*) judge; direct, turn; arrange (2857); be attentive to (10448); **zugrunde richten** ruin

sich richten be erected (11122)

der Richter, — judge

die Richterin female judge

richtig correct

die Richtung direction

riechen smell

der Riegel, — bolt; **Riegel auf!** unbolt the door; **Riegel zu!** bolt the door

der Riese, -n giant

rieseln purl; gurgle; drizzle;

trickle, dissolve in a drizzle (5979)

die **Riesenfichte** giant fir

riesengroß gigantic, immense

riesenhaft gigantic, in gigantic size

der **Riesenleichnam** gigantic corpse

das **Riesenschild** gigantic shell

die **Riesenschildkröte** gigantic tortoise

der **Riesige, –n** giant

das **Rind** ox; (= **Rindvieh**) cattle (9535)

die **Rinde, –n** bark

der **Ring, –e** ring, circle; chain

ringen, a, u struggle

das **Ringerspiel** wrestling match

rings all around, everywhere, on all sides

ringsherum round about

das **Ringspiel** tilting at the ring

ringsum all around, everywhere, on all sides

ringsumher all around, everywhere, on all sides

der **Ringverein** ring dance

rinnen flow, run

Rippach Rippach (= Podunk)

die **Rippe, –n** rib; jutting projection (3938)

der **Ritter, —** knight, cavalier (4141)

der **Ritterkragen** lace collar of a cavalier

ritterlich knightly, chivalric

der **Rittersaal** hall of the knights

der **Rittersänger, —** courtly minstrel; poet of the Romantic movement who treats medieval subjects (5295)

das **Rittertum** chivalry

die **Ritze, –n** crack

der **Rock, ⸗e** coat, skirt, gown

roh rude, impolite, unrefined, coarse, primitive, unworked (9020–1)

das **Rohe** coarseness

das **Rohr, –e** reed, thicket of reeds

das **Rohr** quill (6578)

das **Röhrenwasser** water conducted through a pipeline

das **Rohrgeschwister** sister reeds

das **Röhrigflöten** reedy piping

die **Rolle, –n** scroll (678); roll (*of coins* 5012, 5718)

die **Rolle** role, part

die **Rollekutsche, –n** light carriage

rollen (*wk*) roll, revolve (2404); roll up, turn up (*at the edge* 6394)

das **Rollen** whirl (1755)

der **Rollstuhl** wheel chair

Rom Rome

der **Roman** novel, romance

romantisch romantic

der **Römer, —** Roman

der **Römerzug, ⸗e** journey to Rome

römisch Roman

die **Rose, –n** rose

der **Rosenhügel** rose-covered hill

die **Rosenknospe, –n** rosebud

das **Roß, Rosse** horse, steed

der **Rost** rust, patina

das **Rot** red

rot red

röten (*wk*) redden

sich röten grow red

rötlich reddish

die **Rübe, –n** turnip

der **Rubin, –en** ruby

der **Ruck: auf einen Ruck** with one quick stroke, all together

der **Rücken** back; ridge (9526); **im Rücken** behind

rücken move

die **Rückkehr** return

das **Ruder** oar

rudern (*wk*) row

der **Ruf** call; fame, reputation

rufen, ie, u call, summon; cry, say loudly

die **Ruh(e)** rest, peace, quiet, sleep, silence (5675); leisure (2642); peace of mind (3349, 3626)

das **Ruhebett** bed of ease (resting place = grave)

ruhen (*wk*) rest, lie; be idle (4223); repose (10018)

der **Ruheplatz** bed, bedroom, chamber

ruhig quiet, still, peaceful, undisturbed, calm, serene (8037)

ruhigscheinend seemingly peaceful

der **Ruhm** renown, fame, glory

rühmen praise, commend (6257, 8787); mention boastfully (526)

der **Ruhmesgewinn** harvest of glory

rühmlich glorious

rühren (*wk*) move, stir up (4684); touch

sich **rühren** stir, move; be busy, be active (11534)

rührig busy, alert

die **Rumpelkammer** storage room, old attic

der **Rumpf** trunk, body

rümpfen (*wk*) turn up (one's nose) in contempt

das **Rund** circle; round server (8573)

rund round, rounded off

das **Runda: singt Runda** let's sing a round

die **Runde** circle, surroundings; all around (7040)

rṻnden form a circle

der **Rundreim** refrain

rundumschrieben orb-shaped

rupfen pluck (*petals*)

ruschen whiz about

rüsten prepare, arm

sich **rüsten** get ready, prepare oneself, arm oneself

rüstig alert, nimble

die **Rüstung** armor; equipment (10325)

die **Rute, –n** baton; whip; discipline (6724)

rutschen slide

rütteln (*wk*) shake

S

's = das, es

der **Saal, Säle** hall; lecture hall; room

die **Saat, –en** young grain, field of grain, crop

die **Sabbatstille** quiet of Sabbath

der **Sabiner** Sabine (*native of Samnium, district in central Italy*)

die **Sache, –n** thing, matter; object; cause, affair; **alle Sachen** everything

das **Sächelchen, —** pretty little thing, knicknack

der **Sachse, –n** Saxon

sacht gently, softly; cautiously, slowly (1975, 5921)

der **Sack,** ⸚e sack

der **Säckel** purse

säen sow, scatter (10816)

der **Saft,** ⸚e fluid, elixir, juice, syrup; vital juice (1633)

saftig liquid, succulent, juicy

die **Sage, –n** fable, myth, legend

sagen (*wk*) tell, say, talk, speak (4574)

die **Saite, –n** string

das **Saitenspiel** harp, stringed instrument; music on (a) stringed instrument(s) (9679)

das **Sakrament, –e** sacrament

die **Sakristei** vestry

der **Salamander, —** salamander

die **Salbe** salve

Salomon Solomon

der **Salpeter** saltpeter

salutieren salute

das **Salzregal** royalty derived from salt monopoly

der **Same, –n** seed, nucleus, germ

sammeln (*wk*) gather, assemble, collect; **gesammelt** in a group (4634); in composure (10976)

sich **sammeln** (*wk*) gather

der **Sammet** velvet

die **Sammetmatte, –n** velvetlike meadow

der **Sammler** collector

die **Sammlung** collection

Samothrace Samothrace (*island in the Aegean Sea*)

der **Samstag** Saturday

samt along with, together with, including

sämtlich all together, all, all of

Sancta Simplicitas (*Latin*) holy simplicity, holy innocence

der **Sand** sand; dust (**Trüber Tag** 20); beach (11256)

sanft soft, calm, gentle

sanfthingleitend floating along gently

der **Sang** song, music; singing

der **Sänger** singer, serenader

Sankt Saint

Sanssouci Sanssouci (*French: "free from care"*)

Sardanapal Sardanapalus (*king of Assyria*)

der **Satan, –e** Satan, devil

satanisch satanic, hellish

der **Satansmeister** Master of all devils, Lucifer (*Mephistopheles*)

der **Satiriker** satirist

satt satiated, full; **sich satt sehen an** get tired of gazing at, get one's fill of looking; **satt sein** be tired of; **sich satt weiden** feast one's eyes to satisfaction; **satt haben** be tired of (4925)

sättigen satiate, satisfy

Saturn Saturn (= lead *in alchemy*)

der **Satyr** satyr

das **Satyrvolk** (folk) crowd of satyrs

der **Satz** leap

die **Sau,** ⸚e sow

sauber neat, nice

sauer sour, bitter; hard

die **Sauerei** swinishness

der **Sauerteig** leaven

der **Sauertopf** kill-joy, querulous person

saufen (äu), o, o drink (*heavily or greedily*)

saugen, o, o, draw, suck

der **Säugling** infant, suckling

das **Säulchen,** — small column or pillar

die **Säule, -n** column, pillar

der **Säulenschaft** shaft of a column

der **Saum** crest; edge

säumen (*wk*) hesitate, tarry, linger; **ohne Säumen** without delay

die **Säumnis** delay

die **Säure** acid, sourness

der **Saus** reveling gaiety

säuseln whisper, rustle pleasantly

das **Säuselschweben** evanescent rustling

sausen (*wk*) whiz, roar, rush, buzz; send up with a roar

die **Schachtel, -n** box

der **Schade** harm, injury, misfortune (8193); damage (11034); **schade!** it's a pity; **zu Schaden kommen** become a detriment to (6565); **zu Schaden sein** be a detriment to (7130)

der **Schädel** skull

das **Schädelspalten** splitting a skull

schaden inflict damage, do harm; **es schadet nichts** there's no harm

schädigen inflict damage, injure

schädlich dangerous, detrimental, injurious

der **Schäfer** shepherd

der **Schäferknecht** shepherd's boy

die **Schäferstunde** happy hour of lovers, pastoral hour

schaffen (*wk*) be active, work, achieve, manage; manage to get, get, procure, obtain; do; wish, desire, order; **vom Leibe schaffen** get rid of; **zur Seite schaffen** remove; **ans Land schaffen** put ashore

schaffen, u, a create; **schaffend** creative; **Geschaffenes** Creation

die **Schaffnerin** stewardess, housekeeper

die **Schafsnatur** sheep nature; **Schafsnatur!** Sheep that they are!

schafwollig of sheep's wool

schäkern sport, flirt

schal flat, insipid

die **Schale, -n** bowl, vessel; shell (4661); outer surface (5607)

der **Schalk, ⸚e** jester, rogue; villain, Judas

der **Schall** sound

schallen, o, o sound, peal, resound

schalten have power over, hold sway (4784), rule (8181)

das **Schalten** behavior (6380)

die **Scham** modesty

sich **schämen** be ashamed

schamlos shameless, impudent

schamrot flushed (red) with embarrassment

die **Schande** shame, dishonor, disgrace

der **Schandgesell(e)** scoundrel

schändlich shameful, abominable, foul

die **Schar, -en** host, crowd, group; gang

die **Scharade, -n** charade

sich **scharen** flock together

scharenweise in hordes

scharf sharp, keen, cutting; strict (6673); piercing, acute; violent

scharfangeschlossen tight-drawn

die **Schärfe** sharpness; keen blade (4594)

schärfen (*wk*) sharpen; intensify, make keener (10206)

scharfsichtig sharp-eyed

der **Scharlatan** charlatan

scharren rake, scrape

der **Schatten,** — shadow, illusion (1249); shade (10165); phantom (11388)

schattenhaft shadowlike, phantomlike

der **Schattenkreis** shadowy circle

das **Schattenreich** realm of shades, Hades

die **Schattenruh** shady resting place

schattig shady

der **Schatz,** ⁻e treasure, riches, wealth; treasury (6137); possessions (11070); sweetheart, beloved (2991)

schatzbewußt sensitive to the presence of treasures

das **Schätzchen** sweetheart

schätzen appreciate, esteem, value, consider (2400); appraise (4150); respect (10203)

das **Schatzgemach** treasure house

das **Schatzgewölb(e),** — treasure vault

der **Schatzmeister** treasurer

das **Schatzrevier** hunting ground for treasures

die **Schau** display (6403, 11210); look (9293); exhibition (11210); **zu malerisch-ent-**

zückter Schau (7557) for the rapt gaze of a painter (?), as a picturesque and delightful spectacle (?); **zur Schau kommen** become visible; **zur Schau bringen** represent

das **Schauerfest** weird festival

das **Schaudergrauen** terrifying horror

schauderhaft weird, eery, uncanny

schaudern tremble, start (*with a shudder*); be struck with awe; shudder (6265); **mir schaudert** I have a horror, I feel horror; **es schaudert mich** I shudder (to)

schauen (*wk*) look, gaze; see, behold

das **Schauen** vision (592); **zum Schauen** to watch and contemplate (11289)

der **Schauer,** — shower (909, 4724)

der **Schauer** awe, feeling of devotion and inspiration, feeling of fear and anticipation (473, 2757, 4405); atmosphere of weird foreboding (6620); a cold shiver

schauerlich dreadful; repulsive

schauern (*wk*) shudder; bring a shudder

schauervoll ominous, full of foreboding

das **Schauerwindchen** little squall

die **Schaufel, -n** shovel

schaukeln rock; **schaukelnd** undecided

der **Schaum,** ⁻e foam, spray; froth (6758)

das **Schaumbild** mocking illusion

schäumen foam; (= **abschäumen**) skim off (2337)

der **Schaumlöffel** skimming ladle

der **Schauplatz** scene

das **Schauspiel** play, spectacle (454)

das **Schaustück** showpiece, pocket piece; lucky coin

scheckig spotted, pied

die **Schedel** bill, paper money

Scheherezade Scheherezade (*the storytelling woman in Arabian Nights*)

die **Scheibe,** –n (window) pane; disk (3851)

die **Scheide** sheath

der **Scheidegruß** farewell greeting

scheiden, ie, ie separate, part company, leave, tear oneself away from (4202); divorce oneself from (8931)

sich **scheiden** separate

das **Scheiden** departure, separation

der **Schein** light, brilliance, radiance, gleam, shine; aspect (*in astrology*); appearance; outward appearance, illusion, delusion

scheinen, ie, ie shine; seem, appear; look like

das **Scheit,** –e stick of firewood

der **Scheitel** (top of the) head

der **Scheiterhaufen** stake, pyre

scheitern be stranded, suffer shipwreck

schellenlaut noisy (*with the tinkling bells of a fool's cap*)

der **Schelm,** –e rogue, scoundrel

die **Schelte** scolding

schelten (i), a, o curse (3717); scold, denounce, call (names 5274); deprecate (6201); abuse

das **Scheltwort** invective

der **Schemeltritt** footstool

der **Schemen,** — phantom

der **Schenk** cupbearer

schenken (*wk*) grant, give, present (2828); bestow on (2571); give presents (2674)

schenken pour (2582)

die **Scherbe,** –n broken piece of glass or china

der **Scherben,** — flower pot (3608)

die **Schere,** –n scissors, shears

das **Scherflein** mite, small share

der **Scherz,** –e fun, joke, sport; entertainment (5988); game (6879); prank (8228)

scherzen joke, have fun, sport

das **Scherzergötzen** sportive diversion

das **Scherzgeschrei** sportive shouting

scheu shy, bashful

scheuen have fear of, be afraid of

sich **scheuen,** shun, fear, avoid, be afraid of

das **Scheusal** monster, hideous creature

die **Schichtung** deployment, disposition

schicken send

sich **schicken** (*wk*) adjust oneself to; turn out well (8258)

schicklich properly

das **Schicksal** destiny, chance, fate

schicksalschwer fateful

schieben, o, o shove, push; postpone (11464)

sich schieben, o, o shuffle along

schief slanting, crooked; sloping; distorted (11476); ein schiefes Maul ziehen make a wry face; es steht schief darum something is wrong with it

der Schiefer slate

schiefgesenkt bowed sideways

die Schiene, –n legpiece (*of armor*)

schier almost, nearly; fully (9784)

Schierke Schierke (*a town*)

schießen shoot

das Schiff, –e ship, boat; nave (11010)

die Schiffahrt navigation

der Schiffbruch shipwreck

der Schiffer, — sailor, skipper

der Schifferknabe, –n young sailor, apprentice seaman

das Schifflein, — shuttle (1925)

der Schild, –e shield; escutcheon (9031, 9033); disk (7924)

schildern describe

die Schildkröte tortoise

das Schilf reed, sedge

das Schilfgeflüster whisper of reeds

schilfumkränzt ringed with reeds

der Schimmer gleam

schimmern gleam, glitter

der Schimpf insult; ohne Schimpf und Spaß seriously

schimpfen scold, curse

schimpflich ignominiously

schinden: geschunden flayed, skinned

die Schirmung protection, shelter

die Schlacht, –en battle

schlachten slay, (*as an offering*) sacrifice

schlachterzogen brought up through battles or during war

das Schlachtfeld, –er battlefield

der Schlaf sleep

die Schläfe temple

schlafen (ä), ie, a sleep; schlafend asleep

der Schläfer sleeper, sleeping person

schläfern grow drowsy

der Schlafrock dressing gown

schlafsuchend trying to sleep

der Schlag, ⁔e stroke, blow; shock (2324); kind, type (281); (= Handschlag) handshake; auf einen Schlag at one blow, all at once, without difficulty; nach deinem Schlag after your liking; Schlag auf Schlag hand on hand (*to seal a wager*); Schlag um Schlag blow upon blow

schlagen (ä), u, a strike, beat, knock, smash (3359); sound (149); aus dem Felde schlagen eliminate; Rad schlagen turn cartwheels; ein Schnippchen schlagen snap one's fingers

der Schlamm mud, mire

die Schlange, –n snake; hydra (7227)

schlängeln meander; coil, sneak

schlangenartig snakelike

schlangenhaft snakelike

der Schlangenrüssel snakelike trunk

schlank slender, slim, slight; long

schlapp limp

die **Schlappe** slap

schlau sly

der **Schlauch,** ⁻e wineskin (10038); bag; paunch, potbelly; fat devil

schlecht bad, poor, dim (3853); evil, wicked (10176); **es geht ihm schlecht** he's getting on badly; **mir war es vor den Augen schlecht** it went black before my eyes

schleichen sneak, creep, prowl, steal along

schleichend insidious (740)

der **Schleicher,** — one who creeps; plodder (521); intriguer (9488)

der **Schleier** veil

schleifen slide (*on dance floor*)

sich **schleifen** drag oneself

schleppen drag

die **Schleudermacht** power to hurl

schleudern (*wk*) hurl, toss

schlicht simple, unpretentious

schlichten adjust, arrange

schließen, o, o shut, close, lock (in); conclude; **geschlossen** fettered, locked in chains (4186); **einen Kreis schließen** form a circle

sich **schließen,** o, o (an) form a chain, link oneself to, draw together

schlimm bad

die **Schlinge,** –n snare, trap, noose

schlingen, a, u intertwine

sich **schlingen,** a, u move sinuously

das **Schloß** castle

das **Schloß, Schlösser** lock

die **Schloßwarte** lookout tower of a castle

schlottern shake

die **Schlucht,** –en gorge, ravine

der **Schluck** gulp, swallow

das **Schlückchen** little sip

der **Schlummersaft,** ⁻e sleeping potion

der **Schlund,** ⁻e gorge, abyss; gullet

schlüpfen slip

schlürfen sip, drink slowly and luxuriously

der **Schluß** conclusion, end; **am Schluß** in the end; **zum Schluß** in conclusion

der **Schlüssel,** — key

das **Schlüsselchen** little key

das **Schlüsselloch** keyhole

der **Schlußerfolg** final result

der **Schlußstein** keystone

die **Schmach** shame; insult (6310); disgrace (9257)

schmachten languish

schmächtig languishing (3655); slim, delicate (7756)

schmähen (= **verschmähen**) disdain (7204)

schmählich disgraceful, vile (7771); ignominious

schmal narrow

schmälen criticize

schmälern (*wk*) reduce, narrow

der **Schmalpfeiler,** — thin Gothic pillar

schmauchen (*wk*) produce dense smoke

der **Schmaus** banquet, feast; food served at a banquet

schmausen feast, banquet, eat with satisfaction

schmecken taste; taste good

der **Schmecker** epicure, gourmand

die **Schmeichelglut** ingratiating glow, pleasant warmth

schmeichelhaft ingratiating

das **Schmeichelkätzchen,** — wheedling kitten

die **Schmeichelkraft,** ⸗e power of flattering persuasion

schmeicheln (*wk*) flatter; **schmeichelnd** by means of flattery

schmeichelnd-lüstern ingratiatingly lascivious

der **Schmeichelton** ingratiating and pleasing sound

der **Schmeichler** flatterer

die **Schmeiße,** –n blowfly

schmelzen (i), o, o melt

der **Schmerbauch** paunch, potbelly

der **Schmerz,** –en pain, grief, affliction

die **Schmerzenreiche** (deeply afflicted) Dolorosa

schmerzenvoll agonizing; filled with grief

schmerzlich painful, tantalizing; grievous

der **Schmetterling,** –e butterfly

schmettern blare, ring; **schmetternd** loud and shrill

die **Schmiede** smithy, forge

schmieden (*wk*) forge; weld

sich **schmiegen** nestle, cuddle

schmiegsam caressing (6910)

schminken (*wk*) make up (*face*), paint

schmollen sulk

der **Schmuck** adornment, jewelry, finery; decoration (5565); neatness

schmuck trim, elegant

schmücken (*wk*) adorn, decorate, dress

sich **schmücken** (*wk*) attire oneself in fine clothes, get all dressed up, become radiant (6797)

das **Schmuckkästchen** little jewelry box

schmunzeln smirk, smile

der **Schnabel,** ⸗ beak, bill; prow (of a ship 8539); **die gelben Schnäbel** (= **Gelbschnäbel**) young bird, immature person (6745)

der **Schnack** prattle

die **Schnake,** –n jest

schnapps! snap!

schnarchen snore, snort

der **Schnarcher,** — "Snorer" (*rocks in the Harz Mountains*)

schnarren snarl

schnatterhaft chattering

schnaufen pant, snort

die **Schnecke** snail

das **Schneckenhaus,** ⸗er snail shell

der **Schneckenkreis** spiral

der **Schneckeschnickeschnack** nasal bleatings of a (soap bubble) bagpipe

der **Schnee** snow

schneiden cut; **Gesichter schneiden** make faces

der **Schneider** tailor

schnell fast, rapid, quick, swift (2431); sudden (5475)

die **Schnelle** speed

schnellempfunden quickly felt

schnellen toss

die **Schnelligkeit** swiftness

die **Schnellkraft** elasticity

das **Schnippchen: ein Schnipp-chen schlagen** snap one's fingers

schnippen snap

schnippisch pert

der **Schnitt** cut; **vom neusten Schnitt** after the latest style, up-to-date

das **Schnitzel,** — (*sg*) piece of paper; (*pl*) chips, shavings, leavings

schnopern sniff, scent; nose around

schnörkelhaft ornamented with scrolls and spirals, over-ornate

schnuffeln sniff, have one's nose in

das **Schnürchen** little string

schnüren (*wk*) lace; **geschnürten Leibs** wearing a corset

der **Schnurweg, –e** straight road-way bordered with trees

der **Scholastikus** university student

die **Scholle** lump of earth; native soil

schon already; all right; **schon und aber schon** again and again (8451)

schön beautiful, fair, handsome, pretty, nice; **die Schöne** beautiful woman

der **Schönbart, ⸗e** mask, mummery

die **Schöne** beauty

schonen (*wk*) spare; be indulgent, be considerate

die **Schöngestalt** beautiful figure

die **Schönheit** beauty

die **Schönheitliebende, –n** lover of beauty

der **Schönheitsfreund** lover of beauty

die **Schonung** mercy

der **Schopf** top of the head, fore-lock; brain (6748); **beim Schopfe fassen** seize by the forelock or by the hair of the head

schöpfen draw

schöpferisch creative

die **Schöpfung** creation, creative activity (1560)

der **Schornstein** chimney

der **Schoß** lap; womb (8649); center (8674); **in den Schoß nehmen** take to one's bosom; **im Schoß** within itself (9336)

die **Schranke, –n** bounds, boundary; limit (5303); limitation (6114)

die **Schraube, –n** screw

schrauben screw; heckle, bait (2180)

der **Schreck, –en** fear, fright, terror

das **Schreckbild** frightful spectre

schrecken (*wk*) scare, frighten

der **Schreckensgang** dreadful mission

die **Schreckenshand** hand of terror

Schreckensläufte epochs (ages) of terror

die **Schreckgestalt, –en** frightening phantom

das **Schreckgetön** frightening noise

schrecklich terrible, dreadful, horrible, awful

schreiben, ie, ie write

der **Schreiber,** — clerk

schreien, ie, ie shout, cry; **irre**

schreien confuse by screaming

der Schrein closet, cupboard; chest

schreiten stride, step out; walk, proceed (5813)

die Schrift, –en publication, writing (5346); (hand)writing, signature (10966)

der Schritt, –e pace, step; walk; Schritt und Tritt every movement; Schritt vor Schritt step by step

schroff steep, precipitous, rugged

schröpfen cup, bleed; drain (5850)

schrumpfen shrink, shrivel

schüchtern timid

der Schuft, –en rascal

der Schuh, –e shoe

der Schuhu (= Uhu) owl

schuld: schuld sein to be blamed

die Schuld, –en guilt, fault, debt; in eurer Schuld indebted to you

schuldenfrei free of debt

schuldig guilty; due (9208); duly, as is one's obligation; schuldig sein owe (4821, 6307)

der Schuldner debtor

der Schüler, — pupil, student

die Schulter, –n shoulder

schüren stir

schürfen burrow, dig down

der Schurke villain

der Schurz apron, loincloth

die Schürze apron

sich schürzen gird up one's loins

der Schuß shot

die Schüssel, –n bowl

der Schutt rubble

das Schütteln earthquake

schütteln (wk) shake

sich schütteln (wk) shake oneself, shiver

schütten (wk) throw, pour

schüttern shake, tremble

der Schutz protection; rampart (9467); in Schutz nehmen take under one's protection, defend (4745)

schützen (wk) protect, defend

sich schützen defend oneself, act in self-defense

schwach feeble, weak; faint; inadequate

die Schwäche feebleness, faintness

die Schwachheit weakness, frailty

der Schwaden, — layer of gas or smoke

schwadronieren talk big, swagger

der Schwager, ⸚ brother-in-law; male relative (5238)

der Schwall throng; surging flood (10733)

der Schwan, ⸚e swan

schwanerzeugt swan-bred

schwanger heavily laden

schwangleich swanlike

der Schwank farce; trick

schwank gentle (4656); wavering, swaying (7023); uncertain

schwanken waver, falter, sway, hover; become dizzy (2457); hesitate, move to and fro (5082); be undecided (5701)

die Schwankung wavering

der Schwanz tail

der **Schwarm** swarm

schwärmen (*wk*) roam around, move about, lead a gay or riotous life

der **Schwärmezug,** ⁀e long extended swarm

schwarz black, sinister, dark

schwarzborstig with black bristles

schwärzen (*wk*) blacken; smuggle (4914)

schwatzen talk, prattle, gossip

schwätzen babble, talk nonsense, chatter

schweben (*wk*) hover, soar, be suspended, dangle (1864); drift (11992, 12032); float; im **Schweben** in suspense (8959)

der **Schwedenkopf** "Swedish haircut," hair shorn short

der **Schwefel** sulphur, brimstone

die **Schwefelrute,** –n sulphur torch

die **Schwefelsäure** (? 10083) *see* **Schwefelstank**

der **Schwefelstank** smell of sulphur; **von Schwefelstank und -säure** with the acid stench of sulphur

der **Schweif** tail

schweifen roam, ramble; move aimlessly (4663, 5511); float (10585)

schweigen, ie, ie be quiet, hush (3142); be silent, grow silent; **hier schweigt mein Amt** I need not speak officially, in my official capacity (6451)

die **Schweignis** silence

schweigsam silent

die **Schweigsamkeit** silence

das **Schwein,** –e pig; swine

der **Schweiß** sweat

schwelgen enjoy, revel

die **Schwelle,** –n threshold

schwellen (i), o, o swell up, extend; puff up (7304); rise (7512); become filled (10083, 10108)

schwenken swing

schwer difficult, with difficulty (203); hard, heavy; grave, bad; bitterly (4339); direly (11356)

Schwerdtlein Schwerdtlein

die **Schwere** weight, heaviness

schwergelöst severed with difficulty

schwerlich with difficulty

das **Schwert,** –er sword

die **Schwester,** –n sister

das **Schwesterchen** little sister

das **Schwesterlein** little sister

schwesterlich like a sister, as a sister

schwimmen swim, float

die **Schwimmgebärde,** –n gesture suggesting swimming

die **Schwimmlust** joy of swimming

der **Schwindel** dizziness

die **Schwindelstufe,** –n dizzy height

schwinden, a, u vanish, disappear, dwindle; grow thin and disappear (9236); diminish (11089)

die **Schwinge,** –n wing, pinion

schwingen swing

schwirren whiz

schwitzen (*wk*) sweat, perspire

schwören, u, o swear (by), promise

schwül sultry

der Schwung enthusiasm, verve, sweep; kreisender Schwung sweeping circle

Scylla Scylla (*a monster*)

sechs six

der See, –n lake

der Seedurchstreicher seafarer

seeisch maritime

das Seelchen little soul

die Seele, –n soul (*individual*), mind, inner eye, heart

das Seelenflehen heartfelt supplication

die Seelenkraft spiritual energy, spiritual faculty

die Seelenliebe true love

der Seelenschatz spiritual treasure

die Seelenschönheit spiritual beauty

seeverwandt akin to the sea

das Segel, — sail

segeln sail

der Segen blessing, beneficial quality (2822); harvest, yield (4615)

segenduftend fragrant with benediction

segnen (*wk*) bless, praise, express satisfaction with; bestow benediction upon (6425)

sehen (ie), a, e see, behold, look; perceive, watch, observe

die Sehne, –n sinew

sich sehnen (*wk*) yearn, long for

das Sehnen yearning, ardent desire

sehnig sinewy, tough

die Sehnsucht yearning

sehnsüchtig longing

sehnsuchtsvoll yearning, longing

sehr very; most, very much, a great deal; greatly, plenty

seicht shallow, running low

die Seide silk

der Seidenfaden, ⸗ silk thread

die Seidenflocke, –n silk waste, bits of silk

die Seifenblase soap bubble

das Seil rope; am Seile führen lead on a leash

sein (ist), war, gewesen be; exist, live, be alive; happen

sein his, its; Sein your

seinerzeit in due time, at the proper time

seinesgleichen his equal, the like(s) of him

Seismos Seismos (*god of earthquakes*)

seit [*adv*] since; for

seit [*conj*] since (8146, 8510)

seitab aside, out of the way

seitdem since

die Seite, –n side, part, direction, quarter; zur Seite at his side (9192), within call (9590); mir zur Seite at my side; nach allen Seiten in all directions

die Seitentür side door

seitwärts to the side, aside; over there, on the side; seitwärts gehen disappear, scram

selber self, -self

selbst in person, -self; even; selbst wenn even though, even if

selbständig self-reliant

selbstbewußt proud, sure of oneself

selbstgefällig pleased with oneself

selbstgesteckt chosen for one-self, set for oneself

die Selbstsucht egoism

selbstverirrt self-confused

selbstwillig stubborn

selig happy, blissful; blessed; gratifying (6489); blithe (7567); joyous (11726); selig machen be a source of salvation

die Seligkeit eternal bliss, salvation; happiness, satisfaction

seligmachend saving (souls), leading to heaven

selten seldom, rare, unusual

seltsam strange

senden, a, a (wk, irreg) send; Gesandte ambassadors (angels 11676)

senken (wk) lower (10636)

sich senken (wk) descend, sink down; sag (6696)

senkrecht vertical

seraphicus seraphic; Pater Seraphicus, St. Francis of Assisi

Servibilis servant, stagehand

der Sessel, — easy chair, armchair, throne (7569)

setzen (wk) put, set, seat; stake (2401); ein Ziel setzen terminate, put an end to; in Furcht setzen scare; in Verwirrung setzen confuse; gesetzt, daß ... granted that...; Fuß setzen auf put on (buskins 1808)

sich setzen (wk) sit down; sich in Besitz setzen occupy, seize; be placed (10486)

die Seuche plague

seufzen sigh

der Seufzer, — sigh

die Sibylle prophetess (2577, 8957)

Sibylle Sibyl (3546)

die Sibyllengilde guild of prophetesses

sich -self, -selves; one another, each other

sicher certain, certainly, secure, safe, sure; steady (4984)

die Sicherheit security, safety; certainty

sicherlich certainly

sichern (wk) assure, secure, fortify; make safe (8976); take care of (10286); gesichert safeguarded

sicherstellen make secure, safeguard

sichtbar visible

sichten sort, search out

sie (ihrer, ihr) she, her, it

sie (ihrer, ihnen) they, them

das Sieb sieve

Siebel Siebel

sieben seven

Siebenmeilenstiefel seven-league boots

Siebensachen all sorts of things; feminine charms (euphemistically 2031)

sieden seethe, boil

der Siedequalm seething vapor

der Sieg victory, triumph

das Siegel, — seal

siegen (wk) be triumphant, be victorious; zum Siegen for victorious battle (9853)

der Sieger victor

die Siegerschar host of victors

der Siegesglanz glory of victory

die Sieglung procedure of affixing a seal

das **Signal, –e** sounding of signals

die **Signatur** signature

das **Silber** silver

der **Silberbach** silvery brooklet

der **Silberlaut** silvery tinkling

silbern silvery; hoary (3238)

der **Silberrand** silvery edge

die **Silberwelle, –n** silvery wave

Silenus Silenus (*deity of harvest, companion of Dionysus*)

simulieren ponder, rack one's brains

singen, a, u sing; chirp (290); resound (6448); sing about (9912)

der **Singsang** singsong

sinken sink, go down; fall (4614, 6631); fail, grow dim (2781)

der **Sinn, –e/–en** sense; soul; meaning; meaningfulness (151); thought (1229); sensitive faculty (4347); disposition (5914); creative spirit, Mind (6288); style (6819); intention (8526); idea (7088, 11573); conviction; **bei Sinnen sein** be in one's right mind; **ihr vergehen die Sinnen** she will faint, she will be confused; **nach meinem Sinn** according to my wishes or liking; **aus dem Sinn** out of mind; **zu Sinn nehmen** observe, take cognizance of

sinnen, a, o meditate, reflect; speculate, plan, scheme (8537)

das **Sinnenspiel** play of the senses

der **Sinnentanz** play or confusion of the senses

sinnig judicious; contemplative

sinnlich sensual, sensuous

die **Sinnlichkeit** voluptuousness

sinnlos senseless, thoughtless

die **Sippschaft** kin, clan

die **Sirene, –n** siren (*sea nymph enticing through song*)

die **Sitte** custom; decency (10034)

sittelos unmannered

sittenreich well-mannered

sittig well-mannered

die **Sittlichkeit** morality, decency

sittreich well-mannered

der **Sitz** seat, place to sit; place where someone lives, residence; throne

sitzen, a, e sit, be seated; **sitzen lassen** abandon, give up; **obenauf sitzen** be master, be in command

Sizilien Sicily

der **Skeptiker** sceptic

skizzenweise sketchy, fragmentary

die **Sklaverei** slavery

der **Skolar** student, pupil

der **Skolast** student (*beyond the bachelor degree*); scholar

der **Skrupel, —** scruple

Skylla Scylla (*a monster*)

der **Smaragd** emerald

so so, like that, in this manner, as, thus; then, this way; as well as; **so ein** such; **so... als** not only... but also (6252)

sobald as soon as

die **Socke, –n** sock (5546)

der **Socke, –n** soccus, sock of comedy

sodann then, after that; second (6897)

soeben just now, a minute ago

sogar even

sogleich instantly, at once, on the spot, quickly, soon, right away, before long; immediately, directly, right

die **Sohle**, –n sole

der **Sohn**, ⁺e son

Sol Sol, Phoebus Apollo (*god of the sun*)

solang as long as

solch such (a), so, of that kind (sort)

der **Sold** wages, pay, reward

der **Soldat**, –en soldier

soldatenhaft soldierlike

solid substantial, respectable

sollen, o, o (*wk, irreg*) shall, be to; should, ought to; be compelled to, be supposed to, be said to; **Was soll's?** What's the matter?

solo solo (*musical performance*)

der **Sommer** summer

der **Sommerfeiertag**, –e summer holiday

die **Sommernacht** summer night

der **Sommervogel**, ⁺ butterfly

sonder without

sonderbar strange

sonderlich especially

das **Sondern** separation, analysis

sich **sondern** separate

sonnbeglänzt radiant with sunlight

die **Sonne**, –n sun; year (6756)

sonnedurchstrahlt irradiated with sunlight

sich **sonnen** bask in the sun

der **Sonnenblick** ray of sunlight

der **Sonnenglanz** radiance of sunlight

der **Sonnengott** Helios, Apollo (*god of the sun*)

sonnenklar as clear as daylight

der **Sonnenschein** sunlight

der **Sonnentag**, –e solar day (*24 hrs.* 7244)

der **Sonntag**, –e Sunday

sonst otherwise, else, in other respects; formerly; usually

sonstig other

der **Sophist(e)** sophist

die **Sorge**, –n care, worry; trouble; Dame Care

sorgen (*wk*) worry, take care of; **sorgen für** look after, provide for; see to it; attend to (work 3145)

sorgenfrei carefree

sorgenlos without worries

sorglich careful; anxious (10037)

sorgsam careful

sorgvoll anxiety-filled

die **Sorte** sort

das **Souffleurloch** prompter's box

sich **soulagieren** get relief

soviel as much (as), so much, such a great deal; that much

sowie as soon as, as long as, as well as

spähen watch for, look searchingly; behold

die **Spalte** gap

spalten split, crack; **gespaltene Klauen** cloven hoofs

sich **spalten** (*wk*) crack open

der **Span** long and thin piece of wood; haggard fellow

die **Spange** buckle, clasp

Spanien Spain

spanisch Spanish

sparen (*wk*) save; use sparingly (6228, 6739); put away (7187); hold back (7674)

Sparta Sparta (*chief city of the ancient Greek province of Laconica in the Peloponnesus*)

der Spaß fun, joke, amusement; child's play (8305); Spaß machen entertain, amuse; aus dem Spaß lassen leave unmentioned

spaßen joke, play jokes

spat late

spät late

der Spaten, — spade

spazieren take a walk

der Spaziergang promenade

der Spaziergänger, — promenader

ad spectatores aside, to the spectators

der Speer, –e spear

die Speise food, diet, nourishment; fruit (9548)

speisen (*wk*) eat, dine; provide food for (803)

spekulieren speculate

die Spende liberality, bounty

spenden (*wk*) give, give off, scatter liberally, bestow

spendieren (*wk*) provide lavishly

sperren (*wk*) spread apart, open

sperrig wide open

die Spezerei, –en spices and ointment

die Sphäre, –n sphere

der Sphärenlauf course of spheres

der Sphinx, –e Sphinx (*a monster*)

der Spiegel mirror; surface of water (6912)

die Spiegelflut calm surface (*of the sea*)

das Spiegelglas large mirror, pier glass

spiegelglatt smooth as a mirror

spiegeln (*wk*) reflect

sich spiegeln be reflected

das Spiel, –e play, game, sport; show; ein Spiel von ... sein be at the mercy of ...; mir zum Spiel for my amusement

spielen (*wk*) play, act; play the role of (2010)

der Spielmann fiddler

die Spindel spindle

spinnen, a, o spin

sich spinnen, a, o develop into

der Spinnenfuß spider leg

das Spinnewebe, –n spider web

das Spinnrad spinning wheel

spionieren (*wk*) spy around

spitz sharp, pointed; licking (*flame*)

spitzbögig having a pointed arch

spitzbübisch roguish

die Spitze, –n corner, point; head; an die Spitze at the head

spitzen (*wk*) sharpen

der Spitzenkragen lace collar

spitzig sharp, poignant

splittern splinter

sponsieren: sponsieren gehen go out to pick up a girl

der Sponsierer, — lady's man, flirt; suitor (5187)

der Spott mockery, ridicule; jeers; zu Spott machen make ridiculous (8191)

spotten hold up to ridicule, make fun of

die Spottgeburt monstrosity

spöttisch sarcastic, mocking

die **Sprache** language, speech

das **Sprachrohr** megaphone

die **Sprechart** manner of speech

sprechen (i), a, o speak, talk; say (212); converse; see and talk to, visit (1870, 2192); tell

sprengen burst, force open; crack

das **Sprichwort** proverb

sprießen sprout, spring up

springen, a, u jump, leap, dive; skip (2598); dance (4125); rush, run (4302); crack (6624); burst open (6669); spring up, originate (6840); gush (9530)

spritzen (*wk*) splatter, splash; spurt, throw up spray

sprossen (*wk*) spring up, appear; sprout, shoot up (1471)

der **Spruch,** ⁻e formula (1272); saying (2049); phrase

das **Sprüchwort** proverb

sprudeln bubble; gush, flow forth

sprühen fly (*sparks*); spray (5928, 10029); throw up spray (10650); **es sprüht** sparks are flying

der **Sprung** jump, leap

der **Spuk** spook, apparition

spuken haunt; **es spukt** there are ghosts (4161); **es spukt mir durch alle Glieder** I feel in my bones

die **Spur,** –en track, trail, trace; sign (4988); footsteps (4393)

spüren (*wk*) notice, feel; sense (2821); scent, be on the track of (4322); recognize (6459); inquire (7059)

Squenz, Peter Squenz (*character in Shakespeare's "Midsummer Night's Dream," Peter Quince, a carpenter*)

st—t = stinkt (3961)

der **Staat,** –en state

die **Staatsaktion** play dealing with affairs of state

der **Staatsrat** State Council

der **Stab** staff, baton, (supporting) stick (10012)

das **Stäbchen** small staff, judge's wand; **das Stäbchen bricht** the rod breaks (*official signal to proceed with the execution*)

die **Stadt,** ⁻e city

Städteverwüstende people destroying cities

die **Stadtmauer** city wall

die **Stadtplage** public nuisance; **Stadt- und Landesplage** curse of city and of state (5356)

der **Stadtrat** city council

das **Stadttor** city gate

der **Stahl** steel

der **Stamm,** ⁻e tree trunk; tribe (9515); kin (11812)

der **Stammbaum** family tree

das **Stammbuch** memory book, autograph book

stammverwandt akin, distantly related

stampfen stamp one's foot

der **Stand** position, stand

die **Standarte,** –n standard, banner

standhalten (ä) hold out, stand firm

die **Standsgebühr: nach Standsgebühr** in accordance with the social position of the person or persons involved stark strong, vigorous; powerful; heavily (10339)

die Stärke strength

stärken (wk) strengthen

sich stärken be intensified

starr stiff; staring, fixed (4192); rigid (7021); extending unyieldingly (7952); rugged (10370)

starren become numb, become stiff; be dried up (6574); be packed in (8987); be packed full of (10111); stand up rigidly (9542)

starrsinnig stubborn

die Statt place, stead

statt instead of

die Stätte place

stattfinden take place

das Statut statute

der Staub dust

staubend dust-raising

staubig dusty

stauchen recoil, back up suddenly

die Staude, –n shrub, bush

staunen marvel, be astonished, be amazed

stechen (i), a, o sting, bite; prick, stab (7888)

stecken (wk) stick, put (3587); be, find oneself; be hidden (1293); dir steckt der Doktor im Leib you have the doctor in you; Grenzen stecken draw boundaries (11004)

sich stecken hide (3205)

der Steg narrow wooden bridge

stehen, a (stände/stünde), a stand, stop; be becoming; stand up against (4907); der Gaumen steht euch darnach you have a taste for (543); geschrieben steht it is written (1224); es sollte stehen it should read (1233); was steht dir zu Diensten? what can I do for you? zu Diensten stehen be handy; es steht uns frei we are free to choose; die Uhr steht the clock has stopped; es steht um... things are with regard to...; in Gunst stehen be highly favored; es steht in einem andern Buch that's in another book, that's a different matter (2349); was gehen und stehen mag what is possible (2639); wie steht es mit...? how about...? (3006); es steht schief darum something is wrong with it; wo steht dein Kopf? where is your reason? (3784); obenan stehen rank high (4079); stehen lassen pay no attention to (4189); stehen bleiben stop (5560, 8079); es steht gut um things are flourishing (5650); Wort stehen answer charges, account for (6180); wie steht's? how are things? (6879); Rede stehen answer (7195); jemandem stehen stop and face someone (7201, 8156); voll stehen be crowded (10787)

stehlen (ie), a, o steal

steif stiff

steigen, ie, ie rise; climb; alight (5682)

steigern increase

sich steigern increase, evolve

steil steep, precipitous

der **Stein, –e** stone, rock

das **Steingeklipp** rocky cliffs

das **Steingerüst** stone structure

der **Steiß** buttocks, behind

die **Stelle, –n** spot, place; court (10946); **auf der Stelle** instantly, on the spot (1645); **von der Stelle** from here, from this spot (3649); **an . . . Stelle** in (his) place (4737, 6526); **zur Stelle bringen** produce (6208); **zur Stelle** at the appointed spot (7462)

stellen (wk) lay; put, place; set up (10527); **ein Bein stellen** trip (6792)

sich stellen (wk) place oneself; act (as if); **sich in die Reihe stellen** join the ranks (10508)

die **Stellung** position

sich stemmen brace oneself

das **Stemmen** resistance

der **Stempel** stamp, trade-mark

stempeln (wk) stamp

das **Sterbebett** deathbed

die **Sterbeklage, –n** death wail

sterben, (i), a, o die; **um Lebens oder Sterbens willen** in case something happens to you

sterblich mortal

der **Stern, –e** star

die **Sternblume** star flower, aster

das **Sternelein, —** little star

der **Sternenkranz** starry wreath, halo of stars

die **Sternenstunde** sidereal hour; astrological aspect

sterngegönnt granted by the stars

der **Sternschein** sparkling radiance

die **Sternschnuppe** shooting star

stet constant, persistent

stets always, ever; constantly

die **Steuer** tax

der **Stich** sting, prick; **im Stiche lassen** abandon, leave in the lurch (4606); **Stich halten** hold out, stand up (11376)

die **Stichelrede, –n** taunting

der **Stiefel, –n** boot; **spanische Stiefel** *instrument of torture used by the Spanish Inquisition*

der **Stiel, –e** stem

der **Stier** bull, ox

stiften bring about, cause, excite; give, donate (10996)

still still, quiet, calm, peaceful; silent, tranquil; secret (9446); **Still! hush!;** **im stillen** quietly, secretly; **im allerstillsten Stillen** in deepest secrecy

stillbewußt quietly conscious

die **Stille** peace

stillen (wk) appease, satisfy; calm, quench

stillschweigen be silent

das **Stillschweigen** silence

stillstehen stop

die **Stimme, –n** voice

stimmen (wk) tune

stimmig in accord

die **Stimmung** frame of mind; (elevated) mood

stinken stink

die **Stirn(e), –n** forehead, brow

der **Stock** cane; vine (2319); sticks (3960)

stocken stop short, get stuck, congeal (1633, 6578); be arrested (8233); **das Wort stockt** words won't come

der **Stoff, –e** matter, material

stolpern (wk) stumble

der **Stolz** pride
stolz proud, haughty; imposing, impressive; lofty
stopfen (*wk*) stuff; gag, silence
die **Stoppel** stubble
stören (*wk*) disturb; stir, irritate
die **Störung** disturbance
der **Stoß**, ⁻e push, bump
stoßen (ö), ie, o push, knock (against)
strack straight
stracks straight, straightway
die **Strafe** punishment
strafen punish
straff stretched, tense
sträflich severe
der **Strahl**, –en beam, ray; (= **Bannstrahl**) excommunication (10986)
der **Strahlblitz** flash of lightning
strahlen be radiant
der **Strahlenblick** radiant glance
strahlenreich radiant
der **Strand** shore, beach; sands (*shallow place* 7378)
die **Strandeszunge** narrow sandy peninsula
der **Strang** thread, skein of thread
die **Straße**, –n road, path, street
sträubig-hoch rearing up in rebellion
der **Strauch**, ⁻e bush
der **Strauß** bouquet (3179)
der **Strauß** struggle (4623, 6363)
streben (*wk*) strive, aim at, aspire; push (4116); tend
das **Streben** striving, effort, ambition, tendency
strebsam ambitious
die **Strebsamkeit** ambition
die **Strecke** extent, stretch

strecken (*wk*) stretch (out); lay low (11365)
sich **strecken** (*wk*) stretch out; **sich aufs Lager strecken** lie down
der **Streich**, –e blow, stroke; irresponsible act (11372); prank (6235)
streicheln (*wk*) stroke
streichen move about (unsuccessfully 2032); stroke (3628); steal (3657); run in veins (5899); move past (6244); draw (6349)
sich **streichen** steal
der **Streifen**, — streak, stripe
streifen roam
streifig in streaks
der **Streit**, –e quarrel; battle, struggle; strife
streiten argue; contend; fight
sich **streiten um** quarrel about, fight for
streitig: den Rang streitig machen compete with for
die **Streitkraft** military force
streng stern, austere; strict; stringent, severe
die **Strenge** sternness, severity
strengen wrap tightly
streuen (*wk*) strew, scatter
der **Strich** stroke, streak
stricken knit
das **Stroh** straw
der **Strohmann** scarecrow, dummy
der **Strom**, ⁻e stream, current; flood, crowd
strömen stream; flock; flow; rush (3955)
die **Stromespappel**, –n poplar by a river

der **Strudel** whirlpool, whirling crowd

die **Strudelei,** **-en** impetuous activity

strudeln whirl; **strudelnd** on its swirling eddies (7483)

das **Strumpfband** garter

die **Stube** small room

das **Stück,** **-e** play, piece, show; item (6580); **in allen Stücken** about everything, in every way (3113)

das **Stückchen** little piece, part

der **Student,** **-en** student

studieren (*wk*) study

das **Studierzimmer** study

das **Studium** study; **Studien** studies

die **Stufe,** **-n** step; **Stufe für Stufe** step after step, one on each step (*stairs* 9178)

stufenweis step by step, in tiers

der **Stuhl,** **-e** chair; confessional (2623)

stumm silent, mute

stümmeln (*wk*) (= **verstümmeln**) mutilate

stumm-freundlich in friendly silence

stumpf blunt, dull, without a point (10707); flat

der **Stumpfsinn** idiocy, stupidity

das **Stündchen** good little while, cozy hour

die **Stunde,** **-n** hour; class (1956)

der **Sturm,** **-e** storm

stürmen (*wk*) storm, assault

sturmerregt storm-tossed

die **Sturmgewalt** fury of the storm

stürmisch stormy

der **Sturz,** **-e** cataract; plunge; crash

stürzen (*wk*) fall, rush, crash down; rush away; dump; **ins Verderben stürzen** ruin

sich **stürzen** (*wk*) rush down, hurl oneself

stutzen stop short, be taken aback

stützen support

sich **stützen** rely (on)

stygisch Stygian (*pertaining to the Styx, the nether world*)

Stymphaliden Stymphalides (*monstrous birds, killed by Hercules*)

Subsidien subsidies

suchen (*wk*) seek, look for; try

die **Sucht** mania, lunacy

der **Sud** seething broth

die **Sudelköcherei** slovenly cooking, witches' brewing

der **Süden** south

südöstlich southeast

der **Sultan** sultan

summen (*wk*) hum, buzz

das **Summen** droning sound

der **Sumpf,** **-e** swamp

die **Sünde,** **-n** sin

der **Sünder,** — sinner, transgressor

das **Sünderhemdchen** sinner's shirt (*worn to do penance*)

die **Sünderin,** **-nen** sinner

sündig sinful, iniquitous

der **Supernaturalist** supernaturalist

süß sweet, charming, lovely

der **Sylphe** sylph

symmetrisch symmetrical

das **Symptom,** **-e** symptom

das **System** system
die **Szene,** –n scene

T

der **Tadel** censure, blame
tadeln (*wk*) blame, reprimand
die **Tafel** table; **bei Tafel** at table
der **Tag,** –e day, daylight; **der jüngste Tag** the day of final judgment, doomsday
tagen dawn; **es tagt** day is breaking
der **Tagesblick** light of day
das **Tageslicht** light of day
Tageslüfte (*pl*) day-lit air
die **Tageswelt** world of every-day, world of fact
die **Tageszeit** daytime
das **Tagewerk,** –e: **alle sechs Tagewerk'** "all creation" (3287)
täglich daily, every day
der **Tagslauf** daily course
der **Takt** measure, beat, regular motion
das **Tal,** ⸚er valley, dale
der **Taler,** — thaler (*a coin*)
das **Talent,** –e talent
das **Talgebirg** massif (*mountain range distinguished by deeply-cut valleys*)
der **Tand** trifle, knickknack
tändeln dally
die **Tanne,** –n fir, pine
der **Tanz,** ⸚e dance
tänzeln walk with mincing steps; **tänzelnd gehen** skip along with dancing steps (3143)
tanzen (*wk*) dance
der **Tänzer,** — dancer

der **Tanzmeister** dancing master
der **Tanzplatz** dancing place
die **Tapete,** –n tapestry
tapfer valiant, brave; strong, hearty
die **Tapferkeit** bravery
tappen grope about
täppisch clumsy, awkward
tara: a! tara lara da! [*warming-up exercise for the voice*] do : mi : sol : do
die **Tasche,** –n pocket
die **Taschenspielersache,** –n tricks of legerdemain, magi-cian's tricks
die **Tasse** cup
tasten feel one's way, touch (4918); **tastend** uncertain, groping (4067)
die **Tat,** –en deed, action, feat
der **Tatensturm** tumult of ac-tivity
tätig active
tätig-frei free and active
die **Tätigkeit,** '–en activity, action
tätig-klein active little, active and little
die **Tatze,** –n claw
der **Tau** dew
taub deaf
die **Taube,** –n dove
die **Taubenpost** carrier-pigeon mail service
tauchen dip
taugen (*wk*) be good for, be suited
der **Taumel** frenzy
taumeln stagger, reel
taumlich giddy
der **Tausch** barter, trade
tauschen exchange, swap

täuschen (*wk*) deceive

tausend thousand

tausendblumig of a thousand flowers

Tausend Eine (Nacht) Thousand and One (Nights)

tausendfach thousandfold, in a thousand ways

tausendfältig thousandfold, in a thousand ways

tausendfärbig in many shades

der **Tausendkünstler**, — versatile artisan

tausendmal a thousand times

tausendstimmig with a thousand voices

der **Taygetos** Taygetos (*mountain range in Peloponnesus*)

Tegel Tegel (*town north of Berlin*)

der **Teich** pond

der **Teig** dough

der **Teil**, –e (*also* **das Teil** 2967, 2978, 6272, 6659) part, share; attribute; **an meinem Teil** on my own behalf

der **Teilbesitz** partial possession

teilen (*wk*) share, divide

sich **teilen** separate, dissolve

teilhaftig sharing

teilnehmen (i), a, o participate

Telchinen Telchines (*sea deities, skillful brassworkers*)

der **Teller**, — plate

der **Tellerlecker** valiant trencherman

der **Tempel**, — temple

der **Tempelbau** temple

das **Tempelhaus** sacred lodge

die **Tempelstadt** sacred city

der **Teppich**, –e rug; cover

(2705); carpet, tapestry (6373)

das **Terrain** terrain

die **Terrasse**, –n terrace

das **Testament** Testament

teuer dear; **die Teuren** highly esteemed gentlemen (10957)

der **Teufel**, — devil, Devil, Satan

das **Teufelchen** little devil

die **Teufelsbrücke** Devil's Bridge

die **Teufelsfaust** devil's claw

das **Teufelsfest**, –e festivity of the devil

das **Teufelsliebchen**, — devil's sweetheart

das **Teufels-Korn** *see* **Teufels-schrot**

das **Teufelspack** confounded crowd

das **Teufelsschrot: von altem Teufelsschrot und Korne** having the old sterling qualities of the devil

der **Teufelsstein** Devil's Rock

der **Teufelstanz**, ⸚e dance of the devil

der **Teufelsteil**, –e part (member) of the devil

teuflisch devilish

der **Thalamos** bedchamber

Thales Thales (*Greek philosopher*)

das **Theater** theater; show; scene; stage

der **Theaterdichter** playwright

der **Theatermeister** stage manager

Theben Thebes (*city in central Greece*)

die **Theologie** theology

Theophrast Theophrastus (*ancient botanist, pupil of Aristotle*) die **Theorbe,** –n lutelike instrument

die **Theorie** theory

Theseus Theseus (*king of Athens*)

thessalisch Thessalian (*from Thessaly in northern Greece*)

Thetis Thetis (*a Nereid, mother of Achilles*)

der **Thron,** –e throne

thronen sit enthroned; rule; reign; dwell (8207)

Thule (Ultima) Thule (*the northernmost part of the habitable world, a very distant and very mysterious land*)

die **Thyrsusstange** thyrsus (*staff decorated with ivy and vines*)

tief deep; heavy (*sleep*); remote, hidden (9975); low (11866); **im tiefsten Grunde** utterly, completely (9374)

tiefauflauernd lurking in the depth

tiefbewegt deeply moved

die **Tiefe,** –n depth; lower region (4689)

tiefersteigen descend

tiefsinnig profound

tiefstens most humbly

tiefverrucht most ungodly, most infamous

das **Tier,** –e animal, beast

die **Tierbrut: die Tier- und Menschenbrut** spawn of beast and man

das **Tierchen** little animal

das **Tiergerippe** animal skeleton

die **Tierheit** bestiality

tierisch beastly

tinke! tinke! clink clink! **ein Tinke, Tinke!** a clinking of glasses (5292)

die **Tinte** ink

Tiresias Tiresias (*ancient seer*)

der **Tisch** table

der **Tischrand** edge of the table

Tisiphone Tisiphone (*one of the Furies*)

der **Titan,** –en Titan

Titania Titania (*queen of the fairies*)

der **Titel** title

toasten toast, drink to a person's health

der **Toback** tobacco

toben (*wk*) rave, rage; romp (5233)

das **Toben** uproar

die **Tochter,** – daughter

der **Tod** death

die **Todesnot** death agony

der **Todesschlaf** sleep of death

tödlich deadly, fatal

tödlich-fein deadly and delicate

der **Tokayer** Tokay wine

toll mad, absurd, wild; **das ist zu toll** that is too much; **Tolles** freakish trick

die **Tollheit** folly

der **Ton** clay (2414, 5781)

der **Ton,** –e sound, tone, strain, tune

tönen (*wk*) make a musical sound, ring; emit sounds (243); resound (4667)

der **Topf,** –e pot

topp! agreed! it's a bargain

das **Tor,** –e gate

der **Tor,** –en fool

die **Torheit** folly

töricht foolish

törig foolish

tosen roar

das **Tosen** uproar

tot dead

der **Tote** dead person

töten (*wk*) kill

das **Totenbein** skeleton

die **Totenglocke** knell, funeral bell

der **Totenkopf**, ⸚e skull

das **Totenreich** realm of the dead

der **Totenschein** death certificate

der **Totentanz**, ⸚e Dance of Death

totkämpfen (*wk*) slay in (single) combat

der **Totschlag** slaughter; manslaughter (10268)

totschlagen (ä) slay, put to death

der **Trab** trot

der **Trabant**, –en follower, bodyguard

trachten have one's eyes fixed on, strive to penetrate

trächtig pregnant, heavy, full

der **Tragaltar** portable altar

die **Tragebutte**, –n portable butt or trough

tragen (ä), u, a bear, carry, wear

der **Träger**, — porter

das **Tragewerk** conveyance

die **Tragödie** tragedy

das **Trallern** warbling

die **Träne**, –n tear

die **Tränenlust** desire to weep

der **Trank** drink, potion

tränken give to drink, nurse

transpirieren perspire

die **Traube**, –n grape

trauen (*wk*) trust, have confidence in (4653); give in marriage (8856)

der **Trauergesang** dirge

die **Trauerhöhle** desolate den

trauern mourn

das **Trauerspiel** tragedy

traulich close; intimately; confidently (4705, 12023)

der **Traum**, ⸚e dream

das **Traumbild** apparition

träumen (*wk*) dream; **sich träumen lassen** dream, imagine

die **Träumerei**, –en revery

das **Traumgespinst** web of dreams

die **Traumgestalt**, –en apparition, vision

die **Traumsphäre** sphere of visions

traun! truly!

traurig sad, dreary

traut dear, beloved; intimate

treffen (i), a, o hit; strike; meet; find; hit upon; catch (3206); touch (4678); **es trifft sich** it so happens; **(ihn) treffe keine Schmach** let no disgrace befall (him) (9257); **Erstaunen trifft mich** I am seized with astonishment (9366)

trefflich excellent, fine, exquisite, wonderful; very well

treiben, ie, ie drive, urge; do; carry on (159); **sein Wesen treiben** carry on

trennen (*wk*) separate, sever

sich **trennen** (*wk*) separate

die **Treppe** stair

treten (i), a, e enter, step; **in die Ehe treten** enter into matrimony; **ins Leben treten** come to life; **mit Füßen**

treten kick; **zur Hand treten** assist

treu faithful, true, honest, loyal

die **Treue** fidelity, faithfulness, loyalty

treu-gemein faithful common

treulich truly, conscientiously, faithfully

der **Tribut** tribute

der **Trident** trident

der **Trieb, –e** urge, desire; impulse; bent (11870)

triefen drip

die **Triglyphe** triglyphe (*part of the frieze in a Doric temple*)

trinken, a, u drink; drink in (6511)

der **Trinker** drinker

trippeln walk in short steps, trip

der **Triton, –en** Triton (*sea god*)

der **Tritt, –e** step; **Schritt und Tritt** every movement; **Tritt und Schritt** every step

der **Triumph** triumph

triumphieren triumph

trocken dry; dried up (10720)

trocknen (*wk*) wipe dry

der **Trödel** junk

die **Trödelhexe** huckster witch

der **Trog** trough

troglodytisch troglodytic (*in the fashion of cave dwellers*)

Troja Troy

die **Trojanerin, –nen** Trojan woman

die **Trommel, –n** drum

trommeten sound the trumpet; **es trommetet** the trumpets sound

die **Trompete, –n** trumpet

der **Tropf, ⸚e** wretch, dolt, numskull

das **Tröpfchen** little drop

der **Tropfen, —** drop

das **Tropfenei** oval pearl

das **Tröpflein** little drop

der **Trost** consolation

trösten (*wk*) console

tröstlich cheerful, comforting

trotz in spite of

trotzen (*wk*) bid defiance

trüb dim, indistinct; gloomy, clouded (4094); muddy (6721); **im Trüben fischen** fish in troubled waters

sich **trüben** (*wk*) grow dim or turbid; **getrübt** troubled, perturbed

die **Trübsal** misery

trübselig melancholy

der **Trübsinn** low spirits

der **Trug** deception, delusion; illusion, sham

trügen deceive

das **Truggesicht, –er** mask, deceitful face

Trümmer ruins, remains

der **Trunk** drink, draught

trunken intoxicated, inebriated; elated

der **Trunkne** intoxicated person

der **Trutz** defiant defense; **zum Trutz** in defiance of

trutzen bid defiance

das **Tuch, ⸚er** cloth

tüchtig strong, robust; extensive (4102); excellent, efficient, vigorous, active (11578)

das **Tüchtighafte** practical efficiency; **am greiflich Tüchtighaften** in the matter of substantiality

die **Tücke** malice, spite

tückisch malicious, mischievous

die **Tugend** virtue
tugendlich virtuous
tugendreich virtuous
der **Tumult, -e** tumult, disturbance
tun, a, a do, make, perform, effect, act; **tät(en)** did (*with an infinitive, as an auxiliary of a past tense*); **es ist um ... getan** it's all up with ... (10722)
das **Tun** activity, action
das **Tüpfchen** dot
der **Tupfen, —** spot, freckle
tupfen: getupft speckled
die **Tür(e)** door
der **Turban** turban
die **Türbank** bench in front of the house door
das **Türchen** small door
der **Türflügel, —** wing of a folding door
die **Türkei** Turkey
türkisch Turkish
der **Turm, ⸗e** tower
turmbeladen laden with a tower
sich **türmen** rise to towering heights
der **Türmer** watchman on a tower
der **Turmwächter** watchman on a tower
der **Turmwärter** watchman on a tower
der **Türner** keeper, warden
das **Turnier** tournament
der **Türpfosten, —** doorpost
tutti all
Tyndareos Tyndareos (*Greek king, husband of Helen's mother*)
die **Tyrannei** tyranny

die **Tyrannenart** way (behavior) of tyrants

U

das **Übel, —** evil, calamity
übel evil, bad; **übel dran sein** be badly off; **übel nehmen** take amiss, blame; **übel gehen** (things) go badly; **Übel's** anything bad
übelfertig evil-minded
übelnehmen (i) take amiss, blame
üben (*wk*) practice, exercise; handle (6650); **heilsam und übende** bringing salvation (760)
über over, above, about; **diese Zeit über** all this time
überall everywhere, in all places
überallmächtig omnipotent
überbleicht overcast with ashy paleness
sich **überbreiten** spread out profusely
sich **überbrüten** engender prolifically
überdringen, a, o overpower, descend upon
der **Überdruß** weariness; more than enough
überdrüssig bored
sich **übereilen** (*wk*) be overhasty
übereinander one over another, one on top of the other
sich **überessen (i), a, übergessen** overeat, gorge oneself
überfallen (ä) overtake, seize
überfliegen transcend, soar beyond
überfließen, o, o overflow

überflüssig flowing over

überfüllen (*wk*) fill beyond capacity; **überfüllt** crowded

übergeben (i), a, e hand over

sich übergeben (i), a, e surrender

übergehen change (10782); **die Augen gingen ihm über** his eyes filled to overflowing (with tears)

überglänzen (*wk*) outshine, eclipse

der Überhang cornice, overhang

überhaupt altogether

überirdisch supernatural, spiritual, heavenly

überkleistern paste over

überladen overloaded

überlassen (ä), ie, a cede; leave to

überlästig overweighted

überlaufen (äu), ie, au come over; run over, spill over

überlaufen (äu) (*insep*): **mich überläuft's** a cold shudder comes over me

überleben (*wk*) outlast

überlebendig over-lively

überlegen consider, reflect about

überlustig overly merry

übermächtig immense, most powerful

übermannen overwhelm

das Übermaß profusion; excess

der Übermensch superman

übermorgen day after tomorrow

der Übermut exuberance of spirit; pride; excessive daring (9895); arrogance (10202)

übermütig bold, arrogant

übern = **über den**

übernehmen (i), a, o take upon oneself; take possession of (6471)

sich überneigen bend over

überquer crosswise, diagonally (past)

überraschen (*wk*) surprise

die Überraschung surprise

die Überredung persuasion

überreichen present

übers = **über das**

überschauen survey

sich überschlagen (ä), u, a topple over, turn a somersault

überschnappen snap, crack; break down

überschreiten step across

überschweifen overlap

die Überschwemmung flood

überschwenglich superabundant, profuse

übersehen (ie), a, e look over, survey

übersetzen translate

übersinnlich metaphysical, "platonic"

übersittlich too modest

überspähen scan searchingly

überspringen, a, u leap over, skip

überstechen (i), a, o excel, eclipse; blind (9521)

überstehen, a, a endure, go through, survive

übersteigen, ie, ie surmount; excel; (*intrans*) overflow (3308)

überströmen flood, spread flood-like

übertäuben deafen

überteuflisch supersatanic

überthronen have sovereignty over

übertischt lavish, overly heavy (*meal*)

übertragen (ä), u, a entrust; translate (1223); convey (8013)

übertreiben, ie, ie overdo, exaggerate

übertrümmert covered with debris

über-überwallen billow flowingly above

übervoll too full, overflowing

überwachsen (ä) grow greater than

überwalten prevail, rule

überwiegen prevail (7370); outweigh (8131)

überwinden, a, u conquer

überzählig supernumerary, having too many

überzeugen convince

die Überzeugung conviction

überziehen flow across

übrig over, left over; **das übrige** the rest; **alle übrigen** all others; **im übrigen** as for the rest

übrigbleiben, ie, ie remain, be left over

das Ufer, — bank, shore

ufernetzend lapping the shore

der Uferzug sweep of the shore line

die Uhr clock

uhu! *call of the owl*

Ulyß Ulysses (*Odysseus, Greek hero*)

um around, about, at, for; in order; **um und um** all around, round and about, everywhere, on all sides

umändern (*wk*) change

umarmen embrace

sich umarten pass through metamorphosis, change in form; transform

umbaumt surrounded by trees

umbestellt rearranged

umbringen, a, a (*wk, irreg*) kill

umbuscht surrounded by bushes

umdrängen crowd around

sich umdunkeln (*wk*) grow dark, be veiled in dark clouds

der Umfang extent

umfangen (ä), i, a embrace; surround; hold captive (7444)

umfassen embrace, encircle

umflechten (i) encompass, weave a net about

umfreit surrounded by suitors

umfriedet enclosed, fenced in

umführen lead around (*in a procession*)

der Umgang round, procession

umgarnen (*wk*) ensnare

umgaukeln surround with illusions

umgeben (i), a, e surround

die Umgebung surroundings

umgehen have traffic with; handle (2453)

die Umgestaltung transformation

der Umhang curtain

umher all around, on all sides

umherblicken look around

sich umherdrehen revolve

umherklingen ring out

sich umherlagern take up position(s) round about

umherliegen lie around

sich umhersammeln gather around

umherschauen look around

umherschnippen go about snapping one's fingers
umherschweifen float about at random
umhersehen look around
umhersenden, a, a (*wk, irreg*) distribute
umherspazieren (*wk*) stroll around
umherspüren sniff around
umherstehen stand around
umhertreiben, ie, ie force to move around
umherziehen move about
umhüllen (*wk*) envelop
sich **umhüllen** (*wk*) wrap oneself, cover oneself
umkehren (*wk*) turn around
sich **umkleiden** change one's clothes
umkreisen circle around
umlagert besieged
umlaubt surrounded by foliage
umnebeln surround with a haze
umrascheln (= herumrascheln) rustle about
umrauschen go rustling around
umringen, a, u surround, envelop
umrinnen, a, o surround, envelop
ums = um das
umschauen (*wk*) look around
sich **umschauen** turn around and look
umschlagen (ä), **u, a** wrap around; turn the pages of a book (460)
umschließen, o, o enclose; gather closely around (5872)
umschlingen engulf
umschranzen fawn around

umschreiben limit, restrict
umschuppt scale-covered
umschwärmen swarm around
umschweben (*wk*) hover around, surround, float about; **umschwebt von Bildern** surrounded by hovering images (6289)
umschweifen circle, roam about
sich **umsehen** (ie) look around
umsonst in vain; free, for nothing (3677)
umspannen encompass
umspringen jump around in circles
umstecken surround (*objects stuck away*)
umstellen (*wk*) surround (*objects standing*)
umstricken (*wk*) ensnare
umstürmen (*wk*) assail from all sides
umsummen buzz around
umtoben surround uproariously
umtun, a, a put on (10410)
sich **umtun, a, a** make inquiries (1874)
umtürmt surrounded by towers
umwallen surge about
umwandeln (*wk*) transform
umwehen (*wk*) flood about (689); **umweht** gently fanned (*by breezes* 8362)
umwenden reverse; turn into
umwerben (i), **a, o** court, woo
umwimmeln (*wk*) surround in swarms
umwinden, a, u entwine (741); wrap around, surround
umwittern (*wk*) envelop
umwölkt surrounded by clouds
umziehen, o, o surround; circle

around (10631); hem in (11543)
umzieren frame decoratively
umzingeln encircle
umzirken (*wk*) surround
Una Poenitentium one of the penitents
unabhängig independent
unanständig unbecoming, immodest; indecent (2513)
unaufhaltsam irresistible
unausgesprochen ineffable
unaussprechlich inexpressible
unausweichlich unavoidable
unbändig unmanageable
unbarmherzig merciless
unbedeutend without significance
die Unbedeutenheit insignificance
unbedingt unconditional, absolute, unlimited
unbefriedigt unsatisfied
unbegreiflich incomprehensible, inconceivable
unbegrenzt unlimited
unbehaust homeless
unbehülflich clumsy
unbekannt unknown
der Unbekannte stranger
unbelohnt unrewarded
unbemerkt unnoticed
unbequem troublesome; uncomfortable
unberührbar untouchable
unberührt untouched
unbeschreiblich indescribable, ineffable
unbesiegt unconquered
unbesonnen heedless
unbesorgt unworried, carefree
unbestimmt indistinct

unbestritten uncontested
unbetreten unexplored
unbeweglich motionless
unbewußt not knowing what one says or does
unbezwinglich invincible
und and; even though (9418)
der Undank ingratitude
die Undene Undine (*a water sprite*)
die Undine, –n Undine (*a water sprite*)
undurchdrungen inscrutable
unendlich infinite, unending, endless
die Unendlichkeit infinity, immenseness
das Unerbetene that which has never been gained by entreaty
unerfahren inexperienced
unerforschlich inscrutable
unerforscht unexplored
unerfreulich disagreeable
unergötzlich ungratifying
unerhört outrageous; unheard of; what has never been heard (4674)
unerklärt inexplicable
unerlaubt not permissible, scandalous
unermeßlich immeasurable
unermüdet unwearied
unerobert unconquered
unerquicklich unedifying, annoying
unerreichlich unattainable
die Unersättlichkeit insatiability
unerschlossen unrevealed
unerschöpft inexhaustible
unerschüttert unshaken
unersteiglich inaccessible; impregnable

unerträglich unbearable
unerwartet unexpected, sudden
der Unfall accident
der Unflat filth
unfruchtbar unproductive, barren
die Unfruchtbarkeit unproductiveness, barrenness
der Unfug disturbance
ungebändigt untamed, unbroken, unsubdued
ungebunden unrestrained
die Ungeduld impatience
ungeduldig impatient; rash (11341)
ungefähr about; von ungefähr by accident
das Ungeheuer, — monster
ungeheuer immense, awful, enormous; tremendous (7570); dreadful (10441)
das Ungeheure vastness, the infinite; ins Ungeheure to tremendous proportions
ungekannt unknown
ungekränkt untouched, uninjured
ungeleitet unescorted, by oneself
ungemessen unbounded, unmeasured
ungemischt unmixed; unvaried (2357)
ungemünzt uncoined
ungenügsam insatiable; not easily satisfied, hard to please
ungenutzt unused
ungenützt not taken advantage of
ungerecht unjust
ungern reluctantly
ungesäumt without delay, forthwith

das Ungeschick disaster
ungeschickt awkward
ungeschlacht uncouth
ungescholten without reproof
ungesehen unseen
das Ungesetz lawlessness
die Ungestalt, -en monster, misshapen creature
ungestalt misshapen
ungestört untroubled, undisturbed
ungestraft unpunished
das Ungestüm impetuousness, violence
ungestüm impetuous
ungetrennt unbroken
ungetröstet uncomforted
das Ungetüm monster
ungewiß uncertain, dim
das Ungewisse uncertainty
das Ungewitter violent storm
ungezogen naughty, illmannered
ungleich unequal
das Unglück bad luck, misfortune
unglücklich unhappy
die Unglücksbotschaft bad news, evil tidings
unglückselig miserable, unfortunate
der Unglücksmann man of ill fortune
ungreifbar intangible
unharmonisch unharmonious, discordant
das Unheil misfortune, mischief
unheilig impious
unheimlich spooky, sinister
unhöflich impolite, rude
unhold ungracious
unison (*singing*) in unison

unleidlich intolerable

unmäßig excessive

der Unmensch brute, monster

unmittelbar directly

unmöglich impossible

unmündig under age, infantile

unnütz useless, unprofitable

das Unrecht wrong; unrecht haben be wrong

unruhig restless

unruhvoll restless

unsäglich unspeakable, indescribable

unschätzbar invaluable

die Unschuld innocence

unschuldig innocent

unselig unfortunate, fatal; cursed (11487); Unseliges seeds of misery (5379)

unser our, ours; of us

unsereins we, such people as we, people of our sort

unsicher uncertain, wavering; insecure (9266)

unsichtbar invisible

der Unsinn nonsense

unsinnig foolish

unsterblich immortal; die Unsterblichen the gods; das Unsterbliche the immortal part, soul

die Unsterblichkeit immortality

die Untätigkeits-Entschuldigung apology for being inactive

unteilbar indivisible

unten below; downstairs; down

untenhin down below

unter under, below; among

der Unterbacken, — lower jaw-bone

unterbrechen (i), a, o interrupt; unterbrochen irregular (9532)

untere low, deep (4987); lower (7249)

das Untere lower sphere (*material world*); das Unterste bottommost (10090)

sich unterfangen (ä), i, a venture

der Untergang ruin, destruction; death (6242)

untergehen perish; set (*sun*)

untergraben undermine

unterhalten (ä), ie, a entertain

die Unterhaltung maintenance

der Unterirdische, –n inhabitant of the nether world

das Unterkommen shelter, accommodation

unterm = unter dem

untermengt intermingled

untern = unter den

unternehmen (i), a, o undertake

die Unternehmung enterprise

das Unterpfand pledge, guarantee

der Unterricht explanation

unters = unter das

unterscheiden distinguish

der Unterschied, –e difference

unterschreiben, ie, ie sign

unterschworen festered internally

sich unterstehen dare, presume

untertan subject

untertänig submissive

unterweil now and again; meanwhile

unterweisen instruct

die Unterwelt nether world

sich unterwinden venture, make bold to

unterzeichnen sign

das Untier monster

ununterbrochen uninterrupted, ceaseless

unveraltet ageless

unverändert unchanged

unverdrossen cheerful; untiring, indefatigable

unvergleichlich matchless, unique (8202)

unverletzt safe and sound

unverloren preserved

unvermeidlich unavoidable

unvermerkt imperceptible

unvernünftig unreasonable

unverschämt impudent

unversehrt untouched

unversöhnlich irreconcilable

der **Unverstand** lack of common sense

unverständig foolish, silly

unverzüglich promptly, instantly

unvollkommen incomplete; gibbous, past full (*moon*)

unvorbereitet unprepared

unvorgesehen caught unawares

unvorsichtig careless

unweigerlich unquestioned

unwiderstehbar irresistible

unwiderstehlich irresistible

unwiederbringlich irreparable

unwillig annoyed

unwillkommen unwelcome

unwissend ignorant

die **Unzahl** immense amount

unzählig innumerable, incalculable

unzufrieden discontented

unzugänglich inaccessible

unzulänglich inadequate, insufficient, imperfect

üppig exuberant

uralt very old, primeval, ancient

der **Urbeginn** first beginning

das **Urgebirg** primeval mountains

Urian: Herr Urian Mr. What d'ye call him; Satan

urkräftig irresistibly powerful, strong and spontaneous

die **Urmenschenkraft** might of primitive man

der **Urquell** prime source, fountainhead

der **Ursprung** origin

ursprünglich original

der **Ur-Urahn, –en** ancient ancestor

die **Ur-Urälteste** extremely old woman

die **Ur-Urenkelin** great-great-granddaughter

der **Urväter-Hausrat** ancestral rubbish

urväterlich ancestral

urverworfen condemned from the beginning

V

Valentin Valentine (*brother of Gretchen*)

der **Vampir** vampire (*bloodsucking demon*)

der **Vampiren-Zahn, ⸚e** tooth of a vampire

der **Vasall, –en** vassal

der **Vater, ⸚** father; ancestor; Father

die **Väterburg** ancestral castle

das **Väterchen** daddy

die **Vaterfreudenstunde** hour of paternal joy

das **Vaterhaus** house of the father

die **Vaterkraft** paternal strength, maturity

das **Vaterland** fatherland

vaterländisch native, belonging to one's fatherland

väterlich fatherly

der **Vätersaal** ancestral hall

der **Väterthron** grandfather's chair

der **Vaterwille** will of the father

das **Vehikel** vehicle (*of faith*); medium

venedisch Venetian, from Venice

das **Venerabile** Holy Host

Venus Venus (*Aphrodite, goddess of beauty and love*); planet Venus

verachten (*wk*) despise

verächtlich contemptible

die **Verachtung** contempt

veränderlich changeable

verändern change

verauktionieren (*wk*) auction off

verbergen (i), a, o hide, conceal; **verborgen** secret

sich **verbergen** hide

verbessern improve

die **Verbeugung** bow, reverence

verbieten, o, o forbid

verbinden, a, u combine (1798, 10431); oblige (4054); unite (4234, 5369, 9705)

sich **verbinden, a, u** obligate oneself (1656, 1672); flirt with (1683); join in holy wedlock (8879); attach oneself to, ally oneself with

die **Verbindung, –en** connection

verbitten deprecate; **den Namen verbitt' ich mir** I won't tolerate that name

verbleiben, ie, ie remain; be left

verblenden blind

verborgen rent out (9961)

verborgen-golden hidden . . . of gold

das **Verbot** prohibition, order not to do so

verbräunt browned

das **Verbrechen** crime

der **Verbrecher** criminal

verbreiten (*wk*) spread

sich **verbreiten** (*wk*) spread

verbrennen, a, a (*wk, irreg*) burn; perish in flames (5943)

verbringen, a, a (*wk, irreg*) spend

verbündet allied

der **Verdacht** suspicion

verdächtig suspicious

verdammen (*wk*) condemn; **verdammt** confounded, damned

verdanken owe; render thanks

verdauen digest

verdeckt covered

verdenken, a, a (*wk, irreg*) hold against

das **Verderben** destruction, ruin

verderben (*wk*) go to waste, go to perdition; be destroyed; **verderbt** depraved

verderben (i), a, o corrupt, spoil; waste (10336)

sich **verderben** decay (6693)

der **Verderber** destroyer

verderblich malign, baleful

verdichten render impenetrable

verdienen (*wk*) deserve; earn

das **Verdienst, –e** merit, desert

verdienstlich meritorious

verdoppeln duplicate; double, hasten (11636)

das **Verdoppeln** reverberation (10004)

verdrehen (*wk*): **verdrehten**

Halses spähen look over one's shoulder

verdrießen, o, o annoy, trouble; discourage

verdrießlich annoying; unpleasant; annoyed (7214, 11039)

der **Verdruß** grief, worry; annoyance

verdunkeln (*wk*) eclipse

sich **verdunkeln** grow darker

verdüstern cast a shadow over, becloud

verehren (*wk*) respect; worship; revere, honor; **verehrend** respectful (8662)

der **Verehrer** admirer

die **Verehrung** admiration, reverence, respect

der **Verein** union

vereinen (*wk*) unite, combine

sich **vereinen** (*wk*) unite, combine

vereinigen (*wk*) unite

sich **vereinigen** unite (10693, 10905)

sich **vereinzeln** be separated, be isolated

verengen make narrow, narrow down; block (10550); oppress with anxiety (10862)

verfahren proceed

verfangen operate, work (5195); **nichts verfangen** do no harm (6719)

verfänglich embarrassing (10354); vulnerable (10655)

verfaulen (*wk*) rot

verfehlen (*wk*) neglect; miss (9207)

verflechten (i), **o, o** entangle; intertwine; involve

verfliegen, o, o fly past

verflucht accursed, confounded, damned

verflüchtigen (= sich **verflüchtigen**) evaporate, dissolve into nothingness (11863)

verfolgen pursue

sich **verfügen** betake oneself

verführbar: leicht verführbar easily led astray

verführen (*wk*) seduce; mislead

der **Verführer** seducer

sich **vergaffen** become enamoured

vergällen (*wk*) make bitter, turn into gall

die **Vergangenheit** past

vergänglich transitory

vergeben (i), **a, e** forgive

ins **Vergebene** in vain (8833)

vergebens in vain, of no avail, for nothing

die **Vergebung** forgiveness, remission

vergehen, i, a pine away, die, melt away; pass (6230); **mir verging die Kraft** I had no strength (10835)

sich **vergehen, i, a** transgress, overstep the bounds

vergessen (i), **a, e** forget

vergeuden waste

vergießen, o, o spill, shed

die **Vergifterin** poisoner

vergilbt turned yellow

vergleichbar comparable

vergleichen compare

sich **vergleichen** be comparable

verglimmen, o, o die away (*fire*)

das **Vergnügen** pleasure, delight; amusement

vergnügen (*wk*) satisfy; ver-
gnügt delighted, satisfied
sich vergnügen amuse oneself
vergnüglich with delight
vergönnen (*wk*) grant, permit
vergraben (ä), u, a hide, bury
vergriffen well worn
die Verguldung gilding
verhaftet attached, bound
verhallen die away
sich verhalten (ä), ie, a keep
das Verhängnis doom
verhängnisvoll fateful
verharrend remaining; arrested
(8034)
verhaßt hated, hateful, odious
verheeren (*wk*) devastate
verheimlichen (*wk*) conceal
verheißen, ie, ei promise
verhindern hinder, prevent
verhöhnen (*wk*) deride, sneer at,
mock
verhüllen (*wk*) cover over, conceal; veil
verhungern starve
sich verirren (*wk*) go astray,
stray; verirrt lost
verjagen (*wk*) dispel, drive
away
verjährt age-old, venerable
verjüngen rejuvenate
verkappt disguised
verkehren (*wk*) turn; have
traffic with (6231)
verkennen mistake, fail to recognize
sich verketten link together
verklagen (*wk*) accuse, charge
verklären (*wk*) transfigure,
glorify, illumine, flood with
light (8165, 8474); enlighten
(7453); der Verklärte one

transfigured after rising from
the grave; a Blessed Soul
verklingen, a, u die away
(*sound*)
verkörperlicht provided with a
body
verkörpern provide with substance, make material
verkümmern spoil, interfere
with; be consumed
sich verkümmern pine away
verkünden (*wk*) announce, proclaim; prophesy (8596)
verkündigen announce, proclaim
die Verkündung announcement
verkürzen (*wk*) shorten
verlangen (*wk*) demand, desire;
es verlangt mich I very much
desire (9983)
das Verlangen desire
verlängen (*wk*) extend, stretch
out
sich verlängen grow longer, be
extended
der Verlaß reliance; auf Parteien
ist kein Verlaß no reliance is
to be placed in parties
verlassen (ä), ie, a leave,
abandon
verlästern slander
der Verlaub permission
verleben (*wk*) spend, wear out
verlechzt parched; languishing
sich verlegen auf devote oneself
to
verlegen embarrassed
die Verlegenheit, –en embarrassment
verleiden spoil, mar
verleihen, ie, ie give, present,
grant, lend (5740, 7165, 8291);
bestow upon (10876, 11036)

verleiten lead astray

verlernen (*wk*) forget

verletzen (*wk*) injure; offend (5794)

verleugnen disavow

sich **verleugnen** deny one's identity

sich **verlieben** (*wk*) fall in love; **verliebt** in love; **Verliebte** lovers

verlieren, o, o lose; **das Trallern ist bei mir verloren** trills are wasted on me; **verloren geben** give up for lost, give up hope for (3127)

sich **verlieren**, o, o get lost; wander off; disappear (5996)

verlocken entice

das **Verlocken** enticement

verlöschen (i), o, o grow dim (4650); go out, be extinguished (5639)

der **Verlust** loss

verlutieren seal up with clay

vermählen (*wk*) wed; (= *combine* 1043)

sich **vermählen** wed

vermaledeit cursed, confounded

vermehren (*wk*) increase, augment

sich **vermehren** (*wk*) increase

der **Vermehrer** propagator

vermeiden avoid

sich **vermessen** (i), a, e presumptuously venture; **vermessen** presumptuously

vermissen (*wk*) miss

vermitteln (*wk*) bring about, bargain for, arrange

sich **vermitteln** be brought about

das **Vermögen** fortune, estate

vermögen (a) be able to, be in a position to do, can

vermummen (*wk*) mask, masquerade

sich **vermummen** veil oneself, wrap oneself in disguise

die **Vermummung**, –en masquerade

vermuten suspect

vernarrt sein be infatuated, make a fool of oneself

vernehmen (i), a, o hear

vernehmlich audible

verneinen negate, deny; **Geister, die verneinen** spirits of negation

vernichten (*wk*) crush, annihilate, destroy

die **Vernichterin**, –nen destroyer

vernichtigen destroy

die **Vernichtung** destruction, annihilation

die **Vernunft** reason

vernünftig sensible, reasonable

verpassen let slip by

verpesten infect

verpfänden (*wk*) pawn; pledge (10474); engage, make a deal with (7773)

sich **verpfänden** sign oneself away

verpflichtet obligated; pledged (6046)

verprassen (*wk*) squander in revelry

verpuffen set off like fireworks

sich **verquälen** consume oneself in torment

verrammeln (*wk*) barricade

verraten (ä), ie, a betray

der **Verräter** traitor

verräterisch treacherous

verrennen, a, a (*wk, irreg*) block
verriegeln (*wk*) bolt
verrucht infamous, atrocious
sich **verrücken** change one's location, move
verrückt crazy, insane, deranged
verrufen ill-famed, notorious
versagen (*wk*) fail; refuse (5828); deny (9608)
sich **versagen** deny oneself
sich **versammeln** (*wk*) assemble
versäumen (*wk*) neglect; miss
das **Versäumnis** neglect, negligence
verschaffen provide
verschallen, o, o die, pass away; **verschollen** dead, passed away
verscherzen (*wk*) forfeit, lose through one's own folly
verscheuchen (*wk*) scare away
verschieben, o, o dislocate, dislodge (6625)
sich **verschieben, o, o** get out of place
verschieden different, various (10325)
verschimmeln (*wk*) grow mouldy
verschleiert veiled
verschließen, o, o lock up, close up (11572); **verschlossen** taciturn (6313)
sich **verschließen, o, o** hide; lock oneself in; be inaccessible
verschlingen, a, u devour, swallow
verschlingen, a, u join, entwine (8381, 11926)
sich **verschlingen** wind around (12013)
verschmachten languish
verschmähen (*wk*) scorn, reject, jilt

verschollen no longer heard; departed, forgotten
verschonen (*wk*) spare
verschränkt interlocked (6442); intertwined (7258); laid one across the other (10443)
verschreiben, ie, ie sign away
sich **verschreiben** sign oneself away
verschrumpft shrunken
verschüchtert frightened, intimidated
verschüttet buried
verschweigen pass over in silence, leave unmentioned
verschwemmen (*wk*) wash down
verschwenden waste
verschwenderisch wasteful, prodigal
die **Verschwendung** prodigality, extravagance
verschwinden, a, u disappear; pass away
das **Verschwinden** disappearance
sich **verschwören, u, o** conspire; **verschworen sein** be in a conspiracy
versehen (ie), a, e take care of, provide; **eh' man sich's versieht** before one is aware of it
versenden emit
versengen (*wk*) singe, scorch
versenken (*wk*) lower, submerge
versetzen (*wk*) put, place; transport (7184); **den Atem versetzen** take (one's) breath away; **in Schweiß versetzen** make (one) sweat (6164)
sich **versetzen** (*wk*) imagine oneself, put oneself
versichern assure
versiegen run dry

versinken, a, u sink; be swallowed, be submerged

sich versitzen waste one's life in idle sitting

versöhnen (wk) reconcile, conciliate

sich versöhnen (wk) make up; become reconciled

versorgen (wk) supply (10912); take care of (11608)

verspotten mock

versprechen (i), a, o promise

das Versprechen promise

verspüren (wk) feel

der Verstand understanding, mind; senses (6569); good sense (6764)

verständig intelligent; prudent (5333); rational (6379, 6858); sensible (8842)

verständlich intelligible

verstärken strengthen

sich verstärken reinforce oneself

verstecken (wk) hide

sich verstecken (wk) hide

verstehen, a, a understand, know how; das versteht sich that's understood, that goes without saying

verstimmen put out of humor

verstopfen (wk) plug, use as a plug

verstrahlen radiate

verstümmeln (wk) mutilate

verstummen grow silent

der Versuch attempt

versuchen (wk) try, attempt

sich versühnen (= sich versöhnen) balance one's accounts (by doing penance 5051)

sich versündigen (wk) sin, transgress

vertauschen (wk) barter

vertausendfacht multiplied a thousandfold

verteidigen defend

verteilen (wk) distribute; allot (6433); verteilt dispersed

sich verteilen disperse

verteuern make more expensive, raise the price of

vertiefen (wk) hollow out, dig out

vertrackt preposterous

sich vertragen get along

vertrauen (wk) have confidence; entrust (5318)

das Vertrauen confidence

vertraulich full of confidence (2029); friendly (5198)

vertraut intimate

vertraut-bequem comfortably cosy

der Vertraute intimate friend

vertreiben, ie, ie drive away; die Zeit vertreiben while away the time (1433)

vertreten bar

vertrinken drink away

vertrocknen wither, parch

vertun, a, a play one's part (4759); lay waste (4828); spend (5057); squander (11837); (intrans) der hat vertan he's done for

verüben practice

verwahren (wk) keep, take care of

die Verwaltung management, administration

verwandeln (wk) transform

sich verwandeln (wk) change, turn into, transform oneself

verwandt akin, related

der **Verwandte** relative

die **Verwandtschaft** kinship

verwebt closely interwoven

verwegen rash, audacious, daring, foolhardy; hazardous; **ins Verwegene** to the point of temerity

verwehren prevent

verweigern deny, withhold from, refuse

verweilen (*wk*) linger, abide, stay

das **Verweilen** sojourn, existence (7566)

verwerfen *see* **verworfen**

verwerflich reprehensible

die **Verwesung** corruption, decay

verwickeln entangle, envelop

verwirken (*wk*) forfeit

verwirren (*wk*) confuse, entangle

die **Verwirrung** confusion

verwöhnen (*wk*) spoil

sich **verwöhnen** overindulge, pamper oneself; spoil one's taste (7156)

verworfen infamous, cast out

verworren confused, out of order

das **Verworrene** confusion

verwunden (*wk*) wound, injure; hurt (11152)

die **Verwundrung** amazement

verwünschen (*wk*) curse

die **Verwünschung** curse

verzagen grow despondent

verzapfen tap

verzehren consume

die **Verzehrerin**, **–nen** consumer; you who feed upon (8781)

verzeihen pardon, excuse, forgive

das **Verzeihen** pardon

verzetteln (*wk*) squander

Verzicht leisten auf renounce

verziehen change; **Gesicht verziehen** betray emotion by a change of expression

verzieren decorate

verzweifeln despair

die **Verzweiflung** despair

die **Vettel** old hag

der **Vetter**, **–n** cousin

das **Vieh** beast(s); live stock (6167)

viel much, many, a great deal, a great number

vielfach manifold

vielfältig manifold

vielgeliebt well-beloved, popular (94)

vielgeschaukelt much tossed

vielgestaltet in many shapes, polymorphous

vielgewandt widely experienced, skilled in many things

vielleicht perhaps, maybe, perchance; by any chance, by some chance

vielverworren much confused

vier four; four o'clock

vierbespannt drawn by four horses

vierfach fourfold

das **Viergespann** chariot drawn by four horses, quadriga

vierte fourth

das **Viertelstündchen** brief quarter of an hour

vierundzwanzig twenty-four

vierzehn fourteen

vierzigjährig lasting forty years

die **Viktoria** Victoria, victory

die **Viktorie** Victoria, victory

der **Virtuos** professional performer, virtuoso

visieren (*wk*) look around

das **Vlies** fleece, fur; **das goldene Vlies** the Golden Fleece

der **Vogel,** ⸗ bird; (= girls? sailors? 11217)

der **Vogelfang** birdbaiting

vogelfrei outlawed, not protected by law

der **Vogelsang,** ⸗e bird song

die **Vogelschar** flock of birds

der **Vogelsteller** fowler, birdbaiter

das **Vöglein** little bird

Voland: Junker Voland His Satanic Highness

das **Volk,** ⸗er people, common people; nation; herd (4144); troop (5815); **das junge Volk** young people; **Volk** (*in stage directions*) crowd

das **Völkchen** little company; poor simple-minded people (2181)

die **Völkerschaft** group of people, nation

die **Volkeswoge,** -n wave of warriors, host, legion

das **Volksgedränge** throng (*of common people*)

die **Volksgefahr** national emergency

das **Volksgewicht** mass of troops

voll full, complete, full of; **voller** full of (3678, 6454); **für voll halten** take seriously (6359); **für voll gelten** enjoy full equality (10276)

vollbringen, a, a (*wk, irreg*) complete, accomplish, achieve, finish

vollenden (*wk*) complete, perfect, finish

vollerteilen grant fully

vollführen carry out, accomplish (9003)

vollgepfropft stuffed full

der **Vollgewinn** total gain

vollgültig conclusive; fully valid (9991)

völlig complete, full, total

vollkommen perfect, complete, total

vollstimmig full-voiced, with the entire orchestra

vollziehen execute, perform

das **Volum** volume

vom = von dem

von from, of, by, about

vor before, in front of, for, on account of; ago; in preference to; **vor der Stadt** (just) outside the city; **vor einen Felsen rennen** run into a rock

voran ahead of time (1445); forward (10536); at the head (11511)

vorangehen go ahead; lead on (9077); proceed (10796)

voranschweben hover before (one)

vorantönen: dem Helden tönt sein Name voran the hero's fame precedes him

voraus in advance, in the lead (3979)

voraussagen (*wk*) foretell

voraussehen anticipate, expect

voraussenden, a, a (*wk, irreg*) send ahead

vorausspeisen consume in advance

sich **vorbehalten (ä), ie, a** reserve for oneself

vorbei past, along, over and done with

vorbeiführen lead past

vorbeigehen, i, a walk past

vorbeikrächzen go croaking past

vorbeilaufen (äu), ie, au run past

vorbeireisen (*wk*) pass by (*without visiting*)

vorbeischleichen, i, i move stealthily past

sich **vorbeischmiegen** flow past closely

vorbeiziehen, o, o move past, pass by

vorbereiten (*wk*) prepare

vordem before

vordere foremost, leading

voreilen rush ahead

voreinst formerly, once

vorempfinden feel beforehand

vorerst for the time being

voressen (i), a, e eat in advance; **vorgegessen Brot** bread eaten before it is paid for

vorflammen precede flaming

vorfühlen anticipate

das **Vorgebirg** promontory, headland

das **Vorgefühl** anticipation

vorhalten (ä) hold in front

vorhanden on hand, existing

der **Vorhang** curtain

das **Vorhängel** small curtain (*at a peep window*)

vorher before, before that

der **Vorhof** courtyard

der **Vorige, –n** the former, preceding

vorkommen appear, look, seem

vorlallen (*wk*) murmur, speak haltingly

vorlegen (*wk*) produce (101); submit (11022)

vorleuchten show the way with a light

vorlügen, o, o falsely present (1528)

sich **vorlügen, o, o** falsely imagine (3298)

vorm = vor dem

vormachen deceive with plausible stories

vormals in former days

vorn(e) in front; **von vorne wieder anfangen** start all over again (6959); **von vorn anfangen** make a fresh start (8322)

vornehm grand, genteel; lordly, elegant (10145)

das **Vornehmtun** superior airs

vornehm-willkommen distinguished and welcome

vornen in front

vornenan in the first row, in front

vorpreisen, ie, ie praise publicly

das **Vorrecht** privilege

vorsagen recite

der **Vorsatz** design, plan

vorschieben, o, o (Riegel) shoot (bolt)

vorschnell precipitate, headstrong

vorschreiben, ie, ie prescribe

vorschreiten, i, i progress

die **Vorschrift** prescription

vorschweben hover in front of

sich **vorsehen (ie), a, e** plan, consider carefully beforehand

die **Vorsicht** caution, foresight

vorsichtig cautious

das **Vorspiel** prelude

die **Vorstadt,** ⸗e suburb

vorstehen project

vorstellen (*wk*) represent, portray

sich **vorstellen** (*wk*) imagine (3369)

vortanzen dance in front of

der **Vorteil** advantage; **Vorteil ziehen** take advantage (1014)

vorteilhaft advantageous

vorteilsuchend seeking advantage

der **Vortrag** lecture; style of delivery (546); **zum Vortrag kommen lassen** give a chance to speak (5294)

vortragen (ä) present

vortreten (i) step forward, step forth; call (*at someone's house*)

vorüber past, finished

vorübereilen (*wk*) hasten past

vorübergänglich temporary, for the time being

vorübergehen walk past

vorüberrücken move past

vorüberschleichen steal past unnoticed

vorüberschweben float past

vorüberspazieren promenade past

vorüberziehen pass by

vorwärts forward

vorwärtsdringen press forward

vorwärtsgehen walk forward, make progress

vorwärtsgelangen advance

vorwärtsschauen look forward

vorwärtsschreiten walk forward

die **Vorwelt** former age, former generation(s) (2695); past;

prehistoric time (3238); earlier times (6810)

das **Vorwerk** farm adjacent to manor

der **Vorwurf** reproach, self-reproach (4624)

vorzeigen present, show

vorziehen, o, o prefer

vorzüglich principally, chiefly

W

wach awake

wachbleiben, ie, ie remain awake

die **Wache** guard

wachen (*wk*) wake, be awake, sit up waiting; watch, guard (**Trüber Tag** 64)

das **Wachfeuer,** — campfire

das **Wachs** wax

wachsen (ä), **u, a** grow, increase; grow up (8500)

der **Wachspfropfen** wax plug

das **Wachstum** growth; adolecence (6476)

der **Wächter,** — watchman, night watchman (4426)

wackeln wag loosely, shake

wacker valiant, brisk; stalwart, capable

die **Wade, -n** calf of the leg

die **Waffe, -n** arm, weapon; suit of armor (10764)

der **Waffensaal, -säle** armory

die **Wage** balance, scales

der **Wagen** carriage, chariot

wagen (*wk*) venture, dare, risk, attempt; **gewagt** venturesome, risky, hazardous

sich **wagen** (*wk*) venture

wägen weigh

der **Wagenlenker** charioteer

der **Wagenthron** throne mounted on wheels (*chariot*)

wagerecht horizontal

Wagner Wagner

das **Wagstück** venture, daring enterprise

die **Wahl** choice

wählen choose, select

die **Wählerin, –nen** fastidious chooser

der **Wahn** false or fantastic notion, delusion, fanciful idea

wähnen imagine, believe erroneously

der **Wahnsinn** delirium

wahr true, real

wahren (*wk*) keep, keep to oneself (591); keep for oneself (2739); preserve (9984)

währen last, endure, keep on

wahrhaft truly

wahrhaftig truly, really, indeed

die **Wahrheit** truth

wahrlich truly, honestly, in truth, to tell the truth

wahrnehmen observe

wahrscheinlich probable

der **Wald, –er** forest, wood

das **Waldestal** wooded valley

das **Waldgebüsch** underbrush

die **Waldquelle, –n** forest spring

die **Waldung** arbor, grove

das **Waldvöglein** forest bird

der **Wall, –e** rampart

wallen wander (10007, 10011, 11894)

wallen boil (5712); undulate (5980); billow (6008); curl (8698)

der **Wallestrom** river on its undulating pilgrimage (to the sea)

Walpurgis = Walpurgisnacht (2590)

die **Walpurgisnacht** *night of April 30–May 1, occasion of annual witches' convention*

der **Walpurgisnachtstraum** Walpurgis Night's Dream

walten prevail, rule, govern

die **Walze** cylinder

wälzen roll

sich **wälzen** roll

das **Wälzen** torrent

das **Wams** doublet

die **Wand, ⁀e** wall

der **Wandel** walk

wandeln travel, go, walk; wander

wandeln change, transform (3246; **Trüber Tag** 14, 15, 19; 5782, 5983, 10046)

sich **wandeln** become, change (to) (5386, 5937, 6302, 9572)

Wanderjahre journeyman's years

wandern walk, wander (2995)

die **Wanderschaft** pilgrimage

der **Wandersmann** traveler

der **Wandrer** wanderer; pilgrim (10120)

die **Wandrung** walk

die **Wange, –n** cheek

das **Wangenrot** redness of cheeks

das **Wänglein, —** delicate cheek

wanken waver; totter (11474)

wann when; **dann und wann** now and then

der **Wanst, ⁀e** paunch

wanstig paunchy

die **Wanze, –n** bedbug

das **Wappen, —** coat of arms, escutcheon

die **Ware, –n** ware, article, commodity; (*pl*) goods

warm warm, ardent (1799)
wärmen warm
sich wärmen warm oneself
der Warnegeist warning spirit
warnen (*wk*) warn
warten wait, wait for
die Wärterin, –nen nurse
warum why, for what reason
warum (= worum) for which (3218)
was what, why, whatever; was für (ein) what kind of? what a! (2709); (= etwas) something, anything
waschen wash
der Waschtrog washtrough
das Wasser water
der Wasserboden reclaimed land
der Wasserdrachen sea dragon
der Wasserfall, ⸚e waterfall
das Wasserfräulein, — water sprite
die Wasserfülle ample waters
der Wasserhof Wasserhof (*inn, place of amusement*)
der Wasserkrug, ⸚e water jug
die Wasserlüge, –n water illusion
wässern irrigate
die Wasserschlacht water fight
der Wasserstrahl, –en water jet, (thin) stream of water
der Wasserstrom stream of water
der Wassersturz waterfall
der Wasserteufel water devil
waten (*wk*) wade
weben weave; make; float; hover; webe hin und her weave back and forth (503)
der Weber, — weaver

das Weber-Meisterstück masterpiece of weaving
der Webstuhl loom
der Wechsel change of phases
die Wechseldauer permanence of form persisting through change of substance
der Wechselgesang a song with stanzas sung in turn by two or more singers
das Wechselgeschrei shouting in turn by members (of the multitude)
wechseln (*wk*) exchange, alternate
die Wechselnot dire vicissitude
die Wechselrede dialogue in rimes
wechselseitig mutual, reciprocal, in turn
der Wechselstreit conflict, argument
wechselsweis alternately
der Wechsler money-changer
die Wechslerbank, ⸚e money-changer's table
wecken awaken, arouse
der Wedel fly brush
wedeln wag
weder neither; weder ... noch neither ... nor; weder ... weder neither ... nor (2607, 5499)
der Weg, –e way, path, road; method (11616); der halbe Weg halfway mark; woher des Wegs which way, whence
weg away, gone; away with (7166); hier weg away from here
sich wegen (= sich bewegen) move

wegfluchen (*wk*) drive away by curses

wegführen (*wk*) take away, lead off

weggehen, i, a go away

wegjucken scratch, remove by scratching

sich **wegkehren** turn away

wegkrümmen (*wk*) wriggle away

weglaufen (äu) run away

wegnehmen (i), **a, o** take away

wegpaschen (*wk*) make off with . . . fraudulently (11831)

wegraffen (*wk*) carry off

wegräumen (*wk*) clear away

wegschaffen remove, clear away

wegschieben (*wk*) shove away

sich **wegschleichen** steal away

wegschnappen (*wk*) snatch away

wegschwemmen wash away

wegsinken sink out of sight

wegweichen get out of the way, step aside

wegwerfen (i) throw away

das **Weh, –e** woe, misery, calamity; pang, throe (51); **Weh und Ach** complaining and lamenting

weh(e) alas; woe (is); **weh tun** hurt; **wie weh**(e) **wird mir im Busen** how heavy with woe my heart becomes (3603–4)

wehen blow, float; **wehe hin und her** float to and fro

wehren prevent (4463)

sich **wehren** defend oneself

das **Weib, –er** woman, wife

das **Weibchen, —** female; little wife (5184, 5271)

das **Weibergeklatsch** women's gossip

die **Weiberkunst, ⁻e** woman's trick

weiblich feminine

das **Weibsgebild** female

das **Weibsgeschlecht** females

weich soft

die **Weiche, –n** side

weichen, i, i yield, give ground, retreat; (**von**) shun

weichlich effeminate; soft

der **Weichling** softy

weichwollig soft and downy

die **Weide** meadow, pasture land

die **Weide, –n** willow (9977)

weiden graze

sich **weiden** feast, feed; gloat (**Trüber Tag** 39)

der **Weidenstrauch, ⁻e** small willow tree

weidlich thoroughly

die **Weife** reel

weifen reel (*thread*)

die **Weihe** consecration

weihen (*wk*) dedicate, consecrate

sich **weihen** (*wk*) dedicate oneself, devote oneself

der **Weiher** pond

der **Weihetag** day of consecration

der **Weihrauchduft** fragrance of incense

der **Weihrauchsdampf** smoke of incense

der **Weihrauchsnebel** cloud of incense

weil because, since

weiland of old

die **Weile** while, leisure (7871); **nächtlicher Weile** during the night (**Trüber Tag** 16), of the night (4626)

weilen stop, linger, stay; be

der **Wein, –e** wine

der **Weinberg, –e** vineyard

weinen weep, cry

das **Weinfaß** wine cask

der **Weinstein** tartar

der **Weinstock** grapevine

weise wise, sagacious

der **Weise, –n** wise man, sage, philosopher

die **Weise, –n** way, manner, mode; way of acting (2169); melody, strain (10782)

weisen, ie, ie show, point out

sich **weisen, ie, ie** show oneself, be revealed

die **Weisheit** wisdom

weislich discreetly, prudently

weiß white; **schwarz auf weiß** in black and white, in writing

weissagen foretell, forebode; have a premonition of

das **Weißnichtwie** marvel; je ne sais quoi

weit far, distant, far away; wide, extended; **weit und breit** far and wide; **weit ins Weite** far afield

die **Weite, –n** distance; **feuchte Weite** vast watery domain

weitereilen hasten on

weitergehen go further, go on

weiterhin farther down

weit-eröffnen open up wide

weiterschreiten progress; walk, stride on (10067)

weiterziehen move on

weitgedehnt widely spread, extended

weithinleuchtend shining into the distance

weitläufig extensive, distant

(7987); at great length, in a roundabout way (10747)

weitsichtig farseeing

weitumsichtig very circumspect

welch which, what, what a, which one; who; some

welk withered, dried, shriveled

welken wither

die **Welle, –n** wave

wellen ripple

wellenförmig wavy

das **Wellengeflecht** tissue of waves

das **Wellenreich** realm of the waves

der **Wellenspiegel** mirror of waves

welsch French, Italian

das **Welschhuhn, ⸚er** turkey

die **Welt, –en** world, life, humanity; **die große Welt** high society; **alle Welt** everybody

das **Weltall** universe

der **Weltbesitz** possession of the world

der **Weltenraum, ⸚e** vast cosmic space

die **Weltgegend, –en** clime

welt-gemäß appropriate to the (material) world

weltgewandt worldly-wise

das **Weltkind** worldly-minded person

weltlich worldly; lay, secular (10976)

weltweise sophisticated

der **Wendehals** wry-neck

wenden, a, a (*wk, irreg*) turn, bend (2747); **gewendet** turned; **gewandt** skilled, apt, clever, nimble; with a bent for

sich **wenden, a, a** (*wk, irreg*)

turn; apply, have recourse; turn around (522)

wenig little, small, few; scarcely

wenigstens at least

wenn if, when, whenever; **wenn auch** even if, even though; **als wenn** as if

wer who, whoever; someone, anyone

werben woo, court

der **Werber** matchmaker

die **Werdelust** joy of entering a new phase

werden (i), a/u, o become, come to be, develop; be; will/shall; be (*passive*); **werden zu** change into (2298)

werfen (i), a, o cast, throw; **keine Falten werfen** fit perfectly

sich **werfen (i), a, o** throw oneself; **sich werfen auf** break out on, attack (11814)

das **Werk, –e** work

das **Werkzeug** tool

der **Wert** value, worth

wert worthy, worth, esteemed, dear; **wert sein** deserve

wesen exist, have one's being

das **Wesen, —** being, thing, creature; nature, essence; affair; state, activity, arrangement; goings-on (5929)

die **Wesenheit** essence, characteristic nature

weshalb for which reason

das **Wespennest** wasps' nest

der **West** west wind

der **Westen** west

die **Wette** wager, bet; **um die Wette** in competition, in emulation

wetten bet, wager

Wetterbuben confounded lads

wetterleuchten flash ominously

das **Wetterleuchten** heat lightning

das **Wettern** approaching thunderstorm

der **Wettgesang** singing contest; **in Wettgesang** in rival song

das **Wichtchen** little fellow, little wight

wichtig important, significant

die **Wickel, –n** diaper; (*pl*) swaddling clothes

der **Widder, —** ram

wider contrary to, against; **hin und wider** to and fro, back and forth; **wider mich** in spite of everything I can do (3797)

der **Widerdämon** hostile demon (*who brings misfortune*)

widerdonnern echo, resound

widerhallen re-echo

der **Widerklang** echo; resounding

widerklingen re-echo

widerlich loathsome, disgusting, repulsive

widern be repugnant, be repellent

der **Widersacher, —** adversary

widerschallen re-echo

der **Widerschein** reflection

widersinnig paradoxical, full of contradictions

widerspenstig restive; obstinate; resisting (9797)

widersprechen (i) contradict

der **Widerspruch** contradiction, discrepancy

der **Widerstand** resistance

widerstehen, a, a be distasteful

to (2337); resist, stand up
against (10538, 11269, 11591)
widerstreben (= hin- und widerstreben) surge back and forth
der Widerstreit opposition
widerwärtig unpleasant, repulsive, disagreeable; hostile, resisting (9798); sich widerwärtig gebärden act horrified
wider-widerwärtig most unpleasant
der Widerwillen abhorrence
widmen devote, bestow
die Widmung dedication, homage
widrig unpleasant, repulsive;
hostile
das Widrige opposites, things
mutually incompatible (1041)
wie how; as; like, as if, such as;
when; as well as (7358); wie
viel how much, what
wieder again, once more; back,
in return
wiederaufstehen, a, a get up
again
wiederfinden find, meet, find
again
sich wiederfinden meet again
wiedergeben (i) give back, return
das Wiedergehen (= das Hin-
und Wiedergehen) walking
back and forth
wiederhaben have again
wiederherkehren return hither
wiederholen (wk) repeat; wie-
derholt repeatedly
sich wiederholen (wk) recur,
happen again
wiederkehren return, come back
again

wiederkommen come back, return
die Wiederkunft return
das Wiederlaufen (= das Hin-
und Wiederlaufen) running
back and forth
wiederrennen (= hin- und
wiederrennen) run back and
forth
das Wiederrutschen (= das
Hin- und Wiederrutschen)
sliding back and forth
wiederschwanken (= hin- und
wiederschwanken) waver to
and fro, sway back and forth
wiederschweben (= schwebet
hin und wieder) float back
and forth
wiedersehen see again; Auf
Wiedersehen Good-bye, Au
revoir
sich wiedersehen see each other
again
wiederstreben (= hin- und
wiederstreben) surge back
and forth
wiederum again
die Wiege cradle
wiegen rock (to sleep), lull
sich wiegen rock back and forth;
sleep happy in the thought of
(6171)
die Wiese, –n meadow, pasture
das Wiesengras meadow grass
wieso how so? what do you
mean?
das Wild game
wild wild, undisciplined, noisy,
uncultivated
das Wildbret game, hunted
animal
wildentbrannt burning fiercely

die **Wildernis** wilderness

der **Wildgesang** singing of savages

das **Wildschwein, –e** wild boar

der **Wille** will, wish; **euch zu Willen** for your sake, to please you

um ... **willen** for the sake of; in case of (1714); **um Gottes willen** for nothing, out of sheer benevolence (1652); **um Lebens oder Sterbens willen** to provide against any and all contingencies

willenlos will-less

willig willing, voluntary, glad

die **Willigkeit** willingness

der **Willkomm(en)** welcome; by way of greeting

willkommen welcome

wimmelhaft in a teeming swarm

wimmeln teem, be alive

die **Wimmelschar, –en** swarming host

wimmern wail

das **Wimmlen** teeming throng

der **Wimpel, —** pennant

der **Wind, –e** wind

die **Windel, –n** diaper; (*pl*) swaddling clothes

winden, a, u twine, twist, writhe

sich **winden, a, u** turn, twist, writhe

die **Windesbraut** gale; speed of the whirlwind (5612)

die **Windfahne** weather vane

das **Windgetüm** monstrous wind (*line squall*)

die **Windsbraut** gale, tempest (3936)

der **Wink** sign, signal, nod

der **Winkel, —** corner, angle

winken beckon, signal, nod

winseln whine

der **Winter** winter

winterlich wintry

die **Winternacht, ⸚e** winter night

der **Winterwind** winter wind

der **Winzer** winegrower

der **Wipfel, —** treetop

wir we

wirbeln reel

der **Wirbelrauch** whirling smoke

der **Wirbeltanz** whirling dance

wirken (*wk*) work, operate, be active; accomplish, produce; effect; **wirken auf** affect

die **Wirkenskraft** effective energy

wirklich really, actually

die **Wirklichkeit, –en** reality

die **Wirksamkeit, –en** virtue, effective power

die **Wirkung** effect, result

der **Wirrwarr** confusion, chaos

der **Wirt, –e** host, tavern keeper

die **Wirtin** innkeeper's wife

die **Wirtschaft** establishment, household

das **Wissen** knowledge, information, learning

wissen (ei), u, u (*wk, irreg*) know, know how to, be informed

der **Wissende, –n** knowing (person), initiated

die **Wissenschaft** science; knowledge, wisdom

wissenschaftlich scientific, scholarly

der **Wissensdrang** urge to know, desire for knowledge

der **Wissensqualm** fog of scholarship

wissenswürdig worth knowing

wittern smell, perceive by smelling (7036); seek out (6263); suspect (11725); **es wittert nach** it smells like, it reminds me of (6229)

das **Wittern** atmospheric disturbance (6623, 7254, 7524)

die **Witterung** weather

die **Witwe** widow

die **Witwenschaft** widowhood

der **Witz** wit, ingenuity; good sense

witzeln crack jokes

witzen (*wk*) make intellectual efforts

wo where, wherever; if, when; **wo ein noch aus** which way to turn (5893)

woanders elsewhere

die **Woche**, –n week

das **Wochenblättchen** (weekly) newspaper of a small town

wodurch how, by what means

die **Woge**, –n billow, wave; surging mass (9204)

wogen (*wk*) surge, billow (6441); heave (8412); heave and sway (*like the sea* 11875)

wogenhaft like a wave

woher from where, whence

wohin to where, whither, where, wherever

das **Wohl** welfare, weal, prosperity; **zu Wohl und Weh** for better or worse, as a last resort

wohl well; carefully; in good health; indeed, probably, presumably; to be sure, I dare say

mit **Wohlbedacht** after careful consideration

wohlbedächtig with deliberation

sich **wohlbehagen** feel comfortable

das **Wohlbehagen** feeling of comfort

wohlbekannt well-known, familiar

der **Wohlempfang** festive reception

wohlerwogen well-considered

wohlerworben well-acquired

wohlfeil reasonable, cheap

wohlgebaut well-built

wohlgebildet well-shaped

wohlgefallen (ä) please

das **Wohlgefallen** satisfaction

wohlgehen: dem wird es wohlgehn he will fare well

wohlgemeint well-meant

wohlgemessen fair

wohlgemut cheerful, in good spirits

wohlgenährt well-nourished

wohlgeputzt well-dressed, all dressed up

das **Wohlgericht** well-prepared dish or course

der **Wohlgeruch** fragrance

wohlgeschliffen well-sharpened

wohlgesinnt well-meaning

die **Wohlgestalt** beauty, beautiful form

wohlgestaltet well-formed, well-shaped

wohlgestimmt well-tuned, harmonious

wohlgeweiht duly consecrated

der **Wohlstand** opulence

wohlstimmig concordant, harmonious

die **Wohltat** benefit

wohltätig beneficent

wohltun, a, a do good, benefit;
  wohlgetan well-done
wohlverwahrt well-guarded,
  well-concealed
wohnen live, dwell
der **Wohngewinn** gain in habitable area
wöhnlich persistent
die **Wohnung** house, habitation,
  abode
das **Wölbedach** vaulted roof
wölben vault
sich **wölben** arch
die **Wölbung, –en** vault, arch
der **Wolfesgrimm** wolflike fury
das **Wölkchen,** — little cloud
die **Wolke, –n** cloud
sich **wölken: es wölkt sich**
  clouds are gathering
die **Wolkenart** manner of clouds
der **Wolkenkranz, ⁻e** wreath of
  clouds
der **Wolkenzug, ⁻e** strip of clouds
wollen (i), o, o (*wk, irreg*) wish,
  be willing, desire; be about to;
  allege, claim to; **(wir)** let us;
  wollte nicht just wouldn't
die **Wollenherde, –n** fleecy herd
womit with which
womöglich if possible
wonach for which
die **Wonne** bliss, rapture, ecstasy
der **Wonnebrand** burning fire of
  bliss
der **Wonnegraus** ecstatic dread,
  dreadful ecstasy
wonnevoll blissful
die **Wonnezeit** time of festivities
wonniglich rapturous
woran to which (5375); on
  which (6585)
worauf upon which

woraus from which, out of
  which
worin in which
wornach for which
das **Wort, –e** word, saying;
  promise; command; answer,
  key word (5542); **Wort stehen**
  give an accounting
das **Wörtchen** brief remark
der **Worthauch** whisper, breath
  of speech
wozu why, for what purpose,
  toward what (10788)
die **Wucherklaue, –n** usurer's
  claw
wuchern produce abundant in-
  crement
wühlen burrow; rage
wulstig bulging
wund wounded
die **Wunde, –n** wound
das **Wunder,** — wonder, miracle
wunderbar amazing, wonderful,
  wondrous, strange
das **Wunderding, –e** marvel
der **Wunderflor** marvelous
  flowering
der **Wunderflug** miraculous
  flight
der **Wundergast, ⁻e** strange or
  miraculous guest
die **Wundergestalt, –en** strange
  figure
der **Wunderglanz** miraculous
  splendor
der **Wunderklang, ⁻e** strange
  or miraculous sound
die **Wunderkraft** miraculous and
  supernatural force
wunderlich peculiar, strange,
  singular
der **Wundermann** miracle man

wundern astonish; **es wundert mich** I am surprised

wundernswürdig admirable

wundersam strange, astonishing

der **Wunderschatz** miraculous treasure

wunderschön wonderfully beautiful

der **Wunderschoß** mysterious lap

wunderseltsam wonderfully strange

wunderwürdig marvelous, astonishing

der **Wunsch**, ⸚e wish

die **Wünschelrute** divining rod

wünschen (*wk*) wish, wish for, desire; express the wish

wünschenswert desirable

die **Würde**, –n dignity, honor; office; **nach Würden** worthily, as his position requires

würdig worthy, estimable, respected; dignified, with dignity

würdigen deign

der **Würfel**, — dice

würfeln play at dice

das **Würfelspiel** dice game

sich **würgen** (*wk*) be thrown up, retch

der **Wurm**, ⸚e worm; **Würmer aus der Nase ziehen** get information from, pump

das **Würmchen** poor little thing

die **Wurzel**, –n root, medicinal root

wurzelauf up from the roots

die **Wurzelkraft**, ⸚e (healing or magical) power of roots

wurzeln be rooted

das **Wurzelweib**, –er woman dealing in magic charms prepared from roots

würzen give spice to

der **Wust** chaos; dirty confusion

wüst disorderly, wild; waste, uncultivated

die **Wüste**, –n desert

die **Wut** rage, violence

wüten be furious, rage, be violent

das **Wüten** fury, rage, raging

wütend furious, violent, mad

X

Xenien Xenia, "presents" (*collection of satirical epigrams by Goethe and Schiller*)

Z

sich **zacken** branch off abruptly

das **Zackenhaupt** jagged mountain top (summit)

zackig in a zigzag line; jagged (10039)

zagen be afraid, be fainthearted

die **Zahl** number

zahlen pay, pay for

zählen (*wk*) count, take a census

der **Zahler** payer

zahm tame, docile; not belligerent, not quarrelsome

der **Zahn**, ⸚e tooth

die **Zange** pair of tongs

zappelfüßig jerky-footed, fidgety

zappeln (*wk*) writhe, twitch, kick convulsively

zart tender, delicate, soft, gentle

zärtlich sensitive, gentle, delicate

der **Zauber** magic, magic power

das **Zauberbild** image produced by magic

das **Zauberblatt,** ⁓er magic sheet

das **Zauberblendwerk** magician's illusion

das **Zauberchor** chorus of magic spirits

der **Zauberduft** magic fragrance (haze)

die **Zauberei, –en** witchcraft, sorcery

der **Zauberer,** — sorcerer, wizard

der **Zauberfluß** magical stream

die **Zauberfrau, –en** witch, sorceress

der **Zaubergesang** incantation, magic spell

der **Zauberhauch** atmosphere of magic

die **Zauberhülle, –n** magic wrapping

der **Zaubermantel** magic cloak (*giving its owner power to fly*; = *magic carpet* 1122)

das **Zauberpferd, –e** magic horse

die **Zaubersphäre** sphere of magic

der **Zauberspiegel** magic mirror

die **Zauberspiegelung** magic mirroring

das **Zauberspiel** illusion

der **Zauberspruch,** ⁓e charm, incantation

zaubertoll full of mad sorcery

das **Zaubervolk** band of sorcerers

das **Zauberwerk, –e** work of witchcraft

das **Zauberwesen** magic

das **Zauberwort, –e** magic word, charm, spell

zaudern hesitate, be irresolute

der **Zaum** rein; **in Zaum halten** check, restrain

die **Zeche** revel, drinking party; **auf der Zeche** charged against one

der **Zecher** reveler

die **Zehe** toe

zehen ten

zeh(e)njährig ten years old

zehn ten

zehnfach tenfold

zehntausendmal ten thousand times

zehnte tenth

der **Zehnte** tithe, tenth part

zehren gnaw, consume; feed (6585)

das **Zeichen,** — sign, symbol, mark; token; symptom (4997)

zeichnen (*wk*) draw; characterize (6842); (= **bezeichnen**) designate (8580)

zeigen (*wk*) show, reveal, display; point out

sich **zeigen** (*wk*) appear, reveal oneself; behave (85, 10883)

der **Zeiger** clock pointer (*on water clock: rising for 24 hours, then dropping back to starting point*)

die **Zeile, –n** line

die **Zeit, –en** time, age; festival (10987); **in Zeiten** betimes, in good time (3095); **auf Zeiten lang** for quite a while

der **Zeitenstrudel** whirlpool of time

zeitig early (4431); betimes, in time (6789); opportune, the right time (7658)

der **Zeitvertreib** fun, amusement,

pastime; **zum Zeitvertreib** to pass the time

die **Zelle** cell

das **Zelt, –en** (7010, 7033), **–e** (11121) canopy, tent

zeltartig tentlike

der **Zenith** zenith

der **Zentner, —** hundredweight

die **Zentnermasse, –n** extremely heavy mass

zentralisch in the center, central

der **Zepter** scepter

zerbrechen (i), a, o break (in pieces), smash

die **Zeremonie** ceremony

zerfallen (ä), ie, a fall apart, collapse

zerfließen melt away, evaporate, disperse (4723)

zerknirschen crunch, crush

zerkrachen crash

zerkratzen (*wk*) scratch violently

zernagen (*wk*) gnaw violently

zerpflücken pick to pieces

sich **zerplagen** torment oneself to distraction

zerquetschen (*wk*) squash

zerreißen, i, i tear to pieces; mangle, lacerate (10633); break (1748, 9941, 12026)

zerren pull, drag

zerrinnen, a, o melt away; disappear

zerrütten (*wk*) shake to pieces

zerscheitern be completely wrecked

sich **zerschellen** break to pieces

zerschlagen (ä), u, a shatter, destroy

sich **zerschlagen (ä), u, a** disperse

zerschmettern shatter, smash

zerspalten break up

zersprengen (*wk*) burst; rout, disperse (9457)

zerstieben, o, o be scattered (*like dust*)

zerstören (*wk*) destroy

die **Zerstörung** destruction

zerstreuen (*wk*) disperse, scatter; distract; **zerstreut** distracted, without clear purpose

sich **zerstreuen** (*wk*) scatter, break up

die **Zerstreuung, –en** distraction, diversion

zerstückeln dismember, partition

zerstückt distracted

zertreten (i), a, e crush under foot

zerzausen (*wk*) maul roughly

zerzerren (*wk*) tear badly

der **Zettel** piece of paper

das **Zeug** stuff, material, nonsense (2533)

der **Zeuge, –n** witness

zeugen (*wk*) testify (7122)

zeugen (*wk*) beget, produce

das **Zeugnis** certificate; testimony; **Zeugnis leisten** bear witness

Zeus Zeus (*Jupiter, father of the gods*)

zickzack zigzag

die **Ziege** goat

der **Ziegenbock** he-goat

der **Ziegenfuß** goat's foot

der **Ziegenfüßler, —** goat-footed one, satyr

die **Ziegenfüßlerin, –nen** goat-footed one, female satyr

ziehen, o, o pull, attract; draw; move; train (1174); go, come sich ziehen, o, o move; extend

das Ziel goal; limit (8845); Ziel setzen check, set bounds to (1000, 1760)

ziemen (wk) be proper, suit, become

sich ziemen (wk) be fitting

ziemlich fairly, rather; so ziemlich rather, fairly, fairly well

die Zier ornament, adornment

die Zierde adornment

zieren adorn

der Ziergarten ornamental garden

zierlich dainty, pretty, elegant, neat, graceful

zierlich-stolz graceful and proud

zierlich-zart graceful and gentle

das Zigeunerwesen gipsy doings

die Zikade, –n locust

der Zikadenschwarm swarm of locusts

die Zimbel, –n cymbal

das Zimmer room

die Zinke cornet

die Zinne, –n battlement, spire

der Zins, –en interest, annuity

der Zipfel, — tip, corner (of a cloth or garment); an allen Zipfeln anpacken seize wherever possible (5736); an einem andern Zipfel haben find things turned around (10087)

der Zirkeltanz whirling dance

zirken have its boundaries

zirkulieren circulate

zischen (wk) hiss

die Zither cittern, lute, guitar

zittern tremble, quiver

die Zitterperle trembling pearl

die Zitterwelle, –n trembling wave

die Zitterwoge, –n trembling wave

die Zofe lady's maid

Zoilo-Thersites Zoilo-Thersites, compounded mask of Zoilus (a severe critic of Homer) and Thersites (a maligning character in Homer's Iliad)

der Zoll tribute; toll (10947)

zollen pay (homage)

der Zopf, ⸚e queue, pigtail, braid

der Zorn anger, wrath

zu to, in, at, along with, in order to, as; too

zubereiten prepare

zubringen, a, a (wk, irreg) offer, drink as a toast; bring (7318)

züchtig decorous

zucken (wk) move jerkily, twitch; flash (481)

zücken move swiftly

sich zudecken conceal oneself, disguise oneself

zudenken, a, a (wk, irreg) propose for, confer upon

sich zudrängen press forward

zudringlich officious

zudringlich-zahm importunate and tame

zudrücken press shut; ein Auge zudrücken pretend not to see

die Zueignung dedication

zueilen hasten toward

zuerst first

zufahren rush toward

der Zufall, ⸚e chance, accident

zufallen (ä), ie, a fall toward, fall to one's share

zufällig by chance

das Zufallswörtchen casual word

zuflüstern whisper to

zufrieden contented, satisfied

die **Zufriedenheit** contentment

zufriedenstellen satisfy

der **Zug,** ⸗e movement; motion, journey; pull, draught; stroke, line; procession; **in letzten Zügen** with his last gasp, in his last moments

die **Zugabe,** –n appendage, person attached to another in constant attendance

zugeben grant, assign

zugegen present

zugehen, i, a happen, be going on; **es geht zu** things are going on; **es geht nicht mit rechten Dingen zu** there's something wrong about this, things like this don't happen by proper means

der **Zügel,** — bridle, rein

zügeln check

zugesellen (*wk*) assign to the company of

zugestalten (*wk*) shape in the image of

zugestehen concede, admit

zugleich at the same time; in addition

die **Zugluft** draft

zugreifen fall to, start, help oneself

zugrunde gehen be ruined, be destroyed; **zugrunde richten** ruin, destroy (7919, 9721)

zugut(e) for the benefit of (7498); **zugute kommen** benefit (5913, 10859); **sich was zugute tun** be proud of something, think oneself of importance (7144)

zuhanden sein be at one's disposal (6161); be at hand, be available (11087); **zuhanden sein durch** owe one's existence to (7855)

zuhauf plentiful, in large number, piled up; **zuhauf rollen** roll into a heap (10273)

zuhorchen (*wk*) eavesdrop

zuhören (*wk*) listen to

zukehren turn toward

die **Zukunft** future

zulaufen (äu), ie, au (come) running up to

zulegen (*wk*) add

zuletzt finally, in the long run, after all; **noch zuletzt** finally, in the nick of time

zulieb(e) as a favor, to please (*a person*)

zulispeln whisper to

zum = zu dem

zumachen close

zumal all at once, together at once

zumeist most of all

zumute: dir ist schlecht zumute you feel bad

zunächst next; first of all, above all; next time (1419); next to, after (7955); next to (10950)

zünden set (something) afire

die **Zunft** guild

die **Zunge,** –n tongue

züngeln (*wk*) lick (*flames*)

das **Zünglein** pointer, small tongue (*of the scales of Fate*)

zunicht(e)werden cease to exist; be destroyed utterly, be undone (519); become completely ineffective, lose all meaning (11388)

zupfen pull, tug

zur = zu der

zurechtelegen fix comfortably

zurennen run along

zurichten (*wk*) prepare (*as one prepares a dainty dish* 2651); arrange (*as for theatrical setting* 9341)

zurieseln come purling to

sich zuringen, a, u struggle toward

zürnen be angry

das Zürnen anger

zurück back, back again; stand back! go back! behindhand (547)

zurückblinken beckon glitteringly back

zurückdrängen (*wk*) crowd back

zurückehalten (ä), ie, a hold back

zurückelassen (ä) let out again

zurückeschlingen reabsorb

zurückestoßen (ö), ie, o repulse

zurückfliegen fly back

zurückgeben (i), a, e give back, restore; return (3206)

zurückgehen go back

sich zurückgewöhnen give up, wean oneself of

zurückhalten (ä) hold back, restrain

zurückkehren return

zurückkommen come back, return

zurücklassen (ä), ie, a leave behind

zurücklehnen push back

zurücklenken hold back, restrain

zurückprallen rebound, be thrown back

zurückrollen (*wk*) roll back

zurückrufen call back, recall

zurückschauen look back

zurückschlingen, a, u swallow again

zurücksehen look back

zurücksinken sink back

zurückstoßen (ö), ie, o repulse

zurücktragen (ä), u, a carry back

zurücktreten (i) step back

zurückweichen give way, retreat

zurückwenden turn back

zurückwünschen wish (a thing to come) back

zurückziehen, o, o draw back, retreat, withdraw

sich zurückziehen, o, o withdraw

zusagen be to one's liking

zusammen together

zusammenbrechen (i) collapse

sich zusammendrängen crowd together

zusammenfahren start

zusammenflackern (*wk*) flare up in one flame

zusammenfließen flow together

sich zusammenfügen integrate, fit itself together

zusammengehen go together

zusammengießen, o, o pour together

zusammenhalten (ä) hold together

zusammenleimen paste together

zusammenpassen fit together

zusammenraffen scrape together

zusammenschichten heap up, arrange in layers

zusammenschmeißen smash to bits

sich zusammenstellen join

zusammenstürzen (*wk*) descend,

fall crushingly; collapse (4733)

zuschanden ruined, done for; **sich zuschanden denken** wear oneself out with (futile) thinking

der **Zuschauer,** — spectator

zuschlagen strike, begin to fight

zuschließen lock

zuschnüren lace up; **schnürt mir das Innere zu** ties me all up inside (3493)

zuschwören swear to

zusehen look on, watch

zuspitzen (*wk*) point

zusprechen award, bestow

der **Zustand** state of affairs

zustandebringen (*wk*, *irreg*) bring about

zustandekommen, a, o come into being

zustoßen (ö), ie, o attack, lunge (*in a swordfight*)

zutage to light

zutal downhill

zuteilen (*wk*) apportion, allot

zuteilwerden fall to one's share

zutrauen believe one to be able to do a thing

zutreten step to, join

der **Zutritt** admission

zutun: zugetan devoted, attached

zuverlässig dependable

zuviel too much

zuvor: (als) wie zuvor as before

zuvörderst at first; first and foremost

zuweilen at times, every now and then

zuwenden, a, a (*wk*, *irreg*) turn toward

zuwider contrary; **zuwider sein** be repulsive

zuwogen surge toward, approach in a wavelike motion

zwacken pinch

sich zwängen squeeze

zwanzig twenty

zwar to be sure; I admit; of course

der **Zweck** aim, purpose, goal

zwecklos purposeless

zwei two

zweibeinig two-legged

zweideutig ambiguous

der **Zweifel,** — doubt

die **Zweifelei** skepticism

zweifelhaft uncertain, full of doubts (9145); doubtful

zweifeln doubt, be suspicious (1164)

der **Zweifler** skeptic

der **Zweig, –e** twig, branch, bough; ridge (7814)

zweighaft with (many) branches

zweigleinbeflügelt with small twigs for wings

zweimal twice

zweite second

der **Zwerg, –e** dwarf

die **Zwerggestalt, –en** dwarfed figure

die **Zwergin** female dwarf

das **Zwerglein** little dwarf

zwicken pinch

die **Zwiebel, –n** onion

die **Zwienatur** dual nature

die **Zwietracht** discord

das **Zwillingspaar** pair of twins

zwingen force; control, master

sich zwingen zu press toward, press to

der **Zwinger** enclosed space adjacent to city walls

zwischen between, among, betwixt

zwischendrein in between, in the midst of, among

die **Zwischenkunft** intervention

der **Zwist** dissension, quarrel

zwitschern twitter

das **Zwitterkind** hybrid, crossbreed

der **Zyklop, –en** Cyclops (*a one-eyed giant*)

zyklopisch Cyclopean

Zypern Cyprus (*an island*)

die **Zypresse, –n** cypress tree

Zypria (**–ens**) Cypria, Aphrodite, Venus